THE BASIN OF MEXICO
Ecological Processes in
the Evolution of a Civilization

This is a volume in

Studies in Archaeology

A complete list of titles in this series appears at the end of this volume.

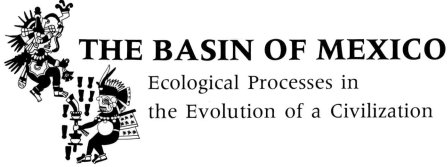

THE BASIN OF MEXICO
Ecological Processes in
the Evolution of a Civilization

WILLIAM T. SANDERS

Department of Anthropology
Pennsylvania State University
University Park, Pennsylvania

JEFFREY R. PARSONS

Museum of Anthropology
University of Michigan
Ann Arbor, Michigan

ROBERT S. SANTLEY

Department of Anthropology
University of New Mexico
Albuquerque, New Mexico

ACADEMIC PRESS   New York   San Francisco   London
A Subsidiary of Harcourt Brace Jovanovich, Publishers

ACADEMIC PRESS, INC.
111 Fifth Avenue, New York, New York 10003

United Kingdom Edition published by
ACADEMIC PRESS, INC. (LONDON) LTD.
24/28 Oval Road, London NW1 7DX

Library of Congress Cataloging in Publication Data

Sanders, William T
    The Basin of Mexico.

    (Studies in archaeology)
    Bibliography: p.
    1. Indians of Mexico––Mexico, Valley of––Antiquities.
2. Land settlement patterns, Prehistoric––Mexico––
Mexico, Valley of. 3. Human ecology––Mexico––Mexico,
Valley of. 4. Mexico, Valley of––Antiquities. 5. Mex-
ico––Antiquities. I. Parsons, Jeffrey R., joint author.
II. Santley, Robert S., joint author. III. Title.
F1219.1.M53S23   972'.5   79–11697
ISBN 0–12–618450–X

Dedicated to Manuel Gamio and George C. Vaillant,
pioneers in the archaeology of the Basin of Mexico

Contents

4

The Natural Environment of the Basin of Mexico

5

Settlement History of the Basin of Mexico

6

Demographic History of the Basin of Mexico

E

Sampling Strategies and Surface Survey in the Basin of Mexico   491

Preface

This book represents the results of field research conducted over a period of 15 years, from 1960 to 1975, in the Valley of Mexico, more properly the Basin of Mexico. This research was a combination of archaeology, ethnohistory, ethnography, and geography. Most of it was conducted as part of a planned long-range project, the Basin of Mexico Survey Project, but we have included a variety of data from a great number of other major projects. In Chapters 1 and 2 we discuss these other sources, but here we would like to emphasize the major contributions to our study. These are René Millon's Teotihuacan Mapping Project, two closely related projects at Tula directed by Richard A. Diehl and Eduardo Matos Moctezuma, Pedro Armillas' studies of the chinampas of the southern lakes, and Angel Palerm's studies of contemporary and sixteenth-century irrigation systems.

In terms of sturcture, the book falls into five major parts. Chapters 1 through 3 deal essentially with the methodology of the Basin of Mexico Survey Project and the conversion of the raw data collected to our series of settlement history maps. Chapters 4 through 7 are essentially data chapters, with a minimum of interpretation, and focus on geography, settlement, demography, and resource utilization. Chapter 8 reconstructs the history of socioeconomic systems based on a combination of the data from survey with excavations. In Chapter 9 we discuss the implications of our project in terms of broad theoretical concepts in anthropology. Chapter 10 is essentially a plea for future research to expand the considerable data base our surveys have produced, with very specific recommendations as to what that research should be. Unfortunately, because of the extraordinarily rapid acceleration of two processes in recent years, industrialization and mechanization of agriculture, this will have to be conducted in the very immediate future. Finally, we have presented a number of Appendixes with topics of a more specialized nature. References to Maps 1–25, which occur throughout the volume, direct the reader to the accompanying box containing the large survey maps.

In a work of complex authorship, in terms of data collection and writing, we feel an obligation to the readers and the authors to acquaint the reader more specifically with the background of its production. In Chapters 1 and 2 we discuss in some detail the data collection credits; here we will confine ourselves to the actual writers of this book. Chapters 1, 2, 5, 6, and 10 were written by Sanders and Parsons. Chapters 3, 4, and all of the Appendixes were written by Santley, who also produced virtually all of the drawings, including the large survey maps. Most of Chapter 7 (the exception being the section on hunting and gathering, written by Santley) and Chapter 9 were written by Sanders, and Chapter 8 was written by Santley and Sanders. It should be noted, however, that some contribution to each of the chapters was made by all three authors. The typing of the manuscript was done by Carol Leathers, Rebecca Storey, and Kathleen Sanders.

We wish to offer our gratitude to the Instituto Nacional de Antropologia e Historia in Mexico for permission to conduct the many campaigns of fieldwork that produced the data for this study, and the following institutions for their financial support for the research: The Pennsylvania State University, the University of Michigan, the Pan-American Union, and most particularly, the National Science Foundation.

Aside from its professional value, the study of one of the most exciting and impressive human achievements—the evolution of the prehispanic civilization of the Basin of Mexico—has been an enormously stimulating personal experience for all of us, and we hope that the book conveys this message to our readers.

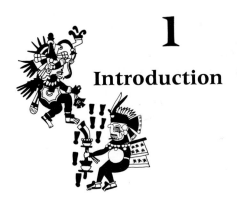

1
Introduction

This book is about a long-term archaeological project in the Basin of Mexico: a settlement pattern survey that began in 1960 and ended in 1975. We will try to explain why we started the project, how we did the fieldwork, what we thought we were trying to do at various stages of the research, what we now think has been accomplished during the years since 1960, and what we feel most needs to be done in the future. This book is not intended to be either a justification or an apology for what we have done. Obviously, we believe the work was quite worthwhile. It will be equally apparent to the reader that we now think some of the work was not carried out as effectively as it might have been: Some important things were left undone or underdone; some unnecessary energy was expended; and at some points we muddled about, conceptually and physically, in situations where more incisive thinking and action would have been desirable. An important aspect of this book, for Sanders and Parsons, is the opportunity it provides to reflect back over nearly half a lifetime of intensive involvement with the prehistory of a small piece of the world that has loomed rather large in the personal and professional experience of both. With the advantage of hindsight we hope to be able to convey something of this experience to the reader.

In the evolution of the civilization of a major culture area there have always been a number of small regions that have played unusually significant roles in the development of the larger unit—such a region is the Basin of Mexico. At the time of the Spanish Conquest it had the densest population, the largest and most highly differentiated urban centers, and the most complex political and economic organization in the history of Mesoamerican civilization. After the Conquest it has continued to function as the economic and political heartland of both the Spanish colonial empire and the modern Republic of Mexico. Moving backward in time, the most expansive, urban, and institutionally most complex society in Mesoamerica in the first millennium A.D. was located in this same area, and it was one of the major areas of cultural development during the first millennium B.C. Obviously, our understanding of the cultural development of Mesoamerica as a whole would be severely impaired if we lacked an understanding of how the Basin of Mexico had attained this nuclearity. For the archaeologist to reconstruct the culture history of prehispanic Mesoamerica without a knowledge of this area would be comparable to a historian writing the history of Colonial and Republican Mexico without access to the documents of the Archivo General in Mexico City (see Figure 1.1).

During the period from the end of the nineteenth century to 1960 there had been considerable archaeological and documentary research in the Basin. This research produced a basic chronology of ceramics, architecture, and to a certain extent, lithic artifacts. It has also provided us with a detailed

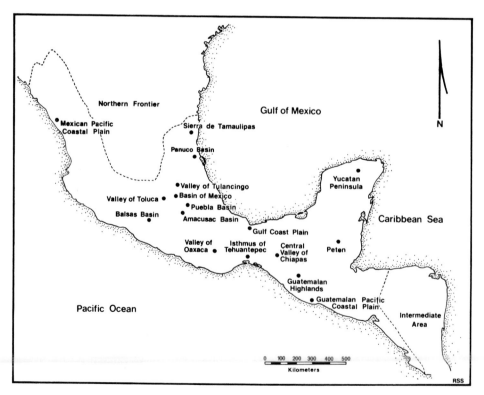

Figure 1.1. Mesoamerica, showing location of the Basin of Mexico in relation to other geographical regions.

knowledge of the technological and artistic characteristics of a sequence of cultural centers from Tlatilco to Cuicuilco, Teotihuacan, Tula, and finally Tenochtitlan; and some idea of the interrelationships between these centers and other areas of Mesoamerica.

In 1960 Eric Wolf, realizing the need to stimulate and coordinate archaeological research in this key area of Mesoamerica, received a National Science Foundation grant to support a conference on the Basin of Mexico. The main purpose of the conference was to bring together a number of Mesoamerican specialists with specific interests in the Basin. The conference had two primary objectives: (*a*) to assess our present state of knowledge and the development of the field, and (*b*) to plan further research. The meeting took place in June, 1960, at the University of Chicago. The following persons were present: Robert Adams, Pedro Armillas, Pedro Carrasco, Michael Coe, Edward Deevey, William Mayer-Oakes, René Millon, Angel Palerm, Roman Piña Chan, William Sanders, and Eric Wolf.

The overall objective of the proposed meeting was to foster research leading to an understanding of the role of the Basin of Mexico in the cultural development of Mesoamerica as a whole. In Wolf's original NSF conference grant the following specific research objectives were listed:

1. Changes in the natural and man-made environment of the Basin of Mexico over time and the possible correlation of these changes with cultural factors
2. The antiquity, development, and relative importance of major and minor patterns of land use over time
3. The characteristics of settlement in the Basin and changes in settlement patterns over time and related population problems
4. The nature of the relationships between hamlets, villages, towns, cities, and similar units at various periods and of relationships between specific sites
5. Problems of urbanization
6. The characteristics of symbiotic regions in the Basin in various periods of time and their social consequences
7. The relevance of environment to agriculture and settlement patterns and to problems of social control at various levels
8. Patterns of ceremonial control at various time levels
9. Patterns of political control at various time levels
10. Patterns of warfare in the prehispanic period
11. The effects of the Spanish Conquest and colonization on social and cultural groups in the Basin of Mexico
12. Casual or functional relationships between various cultural patterns at different time levels

Discussion at this conference made it painfully apparent that there was very little real information about any of the topics Wolf had outlined. The conference participants designed a loose, informal organization in which research, oriented at common objectives, could be planned and undertaken by individual investigators. The Basin of Mexico settlement pattern survey, which Sanders began in June, 1960, was the first such project to be undertaken within this new framework. The project had actually been conceived by Sanders prior to 1960, when, on the basis of ethnohistoric studies and available archaeological data, he had defined the Central Mexican Symbiotic Region (Sanders 1956). This area included the Basin of Mexico, together with adjacent areas of southern Hidalgo, western Tlaxcala–Puebla, and Morelos. This region, containing a diversity of natural environments, was seen as the nuclear region in which could evolve a complex Mesoamerican civilization founded on high productivity, dense population, and intensive specialization and exchange. With the Central Mexican Symbiotic Region defined as the postulated locus for the formation and development of a Mesoamerican civilization, it became necessary for Sanders to design an archaeological strategy for describing and explaining cultural evolution in this area. The reader in the late 1970s should recall that 20 years before most of Central Mexico was very nearly an archaeological blank, with only a few unusual sites being known in any detail.

The basic assumptions that underlay the planning of the project were few and broadly conceived. Civilization was seen as a socioeconomic system, characterized (a) by centralization of political authority, and (b) by considerable internal differentiation, based on economic specialization and differential access to economic and political power. A major research problem, then, was to design archaeological methods that would measure centralization and differentiation. It was evident at the outset that the problem of describing a prehispanic civilization and explaining cultural change through time levels was very much a regional problem, in which a large area and many sites would have to be systematically examined and analyzed. In 1960, Sanders felt that the only way that he could begin to realize his overall objectives would be to carry out an extensive regional settlement pattern survey, of the type earlier pioneered by the Viru Valley Project in Peru (Willey 1953). The original plan was to survey the entire Central Mexican Symbiotic Region. As it turned out, this plan proved to be too vast an undertaking for any single project, and we have confined our efforts to the Basin of Mexico alone.

A second major assumption was that a materialist paradigm was the most useful framework in which to explain why centralized and internally differentiated societies emerged in the region. The perspective Sanders favored at the outset of the project was Steward's (1955) cultural core model, in which civilization develops in an area as an adaptive response to the environmental circumstances of the region. This meant that data on resource exploitation would be required, and, again, it was felt that systematic regional settlement pattern survey was a necessary first step in developing hypotheses about such exploitation.

Even the most ambitious projects have to begin somewhere, and, in 1960, Sanders faced the problem of where to actually start his regional surveys. The Teotihuacan Valley was selected as the starting point for a variety of reasons. Most importantly, René Millon was planning an intensive survey of the large Teotihuacan site, one of Mesoamerica's principal prehispanic urban centers. It was felt that a combination of urban and rural data would provide insights into the structure of prehispanic society that would not be apparent were either project to be carried out in isolation.

Second, unlike some other parts of the Basin of Mexico, the Teotihuacan Valley was still, in 1960, an essentially rural area with many surviving traditional patterns of resource exploitation and settlement that could provide interpretative analogues for prehispanic times. The same rural condition also suggested that site preservation would be better than in regions closer to Mexico City—an important consideration in the pioneer phase of the project. With its arid climate and large functioning irrigation system, the Teotihuacan Valley also seemed an ideal area in which to test the hypothesis, so new and challenging to archaeologists in 1960, that the evolution of a state in central Mexico was closely related to the development of hydraulic agriculture. Finally, because of his studies of contemporary agriculture and settlement in the Teotihuacan Valley in 1955, Sanders had a close familiarity with the area that enabled him to design his investigation there more effectively.

In 1960, Sanders initiated the Teotihuacan Valley project with a set of four specific objectives that he hoped to achieve, largely by means of systematic settlement pattern surveys:

1. To trace the development of agriculture, with a special focus on irrigation and terracing
2. To define and trace the development of different settlement types
3. To construct, as precisely as possible, a population profile
4. To explore the relationship between such phenomena as settlement patterns, agricultural techniques, and demography so as to illuminate the general process of cultural evolution in the Teotihuacan Valley, the Basin of Mexico, and the Central Mexican Symbiotic Region

The decision to begin our work in the Teotihuacan Valley was a logical and reasonable outcome of events during and just prior to 1960. However, one unforeseen consequence of this decision has proved to be rather unfortunate in terms of our general objectives within the Basin of Mexico: Mexico City, in the southwestern basin, continued to expand at a rapid pace throughout the 1960s and 1970s. By the time the Teotihuacan Valley project was completed, several key areas on the fringes of the modern metropolis, where good settlement data could have been collected prior to about 1965, had been destroyed. This is most particularly unfortunate in the case of the Cuicuilco area, in the far southwestern Basin, and we have long lamented the physical obliteration of this key site (apart from a few large ceremonial structures).

As will be detailed in subsequent chapters, during the 15 years after 1960, settlement pattern survey in the Basin of Mexico proceeded intensively under the direction of several individuals. By the mid 1970s most of the entire area had been systematically examined. The only large blank was the area obscured by the modern metropolis of Mexico City in the southwestern Basin. During this passage of years we did a lot of fieldwork, but we paused occasionally to think and write about our data (Blanton 1972a, 1972b, 1976; Parsons 1968, 1971, 1972, 1974, 1976a, 1976b; Sanders 1965, 1968, 1970a, 1970b, 1975, 1976a, 1976b, 1976c). Other people have also used portions of our field data for a variety of purposes (e.g., Alden 1978; Brumfiel 1976; Earl 1976; Kottak 1978). Several investigators have undertaken comparable research in other parts of Mesoamerica (e.g., Blanton *et al.* 1978; Hirth 1974; Kowalewski 1976) and in Peru (Blanton and Kowalewski n.d.; Browman 1970; Parsons 1976c; Parsons and Hastings 1977). All of this work took place during an era in which there were some rather important advances in archaeological method and theory.

A good way to end this general introductory chapter might be to consider, in a general way, how our own research was affected by the general intellectual milieu in which we, as professional academic archaeologists, worked between 1960 and 1975. Near the end of this book we will attempt the converse of this, and consider how our own work has contributed to certain aspects of general anthropological theory.

In 1960 regional archaeology was still very much in its infancy. The classic Viru Valley monograph (Willey 1953) was virtually the only investigation whose objectives were comparable to our own. However, because of the unique environment and survey techniques employed there, the Viru Valley survey could serve only as a general kind of model for our own work. Similarly, the innovative surveys of Bullard (1960) and Adams (1961) in the Maya area were carried out in different ways and for somewhat different purposes than our own proposed research. Just as significantly, there had been little explicit thinking about how an archaeologist might approach a region in order to define and describe cultural systems on the ground at different periods of time. It was obvious to everyone, of course, that if you could locate and describe all sites within a designated region, you would be well on your way toward achieving this goal. The problems, of course, involved the proper designation of a region so that a series of "cultural systems" would fall within it, as well as the more practical matters of actually locating and describing sites and finding funds to support such work.

The Viru Valley Project, with its primary reliance on aerial photography to locate sites, produced a settlement sample heavily biased toward locations with preserved architecture visible on the photographs. Architectural preservation was very poor in our survey area, and, in any event, we wanted to avoid the bias inherent in their methodology. Vescelius' (1960) pioneering paper on sampling techniques based on probability statistics appeared at the beginning of our project. We were not aware of it then, and, in any event, it was most applicable to the single site, already located. The whole sampling revolution, initiated by Binford's 1964 article, was still years away, and we were not involved in the making of that revolution.

As will be spelled out in the next chapter, we opted for 100% survey coverage, and this continued, with very few exceptions, to be the procedure followed for the entire period of our surveys. In 1960, as we began our work, we couldn't think of any reasonable alternative. We felt rather strongly that in order to be able to adequately describe a cultural system on the ground, we needed a map that would show us the complete configuration of human settlement at any one period of time.

During the later 1960s and into the 1970s, however, the archaeological literature was full of papers, symposia, and books about archaeological sampling. And, through it all, season by season, we kept on grinding out 100% surveys. Some of us had mixed emotions, and Parsons (1972) once even came close to apologizing for the absence of any kind of sampling strategy in our research. Sometimes it seemed that our work was less rigorous, less scientific, unnecessarily costly, and perhaps even less useful because we had no sophisticated sampling design. And yet, the data were exciting, and new ideas were generated during and after each fieldseason. New problems clearly defined themselves as the years went by, and the questions we were asking kept getting better. The National Science Foundation kept on supporting our work. Other people asked to use our data. Clearly we were getting good and useful information. And, when we periodically reexamined our principal objectives, a complete survey always seemed the best way to proceed.

From the perspective of the late 1970s we believe, more firmly than ever, that our original decision to do 100% surveys was one of the best decisions we made. In the next chapter we will go to some length to explain why we feel this way. We now realize that many things can be done with a complete settlement map that we hadn't even thought of doing when we started out. Some of these things would be difficult, or even impossible, to do in any reasonable way with a fractional sample, however systematically designed or statistically valid. We are sure that the only serious arguments that would be raised against our position would involve the greater economic costs of complete survey. We will try to address this matter as well in the next chapter.

Another aspect of the foregoing discussion about sampling is that throughout much of our fieldwork we had not adequately conceptualized some of the problems we were grappling with. This probably accounts for some of the agonizing some of us did along the way about some of our procedures and methods. Our objectives, spelled out in most of our grant proposals, were pretty broad statements, wholly worthwhile, but with limited explicit reasoning about how archaeological remains were going to get translated into agricultural systems, population, patterns of specialization and exchange, political differentiation, social variability, hostility, the interrelationships between all these, and other matters. It can be reasonably argued that our models were deficient, and that our reasoning was very largely inductive—more so, perhaps, than it needed to be most of the time. In many ways we knew what we wanted, but we often had failed to fully think through what our hypotheses were and what we might expect to find in the way of artifact configurations if one or another alternative proposition held.

On the other hand, it should also be kept in mind that we had to cope with another major difficulty, especially in the earlier years of the project, and that was the fact that our survey area was all but an archaeological blank except for isolated data on architecture, ceramics, and art. We knew almost nothing, until our own surveys had progressed for a while, even about such basic factors as settlement distribution and relative population. What we had to do, in other words, was to define many of our problems ourselves. Before the problems are properly defined, how can an archaeologist help but do a lot of inductive thinking? Perhaps one of our major contributions in the chapters that follow will be to give the reader some idea of how we would now proceed if we had to do it all over again.

From the outset we were also aware that our research enjoyed some enormous advantages. Because we started out working in a near-vacuum of information, every bit of data we collected made a significant contribution. And, the data were abundant and easily obtained—remains of human settlement almost literally jumped out of the ground at us. Mounds and surface pottery were visible almost everywhere; all we had to do was put them into a map and sort them out in time. There are probably few other areas in the world so conducive to rapid, productive surface survey as the Basin of Mexico was. And yet, at the beginning of our project there was no established methodology for recording settlement data in the way we wanted to. We had to create such a methodology largely from scratch, and, as will be detailed in the next chapter, we spent some time in experimentation with a variety of techniques, some of which did not work out so well. Because we had to innovate and improvise, the earlier stages of our survey were less efficiently done than the later. The watershed years were our 1963 and 1964 fieldseasons. During these months our basic survey methodology was laboriously hammered out, and it has been modified only very slightly since. It has been quite pleasant to find out from a number of people who worked with us at different times that our basic methodology has been transplanted to other areas where it has proven useful and productive (e.g., Blanton *et al.* 1978; Hirth 1974; Parsons and Hastings 1977; Whalen 1977).

Another great advantage to our research was the ease with which a meaningful survey area could be defined on the basis of natural topography. Although this may seem like a fairly small matter, it is actually of considerable consequence. If we wanted to define cultural systems on the ground, how much ground would we need to cover in order to be reasonably confident that we had included all the components of a complex society? Carried to its logical extreme, one might have to include the whole of Mesoamerica in such a survey. However, with the Basin of Mexico measuring some 7000 km^2 in surface area, we had a well-defined natural region that was small enough to deal with on a practical basis, but which, at the same time, was large enough to provide at least the heartland zone for several major cultural systems. High mountains on three sides and an arid northern frontier provide significant obstacles to human settlement that still affect modern occupation. We know of few other areas in the world where cultural and natural borders coincide so well. Regional surveys in most other parts of the world (e.g., Adams and Nissen 1972; Parsons and Hastings 1977; Puleston 1973) have had to draw rather arbitrary borders around their study areas. This may have a significant, though largely unpredictable, effect on impressions about settlement patterns, particularly in more complex kinds of societies where the location of a single important settlement can have a rather profound impact upon many others. For us, the Basin of Mexico was a made-to-order survey area, and we did not even have to think very much about where to draw our survey limits: In most cases we just stopped at the bases of the steep, forested slopes of the surrounding mountain ranges.

Throughout the entire course of our work one of our major sources of stimulation and edification was the presence of several other archaeologists and ethnohistorians working contemporaneously in the Basin of Mexico. Some of the details of these complementary investigations will be discussed in later chapters. For the moment it suffices to note that we benefitted immensely from these contacts. From René Millon's intensive survey of the Teotihuacan center (e.g., Millon et al. 1973) we annually received new ideas for making sense of our own growing corpus of rural settlement data as affected by the presence of the great city. James Bennyhoff, and later Evelyn Rattray and Darlena Blucher, all of Millon's project, provided an increasingly refined ceramic chronology for Teotihuacan which helped us considerably in phasing our own sites. Paul Tolstoy, working with Formative ceramic chronology and economy in the southern basin (e.g., Tolstoy 1975; Tolstoy and Fish 1975; and Paradis 1970), gave us new insights into our unexcavated Formative sites throughout the Basin. Thomas Charlton's work with colonial archaeology (e.g., Charlton 1969, 1972a, 1972b) made us realize that some of our Aztec sites probably had significant post-Conquest occupations. Pedro Armillas' pioneering work in the chinampa area (e.g., Armillas 1971) provided a much-needed baseline for our own survey of that region. Angel Palerm's ethnohistoric researches into prehispanic and colonial hydraulic engineering (e.g., Palerm 1973; Rojas et al. 1974) greatly clarified our thinking about the physical remains of dams, dikes, and causeways we encountered in various places. Charles Gibson's monumental synthesis of historical documentation (Gibson 1964) became a veritable bible for us as we searched for historic analogues of prehistoric patterns. Edward Calnek's archival-based reconstructions of Aztec Tenochtitlan (Calnek 1972, 1973, 1976) gave us the first good view of this key center, almost wholly invisible to archaeologists under the huge mass of colonial and modern Mexico City.

By the early 1970s a substantial quantity of information about prehispanic life in the Basin of Mexico had been collected. Much of it bore directly upon the topics Wolf had in 1960 proposed as significant research objectives (see the preceding discussion). Other data were relevant to significant matters that nobody had even thought of in 1960. It was clear to everyone concerned that during a little more than a decade there had been a quantum jump in our knowledge about prehistoric society in the Basin of Mexico. Feeling that it was time to take stock of what had been learned and where future research efforts might best be directed, a second conference on the Basin of Mexico was held in April 1972, under the auspices of the School for American Research in Santa Fe, New Mexico. Eric Wolf again acted as conference chairman. Some of the substantive results of this meeting were subsequently published in book form (Wolf 1976).

Everyone at the 1972 meeting was impressed with how much had been learned since 1960. In contrast to the earlier meeting, when most discussions had revolved around what we would like to know, the 1972 meeting consisted of four exhausting days in which substantive information flowed out in an almost endless stream. It could easily have gone on far longer. Perhaps the most telling sign of how far we had progressed since 1960 was the fact that a significant portion of the 1972 conference was spent in arguments about how data were to be interpreted or how data bore upon general theoretical problems. Although many different arguments arose on a variety of occasions, most of them revolved around two basic questions: (1) Was population pressure the principal driving force behind cultural evolutionary change in the Basin of Mexico between 1000 B.C. and A.D. 1520? (2) Is the materialist paradigm, especially when phrased in terms of the hydraulic hypothesis, adequate to explain the development of the Teotihuacan urban system? In both arguments, regional settlement pattern data figured prominently, on all sides of these principal issues.

The 1972 conference failed to resolve these matters. Later on in this book, we will address these, and other related questions, again. They are actually specific variants of more general questions being asked by many social scientists interested in cultural evolutionary change.

2

The Strategy and
Tactics of Fieldwork

HISTORY OF THE BASIN OF MEXICO
SURVEY PROJECT

Fieldwork in the Teotihuacan Valley began in June 1960. The most recently completed survey, in the Temascalapa region, terminated in September of 1975. (See Map 4 for the locations of the various survey regions.) The fieldwork of the Teotihuacan Valley project, under Sanders' general direction, extended over five seasons: three 3-month seasons during 1960, 1962, and 1964, and two 6-month seasons in 1961 and 1963, with one or two graduate students remaining in the field during the balance of each year from 1961 to 1963. During the first three fieldseasons in the Teotihuacan Valley, and particularly in 1961 and 1962, a considerable amount of excavation was carried out. Most of the settlement pattern survey was done in 1963 and 1964.

No fieldwork was conducted in 1965, but in 1966 Parsons, who had worked for four seasons with the Teotihuacan Valley Project, returned to that area for 3 months to survey a number of sectors that had been omitted in the previous field seasons. Richard Blanton, who was later to carry out independent surveys in the Ixtapalapa region, and Mary Hrones, who was to be Parsons' principal coworker during all his subsequent fieldseasons, were field assistants in the 1966 season. With this additional experience, Parsons designed and completed the Texcoco region survey project over a 7-month period in 1967, with Blanton and Hrones as his principal assistants.

Two survey projects were carried out in 1969: Blanton's 4-month investigation of the Ixtapalapa region, and Parsons' 3-month coverage of the Chalco region. These activities were followed by a 2-year gap, but in 1972 Parsons spent 10 months completing surveys in the Chalco–Xochimilco region. During that same year Sanders conducted studies of contemporary peasant agriculture in the vicinity of Texcoco. In 1973 Parsons carried out 7 months of fieldwork in the Zumpango region. Sanders, assisted by Santley, surveyed for 8 months in the Cuautitlan region in 1974, and during 1975, Sanders spent 3 months on a partial survey of the Temascalapa region.

Information about site location from two other projects has been incorporated to complete our settlement pattern data. Thomas Charlton worked with the Teotihuacan Valley project in 1963 and developed an interest in Colonial-period archaeology. He resurveyed large sections of the upper Teotihuacan Valley in 1968, primarily in a search for Early Colonial sites (Charlton 1972a, 1972b). In the process, a number of sites, missed in the original Teotihuacan Valley survey, were located, and these have been included in our maps. In 1974 and 1975, Alexander, working in conjunction with Angel Palerm's ethnohistoric research project, carried out intensive surveys and excavations to test the hypothesis that the Colonial-period dike separating Lakes Xaltocan and Texcoco was built over an older prehispanic dike. In the process he surveyed large sections of Lake Xaltocan and the lower western flanks of Cerro Chiconauhtla. His settlement data have not been included in the preparation of our maps.

An important component of our research has been the long-term continuity of personnel who have been most directly involved in data collection and analysis. William Sanders, Jeffrey Parsons, Richard Blanton, and Mary Hrones Parsons have all worked together rather closely before carrying out their various independent investigations. This has lent a degree of stability and consistency that we might not otherwise have achieved.

GENERAL RESEARCH STRATEGY

This project has had two primary objectives: (1) to describe the socioeconomic institutions of cultural systems at different time periods between about 1000 B.C., when the Basin of Mexico was first inhabited by sedentary agriculturalists, until the Spanish Conquest in A.D. 1521; (2) to explain, within a materialist paradigm, the ecological processes of evolutionary change by which these cultural systems evolved and became increasingly centralized and differentiated.

The basic problem was conceived of as a regional one: We knew we were dealing with a series of large, complex societies whose description would require the recovery of varied components over a sizable area. The Basin of Mexico is an area small enough to deal with directly and large enough to provide the setting for the most important components of the cultural systems we wanted to describe. As in the case of most archaeologists, our ability to control for time was critical. To control for space it was necessary to conduct a large regional survey; thus surface data would have to provide most of the information. In a large area, with potentially thousands of sites, one could not possibly hope to excavate at more than a tiny fraction of these sites. The study area, so well defined by nature, lay clearly before us. The major problem was how to decide what kinds of archaeological remains within it constituted adequate data.

To control time it was necessary, at least initially, to refine the existing ceramic chronology. This demanded some excavation. Since excavation was a secondary aspect of our project, we will first discuss our excavation strategy, and then move to a more extended consideration of our survey.

Excavation Strategy

Excavation was a major activity of the Teotihuacan Valley projects in 1961, 1962, and 1963. During the 1961 and 1962 fieldseasons most of the project's energy and resources were dedicated to this activity. At this time excavations were conducted in 21 sites dating to all major time periods. These excavations ranged from small test pitting to complete exposure of apartment-house compounds. The purposes of these excavations were twofold. First, although previous research had provided a broad ceramic chronological framework for the Basin of Mexico, little of this sequence had been published in any useful detail. Furthermore, much of it was based on grave lots or decorated pottery, and thus was only marginally useful for the dating of surface samples from small residential sites. Our own ceramic analysis, based on a combination of excavated and surface materials, is based on a full range of ceramic wares. Unexpectedly, some of the undecorated wares (that usually comprise a large proportion of our surface collections) were extremely sensitive time markers. Jars from the Teotihuacan period, for example, were excellent indicators of phase differentiation.

Second, in the 1960 preliminary season numerous archaeological structural remains in the form of mounds of varying size were encountered. The mounds with a high height to base proportion were identified as temple platforms, and most of the lower mounds were classified as domestic residences. These preliminary functional inferences needed to be corroborated by excavation, and some of our excavations were designed for such a purpose. This was particularly desirable as so few prehispanic houses had ever been excavated. No published excavation of any Formative-period houses, and no rural Teotihuacan, Toltec, or Aztec residences had ever been reported. Vaillant (1941) had excavated what he called a "palace" at the Aztec town of Chiconautla. Portions of several urban residences at Teotihuacan had been excavated by several people (Armillas 1950; Linné 1934, 1942; Sejourne 1959, 1966a, 1966b). Charnay (1884), in the nineteenth century, had excavated portions of several residences at Tula. Incredibly enough, in 1960 this was the sum total of our knowledge about prehispanic residential architecture in the Basin of Mexico.

A few of our excavations were the type of deep stratigraphic pit that Flannery (1976) has referred to as "telephone booths," but most of them were lateral excavations, where we test pitted to a floor level, and then expanded laterally to clear as much of the floor plan as possible. In fact, many of our "telephone booths" were perforations of floors exposed by lateral excavation to test for the presence of earlier floors. Our chronology is thus based primarily on residential ceramics, and it can be directly compared to our surface samples from residential sites.

In subsequent years, Millon's project at the Teotihuacan urban center performed a series of small stratigraphic excavations in order to clarify ceramic chronology. The unpublished results of these excavations were available throughout the course of our own work, and we made some use of them. No additional excavations, for any purpose, were carried out by our project after 1963, until the 1974 season near Cuautitlan (see Chapter 8). Thus, we continued to depend, almost exclusively, on our early chronological work in the Teotihuacan Valley. We have always realized that this may have created some unforeseen chronological problems for us as we moved further afield from the Teotihuacan area over the next decade. However, the working assumption was that the *general* ceramic sequence is uniform throughout the entire Basin of Mexico, and this does not seem unreasonable even today.

Survey Strategy

We have already noted that we early decided to do a 100% survey, and we continued to do this throughout our entire project (in reality certain factors prevented us from achieving a full 100% coverage in some places, and these problem areas and the reasons for this less-than-complete coverage are discussed in Chapter 3). We will now attempt to justify this decision. We strongly believe that economic cost is the only reason why a 100% survey is not always preferable to a systematically designed sampling procedure. However, we hope to suggest, through the course of this book, that even though complete surveys are more expensive in the short run (which, unfortunately, is what most archaeologists have to cope with), in the long run they may actually be cheaper in some areas and for some purposes. It is not our interest to get into an extended discussion over the complex problems involved in archaeological sampling. We will stay close to our own particular area, problems, and data.

Earlier work in the Basin of Mexico, including our own preliminary season in 1960, revealed that surface remains of prehispanic occupation, in the form of mounds, surface pottery, lithic materials, and rock rubble debris, were readily visible on the ground surface for all time periods after about 1000 B.C. We were confident that we could quickly and accurately locate and delineate the remains of ancient settlements where people had resided for any significant length of time. We also felt that we could use surface remains to infer a great deal about a settlement's architectural complexity, and something about its occupational density. We hoped that some information could also be derived about specialization and status within and between settlements, on the basis of how architecture, ceramics, and stone tools were differentially distributed over the ground surface. As it turned out, we were a little overly optimistic: It was possible to say quite a bit about site size, architectural complexity, and occupational density, but much less about differences in status or specialization.

Our most basic premise was that the way in which people distribute their residences over the ground surface is a sensitive indicator of how they interact with their natural environment and with other human beings. Thus, if one could determine how residences were distributed at various points in time, it should be possible to make some significant inferences about how people interacted with one another and with their natural surroundings. Since a major objective was to measure temporal differences in societal centralization and differentiation within prehispanic cultural systems contained within the Basin of Mexico, it seemed that settlement patterns were one good way of getting at these matters. The problem with this reasoning, of course, is that once the distribution of residences for various prehistoric time periods had been described, how were we then to infer what these meant in terms of interactions with natural environment and with other humans. This was the point at which we floundered, and are still, to some extent, floundering. This, in essence, is what settlement pattern archaeology is all about. What we failed to do, and what no one has really ever done adequately, is to develop a series of models, by means of which the archaeologist can make reasonable sociological inferences from settlement pattern data. Nevertheless, our work should have great value in this model building—indeed, without data such as our own, compiled systematically and in large quantity, the task of model building in settlement archaeology may be largely a futile exercise. We will have more to say on this general matter later in the book.

In any event, our immediate objective was to recover a variety of data on where people had lived during the prehispanic past in the survey area. We reasoned that the basic artifact for our subsequent analyses would be the localities where enough people had spent enough time to leave some obvious, enduring physical traces on the present ground surface. The survey thus focused on settlements—places to which such labels as camps, hamlets, villages, towns, cities, and so on, intuitively seemed appropriate. We did not feel that we could locate or identify anything much more ephemeral (e.g., a place where a person had sharpened a stone point while hunting or working in the field; a place in a formerly forested area where somebody had cut down a tree, etc.). What we were most interested in was where such a point sharpener or woodsman ate, slept, procreated, kept his possessions, engaged in craft production, formed part of a household, and from which he confronted the outside world on a fairly enduring basis. We realized that not all such activities would necessarily always be concentrated at the same place, but thought that, in most cases, a great many of them would be. What was known about ethnographically defined sedentary agriculturalists suggested that this was a reasonable assumption. In our most optimistic moments we even thought that we might be able to tell whether a particular place had been the home, or workshop, of a point sharpener, or a woodsman, or a potter, etc., by estimating the content of artifact debris on the ground surface. At such moments we also felt that by estimating the density of such artifact debris we might be able to estimate the number of persons who had resided at a location.

How were we then to translate mounds and concentrations of artifact debris into sociological phenomena for which such terms as camp, hamlet, village, town, and city might be applicable? Before we could even start this, of course, we needed to know which mounds and which masses of surface debris at a particular locality were contemporaneous. This would be most difficult in places where there had been occupation during several time periods, whether continuous or intermittent. Thus, it was necessary to make collections of surface pottery for chronological control, particularly where more than one period was represented. Some places, occupied continuously for more than a millennium, were sure to be hard to deal with in this regard. In the earlier stages of the project it was assumed that these collections, made for chronological control, could also serve for making some inferences about status and function. We soon found that this was not really possible, and by the mid 1960s we had just about abandoned the hope of obtaining any really meaningful data on status and function.

We also knew that we would need to measure both the area over which contemporaneous archaeological remains extended at a particular locality, and the internal variability in mound and artifact density within such an area. The definition of a *site* would serve as a preliminary step in inferring its sociological meaning. This meant defining site limits, as well as describing the internal character of the site itself (as this could be read from the ground surface). For small sites this would be easy enough to do, but for larger sites proper definition and description would involve walking about over a considerable area. Once again, localities of multicomponent occupation would be troublesome to deal with, and special care would have to be taken to designate properly overlapping occupations of different time periods. One of our basic expectations was that a human settlement would be physically coherent: a fairly discrete cluster of archaeological remains surrounded by a large amount of empty space. In general this assumption was correct, and sites could be easily defined throughout our survey area. There were, however, a few exceptions, and we still do not know how to deal with some of these. A major assumption was that intersettlement distance would be a good measure of some significant aspects of societal organization. This required the certain knowledge that a blank on the settlement map for any particular time period was the product of a lack of settlement rather than a lack of survey.

The final step in our settlement description would be settlement classification. This would be a critical and complex component of one of the major objectives of the project—the measurement of centralization and differentiation over space and through time. Nevertheless, our thinking about it has always been a little sloppy. We have often disagreed among ourselves about how to label some sites, and it took us a long time to realize that this was because we did not always have the same criteria in mind in making up and assigning labels for sites. Our inconsistency and lack of precision in this matter is an aspect of the general problem mentioned earlier: As with most archaeologists, we have not adequately faced up to the problem of model building as we attempt to translate archaeological data into cultural behavior.

Nevertheless, we used an intuitive, basically implicit line of reasoning that has served us reasonably well. This reasoning was somewhat as follows. The areal extent of continuously distributed surface artifact debris was a good measure of site size. Small mounds probably represented domestic buildings, while large mounds could reasonably be categorized as ceremonial–civic architecture. The relative density of surface artifact debris and mounds would be an indication of how many people had resided in an area during a period of time. Differential concentrations of stone tools, specific pottery types, and such nonperishable items as kilns, and so on, would be indicative of where specialized tasks had been carried out. Similarly, the differential distribution of exotic artifacts, larger houses, and ceremonial–civic architecture might enable us to say something about the loci of influence and power.

These were the elements that we hoped could be measured adequately. Large, complex, densely inhabited sites with ceremonial–civic architecture and good indications that important people and craft specialists had resided there, would be obvious central places. Small, uniform sites, with few people and unimpressive, generalized remains of architecture and artifacts, would be dependent hamlets and so on. As it turned out, the site classification (see Chapter 3) had to be constructed without any significant input concerning function and status. As already indicated, we soon found that we were unable to cope with these problems within the scope of our project. The adequate definition of this kind of differentiation within and between sites demanded far greater inputs of time and effort than our resources permitted.

We believed that the settlement data we required could be collected in a reasonable way by systematically walking over the ground surface, locating architectural remains and areas of artifact concentration by visual inspection, plotting these remains on a map, making systematic collections of surface artifacts, and describing these archaeological features in a notebook and in a photographic record. As will be detailed in the next section, a procedure was worked out in which these archaeological remains were plotted initially on vertical airphotographs at a scale of 1:5000, and were ultimately transferred to maps traced from the airphotographs. When sets of such remains were closely spaced, and could be dated as contemporary in terms of major blocks of time (Formative, 1500 B.C.–A.D. 0; Classic or Teotihuacan, A.D. 0–750; Toltec, A.D. 750–1150; Aztec, A.D. 1150–1519), they were defined as sites. The initial dating was based on surface impressions in the field. In the case of multicomponent sites, each chronological component at a location was separately classified as a site. As the surface collections were analyzed in more detail, the major blocks of time were divided into phases, and each phase component was given a final site number.

From the outset of the project we felt we needed a 100% survey coverage of the Basin of Mexico to achieve our objectives. First of all, the Basin is environmentally very heterogeneous (see Maps 1, 2, and 3). Any sampling procedure would have to be suitably stratified so that this natural diversity could be properly taken into account. This might have been useful and successful for some purposes, but any stratified sampling method presupposes that the researcher understands what the significant environmental variables were that might affect population distribution. This is no easy matter, and we doubted that we had such an understanding. For example, even though Sanders was, in 1960, very familiar with the Basin of Mexico, the various studies of contemporary agriculture undertaken subsequently constantly modified our view of the significant agricultural variables. This may be further compounded by the fact that practically all our understanding about agricultural productivity is based upon knowledge derived from cultivation systems which employ draft animals and plows to work the soil. Cultivation systems based wholly upon human labor in the same area may have some significantly different requirements and priorities which are largely unknown to us now. Furthermore, although stratified sampling might be effective in controlling for the affects on settlement of major environmental zones, we questioned its effectiveness in controlling for the highly variable and localized distribution of some key resources such as ceramic clays, obsidian, basalt, water, and so on, all of which could have had significant effects on settlement distribution.

Another characteristic of the Basin of Mexico that presents serious problems for sampling procedures is the fact that it was occupied, after about 500 B.C., by large, politically centralized, internally heterogenous societies. Some sites, therefore, were central places, and this kind of site, because it was a focus of centralized functions, would be rare. A sampling procedure might well miss such a site. As Flannery (1976) points out, a capable archaeologist would not miss a Teotihuacan or a Tula, nor would he fail to include such sites in his reconstruction of cultural evolution in his area. But, many central places in the Basin of Mexico are relatively small and unobtrusive, and they could easily be missed in a fractional sample. For example, documentary sources indicate that there were six Aztec-period provincial centers in the Teotihuacan Valley in the early sixteenth century. Our surveys showed that these centers ranged in size from 30 to 200 hectares (ha). Furthermore, they are not physically apparent until one walks directly onto them. All could conceivably have been missed in a fractional sample (after all, they constitute only a tiny percentage of all Aztec-period sites), and yet knowledge of their location is critical to our understanding of the Aztec-period settlement system. Scores of comparable examples abound for wholly prehistoric periods where we have no documentary leads about the placement of important sites. A related matter is that for the Basin of Mexico there was a marked tendency over most of the prehispanic era for a majority of the population to reside in a few large sites. Such sites are usually not particularly visible until one is standing directly atop them, and they could easily be missed in a sampling strategy.

Aside from the matter of central places, the highly localized nature of some resources could have stimulated considerable local specialization by rural settlements. Since the locations of very few such resources were known, they could not be properly considered in designing a sampling strategy. For example, one village in a region might have supplied all the metates for the particular region. A sampling technique could miss such a site, and could conceivably even miss all, or most, of the rural settlements that had occupational specializations.

An additional major advantage of a complete survey is that negative data become highly useful. If, for example, one can say with considerable assurance that in a particular region there were no Formative-period sites, then this is a valuable piece of information if one is interested, as we were, in determining intersite distances for the Formative period. A fractional survey would not permit us to make such a measurement with any degree of confidence or accuracy.

Much of the essence of the foregoing statements concerning our feelings about the advantages of complete survey coverage in our research can be generalized in a single statement: The single most important factor affecting the location of any particular settlement, perhaps especially in more complex societies, is the location of other settlements within the region. This is an aspect of the total environment affecting settlement distribution that cannot be anticipated and controlled for in the same way as can factors like land form and soil type, when an archaeologist is designing a regional survey.

The matter of economic cost is a final consideration in our discussion of survey strategy. This relates particularly to the justification of our decision to do a 100% survey. Our research has certainly not been inexpensive. It has involved about 65 individuals (exclusive of local workmen) over a 15-year period, and we still lack data on some subregions of the Basin of Mexico. Seeing these figures, advocates of a sampling strategy could point to our work as excessively expensive. There are several additional considerations, however. First, it should be noted that we did not survey continuously for 15 years, and very little survey was done at all until 1963, the third year of the Teotihuacan Valley project. With respect to actual survey time, we estimate that all the projects together involved about 50 field months with two to six survey teams, each team with two or three fieldworkers. The total cost was probably in the neighborhood of 500 man-months of time, and less than $200,000 (uncorrected for inflation) for fieldwork costs and some initial analysis. One very major factor in holding down costs was the dedication of a large number of students, who worked very hard for very little money.

Perhaps even more important than these absolute costs, however, is the matter of the utility of archaeological survey data, not only for the immediate needs and objectives of the researchers, but for general anthropology over the long run. A systematic complete survey, if it can be properly published, is analogous to a good site map in terms of long-term utility: It can be used over and over again by different people for new and different purposes that antecedent investigators (including the people who originally made the map or carried out the survey) may not have even considered or thought of. In the introductory chapter we noted some instances of this in terms of our own data. This means that the costs of the complete survey, in terms of dollars per unit of useful information gained, will decrease steadily through time as more and more people make use of the same data for different purposes. It seems to us that a site map or settlement survey done according to a sampling procedure and showing only a partial distribution of features, will have a much more limited use to other investigators whose interests are not identical to those of the original workers. Thus, while the initial costs are lower for such a survey, the long-run price for useful information will actually be higher. We admit that this reasoning did not enter into our own survey strategy. Nevertheless, we hope that by making a point of it here, other archaeologists may be encouraged to do complete surveys in areas where such work is practicable. We readily grant that for regions where prehistoric settlement is badly obscured or where the surface remains of occupation are very subtly expressed, complete surveys are prohibitively expensive and should probably not even be considered until some useful remote-sensing technique becomes available to reduce the high cost of data collection.

Survey Tactics

Survey tactics were developed, largely by means of trial and error, during the 1963 and 1964 fieldseasons. Some additional modifications were made during 1966 and 1967, and again in 1974 and 1975. We do not believe that the changes and modifications affected the resultant data in any significant way, but they did improve the efficiency and consistency of data collecting.

In our initial 1960 season a number of small areas were selected where survey procedures could be tested. Using modern fields, visible on airphotographs, as survey observation units, we attempted a field-by-field survey, in which each modern field was numbered and described. It soon became clear that this approach was extremely time consuming and sometimes involved difficult problems: Some areas were uncultivated and thus

Figure 2.1. No hay nada aquí.

lacked fields, and some fields had shifting and variable borders so that the airphotograph did not correspond very well with the actual on-the-ground situation. By the end of our work in 1960 we had realized that our procedures would have to be changed if we were to be able to complete a survey of the Teotihuacan Valley within our proposed timetable.

In 1961 and 1962 much of our energy was spent on excavation, but we did conduct what we called a "general survey." Here, a small team, seldom consisting of more than two persons, and generally only a single individual, walked quickly over the ground surface, making broad traverses along ridges and across low ground, guided by a 1:25,000 airphotograph. Sites encountered during these traverses were plotted on the airphotograph, and dated on the basis of visual inspection of surface pottery in the field. Such traverses were intended to locate most sites and provide an initial impression of a region from which more intensive survey could then proceed at a later date. Since this general survey involved no surface collecting or detailed site description, a lot of ground could be examined. By the end of the 1962 season, our general survey had completely covered the piedmonts of the lower and middle Teotihuacan Valley, and large areas of its alluvial plain.

The excavation projects were reduced substantially in 1963, and the 1963 and 1964 fieldseasons were dedicated primarily to survey. The general survey was continued to include the rugged Patlachique range, along the southern edge of the Teotihuacan Valley, and part of the unexamined upper valley. Simultaneously a new phase of intensive survey of the sites previously located by the general survey was initiated. The intensive survey was intended to provide detailed descriptions and systematic surface collections from these sites for which, up to then, we had little information apart from mere location. Originally we did not see the intensive survey as an important way of locating new sites, although we expected that some new sites would be found in the course of such work. The basic procedure was to go out to a specific, located site in teams of two people (one archaeologist and one workman). The site's architectural features and areas of substantial artifact concentration were plotted on 1:5000 airphotographs. For each site a descriptive report was prepared in the field that included data on the natural environment, contemporary land use, and the archaeological remains (see Appendix A). Since few of the project personnel knew the complete ceramic chronology well, several survey teams were formed and each team was assigned responsibility for sites of a particular period. One archaeologist led the team that was to survey all Formative-period sites; two archaeologists surveyed all the Classic-period sites; one worked with the Toltec-period sites; and three surveyed the Aztec-period sites. In the cases of multicomponent sites, the same locations were examined as many as three times, once by each appropriate team. The local workmen acted mainly to make and carry the surface collections.

As we worked along through the 1963 season, it became more and more obvious that our survey methodology was not working too well. There were three main problems. First, the survey teams were too small to make and transport efficiently the numbers of surface pottery collections that had to be made on most days. For example, Parsons vividly recalls a hot, dusty afternoon in mid July, 1963, when Charles Kolb, one of the project's more resourceful fieldworkers, staggered up to a previously arranged meeting place with eight bulging cloth bags of pottery tied and draped imaginatively over his body. These collections had accumulated inexorably through the day over a distance of many kilometers. This was not a procedure we cared to repeat very often, but our only alternatives were to slow down our work or make fewer collections, neither of which seemed particularly desirable.

Our second major problem was in locating the sites plotted on the general survey maps. These maps were 1:25,000 airphotographs on which it was easy to make locational errors, especially in rugged terrain. When different people later tried to find these sites again, it was sometimes hard to relocate the precise spot on the ground, particularly if any significant error had been made in its original placement on the 1:25,000 airphotograph. On the very first day of the 1963 intensive survey, Sanders returned late in the afternoon to report that he had been unable to locate the site he had intended to examine despite 6 or 7 hours of careful searching over an eroded hillslope. This is an extreme example, but comparable experiences were not infrequent.

A third problem, more serious yet, was our discovery that many sites had not been found during the earlier general survey, and that some occupational components on multicomponent sites had not been recognized. Looking back, this is not at all surprising given the large distances between survey traverses and the rapid appraisal of site chronology that we had used in the general survey. After several weeks of intensive survey in 1963 we had located such a large number of previously unrecorded sites that our operating procedures were getting rather bogged down as these new sites had to be recorded and arrangements made for their resurvey.

Working with extremely dispersed rural Aztec-period settlements during 1963 and, especially, 1964, Sanders and Parsons began to improvise some different survey procedures. This involved the use of 1:5000 airphotographs to guide systematic walking over the ground surface, making survey tranverses at much closer intervals than for the earlier general surveys. Since teams were still composed of only a single archaeologist, this was a tedious procedure, although it did permit us to locate and describe more effectively all the prehispanic occupation within a region.

By 1967, as Parsons' survey in the Texcoco region got underway, survey methodology had been redesigned to a point where everyone concerned was reasonably satisfied. From this point on there were only minor modifications in the technique. It was of considerable significance to our survey that by the mid 1960s the ceramic chronology for the Teotihuacan Valley was fairly well understood, and, with minor modifications, was seen to be applicable to the Basin of Mexico as a whole. Parsons' first change from the older survey procedure was to eliminate the general survey completely and proceed directly to the intensive survey. He organized the survey in teams of two to four archaeologists (which included at least one person familiar with survey procedures and the complete ceramic chronology) and one Mexican workman. He found that a team of three archaeologists and one worker was ideal in terms of coordinating movements in the field, examining a reasonable amount of terrain in a reasonable length of time, and providing enough people to properly collect and carry around a day's worth of surface pottery collections.

Each team walked in tandem across a section of terrain, with movements directed by one member who carried a 1:5000 airphotograph, about 50 cm on a side, mounted on a plywood board. This individual, the "centerman," walked at the center of the moving line of surveyors. The centerman received a fairly continuous flow of verbal comments from his team members on either side who called over information on the density and chronology of surface pottery (or the lack of it) in their pathways. All this information, together with what the centerman observed in his own pathway, was recorded, in a simple code, directly onto the airphotograph in its proper location. Although we had earlier made some attempt to quantify precisely the differential density of surface pottery by counting sherds within selected 1-m squares, this procedure was soon abandoned as unproductive. Instead, we relied on a subjective visual approximation of sherd density which proved reasonably effective and quite rapid when properly used. The team as

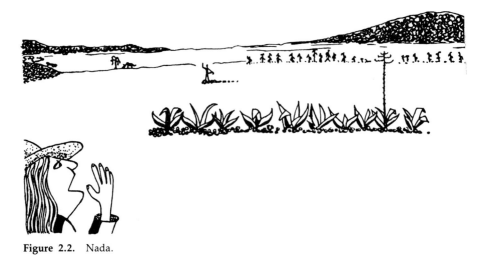

Figure 2.2. Nada.

a whole moved at the pace of the slowest individual, and personnel were responsible for adjusting their direction and speed so as to maintain a proper distance from the centerman. After some experimentation with the spacing between surveyors, it appeared best not to insist on a rigid interval, but to vary distance between individuals according to common sense considerations of topography, drainage, vegetation, modern occupation, complexity of prehispanic occupation, and wind strength (in a strong wind it becomes quite difficult to communicate by voice with team members more than about 25 m away). Such intervals were seldom more than about 75 m, normally were about 40–50 m, and occasionally were as little as 15–20.

When it became apparent, on the basis of surface remains, that the team was getting into an archaeological site, the forward movement slowed considerably as artifacts were inspected and decisions made about chronology and occupational complexity. If it was clear that a site had been encountered, the centerman made a decision about when and where to stop and make a surface collection. When such a decision was made, the centerman told everybody to stop, and the team gathered together at the designated spot. The worker and two team members proceeded to make the surface collection over a designated area (see the following), while the third archaeologist made notes on the locale's soil depth, modern land use, and archaeological remains. A photographic record was also made.

Unless the site was obviously fairly small and simple, there was usually no attempt to define site limits in the field. Rather, when collection and note taking had been completed, the team members returned to their original places and the survey traverse continued as before (although commonly the spacing between surveyors might be reduced significantly if the occupation was complex). If the site continued for any significant distance, or if the occupation became obviously more complex or more questionable, another stop would be made and additional surface collecting and note taking done.

58494

Figure 2.3. Lost.

The only sites not sampled in this fashion were those very abundant locations where occupation was obviously restricted to the last major phase (Late Aztec) whose ceramic traits were so well defined that a simple visual inspection usually sufficed to make accurate chronological inferences. Each team was responsible for evaluating all time periods within the region assigned to it, and there was no chronological division of labor as there had been in earlier years.

Once the survey had been completed for two or three adjacent airphotographs, survey data were traced from these photographs onto a large roll of paper. After the tracing was made, we defined sites and prepared descriptive site reports from our field notes and photographs. Occasionally we noted that for some sites there had been inadequate sampling or imprecise definition. In such cases an additional field check would be required, and we did these checks when convenient throughout the season.

When carried out by experienced people, this general survey method permitted us to cover large areas fairly rapidly, with good accuracy and consistency. It was employed by all of us from 1967 through 1975. In his Cuautitlan–Tenayuca–Temascalapa surveys in 1974 and 1975, Sanders introduced a few modifications to provide better ecological controls. Here, each agricultural field was numbered and a field survey schedule (see Appendix B) designed to record natural environmental features, contemporary land use, and some minimal archaeological observations, such as density of artifact debris, presence of mounds, and occupational chronology. These data were

Figure 2.4. I got a mound.

recorded, for each field, by one member of the survey team, while another recorded archaeological data onto the airphotograph. From these data, sites were subsequently defined and descriptive site reports prepared. In many cases site reports were completed during revisits to the site so as to have first-hand observations at the time of writing.

A very major aspect of field tactics in any regional survey has to do with how the archaeologists cope with the modern inhabitants of their survey area. This is seldom discussed in published reports, but we feel that a few comments here might be appropriate and even illuminating. The Basin of Mexico is one of modern Mexico's most densely populated areas. We encountered people almost everywhere we walked, and, in some cases, we almost literally had to go through backyards of *campesino* households. We had authorization documents from the Instituto Nacional de Antropologia e Historia in Mexico City, and we generally made the additional effort to obtain comparable letters from the office of each municipal president. However, we simply lacked time to talk with each of the innumerable small landowners and tenants before going onto their land. This meant, of course, that we often arrived, unannounced and totally unexpected, in fields where people were going about their normal cultivation activities.

Looking back on it all, we were amazed and much impressed with the equanimity and goodwill with which we were received by most of the people we encountered in this fashion over the years. The vast majority of them undoubtedly took us for harmless lunatics, but were usually courteous and cooperative in granting us access to their lands. Very rarely we were accosted by suspicious and belligerent people. Much more often we encountered politely curious people, who wondered what we were doing, and even volunteered useful information about sites and artifacts once they found out who we were. We can recall invitations to share food and drink, offered spontaneously by truly hospitable people, with few material possessions, who worked incredibly hard for a meager leaving. Some of our most vivid and lasting impressions of rural Mexican people and society were formed during those years. We retain a lot of good memories that vastly outweigh the bad ones.

If our relationships with people were generally quite good, our relationships with their numerous and omnipresent dogs often were not. While it was true, as Kent Flannery once put it, that some Mexican dogs "are so weak that they have to lean against a fence to bark," many dogs were also in much better shape. Since we usually encountered dogs several minutes before we met their human owners, we had many, many tense moments filled with vicious snarling and barking (canine in origin), flying rocks and thudding sticks (human in origin) as we intruded across many hundreds of canine territorial borders. By some miracle, only one person was ever bitten, and this occurred when he stepped onto a sleeping dog hidden in a deep plow furrow.

We will conclude this section with a discussion about our approach to surface collecting. Among other things, our research strategy called for reasonable ways of inferring (a) the chronological placement of settlements, (b) the distribution of specialized activities, and (c) the distribution of higher and lower status. These objectives required making systematic surface collections of ceramic and lithic artifacts from all sites. Visual inspection of the ground surface in the field was adequate for making general inferences about site chronology (subject to later revision) and perhaps for some initial impressions about status and function. But, any real understanding of these matters clearly demanded a more refined artifact analysis. Logistical considerations made it impossible to take large numbers of surface collections from most sites. Because we had only a few survey vehicles (and indeed, lacked any vehicle for much of the 1964 season when our survey was facilitated by local bus and taxi service), and because most of our survey was carried out far from any drivable roadways anyway, collections would almost always have to be hand carried throughout the day. Because the survey teams could seldom include more than three or four people, one of whom had to manipulate a large airphotograph almost constantly, the "carrying capacity" of any one team was quite limited. Because of the difficulty involved in getting to some sites, few sites could be readily revisited to make additional collections. Furthermore, surface collecting was a very time consuming activity, and it took little foresight to realize that we would have to restrict it rather severely in order to cover enough terrain to make our work worthwhile.

In other words, we had to compromise continually between the conflicting demands of (a) understanding the variability of artifact distribution within and between sites, and (b) understanding the regional spatial configuration of contemporary settlements. As work went on, we came to realize more and more clearly that the second category of demands weighed more heavily upon us than the first. Soon we understood that the most we could reasonably expect to accomplish with respect to artifact analysis was to establish settlement chronology. And, it took only a little longer to realize

Figure 2.5. Surface collecting.

that what we were actually doing in the Basin of Mexico was an initial stage of the long-term research program that would be necessary to achieve our general objectives. Once this was clear in our minds, the tactics of surface collecting were simplified. All we had to do was to deal with settlement chronology in terms of our general phases of 200–300 years in length. We could then focus on ceramics, and leave aside any systematic treatment of lithics. Our need to infer general settlement chronology could be realized in a much less rigorous way than could inferences about status and function.

In keeping with all these varied considerations, a fairly standardized system of surface collecting use developed, which has served reasonably well over the years. Once again, it was a flexible procedure, in which different kinds of occupation could be handled somewhat differently. From each collection we needed a large enough sample for analysis, but since this sample often had to be hand carried for some considerable distance in the field, it also had to be small enough to be readily transportable. We found that a strong cloth bag, about 40 cm long and 25 cm wide, about two-thirds full of sherds, would serve the purpose pretty well. On the average, such a bag would contain about 60 and 120 sherds. A procedure had to be devised whereby an adequate number of representative collections of 60–120 diagnostic sherds could be taken and carried away from enough places within a site, such that the site could be properly defined on our map.

It was easy enough to define the size of a collection area: Where sherd cover was relatively greater, a small area was marked off, and all diagnostic sherds collected from within it. Where sherd cover was relatively lower, a larger area would be similarly defined and collected. A modal collection area might be about 10 to 20 m². A few collections were made in an area as small as 1 or 2 on a side. A fairly large number of collections were made from areas between 50 and 100 on a side. A typical surface collection might occupy two or three people for a period of about 20–40 minutes.

Decisions about the frequency and placement of such collections were much more complex matters. We had problems in making these decisions because we generally had no good idea about site extent or complexity when we were on the ground within an undefined site (as we were most of the time). We thought for awhile that the first step we should take would be to define the site borders. This was easily done when the site was small and simple, but very difficult to do if the site was large, with multicomponent occupation (in which each occupational component would have to be defined separately as a site). These latter kinds of sites often wandered around in irregular and unpredictable ways over such large areas that they extended off the airphotograph onto adjacent photographs that had not been brought with us into the field that day. Because we often did not know what kind of a site we were in until we had defined it on the traced map several days later, we sometimes made poor decisions about the placement and frequency of surface collections. Where structures were numerous, we tended to select most of our samples on and around these architectural remains. Our expectation was that by doing this we would have better control over the population history of the site. It remains to be seen whether this expectation is a reasonable one.

Occasionally, when a site had been defined on a map, we found that we had neglected to sample some sizable sector of it. In such a case, we either revisited the site for additional collections, or ignored the deficiency and hoped for the best. Although about 70 surface collections were made on one large site, very few of our largest sites had more than 6 to 8 surface collections, and for most of the smaller ones 1 or 2 collections were taken. As mentioned earlier, only a fraction of the numerous single-component Aztec-period sites were collected. This was done to increase the speed of our survey since we felt that Late Aztec chronology could be adequately controlled by visual inspection while walking over the ground surface.

One additional problem is presented by the nature of the surface collections: There is an inherent sampling bias in all of them. This is because a rigorous, statistically valid method of collecting sherds was not designed. Rather, we collected what previous studies of excavated materials had shown to be chronologically diagnostic items: all rims, decorated body sherds, supports, handles, and basal angles. Such a sampling bias would probably not affect chronological assessment of a site as long as the chronology consisted of periods of 200–300 years duration. It would probably become a serious problem if one attempted to phase the sites on a more refined time scale.

ADJUNCT STRATEGIES

A number of strategies of a nonarchaeological nature were utilized throughout the various projects, to provide a series of analogues for the interpretation of the archaeological data. One of these concerned studies of contemporary ecology. They were initiated by Sanders as early as 1953 with his studies of the chinampas of Tlahuac and Atlapulco, followed by preliminary studies of the Teotihuacan Valley in 1955 (Sanders 1956).

This latter study was considerably expanded by Charlton in 1963, when he worked with the Teotihuacan Valley project (Charlton 1970b). Sanders did a comparable study of the Texcoco region in 1972. Angel Palerm, an ethnohistorian and cultural anthropologist, has been engaged in a much broader program of anthropological research in the Texcoco region, since the mid 1960s. A major result of these projects has been to provide ecological models for our analysis of the prehispanic periods. Although we recognize the fact that peasant technology has changed since 1519, that some changes have occurred in the natural environment, and that important feedback effects on peasant ecology have developed as the superstructure of Mexican society has changed, these studies have nevertheless been exceedingly useful.

Ethnohistoric data have been assembled by each of the specific survey projects for their particular region. These data have been invaluable for the interpretation of the Aztec settlement system, but the data have also been of considerable value in the interpretation of the settlement system of the pre-Aztec periods as well.

Finally, since a major objective was the study of agricultural adaptation to the Basin over a period of 3000 years we need to know something about changes in the natural habitat over this long period of time. With this objective in mind, Anton Kovar, a plant ecologist from Pennsylvania State University, initiated a series of palynological studies in 1963. Aside from providing control on the climatic history of the Basin we hoped that these studies would provide us with insights as to man-induced changes in the habitat.

RELATED PROJECTS

Since the 1960 meeting an enormous mass of new information on the Basin of Mexico and nearby regions in the Central Plateau has become available through the efforts of a great number of researchers, and many of the results of this research are incorporated in this study. Three of these projects involved settlement surveys within the Basin, very similar to our own. For example, Harold McBride in 1968 excavated a Late-Terminal Formative period site at Cuautitlan and conducted settlement surveys in the Cuautitlan region, based on the methodology described by Parsons in his Texcoco monograph (McBride 1974).

McBride used a sampling strategy in his survey, and Sanders, in his 1974 season, reexamined McBride's sites and surveyed the remainder of the region. In 1974, and again in 1975, Alexander, working in conjunction with the ethnohistorian Angel Palerm, was engaged in intensive survey and excavations to test the hypothesis that the Colonial dike that separated Lakes Xaltocan and Texcoco was built over an older Aztec dike. In the process he has surveyed large sections of the bed of Lake Xaltocan and the west piedmont of Cerro Chiconauhtla. Unfortunately, these data are not available for inclusion in our maps.

Between 1965 and 1967, Pedro Armillas completed an intensive survey, accompanied by excavation, of the lakebeds of Chalco–Xochimilco to collect data on the history of chinampa agriculture (Armillas, 1971). His survey has located a number of nucleated Aztec villages on islands in the lake, and great numbers of house sites dispersed throughout the lakebed, in association with fossil chinampas. More recently he has been engaged in an intensive study of the northern lakes and their utilization for chinampa agriculture.

Along with these regional surveys there have been a number of intensive surveys, combined with excavations, of the two large urban centers of Teotihuacan (Millon 1967a, 1967b, 1970, 1976; Millon et al. 1973) and Tula (Diehl 1974, and Matos, 1974, 1976, in two separate but closely related projects). Calnek has completed a study of ethnohistoric documents that will enable him to reconstruct the settlement pattern of Aztec Tenochtitlan in considerable detail (1970, 1972, 1973, 1976). These various projects have provided a mass of excellent and valuable data without which it would be impossible to understand the results of the regional surveys.

Finally, we now have abundant data from regional surveys in those areas around the Basin of Mexico that were considered by Sanders as parts of the Nuclear Area. These include a survey of a 1000-km² region around Tula by Mastache and Crespo (1974), a region that directly adjoins Parsons' Zumpango region; surveys of Tlaxcala and western Puebla, primarily directed by Garcia Cook (Abascal et al. 1976; Garcia Cook 1972, 1973, 1974; and Snow 1969) and a survey of a 500-km² area around Chalcatzingo, in Morelos, by Hirth (1974), working with David Grove's Chalcatzingo project. Hirth has returned to Morelos and is presently conducting surveys around Xochicalco.

Besides these various settlement survey projects there have been a number of research projects in the Basin of Mexico that have produced data useful to our objectives here. These include Paul Tolstoy's excavations of Formative Period sites to refine and amend the early portion of the ceramic sequence (Tolstoy and Paradis 1970; Tolstoy and Fish 1975; Tolstoy n.d.); excavations at Cuicuilco by Muller; excavations at Tlapacoya by various

Mexican archaeologists, under the direction of Lorenzo (Niederberger, 1976); excavations by Santley (1977) and Rosa Reyna at the Late Formative site of Loma Torremote, near Cuautitlan; excavations by Manzanilla and Frangipani, at the Late Formative site of Cuanalan; excavations at the Terminal Formative site of Temesco, by Dixon, and finally, the massive excavations and reconstructions at the site of Teotihuacan, by virtually the entire staff of the Instituto Nacional de Antropologia e Historia (I.N.A.H.), under the direction of Ignacio Bernal (Acosta, 1964; Bernal 1963).

   In 1975, under the direction of Eduardo Matos, a program of salvage archaeology of the Basin was initiated and the first season included excavations at an Aztec chinampa village in Lake Xochimilco; at the multicomponent site of Cerro de La Cruz, Ecatepec; at Azcapotzalco; at a Early Toltec site, on the west flank of the Cerro de la Estrella. The Instituto de Estudios Antropologicos at the Universidad Nacional Autonoma de México (U.N.A.M.), under the direction of Litvak King, is involved in extensive excavations in Formative Period sites in Lakes Chalco and Xochimilco. Finally, in 1977, the Departamento de Salvamiento of the I.N.A.H. conducted excavations with Tenochtitlan in the contemporary barrio of Tepito and in a small Teotihuacan village near Coyoacan.

3
The Settlement Pattern Maps

One of our most formidable tasks was the transformation of raw survey data into a series of finished regional settlement pattern maps for each time period. Until this transformation could be carried out, our impressions of patterns and trends remained on a subjective and tentative level. As the years went by, and more surveyed areas and sites had to be incorporated into the ever-expanding general maps, this process of map making became increasingly complicated and time-consuming. A particularly critical problem has been the maintenance of continuity and comparability over a dozen years and between three principal investigators. Even at the time of this writing, our map-making procedures have not been fully developed to our own satisfaction. Nevertheless, the settlement pattern maps have been one of our basic means for illuminating processes of ecological adaptation and sociopolitical evolution. It thus seems especially desirable that we inform the reader about the procedures we have used to go from concentrations of surface debris to the maps that accompany this volume. We will try to do this in the present chapter.

Aside from the relatively straightforward matters of placing prehistoric settlements in time and delineating them in space, we also have had to cope with the more complex problems of inferring which sites were to be considered as similar or different with respect to their *general* roles within prehistoric settlement systems. That is, we had to develop a settlement typology that, on the one hand, would not exceed the limitations of our survey, but which, on the other, would facilitate the organization and analysis of our large body of data. In developing such a typology we wanted most of all to be able "to delineate areas of occupation on the ground which correspond to prehistoric social communities [Parsons 1971:21]."

From the very outset of the survey, we tried to explicitly conceptualize what our basic analytical "artifact" should be. This "artifact" was the *site*, for our purposes defined as:

> any localized area that shows signs of alteration by man as observable by archaeological method. This would include anything from an isolated house . . . or ceremonial structure, dams, canals, terrace systems, to a city of 100,000 inhabitants. The important point is that a site is "a spatially isolatable unit." A spatially isolatable unit should have some cultural significance to the prehistoric population and not be simply an archaeological abstraction if such units are to be used conveniently in settlement pattern analysis [Sanders 1965:12–13].

In the following sections of this chapter we will discuss how we isolated archaeological features that could be labeled *sites*, and how we went from *site* to *community* or *unit of cultural significance to the prehispanic population*. We had real problems in all procedures. A principal cause of our difficulty was our lack of a completely sound conceptual basis for making critical assumptions about the sociological meaning of site size, architectural complexity, and artifact density. Two problems were particularly severe: measuring relative occupational intensity at multicomponent sites, and estimating the absolute population of settlements. Both these matters will receive special consideration in the following pages.

Because population size became such a key attribute in our site classification, we will begin with a discussion of the procedures we used to estimate population from archaeological remains. This will be followed by a general discussion of the settlement typology we developed and used, and a consideration of the specific limitations of the survey. The chapter will end with a brief comment on how we prepared our base maps upon which sites have been plotted.

RECONSTRUCTION OF
PREHISTORIC POPULATIONS

A major methodological problem is the reconstruction of the demographic characteristics of a prehistoric population. Since much evolutionary theory in anthropology assumes that population pressure was a causal factor, this is more than an academic question. It is our contention that given not necessarily ideal, but at least reasonably good site conditions, and proper *excavation* strategies and techniques, archaeologists can provide almost as much data on the demographic characteristics of a prehistoric population as the ethnographer can for a contemporary one. In the final part of this section we present a case example illustrating the method and compare the results with the method used in reconstructing sites populations from the regional survey data alone.

At this point several questions arise. Why attempt to estimate absolute prehistoric populations, since it is so complex and uncertain a procedure, using archaeological surface remains alone? Why not just compare settlement area, which can be fairly readily and objectively measured, as several archaeologists working in the Middle East have done (e.g., Adams 1965; Wright and Johnson 1975). Would not this provide a more meaningful index of demographic intensity? To these very justifiable questions, we would answer as follows. First, we regard all our estimates as provisional and tentative. Second, an estimate of absolute population is very interesting and useful for its own sake. This is particularly the case where others might want to make use of our demographic data for their own purposes (e.g., for cross-cultural comparisons). Since it is very likely that we possess good insights into deriving absolute population from our survey data, it is probably better, if such absolute estimates are to be made at all, that we make them, rather than others who are less familiar with the material. Third, as will be further discussed later, we believe we have a good basis for making reasonable estimates of absolute population from archaeological remains. Fourth, in our survey work we soon became convinced that simple site surface area could not be used directly as a measure of even relative occupational intensity, unless it were somehow modified to account for the great variability we often observed in the density of surface remains within the borders of different sites. We will argue later that such variability, in most cases, relates directly to the number of people living at a site. Our estimates of absolute population are, in essence, attempts to modify site area so that we can make direct comparisons between sites of different occupational density.

The methodology used in the calculation of the population of the survey regions in the Basin of Mexico is on the one hand complex, but on the other hand simple. It has sometimes been misunderstood by our colleagues. In part this is our own fault for not making it more explicit, but it is also because reviewers have not examined the complete set of published monographs on the surveys; most particularly they have not read Sanders' original formulation of the method (Sanders, 1965). We will therefore present a detailed discussion of the method step by step.

First, the basic control for archaeological estimates is population data from the post-Conquest sixteenth-century civil tax censuses and ecclesiastic documents (see Borah and Cook 1963). Sanders has published a detailed discussion of this data (Sanders 1966a, 1970c, 1976) and we will briefly summarize the results of the analysis here. From A.D. 1560 to 1610 taxes were exacted at a uniform rate of one-half peso per year per taxpayer. Taxpayers included married males, married females (actually in these two cases the married couple was taxed one peso), unmarried men over 14 years of age, unmarried women over 10 years of age, widowers, and widows. Censuses were made in most cases of taxpayers only (in actuality, of taxes collected, in terms of number of pesos), so we are faced with the problem of estimating total population from this element in the population. Fortunately, however, there are enough censuses of total populations of communities to enable one to make reasonably good extrapolations to large regions. During the period from A.D. 1560 to 1600 frequent censuses were taken and constant attempts made to verify them. Furthermore, the civil censuses had a different purpose than the ecclesiastic censuses and hence one can be used as verification for the other. On the basis of these censuses one could establish a history of population from A.D. 1560 to 1610, and it reflects a marked decline.

On the basis of a multiplicity of qualitative statements it is clear that the entire period from A.D. 1519 to 1610 was one of population decline. Prior to 1560, when the private encomienda system was at its peak, there was no consistent head tax, and hence it is very difficult to calculate ratios between taxpayers and amount of tax collected: thus, it is virtually impossible to relate tax amounts to population. There are, fortunately, a number of surveys of the population of selected regions or communities, some with complete census data, that were taken during this period, and these can be used as control points to estimate the amount of decline between A.D. 1519 to 1560. On the basis of these data, Sanders reconstructed several alternate curves of population decline from A.D. 1519 to 1610. The most conservative estimate from the 1519 population must be considered as an absolute minimum, considering the nature of legal disputes, and qualitative statements about population decline that literally fill the national archives.

The 1560 population of the central plateau is very close to the rural population between A.D. 1900 and 1940 for the same region. After 1940, urbanization at major population foci, such as metropolitan Mexico City, Puebla, and Cuernavaca, make it difficult to establish the degree of ruralness of even people living in nearby villages. The bulk of the villagers between 1900 and 1940 did derive most of their income from agriculture and most of the argiculture involved the production of staple crops. Our estimate of absolute carrying capacity of the Basin of Mexico, based on a study of contemporary practices and productivity, and correcting for changes in both parameters, is very close to our estimates of the population of the same area in 1519, based on the documentary sources. What these figures clearly indicate is that our estimates from documentary sources are reasonable.

The next step was to divide up the history of the Basin into time units of comparable length and calculate the total residential areas of all of the sites occupied during each block of time. The results would provide a set of ratios between each of the earlier phases and the Aztec period, on the basis of which we might be able to calculate the earlier populations as a particular fraction of our population figures for the Conquest. For example, if in a given survey area there were a dozen Aztec-period sites, whose residential areas totaled 100 ha, and a single Middle Formative site that occupied 5 ha, then we might estimate the Middle Formative population at one-twentieth the size of the Aztec.

However, in making these estimates we were immediately confronted with the problem that in cases where surface domestic architecture was preserved, the density of such remains varied considerably, suggesting a great range of population density from site to site. Numerous Aztec-period sites had fairly well preserved surface architecture, and showed a range of 1 or 2 houses up to 20 per hectare. We also noted in those same sites that artifact densities were closely related to house densities. This was a significant fact because in many sites architectural remains were not preserved, and in these sites the surface densities of sherds and other artifacts showed a comparable range. The implication was clear: Artifact densities on residential sites closely reflected house densities. The problem then was to establish a relative scale based both on houses and artifact densities and then to convert this relative scale to population densities. One could of course use the standard archaeological procedures of applying some mean family size to each house in those sites with preserved architecture, multiply this by the number of houses in the site, and then extrapolate these figures for sites without architecture—a procedure which in fact we did apply. This is of course always the problem of contemporaneity of houses and of the validity of our use of postulated average family size. We needed an additional approach to verify this method.

A clue was provided by Sanders' 1954 studies of contemporary settlement patterns in the Basin of Mexico, a study that was amplified by Diehl (1970) and Charlton (1970a) during the Teotihuacan Valley project. These studies revealed a comparable range in residential density among contemporary rural settlements from 4 to 24 houses per hectare or, in terms of population, from 20–130 people per hectare or 200–13,000 per square kilometer. Although the range was, in fact, a continuous one, the villages from the Teotihuacan Valley seemed to group into a series of modes. One group clustered at 4000–5000 per square kilometer, another at 1250–2500 per square kilometer, at 500–800 per square kilometer, and finally a few at 200 per square kilometer. Chinampa villages in the southern part of the Basin of Mexico tended to cluster at 7000–10,000 per square kilometer, with a few cases as high as 13,000 per kilometer.

In his studies Charlton demonstrated a relationship between settlement density, household size, and land tenure, suggesting that these ranges were of considerable significance. His studies also showed a relationship to the productivity of the general area in which the community was located (which in turn related to land tenure) and showed two different growth patterns. On the one hand, for those communities with lower population densities, as the village expanded in size, it expanded in area. On the other hand, in those cases where the settlement densities were high, population increases produced an increase in density. The various modes were classified into a series of community types including rancherias (density below 500 per square kilometer), scattered villages (500–1000 per square kilometer), compact low-density villages (1000–2500 per square kilometer), and high-density compact villages (2500–5000). The chinampa villages were judged to be special cases and not included in the typology.

These various sets of data were applied to a number of test areas in the 1965 preliminary report of the Teotihuacan Valley project. A number of areas of heavy Aztec period settlement were selected, population estimates made on the basis of house mound counts and on the basis of refuse densities. An estimate was made, on the basis of the modern community typology, and a comparison of these results with the archaeological estimates, and with the ethnohistoric estimates from the tax data, indicated a discrepancy of no more than 20–30%. Although we did not conduct an organized and explicit test, we did note frequently in our field notes data on modern refuse densities when our archaeological survey was conducted within the contemporary village, and these data indicate a very close correlation between modern refuse density and house densities.

In later publications on the Basin of Mexico surveys, by Parsons and Blanton, the method was reduced to calculations of people from the surface density of artifacts alone, but in a number of cases these estimates were again checked against sites with preserved architecture. Recently Sanders has compared his estimates of regional population, based on the sixteenth-century tax data, with those by Parsons and Blanton, based on archaeological calculations for those same regions for the Aztec period, and the comparisons indicate that the minimal estimates from the ethnohistoric data are approximately 20% higher than the maximal estimates from the archaeological data. Considering the nature of the survey procedures, and the great number of factors that affect site occupational densities and site preservation, this is a remarkable level of agreement.

In summary, the most direct way of estimating population of archaeological sites is to multiply the number of house mounds (i.e., family residences) by some derived figure of mean family size. Indeed, for the few sites where preservation of domestic architecture is reasonably good, we have applied this method. However, in most cases, both because of ancient and modern disturbances, surface architecture has been obliterated, so that all that remained are concentrations of surface pottery and, sometimes, rock rubble. In these instances the amount of surface scatter has been recorded using the following rank scale of estimation, adapted from Parsons' (1971) Texcoco survey.

Absent.   No surface pottery visible.

Scanty.   A wide scattering of surface debris so that only one or two sherds may be present every few meters.

Scanty-to-light.   A wide scattering throughout most of the occupational area, but with a few localized concentrations where sherds are visible at intervals of 20–30 cm.

Light-to-scanty.   Over much of the area sherds occur every 20–30 cm. Zones of scanty occupation appear intermittently.

Light. A continuous distribution of sherds every 20–30 cm, but with no significant buildup in sherd density beyond that point.

Light-to-moderate. Although most of the area contains light surface remains, delimited areas of substantial buildup containing as many as 100–200 sherds per square meter consistently appear.

Moderate. A continuous layer of sherds, so that any randomly placed 1-m square might yield 100–200 pieces of surface pottery.

Moderate-to-heavy. Over most of the area occupation occurs in moderate densities, however, in a few localized areas a 1-m square might contain 200–400 pieces of surface pottery.

Heavy. Densities of 200–400 sherds per 1-m square are continuous. At some sites sherds are literally one atop another, so that a randomly placed 1-m squared might produce as many as 400–800 pieces of pottery.

In transforming these estimates of surface occupation into demographic figures we have assumed that the correspondences between refuse density and population, observable both in rural villages today and at Aztec period sites, were applicable to pre-Aztec communities as well.

Scanty-to-light occupation. Typical of the "compact rancheria" settlement type. Population numbers 200–500 persons per square kilometer (2–5 persons per hectare).

Light-to-scanty or light occupation. Equivalent to the "scattered village" settlement type. Population levels characteristically run about 500–1000 persons per square kilometer (5–10 persons per hectare).

Light-to-moderate occupation. Closely resembling the "compact low-density village" settlement type. Population densities are typically about 1000–2500 persons per square kilometer (10–25 persons per hectare).

Moderate occupation. Associated with the "compact high-density village" settlement type. Population densities are generally 2500–5000 persons per square kilometer (25–50 persons per hectare).

Moderate-to-heavy or heavy occupation. Typical of the upper range in population density found in the compact high-density village settlement type. Modal population density is about 5000–10,000 persons per square kilometer (50–100 persons per hectare).

We would be the first to admit that the population estimation procedure we have just outlined has its limitations and should not be used without a certain flexibility and skepticism. Perhaps the most serious problem is that of estimating sherd densities for any particular phase, in a multicomponent site occupied during several archaeological phases. This is such a critical matter that it will be discussed at some length later. Furthermore, we emphasize that our appraisals of sherd density, both prehistoric and modern, are based upon subjective visual inspection of the ground surface. A brief attempt early in the survey to quantify these visual impressions was soon abandoned, after we realized that meaningful results would demand a huge outlay of time and energy. Our estimates have remained subjective, and thus subject to an inherent inconsistency, as different fieldworkers have somewhat different impressions about sherd densities. Since we made only very casual observations of the concentration and distribution of modern refuse, our equations of sherd density and population density remains the weakest link in our reasoning. A series of other problems (e.g., differential treatment of the ground surface by modern cultivators, differential erosion and alluviation, the possibility of temporary or seasonal occupations, and the inability to demonstrate full contemporaneity within and between sites of the same time period) also have a potentially serious effect on our ability to estimate sherd density for any given slice of time, and thus upon our ability to estimate population density. These and other matters will be addressed in our discussion of survey limitations. However, despite all these undeniable problems, we still feel that our population figures are reliable in a relative sense. And, as the following discussion will suggest, there is reason to believe that they may be valid in an absolute sense as well.

The reader is directed to Figures 3.1–3.5 to obtain a clearer picture of how our field observations were translated into map form.

The Loma Torremote Test Case

In the introduction to this discussion of population reconstruction we stated that under ideal site conditions, and using proper excavation procedures, a very accurate estimate of population can be derived by archaeological methods. The conditions at the Late Formative Loma Torremote site near Cuautitlan were almost ideal. Our excavations here in 1974 showed that the prehistoric population lived in walled house compounds, within which were houses, a patio and a garden area; they had the custom of burying their dead (all ages and both sexes) within the house compound; they rebuilt the house floor every 15–20 years, and they stored their food in underground storage pits that were abandoned after short periods of use. By extensive lateral excavations we were able to associate seven, sometimes eight, stratigraphic levels of house floors, patio floors, burials, refuse deposits, and storage pits, over a total time span of no more than 100 years, in three adjacent house compounds.

In this discussion we will first attempt to reconstruct household sizes for each of the levels of a house compound from the burial data. These calculations will then be compared to calculations based on house floor areas, and the two estimates compared to artifact consumption ratios and storage pit usages. In the case of the burial data we will also compare the results to several other Formative sites to amplify our admittedly small sample.

Since the data base comes from excavation, the population estimates so derived may be considered independent of those based on surface occupational density. The method we propose uses the frequency distribution of burials found in association with prehistoric households to calculate popula-

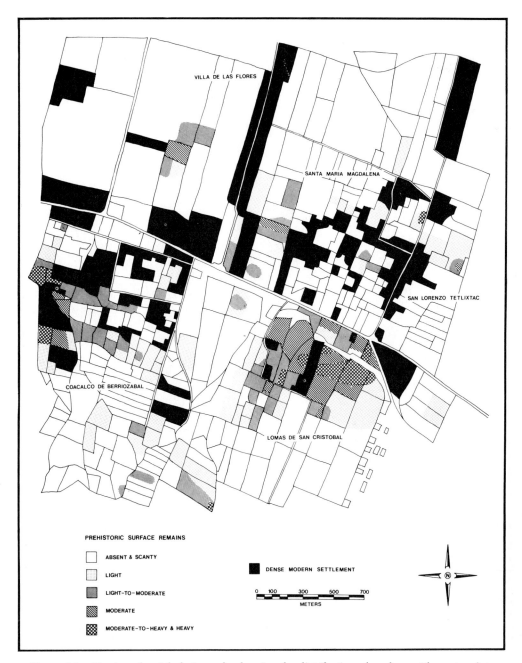

Figure 3.1. Tracing of aerial photograph, showing the distribution of modern settlement and all prehispanic surface remains (Cuautitlan region).

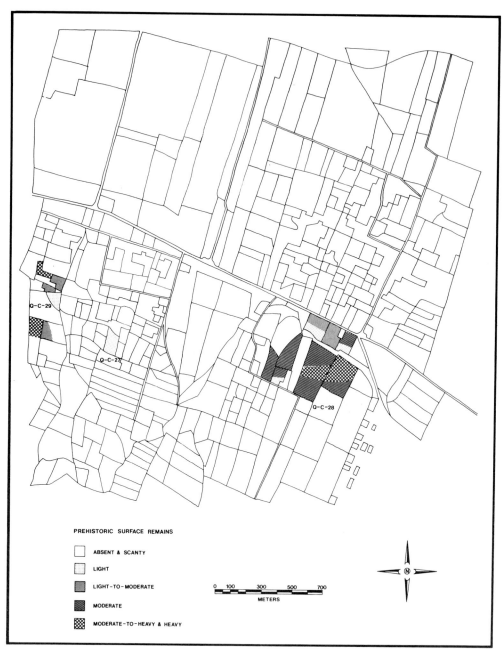

Figure 3.2. Tracing of aerial photograph, showing the distribution of Teotihuacan occupations (Cuautitlan region).

Figure 3.3. Tracing of aerial photograph, showing the distribution of Early Toltec occupations (Cuautitlan region).

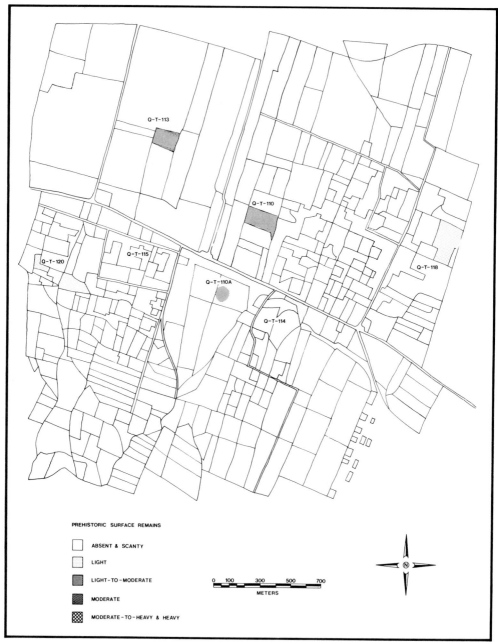

Figure 3.4. Tracing of aerial photograph, showing the distribution of Late Toltec occupations (Cuautitlan region).

Figure 3.5. Tracing of aerial photograph, showing the distribution of Late Aztec occupations (Cuautitlan region).

tion. Our consideration examines four such sites for which there is adequate burial information. The basic tenets of the method are outlined, using data from Loma Torremote—a case where excavations were aimed at determining the distribution of household residential units about the site (Santley 1977). Next, estimates are calculated using the burial data from El Arbolillo, Zacatenco, and Ticoman (Vaillant 1930, 1931, 1935). We conclude by comparing the two independent sets of population calculations.

It is believed that accurate population estimates can be determined when there is excellent control on intrasite household distribution, the frequency distribution of burials, and of such features as storage pits, midden areas, etc., and chronology. The burial data can be used to calculate reliable population figures provided that a Crude Mortality Rate (CMR) can be derived from the skeletal sample.

Demographers have shown that the mortality curve is U-shaped; high in the first year of life; declining rapidly until about age 9; remaining low until middle age; then increasing at a rapid rate during the older years (DeJong 1972:51). The curve of percentage of deaths by age group is also similar. In rural societies, however, the curve climbs to a second peak during middle age and then tapers off since few individuals survive to reach old age. According to the United Nations *Demographic Yearbook* (1967) the CMR today may vary from as low as 5 to as high as 40 persons per 1000 per year. In rural Morelos the CMR is high—about 30 per 1000 per year—with 57% of all deaths occurring by age 5 (Lewis 1951: Table 8). Regrettably, these statistics are for populations that have at least some benefits of modern medical and public health technologies. It would seem, in consequence, that in preindustrial settings (*a*) the CMR was probably quite high, and (*b*) of that total the most substantial portion of all deaths was contributed by the youngest age groups.

To calculate the CMR from the skeletal sample we have used the procedure offered by Ubelaker (1974) and Acsádi and Nemeskéri (1970). This method assumes that within the excavation area the skeletal sample is complete, that the ages at death can be accurately determined, and that the size of the contributing population and their death rates remain constant during the time interval represented by the skeletal sample (Ubelaker 1974:59). The CMR is derived using the skeletal population from El Arbolillo, Zacatenco, and Ticoman (Vaillant 1930, 1931, 1935). These sites are located quite close to one another, have considerable burial populations, and date to the same general period of time (the Formative period). It is assumed, therefore, that the CMR effecting each of these populations is comparable.

To calculate the CMR a 5-year age interval (x) is used. The total number of deaths (Dx) in each group is first summed and then expressed as a percentage of deaths for each age interval (dx). Then:

> The number of survivors at each age interval (lx) is calculated by subtracting the percentage of deaths (dx) in each age interval from the number of survivors entering that interval, beginning with an initial number of 100

survivors. Survivorship values in the life table directly reflect mortality and correspond to the survivorship curves discussed earlier.

Calculations of life expectancy values ($e^{o}x$) necessitate initial determinations of (1) the total number of years (Lx) lived between age interval x and the following interval, and (2) the total number of years (Tx) lived by all survivors of age interval x. The value of Lx is determined by the formula

$$Lx = \frac{5(lx + lo)}{2}$$

where lo is the number of survivors of the age interval following interval x. The factor of 5 is introduced, since the life table is abridged to a 5-year age interval.

The value of Tx is derived from the Lx value by the formula

$$Tx = \text{Sum}_x{}^{w-1} (Lx)$$

The value expresses the total number of years that can be lived by the survivors of each interval. The Tx value has no demographic significance in itself, but is used to calculate life expectancy by the formula

$$e_x{}^o = \frac{Tx}{lx}$$

Consequently life expectancy at birth is computed by the formula

$$e_o{}^o = \frac{To}{lo}$$

Assuming a constant rate of deaths, the crude mortality rate can be calculated directly from the life table by the formula

$$M = \frac{1}{e^o}$$

where M is the crude mortality rate and e^o is life expectancy at birth [Ubelaker 1974:62–65].

Using the burial sample from all three sites we calculate a CMR of 40.29 deaths per 1000 inhabitants per year (Table 3.1). If we only apply the sample from El Arbolillo where the percentage of infant deaths in greater, the CMR becomes 47.55 deaths per 1000 persons per year (Table 3.2). The same series of operations, this time using data from the La Ventilla apartment complex at Teotihuacan (Serrano and Lagunas 1975), indicates that during the Teotihuacan period the CMR was likewise high: circa 35 per 1000 per year. These estimates are near the upper range in the CMR for societies observed in the ethnographic present. The CMR values are also quite similar to the rates recently proposed by Ubelaker (1974:65) for two ossuaries in southern Maryland. Of note is the relatively low number of deaths under 15 years of age in the Vaillant samples (i.e., 31–40% of the skeletal sample). This stands in contrast with the figure of 57% for the 0–5 age group in contemporary rural Morelos. The percentages, however, are very similar to those presented by Salzano (1972:Table 13, p. 4) for a sample of 13 New World hunter–

TABLE 3.1

Life Table Reconstructed from the Age Distribution of the Burial Populations at Ticoman, El Arbolillo, and Zacatenco

Age interval (x)	Number of deaths $(Dx)^a$	Percent-age of deaths (dx)	Survivors (lx)	Total number of years between x and x+5 (Lx)	Total number of years lived after lifetime (Tx)	Life ex-pectancy (e°x)	Mortality rate (M)
0	0	0.00	100.00	472.03	2481.62	24.82	40.29
5	15	11.19	88.81	414.20	2009.59	22.63	
10	16	11.94	76.87	365.70	1595.39	20.75	
15	10	7.46	69.41	320.93	1229.69	17.72	
20	14	10.45	58.96	283.60	908.76	15.41	
25	6	4.48	54.48	242.55	625.16	11.48	
30	16	11.94	42.54	117.25	382.61	8.99	
35	19	14.18	28.36	113.83	205.36	7.24	
40	15	11.19	17.17	61.60	91.53	5.33	
45	13	9.70	7.47	24.30	29.93	4.01	
50	7	5.22	2.25	5.63	5.63	2.50	
55	3	2.55	0.00	0.00	0.00	0.00	

$^a N = 134.$

TABLE 3.2

Life Table Reconstructed from the Age Distribution of the Burial Population at El Arbolillo

Age interval (x)	Number of deaths $(Dx)^a$	Percent-age of deaths (dx)	Survivors (lx)	Total number of years between x and x+5 (Lx)	Total number of years lived after lifetime (Tx)	Life ex-pectancy (e°x)	Mortality rate (M)
0	0	0.00	100.00	456.90	2103.47	21.03	47.55
5	10	17.24	82.76	375.00	1646.57	19.90	
10	9	15.52	67.24	318.95	1271.57	18.91	
15	4	6.90	60.34	267.23	952.62	15.79	
20	8	13.79	46.55	224.13	685.39	14.72	
25	2	3.45	43.10	189.65	461.26	10.70	
30	6	10.34	32.76	133.63	271.61	8.29	
35	7	12.07	20.69	77.60	137.98	6.67	
40	6	10.34	10.35	38.83	60.38	5.83	
45	3	5.17	5.18	17.25	21.55	4.16	
50	2	3.45	1.72	4.30	4.30	2.50	
55	1	1.72	0.00	0.00	0.00	0.00	

$^a N = 58.$

gatherer and simple agricultural populations. The Morelos data may thus be somewhat aberrant, the result, perhaps, of the effects of density-dependent diseases.

Before calculating population figures for entire sites we must first arrive at estimates for individual households. At Loma Torremote several kinds of data have proven to be of paramount import: (a) the number of excavated and expected burials per house compound; (b) the burial pattern; (c) average compound size; (d) the length of occupation; and (e) the percentage of burial space excavated within each household compound. At Loma Torremote individuals are interred directly under house floors, in defunct tronco-conical pits in the neighboring household patio, or in simple burial pits within several meters of the residence. Because no burials occur in the small garden inside the compound, interments tend to cluster. This area within which burials are aggregated is called the "burial space." Sixteen burials are associated with the three excavated compounds: nine in Compound A-1 (42% excavated); four in Compound A-2 (18% excavated); and three in Compound A-3 (12% excavated). All burials date to the Atlamica subphase (ca. 650–550 B.C.) of the Late Formative phase. Mean compound size is about 550 m².

The total number of expected burials within each compound (ΣB_e) can be calculated using the formula

$$\Sigma B_e = \frac{b_{ex}(\Sigma bs)}{bs_{ex}}$$

where b_{ex} is the total number of excavated burials, Σbs is the total burial space expressed as a percentage (100%), and bs_{ex} is the percentage of burial space excavated.

These data can be transformed into population figures by applying the mortality rates derived from the skeletal population and then comparing the resultant calculation of the number of expected deaths with the total number of expected burials. The number of expected deaths (ΣB_M) assuming a constant CMR can be derived by the formula

$$\Sigma B_M = M \ (P_x) \ (T)$$

where M is the Crude Mortality Rate, P_x is a hypothetical population of any size, and T is the time range in years represented by that population. A population estimate for the individual household is then computed by the formula

$$P = \frac{\Sigma B_e(P_x)}{|\Sigma B_M|}$$

Application of these formulae generates the following population figures. Compound A-1 contained from 4.4 to 5.2 occupants on an average basis. The estimate for Compound A-2 is somewhat higher—from 4.6 to 5.5 residents. Compound A-3 had from 5.3 to 6.2 inhabitants, the largest of all three excavated Atlamica Phase households.

Per capita roofed-over space has also been proposed as a reasonably accurate predictor of population size (Casselberry 1972; Clarke 1968; Cook, 1972; Naroll 1962). Taking the Naroll formula, for instance, we can calculate population levels for each household by simply assuming that each occupant requires approximately 10 m² of residence space. Since the houses associated with Compound A-1 are much larger in size, the population figures derived for these residences are correspondingly much higher. The number of artifacts and storage pits used by these same households can also be estimated. Depending on the household, these undergo considerable variation. Moreover, implement and storage pit consumption varies through time. During our earlier levels the rates are fairly comparable between compounds, but by the end of the occupational sequence Compound A-1 appears to be using more pottery vessels and obsidian implements and it has at its disposal a greater number of underground storage pits. These differences—at least for obsidian and for storage pits—are still very apparent after correcting for changes in population size. The fact that they remain in evidence suggests that the relative status position of each consuming household has an effect on the number of artifacts available to each compound.

Indeed, as we will demonstrate in a later chapter, Compound A-1 is the household of the lineage chief whose duties involve a number of redistributory functions. This, of course, accounts for the greater amount of obsidian and storage loci in Compound A-1, and it may also explain why, during the latter part of its history this same household was utilizing a greater number of pottery vessels. Following this, it might be postulated that because of prestige distinctions individual per capita figures of roofed-over space will also fluctuate. If it is assumed that per capita roofed-over space is directly related to status and that status can be measured by the total amount of pottery vessels a particular household is using, then we would discover that on the average Compound A-1 consumed nearly double the number of vessels that Compound A-2 did. We might therefore conclude that the average per capita figure for the ranked compound would have been about twice that for low status households.

The frequency distribution of burials indicates little variability in mean population size between households. There is, however, considerable variation in residence size for these same households. The amount of refuse accumulation, although closely tied in with changes in population size, consequently appears to be household specific. What this means is that any common denominator of roofed-over space should be applied with extreme caution, as the exact per capita figure can fluctuate widely between neighboring households, depending on their relative status position. In fact, the estimate for Compound A-1 (ca. 23 m² per person) is more than twice that computed for nearby compounds (Santley 1977). This agrees quite favorably with the amount of difference we would expect based on the level of pottery consumption.

Estimates of population size and population density for the site may now be undertaken. Excavation, combined with data obtained from 12 km of roadway profiles crisscrossing the site, indicates a residential density of 16–19 household compounds per hectare. All these households are contemporaneous, that is, each one was continuously occupied throughout the Atlamica Phase. The estimate of 5–6 occupants per household suggests a density range of 80–114 persons per hectare. Total population for the entire 25-ha area covered by Formative household units would therefore be about 2000–2850 individuals.

These figures (the density calculation in particular) are somewhat high, but nonetheless they are within the range for nucleated communities found today in the Basin. The high population density is of course closely related to the high density of contemporaneous households. In the Teotihuacan Valley, where many of our estimates of modern population density were originally derived, the area covered by household residential units tends to be larger, and only in one community—El Calvario Acolman—does the density of households approach the level observed at Loma Torremote (Diehl 1970: Table 24).

At El Arbolillo, Zacatenco, and Ticoman, the quality of household residential data is sharply reduced, so population can only be calculated in a very general manner. In these instances, since the occupations are multicomponent, the burial sample must first be phased by chronological period. The number of expected burials can then be estimated by multiplying the number of excavated burials (b_{ex}) by the total potential burial space in square meters (Σbs) divided by the excavated portion in square meters of that burial space (bs_{ex}). The number of expected burials (ΣB_e) can then be compared with the number of expected deaths derived from the CMR (ΣB_M) to compute total population. The total potential burial space is defined here as roughly 50% of the total site area (Santley 1977).

We are now in a position to evaluate the accuracy of survey techniques for estimating population density. Table 3.3 summarizes length of occupation and population density (as derived from the density of surface refuse) for 13 archaeological components at El Arbolillo, Zacatenco, Ticoman, and Loma Torremote. The table also presents our appraisal of population density based solely on the frequency distribution of burials. In only one case (the Late Middle Formative occupation at Zacatenco) have the excavated remains indicated a density that would be predicted based only on surface scatter. In five additional cases the burial estimates are below the surface refuse figures, but interestingly, not by much, so it seems that for these components there is a fair degree of congruence between the two techniques. What is surprising is that for seven components the burial data forecast a higher density figure. At Loma Torremote the burial density is abnormally high. For the remaining six cases, however, the amount of over-estimation is approximately 26%. This agrees quite closely with Sanders' judgement from the documentary sources (mentioned earlier in this section) that the survey figures should be revised upwards about 20%.

To conclude, it appears that the reliability of surface refuse as a means for reconstructing population is reasonably high. In certain cases, for example at Loma Torremote, occupational density does not appear to be a good indicator. In most cases the closeness of fit of the two sets of calculations is striking. If anything, our estimates would seem to be too conservative. Therefore, if we are to rely on occupational density, we would suggest use of the higher figures from that range as predictors of past momentary population.

TABLE 3.3

Estimates of Population Density and Size at the Formative Sites of El Arbolillo, Zacatenco, Ticoman, and Loma Torremote

Phase	Population density (per hectare)				Total population size			
	El Arbolillo	Zacatenco	Ticoman	Loma Torremote	El Arbolillo	Zacatenco	Ticoman	Loma Torremote
Tlalnepantla	23 (SNV)[a]	—	—	8 (H)	117 (SNV)	—	—	18 (H)
Aguacatitla	53 (LNV)	3 (H)	—	8 (H)	530 (LNV)	5 (H)	—	18 (H)
Ecatepec A	60 (LNV)	3 (H)	—	10 (H)	600 (LNV)	5 (H)	—	60 (H)
Ecatepec B	65 (LNV)	16 (H)	—	10 (H/SDV)	651 (LNV)	22 (H)	—	100 (H/SDV)
Atlamica A	—	3 (H)	18 (SDV)	55 (LNV)	—	5 (H)	203 (SDV)	1367 (LNV)
Atlamica B	—	3?(H)	21 (SNV)	97 (LNV)	—	5?(H)	239 (SNV)	2425 (LNV)
Cuautlalpan A	—	—	59 (LNV)	35 (SNV)	—	—	662 (LNV)	175 (SNV)
			34 (SNV)				388 (SNV)	
Cuautlalpan B	—	—	74 (LNV)	35 (SNV)	—	—	832 (LNV)	175 (SNV)
Tultitlan	—	—	13 (SDV)	8 (H)	—	—	143 (SDV)	15 (H)

[a] Settlement types based on Basin of Mexico survey: LNV = large nucleated village, SNV = small nucleated village, SDV = small dispersed village, and H = hamlet.

SETTLEMENT TYPOLOGY

In classifying sites we considered the following variables as our main definitive criteria: (*a*) site size; (*b*) occupational density; (*c*) architectural complexity; (*d*) population; (*e*) and location with respect to other contemporary sites. Since population is usually a product of site size and occupational density, it seldom represents an independent variable. The surface area (in hectares) of each site was obtained from measurements on the 1:5000 air photographs, and in the case of multicomponent sites the surface collections were used to provide control on the spatial extent of each occupation. Undoubtedly, postdepositional factors such as erosion and plow agriculture have served to scatter and redistribute surface pottery over a much larger area than it originally occupied. Regrettably, our surveys have not attempted to compensate for this problem.

Occupational density was based on the field observation. In assigning values to sherd density in the field, we applied a rank scale of estimation: absent; scanty; scanty-to-light; light-to-scanty; light; light-to-moderate; moderate; moderate-to-heavy; and heavy. At multicomponent sites the observed density was reduced to account for the proportionate lesser occurrence of material dating to any one phase.

At such sites, occupations of different phases were proportionately ranked into primary, secondary, and tertiary components. The relative weighting for each component was derived from the proportions of ceramic types in our surface collections. For example, at a multicomponent site where the overall density of surface pottery was consistently "moderate" and where the primary component comprised about 70% of all sherds collected, and two secondary components amounted to about 15% each, the revised surface sherd densities would be "moderate" for the primary component and "light" for each secondary occupation. This procedure, when combined with the data from single-phase occupations, resulted in a listing by density and location of all contemporaneous settlements. We faced a somewhat more complex problem when trying to assess the chronological placement of architectural remains at multicomponent sites. As a general rule of thumb, we assigned visible architecture to the dominant phase, especially if that phase was highly dominant. When ceramics from two phases were about equally represented in our surface collections, we had to evaluate each site individually, and often we were unable to reach any satisfactory conclusion. Sometimes such a dilemma was provisionally resolved by assigning visible architecture to the more recent phase. On a very few occasions, we decided that architectural remains might most reasonably be placed with a secondary component (e.g., an isolated temple platform, or high mound, with a few Aztec-period sherds, lying in a small site dating to an earlier period). When isolated architecture occurred outside residential sites and without surface pottery (e.g., an agricultural terrace), we either left chronological placement open, or assumed an association with the dominant occupational phase in the local area. While we felt that larger, relatively low mounds might be a reasonable indication of elite status, it was only rarely that our survey data permitted us to make inferences about elite versus commoner residences. For our survey area generally there were very few preserved mounds, especially for periods before the Aztec. This is probably due to the more severe erosion of older sites, and to the location of many sites on intensively cultivated land where centuries of posthispanic plowing has leveled the ground surface and obliterated all but the most substantial traces of architecture. In some areas, particularly the Cuautitlan, Tenayuca, and Ixtapalapa regions, the rapid growth of Mexico City has covered large zones with nucleated recent urban and suburban sprawl.

Architectural complexity refers to the presence or absence of mounds, to the total number of mounds, when present, and to the number of different kinds of mounds and their spatial arrangement to one another. Counting the total number of mounds was a relatively straightforward matter, since such constructions can be observed in the field as rises above the contemporary ground surface. In designating mound types (i.e., whether the structure was a residence or civic–ceremonial structure), we generally relied on mound size and proportion (height to lateral dimensions) as our main criteria. The relative abundance of surface pottery also proved to be a useful indicator, because higher mounds, to which we attributed a civic–ceremonial function, were commonly associated with less surface pottery. The determination of whether a domestic structure was an elite or commoner residence was based again on mound total size, combined, in some instances, with the amount of more finely decorated pottery. In areas of recent urbanization, destroyed residential mounds were frequently encountered as circular configurations of dense surface scatter. The location of obliterated civic–ceremonial structures was more difficult, due to the absence of much surface refuse. In some cases we were able to obtain the location of destroyed large mounds from local informants; in many other cases we acknowledge this as a major lacuna in our data.

Population was derived from site size and the adjusted occupational densities. At sites where occupation was consistently light-to-moderate, moderate, and moderate-to-heavy, we used population figures of 10–25, 25–50, and 50–100 persons per hectare of settlement, whereas at sites where the density of surface material was generally light or light-to-scanty, we were guided by figures of 5–10 and 3–5 persons per hectare. Most densities of less than light-to-scanty were considered as derived from areas of denser occupation located nearby. Minimum site population was assumed to be 7 persons: a total equivalent to the average size of the Aztec-period extended family.

For most time periods we have had relatively little difficulty in distinguishing "spatially isolatable units" which could be interpreted as prehistoric social communities. In these cases, zones of denser refuse accumulation were surrounded by extensive areas of little or no occupation, so that the spatial definition of most sites was readily apparent and clear-cut (see Figures 3.1–3.5). For the Aztec period, however, particularly in the Teotihuacan, Texcoco, Chalco, and Zumpango regions, we were confronted with the problem of having to deal with nearly continuous distributions of dispersed occupation over wide areas. In these situations we generally defined site borders either (a) on the basis of association with small civic–ceremonial complexes, the probable residences of *calpulli* headmen and their families (see page 160); or (b) where natural boundaries (barrancas and hills) appeared to reinforce an actual fade-out of occupational density (Parsons 1971:21). In actuality, however, many of our "site" borders for these dispersed Aztec-period occupations are quite arbitrary. Consequently, we have seldom taken such sites too seriously as meaningful sociological communities. We have long been puzzled and frustrated by this kind of occupation as it so perversely defies our standard practices of site definition. We are now wondering if the main reason for our methodological and conceptual problems might be the fact that such occupation does not represent communities at all, but rather reflects some very different kind of sociological category. The status of *mayeque* or *Tlalmaitl* (e.g., Carrasco 1971), described in sixteenth-century documents as landless tenants dependent on their landlords, comes to mind as a distinct possibility. We will have more to say on this matter in a subsequent chapter. For the moment, however, we have "forced" this kind of occupation into our standard site categories, realizing that the fit is poor and that we will ultimately need to develop another category to account adequately for this segment of our settlement data.

Our present settlement typology is explicated in the following paragraphs. It is based upon our most recent assessments of site size, occupational density, population, architectural complexity, and, to a more limited degree, presumed intersite relationships. As intimated earlier, the single greatest weakness of this typology is that we do not control site function in any systematic way. Our settlement typology attempts not to go beyond this limitation. However, we suspect that it fails in this attempt on one major point: Some sites, particularly some of the smaller "villages" and "hamlets," may actually be remains of temporary, or seasonal, or even nonresidential occupations. At the moment we have no way of resolving this, and their estimated populations and surface areas have been computed and added into the totals for various periods. On the other hand, because the populations and areas of such sites probably amount to only a very small percentage of the total population and settlement area for any given period, we are not too concerned about the *general* validity of our inferences based upon demographic variables. The reader will note that there is a general conformity between the settlement typology we are employing here and that used in the several monographs published to date (Blanton 1972a; Parsons 1971; Sanders *et al.* 1975). However, in a few places we have modified our original typlogies for purposes of greater clarity and uniformity.

Supraregional Centers. This is a special kind of site within our survey area. In fact, there are only three such sites in the entire Basin of Mexico: Teotihuacan during its peak growth, Tenochtitlan during the Late Aztec phase, and Texcoco, a much smaller Late Aztec center. Tula, a major Late Toltec center, lies just beyond the northwestern edge of the Basin. None of these sites, except the fragmentary remains of Texcoco and some of the peripheral sections of Teotihuacan, were actually surveyed by us. Our understanding of these sites is based very largely on documentary sources (in the case of Texcoco and Tenochtitlan), and upon the work of other archaeologists (Teotihuacan and Tula). Thus, we know that such centers were large, urban communities, whose monumental architecture reflects a highly developed social stratification, and whose populations contained many non-food-producing specialists. Texcoco, the smallest of these supraregional centers, probably contained at least 25,000 inhabitants (Parsons 1971), whereas both Teotihuacan and Tenochtitlan contained more than 100,000 inhabitants at the peak of their influence (Calnek 1972, 1973; Millon *et al.* 1973). Furthermore, we know (independently of our survey data) that these centers were the foci of farflung polities that had wide impact over large parts of Mesoamerica.

Provincial Center. A large, nucleated community, with a population of 1000–10,000, with distinct civic–ceremonial–elite architecture, dating to a period when the Basin was under the hegemony of Teotihuacan (Teotihuacan period), Tula (Late Toltec period), or Tenochtitlan (Late Aztec period). The presence of civic–ceremonial and/or elite architecture implies the presence of individuals who occupied offices and carried out roles within the higher levels of a sociopolitical hierarchy. We presume, but can seldom actually demonstrate, the existence of craft specialization.

Regional Center. A large, nucleated community, with a population of 1000–10,000, with distinct civic–ceremonial–elite architecture, dating to a time period when local regions were largely independent of control from supraregional centers. Chronologically, regional centers associate with the various phases of the Formative period, the Early Toltec phase, and the Early Aztec phase. The presence of civic–ceremonial–elite architecture implies the presence of individuals occupying important roles in a hierarchical sociopolitical organization. We presume, but can seldom actually demonstrate, the existence of craft specialization.

Large Nucleated Village. A substantial community, with light-to-moderate or moderate concentrations of surface pottery, little or no indication of ceremonial–civic–elite architecture, and an estimated population of 500–1000+ people. Several sites in this category (e.g., Loma Torremote, Tlatilco, and Chimalhuacan, or Tx-MF-13, Parsons 1971) have estimated populations well in excess of 1000 people. These latter sites have not been labeled regional centers because they apparently lack the civic–ceremonial-elite architecture which we regard as evidence for the individuals and institutions associated with the upper levels of a sociopolitical hierarchy. We suspect that most inhabitants of most large nucleated villages were agriculturalists, but we rarely have any good insights into function and specialization.

Small Nucleated Village. A relatively small community, with light-to-moderate or moderate concentrations of surface pottery, little or no indication of civic–ceremonial–elite architecture, and an estimated population of 100–500 people. We suspect that most inhabitants of most small nucleated villages were agriculturalists, but we rarely have any good insights into function or specialization.

Large Dispersed Village. Similar to the large nucleated village, but with a lower concentration of surface pottery (generally light, occasionally light-to-moderate). Indications of civic–ceremonial–elite architecture are rarely, if ever, present.

Small Dispersed Village. Similar to the small nucleated village, but with a lower concentration of surface pottery (generally light, occasionally light-to-moderate).

Hamlet. A small site with less than 100 people. Remains of simple domestic residences sometimes occur, but evidence of civic–ceremonial-elite architecture is entirely lacking. The density of surface pottery varies between light and moderate. A large number of hamlets seem to be occupied by fewer than about 20 people, and some of these may not be permanent residences. We rarely have good insights into function or specialization, although we generally tend to assume that most hamlets are inhabited by agriculturalists. Hamlets are the single most numerous settlement type during most time periods.

Tezoyuca Hilltop Center. This is a rather special kind of site for several reasons. First, such sites are always situated on the tops of distinct hills or ridges. Second, they are geographically restricted to the southern flank of the Teotihuacan Valley, the Texcoco region, and two sites west of Lake Texcoco in the Tenayuca region. Third, they are chronologically restricted to the Terminal Formative phase, and contain substantial proportions of a ceramic complex we call the Tezoyuca complex (see Appendix C). Fourth, relative to other sites of the same period, they contain an unusual amount of civic–ceremonial architecture, in the form of isolated pyramidal structures or complexes of such structures, compared to the size of the residential area. Residential occupation also occurs, generally clustered on terraced slopes below or around the civic–ceremonial architecture.

As noted, the residential areas of Tezoyuca hilltop sites are small, cover only a few hectares, and probably had only a few hundred inhabitants. Parsons (1971) earlier called these sites "segregated elite districts," a term we have found useful, but which we prefer not to use here in order to avoid the specific connotations of status and function it implies.

Large Ceremonial Precinct.   These sites are commonly found on isolated hilltops or on ridge crests, although a few do occur on low ground. Generally there are several obvious pyramidal mounds, often arranged around a plaza or set of plazas. The absence of much surface pottery suggests a lack of significant residential occupation. We believe that such localities served as foci of ritual, and perhaps also as cemeteries for a few elite individuals. The key aspect of their definition is that they occur isolated from significant residential occupation.

Small Ceremonial Precinct.   Similar to the large ceremonial precinct, except for smaller scale. Usually there is only a single isolated pyramidal mound, or, more rarely, a stone sculpture or carving. Most such sites are found on the tops of hills and ridges, although a few occur on lower ground. We have had some problems with the latter situation where isolated pyramidal structures of later periods appear to have been built on ground occupied earlier by a residential community.

Salt-Making Station.   This is a site category defined on the basis of somewhat specialized and unique features. Each site consists of a low mound, of highly variable size, and homogeneous earth fill, distributed along the shore of Lake Texcoco, approximately in the strip that is seasonally inundated and exposed. Apparently, the process of salt extraction involved leaching of the salt from the highly salinized soils, and the mounds are the accumulated debris of this process. Only rarely are there associated architectural remains, except in the form of house mounds on the summit of the larger mounds. Another essential characteristic of sich sites is that the artifactual remains consist almost exclusively of moderate to heavy concentrations of Texcoco Fabric Impressed pottery (see Appendix C). Other ceramics occur only in very minor percentages, except in cases of the larger mounds with summit house mounds, but even in those cases Texcoco Fabric Impressed pottery runs well over 50% of the total sample.

We have reasonable evidence (e.g., see Blanton 1972; Charlton 1969; Parsons 1971; Tolstoy 1958) that Texcoco Fabric Impressed pottery was used in the production of salt. Most of these sites do not represent permanent settlements. Since Texcoco Fabric Marked pottery is confined to the Early Aztec and Late Aztec phases (and probably mainly to the latter period), all our designated salt-making stations date very late in our sequence. However, the occasional presence of earlier pottery at these locations suggests that some of them may contain minor Teotihuacan and Formative period components as well.

There are also good indications (from the surface distribution of high concentrations of Texcoco Fabric Marked pottery) that salt making was being carried out within parts of other Late Aztec sites that we have designated as hamlets and villages.

Quarry. Locations of limited occupational debris at obvious sources of basic raw materials (e.g., obsidian, lime, or basalt). Such sites are not always very obvious, and we have defined only a few. All our defined quarries are in the Teotihuacan Valley where some seem to be associated with obsidian extraction. We predict that more quarry sites will eventually be identified elsewhere (e.g., in the area of rich lime deposits around Apaxco in the northwestern Basin) once we have determined what artifacts constitute proper evidence for quarrying activities. Heavy modern industrial use of some resources (e.g., the above-mentioned lime deposits) also renders quite difficult the location and identification of prehispanic quarries in some places. Beyond the northeast corner of the Basin, northeast of Pachuca, a large number of obsidian quarries have been found (Charlton 1977; Spence and Parsons 1972).

Royal Retreat. A special site category whose definition is based upon a correlation of archaeological and documentary information. Several sixteenth-century documentary sources tell us that a number of locations functioned as rural residences, ritual foci, and pleasure gardens for the uppermost ruling elite in the Basin of Mexico during Late Aztec times. Documents also tell us that at three of these places—Chapultepec, Tetzcotzingo (Tx-A-62, Parsons 1971), and Tepetzinco, baths were attached to the residental complex. We have not attempted to use this site designation for any period prior to the Late Horizon.

Indeterminate Site. In a large number of cases some information is available for rural sites situated in areas that have not been intensively surveyed. In other cases where surveys have been conducted, we were not able to proportionately sort out certain components because of dense over-burden from later occupations. Thus, although we can locate and periodize these sites on our settlement maps, we cannot as yet determine precisely where these sites fit into our community hierarchy. Three categories of indeterminate sites appear on our settlement maps.

1. *Excavated site.* These are sites outside of our surveyed areas that are known exclusively from excavation. Examples of this type include the sites of Cuicuilco, Copilco, Cerro Tepalcate, Contreras, Tetelpan, and Melchor Ocampo. Excepting those of the Aztec period, each of these sites is depicted as a hexagon. The size of the hexagon denotes our appraisal of relative importance.

2. *Ethnohistoric site*. These are Late Aztec sites, again outside of our intensively surveyed area, which occur on Gonzalez Aparicio's (1973) map, *Plano Reconstructivo de la Region de Tenochtitlan al Comienzo de la Conquista*. Although data on occupational density are lacking, these sites appear to be substantial settlements, probably corresponding to the village level in our settlement hierarchy. Several ethnohistoric sites are also located in the Teotihuacan region. The placement of these is based on Sanders' (1965) study of Late Aztec settlement in the Teotihuacan Valley.

3. *Surveyed site of unknown occupational density*. All sites falling into this category date from the Early Aztec phase in the Cuautitlan, Teotihuacan, and Tenayuca regions. Most of these occupations are obscured by dense Late Aztec settlement, but generally they appear to be small dispersed communities, probably hamlets and small villages. The Early Aztec settlements of Ecatepec and Coacalco may be larger, more substantial communities.

In defining sites we also considered trace occupations. These occupations consisted of limited presences of material, generally several isolated sherds, dating from a particular archaeological phase. Although commonly found at settlements dating to earlier or later time periods, such occurrences were also present in isolation unrelated to any permanent habitation sites. We interpret such ceramic traces as probable evidence for certain unspecified kinds of exploitative activities that are spatially detached from residential sites, for example, planting or harvesting in agricultural fields. We also think that some ceramic traces are probably accidental and fortuitous occurrences. We regard both probabilities as relatively meaningless for our purposes here, and we have made no effort to designate pottery traces as sites or to show their locations on our settlement pattern maps.

Upon completetion of the site tabulation all occupations were given a site number. In numbering sites we utilized a three unit system. The first unit was a alphabetic character denoting the survey region (e.g., T = Teotihuacan region; Tx = Texcoco region; Q = Cuautitlan region). The second unit designated the archaeological period and phase: EF = Early Formative; MF = Middle Formative; LF = Late Formative; TF = Terminal Formative; EC = Early Classic or Teotihuacan; LC = Late Classic or Teotihuacan; ET = Early Toltec; LT = Late Toltec; and A = Aztec. In the Teotihuacan, Temascalapa, Cuautitlan, and Tenayuca regions the basis for chronological indication was more general: F = Formative; C = Classic or Teotihuacan; T = Toltec; and A = Aztec. The third unit was an Arabic numeral: the specific number for each site within each time period. These chronological designations were developed fairly early in our survey when our older chronological terminology was still in general use. We have retained these designations for reasons of overall continuity between older and more recent surveys.

Our breakdown of the Early to Middle Formative into four phases or subphases was based on Tolstoy's (1975) reanalysis of the Parsons–Blanton surface samples from the Texcoco, Ixtapalapa, Chalco, and Xochimilco regions, on Sanders' *et al.* (1975) evaluation of the Middle Formative occupation in the Teotihuacan region, and on Santley's (1976c, 1977) study of the

Formative occupations in the Cuautitlan and Tenayuca regions. We also had the benefit of Tolstoy's (1975) reexamination of excavated lots from Cuicuilco, Tetelpan, Copilco, Contreras, Tlatilco, and Azcapotzalco, all in the unsurveyed western part of the Basin, in addition to his own comparative material from El Arbolillo, Tlapacoya, and Coapexco (Tolstoy and Fish 1973; Tolstoy and Paradis 1970). Both Sanders' and Santleys' phasing of the Early and Middle Formative were accomplished directly at each site in the field, so that data were available on the spatial extent and occupational density of each component. Tolstoy, dependent upon laboratory analysis of scattered sherd collections, could not be as discriminant. He divided the surface and excavation samples into three general categories: bulk of occupation dating from phase; definite occupation dating from phase; and possible occupation dating from phase (Tolstoy 1975:335). In order to operationalize Tolstoy's periodization of surveyed Formative sites, the following set of simplifying assumptions was introduced. If the bulk of an occupation dated to a particular phase in the Tolstoy sequence, this component was assumed to equal the maximum refuse density for the period as reported by the survey. Surveyed sites with several "definite" secondary components were assumed to equal approximately one-half of the density of the primary occupation. If a surveyed site had two substantial components (i.e., the bulk of all occupation dating from two phases), the densities observed in the field were each reduced by one-third. All "possible" occupations were ignored. All sites not encountered by our surveys but visited by Tolstoy were designated as indeterminate.

LIMITATIONS OF THE SURVEYS

During the course of the various survey projects a number of serious (or at least potentially serious) problems were recognized in our data base. These limitations have direct bearing on the level of accuracy of the reconstruction presented in this study, as well as raising questions for future research. They are considered under the following general headings: (a) problems associated with incomplete survey coverage, (b) problems deriving from the assumption that all sites occupied during a particular phase are contemporaneous, and finally (c) the Cuicuilco problem.

Incomplete Survey Coverage

The problem of incomplete areal coverage is perhaps the greatest inadequacy of our surveys. A variety of factors has contributed to our inability to obtain a 100% sample of prehistoric sites. Erosion, alluviation, and dense crop or undergrowth have restricted survey reliability even in areas relatively unaffected by the recent growth of Mexico City. Other areas, most notably the Tacuba region and a portion of the Ixtapalapa and Tenayuca regions, are currently under Mexico City and hence have not been surveyed. Beside these regions, many large towns, for example, Chalco, Xochimilco, Texcoco, Cuautitlan, and Ecatepec have also witnessed much recent growth, making intensive (or even spot) survey extremely difficult if not impossible. Moreover, there are still small surveyable sections of the Basin where no systematic surveys have been conducted. Last, and on a more particular level, our degree of control for estimating phase-specific occupational densities at multicomponent sites is still largely subjective.

In areas that have been intensively surveyed, the problem of an incomplete sample of prehistoric habitation sites is most serious on parts of the alluvial plain. The problem is twofold. First, much of this area is densely planted in large fields of maize and alfalfa which obscure much evidence of prehispanic occupation. This is compounded by the fact that many of our surveys were conducted in the summer and early fall months when field crops were at their maximum growth. We have attempted, in some cases, to return to these problem areas, but we have as yet only succeeded in revisiting a few fields. The second problem concerns the effectiveness of our surface surveys in detecting habitation sites, particularly small rural sites, in areas of deep soil even when ground cover was not a problem. The survey data suggest that the Basin floor was largely avoided for extensive settlement until the Late Aztec phase, yet recent studies of contemporary agriculture indicate that these lands are among the most productive areas of the Basin in terms of agricultural potential. An important example of a completely buried archaeological site was the partial remains of a prehistoric floodwater irrigation system near Santa Clara Xalostoc (Sanders and Santley 1977). These features are located in the profiles of two large clay pits, the deepest part of which is situated 7–8 m below the modern ground surface. In a number of cases we detected residential sites only because we noted ceramics in the fill from canal excavations. On the other hand, we do have a fairly large sample of sites from most time periods that we did detect on the surface in deep soil areas, so the effects of alluviation seem to have been highly localized. In this regard, we have been particularly impressed with the number of small sites (dating from Late Pleistocene through Late Aztec times) that show up clearly over the entire surface of Lake Chalco–Xochimilco, and around the shoreline of Lake Texcoco. A major research project, using infrared aerial photographic techniques, plans to address this problem of potentially invisible sites in considerable detail in the near future.

On the piedmont this problem is directly the reverse. Thus, rather than being covered by alluvial sediments, many sites have been subjected to various degrees of sheet erosion. We suspect that only in rare instances has erosion obliterated entire sites. On the other hand, there is evidence indicating that erosion has washed away much if not all of the intervening soil mantle, so at many sites virtually all refuse that has accumulated during their occupational history is visible on the surface. Thus we may have consistently overestimated occupational density at a large number of piedmont sites.

Unfortunately, we have no way of determining the amount of soil that has been removed through the erosion process. This is a major limitation of our survey, one certainly deserving further consideration if we are to place much confidence in our density estimates.

The beds of the former lakes (Zumpango, Xaltocan, Texcoco, Xochimilco, and Chalco) created a special set of survey problems. The vast wasteland of former Lake Texcoco posed a particularly severe barrier to effective reconnaissance. When we tried to maneuver within it, we became hopelessly lost on its featureless surface, and our vehicles got hopelessly bogged down in its slippery silt deposits. Since we knew (from Cortes' eloquent descriptions) that the saline waters of Lake Texcoco were several meters deep in the sixteenth century, we assumed that no significant human occupation had ever existed in the central part of the lake (except, of course, on a few well-known large islands). Therefore, we ignored most of the former Lake Texcoco lakebed, and concentrated our efforts on the shoreline zones where we felt that salt-making stations and fishing and birdhunting camps could have existed, or where local springs might have permitted some chinampa-like cultivation.

The northern lakes, Xaltocan and Zumpango, presented more complex problems. Here we were uncertain about the character of the lacustrine system. Most writers have assumed the presence of a single large sheet of saline water, and have even drawn it up to the 2250-m contour line. We have reduced it to the 2238-m contour in keeping with our observations of salinized soils visible on the aerial photographs. An intensive survey by Pedro Armillas (personal communication) has revealed that, in fact, there were probably a number of separate ponds most of the time, and only under exceptional circumstances did they form a single lagoon. This strongly suggests that we might reasonably expect to find sites in unexpected places over almost any part of the Xaltocan–Zumpango lakebed. As it now stands, we have surveyed only part of the western half of the Xaltocan–Zumpango lakebed (we had to leave unexamined a large area of standing water southwest of the present town of Zumpango, measuring about 6 km long and 3 km wide, in which local inhabitants told us there were several large mounded sites accessible only by canoe). We made an examination of Xaltocan island, but elsewhere in Lake Xaltocan our principal reconnaissance techniques consisted of examining anomalous features on the aerial photographs and spot checking visible mounds.

The entire lakebed of Lake Chalco–Xochimilco (except for the western end of Lake Xochimilco, now covered by urban sprawl) was systematically surveyed. Since even Early Formative sites occur here, with excavated features only a few centimeters below the level modern ground surface (Tolstoy et al. 1977), we feel fairly confident about the reliability of our survey in this area.

Large sections of the Tenayuca and Ixtapalapa regions have recently been covered by suburban growth from Mexico City. This problem is most serious at lower elevations where dense modern settlement is literally continuous. In the Tenayuca region, for example, the settlement pattern data show a distinct tendency for many prehistoric sites to prefer alluvial locations, from Late Formative times onward. This is also an area favored by modern settlement, so that there is good reason to believe that our survey coverage is far from reliable. This problem is also serious on the neighboring lower piedmont, another area of heavy modern settlement, and such well known sites as Ticoman, Zacatenco, and El Arbolillo are today all but destroyed. In the Ixtapalapa region the dampening effect of modern settlement on survey reliability is quite comparable, especially in the more densely settled western part of the peninsula. Fortunately, Blanton surveyed the region before the very heavy recent utilization obliterated many sites in the central and eastern portions.

Our surveys within the large number of modern towns which dot the Basin are also deficient. For the most part, our decision not to survey within many of these communities stems from the fact that in most cases they are densely nucleated settlements, often with paved streets and a great amount of recent bulldozing and other modification of their landscape. Nonetheless, it should be borne in mind that areas favored for modern settlement were probably also loci of intense prehispanic occupation. For the Late Aztec phase we have some control on the location of most major settlements, from the documentary sources. The major inadequacy in our data base here pertains to the possibility that pre-Late Aztec sites may also occur at these same locations. Small sites within such communities could easily be missed, but spot surveys in vacant lots, sewer trenches, and the like should be sufficient to establish the presence–absence of substantial components. Just where these occupations fit into our settlement typology hierarchy, however, we see no means of determining at present.

Another annoying limitation of the survey is the great decrease in the reliability of eyeball observations on multicomponent sites, especially where one component is greatly predominant (Parsons 1971:23). At large sites we have tried to make our assessments more objective by revisiting settlements and carrying out independent sets of observations using different survey teams. In many cases we have also collected numerous surface samples, and later proportionately ranked the various components, based on the observed occupational densities. Despite these "refinements" in methodological rigor, we still feel that at many sites, particularly at those done relatively early in the survey, we may have erred in estimating the density values for less common secondary and tertiary components.

In the final analysis, our ability to plot the surface areas of occupation for separate phases, at any multicomponent site, depends upon the quality of our surface collections. As indicated in Chapter 2, we were seldom able to make our collections large enough, or often enough, to deal fully adequately with multicomponent sites. In particular, our surface collections are deficient because both their placement and their content is biased: Their placement is biased toward ad hoc localities often decided upon before the full extent or complexity of a site became wholly apparent; their content is biased toward ceramic categories we regarded as diagnostic at the time of fieldwork. These limitations and biases conspire against us when we have to deal with multicomponent sites, especially if one or more secondary components were not recognized at the time of survey. It often becomes difficult to make meaningful quantitative comparisons between collections at different sites, or even within the same large site. Thus, we have sometimes been reduced to crude approximations and intuitive estimates when attempting to distinguish and quantify secondary and tertiary occupations throughout our survey area.

Our ability to make reasonable estimates of occupational density and population depends very largely, of course, on the consistency of our visual impressions of sherd density on the modern ground surface. If our transformations of sherd density to population figures are to have any meaning, it is critical that, for example, a "moderate" sherd density in one area or at one time have the same demographic implications as a "moderate" sherd density in another area or another time period. As we mentioned earlier, it is not always easy to achieve complete consistency in these visual estimations at various times of the year and of sherd density made by different people on separate field projects during different fieldseasons. This problem is serious enough, but it is compounded by the differential treatment of modern ground surfaces by present-day inhabitants. Such differential treatment significantly affects how surface pottery is produced at the ground surface and how it appears to the observer. We have already noted the problems produced by differential alluviation, erosion, and modern crop cover. Related to these is the manner in which modern agriculturalists modify the ground surface. Surface pottery on a recently plowed field usually has a different visibility and appearance to the eye than the same surface pottery in the same plowed field after several weeks have elapsed. Ground that has rarely, or never, been plowed usually will have very little surface pottery, even though occupation there may be quite intense. Fields which are alternated between pasture and crops will tend to show different concentrations of surface pottery than fields which are always under cultivation—and such differences may be more a product of differential modern land use than of differential prehispanic occupational density.

We have never dealt systematically and rigorously with these potentially serious problems. However, we have always been aware of these difficulties, and have tempered our observations in view of the more obvious limitations of our method. For example, we once found a site on a large expanse of nearly level ground atop a large, steep-sided hill. This land had apparently never been cultivated. There were numerous large mounds scattered over an area of about 30 ha. Surface pottery was absent except in a few places where rodent burrows had exposed handfulls of sherds. Such rodent burrows were not numerous, but each one we found had a few fragments of pottery around it. We did not classify the site as an uninhabited ceremonial precinct. Rather, we assumed that the isolated sherds exposed by burrowing rodents were indicative of the presence of substantial subsurface residential debris throughout the site, and we called the site a regional center. On the other hand, we would have faced a potentially much more confusing situation had the rodents neglected to inhabit this particular locality.

In other cases, we have observed numerous sites at different seasons, during different years, and under different conditions of surface treatment. Such visits have convinced us that *most* sites would be interpreted in an identical, or very similar, manner provided adequate care was taken in making our survey observations. Furthermore, we enjoy a tremendous advantage in that *most* land is intensively cultivated *most* of the time over *most* of our survey area. Thus, most of our allowances and special considerations have to be made for seasonal difference and for the small proportion of land that has not been cultivated in recent times. In other words, while we are prepared to admit that problems of differential modern land use and seasonal variation have almost certainly produced some inconsistency and error in making inference about occupational density and site character, we believe that such errors and inconsistencies have not significantly affected our general conclusions.

Contemporaneity of Surface Occupations

The problem of contemporaneity of surface occupations within each chronological phase places additional constraints on the reliability of our settlement pattern reconstructions. Basically, this problem stems from the assumption that all sites assigned to a particular chronological phase were in fact all occupied throughout all of the time period in question. As Tolstoy (1975:337) notes, site tallies and the demographic estimates derived from them tend to be inflated when the basis for periodizing surface remains is excessively gross. Tolstoy's reanalysis of our surface collections suggests that the amount of inflation—at least during the Early and Middle Formative— appears to vary from 18 to 25%, although shrinkage of these overestimates can be achieved through the application of finer chronologies. Although the chronological scheme used in this discussion is more fine-grained than that originally applied during the Teotihuacan or Texcoco surveys, our phasing is still quite general—each representing a summary of 150–250 years of occupation. While excessive site counts are still expected, we believe that this problem most concerns coevality at small sites (e.g., hamlets) where the combination of limited demographic size, extensive forms of land use, and ties with larger settlements tend to make these occupations more short-term and transitory. At larger sites (ca. 10 ha or more) both Tolstoy's study and our phasing of surface remains suggest that most were inhabited continuously for long periods of time. The question that then remains is the proportion of each larger site (i. e., area in hectares) that was occupied on a contemporaneous basis. This is a problem of some significance, one to which the following case examples have direct bearing.

Using the generalized system of chronological phasing, surveys in the Cuautitlan and Tenayuca regions indicate the following history of settlement during the Formative period. Initially, settlements tended to favor a few choice localities near permanent streams where crop security is high. During the Middle Formative the Guadalupe Range eastern and southern piedmont became the major locus of settlement in the Tenayuca region, with the bulk of all occupation residing in three large villages. In the Cuautitlan region, on the other hand, there was some growth along the upper drainage of the Rio Cuautitlan, but for the most part populations tend to inhabit small dispersed settlements. By Late Formative times population appears to be equally balanced in the two survey regions. During Terminal Formative times, however, the Tenayuca region witnessed considerable population loss. Population levels also drop in the Cuautitlan region, ostensibly because of the virtual abandonment of Loma Torremote, and the vast majority of all occupation was nucleated at San Jose—now a regional center. The Early Teotihuacan period was one of almost total depopulation in both the Cuautitlan and Tenayuca regions. In fact, it is not until Late Teotihuacan times that settlements reappeared in appreciable numbers. (See Figures 3.6 and 3.7.)

When a finer system of chronological phasing is applied to the survey data, several of the patterns described above turn out to be fallacious. The reconstruction based on the generalized dating scheme, although it correctly portrays the mainstream of settlement history, does not fully depict the process of population ebb and flow in the Cuautitlan–Tenayuca region. Moreover, both population levels and site numbers emerge as grossly exaggerated—perhaps by a factor as high as 30–40% for certain phases. There are two major problem areas. First, the explosive growth that occurred in the Guadalupe Range actually took place during the last half of the Middle Formative phase. The population in this area during Early Middle Formative times remained quite small, with a substantial proportion occupying a single settlement—El Arbolillo. Second, the large Late Formative community at Loma Torremote is not contemporary either with the communities on the eastern–southern side of the Guadalupe Range or with the site of San Jose Cuautitlan. In fact, when Loma Torremote grows considerably in size during the Early Late Formative, it does so at the expense of population at neighboring sites. In other words, for about a century (ca. 650–550 B.C.) practically all of the Early Late Formative population in the Cuautitlan and Tenayuca regions is concentrated at Loma Torremote. The demise of Loma Torremote as a major population locus corresponds with the reoccupation of the Guadalupe Range eastern and southern piedmont and with the first large occupation at San Jose, 4 km to the east. (See Figures 3.8, 3.9, 3.10, and 3.11.)

This reconstruction of population movements, of course, is based on excavation data as well, not on information exclusively derived from the survey. We do not believe that short-term relocations of this kind were ever very common in the prehistory of the Basin. The Loma Torremote case indeed appears to be a truly extraordinary situation, brought about by a variety of factors (Santley 1977). Nevertheless, the example does show that

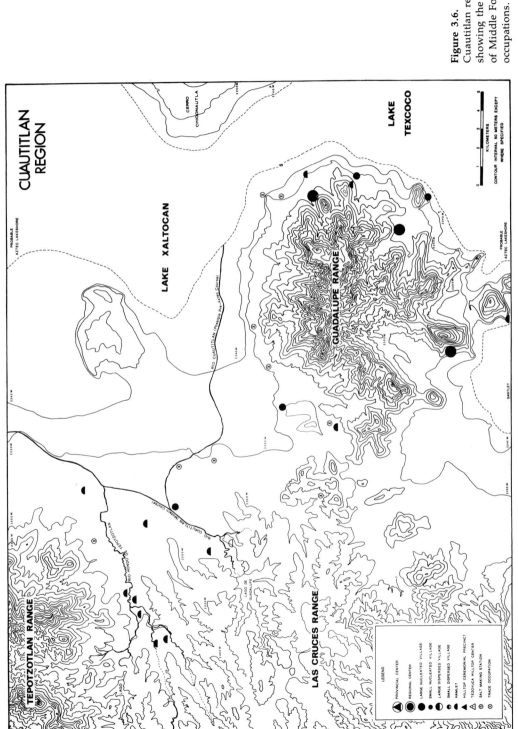

Figure 3.6. The Cuautitlan region, showing the distribution of Middle Formative occupations.

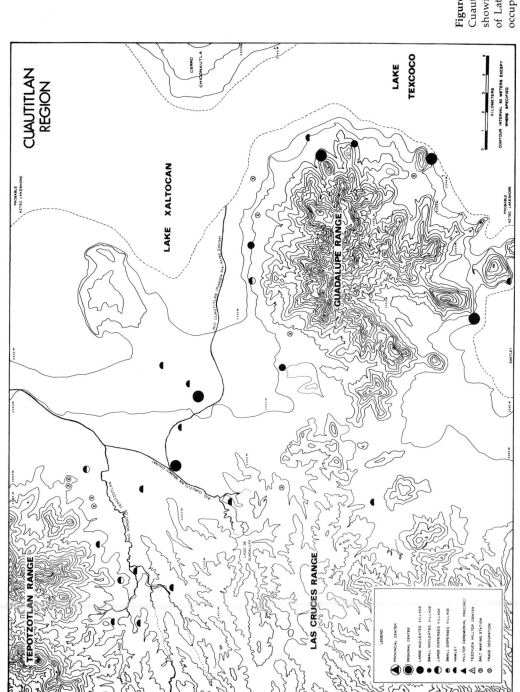

Figure 3.7. The Cuautitlan region, showing the distribution of Late Formative occupations.

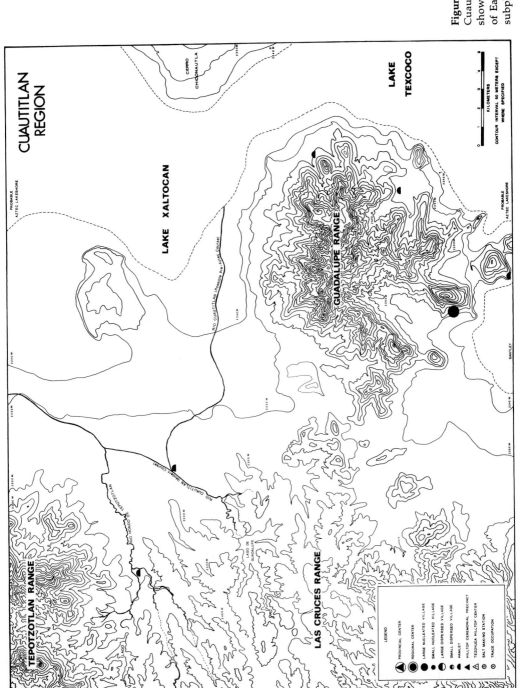

Figure 3.8. The Cuautitlan region, showing the distribution of Early Middle Formative subphase occupations.

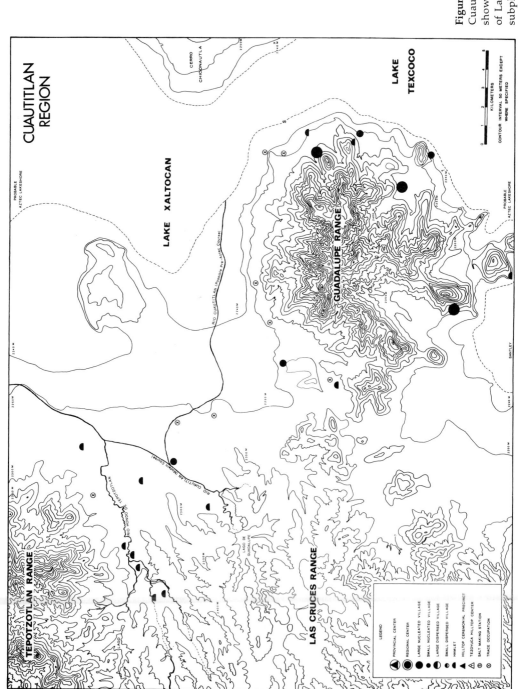

Figure 3.9. The Cuautitlan region, showing the distribution of Late Middle Formative subphase occupations.

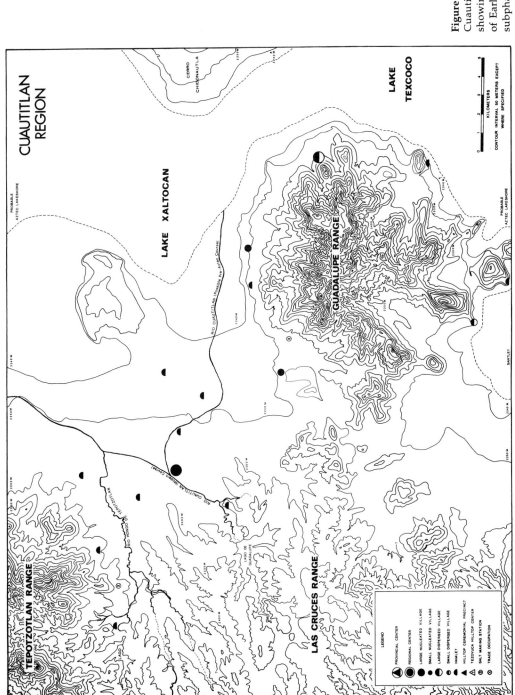

Figure 3.10. The Cuautitlan region, showing the distribution of Early Late Formative subphase occupations.

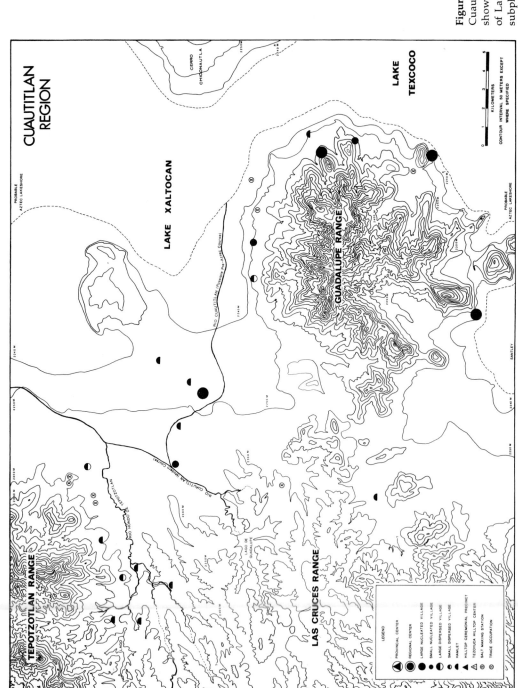

Figure 3.11. The Cuautitlan region, showing the distribution of Late Late Formative subphase occupations.

contemporaneity of larger sites can be a real problem in some cases, especially when the region under consideration is relatively small in size. For much larger areas, like the Basin of Mexico as a whole, where there is a great increase in community sample size, the problem of intraperiod contemporaneity would seem to be less serious.

An even greater shortcoming of the survey has been our inability at this time to phase sites from the final two-thirds of the Teotihuacan period: a period of some 650 years. Since occupations have a much greater chance of not being coeval the more general the chronology becomes, it can be argued that a certain segment of all sites are not contemporaneous. In areas where the period has been divided into several temporal components, we have found that there is always a small portion of sites that do not date to a particular phase. In the Cuautitlan region, to return to the example mentioned earlier, the Teotihuacan period map only illustrates the distribution of sites during the final phase. If a map were to be drawn for the earlier phases, it would show that the vast majority of Teotihuacan sites in this area paralleled the lower reaches of the Rio Cuautitlan. In comparison, the western part of the region—along the upper part of the Rios Cuautitlan and Tepotzotlan—would be shown as relatively unoccupied. Thus, while we have met with some success in phasing the Teotihuacan period in the Cuautitlan and the Tenayuca regions, we are currently unable to carry out a similar operation for sites elsewhere in the Basin. We suspect the most of the Teotihuacan period sites depicted on the settlement map were occupied during the final phase. What is not known, however, is the precise distribution of occupations during the earlier phases.

Despite the fact that nearly 3500 km^2 have been systematically surveyed, there are still small surveyable portions of the Basin where no surveys have been conducted. These are situated in two areas: the northeastern corner of the Basin; and the region west of Lake Texcoco between Cuicuilco and Azcapotzalco (Map 4). The northeastern corner includes that part of the Basin north of the Temascalapa region, east of the Zumpango region, and west of Cerro Los Pitos, plus a small section of the north shore of Lake Xaltocan. The region west of Late Texcoco (the Tacuba region), extending from the lakeshore up to the base of the Sierra de las Cruces, is currently under the suburban sprawl from Mexico City and, therefore, cannot be surveyed on any systematic basis, except for the upper piedmont. The sierra zone, the area to the west of Lago de Guadalupe, and a substantial segment of the interior of Late Texcoco have also been rarely visited as a part of our survey projects.

Although our regional coverage is about 75–80% complete, we do have some strong suspicions concerning the settlement history of the remaining 20–25%. The Tacuba region has long been documented as an area rich in precolumbian sites. A respectable number of Formative-period sites—Tlatilco, Contreras, Copilco, El Tepalcate, to name a few—have been excavated during the past 40 years, so it seems likely that the area had a large

Formative occupation. The area is also noted for Teotihuacan and Early Toltec-period sites, especially in the northern portion, around Azcapotzalco, and Gonzalez Aparicio's (1973) map shows that it was among the most densely settled parts of the Basin during the Aztec period. What is unclear are the absolute number of sites during each time period and the characteristics of size, complexity, and density for specific sites.

Environmentally the Tacuba region is similar to the Texcoco region on the eastern side of Lake Texcoco. This might imply some parallels in general settlement history. For certain periods (the later phases of the Formative period, the Early Toltec and Aztec periods), this indeed seems to be the case. However, it is probable that there are significant differences in occupational intensity and sociopolitical status during Early Formative, Late Toltec, and Teotihuacan times. For these three major periods the Tacuba region seems quite distinct, both demographically and politically, from the Texcoco region where large, complex sites comparable to Tlatilco (one of the major sites in the Basin of Mexico during Early Formative and Early Middle Formative times) and Azcapotzalco (which probably covered at least 200 ha in the Teotihuacan period) are absent. The relative proximity of the Tacuba region to the key Formative site of Cuicuilco (discussed later) is probably a major factor in some of its settlement history.

Unlike the Tacuba region, we have almost no information about the large, unsurveyed northeastern segment of the Basin (the Pachuca region). Nevertheless, we feel justified in making several predictions about what will ultimately be found there. Our confidence in this regard derives from the generally successful predictions we made about prehispanic settlement in the Temascalapa region, along the southern margin of the Pachuca region, where test surveys were conducted in 1975). Our confirmed expectations for Temascalapa were that (a) there would be little or no occupation there during Formative times; (b) there would be substantial occupation dating to the Teotihuacan period, the Late Toltec phase, and the Late Aztec phase; and (c) there would be few sites of Early Toltec or Early Aztec age. Projecting these findings from Temascalapa northward into the as-yet-unsurveyed Pachuca region, we predict the following: (1) That this arid area was essentially uninhabited during the Formative period. If any sites are present, they are probably temporary occupations located near the obsidian outcrops east of Pachuca. (2) Small Teotihuacan sites should occur throughout the area, but these should show distinct preferences for (a) the obsidian sources, and (b) the flanks of the hillslopes, where rainfall and natural runoff are relatively high. (3) During the Early Toltec phase there should either be no settlement at all, or a contraction of occupation to a few favored localities. (4) A proliferation of rural settlement, with several substantial communities, is expectable during the Late Toltec phase. (5) This should be followed by a large population decline, or even total abandonment, during the Early Aztec phase. (6) There should be substantial resettlement of the entire area during the Late Aztec phase.

While we have some confidence that these expectations are reasonable and valid, the area in question does remain an archaeological unknown. Past experience has shown that occasionally surprises do occur, and it is quite conceivable that we could be wide of the mark in some aspects of what we think the Pachuca region represents in the way of prehispanic settlement. Bearing these limitations in mind, we propose the following index of survey reliability. This index attempts to compensate both for sites whose population levels have been miscalculated, for any of the reasons just discussed, and for sites which, because of the problems of sheet erosion or alluviation, were not encountered in the field.

To date systematic surveys have been carried out over an area approximately 3500 km² in extent: circa 75–80% of the agriculturally usable land mass of the Basin. Within this intensively surveyed area we would estimate that about 80% of all spatially isolatable communities have been found. The remaining 20–25% has been accounted for by what we have termed the "survey factor." This factor is based on Sanders' (1976b) calculation that the Late Aztec maximal population figures from the surface surveys are about 20% below the minimal figures derived from the documentary sources. The comparison of population estimates based on occupational density and those derived from the frequency distribution of burials in excavated household contexts demonstrates a similar amount of underestimation in the survey figures.

The estimate of 80% survey reliability, however, varies considerably from survey region to survey region and from environmental zone to environmental zone. An average of 80% or higher is probably most pertinent to communities in piedmont locations and to the northern half of the Basin—two cases where the surveys were able to collect information on a nearly continuous field-by-field basis. There is a marked dropoff in survey reliability in relatively flat areas of deep soil plain, because of dense modern occupation, large stands of alfalfa and thick maize, and substantial alluviation. In this area we estimate that no more than 20–60% of all prehistoric occupation was recorded by the surface survey. The 20% figure applies most readily to the zone around Mexico City—the western portion of the Ixtapalapa region, the Tenayuca region, the Tacuba region, and the western end of the Xochimilco region, where modern occupation literally enamels the alluvial plain. In the Teotihuacan and Cuautitlan regions we would suggest that the surveys are about 40–50% complete in the alluvial plain. For the Texcoco, Ixtapalapa (eastern sector), Chalco, and Xochimilco regions we would hazard a 50–60% estimate for the same environmental zone. However, for most of the Chalco–Xochimilco lakebed, where post-Pleistocene alluviation appears to have been minimal, we feel that an 80% reliability figure is appropriate for this largely open area where continuous field-by-field survey was carried out. As indicated previously, the beds of Lake Texcoco and Xaltocan remain essentially unsurveyed (certainly not more than a 10% coverage), although we feel that this has only a slight impact on our impressions about regional occupation. About half of the Lake Zumpango lakebed was surveyed, and we suggest a reliability factor of perhaps 50–60% for this area.

The Cuicuilco Problem

The site of Cuicuilco presents a special set of problems. Although excavations have been conducted at Cuicuilco since the 1920s, our knowledge of this important center is still woefully incomplete. To a large extent, this inadequacy is the direct result of the fact that most of the site has been covered by the Pedregal laval flow. This is further compounded by our lack of survey coverage along the western rim of Lake Texcoco and Lake Xochimilco—an area, as we have already mentioned, that is now within the modern limits of Mexico City.

Perhaps the most consistent and useful body of data comes from the I.N.A.H. excavations, conducted in 1967 prior to the construction of the Ciudad Olympica, after mechanized equipment had removed portions of the lava overburden. Regrettably, much of this information is either unanalyzed or unpublished, but it is sufficient to permit a preliminary consideration of the site and its impact on rural settlement. The archaeological sequence at Cuicuilco has been reported by Heizer and Bennyhoff in a number of papers and need not be mentioned here in any detail. The site was occupied throughout the Middle, Late, and Terminal Formative phases (Bennyhoff 1966; Muller: personal communication), and there are strong indications that an Early Formative component is present as well (Tolstoy 1975:Figure 2). The major occupations occur during the Late and Terminal Formative phases. In addition, several early ceremonial constructions are associated with Late Middle Formative ceramics. This suggests that Cuicuilco was also a substantial Middle Formative community—in all likelihood the largest and most complex site in the Basin at that time.

The I.N.A.H. excavations have significantly revised our impression of the site. First, we now know that the site was huge. According to Muller (personal communication) Terminal Formative occupation is continuous over an area 1.5 km wide, bisected by the I.N.A.H. trenches. House floors, bell-shaped storage pits (some with burials, others without), and dense domestic refuse repeatedly occur in excavated contexts. Second, the basic unit of settlement appears to be the house compound—a residence and its adjacent patio, all enclosed by a permanent wall. This pattern is repetitive, and individual compounds are situated on streets apparently laid out on a grid and oriented to the main pyramid complex. Smaller pyramids also dot the residential zone, presumably to serve the local populace. At present, we are unsure whether this pattern occurs throughout the estimated 4–5 km^2 that comprise the Cuicuilco site or whether it is restricted to the site core. What is striking, however, is the apparent similarity to the urban configuration of Teotihuacan: a resemblance, of course, which begs a whole series of questions about the character of sociopolitical and economic organization at the site.

Another major point concerns the dating of the Pedregal lava flows and their impact on the viability of the Cuicuilco center to withstand a natural catastrophe of such magnitude. The most widely accepted interpretation of this disaster presumes that the Xitle eruption covered the site sometime near the end of the Formative period. This, in turn, appears to have provided the impetus for the shift in the balance of power to Teotihuacan. The new data have modified this point of view. The excavation of several Early Teotihuacan period pyramids at Cuicuilco indicates that the lava flow which covered the site did not occur until the middle of the Teotihuacan period (Muller: personal communication). More importantly, it appears that there was an earlier eruption: one which did not obliterate the site but did pass nearby during Terminal Formative times. Admittedly, there is still much uncertainty concerning the effects of this earlier eruption on Cuicuilco, but it does seem likely that it severely curtailed the site's agricultural base. This we view to be a factor in precipitating Teotihuacan supremacy in the Basin of Mexico.

It is probable that the impact of Cuicuilco on rural settlement during the later phases of the Formative period was quite comparable to that exerted by Teotihuacan several hundred years later, only on a much more local level. The fragmentary data we possess clearly suggest that the sociopolitical significance of the Cuicuilco center was without parallel in the Basin of Mexico during the Early Terminal Formative phase. Unfortunately, future research is not likely to shed much light on this critical problem. Surveys of the site's immediate sustaining area, now densely covered by modern urban occupation, are certainly out of the question, and any excavations at Cuicuilco itself must first contend with several meters of lava flow, another improbability. Test excavations, in association with modern construction projects, must inevitably suffer from the problems of being small-scale, haphazardly placed, and not integrated by any unified body of research objectives. What is assured, therefore, is that the Cuicuilco problem will continue to be a plaguing concern for a great many years to follow.

PREPARATION OF THE BASE MAP

In constructing the Basin of Mexico base map we relied on quadrant maps published by *Comision de Estudios del Territorio Nacional (Cetenal)* and by *La Secretaria de la Defensa Nacional.* These maps were drawn either to 10-m or to 50-m contour intervals, but because of problems in scale the 50-m contour interval (beginning at an elevation of 2250 m) was selected as the basis for delineating topographic features. With the exception of the Chalco, Xochimilco, and Ixtapalapa regions, we used the *Cetenal* quadrant sheets because of their more convenient scale (1:50,000). Elsewhere in the Basin contour intervals were derived from the National Defense maps, owing to problems in following specific contours on the prepublication blueprints of the *Cetenal* maps for these areas. The 2240-m contour line was also plotted, since it closely paralleled the precolumbian lakeshore. Both the 2240- and 2250-m contours, regardless of survey region, were transcribed from the *Cetenal* quadrant maps, due to errors in their location on the National Defense maps. Our reconsideration of these contour lines was at greatest variance with the National Defense maps in the Teotihuacan, Texcoco, and Cuautitlan regions (for comparison see Parsons 1971; McBride 1974). The border of the prehispanic lake system was based on alignments of Aztec period salt-making stations, plus the distribution of salinized soils; along Lakes Chalco and Xochimilco the shoreline was assumed to be 500–1000 m within the outline of the 2240-m contour interval. Major prehispanic stream courses were extrapolated from modern drainage patterns. The lower course of the Rio Cuautitlan, which currently empties into the Rio Tepotzotlan, was derived from documentary sources (Rojas *et al.* 1974:24).

All settlement localities were plotted on the Basin of Mexico base map, using a system of symbolic notation adapted from Parsons' (1971) Texcoco survey. For the level of supraregional center, however, we attempted as accurately as scale would permit to depict the actual settlement zone of these exceedingly large centers. The borders of Teotihuacan, both during the Tzacualli and Xolalpan phases, were obtained from the *Teotihuacan Map* (Millon *et al.* 1973). For the Late Aztec site of Texcoco we were guided by Parsons' (1971:92) survey of the periphery of this important Aztec settlement. The boundary limits of the Aztec capital, Tenochtitlan, were drawn from Gonzalez Aparicio's (1973) ethnohistoric study of Late Aztec settlement in the Basin. For the Late Toltec center at Tula, directly outside the northwestern corner of the Basin, we had available two maps: one from the *Proyecto Tula* (Matos 1974); the other from the University of Missouri Tula Project (Diehl 1974).

In transferring site locations from the Zumpango and Texcoco regional maps to the Basin of Mexico map, we ran into one minor difficulty. This problem stemmed from the fact that Parsons' survey maps of these regions were based on the National Defense contours, whereas the map of the Basin for these areas reproduced the *Cetenal* contours. As already mentioned, the two sets of government maps differed in terms of the placement of specific contour lines, especially at lower elevations. Thus, not only did particular contour lines change, but we also found that in some cases the army maps had mislocated entire communities. For this reason the precise location of a few prehistoric settlements varied somewhat. This was more a problem on the Basin floor than on the adjacent piedmont where contour lines were more tightly spaced.

In defining major ecological zones, our classification followed the scheme used originally by Wolf and Palerm (1955), Sanders (1965), and slightly later by Parsons (1971). We disregarded several of Blanton's (1972) environmental types (e.g., the Cerro Pino Upper and Lower Slopes, the Lomas and Hoyas), as we felt that a more simplified zoning typology would be sufficient to bring out major settlement pattern–environmental type correlations. Furthermore, had we applied Blanton's more refined ecological classification, we would have been forced to create a wide variety of new zones to account for the obvious diversity that characterizes the Basin today. As it is, we did find it necessary to devise two additional zones: the Thin Soil Alluvium and the Upland Plain. Our general ecological typology should therefore be considered as provisional, since it is based largely on topographic variety. The reader is referred to Chapter 4, where the significant environment variability in the Basin of Mexico is discussed in detail.

The rainfall isoyets in Map 2 are taken from a special publication of Recursos Hidraulicos (see References).

SUMMARY

In this chapter attention has been drawn to both the methods we employed and the numerous problems we encountered during the survey, the data analysis and compilation, and the preparation of the prehistoric settlement maps of the Basin of Mexico. We have attempted to make clear, perhaps at undue length, the various procedures we used in estimating population and have specified the criteria we applied in constructing our community typology. Our most nagging concern is the various limitations of the survey—problems, in many instances, that were not perceived until the survey projects were well under way. We do not believe that such hinderances have greatly limited the general utility of our survey. Hopefully, the following chapters, where we expound on our results and their theoretical implications, will serve as adequate justification and a case in point.

4

The Natural Environment
of the Basin of Mexico

The Basin of Mexico lies near the southern end of the Mexican *Meseta Central,* a broad upland zone formed by Late Tertiary vulcanism. The Basin was formed as volcanoes and their deposits of lava and ash blocked older drainage outlets to the south, and massive walls of high volcanic ridges built up around the western, southern, and eastern sides of a great central depression. Into this depression, for many millennia, poured the alluvial detritus eroded from the surrounding hillslopes. Thus, the Basin of Mexico is today a great elevated plain surrounded on three sides by high mountain ranges (to the east by the Sierra de Nevada, to the west by the Sierra de las Cruces, and to the south by the Sierra de Ajusco), and to the north by a series of low, discontinuous hill ranges. Lateral extensions of the main sierra (e.g., the Guadalupe, Tepotzotlan, Patlachique, and Santa Catarina ranges) divide the Basin into the natural sub-units which have served so conveniently to define our various regional survey areas within the Basin. Before completion of the "Grand Canal" in the eighteenth century, the Basin was a closed hydrographic unit approximately 7000 km² in extent. Springs, meltwater from the two snow-capped volcanoes, Popocatepetl and Ixtaccihuatl, and runoff from the summer rains all flow toward the center of the Basin, and until the nineteenth century most of this water emptied into a series of shallow lakes that traversed the Basin floor.

The Basin presents a number of favorable and unfavorable circumstances for a maize-based agricultural economy. As a whole it fits into Palerm and Wolf's (1960:13) Central Highland Type I, Variant B environmental type.

Winters are characteristically cold and dry, but summers are warm with abundant rain. Precipitation varies from an annual average of 450 mm on the northeastern plains to more than 1500 mm in the southwestern mountains. More than 80% of all precipitation falls between June 1 and October 1. Since this period corresponds with the thermal summer season, conditions are theoretically optimal for maize cultivation. Soils are generally quite fertile, many being able to withstand almost continuous cropping, and a high percentage have a friable texture that is ideal for an agricultural system based on hand tools of wood and stone. There are, however, a number of major problems for maize cultivation.

Perhaps the most serious is the winter frost problem. Frosts are typically severe from November 1 to February 1, but generally they begin in October and last well into February. Historic frosts have produced crop disasters as early as September and as late as March. In prehispanic times this problem would have been particularly acute, as no native cultigens were adapted to the winter frost season. Minimally, this meant a single cropping season and a very careful planning of agricultural activities. (See Figure 4.1.)

The rainfall pattern is monsoonal. Scattered showers occur from November 1 to May 1. Substantial showers begin in May and become consistent from June 1 until mid-September. Generally, there is a lull in precipitation in July–August, the summer *canicula*. The rains taper off in late September and return to the pattern of scattered showers by November. Individual showers, particularly in the drier north, are torrential, falling in the late afternoon–early evening. The rainfall pattern also tends to be localized, with only certain stations receiving notable accumulations on most days. As we have mentioned, precipitation increases from north to south. There is also a rise in rainfall with greater elevation; precipitation in upland zones is commonly about 50% higher than the Basin floor. In addition, the western side of the Basin typically registers greater accumulations than the eastern; the highest rainfall values are achieved in the southwest, the lowest in the northeast (see Map 2).

Although the rainy season has never failed completely, the beginning of the rainy season is frequently delayed until mid-June. Mid-summer droughts lasting up to several weeks are by no means rare, and in the central and northern portions of the Basin rainfall is highly variable from year to year, commonly falling below the requirement for a good maize crop. For example, at the Tacuba station (mean annual precipitation, 578 mm) during the period from 1878 to 1950, rainfall dropped below 500 mm 14 times (see Figure 4.2). Over much of the Basin there is a greater than 50% chance that rainfall will be well below average or have a delayed start; such a pattern places severe constraints on crop security, especially when the system of land use does not involve artificial humidity control.

The major problem is the relative timing of the rains and the frosts. A retarded rainy season combined with early frosts is fatal for the maize crop. The frost–rainfall problem varies considerably in significance from area to

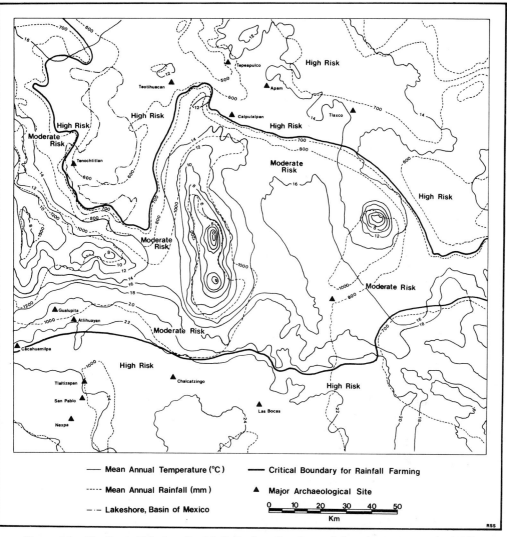

Figure 4.1.   The Central Mexican Symbiotic Region, showing variations in mean annual rainfall and mean annual temperature.

area within the Basin. Above 2700 m the frost season is so prolonged that maize cannot be grown except in a few localized "hot spots." Within the elevation band where maize can be grown (2240–2700 m), the frost–rainfall problem is most severe in the upper piedmont (2500–2700 m) and alluvial plain (2245–2260 m). The problem is less serious in the south, where rainfall is both more abundant and more regular. Near the lakeshore (2238–2245 m) and in the lower–middle piedmont (2260–2500 m) the combination of inadequate moisture and crippling frosts occurs much less frequently and crop

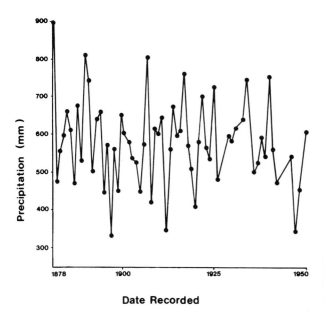

Figure 4.2. Total annual precipitation recorded at the Tacuba Station, Basin of Mexico.

production in these areas is much more secure. Periods of low precipitation, the relatively high percentage of agricultural land that is susceptible to erosion, and declining soil fertility resulting from too short a cropping cycle, present additional obstacles for successful maize cultivation. As we will discuss in the concluding section, the combined effects of these ecological variables are critical to our understanding of the prehispanic settlement history of the Basin.

On the basis of the rainfall–frost regime, plus variation in soil depth and texture, slope angle, amount of natural subsurface moisture, and absolute elevation above sea level, we have divided the Basin of Mexico into nine major environmental zones (see Map 1).

The Lake System. At the time of the Spanish Conquest the Basin floor was covered by an extensive system of large lakes. To the north were Lakes Xaltocan and Zumpango; in the center, Lake Texcoco; and to the south, Lakes Xochimilco and Chalco. The lakes were shallow, ranging in depth from 1 to 3 m, and part of the year consisted of a number of interconnected ponds of varying size. Lake Texcoco, the largest of the five, was located at the lowest elevation (lowest point ca. 2235 m), was the ultimate destination of all drainage, and hence was extremely saline. Lakes Xochimilco and Chalco were about 3 m higher than Lake Texcoco, and Lake Xochimilco drained into it. Because of this outlet, which functioned year round, and because of the presence of numerous springs along the southern shore, the water in Lakes Chalco and Xochimilco was fresh and covered by floating vegetation. Lakes Xaltocan and Zumpango were also situated at a somewhat higher level but drained into Lake Texcoco only seasonally. Consequently, they were more saline than lakes Xochimilco and Chalco, except at the mouths of major perennial streams or near local springs.

In precolumbian times the lakes provided a wide variety of food resources. From the lake itself five kinds of fish, frogs, polliwogs, freshwater crustaceans and molluscs, turtles, and various aquatic insects and their larvae were obtained (Orozco y Berra 1864:162). From the lakeshore gathered plant resources included reeds, wild rice, and a blue–green algae called *Tecuilatl* (Orozco y Berra 1864:153–163; Santley 1977). During the fall and winter months the lake system was also one of the terminal points of the Central Flyway: a migratory route for waterfowl coming down from the prairie marshes of western Canada (Flannery 1968).

The Saline Lakeshore.   Ringing Lakes Texcoco, Xaltocan, and Zumpango was a band of poorly drained saline soil approximately 500–1000 m wide. Although today much of this area remains a barren strip of limited agricultural utility, in antiquity it was the principal zone of salt making. Large, amorphous earth mounds, heavily littered with fragments of Texcoco Fabric Marked pottery (a Late Aztec ceramic type linked with the production of salt) have been found in great abundance around the western, eastern, and southern shoreline of Lake Texcoco. These features bear mute witness to the intensity of prehispanic salt making. Several sixteenth- and seventeenth-century documentary sources (e.g., Peter Martyr Anglerius 1628) indicate that salt making was also carried out around the southwestern shore of Lake Texcoco, at the south edge of Tenochtitlan, in an area now completely covered by modern Mexico City.

Near major freshwater streams the lakeshore was probably overgrown with luxuriant hydrophytic vegetation. For the remainder of this zone, salt-resistant grasses such as *Sporobolus plumbens, Distichlis prostrata,* and *D. spicata* along with the various species of reeds (*Typha*) were probably characteristic (Kovar 1970:22–23).

The Deep Soil Alluvium.   Between the 2240 and 2300-m contour intervals is a relatively flat, expansive zone of soil deposition that we have termed the deep soil alluvium. Geographically, this zone occurs as a band several kilometers wide surrounding the lake system. In a number of places this alluvial zone reaches considerable widths, the larger of which parallel the drainages of Rivers Cuautitlan–Tepotzotlan, Teotihuacan, Papalotla, and Ameca. Somewhat less substantial alluvial zones flank the Rio Hondo near Azcapotzalco and the Avenidas de Pachuca. In general terms, the major expanses of deep soil alluvium are found (*a*) along the eastern edge of Lake Texcoco and Lake Chalco, between Teotihuacan and Chalco, (*b*) in the Tacuba region, along the northwestern corner of Lake Texcoco, and (*c*) in the Cuautitlan region along the southwestern side of Lake Zumpango. Soil depth frequently exceeds 4–5 m. Away from major stream flows loam and clay–loam soils predominate, but along water courses and in more inland areas, soils with a sandy loam texture are common. Except for the more humid southern Basin, the alluvium is agriculturally marginal unless irrigation is applied. This is due primarily to a combination of low rainfall and severe frosts that tend to settle in low-lying areas. The drainage of marshy localities near the lakeshore would have posed additional problems in precolumbian times. With the application of hydraulic techniques, however, the alluvium can be transformed into the most productive agricultural zone in the Basin.

Because of continuous cultivation for at least two millenia, the natural vegetation is difficult to reconstruct. The northern alluvium undoubtedly had scrubby growth, while in the south the increase in precipitation probably brought about a woodland formation of oak and cypress, interspersed with taller grasses and a variety of shrubs. Along the shore, or major streams that bisect the alluvial plain, a gallery association of swamp cypress, *Acacia,* reeds, and representatives of the *Cyperaceae* and the *Compositae* was probably predominant. Game animals such as the cottontail rabbit (*Sylvilagus* spp.), the jack rabbit (*Lepus callotis*), assorted rodents, various species of bird and reptile, and in wetter localities whitetail deer (*Odocoileus virginianus*) were presumably common on the Basin floor.

The Thin Soil Alluvium.   In the northern Basin the combination of lesser relief, lower rainfall, and hence a low rate of soil deposition, has produced a relatively expansive alluvial plain of shallow depth. Soil texture is good (i.e., loams and sandy loams predominate), but because soils are generally less than 1 m in depth, evaporation is high. The only large stream course is the Avenidas de Pachuca. The low incidence of major water flows, combined with the fact that precipitation is low and frosts severe, mean that this area must be considered marginal for both irrigation agriculture and dry farming. The natural vegetation today consists of short grasses and maguey (*Agave* spp.), and in antiquity these were probably augmented by scrub oak. Rabbit and deer are consequently assumed to have been moderately abundant.

The Upland Alluvium.   Near Amecameca, in the southeastern corner of the Basin, there is an expanse of sedimentary deposit that we have termed the upland alluvium. The plain occurs at an average elevation of 2550 m, although parts occur at as low as 2450 m or as high as 2600 m. In general, soils are friable, rainfall is considerable (900–1100 mm), and frosts do not seem to be as much a problem as at lower elevations. The plain is also traversed by a major perennial stream, the Rio de Ameca. Today, intensive rainfall cultivation is practiced on the plain. However, the dispersed nature of prehispanic settlement in the area, up to and including the Late Aztec phase, suggests that relatively extensive techniques were applied in antiquity. This upland area is also situated at the main pass in the sierra leading to Morelos, so that the plain serves as the major artery of communication from the Basin to the south. Virtually all of the area is under cultivation today, but originally the plain must have been in oak forest, perhaps mixed with pine, alder, madrone, and cedar at its upper borders (Tolstoy and Fish 1973:2). Along the Rio de Ameca edaphic conditions probably permitted an oak–cypress–acacia gallery forest. Because of the dominance of oak, whitetail deer were doubtlessly present in appreciable numbers.

The Lower Piedmont. The lower piedmont consists of a band of gently sloping terrain, below 2350 m, which merges with the Basin floor alluvium at approximately 2260 m in most areas. The absolute elevation of this lower boundary varies from place to place. In the upper Teotihuacan Valley the border is at 2300 m, whereas to the south of Lakes Chalco and Xochimilco the line of demarcation is close to the 2250-m contour interval. Likewise, its width varies considerably. In the southern Basin, because of the steep escarpment of the Sierra de Ajusco, the lower piedmont is rarely wider than about 1 km. On either side of Lake Texcoco the band of gently sloping land ranges from 2 to as much as 4 km wide in some places. In the north, because of the absence of major mountain peaks, the lower piedmont is more expansive.

The far northwestern corner of our survey area, north of a line extending through the modern communities of Huehuetoca, Tequisquiac, and Tlapanaloya, actually lies outside the Basin of Mexico drainage. Here the land slopes gently to the north, and is drained by the Rio Salado, a tributary of the Rio Tula. Although this area corresponds quite closely to the general lower piedmont zone we describe here, its elevation descends to a low of about 1950 m at the modern town of Apaxco where our survey terminated. This is some 300 m below the general minimal elevation of the lower piedmont in the Basin of Mexico proper. We are presently unaware of any significant ecological implications of this elevation difference.

Soils are generally sandy loams in texture and thus well-suited to maize-based agriculture with hand tools. Rainfall is also more substantial than on the Basin floor, and frosts are less frequent during the fall season. Soil depth today is quite variable, with deposits of 5–50 cm being commonplace, along with numerous exposed areas of *tepetate,* an indurated hardpan subsoil. Soil depth was substantially greater prior to the Spanish Conquest. Because plant growth is slow and rainfall torrential, any stripping of the natural vegetation can tremendously accelerate soil removal unless proper conservation techniques are applied. The major impediment to agricultural use, therefore, is the high vulnerability of this zone to erosion: a problem that seems to have been serious as early as the Formative period.

Because of this problem, as well as the fact that much of this area is either under cultivation or used for pasture, only remnants of the natural vegetation cover exist. Comparison with refuge areas, principally in the south, suggests that much of this zone was in oak forest. At lower elevations the forest probably resembled a more open woodland, mixed with various shrubs and grasses. In the south, at greater elevations, and along barrancas a more dense association of oak and alder was probably typical, while to the north there was probably a gradual transition to a scrub oak forest. Before extinction in historic times, great numbers of whitetail deer were permanent inhabitants.

The Middle Piedmont.   By middle piedmont we mean the band of moderately sloping ground that occurs between 2350 and 2500 m above sea level. Geographically, this zone is adjacent to the lower piedmont and parallels it in distribution about the Basin. Soil texture and depth are also quite comparable, as is rainfall. Slope angle is slightly greater, however, so sheet and gully erosion are somewhat more of a problem. Where vestiges of the original plant cover remain, a dense, oak broadleaf forest predominates. Near its upper extreme, cypress, alder, and a few conifers are also present. The abundance of oak suggests whitetail deer as the dominant herbivore.

The Upper Piedmont.   At approximately 2500 m an increase in slope angle marks the lower boundary of a transitional ecological province which extends up to the 2700-m contour, the foot of the sierra. Soils tend to be clay textured and very shallow. Over large areas sheet erosion has removed practically all soil, in certain places even cutting into 2–4 m of *tepetate* subsoil (Parsons 1971). Innumerable barrancas, many as deep as 20–30 m, also scar the landscape. Not including the northeastern Basin, precipitation is both heavy and regular, but the severity of frosts during the early fall months means that aboriginally only varieties of fast-maturing maize could survive in this zone. Before erosion became rampant, the upper piedmont was probably covered by a mixed broadleaf-conifer forest of oak (*Quercus* spp.), pine (*Pinus leiophylla*), cypress (*Cupressus Lidleyi*), alder (*Alnus* spp.), tepozan (*Buddleia* spp.), madrono (*Arbutus xalapensis*), and various shrubs and grasses (Kovar 1970:33; Parsons 1971:11; Sears 1952:244; Tolstoy and Fish 1973:2). Presumably, this zone also delimited the upper habitat range of whitetail deer.

The Sierra.   The sierra is a rugged, precipitous area, devoid of any permanent modern settlement, that extends from 2700 m to as high as 5800 m in the southeast. Occasionally cultivated fields occur up to 3000 m, but the major commercial value of the zone is as a source of lumber for construction, fuel, and charcoal burning. As might be expected, the sierra is in conifer forest, with oak and alder occurring up to 2800 m. Three species of pine predominate: *Pinus patula* and *P. Montezumae,* which disappear at about 3500 m, and *P. Hartwegii,* which extends all the way up to the 4000-m timberline (Sears 1952:244). Fir (*Abies religiosa*) and juniper (*Juniperus monticola*) may also be found. Because of its agricultural marginality, large sections of the sierra are now used for pasturing herds of cattle. A few deer and smaller mammals are sometimes hunted, particularly prior to about 1940.

An additional component to the environment of the Basin of Mexico, and one that has produced additional variety in terms of human occupation, is the complexity of its geological history. In Cretaceous times the area now occupied by the Basin was part of a shallow tropical sea. Relicts of this phase of its history occur in the form of a few low hills in the northwest corner. During the Cenozoic, a series of seven phases of volcanism resulted in the elevation of the Basin floor to its present minimum elevation of 2235 m above sea level and produced virtually all of the surface topography visible today.

No traces of the first phase, dating from the Eocene, have been identified. The second phase, dating from the Middle Oligocene, is well represented by low ranges of hills in the northwest corner of the Basin. Phases three and four, occurring during the Late Oligocene and Early Miocene, have left a series of small, isolated topographic features. During phase four (Late Miocene) what Mexican geographers refer to as the "Sierras Menores"—the small ranges—were formed; these include the Sierras of Guadalupe, Tepozotlan, and Patlachique. Phase five, dating from the Pliocene, was one of major volcanic activity and the great Sierras that border the Basin on the east and west (the Sierra Nevada and Sierra de las Cruces) were formed. Although virtually all of the surface topography that had evolved up until this point was of volcanic origin, age and erosion have reduced the cone-like forms so diagnostic of volcanism to less regular forms. Virtually all the hills in the Basin today that have the typical volcano appearance date from phases six and seven, which occurred during the Pleistocene. Phase six witnessed extensive volcanic activity all over the Basin. This involved building on older formations plus the formation of isolated hills such as Cerro de la Estrella, Cerro Chimalhuacan, and Cerro Gordo.

During phase seven, dating from Late Pleistocene times, the massive Sierra Ajusco or Chichinautzin, which delimits the Basin to the south, was formed. Prior to this event, the Basin of Mexico was a broad valley, tilted downward from north to south, that drained into the Balsas River. Also dating from this phase were the great volcanoes of Popocatepetl and Iztaccihuatl and the chain of small volcanoes that form the peninsula of Ixtapalapa. Aside from the indirect effects that this tectonic activity has had on such features as rainfall and temperature, the two components we utilized to define our ecological zones, it has had more direct effects, in the form of surface topography, hydrography, soil formation, and mineral distribution, that directly relate to problems of human resource exploitation. Mooser (1975) has published a detailed geological map of the Basin which we have simplified to illustrate the brief summary of the geological history presented here (Map 3).

To recapitulate, the Basin of Mexico is a complex area geographically, including at least nine major environmental zones. Each one of these zones presents a different set of problems for prehispanic cultivation, and each contains its own particular inventory of faunal, floral, and other natural resources. As subsequent chapters will show, a clear understanding of these ecological–environmental variables is a necessary point of departure for explaining why the Basin attained early preeminence in Mesoamerican prehistory and retained its nuclearity right up to the Spanish Conquest.

5

Settlement History
of the Basin of Mexico

In Mesoamerica, as in other culture areas, archaeologists have defined a large number of local regional chronologies based on changes in ceramic styles. In the older chronologies the various periods and phases were frequently assigned a numerical nomenclature, but more recently the tendency has been to use names. Generally, the period and phase designations have been derived from local place names, or in cases where the phases or periods correlated with historical documents, they have been named after ethnic groups or centers noted in the documents. As the various regional surveys of the Basin of Mexico project developed, a variety of unexpected chronological problems emerged. We say unexpected because this was one of the few areas of Mesoamerica where archaeologists had worked extensively on the local chronology.

In Chapter 2 we pointed out, in our discussion of the purpose of the excavations conducted during the Teotihuacan Valley project, a number of difficulties that arose in the use of the published ceramic sequence for the Basin of Mexico. These included incomplete publication for some phases of the sequence, and very selective reporting (in the sense that only certain kinds of ceramics—primarily decorated burial vessels—were described) of the ceramic complex when phases were well described. A more serious problem was the possibility that nonchronological factors might have operated to produce some of the variety noted in our ceramic samples. Basically, stylistic variability, whether in ceramics or some other medium, is produced by three factors: time, space, and subsocietal differentiation. Most particularly we were concerned with the spatial factor. The Basin of Mexico is a relatively large area, and theoretically there might have existed a variety of ceramic styles that were contemporary with each other and were produced by regional differentiation.

There is no doubt that the spatial factor did operate to produce minor stylistic variety, particularly during the earlier ceramic phases when markets were absent and sociopolitical systems were small. This kind of variety, however, was generally easily accommodated by the master sequence for the Basin as a whole. The major problem was that of possible major variations in style within the same chronological phase or period. This was a critical problem because our settlement survey suggested that certain style complexes, at several points in time, were spatially restricted. We could either interpet this as evidence that the areas outside the distributions were unpopulated or that other ceramic styles, found in those areas, were contemporary. This problem emerges most particularly at two points during the occupational history. One is toward the end of the Formative or Pre-Classic period and involves the precise interrelationships between the Tezoyuca, Chimalhuacan–Patlachique, and Tzacualli ceramic complexes, and the other is the problem of the relationship between the Aztec I and Aztec II ceramic complexes at the end of the sequence.

With respect to the chronological scheme, which will be discussed later, we have generally assumed that there is little variation caused by the spatial factor throughout most of the sequence. Thus, the absence of ceramics dating to a particular phase means that certain sections of the Basin were probably unoccupied during the time period in question. Likewise, all sites containing similar pottery are considered contemporaneous. A number of methodological problems are associated with both of these assumptions. These we will explore in some detail in later chapters.

Aside from the various local chronologies, like the Basin of Mexico sequence, archaeologists have also designed a chronology for Mesoamerica as a whole. Unfortunately the terminology used has stage as well as period connotations and this has produced considerable confusion in the literature. Among those terms which have this double meaning are Formative, Pre-Classic, Classic, Militaristic, Post-Classic, Archaic, and so on. At a seminar of the School of American Research in 1972 a group of Mesoamericanists proposed (Wolf 1976) a new scheme for the culture area as a whole, essentially borrowed from John Rowe (1960), who designed such a scheme for the Central Andes. The new terminology has an advantage in that it is strictly chronological in meaning. We have adopted it for this study and will apply it to the local Basin of Mexico chronology to facilitate comparison with other regions of Mesoamerica. In Table 5.1, this overall chronology is presented, along with its equivalents in the previous general Mesoamerican sequence, and the various local chronologies published for the Basin of Mexico.

TABLE 5.1
Chronological Concordances for the Basin of Mexico

YEARS	MAJOR ARCHAEOLOGICAL PERIOD			ARCHAEOLOGICAL PHASE				
				BASIN OF MEXICO	TEOTIHUACAN REGION	CUAUHTITLAN REGION	TEXCOCO & IXTAPALAPA REGIONS	VAILLANT
1519 A.D.	LATE HORIZON		LATE POSTCLASSIC	TLATELOLCO	TEACALCO	LATE AZTEC	LATE AZTEC	AZTEC IV
1400				TENOCHTITLAN	CHIMALPA			AZTEC III
1300	SECOND INTERMEDIATE	PHASE THREE		CULHUACAN TENAYUCA	ZOCANGO	EARLY AZTEC	EARLY AZTEC	AZTEC I-II
1200			EARLY POSTCLASSIC					
1100		PHASE TWO		MAZAPAN	ATLATONGO	MAZAPAN	LATE TOLTEC	TOLTEC
1000					MAZAPAN			
900		PHASE ONE		COYOTLATELCO	XOMETLA	COYOTLATELCO	EARLY TOLTEC	
800					OXTOTIPAC			
700	MIDDLE HORIZON	PHASE TWO	CLASSIC	METEPEC	METEPEC	TEOTIHUACAN	LATE CLASSIC	TEOTIHUACAN IV
					LATE XOLALPAN			TEO. III-B
600				XOLALPAN	EARLY XOLALPAN			TEOTIHUACAN III-A
500					LATE TLAMIMILOLPA			TEOTIHUACAN II-III
400		PHASE ONE		TLAMIMILOLPA	EARLY TLAMIMILOLPA		EARLY CLASSIC	
300								
200		PHASE FIVE		MICCAOTLI	MICCAOTLI			TEOTIHUACAN II
100					APETLAC			TEOTIHUACAN I
0		PHASE FOUR		TZACUALLI	TEOPAN	TZACUALLI		
100			TERMINAL PRECLASSIC	CUICUILCO V	OXTOTLA		TERMINAL FORMATIVE	VERY LATE TICOMAN
200		PHASE THREE-B		CUICUILCO IV	PATLACHIQUE	TULTITLAN		LATE TICOMAN
300 B.C.		P. THREE-A			TEZOYUCA			
				TICOMAN III				
400	FIRST INTERMEDIATE	PHASE TWO-B	LATE PRECLASSIC	TICOMAN II	LATE CUANALAN	CUAUTLALPAN	LATE FORMATIVE	INTERMEDIATE TICOMAN
500								
600		PHASE TWO-A		TICOMAN I	EARLY CUANALAN	ATLAMICA B		EARLY TICOMAN
						ATLAMICA A		
700		PHASE ONE-B	MIDDLE PRECLASSIC	CUAUTEPEC L. LA PASTORA	CHICONAUTLA	ECATEPEC B		MIDDLE ZACATENCO
800				EARLY LA PASTORA		ECATEPEC A	MIDDLE FORMATIVE	
900				EL ARBOLILLO	ALTICA	AGUACATITLA		EARLY ZACATENCO
1000		PHASE ONE-A						
1100				BOMBA		TLALNEPANTLA		EARLY EL ARBOLILLO
1200		PHASE TWO	EARLY PRECLASSIC	MANANTIAL			EARLY FORMATIVE	
1300	EARLY HORIZON							
1400		PHASE ONE		AYOTLA				
1500				COAPEXCO				
1600	INITIAL CERAMIC			NEVADA-TLALPAN				
1700								

93

The new system includes six major periods: Initial Ceramic, Early Horizon, First Intermediate, Middle Horizon, Second Intermediate, and Late Horizon. The Early, Middle, and Late Horizons are periods marked by the widespread distribution of the Olmec, Teotihuacan, and Aztec art styles over large areas of Mesoamerica. The First and Second Intermediate, as their terminology suggests, are interim blocks of time occurring between the major horizon styles. In both cases, their inception is defined by the disappearance of the preceding horizon style, followed first by a period of regionality in ceramics and other stylistic media, and then by the rapid development of the succeeding pan-Mesoamerican style. Subdivisions of these periods or phases, although applicable to a great part of Mesoamerica, are based largely on the Basin of Mexico sequence.

In assigning a temporal position to sites found during the surface survey we have been guided by the ceramic diagnostics defined by Tolstoy (Tolstoy, n.d.; Tolstoy and Fish 1975; Tolstoy and Paradis 1970), Vaillant (1930, 1931, 1935), Sanders et al. (1975) and McBride (1974) for the Early Horizon and the First Intermediate; by Vaillant (1941), Rattray (1966, 1973), Millon et al. (1973), Parsons (1966, 1971) and Sanders et al. (n.d.) for the later phases. For the most part our periodization is based on excavated sequences of pottery wares, vessel forms and stylistic attributes. The chronological sequence derived from these excavations is particularly fine grained, each phase involving 50–150 years of occupation. Our surface sample phasing is more general, each phase spanning about 150–200 years. With the exception of the Early Horizon and the First Intermediate One phase we have not tried to apply the more refined excavation sequence to the survey data, largely because the refined sequence has only been recently derived, and we have not had access to the surface samples for reevaluation. Finally, many of the excavation phase diagnostics occur in very low frequencies and, considering the nature of our sampling procedures, have a high probability of not being represented in our surface collections. In Appendix C we have presented a detailed discussion of the contents of our ceramic sequence accompanied by the appropriate illustrations for those readers who have a more specialized interest in the archaeology of the area.

EARLY HORIZON (1500–1150 B.C.)

During the overall Early Horizon Period approximately 19 sites were occupied (Maps 5–7). Twelve of these are classified as hamlets, 3 as small villages, 2 as large villages, and 3 others as indeterminate status. Of this sample 9 were occupied during Phase One (1500–1300 B.C.), a sample that includes 4 small villages (2 at Coapexco, and 1 each at Tlapacoya and Tlatilco), 5 hamlets, and 2 sites of indeterminate status. During Phase Two (1300–1150 B.C.), the Coapexco sites were apparently abandoned, Tlapacoya continued as a small village, Tlatilco expanded into a large village, and a large

village was also founded at Tuleyahualco. The number of hamlets i
to 12 and 2 sites of indeterminate status were occupied.

The data suggest relatively slight population increase between
phases, although it could have been more substantial than our data ir...cate.
The problem is estimating the population of Tlatilco, since it lies within the
urban zone of Mexico City. Evidence from burials at Tlatilco, dating from
Phase Two (Piña Chan 1958; Tolstoy 1975), suggests some kind of ranking
structure, but the overall settlement pattern does not indicate very elaborate
political organization.

With respect to population distribution, the pattern is as follows. During
Phase One nearly half the population, perhaps even more, resided at the
villages at Coapexco, in the upland alluvium zone, at an elevation of 2600 m,
very close to the broad, low (2485 m) pass over the Ajusco range to Morelos.
Considering the fact that the ceramics of the Early Horizon generally have a
close resemblance to contemporary ceramics from Morelos, and that Morelos
was more densely settled during this, and the succeeding First Intermediate
One phase, it is tempting to view Coapexco as the locus of initial colonization of the Basin by sedentary farmers from Morelos. Ecologically this sequence of events makes sense. The great majority of the population of
Morelos throughout the prehistoric and historic periods resided at an elevation of 1200–1600 m above sea level, a frost-free altitude. Both rainfall (700–
1000 m) and the temperature present an ideal habitat for wild maize, and
Morelos, along with comparable ecological zones in Oaxaca, Guerrero, and
Puebla, was probably one of the hearths of early maize domestication. As the
result of this initial demographic and cultural precocity population pressure
by Early Horizon times might have been sufficient to stimulate the occupation of such regions of higher elevation as the Basin of Mexico.

The balance of the population during Phase One was concentrated
primarily within the deep soil alluvium (with several settlements on the
shore itself) of the southern part of the Basin. Only one small village (Tlatilco)
and one hamlet were recorded on the lower piedmont, a prime zone for the
First Intermediate period settlement. During Phase Two, although the deep
soil alluvium was still a favored location, the trend toward a preference of
population for lower-middle piedmont settlement is evident. The population
is also more evenly balanced, with nearly all of it concentrated in four large,
well spaced settlements (assuming that one of the indeterminate sites,
Cuicuilco, was at least a small village). These settlements are spaced at
10–15-km intervals.

Viewing the pattern for the Early Horizon generally, there was a clear and
obvious weighting of population westward and southward, correlating very
closely with rainfall patterns in the Basin. There are essentially two kinds of
settlements: (a) substantial nucleated villages with a few hundred inhabitants, and (b) much smaller and more ephemeral sites, which we have called
hamlets. Not all of the latter need necessarily represent permanent occupation. In no case do we have any indication of civic–ceremonial–elite architec-

ture, although we stress again that Tlatilco, probably our largest and most complex site, remains very poorly known, obscured as it is by the overburden of modern Mexico City.

FIRST INTERMEDIATE: PHASE ONE (1150–650 B.C.)

There was a veritable population explosion between the Early Horizon and the First Intermediate One phase (Maps 8–10). Our sample for the overall period includes 8 large villages, 11 small villages (4 dispersed, 7 nucleated), 49 hamlets, 5 sites of indeterminate status and 2 salt-manufacturing stations. The amount of time involved is greater than that encompassed in the Early Horizon (500 compared to 350 years), but even allowing for this difference the population increased at a considerably accelerated rate. Most of this growth apparently occurred during Subphase One B as Table 5.2 indicates. The increase between Early Horizon Phase Two and First Intermediate One A is a modest one. On the other hand, this did involve a substantial geographic expansion since there were hamlets as far north as the Teotihuacan Valley. Subphase B was primarily a phase of filling in of populations within the same physical space. Virtually all of the village settlements were located in the southwestern portion of the Basin, the same region where most of the Early Horizon population was located. Almost all of the settlements in the more arid areas (the Cuautitlan region, the Teotihuacan Valley, and the Texcoco region) were hamlets, and located primarily in the lower and middle piedmont. In the southern region the pattern we described for the Early Horizon persists, with deep-soil alluvium and lower-middle piedmont settlements. Villages are more numerous however, and more closely spaced, that is, at 5–10-km intervals. There was an unusually dense cluster of settlements to the south and east of the Guadalupe Range and the adjacent Tacuba region, located primarily on the lower piedmont, but close to the edge of the deep-soil alluvium.

Thus, the First Intermediate Phase One occupation appears to be an expansion and elaboration of the basic Early Horizon pattern. The four principal changes that occur in the First Intermediate Phase One are (a) substantial population growth in the deep-soil alluvium and lower-middle piedmont zones in the southern Basin; (b) the presence of some very large, nucleated communities, for a few of which we estimate population on the order of 1000 people; (c) the decrease, by a factor of roughly one half, in the intersite distance between substantial villages; and (d) the presence of two distinct kinds of village settlements, one of which is significantly larger than the other. Despite these rather significant changes, however, there is still no indication that any one site (or small number of sites) stood at the top level of a sociopolitical hierarchy of any complexity and scale. There are no sites that stand out as really different or unusual in terms of size and internal complexity. Most particularly, there is no definite evidence of civic–ceremonial–elite

TABLE 5.2
Population Increase during the First Intermediate Phase

	First Intermediate One A	First Intermediate One B
Large villages	2	6
Small villages	6	12
Hamlets	17	47
Indeterminate	3	5
Salt extraction	0	2

architecture. Differentiated burials and the presence of two significantly different kinds of settlements (large versus small villages) clearly imply ranking, but social stratification and hierarchical political dominance seem to be absent from the scene.

FIRST INTERMEDIATE: PHASE TWO (650–300 B.C.)

Unfortunately, although this long period has been subdivided, on the basis of excavations by Vaillant (1930, 1931, 1935), Heizer and Bennyhoff (1966), McBride (1974), and Santley (1977), we have not examined our surface samples with the more refined phasing in mind and hence will have to deal with the phase as a whole—a 350-year time span (Map 11). In length it is comparable, however, to the Early Horizon or First Intermediate One subphases, so we can make significant general comparisons.

The outstanding trends of this period are (a) substantial population growth (approximately a 3.5-fold increase over the antecedent period); (b) the first definite presence of civic–ceremonial architecture (modest in scale, but well defined at some sites, with pyramidal mounds up to about 5 m high at a few of the largest settlements in the southern Basin); and (c) the presence, for the first time, of a well-defined hierarchy of settlements (hamlets and small villages, large villages, and regional centers), whose top level comprised six very substantial sites with definite, or probable, civic–ceremonial architecture. One of the latter sites (Cuicuilco, in the southwest Basin) may have had a population of 5000–10,000 people, while the other five contained between 1000 and 3500 people. The sample also includes 16 large villages (2 dispersed, 14 nucleated), 29 small villages (18 dispersed, 11 nucleated), 105 hamlets, and 3 sites of indeterminate status. When specific subregions are examined, a fair degree of variability is seen. Population growth is most rapid and most substantial in the east and southeast, while in the west-central Basin (a major focus of First Intermediate Phase One occupation) population growth was much more limited, and the far northern Basin remained almost uninhabited. Most population growth occurred within areas already occupied less intensively during the antecedent period. The only newly occupied zone of any size was the upper piedmont and upland alluvium in the far southeastern Basin, south of Cerro Chiconquiac, adjacent to the most densely settled part of the entire Basin. This latter situation almost certainly reflects migration out of the densely occupied alluvium and lower-middle piedmont east of Lake Chalco. Another newly inhabited zone was the saline eastern lakeshore of Lake Texcoco, where a few small sites now occupied marshy ground far away from any suitable agricultural land. These sites probably represent the residences of people specialized (at least seasonally or temporarily) in the exploitation of lacustrine resources.

The relative regularity of spacing between substantial settlements that characterized the First Intermediate Phase One is no longer apparent. While several major sites are consistently separated by intervals of 8–12 km, several others are spaced quite closely. An inspection of our general settlement map (Map 11) suggests the presence of four or five separate settlement clusters that may have sociopolitical significance: (a) around the edges of the Guadalupe Range and into the Cuautitlan alluvium in the west-central Basin; (b) in the lower-middle piedmont of the Texcoco Region; (c) around the edges of the deep-soil alluvium east of Lake Chalco in the southeastern Basin; (d) the Cuicuilco area in the southwestern Basin; and (e) a less well-defined cluster occupying the lower piedmont on the north and south shores of the lakeshore at the juncture of Lakes Chalco and Xochimilco (this may actually belong with either cluster 3 or cluster 4). Nearly two-thirds of the total Basin population resided on the alluvium and lower-middle piedmont around Lakes Chalco and Xochimilco. Most of the remaining third was shared between the Texcoco and Cuautitlan–Tenayuca–Tacuba settlement clusters on either side of Lake Texcoco.

Our data for the First Intermediate Phase Two indicate significantly more societal differentiation and centralization than for the antecedent First Intermediate Phase One. For the first time we have evidence for distinctive civic–ceremonial architecture, for a three-level settlement hierarchy, for several discrete major settlement clusters, and for some suggestion of occupational specialization. The Cuicuilco site probably represents a level of sociopolitical centralization qualitatively distinct from the five other settlements we have called regional centers. This raises the possibility that there was a fourth organizational level, at least in the southern Basin, with Cuicuilco dominating several other smaller regional centers.

FIRST INTERMEDIATE: PHASE THREE (300–100 B.C.)

This phase is a time of major sociopolitical change and striking regional variation in settlement configuration (Map 12). The most pronounced differences relative to antecedent Phase Two are (a) an approximate doubling of total population; (b) the presence of two very large regional centers; and (c) a marked change in the basic configuration of settlement, especially in the Teotihuacan Valley, but also in several other areas. Besides the Tezoyuca hilltop centers and the two large regional centers the sample includes 10 small regional centers, 10 large villages (3 nucleated, 7 dispersed), 37 small villages (10 nucleated, 27 dispersed), 135–150 hamlets, and 4 small isolated ceremonial complexes. Because there is such great regional settlement diversity within the Basin, each major subarea will be discussed separately. At the end of this section we will discuss the special problem of the Tezoyuca hilltop center.

The Chalco region, and especially the segment east of Lake Chalco, stands out as relatively conservative. There was a moderate population decline from the Phase Two level. *Most* substantial Phase Two sites continue to be occupied, and *most* Phase Two large villages and regional centers continue to be important communities in Phase Three times. However, three very substantial Phase Two villages, inland from the northeast corner of Lake Chalco, are no longer occupied in Phase Three, and there is a noticeable clustering of major sites on the piedmont ringing the central part of the deep alluvium east and slightly south of Lake Chalco. This latter area is the only place in the Chalco region where substantial new settlement occurs in Phase Three.

In the Ixtapalapa region, immediately north of Lake Chalco, there is only limited continuity between Phase Two and Phase Three settlement. The major Phase Two regional center was abandoned, and a substantial proportion of Phase Three population resided at a new regional center (Ix-TF-5; Blanton 1972) situated on a pronounced ridge well up on the rugged Santa Catarina massif, surrounded by massive stone retaining walls. An inspection of Map 12 suggests that major Phase Three sites in the Ixtapalapa region form a distinct settlement cluster together with three substantial sites in the far southwestern corner of the adjacent Texcoco region (around the base of Cerro Chimalhuacan) where there had been only limited Phase Two occupation. Within the borders of our Ixtapalapa region survey area, Phase Three population is about 15% less than Phase Two. However, if the buildup of Phase Three population around Cerro Chimalhuacan (formally a part of our Texcoco region survey area) is also considered, then there would have been a modest population increase relative to Phase Two.

In the far southwestern Basin, Cuicuilco reached its maximum size and architectural complexity. Earlier excavations (e.g., Cummings 1933) have shown that massive temple platforms, up to 80 m in diameter and 20 m high, were being built there in Phase Three times (see Figure 5.1). On the basis of scattered data from a number of exposed areas within the site (e.g., Palerm and Wolf 1961e), we estimate a settlement area of at least 400 ha, and a minimal population in the neighborhood of 20,000 people. It is quite possible that the site may actually be significantly larger. The monumentality of its Phase Three public architecture was without parallel in the entire Basin of Mexico, and only Teotihuacan equalled or exceeded it in size and population. There is very limited Phase Three occupation in the Xochimilco region east of Cuicuilco. Similarly, there are no reported Phase Three sites in the Tacuba

Figure 5.1. Oblique aerial view of Cuicuilco Pyramid. (Courtesy of CIA Mexicana Aerofoto S.A.)

region north of Cuicuilco. This paucity of settlement may be more apparent than real, as archaeological remains in the Tacuba region and the western Xochimilco region are so badly obscured by modern settlement. Furthermore, most archaeological investigations in the Tacuba region were carried out at a time (prior to 1960) when Phase Three pottery was poorly defined and inadequately described. Phase Three occupations may thus have gone unrecognized in these early investigations. On the other hand, the fact that so few Phase Three sites have ever been found in the entire southwestern Basin does suggest that a very high proportion of that area's total Phase Three population resided at the main Cuicuilco center itself. We know that a situation quite like this characterized the Teotihuacan area in the opposite corner of the Basin (see later discussion).

In the Texcoco region there was a substantial population increase during First Intermediate Phase Three, and overall population more than doubled, relative to Phase Two. Occupation was concentrated quite densely in three small regional centers and a series of substantial villages in the lower-middle piedmont, and there is an almost continuous band of Phase Three settlement along this strip. Our settlement map shows a distinct break in Phase Three settlement continuity at the southern end of the Texcoco region. North of this break there is a well-defined Phase Three settlement zone that extends up to the Patlachique Range on the southern edge of the Teotihuacan Valley. This Texcoco settlement cluster is comparable in general size and character to the Ixtapalapa and Chalco clusters we have already defined. Each of these three clusters contains several small regional centers (that contain between 1500 and 4500 inhabitants, with modest public architecture), and a total population on the order of 15,000 people. The Texcoco cluster is somewhat different in that it contains several Tezoyuca hilltop centers (see later discussion).

The greatest Phase Three changes occurred in the Teotihuacan Valley. Prior to Phase Three this had always been a distinctly marginal part of the Basin, with low population density and no large communities. During Phase Three times, however, this situation was radically reversed, and the Teotihuacan Valley attained a regional preeminence that it consolidated, expanded, and maintained for another thousand years. The site of Teotihuacan rapidly developed into a very large Phase Three regional center, covering 6–8 km^2, with an estimated population of 20,000–40,000 people, and containing elaborate public architecture (Millon *et al.* 1973). Situated next to a major group of permanent springs in the lower piedmont, at the head of a large alluvial plain, the Teotihuacan center contained over 90% of the total Phase Three population in the Teotihuacan Valley. The balance of the population was dispersed through the lower-middle piedmont, particularly on the southern flank of the valley, in hamlets and small villages. As noted earlier, it seems very likely that Teotihuacan and Cuicuilco were very similar in size, character, and regional impact during the First Intermediate Phase Three.

In the Cuautitlan–Tenayuca region, on the western side of the Basin, two major events occurred in Phase Three times: (*a*) there was a significant decline in population, and (b) most of the remaining population was nucleated at one small regional center at the upper edge of the deep-soil alluvium. The northern third of the Basin (the Zumpango, Temascalapa, and Pachuca regions) may have been occupied for the first time during this phase. Parsons found 21 "Terminal Formative" hamlets in the Zumpango region, most of which occurred in a small linear cluster above the north shore of Lake Zumpango. These sites were somewhat unusual in that their surface pottery contained a very high proportion of jar forms, with the distinctive wedge-shaped rims diagnostic of both Patlachique (First Intermediate Phase Three) and Tzacualli (First Intermediate Phase Four) phases. We are presently uncertain whether these hamlets are chronologically Patlachique, Tzacualli, or both. Sanders' survey in the Temascalapa region, north of the Teotihuacan Valley, detected numerous small Tzacualli-phase hamlets, with a full range of ceramic forms, and no Patlachique-phase occupation. Since the Temascalapa region is much closer than Zumpango to the major Patlachique center of Teotihuacan, the lack of Patlachique-phase occupation there might be taken as evidence that the small phase hamlets on the north shore of Lake Zumpango are Tzacualli phase in date. In any event, the entire northern third of the Basin of Mexico was, at most, only very sparsely occupied even at the end of the First Intermediate Period.

Summary and Conclusions

A number of general processes, some anticipated during First Intermediate Phase Two and others originating wholly within Phase Three, characterize the Basin of Mexico during this latter period. (a) Overall population continued to grow more unevenly and at a significantly slower rate than during previous centuries. (b) This overall growth was accompanied by a distinctive clustering of population into six principal groupings which, in turn, were separated by zones of sparse occupation. Three of these clusters (Chalco, Ixtapalapa, and Texcoco) were somewhat similar in general overall size, population, and character (ca. 15,000 people, dominated by several small regional centers). Two clusters (Teotihuacan and Cuicuilco) were characterized by extreme nucleation of large regional population into a single, very elaborate center of 20,000 or more people. One cluster (Cuautitlan–Tenayuca) is similar to Teotihuacan and Cuicuilco, but at a much smaller scale. (c) A four-level settlement hierarchy is now well defined, with two centers (Cuicuilco and Teotihuacan) so much larger and more complex than 13 other small regional centers, that the latter must almost certainly have been to some extent subordinate to the former. (d) The southern Basin continues to be a major demographic focus. This represents the persistence of a pattern that began back in Early Horizon times, and that seems clearly related to the high productivity of rainfall agriculture and small-scale water-control technologies in the well-watered southern Basin. However, a new demographic focus is also clearly apparent in the more arid east-central Basin (the Teotihuacan Valley and the Texcoco region) where rainfall agriculture is uncertain and earlier developments had been distinctly marginal relative to the southern Basin. The political centralization implied by the size and complexity of Phase Three Teotihuacan was necessarily closely linked to the development of canal irrigation. (e) The characteristic settlement clustering and distinctive settlement hierarchy of Phase Three raises the question of the nature of the sociopolitical organization that produced these material manifestations. The sparsely occupied areas between settlement clusters might suggest the existence of well-defined buffer zones between hostile polities. This same hostility might also account for the observed tendency toward settlement clustering. The unique massive stone retaining walls surrounding Ix-TF-5, a principal Phase Three regional center at the southeastern corner of Lake Texcoco, might be indicative of more intensified hostility, such as that which might characterize high-level confrontation between Cuicuilco and Teotihuacan. In other words, we see Phase Three as a time of transition in which the basic situation was one of political fragmentation and conflict. However, this basic setting also included an overlay of higher-level organization in which two very large centers simultaneously sought to expand their spheres of influence. We will expand and develop this model in a later section.

The analyses of Earle (1976) and Brumfiel (1976) relate to this general matter of sociopolitical organization. They have examined some of our First Intermediate Period data from the 1967 and 1969 fieldseasons (Texcoco region, Ixtapalapa region, and the northern section of the Chalco region). Their results, while necessarily provisional in view of their incomplete sample, complement our own impressions about the significance of settlement configuration in Phases Two and Three of the First Intermediate. Earle used the nearest neighbor statistic to measure the relative tendencies toward aggregation, regularity, or randomness in site spacing. His analysis suggests that political centralization may have been significantly accelerated during Phase Three times. He argues that state formation, involving forced resettlement of regional populations around some centrally imposed local administrative centers, may well have produced the Phase Three patterning he detects. This general view dovetails fairly well with our own impressions, from an expanded data base, of the basic difference between Phase Two and Phase Three settlement configuration.

Using a modified form of catchment analysis, Brumfiel (1976) attempts to measure the relative significance of population pressure during First Intermediate Phases Two and Three. This provides a test of a particularly critical hypothesis, since population pressure has been widely offered as an explanation of cultural evolution. Brumfiel argues that while only some of the larger Phase Two settlements would have had problems in generating adequate subsistence from their immediate hinterland, all large Phase Three settlements over 30 ha in size would have experienced problems in obtaining enough food from within a radius of 5 km. She concludes that such problems in food supply were alleviated by the imposition of tribute demands, and that these tribute relationships were an important factor in the increasing centralization (probably state formation) of Phase Three. While we cannot fully aqree with her rejection of population pressure as a causal factor in political centralization, we do find that she has made another nice case for a significant sociopolitical difference between the organization of Phase Two and Phase Three society.

The Tezoyuca Problem

We have classified 13 sites as Tezoyuca hilltop centers. These are relatively small sites, with estimated populations of 300–600 people, all of which have well-defined precincts of public architecture, and all of which are located atop isolated, steep-sided hills. Nine of these sites occur in a ring around the edges of the Patlachique Range at the juncture of the Teotihuacan Valley and the Texcoco region. Two are found a few kilometers further south, in the central and south-central Texcoco region. Two more occur on the east side of the Guadalupe Range, on the far northwest corner of Lake Texcoco. Their significance has still not yet been adequately assessed despite the fact that we have known about some of them since the very early years of our project. One major problem is that we are still uncertain about the chronological placement of the Tezoyuca ceramic complex. This complex has close resemblances to the pottery of the final subphase of the First Intermediate Phase Two (Ticoman 3, or Late Cuanalan; Sanders *et al.* 1975). Tezoyuca pottery also has clear links to the Chimalhuacan–Patlachique ceramics of the First Intermediate Phase Three. All of this suggested to us initially that Tezoyuca pottery represented an intrusive ethnic enclave (West suggested that it came from Chupicuaro) that was either contemporary with Ticoman 3–Late Cuanalan or with some as yet undefined early subphase of Patlachique–Chimalhuacan (e.g., West 1965).

Recent data have complicated the picture. McBride (1974) excavated the large First Intermediate Two–Three site at Cuautitlan, a site in flat alluvial plain, and the Tezoyuca ceramic complex is well represented there. Resampling of a number of First Intermediate Three sites in the Texcoco region, in gently sloping terrain, revealed considerable numbers of Tezoyuca sherds mixed with the dominant Patlachique material (the Tezoyuca hilltop centers in the same area, however, had only Tezoyuca pottery). Finally, Bennyhoff (1966) reports Tezoyuca ceramics at Cuilcuilco, and Sanders, in a reexamination of several sites in the southern Basin, noted a few Tezoyuca sherds on sites in those regions. At Cuilcuilco and the other southern sites, however, it seems not to be represented in sufficient quantity to say that the ceramic complex as a whole is a well-defined ceramic phase in that area. What these new data seem to suggest is that the Tezoyuca ceramic complex was widely spread in the central, primarily the east–central, part of the Basin and that it seems to be a genuine phase sandwiched between the Ticoman and

Chimalhuacan–Patlachique ceramic complexes. The scattered sherds found in the southern sites we interpret as trade pieces, and a distinctive ceramic complex, probably a late persistence of Ticoman-like ceramics, is the local equivalent in that area.

The suggestion is that even in the north the Tezoyuca may have been an exceedingly short phase and that it ultimately evolved into the Chimalhuacan–Patlachique complex. This perhaps explains its unobtrusiveness except at the few hilltop sites, which were apparently occupied only during this subphase. If this chronological interpretation is correct, then we would seem to be dealing with a situation in which, for a brief time during the early part of First Intermediate Phase Three, there was a cluster of small hilltop centers in the central part of the Basin, and a relatively dispersed regional population that was probably somewhat smaller in size than that of the antecedent Phase Two. The significance of hilltop settlement might suggest that hostility and warfare were important enough to be major factors in selecting for settlement location in settings of maximum defensibility. The short-lived occupation of such defensible locations perhaps indicates that hostility and warfare were somewhat relaxed with the process of political centralization in Phase Three times. During the remainder of the phase, the major political confrontations would seem to have been between the unusually large centers, like Teotihuacan and Cuicuilco. As we have already argued, on the basis of other evidence, political centralization involving those two centers was a major element of Late Phase Three. This view of the Tezoyuca hilltop centers is presently an attractive hypothesis for us.

In an earlier interpretation, Parsons (1971) saw these Tezoyuca hilltop centers as contemporary with the principal Patlachique phase occupation. He called them "Segregated Elite Districts," and suggested they were a spatially discrete component of the basic organization of Phase Three society. We are presently inclined to discard this latter hypothesis in view of the apparent early chronological position of Tezoyuca pottery. However, we still cannot actually demonstrate that the Tezoyuca ceramic complex is chronologically earlier than the Chimalhuacan–Patlachique. Thus, the possibility still remains open that Tezoyuca pottery was being used by only a restricted segment of Phase Three society at the same time when most people were using the Chimalhuacan–Patlachique ceramics. In sum, we regard the Tezoyuca problem as still unresolved, and we will continue to side-step the issue wherever possible.

FIRST INTERMEDIATE: PHASE FOUR (100 B.C.–A.D. 100)

This phase witnessed the most revolutionary change in the life style of the population of the Basin of Mexico since its initial colonization by sedentary farmers 1400 years earlier (Map 13). The obvious and most dramatic event was the emergence of Teotihuacan as a center of extraordinary size and population. As Millon's mapping project has evolved, particularly the analytical state of data processing, the size and population figures of the site during this phase have been steadily revised upward. The earliest estimates were 20,000–30,000 (Millon 1967a, b). This was increased to 45,000 in a later publication (Millon 1970) and finally to 60,000 with a minimal areal extent of 20 km² (Millon 1973). Most recently George Cowgill (personal communication) has expressed the opinion that the site may not have been appreciably smaller during this phase than it was at its peak (with a mean estimate of 125,000 people concentrated in an area of 20 km²) during the Middle Horizon.

These upward revisions have resolved a serious problem that emerged from the Basin of Mexico survey—the small size of the "rural" Phase Four population. Our initial Teotihuacan Valley survey revealed a total of 64 sites of which 63 were hamlets and 1 was a small dispersed village. The maximum populations of these settlements certainly did not exceed 4000–5000 people. Sanders' recent surveys of the Temascalapa region, along the north edge of the valley, revealed an additional 30 hamlets, many of which probably were single-family settlements. The total Temascalapa region population could not have been over 1000 people in an area of 150 km². Parsons' (1971) and Blanton's (1972) surveys of the Texcoco–Ixtapalapa region revealed only nine hamlets, one large dispersed village, a small dispersed village, one small nucleated village, and a large isolated ceremonial precinct: a total population of one to a few thousand. Preliminary examination of the ceramics from the Chalco–Xochimilco indicates that Phase Four occupation in those regions was very sparse. Our Cuautitlan survey revealed only one large dispersed village and seven hamlets, a striking decline from First Intermediate Phase Three values. We suspect, on the basis of our Temascalapa survey, that Parsons' recorded 21 "Terminal Formative" hamlets in the Zumpango region may be of Phase Four date, but even here the total population would probably be less than 1000. For the Tacuba region we are faced with the problem of deficient data. However, the only reported Phase Four pottery comes from the site of Azcapotzalco (Rattray 1968).

The case of Cuicuilco presents a special problem. Formerly we believed that the massive lava flow from Xitle occurred at the end of the First Intermediate Two phase and that the disaster wiped out the town. Later excavations by Heizer and Bennyhoff (1958) revealed the presence of Phase Four ceramics and suggested that the eruption either occurred several hundred years later or destroyed only part of the area. Finally, unpublished excavations by the I.N.A.H. in connection with the construction of the Ciudad Olímpica (Florencia Muller personal communication) have revealed that there was a substantial occupation at the site, along with ceremonial construction, as late as First Intermediate Five times. Geological studies, in connection with the same project, indicate that there were two lava flows, one dating toward the end of Phase Three, that seriously reduced the productivity of the area, and a second, at the end of Phase Five, that reduced the entire area to a rocky wasteland. On the basis of the scale of the Phase

Five architecture it is probable that the community was no more than a small regional center in Phase Four.

In summary, the total First Intermediate Phase Four population of the Basin of Mexico, outside of Teotihuacan, could not have exceeded 15,000 people. Assessing the situation as a whole, the population was substantially lower than that during First Intermediate Three phase. This was the first major phase in the history of the colonization of the Basin by sedentary farmers during which population did not substantially increase. The great majority (80–90%) of the population was nucleated at Teotihuacan—a truly extraordinary event.

Almost as extraordinary is the monumentality and planning of public architecture at this same time. Teotihuacan's great central avenue was laid out, and two major public structures—the Sun Pyramid and the Moon Pyramid—were built along it. The Sun Pyramid, with a volume of about 1,000,000 m^3, was the largest single-phase structure ever erected in the precolumbian New World. This monumentality of public architecture is suggestive of a highly stratified society at Phase Four Teotihuacan, although we still lack supportive data from domestic architecture and burials.

In view of the hostile posture of the settlement pattern we hypothesized for Phase Three, it is tempting to suggest that this massive dislocation of population had a coercive component. Somehow, as we will discuss later, the Phase Four polity was able not only to incorporate the rest of the Basin's population politically, but to relocate them physically as well. The motive for such extreme population nucleation is still unclear to us. Presumably political control was the principal factor involved. However, we know of no other situation in the historical or archaeological record in which so large a sedentary regional population was involved in such a drastic relocation. The Early Dynastic in much of southern Mesopotamia (Adams and Nissen 1972) may approach it, although it was clearly not on the same scale. The apparent substantial Phase Four population decline suggests that this extreme population nucleation was not without a certain stress, manifested in the loss of population. We still cannot say very much about whether this loss of population was produced (a) by conflict in the initial process of nucleation; (b) by declining birth rates and (or) rising mortality rates in a huge nucleated community where the organization of food supply was still incompletely developed; or (c) by a combination of these and other factors.

This last consideration raises the question of the economic structure of Phase Four Teotihuacan and its rural hinterland. Recent studies by Spence (n.d.) indicate that economic specialization, at least in the obsidian trade, was present at the Phase Three center and became further elaborated during Phase Four. He estimates that 2% of the population were obsidian craftsmen. Approximately half of these were producing obsidian artifacts for trade, external to the Basin of Mexico, a very low value. We do not know how many other kinds of craftsmen there were, but if the ratio between obsidian workers and other craftsmen [see the section entitled "Middle Horizon (A.D.

300–750)] was comparable to that during Late Xolalpan times, then no more than 6% of the population were nonfood producing specialists.

All these data suggest that Phase Four Teotihuacan was a highly stratified agrarian community in which more than 90% of a large, nucleated population was engaged in full-time agriculture. There is even a possibility, considering their small size and light occupation, that many rural sites were seasonally occupied settlements, utilized by people residing much of the time at Teotihuacan [see the section entitled "Middle Horizon (A.D. 300–750)"]. This hypothesis implies a tremendous intensification of agriculture in Teotihuacan's immediate hinterland, and it is during this period that we would expect to have a maximal expansion and elaboration of the Teotihuacan Valley irrigation system. This seems particularly expectable as there is still little evidence that Phase Four Teotihuacan (in contrast to the Middle Horizon situation) was able to expand its tributary networks beyond the Basin of Mexico.

FIRST INTERMEDIATE: PHASE FIVE (A.D. 100–300)

This is equivalent ceramically to the Miccaotli–Early Tlamimilolpa subphases at Teotihuacan. We presently cannot sort out components of this phase from the succeeding Middle Horizon. Our overall impression is that many Middle Horizon sites have Phase Five components, but that there are numerous Middle Horizon sites with exclusively Middle Horizon occupation.

MIDDLE HORIZON (A.D. 300–750)

Essentially this is the segment of the Teotihuacan ceramic sequence that includes the Late Tlamimilolpa, Xolalpan, and Metepec subphases. Our map is an attempt to represent the settlement pattern in Late Xolalpan times (A.D. 550–650), the phase of major political and (or) economic dominance of the center, not only over the Basin of Mexico, but over much of Mesoamerica as well (Maps 14 and 24).

In the Basin of Mexico we recorded the following sites, in addition to Teotihuacan itself; 10 provincial centers, 17 large villages (15 nucleated, 2 dispersed), 77 small villages (55 nucleated, 22 dispersed), 149 hamlets, 9 small isolated ceremonial precincts, 2 large ceremonial precincts, 4 indeterminate sites, an obsidian quarry (the Otumba quarry, to which we must add the Pachuca quarries in the northeastern corner of the Basin), 1 isolated gravel quarry for construction (but our survey has revealed numerous construction material quarries located within or adjacent to occupational sites), and several isolated salt-making stations (but again a number of occupational sites were apparently salt-making communities).

The Xolalpan phase center of Teotihuacan, on the basis of data from Millon's Teotihuacan mapping project, was a large, compact center. During this phase it covered 20 km², had an estimated mean population of 125,000 people (Millon *et al.* 1973 suggest a possible maximum of 200,000) and a mean density of 7000 per square kilometer. In terms of the monumentality of civic architecture, degree of planning, and overall size it ranks with the greatest pre-industrial centers of the world (see Figures 5.2–5.4).

On the basis of Millon's survey and excavations (Millon 1976) it seems that approximately one-third of the population were economic, political, and religious specialists, and the evidence favors full-time specialization. Although some of the craft specialization did involve the manufacture of high-status products consumed only by a limited elite clientele (e.g., jade body ornaments), many crafts included the production of basic goods, such as obsidian tools, grinding stones, and ceramic cooking vessels. Approximately 12% of the population was apparently involved in obsidian production during this phase (Spence n.d.). The bulk of the population, at least two-thirds of it, were apparently farmers, who lived in the center but derived their livelihood from agriculture.

We noted that Teotihuacan exhibited architectural planning. Each grid

Figure 5.2. Oblique aerial view of Teotihuacan, looking south. (Courtesy of CIA Mexicana Aerofoto S.A.)

Figure 5.3. Oblique aerial view of Sun Pyramid, Teotihuacan, looking east. (Courtesy of CIA Mexicana Aerofoto S.A.)

unit, or urban block, in the residential area was a single, large multifamily residence (see Figure 5.5). The largest of these may have housed as many as 100 people. The plans, plus burial data and suggestions from other features indicate variation in social structure and composition. Some individual compounds were apparently characterized by little evidence of internal ranking and had an essentially kin-like structure, whereas others suggest a patron–client type relationship among the residents. A comparison of the plans of entire compounds, along with variations in mural paintings and other artifact categories associated with them, also indicate considerable differences in wealth and political power from compound to compound. This is also suggested by striking differences in room size and general spaciousness (i.e., ratios of patio to room space) among the various compounds. Residences along the main avenue are particularly notable in terms of these categories.

With respect to rural settlement a series of significant changes had occurred since the First Intermediate Four phase. First the population of the Basin was at least double that of Phase Four times, possibly triple, depending on the various estimates of the population of Teotihuacan itself. If the estimate of 60,000 people for the population of the Phase Four center is close to the mark, then the period from A.D. 100 to 600 witnessed a doubling of the population of the center and an increase in the countryside of at least seven times the Phase Four level. If the population of the Phase Four center was comparable to that of the Xolalpan center then population growth would be approximately double and have occurred almost entirely in the countryside. In either case the trend toward extreme centralization so diagnostic of Phase Four is reversed.

This last paragraph represents a significant departure from some of our earlier hypotheses about demographic processes during the Middle Horizon (e.g., Blanton 1972; Parsons 1968, 1971). Formerly we believed that the great nucleation of population in the Teotihuacan center had occurred during the Middle Horizon when a fully developed Teotihuacan state had forcibly removed a great many people into the center from over a large region. While we were always uncomfortable with our apparent inability to distinguish much distinctive First Intermediate Phase Four pottery in the eastern and southern Basin, we never actually felt that much of the area was without occupation during that period. Rather, we vaguely attributed our difficulties to regional ceramic variability, in which the southern Basin simply failed to acquire the diagnostic Tzacualli ceramics in vogue at Teotihuacan itself. With the expansion of our survey to the northern Basin after 1972, however, we

Figure 5.4. Oblique aerial view of the Royal Palace, Teotihuacan, looking east. (Courtesy of CIA Mexicana Aerofoto S.A.)

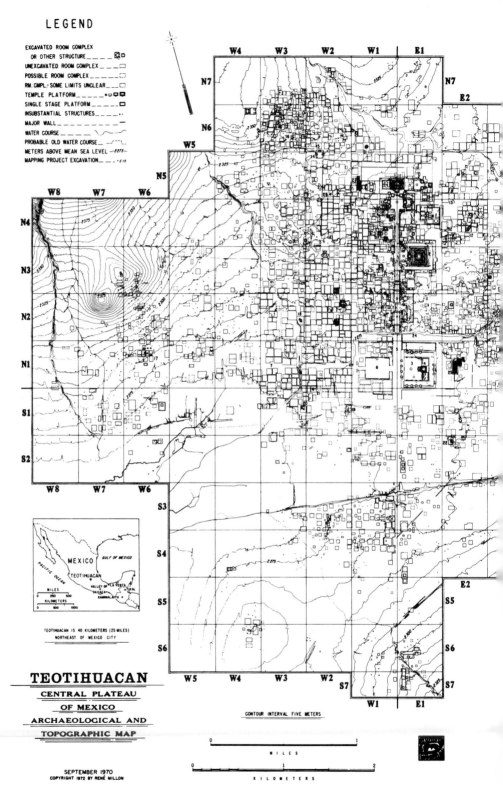

Figure 5.5. Map of Teotihuacan. (From *Urbanization at Teotihuacán, Mexico*, v. 1, *The Teotihuacán Map.* Copyright © 1973 by René Millon, all rights reserved.)

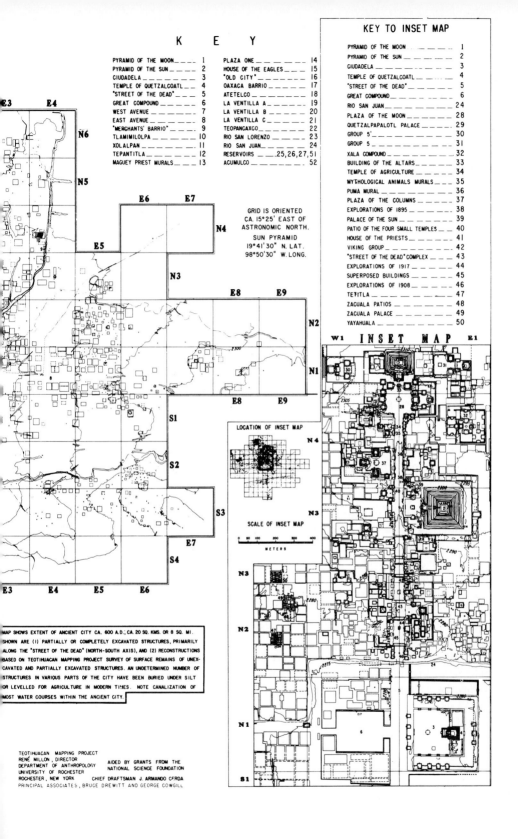

saw a dramatic reversal of the assumed Middle Horizon population decline that we had found everywhere in the south. Instead we saw a large Middle Horizon population increase relative to the antecedent First Intermediate. This, coupled with our realization that Tzacualli phase occupation was in all likelihood very scanty over much of the Basin, has caused us to assign the period of extreme population nucleation to the First Intermediate Four phase. In fact, the First Intermediate Five phase and succeeding Middle Horizon period appear to be a period when rather substantial numbers of people were put back into the rural setting—probably in line with deliberate policies of the Middle Horizon polity centered at Teotihuacan (see later discussion).

Throughout the Basin of Mexico there are some very important character-istics of Middle Horizon settlement configuration that contrast very markedly with the locational and distributional patterns we have noted for First Inter-mediate occupation. First, there was an obvious shift in occupational inten-sity from south to north, and most of this shift was absorbed at a single large center. There had been a steady tendency throughout the First Intermediate Phase Three for population to expand more rapidly in the northern half of the Basin than in the south (the south:north population ratio went from 10:1 in Phase One to about 3:2 in Phase Three). Nevertheless, even during Phase Three the south was more densely inhabited, and the relatively high ratio of population living in the north-central portion of the Basin by Phase Three times was almost entirely due to the presence of the Teotihuacan center. The demographic preeminence of the south was forever ended by the radical changes in Phase Four when perhaps 80–90% of the total Basin population resided at Teotihuacan. Even with the more equitable population distribu-tion achieved in Middle Horizon times, from 50% to 60% of the total Basin population continued to reside at the Teotihuacan center. However, it is noteworthy that the Middle Horizon rural population (i.e., that outside the Teotihuacan center) in the northern half of the Basin exceeded that of the southern Basin by a ratio of nearly 4:1 (although it must be noted that a substantial fraction of this rural northern occupation was concentrated along the northern edge of the Teotihuacan Valley and along the north side of the Guadalupe range (Cuautitlan–Tenayuca regions).

Second, there was a major rearrangement of population within the Basin, and there are several indications that this was a highly structured rearrange-ment, imposed by a central political authority. We have already noted the presence of several distinct First Intermediate Phase Three settlement clusters which were, in turn, completely obliterated by the radical dislocations of Phase Four. In the Middle Horizon, three very distinct demographic zones stand out within the Basin: (1) a major population focus at Teotihuacan itself, together with a substantial rural occupation in the adjacent Temascalapa region on the north side of Cerro Gordo; (2) a secondary focus in the northern Tacuba region and Cuautitlan–Tenayuca region, centering on the poorly known site of Azcapotzalco, but extending northward around the edges of the Guadalupe Range and into the Cuautitlan alluvium; and (3) the rest of the

Basin, where there was a fairly even scatter of rural occupation in hamlets, small villages, and a few more substantial communities.

Some recently completed computer-assisted analyses of settlement data from the Chalco–Xochimilco region serve to amplify our impressions about the structure of Middle Horizon rural occupation. Tables 5.3 and 5.4 show that the mean size and population of Middle Horizon sites in the Chalco–Xochimilco region are substantially smaller than for the antecedent First Intermediate Phases Two and Three. Furthermore, there is significantly less variability of site size and population in Middle Horizon settlements than for the same two earlier phases. These relationships are graphically illustrated in another way by the histograms in Tables 5.5–5.12. There are very few Middle Horizon sites in the Chalco–Xochimilco region that contain more than 500 people or that cover more than 10 ha. The mean site size for Middle Horizon sites is only about 80 people, whereas for First Intermediate Phase Three sites this figure is about 260 persons. The much smaller standard deviations for both site area and population during the Middle Horizon is likewise indicative of comparative settlement uniformity, and contrasts quite markedly with the much more heterogeneous settlement of antecedent phases. Tables 5.5–5.12 suggest another aspect of Teotihuacan's impact on the Chalco–Xochimilco region in Middle Horizon times. In the First Intermediate Phase Three (Table 5.7) there were clearly four or five distinct categories of site area, including two or three categories of well over 35 ha. During the Middle Horizon there may be as many as three categories of site area (Table 5.8). However, these all fall below 35 ha. The incorporation of the Chalco–Xochimilco region into the Teotihuacan orbit after First Intermediate Phase Three resulted in the disappearance of the upper two or three levels in the local settlement hierarchy.

Table 5.10 reveals very clearly the bimodal distribution of site elevation during the Middle Horizon in the Chalco–Xochimilco region. This is antici-

TABLE 5.3
Chalco–Xochimilco Region: Variability in Site Population from Middle Formative through Teotihuacan Periods

Period	Number of sites	Mean site population	Standard deviation	Standard deviation/ Mean site population
First Intermediate Phase One	17	323.5	587.5	1.8
First Intermediate Phase Two	60	403.8	980.3	2.4
First Intermediate Phase Three	72	259.2	675.9	2.6
First Intermediate Phase Five through Middle Horizon	62	83.4	131.2	1.5

TABLE 5.4
Chalco–Xochimilco Region: Variability in Site Area from Middle Formative through
Teotihuacan Periods

Period	Number of sites	Mean site area (in hectares)	Standard deviation	Standard deviation/ Mean site area
First Intermediate Phase One	17	11.5	15.1	1.3
First Intermediate Phase Two	60	11.9	24.2	2.0
First Intermediate Phase Three	72	10.9	21.4	2.0
First Intermediate Phase Five through Middle Horizon	62	4.7	6.4	1.4

pated, to a lesser degree, during the antecedent First Intermediate Phase Three, but, while the elevation modes are similar, the Phase Three peaks are much less well-defined (Table 5.9). The modal elevations of the Middle Horizon are in the upper part of the deep-soil alluvium, at about 2270 m above sea level, and in the middle piedmont, between 2440 and 2460 m above sea level. Since, generally speaking, rainfall varies directly with elevation in the Chalco–Xochimilco region, one might expect to see a clearcut bimodal distribution of site by rainfall as well. However, Table 5.12 shows a distinct trimodal distribution of site by rainfall, with modal peaks at 690 mm, 780 mm, and 900 mm per year. This contrasts rather markedly with the relatively continuous distribution of sites by rainfall during Phase Three of the First Intermediate (Table 5.11).

Because we still understand very little about site function, the meaning we can attach to these various distributional data remains somewhat uncertain. Nevertheless, it seems clear, even at this point, that Middle Horizon settlement in the Chalco–Xochimilco region was more uniform and regular than during the preceding half millenium. We suggest that the placement of settlement between A.D. 100 and 700 in the Chalco–Xochimilco region, and probably elsewhere throughout our survey area, was deliberately structured by Teotihuacan for two main purposes: (a) to put people into the best locations for producing surplus raw materials for consumption in the main center; and (b) to consolidate political control by removing people from older local centers. In the Chalco–Xochimilco region, for example, this site placement apparently focused on the upper edge of the deep-soil alluvium and the middle piedmont, both prime zones for rainfall agriculture and small scale irrigation. The deep-soil alluvium would also have offered the potential dual capacity for the exploitation of lake resources and chinampa-like cultivation.

A third important general aspect of First Intermediate Phase Five–Middle Horizon settlement and demography is its apparent sharply reduced growth

TABLE 5.5
Histogram of Site Population, First Intermediate Phase Three, Chalco–Xochimilco Region

Population (increments of 100)	Percentage	Number of sites	
0	65.3	47	XXXXXXXXXXXXXXXXXXXXXXXXXXXXXXXXXXXXXXXXXXXXXXXXX
100	11.1	8	XXXXXXXX
200	9.7	7	XXXXXXX
300	1.4	1	X
400	2.8	2	XX
500	0	0	
600	0	0	
700	2.8	2	XX
800	0	0	
900	0	0	
1000	0	0	
1100	0	0	
1200	0	0	
1300	0	0	
1400	0	0	
1500	1.4	1	X
1600	0	0	
1700	0	0	
1800	1.4	1	X
1900	0	0	
2000	0	0	
2100	0	0	
2200	1.4	1	X
2300	0	0	
2400	0	0	
2500	0	0	
2600	0	0	
2700	0	0	
2800	0	0	
2900	0	0	
3000	1.4	1	X
3100	0	0	
3200	0	0	
3300	0	0	
3400	0	0	
3500	0	0	
3600	0	0	
3700	0	0	
3800	0	0	
3900	0	0	
4000	1.4	1	X
4100	0	0	
4200	0	0	
4300	0	0	
4400	0	0	
4500	0	0	
4600	0	0	
4700	0	0	
4800	0	0	
4900	0	0	

TABLE 5.6
Histogram of Site Population, Middle Horizon, Chalco–Xochimilco Region

Population (increments of 100)	Percentage	Number of sites	
0	72.6	45	XXXXXXXXXXXXXXXXXXXXXXXXXXXXXXXXXXXXXXXXXXXXXXX
100	14.5	9	XXXXXXXXX
200	3.2	2	XX
300	4.8	3	XXX
400	1.6	1	X
500	1.6	1	X
600	0	0	
700	1.6	1	X
800	0	0	
900	0	0	
1000	0	0	
1100	0	0	
1200	0	0	
1300	0	0	
1400	0	0	
1500	0	0	
1600	0	0	
1700	0	0	
1800	0	0	
1900	0	0	
2000	0	0	
2100	0	0	
2200	0	0	
2300	0	0	
2400	0	0	
2500	0	0	
2600	0	0	
2700	0	0	
2800	0	0	
2900	0	0	
3000	0	0	
3100	0	0	
3200	0	0	
3300	0	0	
3400	0	0	
3500	0	0	
3600	0	0	
3700	0	0	
3800	0	0	
3900	0	0	
4000	0	0	
4100	0	0	
4200	0	0	
4300	0	0	
4400	0	0	
4500	0	0	
4600	0	0	
4700	0	0	
4800	0	0	
4900	0	0	

TABLE 5.7
Histogram of Site Area, First Intermediate Phase Three, Chalco–Xochimilco Region

Site area (in hectares)	Percentage	Number of sites	
0	23.6	17	XXXXXXXXXXXXXXXXX
1	13.9	10	XXXXXXXXXX
2	11.2	8	XXXXXXXX
3	5.6	4	XXXX
4	8.3	6	XXXXXX
5	2.8	2	XX
6	0	0	
7	4.2	3	XXX
8	4.2	3	XXX
9	0	0	
10	2.8	2	XX
11	4.2	3	XXX
12	2.8	2	XX
13	0	0	
14	2.8	2	XX
15	2.8	2	
16	0	0	
17	0	0	
18	0	0	
19	0	0	
20	1.4	1	X
21	0	0	
22	1.4	1	X
23	1.4	1	X
33	1.4	1	X
34	0	0	
35	1.4	1	X
43	1.4	1	X
74	2.8	2	XX
75	1.4	1	X
129	1.4	1	X

rate (compared to the First Intermediate period), over nearly a half a millenium. Although we have plotted settlement in terms of a single long period, our ceramic analyses indicate that most sites were in fact occupied in more or less the same manner during both its earlier (Tlamimilolpa) and later (Xolalpan and Metepec) phases. Apparently following the First Intermediate Four depression there was a relatively rapid recolonization of the rural areas during Phase Five and then stabilization during the Middle Horizon. The only significant population growth during the Middle Horizon itself appears to have occurred at the Teotihuacan center. While the population profile of Teotihuacan itself is still a subject of some uncertainty, there does appear to

TABLE 5.8
Histogram of Site Area, Middle Horizon, Chalco–Xochimilco Region[a]

Site area (in hectares)	Percentage	Number of sites	
0	19.4	12	XXXXXXXXXXXX
1	17.8	11	XXXXXXXXXXX
2	19.4	12	XXXXXXXXXXXX
3	9.7	6	XXXXXX
4	6.4	4	XXXX
5	4.8	3	XXX
6	6.4	4	XXXX
7	3.2	2	XX
8	1.6	1	X
9	1.6	1	X
10	0	0	
11	1.6	1	X
12	0	0	
13	0	0	
14	0	0	
15	1.6	1	X
16	0	0	
17	1.6	1	X
18	1.6	1	X
19	0	0	
20	0	0	
21	0	0	
22	0	0	
23	0	0	
24	0	0	
25	0	0	
26	0	0	
27	0	0	
28	0	0	
29	0	0	
30	0	0	
31	1.4	1	X
32	0	0	
33	1.4	1	X
34	0	0	
35	0	0	

[a]There are no sites larger than 34 ha.

have been some significant population growth there during the centuries after First Intermediate Phase Four. On the other hand, our present view of rural Middle Horizon occupation in the Basin of Mexico is that there was little significant internal population growth at all (once again, the poorly known Azcapotzalco zone becomes critical in this regard). Overall, the Middle Horizon apparently represents the first major demographic plateau within the Basin of Mexico as overall population growth slowed significantly.

TABLE 5.9
Histogram of Site Elevation, First Intermediate Phase Three, Chalco–Xochimilco Region

Elevation (in meters)	Percentage	Number of sites	
2240	5.6	4	XXXX
2250	0	0	
2260	5.6	4	XXXX
2270	9.7	7	XXXXXXX
2280	6.9	5	XXXXX
2290	1.4	1	X
2300	6.9	5	XXXXX
2310	2.8	2	XX
2320	0	0	
2330	4.2	3	XXX
2340	2.8	2	XX
2350	0	0	
2360	4.2	3	XXX
2370	1.4	1	X
2380	0	0	
2390	1.4	1	X
2400	2.8	2	XX
2410	2.8	2	XX
2420	5.6	4	XXXX
2430	2.8	2	XX
2440	6.9	5	XXXXX
2450	2.8	2	XX
2460	1.4	1	X
2470	6.9	5	XXXXX
2480	4.2	3	XXX
2490	0	0	
2500	2.8	2	XX
2510	1.4	1	X
2520	2.8	2	XX
2530	0	0	
2540	1.4	1	X
2550	1.4	1	X
2560	0	0	
2570	0	0	
2580	0	0	
2590	0	0	
2600	1.4	1	X

While it is difficult to be precise about cause and process, it seems reasonable to argue that Teotihuacan's policies were a primary element in fabricating this demographic plateau. Teotihuacan needed to maintain a relatively thin rural population, fairly evenly scattered in fairly small communities. While this policy would have facilitated political control, it would also have discouraged any significant expansion of rural population, and only at the

TABLE 5.10
Histogram of Site Elevation, Middle Horizon, Chalco–Xochimilco Region

Elevation (in meters)	Percentage	Number of sites	
2240	9.7	6	XXXXXX
2250	6.4	4	XXXX
2260	1.6	1	X
2270	11.3	7	XXXXXXX
2280	9.7	6	XXXXXX
2290	4.8	3	XXX
2300	6.5	4	XXXX
2310	1.6	1	X
2320	1.6	1	X
2330	1.6	1	X
2340	0	0	
2350	1.6	1	X
2360	0	0	
2370	0	0	
2380	1.6	1	X
2390	0	0	
2400	3.2	2	XX
2410	1.6	1	X
2420	1.6	1	X
2430	3.2	2	XX
2440	6.5	4	XXXX
2450	1.6	1	X
2460	11.3	7	XXXXXXX
2470	1.6	1	X
2480	0	0	
2490	4.8	3	XXX
2500	1.6	1	X
2510	0	0	
2520	0	0	
2530	0	0	
2540	1.6	1	X
2550	3.2	2	XX
2560	0	0	
2570	0	0	
2580	0	0	
2590	0	0	

center itself was there any possibility for population growth. But, although some population growth could and did occur, logistical factors in supplying the huge center would have prevented any rapid population expansion there. A major impact of the Middle Horizon Teotihuacan polity was thus a significant depression of population growth rates within its own heartland area in the Basin of Mexico.

In terms of exploitation patterns, we can define four basic Middle Horizon settlement zones, each one probably related to a different kind of resource utilization.

TABLE 5.11
Histogram of Site Rainfall, First Intermediate Phase Three, Chalco–Xochimilco Region

Annual rainfall (in millimeters)	Percentage	Number of sites	
620	0	0	
630	0	0	
640	0	0	
650	0	0	
660	1.4	1	X
670	0	0	
680	2.8	2	XX
690	6.9	5	XXXXX
700	4.2	3	XXX
710	0	0	
720	4.2	3	XXX
730	1.4	1	X
740	1.4	1	X
750	1.4	1	X
760	2.8	2	XX
770	1.4	1	X
780	8.3	6	XXXXXX
790	6.9	5	XXXXX
800	1.4	1	X
810	0	0	
820	1.4	1	X
830	0	0	
840	0	0	
850	4.2	3	XXX
860	1.4	1	X
870	1.4	1	X
880	2.8	2	XX
890	2.8	2	XX
900	5.6	4	XXXX
910	0	0	
920	5.6	4	XXXX
930	0	0	
940	0	0	
950	4.2	3	XXX
960	2.8	2	XX
970	1.4	1	X
980	2.8	2	XX
990	9.7	7	XXXXXXX

Zone One is the area that includes Teotihuacan, the lower and middle sections of the Teotihuacan Valley, the Patlachique Range, and the northern half of the Texcoco region. When we initiated the Teotihuacan Valley survey we had accepted Armillas' estimate of 7.5 km² as the extent of the site, had calculated a probable population of the center as 50,000, and assumed that all were non-food-producing specialists. We expected, therefore, to find a great

TABLE 5.12
Histogram of Site Rainfall, Middle Horizon, Chalco–Xochimilco Region

Annual rainfall (in milli- meters)	Percentage	Number of sites	
620	0	0	
630	0	0	
640	0	0	
650	0	0	
660	4.8	3	XXX
670	0	0	
680	4.8	3	XXX
690	8.1	5	XXXXX
700	3.2	2	XX
710	3.2	2	XX
720	4.8	3	XXX
730	0	0	
740	1.6	1	X
750	4.8	3	XXX
760	4.8	3	XXX
770	1.6	1	X
780	8.1	5	XXXXX
790	3.2	2	XX
800	1.6	1	X
810	1.6	1	X
820	1.6	1	X
830	0	0	
840	0	0	
850	0	0	
860	1.6	1	X
870	1.6	1	X
880	0	0	
890	3.2	2	XX
900	8.1	5	XXXXX
910	1.6	1	X
920	0	0	
930	3.2	2	XX
940	0	0	
950	0	0	
960	1.6	1	X
970	0	0	
980	0	0	
990	4.8	3	XXX

number of rural settlements in the Teotihuacan Valley that provided the agricultural surplus to support the center. In fact we found very few settle- ments in the Valley proper until we surveyed the upper valley, and the area on the north periphery of the Valley. Meanwhile, Millon's Mapping Project at Teotihuacan had revealed that the site was much larger than we had assumed from Armillas' preliminary surveys. Later surveys by Parsons revealed that the northern half of the Texcoco region, an area densely settled in Phase Three times, was very sparsely occupied during Phase Four and the Middle Horizon. We then suggested that a substantial percentage of the population of the center were farmers and that this region of sparse rural settlement was directly utilized by the population residing in Teotihuacan. Millon's suggestion, from his independent Mapping Project data, that one-third of the population were economic, political, and religious specialists dramatically supported this reconstruction. Zone One therefore is an inner zone of agricultural and other resources (basalt, clay, construction material) directly utilized by the population of Teotihuacan. The two major obsidian quarries (Cerro de Las Navajas and Barranca de Los Estetes), both outside of this zone, were probably also directly controlled since Middle Horizon settlements have not been reported near the quarries.

Zone Two involves several areas, all in the central portion of the Basin, where rural settlement is relatively substantial, and individual settlements are often large in size. This includes the Tenayuca region, the Tacuba region, the Cuautitlan region, the Temascalapa region, and the northern edge and the upper part of the Teotihuacan Valley. All settlements in these areas are characterized by substantial concentrations of archaeological surface debris, and by clear-cut evidence of the presence of the Teotihuacan type of multi-family houses. Wherever we were able to define the specific community plan, all of the larger settlements were laid out on a grid comparable to that of the city. In two unusually well preserved provincial centers the ceremonial precincts were laid out in a linear fashion, possibly to emulate the linear arrangement at Teotihuacan. A cluster of settlements at Ecatepec along the northwestern shore of Lake Texcoco were probably salt-making communities. The total rural population of Zones One and Two was in the neighborhood of 65,000. This contrasts with the 18,000 in the same area during First Intermediate Phase Three, and possibly 10,000 during Phase Four.

Zones Three and Four form a third settlement pattern found in the southern and northern peripheries of the Basin. In the south this includes the southern half of the Texcoco region, the Ixtapalapa Peninsula, and the Chalco–Xochimilco areas (Zone Three). These regions were major centers of First Intermediate One–Three population—in contrast they were much less densely settled in Middle Horizon times and virtually depopulated in First Intermediate Phase Four. Surveys have revealed approximately 150 hamlets, 20 small village sites, and 1 small provincial center (Tx-EC-32, Portesuelo). Cuicuilco may have functioned as a small center during the First Intermediate Five phase. The total population probably did not exceed 15,000 in an area of 3000 km^2. This contrasts with our estimated 90,000 for the same area in the First Intermediate Phase Two–Three.

We have the distinct impression (although this has not yet been systematically confirmed) that some of the smaller sites lack the full range of ceramic types commonly found on Middle Horizon residential settlements. Furthermore, there are many sites, especially in the southern Basin, where the density of surface pottery is quite low and where the heavy rock rubble (suggestive of the presence of substantial multiroom houses), so characteristic of Middle Horizon sites in the central Basin, is lacking. Many of these settlements are along the shores of Lake Texcoco and Chalco; others are located well up on the piedmont in the southeastern corner of the Basin. We suspect that some of them were occupied on a seasonal, or temporary, basis by people who may have resided permanently in larger local communities, or who may even have been associated with specific residential compounds at Teotihuacan itself. They probably represent special resource exploitation sites, along the lakeshore for lake products, and on the piedmont probably for forest products.

Our model here is very similar to the pattern described for the present day Yoruba in southwestern Nigeria. In the Yoruba case, the bulk of the population is concentrated in large nucleated settlements, whose inhabitants are involved in agriculture, craft specialization, and mercantile activities. The Yoruba reside in large compounds that house corporate lineages. Some segments of each compound occupy exploitation sites permanently, or seasonally, at some distance from the town. The Middle Horizon pattern in the southern Basin of Mexico probably approximated this Yoruba settlement system.

A comparable settlement pattern occurs in the northwestern corner of the Basin, primarily our Zumpango region (Zone Four). The Middle Horizon occupation here consists of one large nucleated village (possibly a small administrative center), plus many small villages and hamlets. This area had been very sparsely inhabited prior to the Middle Horizon. In some contrast to Zone Three, there are proportionately more settlements with a full range of ceramic types and masses of rock rubble suggestive of permanent residence in substantial stone structures. Also, as Map 14 indicates, overall Middle Horizon population density in the Zumpango region was somewhat higher than for the southern Basin. Nevertheless, there are also many small sites with limited surface pottery and no significant rock rubble.

In view of its relatively low agricultural productivity, we were a little surprised to find such a substantial population buildup in the north during Middle Horizon times. However, one aspect of the modern scene gave us a clue to understanding this apparent anomaly. Today there are several major cement plants in the region. These exploit the large lime deposits, of Cretaceous age, that outcrop so abundantly in this corner of the Basin. Many of our Middle Horizon sites are in the Rio Salado drainage where substantial lime deposits have been cut into and exposed at the ground surface. In the fifteenth and sixteenth centuries, several communities in the area earned a living by processing limestone into lime, and carried the processed lime into the Mexico City market (Gibson 1964:336; Montúfar 1897). Considering the massive use of lime plaster at Teotihuacan, it would seem reasonable that the Teotihuacanos settled the population in this area in response to that need. The association of sites with major lime deposits is very close, even to the degree that larger sites are found near major extrusions and smaller sites close to the smaller ones. Thus, even though we cannot presently demonstrate, through artifactual analyses, the existence of specialized Middle Horizon lime working in Zumpango, we have some confidence that our hypothesis about its significance is a reasonable one. We did notice very heavy concentrations of limestone rubble in the fields of those sites located within a kilometer of the lime quarries, suggesting that the material was quarried, transported to, and burned in kilns within the village.

Our model for the Middle Horizon settlement system is that of a single, highly evolved polity that had complete control over its immediate hinterland in the Basin of Mexico. The entire Basin was a core resource area directly controlled by Teotihuacan. The production of the region served primarily for the life support of the center. The major shifts in community and zonal settlement suggest that Teotihuacan had effected a massive recolonization program to more efficiently exploit this core resource area. Virtually all of the basic resources needed by Teotihuacan could have been obtained from the Basin of Mexico: staple cultivated foods, such as maize, beans, and amaranth; animal protein resources such as fish, water fowl, and deer; fibers (from the maguey plant for cordage and clothing, reeds from the lakeshore for baskets and mats); basalt for grinding stones, hammerstones, and digging tools; oak and pine for a great variety of wood tools; salt from the lake; stone and earth for construction material; and clay for ceramics. Within the Basin, Zones One and Two probably provided the city with most of its staple foods, plus fiber, obsidian, basalt, salt, construction material, and clay. Zone Three was primarily a source area of animal protein (primarily fish and waterfowl from the freshwater lake), fibers (reeds from the lake), oak, pine, and wild plants. Zone Four supplied lime for construction, and fine quality obsidian. Some goods, consumed in relatively small quantity by relatively few people, were apparently obtained from outside of this core area. The evidence of such imported goods at Teotihuacan, and the presence of Teotihuacan exports in foreign areas, suggest a very extensive international trade network.

Another shift in the ecosystem was an apparent increase in the percentage of nonfood producers in the center from 6% in the case of the Phase Four center to 33% by Middle Horizon times. This process also involved the shift from part-time to full-time specialization and an enormous increase in foreign trade (for example, the percentage of the population involved in the obsidian export trade increased from 1% to 7%) (Spence n.d.). There is also evidence in Spence's data of a gradual and increasing dependence of the food-producing population on non-food-producing specialists for much of their technology (for example, the obsidian workers servicing the local needs increased from 1% or 2% to 5% between First Intermediate Phase Four and Middle Horizon times).

Our model for the Middle Horizon settlement system bears some superficial resemblance to what some geographers and anthropologists (e.g., Blanton 1976a) have called primate systems. In such systems there is a single, unusually large center which completely dominates a large region, both politically and economically, and whose existence inhibits the development of secondary centers. It is not altogether clear what factors surround the development of such primate systems, although Blanton (1976a, following Johnson 1970 and Smith 1974) notes that primary centers often occur in the modern world in situations where there are great wealth differentials between the inhabitants of central versus peripheral zones. A key feature of historically known primate systems is that most producers within a large region look to the primate center as a place to dispose of their goods and services, and most consumers within a large region are oriented toward the same center as a place to acquire most of the goods and services which a household cannot produce for itself.

Middle Horizon Teotihuacan was, in several ways, a primate center of the first order. With the possible exception of the poorly known center at Azcapotzalco on the west side of Lake Texcoco, all known provincial centers were less than 1/20 the size of Teotihuacan (e.g., Blanton 1976b). Nevertheless, the urban–rural relationships we propose would appear to be very different from those which have been used to characterize modern primate systems: a basic conflict between a wealthy, well-served center and a poor, badly served periphery. For the Teotihuacan system, we see rural settlements (at least within the Basin of Mexico) as economic and sociological extensions of the center, with little of the urban–rural dichotomy which assumes so prominent a role in most sociological models of urban societies. Furthermore, instead of the instability that Blanton (1976a:262) predicts for primate systems because of center–periphery cleavages, we seem to find the Teotihuacan system enduring for some 500 years in a relatively unchanged form.

And yet, at the same time, we cannot help but perceive the Teotihuacan system as economically inefficient and even unsound. Transport costs, particularly for bulky items, were very high everywhere in prehispanic Mesoamerica except in those few places where traffic could move along water routes. Teotihuacan, unlike the Late Horizon capital at Tenochtitlan, was situated well away (more than 10 km) from any navigable body of water. Hence, supplying the Middle Horizon center with subsistence staples and bulky goods would have been a much more formidable task than for Tenochtitlan, a millenium later. Our model proposes that most of Teotihuacan's basic subsistence needs were supplied from a zone within some 20 km of the capital. If significant amounts of food for the central community derived from further afield, the high overland transport costs would have rendered the whole operation relatively inefficient. We have already argued that this inefficiency is manifested by the marked decline in population growth rates during the long Middle Horizon, and by the low *overall* Basin population of this period (less than one-fourth that of the Late Horizon).

Finally, in no modern case example where primate centers occur does such a large proportion of the population reside in the central community. In other words, we find it difficult to relate the Basin of Mexico Middle Horizon settlement system to existing spatial models derived from geography and economic anthropology. We will return to this matter in later sections where we discuss the collapse of the Middle Horizon system and the formulation of new organizational modes in the Second Intermediate period and Late Horizon.

SECOND INTERMEDIATE: PHASE ONE (A.D. 750–950)

The eighth century A.D. was a time of profound change in settlement configuration within the Basin of Mexico (Map 15). Teotihuacan itself was reduced to about one-fifth of its Middle Horizon size. Elsewhere population was redistributed in a radically different manner, with only limited continuity with Middle Horizon occupation. The basic demographic process was a dispersal of population outward from the huge Middle Horizon center into more sparsely occupied parts of the Basin. This is most apparent in the great expansion of occupation in the Texcoco region and, to a more limited degree, in the Chalco and Ixtapalapa regions. However, other areas, at some distance from Teotihuacan, apparently lost significant population (e.g., the Temascalapa region and the Zumpango region), and the Basin as a whole lost one-third of its Middle Horizon population. There are some superficial resemblances to the First Intermediate Phase Three settlement pattern: An overall population of roughly the same size; a tendency toward discrete settlement clustering in some of the same areas; and a fragmented polity, implied by both the discrete settlement clustering and by the absence of any single major center. However, as we hope to make clear below, the Second Intermediate Phase One was by no means a return to First Intermediate Phase Three conditions. The greatest continuity of population, both in terms of population size and location, between the Middle Horizon and the Second Intermediate One phase was in the Tenayuca, Tacuba, and Cuautitlan regions. The total number of occupations breaks down as follows: one large regional center (at Teotihuacan), 14 smaller centers with populations varying from a few thousand to 10,000, 15 larger villages (12 nucleated, 3 dispersed), 40 small villages (18 nucleated, 22 dispersed), and 128 hamlets.

Population in the northern half of the Basin was clustered into three well-defined groupings: the Teotihuacan Valley cluster, the Tenayuca–Cuautitlan cluster, and the Zumpango cluster. Each cluster is separated from other population groupings by virtually empty zones between 10 and 20 km in width. Although well-defined, these settlement clusters were of very dissimilar population size: The Teotihuacan Valley cluster contained well over 50,000 people; the Tenayuca–Cuautitlan cluster had perhaps 20,000 inhabitants; while the Zumpango cluster included no more than 5500 people. The situation in the southern Basin is somewhat more complex. Here we find three or four substantial regional centers, spaced between 7 and 15 km apart. Dispersed rural occupation, in the form of villages and hamlets, is scattered throughout the intervals between these centers. It seems somewhat more reasonable to consider these as three separate settlement clusters (each with populations of between 5000 and 12,000 people) rather than as a single large cluster, with a total population of about 35,000, which is about the same as our estimate for the First Intermediate Phase Three population of the same area (excluding Cuicuilco) and is about three times that of the Middle Horizon.

Alden's (1978) nearest neighbor analysis of these same settlement data supports such a tripartite division. Nevertheless, the rural settlement here is rather more continuously distributed between major centers than elsewhere in the Basin, and there was probably some significant organizational difference between the northern and southern sections of the Basin. Its relative proximity to Cholula, the major Second Intermediate Phase One supraregional center in central Mexico, may have a lot to do with the distinct settlement configuration of the southern Basin at this time. We will refer to the three principal settlement groupings in the southern Basin as the Portesuelo cluster, the Cerro de la Estrella cluster, and the Xico cluster.

The Teotihuacan Valley Cluster. Although a precise measure of the Teotihuacan center must await the final results of Millon's Mapping Project, an independent assessment of the site's borders by our field teams suggests that the Second Intermediate Phase One center was comparable in extent and population to the First Intermediate Phase Three settlement, an area of 5–6 km^2 and a population of 30,000–40,000. This was by far the largest community in the Basin of Mexico at this time. The balance of the cluster's population was concentrated in a series of nucleated villages and regional centers along the edge of the two alluvial plains of the lower Teotihuacan and the middle Papalotla valleys, on both sides of the Patlachique Range. In other words, the population of the cluster was distributed so as to have easy access to the more productive agricultural land, land that had been directly utilized, from a great distance, by the population of the Middle Horizon center. It would appear that as Teotihuacan's political and economic importance declined through the eighth century, the various factors that had produced such an extreme population concentration there were no longer operative. Administrators would have had much more limited roles, wealth and power would have been greatly reduced, and there would have been a great decline in the demand for the products of skilled craftsmen. Many non-food producers would have emigrated to new power centers. It is not difficult to envision why the agricultural population that remained would have moved out into locations more convenient for cultivation activities. The large Middle Horizon population on the north flank of the Teotihuacan Valley and the upper portion of the Valley virtually vanished. All that remained was a small regional center and a few outlying satellite settlements along the Ajuluapan River. We estimate the total population for the Teotihuacan cluster as about between 75,000–80,000, with approximately half residing at Teotihuacan itself. This amounts to about three-fourths of the agricultural population, and a little over half the total Middle Horizon population, for the same area.

The Guadalupe Cluster.   This was the area of greatest continuity with Middle Horizon occupation. Although there were several new centers founded, and a number of substantial Middle Horizon settlements were abandoned or greatly reduced in size, the two periods were quite similar in terms of overall population, general settlement location, and general settlement character. In both periods population was heavily concentrated in a number of large communities along the lakeshore, around the lower flanks of the Guadalupe Range, and at the edge of the deep-soil alluvium in the northern Tacuba region. Most of the Second Intermediate Phase One population resided in seven regional centers, each with a population of several thousand. Only along the fringes of the deep-soil alluvium in the Cuautitlan area, north of the Guadalupe Range, was there a significant population loss relative to Middle Horizon times. We estimate a total population of about 20,000 people for this cluster.

The Zumpango Cluster.   This is one of the smallest Second Intermediate Phase One population clusters in the Basin of Mexico, and it is the only one outside the Teotihuacan Valley in which overall population declined from Middle Horizon Levels. This decline may be related to the marginal quality of agriculture in this area of thin soil and low rainfall. It would also be expectable if most of the Middle Horizon population had been, as we suggested, specialized lime workers whose principal market at Teotihuacan had largely disappeared by Phase One times. This conclusion is justified by the fact that no settlements at all are located near the limestone outcrops. There is a single Phase One regional center, and a broad scattering of small villages and hamlets. Many of the latter occupy the same locations as small Middle Horizon settlements, and it is clear that some Middle Horizon hamlets and small villages continued to be occupied. The Phase One regional center, however, represents a complete break with the Middle Horizon occupation. It lies atop a steep-sided, flat-topped hill (Mesa La Ahumada) that rises more than 200 m above the general level of the surrounding terrain. Middle Horizon ceramics are completely absent there. With more than a quarter of the total cluster population, this regional center is also the only location in the Zumpango region where a full range of Second Intermediate Phase One decorated ceramics occurs, and it is the only site where civic–ceremonial architecture is found. It is possible therefore that the smaller settlements in the area were not permanent peasant communities but exploitation sites. We estimate the total population of the Zumpano settlement cluster at about 5500 people.

The Portesuelo Cluster.   This consists principally of a single large regional center (the Portesuelo site, Tx-ET-18; Parsons 1971:75) with abundant ceremonial–civic architecture, an estimated nucleated population of about 12,000 people, and a full range of Second Intermediate Phase One decorated ceramics. A few small sites in the general region contained a relatively insignificant number of people and again may have been exploitation sites rather than permanent settlements. The principal Phase One center grew out of a much smaller Middle Horizon site (Tx-EC-32; Parsons 1971:60) that probably had served as a small provincial center in Middle Horizon times. Nowhere in the Basin of Mexico was so large a Phase One occupation so tightly nucleated and so isolated from other major settlements: Northward it is nearly 20 km to the southern edge of the Teotihuacan Valley cluster; it is more than 12 km south to the Xico settlement cluster; and the Cerro de la Estrella cluster, at the west end of the Ixtapalapa region, lies nearly 20 km to the west.

The Cerro de la Estrella Cluster.   Here, as in the case of the Portesuelo cluster, we seem to have a single, isolated population concentration (ca. 5000 people at Ix-ET-13; Blanton 1972:91) at a single major settlement. This settlement, on the lower northern flanks of Cerro de la Estrella, had also been the locus of a small Middle Horizon central village. Our inability to adequately appraise prehispanic occupation in the nearby southwestern corner of Lake Texcoco (an area now heavily covered by modern Mexico City) must be kept in mind here. However, for the moment it does appear that the Cerro de la Estrella cluster is another real Phase One occupational isolate, with only limited rural occupation around a single, nucleated center.

The Xico Cluster.   This is a complex occupational unit, and in some ways is actually a kind of noncluster. There is a single principal regional center, of perhaps 3500 inhabitants, on Xico island at the eastern end of Lake Chalco (Ch-ET-13, Parsons n.d.). Some 4 km to the southeast, in the deep-soil alluvium along the southeast shore of Lake Chalco, is another large, nucleated settlement where some 2400 people may have resided (Ch-ET-24, Parsons n.d.). Both these large sites also contain small Middle Horizon occupations. There is another nucleated Phase One settlement, on the southwest shore of Lake Chalco (Ch-ET-31, Parsons n.d.), some 8 km west of Xico, which contained another thousand or so people. Some 10 or 11 km due east of Xico, at the edge of the lower piedmont, is another focus of Phase One occupation, in several small sites, for which our population estimate is about 1200–1500 people. There are, in addition, a few other small settlements scattered rather widely throughout the general Chalco–Xochimilco region. Only the three largest communities, around the Lake Chalco shoreline, contain ceremonial–civic architecture and a full range of Second Intermediate Phase One decorated pottery, again suggesting the possibility that the smaller sites were impermanent exploitation stations.

In summarizing the rather complex Second Intermediate Phase One situation from our regional perspective, several generalizations seem particularly significant. It is now more difficult than before to comprehend the settlement configuration within our survey area by looking at the Basin of Mexico in isolation from the rest of central Mexico. In some respects this is also true for the antecedent Middle Horizon, and we have already indicated how we suffer from a less than adequate view of adjacent sections of the Central Mexican Symbiotic Region in our efforts to understand the Middle Horizon settlement system centered on the Basin of Mexico. However, for the Middle Horizon we do have reasonable control over what we know to be the heartland of a large regional system. For the Second Intermediate Phase One we are much less clear about where the Basin of Mexico lies in terms of core and periphery as new regional systems replace Middle Horizon Teotihuacan. Certainly, within the Basin of Mexico, there was no Second Intermediate Phase One supraregional center comparable in any way to the scale and immensity represented by Middle Horizon Teotihuacan. The situation we do have, a series of very discrete settlement clusters, ranging in population between roughly 5000 and 60,000 people, situated so as to be directly accessible to prime agricultural land, with each settlement cluster focused on one, or a few, major population centers that contained between 5000 and 30,000 inhabitants, is quite suggestive of a fragmented regional polity in which physical distance and nucleation provided a measure of insulation and protection from potentially (or actually) hostile relationships which could not be otherwise resolved at higher levels. The distinct paucity of rural settlement in this period—much more pronounced than at any other time in the Basin of Mexico—may also be an indication of such a politically fragmented system.

A major problem with this political model is the widespread distribution of the Coyotlatelco ceramic complex. First defined by Tozzer (1921) from the Coyotlatelco type site near Azcapotzalco, it was subsequently shown to be not only widely distributed over the Basin of Mexico (Rattray 1966; Parsons 1971; Blanton 1972; Sanders et al. n.d.) but in the Valley of Toluca (Piña Chan 1977) to the west and the southern part of Hidalgo to the north as well (Diehl 1974; Mastache and Crespo 1974). One would expect considerable stylistic regionalism in ceramics during a period of political fragmentation over such a large area. Furthermore, outside the Basin, new supraregional centers were developing in adjacent parts of central Mexico, for example, Xochicalco to the south, across the southern divide of the Basin, in the state of Morelos, and, especially, Cholula to the southeast, just across the Sierra Nevada. Because we know relatively little about these Second Intermediate centers, we find it difficult to relate our own settlement data to them. We feel very strongly that the developing center of Cholula was exercising a major role in central Mexico during and after the period of Teotihuacan's decline.

A major problem in the resolution of this problem has been the state of confusion as to the chronology of Cholula, one of the larger sites in Mesoamerica. It is now apparent that Cholula emerges as small village during the First Intermediate Two–Three Phases, evolves into a regional or a provincial center during the rise of Teotihuacan (where it was clearly under the cultural, and probably political, domination of that center), and underwent explosive growth during the Second Intermediate One Phase when a huge acropolis of plazas and public buildings was constructed (much of the fill of the gigantic lower terrace of the Great Pyramid consists of constructions of this phase). The center during Phase Two was of comparable importance to judge from the fact that the Great Pyramid was constructed at this time, and at the time of the Spanish Conquest it was still a center of 20,000–40,000 inhabitants, although dominated by Aztec Tenochtitlan (see Figure 5.6). Publications on the ceramics of the site have focused on the First Intermediate Five–Middle Horizon when the ceramic complex was closely related to Teotihuacan and during the Second Intermediate Two–Three and Late Horizon when a spectacular polychrome style referred to as Mixteca–Puebla or Cholulteca was characteristic, and say little about the ceramics of the Second Intermediate One phase. Only recently has it become apparent that the ceramic complex in western Puebla and northern Tlaxcala during this phase was, in fact, identical to the Coyotlotelco complex in the Basin of Mexico (Rattry, personal communication in reference to Cacaxtla; Merlo Juarez, personal communication in reference to Cholula; and Garcia Cook and Trejo 1977). If Cholula did exercise political suzerainty over much of the Central Plateau, and was the source of the Coyotlatelco ceramic style, it would go a long way toward explaining the widespread distribution of the style.

Quite obviously we do not have data on hand to resolve these two possible interpretations. In either case, the rapid decline of Teotihuacan is probably causally related to the rise of Cholula, and possibly Xochicalco to the south as well (see Figure 5.7). Some mechanisms can be suggested for this process of decline, based on our model of the growth of Teotihuacan. To recapitulate, we postulated an early explosive growth based on the development of hydraulic agriculture, in which a large population was concentrated in the vicinity of the springs, to form an essentially agrarian community. Much of the later growth can be ascribed to the increasing craft specialization and expansion of trade networks, a growth facilitated by the highly centralized political and demographic systems.

Teotihuacan's political and economic domination of the Central Plateau had a surprisingly long life, but in terms of Central Mexican ecology it was clearly vulnerable. First, the agricultural potential of the Puebla–Tlaxcala region was fully comparable to that of the Basin of Mexico, excepting chinampa agriculture in the southern lakes, which was not a developed system in Middle Horizon times. The only advantage Teotihuacan had was an organizational precocity, but given similar ecological conditions this organization could, of course, be duplicated. A decided advantage that the Puebla–Tlaxcala region did have was closer proximity to regions of very different environments and hence resources, such as the Gulf Coast, Central Oaxaca, and the Maya Lowlands.

There is a strong suggestion, in the form of archaeological evidence of

Figure 5.6. Oblique aerial view of the Great Pyramid at the site of Cholula. (Courtesy of CIA Mexicana Aerofoto S.A.)

Figure 5.7. Oblique aerial view of Xochicalco. (Courtesy of CIA Mexicana Aerofoto S.A.)

intentional burning of Teotihuacan residences in its terminal phase, that the process of replacement of Teotihuacan by Cholula was not a peaceful one. The immediate cause of Teotihuacan's decline was most probably a series of military disasters engineered by nearby central plateau states like Cholula and Xochicalco, but the processual cause was the collapse of Teotihuacan's external trade networks (see Chapters 8 and 9).

SECOND INTERMEDIATE: PHASE TWO (A.D. 950–1150)

The tenth century A.D. is the earliest period to which relatively meaningful references are made in the semilegendary, semihistorical accounts, recorded during the era of Spanish conquest and initial colonization (Figure 5.12 and Map 16). According to most readings of these accounts, the great Toltec center at Tula, or Tollan, was the principal sociopolitical capital in central Mexico from the tenth through the twelfth centuries, and the Basin of Mexico was within its domain. For more than 30 years most archaeologists have equated this quasihistorical Tollan with the archaeological site of Tula, a few kilometers northwest of the Basin of Mexico (Jiménez Moreno 1941; Diehl 1974). We agree with this equation in most respects, but hasten to point out a few complicating factors. First, the semilegendary Tollan is a rather diffuse notion, both in time and space. It is not wholly unreasonable to think of this term, Tollan, as having both a great time depth and associations with more than one center over a long period of time. For example, Teotihuacan could conceivably have been called Tollan by people throughout Mesoamerica during the Middle Horizon and even into the Second Intermediate Phase One. The name could have shifted over to a new center that developed during the Second Intermediate Phase Two.

Second, there is the matter of Cholula on the southeastern edge of the Basin of Mexico. We have already argued that it probably was a major sociopolitical factor in central Mexico during the Second Intermediate Phase One. We also suggested that it had a significant impact on the configuration of settlement, in at least the southern Basin, at that time. Unfortunately, we still know surprisingly little about this key center during Phase Two, but there is good reason to suspect that it continued to have a major influence in central Mexico (e.g., Noguera 1954; Marquina 1970). Indeed, it is difficult to reject the hypothesis that Cholula was as significant a factor as Tula in the configuration of Second Intermediate Phase Two settlement in the Basin of Mexico. Cholula, in fact, is mentioned by the Toltec annals as a place where their great leader Quetzalcoatl Topiltzin Axcitl resided during his hegira from Tula. Archaeological confirmation of this is provided by the fact that the Great Pyramid was apparently constructed during this phase—the largest structure in prehispanic Mesoamerica—and it was traditionally the Temple of Quetzalcoatl.

At first glance, the presence throughout the Basin of a Phase Two ceramic assemblage that can, with little hesitation, be labeled as the general Mazapan complex (Vaillant 1941; Parsons 1971) would seem to argue for primarily Tula associations. However, there is some distinct variation in this assemblage within the Basin (e.g., Parsons and Whalen n.d.), and the Phase Two ceramic assemblage at Cholula itself remains very superficially described. Indeed, Mueller (in Marquina 1970:139) notes a distinct Mazapan influence in Choluteca II pottery (approximately equivalent to Second Intermediate Phases One and Two), and even illustrates (Marquina 1970:140) a very good Red-on-Buff bowl, with tripod hollow supports, that would be lost in any Mazapan-phase collection from the Basin of Mexico or Tula. Until we understand Cholula much better, we cannot neglect its potential impact on the Basin of Mexico in Phase Two times. One could even argue (although we ourselves are not now prepared to do so) that Cholula was Tollan, and Tula was something less during the Second Intermediate Phase Two. If we lacked the quasihistorical (and potentially misleading) documentation about Tollan, the latter reasoning might be more reasonable on the basis of archaeological data alone.

The survey revealed 733 sites. They break down as follows: 10 provincial centers, 19 large villages (10 dispersed, 9 nucleated), 110 small villages (83 dispersed, 27 nucleated), 555 hamlets, 5 salt-making stations, and 2 sites of indeterminant status. One very striking feature of Second Intermediate Phase Two settlement is the very high proportion of hamlets and small dispersed villages. The Second Intermediate Phase Two, with the highest proportion of rural settlement of any prehispanic period in the Basin of Mexico, thus stands in marked contrast with the antecedent Phase One, which had the lowest proportion of such rural occupation (Table 5.13).

The sociological implications of this ruralization will be discussed later, but first we should briefly consider the possibility that it might have increased our survey error by a greater margin than for any other period. Over the years we have wondered how great a proportion of Phase Two sites we were missing simply because so many of them were so small in size and so light in occupational density. We were particularly concerned about our ability to perceive such small sites in the deep-soil alluvium where even a relatively shallow alluvial overlay might render them invisible. Our concern

TABLE 5.13
A Comparison of Sites of the Second Intermediate One–Two Phases

	Second Intermediate One	Second Intermediate Two
Hamlet	5%	26%
Small village	11%	31%
Large village	9%	13%
Small provincial or regional center	39%	30%
Large regional center	36%	0

was intensified when we realized that almost no Phase Two occupation had ever been reported from the unsurveyed Tacuba region (now largely occupied by Mexico City, but from which locale occupation from most other periods had been turned up in some abundance over the years). Could this apparent near absence of Phase Two occupation in the Tacuba region be primarily a product of the low probability that such small rural sites would be noticed within a modern urbanized setting?

Another aspect of this problem emerged when we extended our surveys into the northern third of the Basin. Here we found a rather different settlement pattern, in which overall Phase Two settlement density was much greater, and where large, nucleated sites were more abundant, than in the southern Basin. This has led us to suspect that the still unsurveyed northeastern section of the Basin (the Pachuca region) may also contain a large, relatively nucleated Phase Two occupation. If this is so, then there is some additional reason to suspect that our overall Phase Two population estimate for the Basin as a whole is underestimated relatively more than for any other time period.

On the other hand, we have been able to locate a very large number of small Phase Two sites in most parts of the Basin. Many of these are in low-lying, deep-soil terrain. The only substantial surveyed area where Phase Two sites are quite scarce is the central part of the Texcoco region on the east side of Lake Texcoco. We feel fairly certain that this latter site scarcity is, in fact, a product of a genuine lack of Phase Two occupation. These factors offset, to some degree, our more pessimistic feelings expressed in the preceding paragraph. However, we continue to argue, with ourselves and with each other, about the relative reliability of our Phase Two settlement perception. For example, Sanders thinks that there were many small Phase Two sites in the unsurveyed Tacuba region and that numerous small sites were missed in the surveyed area. With these considerations and the likelihood of a substantial Phase Two occupation in the unsurveyed Pachuca region, the total number of small Phase Two sites in the Basin, he believes, was probably at least twice that which we report. Parsons, on the other hand, feels that significantly fewer small sites have been missed in surveyed areas, and that the lack of reported sites in the Tacuba region probably reflects a real paucity of occupation there (see later discussion). Nevertheless, we all agree that our Phase Two data provide a valid basis for making meaningful inferences about cultural behavior.

During Phase One 75% of the population lived in regional centers, whereas only 30% lived in provincial centers during Phase Two. Only 16% of the population in Phase One lived in settlements with less than 500 people whereas 57% lived in such settlements in Phase Two. A second difference between the two patterns is the much greater number of dispersed settlements during Phase Two. Thirty villages were nucleated during Phase One and 25 dispersed, whereas 46 were nucleated and 93 dispersed during Phase Two. The difference is particularly striking in the large villages, where 12 of the 15 communities of this type in Phase One were nucleated, whereas only 9 of 19 were nucleated in Phase Two. Furthermore, the provincial centers during Phase Two were much smaller and less densely settled than in Phase One. Clearly there was a marked overall trend toward ruralization and dispersion of the population in Phase Two times.

With respect to zonal settlement within the Basin of Mexico, there are striking differences. The Teotihuacan Valley and Cuautitlan–Tenayuca regions had population levels comparable to Phase One, but population was now more evenly distributed. In the Teotihuacan Valley, the upper valley and the northern flank, areas devoid of Phase One occupation, contained substantial Phase Two rural settlement. Much of this population redistribution was probably the result of continuing loss of population from the old Teotihuacan center. We estimate that this latter community had now declined to no more than 10,000–20,000 people—a small provincial center of distinctly secondary importance.

The single biggest surprise in our Phase Two settlement configuration has been the high occupational density in the Zumpango region in the northwestern Basin. Here areal population density was exceeded only by that of the Teotihuacan Valley (Table 6.17). Furthermore, the proportion of population living in nucleated communities was the highest in the entire Basin of Mexico (Table 6.15) during Phase Two times. There are two very sizable provincial centers, the largest of which has an estimated population of roughly 4000 people. These characteristics represent a reversal of most preceding demographic trends in the Zumpango region, although the general population buildup is somewhat analagous to that of the Middle Horizon in the same area (Table 6.18). Looking at the Basin as a whole, it is quite apparent that the demographic gradient of the Second Intermediate Phase Two is essentially the reverse of that which had characterized the area through the First Intermediate period, that is, the northern half of the Basin was now much more densely settled, with a far higher proportion of large, nucleated communities. The southern Basin was distinctly secondary, in demographic terms.

We feel rather strongly that the Second Intermediate Phase Two settlement configuration throughout the Basin of Mexico can only be understood in reference to the development and florescence of the supraregional center at Tula, some 20 km WNW of the northernmost edge of our Zumpango region survey area. The Tula center, as we have already indicated, reached its peak development at this time. All available evidence (Diehl 1974; Matos 1974) indicates that there was a small Second Intermediate Phase One center at Tula, but there is little to suggest that it had more than local significance. One significant factor in the relatively high Second Intermediate Phase Two settlement density in the Zumpango region may have been the importance of this area as a source of lime for Tula, as it probably had been for Teotihuacan during Middle Horizon times. However, we find this hypothesis somewhat less appealing for the Second Intermediate Phase Two than for the Middle

Horizon. Primarily this is because Tula itself lies within an area of abundant lime outcrops which probably would have been quite adequate for its needs. Nevertheless, we do not feel we can wholly reject this idea at this time.

One thing is very clear: We need to know something more about Tula in order to better assess its impact on Basin of Mexico settlement. Fortunately, we have comparable settlement data from a surveyed area of 1000 km² around Tula and adjacent to the Basin of Mexico. The survey was conducted by Guadalupe Mastache and Ana Maria Crespo (1974, 1976), in connection with Eduardo Matos' Tula project, using the same methodology as our own Basin of Mexico survey. We have included a copy of a preliminary map of their survey for comparison (Figure 5.10). Table 5.14 summarizes their data and compares it with the Basin of Mexico.

The total Second Intermediate Phase Two population for the Tula survey region, including Tula itself, is approximately equal to that of our surveyed portions of the Basin of Mexico (an area more than four times its size). It is clear that the Tula region was several times as densely settled as the Basin of Mexico during this period. The total combined Phase Two population of the Basin of Mexico and the Tula region was probably very close to the combined Middle Horizon total for the same two areas. The growth of the center of Tula apparently acted as an enormous magnet, pulling the rural population of the Basin in the northwesterly direction during Phase Two times.

Although the Tula region survey area is relatively small, and its limits are arbitrarily fixed, some aspects of its Phase Two settlement configuration provide extremely useful insights into political and economic organization in Central Mexico for this time period. The Phase Two Tula center covered about 12 km², and probably contained about 60,000 inhabitants (Diehl 1974; Matos 1974) (see Figures 5.8 and 5.9). The Phase Two rural population

TABLE 5.14

A Comparison of Sites of the Basin of Mexico and the Tula Region in the Second Intermediate Phase Two

	Basin of Mexico (Surveyed region: 3500 km²)	Tula region (Surveyed area: 1000 km²)
Supraregional center	0	1 (estimated population 60,000)
Provincial centers	10	0
Large villages		
Dispersed	10	26
Nucleated	9	13
Small villages		
Dispersed	83	18
Nucleated	37	58
Hamlets	555	35
Small ceremonial		
centers	2	1
Salt-making stations	5	0
Indeterminate	2	0

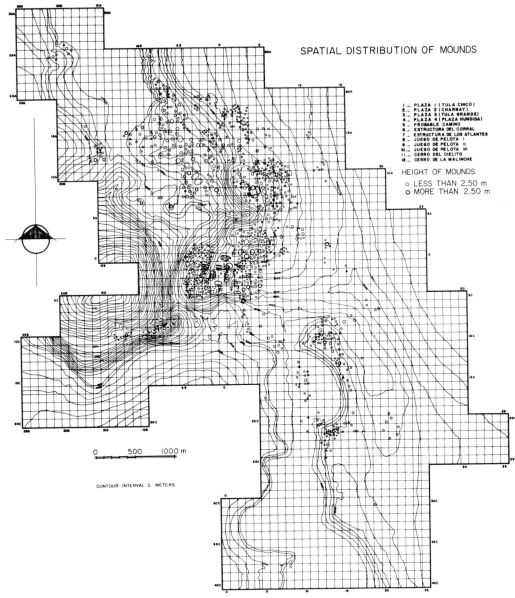

SPATIAL DISTRIBUTION OF MOUNDS

1.— PLAZA 1 (TULA CHICO)
2.— PLAZA 2 (CHARNAY)
3.— PLAZA 3 (TULA GRANDE)
4.— PLAZA 4 (PLAZA HUNDIDA)
5.— PROBABLE CAMINO
6.— ESTRUCTURA DEL CORRAL
7.— ESTRUCTURA DE LOS ATLANTES
8.— JUEGO DE PELOTA I
9.— JUEGO DE PELOTA II
10.— JUEGO DE PELOTA III
11.— CERRO DEL CIELITO
12.— CERRO DE LA MALINCHE

HEIGHT OF MOUNDS
o LESS THAN 2.50 m
O MORE THAN 2.50 m

0   500   1000 m

CONTOUR INTERVAL 5 METERS

Figure 5.8. Map of Tula by the I.N.A.H. Tula Project. (After Matos *et al.* 1974.)

surrounding the center was, as we have just noted, relatively dense and nucleated (see Figure 5.10). Crespo and Mastache (personal communication) also point out that the rural Phase Two settlements around Tula have much more substantial domestic architecture than is usually the case in the Basin of Mexico at this time. This may be taken as an indication of more intensive, permanent, long-term residence than for many Phase Two sites in the Basin

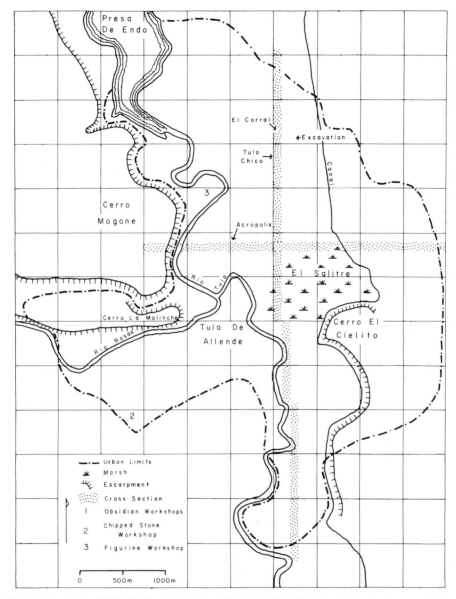

Figure 5.9. Map of Tula by the University of Missouri Tula Project. (After Diehl *et al.* 1974.)

of Mexico. Their estimate for the Phase Two rural population in the Tula region is about 60,000 inhabitants—a figure essentially equal to that of the Tula center. It is quite interesting to note that the combined Phase Two center and rural population of the Tula region is about equal to that of the Teotihuacan center during the Middle Horizon. Crespo and Mastache (1976) also note the absence of Phase Two provincial centers in the Tula region (i.e., large sites with well-defined civic–ceremonial architecture). This may indi-

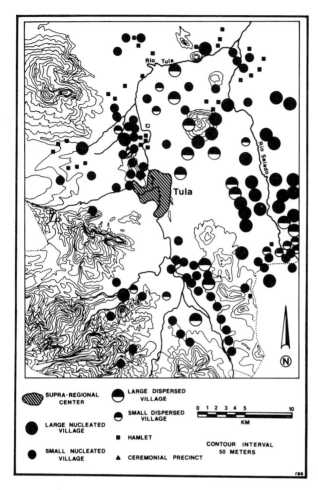

SUPRA-REGIONAL CENTER

LARGE NUCLEATED VILLAGE

SMALL NUCLEATED VILLAGE

LARGE DISPERSED VILLAGE

SMALL DISPERSED VILLAGE

HAMLET

CEREMONIAL PRECINCT

0 1 2 3 4 5   10

KM

CONTOUR INTERVAL 50 METERS

Figure 5.10. The Tula region, showing the distribution of Second Intermediate Phase Two occupations. (After Mastache and Crespo n.d.)

cate a close sociopolitical integration of Phase Two centers and rural population in the Tula area. We believe that the Phase Two situation at Tula
represents a tight integration of roughly the same number of people as at
Middle Horizon Teotihuacan (ca. 125,000), the principal difference being that
whereas the Teotihuacan Middle Horizon was completely nucleated, at Phase
Two Tula there was a broader dispersal of about half the total core population. We would argue that this center–rural dichotomy at Phase Two Tula
represents a physical separation of the non-food producers and agriculturalists, who had been concentrated in a single large center at Middle
Horizon Teotihuacan. We will develop this argument further in the following
paragraphs, and then consider its implications for our Basin of Mexico
settlement data.

The dense rural population in the immediate area of Tula also suggests a
very different *resource procurement* system than at Teotihuacan in Middle
Horizon times. To recapitulate, we noted a very small Middle Horizon rural

population within a 10–15-km radius of Teotihuacan (a radius comparable to that of the Tula regional survey area). On this basis, we suggested that a substantial percentage of the population living in Teotihuacan itself were farmers. The close spacing of rural settlements in the Second Intermediate Phase Two around Tula, on the other hand, suggests that most of the population of Tula itself were not farmers. What little data have been published lend support to our reconstruction. Obsidian workshops, for example, occupy an area at Tula as large as that at Middle Horizon Teotihuacan, a site with twice its population. We have little information on other kinds of craft specialization at Tula, but the obsidian data certainly suggest the existence of many other specialized artisans and craftsmen there.

We have already argued that the overall combined population of the Basin of Mexico and the Tula region survey area were probably roughly the same during both Middle Horizon and Second Intermediate Phase Two times: ca. 250,000 people. We also noted that Millon (1976) has proposed that about one-third of the Middle Horizon population at Teotihuacan were probably non-food producers—that is, about 40,000 people. We have also suggested that some of the rural Middle Horizon population in the Basin of Mexico were non-food producers, most significantly the inhabitants of the Zumpango region who may have been largely oriented toward producing lime. Perhaps 10,000–15,000 Middle Horizon non-food producers might reasonably be added to the estimate of 40,000 for Teotihuacan itself. This would mean that about one quarter (50,000–55,000) of the total Basin of Mexico–Tula region Middle Horizon population were non-food producers. For the Second Intermediate Phase Two we have argued that all the Tula urban population were non-food producers (ca. 60,000 people). We might expect that perhaps another few thousand non-food producers may have resided in the several Phase Two provincial centers in the Basin of Mexico. It thus seems reasonable to argue that the proportion of non-food producers for both the Middle Horizon and the Second Intermediate Phase Two in the Basin of Mexico and the Tula region would have been about the same: roughly one quarter. This might (and probably does) imply some general organizational parallels between the Middle Horizon and Second Intermediate Phase Two. However, the differences in settlement systems make it more difficult to argue for specific organizational isomorphism with the Middle Horizon.

Tula had a number of specific peculiarities when compared to Middle Horizon Teotihuacan or Late Horizon Tenochtitlan. Surveys at Tula have revealed thousands of small mounds, apparently residential units inhabited by nuclear or extended families (Figure 5.8). An extended family residence, interpreted as the residence of a merchant, has been completely excavated, along with portions of several others (Diehl 1974). This pattern of small houses contrasts sharply with the multiapartment blocks at Middle Horizon Teotihuacan, but is comparable to the residential pattern at Late Horizon Tenochtitlan (Calnek 1972). On the other hand, Tula differs from both of these two centers in the absence of major avenues and of an orderly grid system. In this feature it also differs from other major plateau centers such as Cholula. Another feature of Tula's settlement pattern is the contrast between the relatively large residential area, combined with the relatively small scale of its public architecture (see Figures 5.11 and 5.12). This latter feature also contrasts with the picture of Tollan, presented in the documentary sources, of a major capital of a large tributary empire.

Diehl's (1974) and Matos' (1974) projects may offer some explanation for these paradoxes. Apparently, the center grew explosively but collapsed almost as suddenly, the growth and decline perhaps occurring over a period of only 100 years. This would leave little time for the rulers to effectively mobilize labor for public works. As a capital of a rapidly expanding, large empire, the massive concentration of population is expectable but apparently the time was too short for them to engage in an urban renewal program, comparable to that which occurred at Teotihuacan.

Physically, Tula at about A.D. 1100 may have been somewhat similar to Teotihuacan during the First Intermediate Phase Four (Tzacualli phase), or Phase Five (Miccaotli Phase), before the massive architectural reorganization that occurred at the latter site after a few centuries of occupation. Developmentally, however, the archaeological data suggest great differences in the organization of production and redistribution that reflect the more evolved state of political and economic institutions in central Mexico during the period of Tula's growth and florescence.

At the beginning of this section we briefly discussed the center of Cholula. This major supraregional center, situated east of the Sierra de Nevada on the broad Puebla plain, lies about 40 km east of the southeasternmost edge of our Chalco region survey area. It is thus farther away than Tula, and, since it is separated from the Basin of Mexico by a major mountain range, lacks Tula's ready accessibility to our survey area. Nevertheless, because of its relative proximity and apparent close ceramic affiliations with the Basin of Mexico during the Second Intermediate, we feel that Cholula must be considered as a potentially significant factor in the configuration of Second Intermediate Two settlement in the Basin of Mexico.

One outstanding aspect of the distribution of Second Intermediate Two sites in the Basin of Mexico (Map 16) is the extremely low settlement density across the broad lakeshore and piedmont of the Texcoco region east of Lake Texcoco. This is a carefully surveyed area, and we feel quite confident that the paucity of sites here reflects a real Second Intermediate Two occupational gap. Because of modern urban overlay, the situation in the Tacuba region on the western side of Lake Texcoco is poorly understood (for any time period). We earlier noted the fact that very little Second Intermediate Two occupation has ever been reported from this area, despite a fair abundance of reported sites from almost every other period. We remain divided among ourselves as to whether this apparent dearth of Second Intermediate Two occupation in the Tacuba region reflects a very low population density, or is more a product of the relative invisibility of the very small sites that probably existed there

Figure 5.11. Oblique aerial view of Tula. (Courtesy of CIA Mexicana Aerofoto S.A.)

Figure 5.12. Oblique aerial view of the Acropolis at Tula. (Courtesy of CIA Mexicana Aerofoto S.A.)

during this period. In any event, we cannot yet reject the idea that Second Intermediate Two occupation in the Tacuba region was, in fact, very sparse and generally similar to that in the Texcoco region. In this case, there would have been a broad band of very sparse Second Intermediate Two occupation extending across the entire width of the south–central Basin of Mexico.

Two distinctive aspects of Second Intermediate Two settlement in the southern Basin of Mexico are (1) the overall low population density, and (2) the small size of sites. Our estimated population density for the southern Basin (southern Texcoco region, Ixtapalapa region, Chalco region, and Xochimilco region) is about 15 persons per square kilometer. This contrasts sharply with overall population density for the northern Basin (Teotihuacan Valley, Temascalapa region, Zumpango region, and Cuautitlan–Tenayuca region) where we estimate about 45 people per square kilometer at this time. Furthermore, there are only two relatively large, nucleated communities in the southern Basin, and both of these probably contained less than 2000 people (Tx-LT-53, Parsons 1971; Ch-LT-13, Parsons n.d.). This is another pronounced change from the northern Basin where there are many nucleated Second Intermediate Two communities, and several nucleated provincial centers with populations of several thousand people.

In other words, the southern Basin is demographically quite different from the north during Second Intermediate Two times. Furthermore, these two distinctive areas were apparently separated by a broad belt of very limited occupation. The implications of all this are not wholly clear, but we suggest that the following is a reasonable argument at this time. Although we have little information about it, we see Cholula as a major Second Intermediate Two center in central Mexico. Tula was clearly a center of comparable significance at this time. The configuration of Second Intermediate Two settlement in the Basin of Mexico suggests a basic north–south dichotomy in which the population of the northern Basin was affiliated with, and dependent upon, Tula, while the inhabitants of the southern Basin were similarly linked with Cholula. The broad occupational gap in the central Basin reflects a sociopolitical buffer zone of some sort between the two major centers.

The differences between Second Intermediate Two occupation in the northern and southern Basin may reflect important differences in how these areas related to Tula and Cholula, respectively. These differences will only become more apparent as we obtain information about Cholula, to the southeast, analogous to that we are now beginning to have for Tula, to the northwest. We see the northern Basin as an integral component of the Second Intermediate Two Tula settlement system, with a large, regional population closely linked economically and politically with the central core (at Tula). The southern Basin may have had similar links to Cholula, but the lower population size and much greater population dispersal in the south suggest a rather different kind of relationship.

Whatever its precise character, the Second Intermediate Two situation is a logical outgrowth of the Second Intermediate One model we developed earlier. Here, in the wake of Teotihuacan's collapse as a supraregional center, we postulated that a series of relatively autonomous polities developed in the northern Basin where there were no major centers (the Tula region probably was the locus of another Second Intermediate One settlement cluster, of moderate size, probably comparable to that we have in the Zumpango region or in the Cuautitlan–Tenayuca region). In the south, where the settlement lacked the well-defined clustering we had in the north, we suggested that the impact of Cholula, a major Second Intermediate Two center, was probably significant. In the Second Intermediate One, as in Second Intermediate Two, there is every indication of a major occupational gap between the northern and southern sections of the Basin (Maps 15 and 16), and, thus, a strong suggestion of northwest–southeast sociopolitical cleavage during both periods.

SECOND INTERMEDIATE: PHASE THREE (A.D. 1150–1350)

The legendary history written down during the era of Spanish conquest refers to Tula's collapse as a major center during the mid-twelfth century (e.g., Brundage 1972). This collapse was accompanied by frosts, droughts, crop failures, and invasions of "Chichimec" intruders from the north. The two centuries after Tula's decline have long been interpreted, on the basis of these legendary histories, as a troubled era of struggle and conflict between numerous small polities that consolidated within the Basin of Mexico as dominant groups of mobile Chichimec invaders merged with indigenous sedentary agriculturalists. The same documentary sources indicate that this period of political fragmentation ended with the formation of the Tepaneca and Acolhua hegemonies in the later fourteenth century, when large portions of the Basin were brought under the control of Azcapotzalco and Texcoco. Up to this point the archaeological input into the culture history of this era has been minimal. However, we are quite confident that our Second Intermediate Three period (defined by the Aztec I and Aztec II ceramic assemblages) pertains to this era. We will now go on to consider how our archaeological settlement data might complement the traditional documentary-based interpretation (Map 17).

At the outset we have to note that the Second Intermediate Three has been one of the most difficult periods for us to handle. This is primarily because the diagnostic Second Intermediate Three ceramic markers do not readily stand out from Late Horizon surface pottery when an observer walks over a site area where both components are present. Late Horizon is nearly everywhere so predominant over the Second Intermediate Three, when the two occur together, that it is usually difficult to assess properly the presence and relative proportion of Second Intermediate Three occupations unless surface samples are taken fairly frequently. But, because Late Horizon sites are everywhere so numerous, we could only sample a small number of them. Likewise, on large, nucleated Late Horizon sites we found it virtually impossible to take more than a very few surface collections, simply because of time and personnel limitations. However, such sites, we learned, are precisely where Second Intermediate Three occupations are most likely to occur.

Another significant problem in this regard relates to the fact that many modern towns directly and completely overlie major Late Horizon communities of the same name (e.g., Texcoco, Xochimilco, Amecameca, Mixquic, Cuitlahuac, etc.). Often these modern towns are so nucleated and heavily built up that we can see little or nothing of the Late Horizon occupation, even though we know it is there (on the basis of sixteenth-century documentary sources). However, in such cases we do not usually know whether there is also a Second Intermediate Three community of any significance at the same locality. We have determined (where Late Horizon centers are only partly covered by modern towns, e.g., Xaltocan and Huexotla) that this is sometimes the case. However, we can often only hazard a guess or rely upon suggestions from documentary sources (e.g., Azcapotzalco, Cuautitlan, Xochimilco, Amecameca, Mixquic). Despite all these problems, the Second Intermediate Three settlement pattern we have defined seems consistent and reasonable. We believe it is essentially valid.

The southern three quarters of the Basin contains a respectable Second

Intermediate Three population, approximately equal in total size to that of the Second Intermediate One, and sharing some of the same distributional patterns as the latter period: most particularly, a high proportion of the total population residing in a relatively small number of nucleated communities situated on low-lying ground around the lakeshore (Map 17). Nevertheless, there are also some major differences between the Second Intermediate One and Second Intermediate Three settlement configurations: a near complete absence of Second Intermediate Three occupation in the far northern Basin; the much greater number of small, widely scattered Second Intermediate Three sites; and the *generally* less extreme settlement clustering in Second Intermediate Three times.

There is a definite intensification of Second Intermediate Three occupation moving from north to south in the Basin of Mexico. The northern quarter is virtually empty. This is puzzling in view of the relatively heavy buildup of earlier Second Intermediate Two and subsequent Late Horizon occupation in the same area. A similar population decline seems to occur at this time in the Tula region survey area (Mastache and Crespo 1974). We are presently unable to account for this demographic behavior in any reasonable way. At the general latitude of Lake Xaltocan–Zumpango, there are small regional centers at Teotihuacan, Xaltocan, and Cuautitlan. It is unlikely that any of these exceeded 5000 in population. In the central Basin there are two pairs of regional centers: Azcapotzalco and Tenayuca on the western side of Lake Texcoco; and Huexotla and Coatlinchan on the east. These are large centers, probably on the order of 10,000–15,000 people each, which historically are known to have been paramount in the first major post-Tula polities in the Basin of Mexico: the Tepaneca domain on the west, and Acolhuacan on the east (Brundage 1972; Davies 1976; Parsons 1971). The distinctly paired configuration of these centers is unusual, but (particularly for Acolhuacan) probably reflects a north–south dichotomy of administrative control and tributary domain within a loosely structured larger confederation.

The southern end of the Basin, around the Lake Chalco–Xochimilco shoreline, is the most densely populated area in Second Intermediate Three times. We can identify six or seven large nucleated sites here: Culhuacan, Xochimilco, Cuitlahuac, Mixquic, Chalco, Xico, and (further to the southeast) Amecameca. Although it is doubtful that any of these centers (excepting probably Chalco) exceeded 5000 people, their combined population is impressive. Their relatively large size and quite regular spacing (averaging 6–8 km, except for the more distant site of Amecameca) suggest that these sites functioned as small regional centers, each of which dominated small tributary regions within the southern Basin. The intercenter spacing becomes almost completely regular if we could assume that there is a Second Intermediate Three center at Tlalmanalco, about half way between Chalco and Amecameca. Documentary sources (Chimalpahin 1965) indicate that a Late Horizon center existed at Tlalmanalco, but the modern community there almost completely obscures its archaeological remains, and we have no good way of estimating its status in Second Intermediate Three times.

The Chalco–Xochimilco region is additionally interesting because it is here that we find the only large concentrations of Aztec I pottery anywhere in the Basin of Mexico. If we are correct in our belief that the Aztec I and Aztec II ceramic complexes are essentially contemporary, then the presence of so much Aztec I in the south may indicate some degree of economic and/or sociopolitical differentiation from the north. To the east, across the Sierra Nevada in Puebla, the Cholula ceramic assemblage dating to this period apparently contains a considerable amount of Aztec I Black-on-Orange pottery (Noguera 1954). It seems quite likely that the Chalco–Xochimilco region is linked to this nearby major center in a very different way than the more northerly parts of the Basin of Mexico, where Aztec I Black-on-Orange is virtually absent during Second Intermediate Three times. One possibility might be that the southern Basin remained within the larger domain of Cholula, while in the north, where Tula's authority had waned and disappeared, a series of smaller, autonomous polities were developing and consolidating into the Tepaneca and Acolhua domains.

Another significant aspect of Second Intermediate Three settlement is the general discontinuity between major population concentrations of this period and those of the antecedent Second Intermediate Two. Only at Teotihuacan and Xico did large Second Intermediate Two settlements develop into important Second Intermediate Three communities (and at Xico there is actually a physical separation of more than 100 m between the earlier and later occupations). In all other cases, as far as we can determine, Second Intermediate Three centers were established at localities with little or no Second Intermediate Two occupation (although both Tenayuca and Azcapotzalco had major Second Intermediate One occupations: Noguera 1935; Tozzer 1921). Part of this discontinuity almost certainly has to do with the general population growth that occurred during Second Intermediate Three times in most parts of the Basin. Another part of it is probably related to the earliest significant implementation of chinampa agriculture in the bed of Lake Chalco–Xochimilco where, for the first time, we begin to have substantial settlement in the immediate lakebed zone, which had previously been largely nonagricultural terrain (Parsons 1976). It is particularly interesting to note that the greatest Second Intermediate Two–Second Intermediate Three occupational discontinuity of all is in the central Texcoco region on the east side of Lake Texcoco. Here two principal Second Intermediate Three regional centers are located in a zone that had long remained nearly empty during both Second Intermediate Two and Second Intermediate One times. This abrupt change may well be related to the disappearance of a long-standing sociopolitical frontier which had separated the domains of Tula and Cholula between the end of the Middle Horizon and the beginning of Second Intermediate Three.

Where our data are most deficient, because of the methodological problems noted previously, is with respect to smaller sites, since they are seldom recorded in the documentary history. Our best control, at present, is from the Texcoco and Ixtapalapa regions. Beside the three substantial regional centers—Coatlinchan, Huexotla, and Culhuacan—Parsons (1971) and Blanton (1972) record 108 hamlets, 6 small dispersed villages, 2 small nucleated villages, and 1 large dispersed village.

With respect to the other regions our assessment is as follows. At 56 small Late Horizon sites in the Cuautitlan and Tenayuca regions, we noted Aztec II ceramics in our surface samples, or the field crews noted them in their reports. To this total should be added the centers of Tenayuca, Cuautitlan, and Azcapotzalco. On the basis of these scattered data these regions (and the Tacuba region as well) were at least as densely settled as the Texcoco region. The Chalco–Xochimilco region was apparently the most densely settled portion of the Basin of Mexico. Besides the centers of Xochimilco, Cuitlahuac, Chalco, and Amecameca, Parsons recorded 2 large nucleated villages, 1 large dispersed village, 2 small nucleated villages, 5 small dispersed villages, and approximately 150 hamlets.

Finally, with respect to the Teotihuacan region our data are very unsatisfactory, but we did record Aztec II ceramics in 49 localities. Of these, substantial amounts were present at five sites, all of which later evolved into Late Horizon centers: Otumba, Teotihuacan, Acolman, Tepexpan, and Chiconautla. The remaining sites were probably all hamlet-size communities.

LATE HORIZON (A.D. 1350–1519)

For this final phase of prehispanic occupation there is a tremendous potential for new insights into societal organization through the integration of archaeological remains with the wealth of documentary material compiled during the era of Spanish conquest and the early decades of the Colonial period. Although some significant beginnings have been made, this potential is still largely unrealized as ethnohistorians and archaeologists tend to pursue their own particular interests and problems with only limited concern for the implications of each other's data. In this section we hope to contribute to such an ethnohistoric–archaeological synthesis by considering our regional settlement data, together with reconstructions from documentary sources of local and regional organization in the fifteenth and sixteenth centuries. Although the full complexity of sociopolitical organization is beyond the scope of this discussion, we will consider our present understanding of the spatial dimensions of Aztec society so as to provide a frame of reference in which to discuss the implications of our archaeological settlement data. Our principal sources for the summary that follows are Barlow (1949), Calnek (1966, 1970, 1972, 1973, 1976), Carrasco (1961, 1964), Carrasco et al. (1976), Gibson (1964), Kirchoff (1959), Monzón (1949), Moreno (1931), Sanders (1965, Sanders et al. 1970), Sanders and Price (1968), and Soustelle

(1955). Although these ethnohistoric studies indicate several points of major disagreement, we will try to show that our complementary archaeological data clarify some of these long-standing problems which, up to this point, have been attacked almost exclusively from a documentary perspective. (The reader is referred to Map 18 for the discussion that follows.)

In our last section we inferred that during Second Intermediate Three times a series of small polities (with only limited continuity from the antecedent Second Intermediate Two era) developed, each focused on a regional center of modest size: Teotihuacan, Xaltocan, and Cuautitlan in the northern Basin; the paired capitals of Azcapotzalco–Tenayuca and Coatlinchan–Huexotla in the central area; and Culhuacan, Xochimilco, Cuitlahuac, Mixquic, Chalco–Xico, Tlalmanalco (?), and Amecameca in the south. During the Late Horizon about 50 of these semiautonomous localized units existed (Gibson 1964). Each such unit consisted of a fairly discrete territory within which there was an administrative–market center that provided a focus for a dependent rural population. Within most such territorial units, roughly a third of the total population resided in the local centers. Most of these local centers had populations of 3000–4000; many contained 5000–6000 inhabitants; while a few had more than 10,000 people (Xochimilco, Tacuba, Azcapotzalco, Ixtapalapa, and probably several others). Some of the larger centers dominated the territories and affairs of several adjacent smaller centers, and provided serious obstacles to the complete domination of the expanding Triple Alliance empire throughout the fifteenth century. The marked, and often successful, resistance of Chalco to Triple Alliance domination throughout the fifteenth century may relate to this region's long linkage to Cholula (see preceding discussions of Second Intermediate One, Second Intermediate Two, and Second Intermediate Three periods).

The three Triple Alliance centers (Tenochtitlan, Texcoco, and Tacuba) represent a distinctly higher level of sociopolitical organization. This is especially so for Tenochtitlan which, with an estimated population of 150,000–200,000 (Calnek 1972) is so very different, both in terms of size and function, from other Late Horizon centers that it merits some very special consideration. Texcoco, with a population of roughly 30,000, was a distinctly secondary partner in this larger state organization (especially after the mid-fifteenth century). Tacuba's role was probably little more than a formality that acknowledged the previous importance of the Tepaneca domain. From a modest beginning in the early fifteenth century, the military alliance of these three major centers rapidly built up an expanding tributary domain that, within a few decades, extended well beyond the borders of the Basin of Mexico.

Calnek's (1970, 1972, 1973, 1976) archival-based studies of Tenochtitlan have provided a new dimension of understanding for this Late Horizon capital. The urban center apparently covered an area of 12–15 km². Its population density (ca. 12,000–13,000 per square kilometer) was thus far higher than for Middle Horizon Teotihuacan. Its inhabitants, who were almost exclusively nonagriculturalists, were tightly packed into domestic units of extended family size arranged within a fairly regular grid of streets and canals. At one time there had been two discrete centers on adjacent islands; Tlatelolco to the north, and Tenochtitlan to the south. Both centers ultimately merged physically, and late in the fifteenth century the Tlatelolco ruler (*tlatoani*) was forcibly removed and replaced by a governorship installed by Tenochtitlan. Tenochtitlan was divided into four major wards, and Tlatelolco constituted the fifth principal ward of the main center. Each of the five major wards was subdivided into smaller territorial units (*tlaxilacalli*). There were a total of some 80 tlaxilacalli within the urban center, each with its own ceremonial–civic precinct. The uppermost organizational level was manifested by the large precinct at the heart of Tenochtitlan. This included a vast religious enclosure (about 500 m on a side), several royal palaces, and numerous other buildings. There were two major marketplaces (one in Tenochtitlan, and the other, probably the larger, in Tlatelolco). Numerous smaller redistributional locations (which we understand less about) were scattered throughout other parts of the urban zone (see Figures 5.13 and 5.14).

It is interesting to note that while all important Second Intermediate Three centers continued to be significant political centers during the Late Horizon, it is also the case that all three of the Triple Alliance capitals were established at localities which had been unoccupied or insignificant during the earlier Second Intermediate Three period. This is supported by both documentary (in the case of Tenochtitlan and Texcoco) and archaeological (for Texcoco) evidence. The significance of this lack of locational continuity in the locus of primary political power is not wholly apparent to us. However, it does parallel a similar lack of continuity that we have already noted for the Second Intermediate Two–Second Intermediate Three transition. Such spatial dislocations of power and authority over time may reflect organizational changes of considerable magnitude in which new priorities greatly override old considerations. In the case of Tenochtitlan, one of these priorities almost certainly involved maximizing the specialized production and water-borne redistribution of goods from within the entire Basin on a much larger scale than ever before. As we will further elaborate in what follows, the demographic "success" of the Late Horizon clearly reflects the implementation of such a priority.

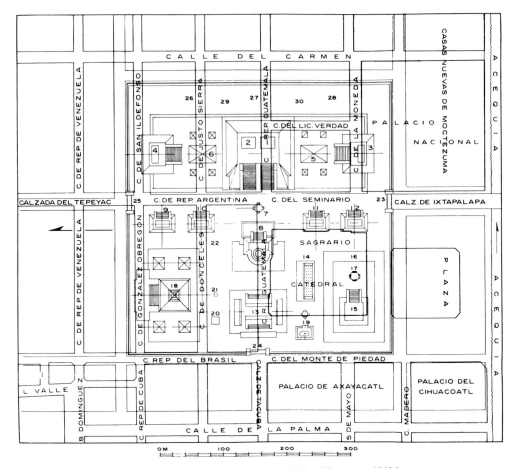

Figure 5.13. Plan of central enclosure, Tenochtitlan. (After Marquina 1960.)

After the early fifteenth century, most local polities functioned as administrative units within the expanding Triple Alliance domain. Many local centers have even survived to the present day as municipal centers. Although archaeological and ethnohistoric evidence indicates that at least 14 or 15 of these local centers had existed during the antecedent Second Intermediate Three period, it is by no means clear how the remaining 35, or so, developed. It is quite possible that many of these local centers came into being in response to the local administrative and redistributional needs of local areas in which population was rapidly expanding during Second Intermediate Three and Late Horizon times. It is also quite possible that some (or many?) local centers were established, or at least expanded and elaborated as such, during the course of Triple Alliance development during the fifteenth century as the administration of expanded tribute and redistribution networks became more complex.

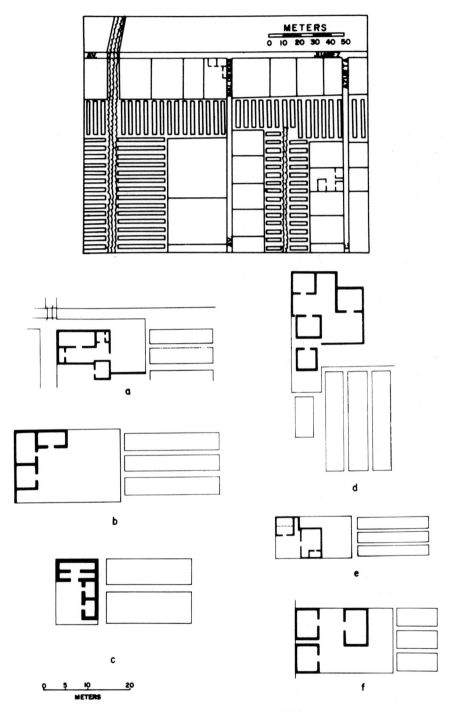

Figure 5.14. House lots at Tenochtitlan. (After Calnek 1972.)

Most local centers had a hereditary ruler—the *tlatoani*—who acted as the head of state. When smaller polities were incorporated into the larger domains of the Acolhua, the Tepaneca, or the Triple Alliance, the native ruling family would often be retained in power. In such cases supralocal political integration would often be facilitated by the establishment of marriage ties between the local ruling lineages and the royal families of Texcoco, Tacuba, and Tenochtitlan. In other cases, the native dynasty in a local center would be replaced by appointees of the dominant ruling elite. Larger centers also had their own hereditary *tlatoani*. These latter individuals wielded vastly more authority over much wider areas, and were surrounded by much larger and more elaborate administrative bureaucracies. In some respects the *tlatoani* of Tenochtitlan (and to a lesser extent of Texcoco and Tacuba) can be seen as local *tlatoani* writ large. However, because these paramount *tlatoani* stood at the head of an expanding conquest state engaged in the forceful extraction of tribute over a wide area, they were also something quite different from local *tlatoani* who related to their small domains on a very different basis (i.e., where the conquest element was wholly or largely absent). Later on we will note that this structural difference in the political roles of major and minor *tlatoani* was only one part of a series of qualitative differences between major and minor centers in Late Horizon times—especially with respect to the huge urban system of Tenochtitlan. These differences become important as we try to understand the implications for societal organization of our Late Horizon settlement data.

The documentary-based reconstructions of local-level organization are more obscure than the outline we have just sketched for state-level organization. Since Late Horizon centers, with only two or three exceptions, are almost always totally, or largely, obscured by modern occupation, our primary archaeological concern has necessarily been with rural occupation. For our purposes the basic problems involve the composition of local communities and their configuration over the landscape. However, we find that the available documentary studies are less useful in this regard than we had originally hoped. It is quite clear that Late Horizon society was highly stratified. A small proportion of the total population (probably somewhere between 5% and 10%) was of noble (*pilli*) status. The noble stratum was itself internally differentiated with respect to access to authority and wealth (in goods and services). The dominant nobility functioned as heads (*tecuhtli*) of patrimonial estates in which they were granted hereditary rights by the Triple Alliance to the produce of certain lands and services of certain commoners in return for their administrative services within the larger state organization. Such *tecuhtli* also had rights to agricultural produce and labor services of local commoners for whom they provided certain local-level administrative and redistributional functions. It is probable that some *tecuhtli*, especially the more powerful, exercised such tight and enduring control over tracts of land and the labor services of commoners living on these lands, that it is not wholly inappropriate to speak of private estates and dependent tenants. However, as several writers have long argued, such "private" estates were probably of minimal importance, and are perhaps best viewed as linked to the roles of their "owners" in the state-level administration, where rights to land, produce, and labor were granted by the central authority to important administrators in the course of the militaristic expansion of the Triple Alliance conquest state. This carving out of tributary estates by the Triple Alliance central authority was a principal factor in the continuous and accelerating erosion of the political autonomy and territorial integrity of the domains of local *tlatoani* within the Basin of Mexico and elsewhere.

The principal *tecuhtli* within a local polity also functioned as its *tlatoani*. In this role the *tlatoani* served to relate his domain to the Triple Alliance state system: A major part of this relationship concerned the assignment and collection of tribute imposed by the Triple Alliance. Several categories of lesser nobles had rights to smaller estates and functioned as lower-level administrators within the Triple Alliance and local organizations. It seems to be generally the case that nobility resided in centers, although the sources are not always clear on this point.

Below the nobility stratum was the great majority of the population: the commoners who paid tribute in goods and services to the nobility. Most commoners fell into two groups: (*a*) the *macehual*, free commoners with direct access to corporately held land, and (*b*) the *mayeque*, consisting mainly of dependent landless tenants who resided on estates of the nobility, and who existed outside the corporate organizations of the *macehual*. There is little doubt that the free commoner (*macehual*) status and corporate social organization have a long time depth in prehispanic Mesoamerica. Certainly the nicely defined spatial divisions at both Monte Alban (Blanton *et al.* 1978) and Teotihuacan (Millon *et al.* 1973) are suggestive of the presence there of well-defined corporate groups during Middle Horizon times. A well-defined spatial patterning also occurs within the urban community of Late Horizon Tenochtitlan (Calnek 1972). However, the recruitment and organization of landless tenants (*mayeque*) are less apparent, and there is some evidence to suggest that this status category may be peculiar to the Late Horizon and to the demographic and sociological dislocations produced by the expanding impact of Triple Alliance military conquest (e.g., Olivera 1976): Some people probably became landless tenants as they were driven from their homelands and physically displaced into areas where they had no local roots or ties. In other cases, some people in areas newly conquered by the Triple Alliance may have found themselves living within "estates" just granted to important Triple Alliance administrators. Such people might have been transformed into *mayeque* in the minds of Triple Alliance authorities without too many other changes in their life styles (excepting, probably, having to work harder). In any event, we know of no documentary-based studies that give us a good basis from which to predict the archaeological manifestations of *mayeque* status in the record of regional settlement. However, as we will try to show later in this section, we do feel that one of our Late Horizon settlement types can be reasonably linked with the *mayeque* group.

At the local level, a significant proportion of the population was or-

ganized into *calpultin* (singular *calpulli*), a term the Spaniards usually translated as *barrio* (ward). Although there is some confusion on the matter
(probably in large part created by the aforementioned sociopolitical disrup-
tions of local organization by the Triple Alliance military conquests and
subsequent organization of state-level tributary domains), the *calpulli* was
apparently a territorial-based corporate group which constituted the basic
organizational element of Late Horizon society at the level of the local domain. The *calpulli* had political functions in that it had an elective, hereditary
headman—the choice limited to a particular lineage—who acted as a local
executive official and as a go-between between the *tlatoani* and the *calpulli*
members. It had economic functions, in that it was a tax-paying unit, and in
that the rural *calpulli* owned land in common. It had educational functions as
well since each *calpulli* had a young man's school, the *telpochcalli*. It had
military functions, as the men of each *calpulli* fought as a unit of the *tlatoani's*
army. It also had religious functions, and each *calpulli* had a small ceremonial
complex where group ritual was conducted.

Although we know that the term *calpulli* referred to a basic sociological
unit of Late Horizon society, we are still a long way from understanding
either the composition or the structure of this basic unit. This often makes it
quite difficult to infer the specifics of societal organization from archaeological settlement configurations with as much confidence as one might expect.
Part of this confusion relates to a rather pronounced rural–center dichotomy
in Late Horizon society, and to the fact that we have rather more information
about one very large center (Tenochtitlan) than for any other segment. It
appears that in most centers the *calpultin* were well-defined, ward-like sections, where nobility and commoners, farmers, artisans, and administrators
might reside together. In Tenochtitlan, and probably in Texcoco and Tacuba
as well, there was a strong tendency for the *calpulli* to be a specialized unit,
where all members shared the same functions (e.g., specific kinds of
craftsmen). In Tenochtitlan the term *calpulli* is sometimes replaced by
tlaxilicalli, suggesting transformed functions. Most rural *calpultin* probably
consisted of spatially discrete settlements of commoner agriculturalists.

Another confusing aspect of the local community is that the term *calpulli*
was used by Spanish administrators to designate several different kinds of
spatial units. In most detailed sixteenth-century censuses, the *calpulli* is
divided into *barrios pequeños,* which are also referred to by the term *calpulli.*
These units may be localized patrilineages within the larger sociological–
spatial unit. These may have been exogamous units, and in the smaller
centers they were probably homogeneous in economic and political status.
Census data indicate that the population of a *barrio pequeño* varied from a few
score to a few hundred, while the larger *calpultin* varied between 500 and
1000 people. To complicate matters still further, however, in Tenochtitlan
(and perhaps in a few other large centers) the larger *calpulli* (or *tlaxilicalli*)
were further grouped into four major wards that were also referred to as
calpulli. These were apparently purely administrative units.

Before we proceed to consider the implications of our Late Horizon settlement data, it will be useful to discuss some special problems we have had in depicting these data on our map. A principal difficulty relates to the great continuity between Late Horizon centers and large, nucleated modern communities. Another major problem (which is also felt for all earlier periods as well) is the near complete obliteration of the ground surface beneath the huge area now covered over by modern Mexico City (principally the Tacuba region), within which Late Horizon occupation was so substantial. In this latter regard, Gonzalez's (1973) settlement map of the European-contact period (compiled from documentary sources) has been an invaluable guide in our reconstruction of Late Horizon rural occupation in the Tacuba region. Using his map, we have been able to locate 138 such sites within the Mexico City area. It is interesting to find that the density of rural sites that Gonzalez reconstructs from documentary sources for the Tacuba region is very comparable to the density of Late Horizon occupation we have defined in other areas by archaeological survey. This suggests that Gonzalez's map is probably fairly accurate. We have also used his map to plot the locations of several Late Horizon sites outside the Tacuba region where the presence of nucleated modern settlement made archaeological survey impossible.

The matter of Late Horizon centers is a particularly critical one since such a large proportion of the total population resided in them. Most of these centers are today covered by large, nucleated towns, often with paved streets and cemented household patios. In such localities even partial surveys are impossible. Such important centers as Ixtapalapa, Amecameca, Chalco, Tlalmanalco, Mixquic, Tlahuac, Xochimilco, Chimalhuacan, Texcoco, Ecatepec, Cuautitlan, Zumpango, and Apaxco are obscured in this way. In some cases the prehispanic center was larger than the modern community, or slightly displaced from it, and we were able to survey the peripheral fields and estimate the surface area of the Late Horizon center, as in the cases of Coatlinchan, Culhuacan, Texcoco, Tlalmanalco, and Chalco. Much more commonly, especially within the metropolitan area of modern Mexico City, even this procedure was not possible, as in the cases of Coyoacan, Mexicaltzingo, Huitzilopocho, Tacuba, Azcapotzalco, and Tenochtitlan–Tlatelolco. More complete surveys were feasible at a few centers where modern settlement was dispersed or absent, as for Tepetlaoxtoc, Xaltocan, Teotihuacan, Acolman, Tepexpan, Huexotla, Tenayuca, Otumba, and Tepozotlan. Our ability to survey most of Late Horizon Tepetlaoxtoc was additionally revealing as it showed that some important centers had a relatively dispersed settlement pattern. We believe such a pattern was also characteristic of several (or most?) Late Horizon centers in the Zumpango region, for example, Apaxco, Tlapanaloya, Huepoxtla, Jilotzingo. We are presently unable to account for the dispersed occupation of these latter centers, except to suggest that the observed lower population density may relate to more marginal agricultural potential in areas of thin soil and small irrigation potential, and more directly to their less urban, in economic terms, character.

Perhaps more than for any other period, our lack of survey in the far northeastern corner of the Basin (the Pachuca region) and in some portions of the Basin's alluvial plain has resulted in the omission of an unusually large number of rural sites. For the Pachuca region, documentary evidence (Montúfar, 1897) indicates substantial occupation. In those areas of the low-lying alluvial plain that we have surveyed, the numerous Late Horizon sites located suggest that many others also exist in environmentally similar places where we have not made observations.

With these documentary-based insights into spatial organization, and the realization that our reconstruction of Late Horizon settlement patterning is plagued by some peculiar deficiencies, we now turn to the specifics of the archaeological settlement record. Perhaps the single most outstanding aspect of this settlement is its omnipresence throughout the Basin. Some 40% of all our prehispanic sites (see Table 6.1) date to this relatively short period (which may be less than 200 years, and is certainly no longer than 250–300 years, even if we allow for the continuation into Colonial times of some ceramic markers) (Charlton 1971). Late Horizon sites occur in all environmental zones, and it is rare to walk over an agricultural field in which at least a few sherds of this period cannot readily be picked up from the ground surface. Our population estimate of about 1,000,000 is at least four times the level attained in the Basin during any earlier period. Comparable population levels were not again attained in the Basin until the present century. This demographic "success" is startling, and some other writers have recently been sufficiently impressed to accord it some special consideration in general discussions of preindustrial demography (e.g., Harris 1977).

Late Horizon occupation is also particularly notable for the uniformity of its ceramic assemblage throughout the entire Basin of Mexico. For no other time period do we see the standardization of vessel form and decoration that so greatly facilitates the recognition of Late Horizon occupation anywhere in our survey area. A detailed description of this ceramic assemblage from one part of the Basin (e.g., Parsons 1966) is essentially valid for the whole. The only significant spatial variation (aside from functionally specific sites and localities) seems to be in the much greater frequency of certain decorated types at centers as opposed to rural settlements. This is a rather substantial change from the antecedent Second Intermediate Three period, and almost certainly reflects the much higher degree of political and economic integration attained during the Late Horizon.

We have defined two basic categories of Late Horizon archaeological settlements: nucleated centers (most of which are mentioned as such in the documentary sources), and dispersed occupation, which we have designated as hamlets and villages of varying size. At least half of the total Late Horizon population resided in nucleated centers—with up to 20% at the single principal capital at Tenochtitlan–Tlatelolco. We have already noted that archival-based reconstructions of Tenochtitlan–Tlatelolco indicate a densely nucleated core, with a "suburban" periphery of relatively more dispersed occupation. Calnek's reconstruction of Tenochtitlan–Tlatelolco and its environs, together with our own appraisals of settlement and population in the southwestern Basin, suggest rather strongly that it is difficult to apply the term *rural* to any part of this "Greater" Tenochtitlan region. We estimate that approximately 400,000 people resided in a 600-km² zone of piedmont, alluvial plain, and lakebed that extended from the Sierra de Guadalupe southward to the foothills of the Ajusco Range, the largest and densest concentration of population in the history of prehispanic Mesoamerica. Included within this zone would be the provincial centers of Tenayuca, Azcapotzalco, Tacuba, Coyoacan, Mexicaltzingo, Huitzilopochco, Ixtapalapa, Culhuacan, and Xochimilco. Several of these centers had populations of more than 10,000. There were also a large number of smaller settlements within this same region. From the air the entire Greater Tenochtitlan area must have appeared as a single gigantic settlement, of varying occupational density, closely tied together by the network of causeways and canals. It is useful, for some purposes, to think of Greater Tenochtitlan as a kind of single great community, economically and politically integrated at several levels, and forming a discrete component, not duplicated elsewhere, of the Late Horizon settlement system. We will return to this matter shortly when we attempt to reconstruct this settlement system in its entirety.

We have some difficulty in reconstructing the physical configuration of smaller, Late Horizon centers where documentary evidence is more scanty than for Tenochtitlan–Tlatelolco, and where archaeological data are usually limited as well. Nevertheless, a general pattern seems to emerge: Most provincial centers, from Texcoco on down, are comprised of (a) a nuclear core, within which most of the site's monumental ceremonial–civic architecture is concentrated, and where population density compares with that of Tenochtitlan (4000–10,000 per square kilometer), (b) a larger periphery of lower population density (ca. 1000–4000 per square kilometer) that merges almost imperceptibly with (c) a zone of much more dispersed rural occupation that radiates for a considerable distance. This pattern is not completely uniform. Coatlinchan, for example, has very little rural occupation in its hinterland, while even the core area of Tepetlaoxtoc was fairly dispersed. Nevertheless, the *general* pattern is unmistakable. In some respect this physical configuration of smaller centers reproduces in miniature, and in a much more simplified form, the settlement configuration of Greater Tenochtitlan (see Figure 5.15).

We have had one outstanding problem in dealing with Late Horizon rural occupation: Much of it is so dispersed that we find it difficult, and sometimes impossible, to define sites according to the same considerations we have applied to other periods—basically, delimiting a discrete spatial cluster of occupational remains, clearly separable from other clusters. In our use of the term *dispersed* to describe Late Horizon rural occupation, we do not mean that communities are widely separated. Rather, there is a very distinct tendency for individual houses, or small clusters of individual houses, to be

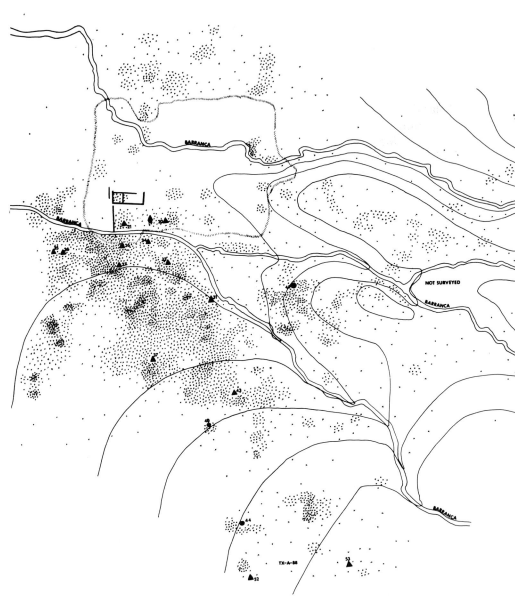

Figure 5.15. Map of the Late Horizon provincial center of Huexotla. (After Parsons 1971.)

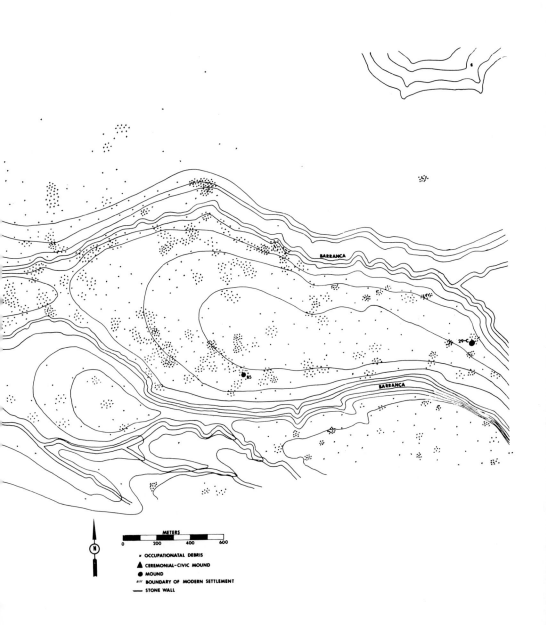

BARRANCA

BARRANCA

29-C

85

METERS
0   200   400   600

× OCCUPATIONATAL DEBRIS
▲ CEREMONIAL-CIVIC MOUND
● MOUND
⌁⌁ BOUNDARY OF MODERN SETTLEMENT
— STONE WALL

165

broadly and continuously dispersed over the landscape. Nucleated villages are quite rare, although nucleated hamlets are rather common. In such cases, where we are faced with a sea of scattered mounds and sherd clusters, it has been extremely difficult to define objectively a coherent cluster of occupation to which the label *site* can reasonably be attached.

Our present Late Horizon settlement map is somewhat defective in that a significant number of the sites depicted are defined somewhat arbitrarily. Ideally, this map should be reproduced at a much larger scale so as to depict the actual distribution of the many thousands of dispersed individual structures and artifact concentrations. This is not economically feasible, so as it now stands the reader must simply accept at face value our evaluations about what to call a site. We have tried to strike a balance between the one extreme of labeling each mound or sherd concentration as a site, and the other extreme of referring to a vast area of scattered mounds as a huge dispersed village. The great difficulty we have sometimes had in attaining this balance may mean that a significant proportion of the Late Horizon population was not organized on a community basis. Whatever the case, this rural settlement pattern is unique in the prehispanic era. This suggests that there may have been something unique about Late Horizon societal organization as well.

Despite our problems with Late Horizon rural occupation, we can define five fairly consistent rural residential settlement types. Furthermore, although examples of each type can be found anywhere within the Basin, there is a distinct tendency for specific types to occur much more frequently within particular subregions. (See Map 18.)

Nucleated Radial Village. This is a very minor settlement type, and is found almost exclusively in highly productive areas. A few occur around the edges of alluvial plains throughout the Basin. A few more occur within and around the chinampa zone of Lake Chalco–Xochimilco. The best example of the latter situation is the community at Xico Island, and this may actually be a detached suburb of the nearby Chalco center.

Dispersed Line Village. Within the Basin as a whole this is not a common settlement type. However, it is encountered frequently in the Teotihuacan Valley and within adjacent sections of the Texcoco and Temascalapa regions where narrow bands of piedmont lie between alluvial plains and rugged hills. In such cases there are almost continuous ribbons of occupation on the piedmont (analogous to the modern linear villages of Tlaminca–Tlaixpan–Purificacion east of Texcoco, and to Chimalhuacan at the southeastern corner of Lake Texcoco). In a number of cases, where the preservation of architectural remains was unusually good, we were able to define semidetached mound clusters of 10–40 structures arranged along terraces. A series of such mound clusters form what we call a line village. Such a mound cluster might correspond to the *barrio pequeño* subdivision of the *calpulli*, while the entire line village might comprise a complete rural *calpulli*. At considerable intervals within such linear settlement bands we often encountered small

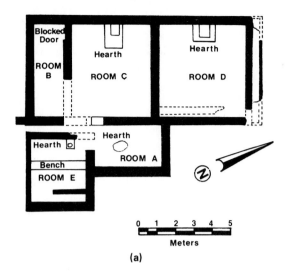

(a)

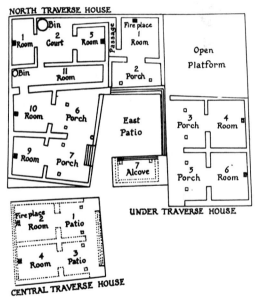

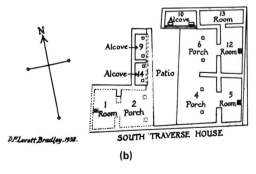

Figure 5.16. Late Horizon residences. (a) From small village site. (After Sanders 1965.) (b) From central core of small provincial center (no scale). (After Vaillant 1941.)

ceremonial–civic precincts formed of distinctive architecture: a small temple platform, several lower platforms, and a large, multiroomed structure that may represent a high status residence (the *calpulli* headman?) or some kind of public building (the *telpochcalli* or young man's school?) Such precincts are probably the architectural manifestations of *calpulli*-level ritual and secular functions. Thus, even though we are almost never able to define precisely the borders of specific *calpulli* units on the ground (because occupation is apt to be so continuous over such large areas), the intermittent presence of such precincts, together with some well-defined housemound clusters, gives us some sense that the ethnohistoric models are essentially valid, and that at least some of the Late Horizon rural population in the northeastern quadrant of the Basin were organized in *calpultin* and *barrios pequeños*. In drawing site borders in areas where unbroken linear settlement extends for great distances, we have been guided by the locations of what we believe are *calpulli* ceremonial–civic precincts. That is, we hope (and expect) that what we have called a village site corresponds roughly to a *calpulli* community.

Dispersed Radial Village.   This is one of our most common settlement pattern types (see Figure 5.17). A majority of rural occupation in the Texcoco region, the Teotihuacan Valley, and (to a somewhat lesser degree) the Zumpango region, falls into this category. This is much the same as our dispersed line village, the principal difference being that for most radial villages the topography is relatively gentle and unbroken, and settlement is often virtually continuous over large areas. Although site definition is much more difficult than for one-dimensional line villages, several of the same guiding principles hold: Mound clusters and the placement of small ceremonial–civic precincts have given us some sense of corporate organization, and sites have been defined in an effort to approximate *calpulli* communities. However, we are usually less than confident about the sociological significance of many of our defined sites, particularly in the cases where widespread sheet erosion has seriously disturbed original architectural configurations.

Zonal Hamlet Pattern.   This is also a very common settlement type (see Figure 5.18). Although it occurs throughout our survey area, it is clearly dominant in the northwestern and southeastern quadrants of the Basin. The zonal hamlet is essentially a more dispersed subtype (in the sense that the occupational clusters are smaller and more widely spaced) of the dispersed radial village. Individual sites sometimes consist of isolated clusters of five or six housemounds. More commonly, where architectural preservation is poor, sites appear as isolated concentrations of light surface pottery covering a few hectares. Ceremonial–civic precincts are generally absent, and there is usually no obvious way in which the isolated hamlets can be linked together in larger units.

Isolated Household Pattern.   While isolated households (i.e., single mounds, or small areas of sherd scatter) have been defined as sites through-

PREHISTORIC SURFACE REMAINS

● Aztec Mound

☐ Absent

Light

Light-to-Moderate

Moderate & Moderate-to-Heavy

0   200   400   600   800
Meters

Figure 5.17. Dispersed Late Horizon village from the Cuautitlan region. Note correlation between prehispanic occupational loci and modern field borders.

169

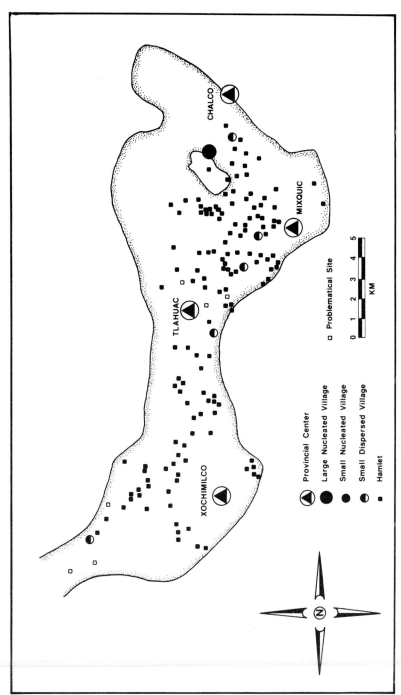

Figure 5.18. Late Horizon settlements in Lake Chalco–Xochimilco.

out the Basin, it is only on the Lake Chalco–Xochimilco lakebed that this is a common and dominant Late Horizon settlement type. This geographic concentration of isolated household sites seems to relate to the organization of chinampa cultivation in Tenochtitlan's breadbasket zone. Pedro Armillas worked in the Chalco–Xochimilco lakebed between the mid 1940s and mid 1960s (Armillas 1971; West and Armillas 1950) during the era before large-scale, mechanized agriculture and modern suburban expansion. For some areas he was able to define rather precisely the original configuration of prehistoric chinampas and Late Horizon rural occupation. He found that nearly the entire lakebed had apparently been covered with garden plots arranged within units of a large grid defined by major canals. In some areas of unusually good preservation it could be seen that each grid unit contained a set of chinampa fields that completely surrounded a single house. This suggested a general pattern in which each housemound was surrounded by the land cultivated by its members. Our own surveys (carried out in 1969 and 1972) indicated that this isolated household pattern was very common throughout the old chinampa district of Lake Chalco–Xochimilco, although small multihousehold settlements were also present. These latter seem to have served as nuclei for more dispersed Zone B settlement.

In essence, these rural residential settlements are of two basically different types: (1) sites that are characterized by dispersed clusters of numerous households, and (2) sites that consist of dispersed clusters of a few households, or of individual isolated households. The former seem particularly abundant in the eastern and northern Basin, while the latter dominate in the south. We feel that this dichotomy reflects some significant organizational variability within the heartland of the Triple Alliance. We will address this variability shortly when we consider the general matter of the Late Horizon settlement system. Before doing this, however, it will be useful to discuss the nonresidential sites we have defined for this period. We located many isolated ceremonial complexes and resource-exploitation sites—not all of which are located on the Late Horizon map.

Isolated Ceremonial Complexes. These generally occur on the summits of small hills within a short distance of residential sites. Usually they are very small in size, primarily a single plaza complex with a small temple platform and associated smaller platforms. In a few cases the temple platforms were 3–5 m high, and several plaza complexes with connecting causeways and associated cemeteries occur. A particularly impressive exception to the generally small size of such sites is the massive temple-causeway complex atop isolated Cerro Tlaloc, along the uppermost edge of the southeastern Basin (Wicke and Horcasitas 1957). Judging from the numerous ethnohistoric references to hilltop Tlaloc shrines, many of these sites must be dedicated to this deity.

Salt-Making Stations. In the course of our archaeological settlement studies, we have rarely been able to confidently and systematically identify the presence of specialized activities or to delineate their distribution in space. Ethnohistoric studies indicate, at a general level, that specialization was a key feature of Late Horizon society. However, the economic structure has remained vague, at least partly because of the very limited input from archaeology (Charlton 1969, and especially Brumfiel 1976, are two of the significant exceptions). Because the development of economic specialization is so vital in our effort to describe and explain the evolution of prehispanic culture in the Basin of Mexico, and because salt making is one of the few specialized activities that we can identify and delineate with some confidence, we will here devote some time to the analysis of this industry. In so doing, it is our larger purpose to clarify some aspects of specialization within the larger Late Horizon economy.

All around the shoreline of saline Lake Texcoco we have identified numerous localities at which a single Late Horizon ceramic type (a coarse, soft, poorly fired ware denoted as Texcoco Fabric Marked: Mayer-Oakes 1959; Parsons 1971; Tolstoy 1958) is extraordinarily abundant on the ground surface. In many of these localities this pottery occurs to the near exclusion of other ceramics, although sometimes it is mixed with ordinary domestic pottery. Occasionally, Texcoco Fabric Marked pottery occurs in small patches on the level ground surface. More commonly it litters the surface of irregularly mounded areas where considerable masses of earth have been thrown up to elevations of a meter or so. Sometimes there are vast earth mounds, up to 3 m high and 200 by 400 m in area, over which this pottery is densely scattered. Archaeologically we have found the greatest density of such occupation around the northern rim of Lake Texcoco, from Tenayuca north to Ecatepec on the northwest, and from Chiconautla south to Tequisistlan and Ixtapan (northwest of Texcoco) on the northeast. We have found similar sites, more dispersed and smaller in size, around the eastern and southern shoreline of Lake Texcoco. When Sanders first visited the area in 1951, there was a continuous band of large mounds littered with Texcoco Fabric Marked pottery extending from the Sanctuary of Guadalupe to Ecatepec. We casually noted many here during the early 1960s, although formal surveys were not carried out until 1974 when most of the area between Tenayuca and Ecatepec had long been covered over by the urban expansion of Mexico City. However, the remnants of these sites can still be seen throughout this zone, and are particularly impressive east and northeast of Ecatepec.

Although none of these sites have ever been excavated, several writers (e.g., Charlton 1969) have already made convincing arguments that they represent the remnants of Late Horizon salt making. A good part of such an argument rests on ethnohistoric information; Ecatepec, Tequisistlan, and Ixtapan are all identified as principal salt-making towns in the Relación of 1580 (Paso y Troncoso 1905). Other historical studies (e.g., Gibson 1964; Mendizabal 1946) refer to many other early Colonial salt-producing towns around the entire shoreline of Lake Texcoco. A little-known passage from the works of Petrus Martyr Anglerius (1628:188) clearly describes (even in this poor English translation) salt manufacture in the area immediately south of Tenochtitlan at the time of Spanish conquest:

> They go from Ixtapalapa to Tenustitan (Tenochtitlan) . . . upon a wall of stone. . . . That wall is instead of a bridge for Ixtapalapa also itself, some part of it stands in a salt lake, but the rest is built upon the land. Two cities founded partly in the water join to one side of that bridge. On the other side stands one, whereof the first they meet with who goes that way, is called Mesiqualcingo (Mexicaltzingo): the second is Coluacaca (Culhuacan?) . . . and the third is called Vuichilabasco (Huitzilop-chco). . . . The cities adjoining to the bridge make salt, which all the nations of the countries use. Of the salt water of the lake, they make it hard, conveying it by trenches into the earth to thicken it, and, being hardened and congealed they boil it, and after make it into round lumps or balls, to be conveyed to markets or fairs for exchange of foreign commodities.

An ethnographic study (Apenes 1944) describes the last surviving traces of traditional salt making on the northeastern shore of Lake Texcoco in about 1940. From this description it can readily be understood how the mounded areas were formed as collected masses of saline soil from the lakeshore zone were discarded after being leached of their salt content. Deep pottery jars and shallow metal evaporating trays are now the principal vessels employed in this process.

In our examinations of these sites we have noted the featureless profiles of deep borrow pits cut into the mounds by modern adobe brick makers. In a few cases, particularly on the larger, higher mounds, there are low undulations where much greater frequencies of normal domestic pottery occur. These localities probably represent residences placed within the immediate salt-making zone. Generally, however, the salt makers seem to have lived at hamlets and villages separated by 50–500 m, or more, from the actual salt-making stations. Ceramic samples from these hamlets and villages contain about 20–30% Texcoco Fabric Marked pottery, and 70–80% standard domestic pottery.

While locational and ethnohistoric data lend strong support to the argument that the sites described above are salt-making stations, some readers might justifiably raise the objection that the function of Texcoco Fabric Marked pottery is still uncertain. Let us now adduce some additional information that bears upon this critical point. First, it is interesting to note that away from the Lake Texcoco shoreline (and the southern part of the Lake Xaltocan–Zumpango) Texcoco Fabric Marked pottery occurs in only minute quantities, although a few pieces of it are apt to be found on almost any Late Horizon site. This holds true for sites within and around the shoreline of freshwater Lake Chalco–Xochimilco. A much more complex problem concerns the manner in which ceramic vessels were actually employed in the salt-making process. Texcoco Fabric Marked pottery is so crumbly and friable that few sherds large enough to tell us much about vessel form are preserved on the ground surface. An examination of 104 rim sherds of this ware collected from several small excavations of Late Horizon sites in the Teotihuacan Valley (Parsons 1966) shows two basic vessel forms: vessels with near vertical walls, and vessels with wide flaring walls. A few basal fragments suggest flat bottoms. Mouth diameter could not be ascertained, and no sherds large enough to indicate vessel depth were found. This inability to define vessel form is perhaps not as serious as it might first appear, since observations of the surviving vestiges of primitive salt making in the Basin and hints of Conquest-period practices suggest that several kinds of vessels can be associated with this activity.

The study by Riehm (1961) of prehistoric salt production along the coasts and at inland salt springs in Western and Central Europe is most enlightening as regards the probable function of Texcoco Fabric Marked pottery. Bronze and Iron Age salt makers in this area utilized a variety of mass-produced, porous, friable vessels for the purpose of molding crystallized salt into various shapes of roughly standard sizes and weights. This sort of pottery occurs in several forms in different areas: large goblet-like vessels; rectangular bowls measuring 8–10 cm deep and between 20 × 30 cm and 40 × 25 cm in size; steep-walled hemispherical bowls with flat bases; and cylindrical vessels 3 to 4 inches in diameter. According to Riehm's interpretation, salt was also marketed and bartered in the same enveloping clay vessels in which it had been originally molded. He also suggests that wall porosity functioned to permit the evaporation of excess water still adhering to the damp, freshly crystallized salt—a process accomplished by heating the newly filled vessels near a fire, or in the open sunlight in warmer areas.

This kind of ceramic material forms a large (although unspecified) proportion of artifact assemblages recovered from prehistoric European salt-making sites from England to the Black Sea coast. Apparently, most of this salt-packaging pottery was made on or in wooden molds. Interestingly enough, vessels of this character from Black Sea coastal sites are fabric marked, "manufactured serially by placing a cloth into a hollowed wooden mold and pressing a thin layer of plastic clay on it [Riehm 1961:190]."

It seems reasonable to argue that Texcoco Fabric Marked pottery functioned partly, or evenly primarily, to mold and package standard units of salt for distribution to consumers. The localized manufacture and use of this cheap, expendable pottery near the loci of salt manufacture would have produced the observed concentrations of this material around the saline lakeshore as numerous broken vessels were discarded in the course of manufacture and use. The very small quantities of Texcoco Fabric Marked ceramics that occur at nearly all Late Horizon residential settlements would represent the consumption of prepackaged salt, perhaps in standardized weights, by the entire Basin population.

Although we strongly suspect that there was substantial salt making around the Lake Texcoco Shoreline in pre-Late Horizon times, it is much more difficult to demonstrate its existence for earlier periods. This difficulty is probably related to less intensive production in cultural systems of much lower overall population size and density. It may also be related to the absence of a highly distinctive ceramic ware associated with the salt-making–packaging process. Furthermore, the great intensity and extent of Late Horizon salt making may be obscuring earlier activity in areas which have never been plowed and cultivated because of highly saline soils, and where any deeply buried materials would have little chance to appear at the ground surface. We found only a very few Late Horizon salt-making stations with traces of pre-Late Horizon sherds. Nevertheless, the very high proportions of a single ceramic type (which is an ordinary domestic ware, rather than the more specialized and distinctive Late Horizon Texcoco Fabric Marked) in several excavations of earlier lakeshore sites suggests the existence of some intensive salt making in pre-Late Horizon times. We have defined a First Intermediate One salt-making site in the Teotihuacan Valley delta near Chiconautla on the basis of the fact that 90% of the rim sherds from our excavation there were bay ware jars. We also defined a nearby mound as a Middle Horizon salt-making locality on the basis of the unusually high proportions there of a few vessel types (Litvak King 1964).

A suspicion that some Late Horizon salt-making stations are superimposed over earlier sites of similar function is justified by Mayer-Oakes' (1959) excavation of such a site at El Risco, near Ecatepec. Here he obtained substantial quantities of First Intermediate Five, Middle Horizon, Second Intermediate One, and Second Intermediate Two pottery, with high proportions of a few ceramic types, from the lower levels of his excavations. On the other hand, we have seen examples of Late Horizon salt-making stations where deeply pitted mounds show nothing but Late Horizon pottery to the bottoms of pits at depths of more than a meter below the modern ground level.

We conclude that salt making was present from the beginnings of sedentary life in the Basin of Mexico, but that it was not until the Late Horizon that salt production was carried out on an intensive, large-scale basis by full-time specialists, most of whom resided around the edges of Lake Texcoco. A possible exception to this generalization is along the southwestern shore of Lake Xaltocan–Zumpango where there are numerous Second Intermediate Two sites with heavy sherd concentrations of a single ceramic type (simple jars, of ordinary utilitarian ware). Such sites may be closely tied to the economic structure of Second Intermediate Two Tula. The absence of a pre-Late Horizon ceramic type analogous to Texcoco Fabric Marked ceramics might indicate a lesser concern with the packaging of standard units of salt, and thus a basically different mode of distribution and redistribution.

Other Resource Exploitation Sites. Quarry sites have often been identified, but have seldom been shown on our map. There are literally hundreds of geological deposits with various kinds of material (e.g., volcanic gravel) that were used in building construction. Many such deposits are still being quarried today. Only more intensive investigation, including excavation, can definitely date earlier quarries at such localities.

Another type of archaeological feature not represented on the map are such agricultural remnants as dams, canals, and terraces. In most cases where we recorded these, they were in direct association with residential settlements and were thus not recorded as separate sites.

Conclusions

Marvin Harris' (1977) recent work is one example of the long-standing interest among general scholars in Late Horizon economy in the Basin of Mexico. The ability of a preindustrial cultural system, with a neolithic technology and with minimal input from domestic animals, to achieve the high levels of productive capacity and redistributional efficiency implied by the large Late Horizon population is an impressive achievement. It becomes even more impressive when one considers that the extremely high cost of overland transport in the highlands of prehispanic Mesoamerica (absence of pack animals, dearth of navigable waterways, and rugged topography) precludes any enduring long-distance movement of bulk subsistence staples. Analyses of Triple Alliance tribute records (Barlow 1949; Molins 1954) have shown that large quantities of foodstuffs for consumption at Tenochtitlan were acquired only from within the Basin of Mexico or from its immediate environs. These studies have also demonstrated that imperial grain tribute could have supported no more than 40,000–50,000 people, only a fraction of the urban population of Tenochtitlan alone. We are thus dealing with a cultural system of some 1,000,000 people whose *basic* necessities (including material goods as well as foodstuffs) were generated within a fairly small area centering on the Basin of Mexico. As we noted before, this population was not exceeded until the present century, and it was at least four times the number of people that had inhabited the same region during any earlier prehispanic period.

Clearly, an understanding of the Late Horizon settlement system demands an understanding of the complexities of a redistributional system which (through mechanisms in addition to imperial and local-level tribute) supplied the necessities of life to huge numbers of non-food producers (most of whom were concentrated in Tenochtitlan), and which likewise channeled to consumers the products of nonagricultural artisans and craftsmen. Obviously our own investigations have not provided answers, or even hypotheses, for many aspects of this redistributional system. Nevertheless, our improved regional perspective permits us to address some features of Late Horizon economic organization which have remained unamenable to purely ethnohistoric research.

The massive buildup of Late Horizon occupation on the low-lying lakeshore alluvium and lakebed indicates a transformation of this previously marginal swampy terrain to highly productive agricultural land by means of large-scale drainage and flood control technology. Particularly significant was the expansion of agricultural activity in the Zumpango, Cuautitlan, Texcoco, and Chalco plains. The *tlatoani* of Cuautitlan actually redirected the

Rio Cuautitlan northward to irrigate the lands west and north of that center and to regulate flooding in low-lying areas (Anales de Cuautitlan 1945). The massive channels that collect and direct the piedmont floodwaters east of Lake Texcoco almost certainly date to the Late Horizon. Drainage agriculture reached its maximal expression, of course, in the conversion of the vast swamps of Lake Chalco–Xochimilco to cultivated fields—the famous chinampas. This was truly a monumental hydraulic enterprise, involving the construction of massive drainage ditches, the implementation of an elaborate flood control apparatus of dikes and sluice gates that closely regulated water levels over a wide area, and a huge outlay of labor in the construction of fields by piling up masses of soil and vegetation. We estimate that some 10,000 ha of chinampa fields were thus created in the southern Basin, and there may have been a few thousand additional hectares in the walled-off southwestern corner of Lake Texcoco, around Xaltocan in the north and Chimalhuacan on the southeast shore of Lake Texcoco. The prehispanic settlement within this chinampa region is very predominantly Late Horizon, and it would appear, as Armillas (1971) originally suggested, that large-scale chinampa cultivation is entirely a phenomenon of the Late Horizon. The production of the agricultural land newly created during the Late Horizon by means of massive hydraulic engineering in swampy lake and lakeshore areas would probably have been sufficient to supply at least a half million people with basic food staples.

Another aspect of Late Horizon productivity is the intensified use of higher, thinner-soil areas in the upper piedmont where earlier occupation was absent or scanty. This is generally true for all areas of the Basin, although less so for the Cuautitlan and Tacuba regions. In several cases Late Horizon occupation in such previously marginal areas can be clearly associated with remnants of floodwater irrigation and terraced hillslopes, clear evidence for the intensification of agricultural production in these newly colonized areas. Perhaps most impressive of all in this regard is the massive reoccupation of the entire Zumpango region piedmont, a large zone in the far northwestern Basin that had contained a large Second Intermediate Two population, but for which there is no trace of Second Intermediate Three settlement. The basis for the Second Intermediate Three abandonment of this region, and the subsequent Late Horizon reoccupation, presently eludes us. However, the Late Horizon population buildup there is consistent with events in the Basin as a whole, and may represent a kind of state-directed resettlement in order to exploit a large block of unused terrain. We will return to this latter point shortly.

Most readers will probably find little to quibble with in our general argument that the Late Horizon population in the Basin of Mexico was able to provide for its own basic subsistence needs. But, we still have not said much about how food, and other necessities, got from producers to consumers, many of whom were specialists and did not provide for all their own basic needs. In addressing this question, it is useful to consider the loci of different kinds of producers and consumers. Ethnohistoric studies indicate that nearly all of Tenochtitlan's 150,000–200,000 inhabitants were non-food producers. Ethnohistoric and archaeological evidence indicates that a great many people clustered in suburban zones around Tenochtitlan's peripheries were also probably specialized in nonagricultural activities (certainly salt making, and perhaps others). We suspect (although there is no real evidence) that some of the other largest centers (Texcoco, and perhaps Tacuba) had very high proportions of non-food producers in their urban populations. However, what of the dozens of smaller centers, most of which are both inaccessible to archaeological investigation and poorly described in documentary sources? We have usually assumed that the densely nucleated core areas of these smaller centers were occupied by non-food producers (craftsmen, administrators, and retainers), while the less nucleated peripheries were inhabited by agriculturalists. This assumption has been based principally on analogies with the better known large centers, and on the fact that much of what limited archaeological evidence there is for craft activity (e.g., spindle whorls, figurine molds) has come from the core areas of the better preserved small centers. We reasoned that redistribution between agriculturalists and artisans would have occurred within a market framework, with larger centers having larger and more frequent markets, while at smaller centers there were fewer and smaller markets. The market component of our model has derived from the eyewitness accounts of Tenochtitlan–Tlatelolco in 1519, and from early Colonial-period references to markets at many of our Late Horizon centers.

Assuming that nearly all the population of Tenochtitlan and Texcoco were non-food producers, and that in the smaller centers about half the population fell into this category, and applying some intermediate value for the larger provincial centers (e.g., Chalco, Xochimilco), then the ratio of food producers to non-food producers within the Basin of Mexico as a whole calculates out to about 2:1 or 3:1. We should stress again that our research has not included systematic archaeological investigation of function, and nearly all our inferences on this key question have been highly tentative (although we ourselves have occasionally lost sight of this uncertainty).

Two recent studies (Calnek 1976; Brumfiel 1976) have provided us with truly new insights into the organization of Late Horizon economy that prompted us to reconsider some of the implications of our settlement data. Calnek's documentary-based study re-emphasized the role of noble estates and landless tenant laborers in the food supply of urban Tenochtitlan. This provided us with the take-off point for thinking that our commonly observed pattern of very dispersed rural Late Horizon occupation, with no apparent corporate or community structure, could be equated with the residences of landless tenants (e.g., Parsons 1976a). From here, it was logical to postulate that areas where such a fragmented settlement pattern is common, or dominant (e.g., the chinampa zone, and parts of the more marginal piedmont areas) represent areas of state-directed agricultural intensification and resettlement by detached or uprooted persons who were directly dependent upon the Triple Alliance administrators for whom they provided a major measure of subsistence. The presence of smaller Second Intermediate Three occupations in some of these same areas suggests that such a process may have been underway, in a much more modest way, for a century or two prior to the formation of the Triple Alliance.

Conversely, the same logic would require us to equate our more clustered rural occupation with corporately organized commoners (*calpulli*). This dovetails with the arguments we have already presented along this line: that such corporate *calpulli* units can be recognized by house clusters and the spacing of ceremonial–civic precincts. In some areas (e.g., the northeastern Basin) we would seem to have a predominance of corporately organized commoners, while in others (e.g., the chinampa area, the Zumpango region, and the southern piedmont) a dominance of dependent tenants is clearly suggested. The basis for this fairly distinctive regional variation is not wholly clear. However, it is interesting to note that areas where we suggest that dependent tenants were dominant are precisely those areas where there was minimal Second Intermediate Three occupation. This suggests that the Triple Alliance moved rapidly to expand, and appropriate for its own use, the productive capacity of areas that were being little utilized in the fourteenth century.

Brumfiel's archaeological study (a rigorous, intensive surface investigation of Huexotla, a well-preserved small Late Horizon center east of Lake Texcoco) offers a potential breakthrough in the understanding of Late Horizon economy. She found little evidence to suggest any *significant* economic differentiation between the Huexotla urban core, urban periphery, and rural hinterland. In essence, during Late Horizon times the dominant (but not exclusive) concern of most Huexotla inhabitants, both urban and rural, was agriculture. Furthermore, there was little, if any, indication that different crops were being cultivated at lower and higher elevations within the Huexotla study area (2250–2600 m). The presence of a few specific indicators of craft activity (e.g., spindle whorls) indicated that some nonagricultural work was being performed, but it was not possible to detect specific zones within which such activity could be construed as full-time specialization.

The near total absence of comparable data from other Late Horizon centers makes it premature, and a bit dangerous, to generalize too widely from the Huexotla baseline. Nevertheless, some of Brumfiel's findings have significant implications for our own concerns, and we will advance some of our thoughts at this point. Her work suggests that agriculture may be the dominant concern of most residents of most smaller Late Horizon centers throughout the Basin of Mexico (urban as well as rural), although we might expect some significant departure from this at centers, such as Otumba, which are adjacent to large concentrations of nonagricultural resources (obsidian, in the case of Otumba). This would mean that full-time non-food producers were proportionately very much more highly concentrated at Tenochtitlan than we originally thought. This might even mean that the basic redistributive unit, in which symbiosis between agriculturalists and artisans, and so on, was structured, was not so much the individual small center and its immediate rural hinterland, but rather that this dichotomy was between Greater Tenochtitlan, on the one hand, and the rest of the Basin of Mexico, on the other. Certainly the demands of Tenochtitlan, with its huge mass of non-food producers, would have placed a great strain upon the agricultural capacity of the entire Basin. Parsons (1976c) has argued that the extraordinarily productive chinampa zone alone was probably able to provide well over half the total subsistence requirements of the Late Horizon capital. However, the remaining fraction was still very substantial, and the generation of such a substantial surplus above the level of local needs would almost certainly have required a very high degree of full-time agricultural productivity by almost all the remaining Late Horizon population in those parts of the Basin where productivity was generally much lower than in the chinampa district.

This hypothesis may be a bit overstated, and the reality of Late Horizon economy may have more closely approached something like the following. Greater Tenochtitlan (including the chinampa district of Lake Chalco–Xochimilco) was a tightly integrated economic unit comprising nearly a half million people. A nucleated core (Tenochtitlan–Tlatelolco), occupied by non-food producers, was surrounded by a suburban core of intensive agriculturalists and some full-time artisans (e.g., salt makers). Further away, within a radius of 20 km (perhaps slightly more within the chinampa district) full-time agriculturalists provided the great majority of the center's subsistence requirements. The remaining subsistence needs derived from tribute and rent (from dependent tenants) from more far-flung areas. Greater Texcoco would have been a smaller version of Greater Tenochtitlan, with a less highly differentiated structure. Smaller centers, down to the level of Huexotla, would have been tiny, greatly simplified versions of the same basic model, with a much less rigid economic structure (e.g., overlapping functions of rural and urban inhabitants, etc.).

However, one major factor argues for the qualitatively different economic role of Tenochtitlan: the overwhelming size of its urban core and suburban periphery. With close to a half million inhabitants, nearly half of the total Basin's population, Greater Tenochtitlan represents such massed energy and power that its economic role must have been correspondingly overwhelming within the Basin. We suspect that future investigations of Late Horizon economic structure will demonstrate that production, specialization, and redistribution throughout the entire Basin were ultimately focused upon, directed by, and directly tied to, the needs, priorities, and constraints of the Triple Alliance capital, so strategically placed that most of the Basin's resources were directly accessible to it by water-borne transport.

Taken from these perspectives, the pattern for the Late Horizon appears to contrast much less with that of Middle Horizon Teotihuacan—the scale is just larger. The half a million or so population of Greater Tenochtitlan, with its mosaic of administrators, craftsmen, merchants, and *calpulli* or tenant farmers, could be the counterpart of Teotihuacan, and the remainder of the population would correspond to Teotihuacan's outer rural settlement. Even the proportions are comparable.

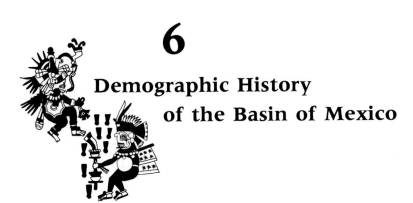

6

Demographic History
of the Basin of Mexico

The overall population profile of the Basin of Mexico, including the Tula region, is a fascinating one, and indicates the complexity of the factors that affect human growth rates. We have postulated a total population of 5000 at approximately 1150 B.C., the end of the Early Horizon. This population either grew from an initial colonization of the Basin by a seed population of farmers from Morelos (presumably first settling at Coapexco and Tlapacoya) around 1500 B.C., or the native, hunting and gathering population of the Basin borrowed crops and ceramics from the people of Morelos at this time.

By 650 B.C., the end of the First Intermediate One, the population had increased to 25,000. This represents an annual growth rate of .33% or a doubling rate of every 225 years. Between 650 and 300 B.C. the population more than tripled, an annual growth rate of .35% and a doubling rate of every 200 years. This same rate continues during the First Intermediate Three phase (300–100 B.C.), when the population doubled again. During the overall period the population increased from perhaps a few hundred people to approximately 145,000, representing a steady annual growth rate of approximately .3%.

If our calculations are correct as to the First Intermediate Four population, this phase witnessed a major disruption of the process, and the population declined to a figure of 80,000–110,000. By A.D. 650, however, toward the end of the Middle Horizon, it had reached 250,000, or an increase of 2.5 to 3.2

183

times the Phase Four level. This means that the doubling rate was either every 600 or 700 years. In either case this represents an obvious slowdown in growth rates to either .115% or .10% per year. We have some evidence of substantial migration out of the Basin of Mexico as Teotihuacan expanded in size (see page 398), so that if the lower figure for the First Intermediate Four population is correct, the growth rate may actually have been very close to the First Intermediate rate.

The period A.D. 750–1250 was one of relative population stability with population fluctuations from the Middle Horizon high to lows comparable to that of the First Intermediate Three phase. Finally, the period A.D. 1250–1519 was one of very rapid population growth from 175,000 to 1,000,000–1,200,000 people. The growth rate during this period was even higher than that during the First Intermediate, involving a .7% annual increase or a doubling rate of every 100 years.

In terms of population distribution by sites, the data are of considerable theoretical interest. Table 6.1 presents a tabulation of types of sites by phase. The total number of habitation sites (i.e., excluding salt stations, quarries, and ceremonial centers) is 3699. They fall into the following categories in terms of percentages: hamlets 68%, small villages 17%, large villages 5%, regional centers 3%, indeterminant 6%, Tezoyuca hilltop and supraregional centers 1%. Also of considerable interest is the tremendous weighting of sites toward the end of the chronological sequence; over 40% of all sites occurred in the Late Horizon, a period of only 200 years (see Figure 6.1). These patterns of site type distribution are of interest, but even more useful is the distribution of actual population in the various types of sites, and by ecological zones.

Figure 6.2 shows in graphic form the distribution of population by settlement type for each phase. Very striking in the graph is the increasing tendency, from the Early to the Late Horizon, for the population to reside in large nucleated settlements: during the Early Horizon and First Intermediate One phases, in large villages; during the succeeding phases, in the various categories of centers. Hamlets, which are the predominant settlement type, never included more than 25% of the population at any time and the range is from 10% to 25%. In all phases over half the population resided in settlements exceeding 500 people (i.e., large villages and centers) and during many phases (First Intermediate One–Four, Middle Horizon, Second Intermediate One, Late Horizon) over two-thirds of the population resided in such communities. If we include the Tula region for the Second Intermediate Two phase (and this is a reasonable procedure since the supraregional center, Tula, was located there) this was true for that phase as well (Figure 6.3).

With respect to the distribution by environmental zone the variability by survey region is so great that a distillation of this variety into a series of summary statements for the entire Basin would seem of little utility. This is best approached by a region-to-region analysis. It is also of considerable utility to analyze variations in population distribution by settlement type by

TABLE 6.1

Basin of Mexico: Number of Sites by Type and Phase

Period	Hamlet	Small nucleated village	Small dispersed village	Large nucleated village	Large dispersed village	Small center	Large center	Indeterminate	Salt site	Quarry	Tezoyuca	Supra-regional center	Small ceremonial precinct	Large ceremonial precinct	Total
EH1	5	4	0	0	0	0	0	2	—	1	—	—	—	—	12
EH2	12	1	0	2	0	0	0	2	—	1	—	—	—	—	18
I11A	17	2	4	2	0	0	0	3	—	1	—	—	—	—	29
I11B	47	6	6	6	0	0	0	5	2	1	—	—	—	—	73
I12	105	11	18	14	2	5	1	3	—	1	—	—	1	—	161
I13	135	10	27	3	7	10	2	0	—	1	13	—	4	—	212
I14	130	1	2	0	2	0	0	1	—	1	—	1	—	1	139
I15	—	—	—	—	—	—	—	—	—	—	—	—	—	—	—
MH	149	55	22	15	2	9	1	4	2	2	—	1	9	2	273
2I1	128	18	22	12	3	14	1	1	2	1	—	—	2	1	205
2I2	555	27	83	9	10	10	0	2	5	1	—	1	5	—	708
2I3	258	4	11	2	2	14	0	105	—	1	—	—	1	—	398
LH	986	31	234	10	79	37	4	137	56	1	—	2	54	5	1636
Total	2527	170	429	75	107	99	9	265	67	13	13	5	76	9	3864

Totals

	All phases	Late Horizon	Pre-Late Horizon
Hamlet	2527	986	1541
Small village	599	265	334
Large village	182	89	93
Regional–provincial center	108	41	67
Indeterminate	265	137	128
Special use	80	57	23
Supraregional center	5	2	3
Ceremonial precinct	85	59	26
Tezoyuca sites	13	0	13
Total	3864	1636	2228

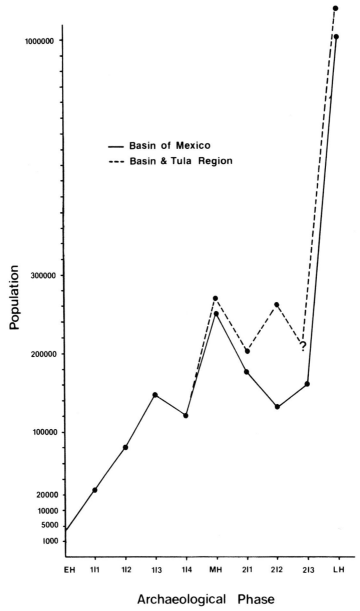

Figure 6.1. Population history of the Basin of Mexico.

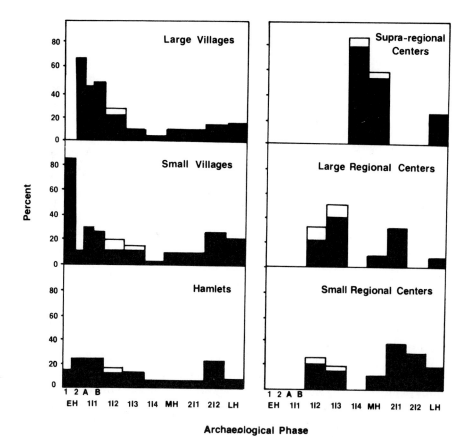

Figure 6.2. Histogram of population distribution by settlement type and phase in the Basin of Mexico.

region, so we will now proceed to an in-depth analysis of demographic patterning on a regional level.

THE SOUTHERN BASIN

A cursory glance at our rainfall map reveals that the southwestern third of the Basin was unusually well-endowed in terms of annual precipitation, with virtually all stations recording over 700 mm of annual rainfall. The highest values are achieved on the middle slope, above Xochimilco, where over twice this minimal amount falls in an average year.

There is also a striking similarity in the population profiles of the survey regions within the southern Basin, Chalco, Xochimilco, and Ixtapalapa. Although we lack survey data from the Tacuba region, on the basis of reported sites, it seems to have had a parallel history (with the exception of the First Intermediate Five–Middle Horizon) and to this general area should be added

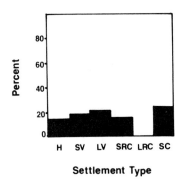

Percent

80
60
40
20
0

H   SV   LV   SRC LRC SC

Settlement Type

Figure 6.3. Histogram of population distribution by settlement type in the Basin of Mexico and Tula region during the Second Intermediate Phase Two.

the Tenayuca region and the southern edge of the Texcoco region, in terms of their overall demographic history. The noted similarities lie in the fact that the initial colonization was early, and that it was the most precocious portion of the Basin during the First Intermediate period. Finally, with the exception of the First Intermediate Four–Five–Middle Horizon town of Azcapotzalco, the area was demographically marginal then, as well as during the Second Intermediate Two phase, was well settled during the Second Intermediate One phase, and was a nuclear area during the Second Intermediate Three–Late Horizon phases.

The early precocity clearly was related to the very favorable conditions for rainfall agriculture. The depression during much of the middle period of occupation was related to the shift of population centers to the north, and the final period of maximum population growth was obviously related to the great expansion of chinampa agriculture. In terms of demographic patterning by region, the situation may be summarized as follows.

Chalco–Xochimilco Regions

We find it convenient to discuss these two regions together because of the somewhat arbitrary way in which the surveys were organized. In 1969 Parsons surveyed the Chalco region, the limits of which were essentially determined by consideration of time and funds. Geographically and ethnically, the area surveyed was the northern half of the old province of Chalco. The remainder of this political district was surveyed by Parsons in 1972, along with the old province of Xochimilco—as the Xochimilco survey region.

Geographically, as we have pointed out, this is an area of high rainfall with a CW climate, in terms of the Koeppen climatic classification, actually expressed every year. A key geographic feature of the area is the great expanse of freshwater lake and swamp, split by the Tlahuac causeway into artificially defined Lakes Chalco and Xochimilco. Prior to the eruption of Xitle, there were two extensive lake shore plains, one east of Lake Chalco and one west of Lake Xochimilco. The latter, after First Intermediate times, became a vast rocky wasteland as a result of the volcanic eruption. The balance of the lake shore is characterized by only narrow ribbons or small deltas of deep soil plain with rugged topography almost abutting on the lake shore. A number of islands, four of large size, were foci of prehispanic settlement (Mixquic, Xico, Tlahuac, and Xochimilco). To the southeast, an extensive gently sloping piedmont area descends as a series of terrace-like steps from the surrounding high sierra to the lake shore plain. The balance of the higher elevations, in the south–central and southwestern portions of the area, consist of a chaotic mixture of great tongues of lava, young volcanos, masses of contorted rock, and small depressions. Much of it consists of surface rock and cinders, and agriculture today is concentrated primarily in a great number of *cañadas,* small spaciously discontinuous pockets of deep fertile soil. Much of this area, furthermore, lies above 2500 and is thus within the more severe frost zone. Finally, in the southeast corner, is a large expanse of alluvium we have referred to as the upland alluvium, which also lies above this contour line. (The reader is referred to Tables 6.2 and 6.3 and Figure 6.4 to clarify the discussion to follow.)

The initial settlement of the dual region occurred during the Early Horizon A when two small villages (near Coapexco) were established at the headwaters of the Ameca River in the southeast corner of the Basin at an elevation of 2550–2600 m above sea level, a very unusual location for settlement this early. They are located at the lower end of the escarpment on the edge of the upland alluvium, and it is possible that the tendencies of frost to settle at lower elevations left these slopes relatively frost-free. The survey also located a hamlet near the same river, at its lower course on the Chalco lake shore plain, and another one on a small island on the lake. There was also apparently a small settlement at Cuicuilco. Parsons estimates the total population at approximately 650 people. Excavations by Tolstoy at Coapexco suggest the possibility that the two small villages may have been part of one

TABLE 6.2
Chalco–Xochimilco Region: Population in Percentages, by Community Types

Period	Population	Area (km²)	Density	Hamlet	Small village	Large village	Small centers
EH	650	650	1.0	17	83	—	—
1I1	6,600	650	10.15	6	16	78	—
1I2	29,100	650	44.77	5	12	48	36
1I3	23,500	650	36.15	9	15	26	49
1I4	Very small	650	—	—	—	—	—
1I5	3,000	650	4.6	—	—	—	—
MH	5,800	650	8.92	33	53	14	—
2I1	11,800	650	18.15	11	11	26	52
2I2	9,650	650	14.85	38	24	19	20
2I3	67,100	650	103.23	6	11	8	75
LH	89,600	650	137.85	10	5	9	75

TABLE 6.3
Chalco–Xochimilco Region: Population in Percentages, by Ecological Zones

Period	Alluvial plain	Lower piedmont	Middle piedmont	Upper piedmont	Island	Upland alluvium
EH	—	—	—	—	17	83
1I1	—	94	6	—	—	—
1I2	1	54	41	—	2	2
1I3	11	60	27	—	—	2
1I4	—	—	—	—	—	—
1I5	—	—	—	—	—	—
MH	26	40	25	—	1	9
2I1	35	26	5	—	34	—
2I2	12	53	10	—	23	2
2I3	28	2	17	—	39	11
LH	19	8	15	—	29	26
			Cuicuilco Population			
1I1	2,500					
1I2	10,000					
1I3	20,000					

large village with substantially larger population than Parsons estimates. At any rate, the total population probably did not exceed 1000 people.

During the period of time that is embraced by our Early Horizon B and the First Intermediate One A subphases, population increased only slightly, and then during the First Intermediate One B phase it increased at a much more rapid rate to 6600, a figure that does not include our guesstimate of 2500 for Cuicuilco. Again excluding Cuicuilco, during Phase Two the population tripled. We estimate a maximum population for Cuicuilco at this time of 10,000, which, if included, would mean a growth of four and one-half times the First Intermediate One B population. During Phase Three, excluding Cuicuilco, the population decreased somewhat; if we include this center then there was a small increase. In either case, the growth rate slowed down considerably and population was relatively stable.

The two regions were virtually depopulated during the First Intermediate Four phase, in our opinion, the result of population movement to Teotihuacan. During Phase Five and the succeeding Middle Horizon, there was a modest reoccupation of the area, with a population somewhat below the First Intermediate One B level. The population then doubled during the succeeding Second Intermediate One phase, and this growth can be explained as part of the process of population movement back into the countryside from Teotihuacan, or as internal population growth from the small Middle Horizon base. The population declined slightly during the succeeding Phase Two, followed by a very rapid growth of population, to reach a peak in 1519, when it was at least twice as high as the previous First Intermediate Two–Three population, to judge only from our survey data. In

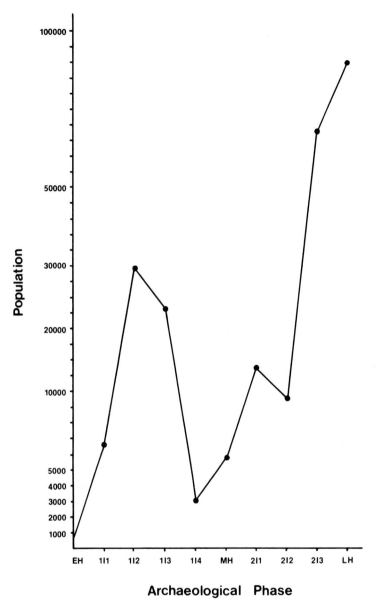

Figure 6.4. Population history of the Chalco and Xochimilco regions.

fact, our estimates from documentary sources would suggest that the population was double our archaeological estimates. This discrepancy lies primarily in our poor archaeological control of major sites such as Xochimilco, Mixquic, Tlahuac, Chalco, Tlalmanalco, Amecameca, and as we shall see at a later point, there was a very strong tendency in the two regions for the majority of the population to reside in major population centers.

In terms of distribution by ecological zones, the pattern is as follows, in each case excluding Cuicuilco. During the Early Horizon 83% of the population resided in the lower escarpment of the upland alluvium plain at Coapexco, the balance on islands in the lake. During the First Intermediate Phase One 94% resided on the lower piedmont, 6% on the middle piedmont. These figures are misleading, however, since all of the 94% lived at the edge of the piedmont, and much of the cultivable land probably lay within the adjacent plain. During Phase Two 95% of the population resided in communities in the lower and middle piedmont; 41% of which resided well above the edge of the plain and were clearly piedmont cultivators, the balance in locations that suggest a reliance on lands found both in the plain and on the piedmont. Two percent resided on islands in the lake, 1% in the Chalco plain, and 2% in the upland alluvial zone, primarily on the edge of that plain. The orientation toward piedmont settlement continues during Phase Three when 87% of the population lived in the lower and middle piedmont, but now 11% resided on the alluvial plain, 1% in the upper piedmont, and 2% in the upland alluvium.

This pattern shifts appreciably during the First Intermediate Five–Middle Horizon with a wide range of niches being used. Twenty six percent lived on the lake shore plain, 1% within the lakebed, 9% in the upland alluvium, 40% in the lower-middle piedmont, and 25% on the upper piedmont. During the Second Intermediate One phase there was a heavy focus on lacustrine locations, with 34% living on islands in the lake (primarily on the island of Xico), 35% in the plain, or 69% in total at lacustrine locations. The balance resided on the lower and middle piedmont. One might predict from these data that this was the phase of inception of small-scale chinampa agriculture, but confirming data are not available. The obvious place to search for such evidence would be at Xico. During the Second Intermediate Phase Two the population shifted basically into higher elevations, and during Phase Three there was a return to a lacustrine focus.

It is very difficult to use the Late Horizon archaeological data in any meaningful way because of our poor control of the population of the large nucleated settlements. Our documentary studies, however, suggest that 44% of the population resided on islands within the lake, either on chinampas or on the immediate lake shore, 24% resided on the southeast piedmont,· an additional 23% within and on the nearby slopes of the upland alluvium, and about 10% in the rugged escarpment around Milpa Alta.

With respect to population distribution by community, the pattern is as follows (again excluding Cuicuilco). During Early Horizon times, most of the population was at the single or dual community of Coapexco. This tendency for most of the population to live in large settlements continued during the First Intermediate One phase when 78% of the population resided in large villages (five of them). During Phase Two 36% resided in seven regional centers and 48% in large villages, or 84% of the population resided in large settlements. During Phase Three this dropped only slightly to 75%, but

Cuiciulco reached its maximum size in this phase. This pattern was also characteristic of the Second Intermediate One and Three phases and the Late Horizon, where in all cases over 70% of the population resided in centers or large villages. The pattern of residence in large settlements contrasts sharply with that of the Middle Horizon, when 76% of the population lived in small villages and hamlets and with that of the Second Intermediate Two phase, when 62% resided in such communities.

Tacuba Region

Although we have no controlled survey for this region, it, along with the Tenayuca region, 'was| one| of| the|most intensively studied portions of the Basin of Mexico prior to our surveys. On the basis of excavation and limited survey, some general patterns may be summarized (see Figure 6.5). In terms of geographic patterning this region consists of a series of parallel north–south zones. The lowest strip is an arm or bay of the great salt lake of Texcoco, which here is studded with small islands. Adjacent to this is the lake shore plain, generally only a few kilometers wide. This is bordered by an extensively dissected piedmont. The balance of the habitation zone, the middle and upper piedmont, is characteristically rugged. A great number of streams traverse the area, and because of the heavy rainfall on the upper slopes, several of them are permanent or semipermanent in nature. Springs are also abundant at the upper elevations. All in all, this is a highly favorable environment for both intensive and extensive agriculture.

The region was well settled throughout the prehispanic period. During the Early Horizon the largest settlement in the Basin, Tlatilco, was located here, and it was one of the most densely settled portions of the Basin during the succeeding First Intermediate One–Two phases. It may have been abandoned during Phase Three, but this conclusion is highly tentative since most researchers who have studied ceramics from excavated sites were not familiar with the Phase Three ceramics. If so, it is tempting to see the depopulation as related to the final period of maximum growth of Cuicuilco.

During the First Intermediate Five–Middle Horizon, there was a major concentration of population in and around Azcapotzalco. The Azcapotzalco site itself is difficult to assess, but there was a continuously densely settled zone of at least 200 ha on the western edge of the contemporary city, in the present barrios of San Miguel Amantla and Santiago Ahuixotla. It extended for an indefinite distance to the east, within the barrio of San Luis, and Middle Horizon ceramics have been reported even further east in the central plaza of the city of Azcapotzalco. The site could have covered 300–400 ha, if all of these occupations were part of one large site. A major concentration of population continues in the same sector during the Second Intermediate Phase One and the region had a heavy concentration of population during the Second Intermediate Phase Three. Very little Phase Two ceramics have been reported, but this may be a result of lack of research. We

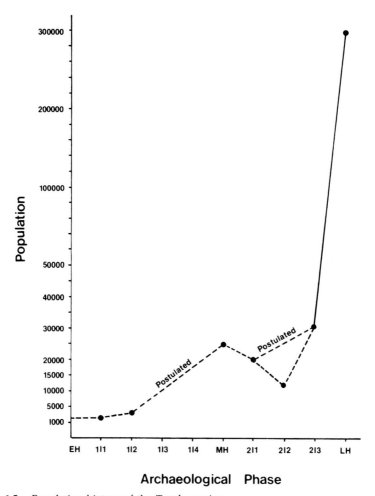

Figure 6.5. Population history of the Tacuba region.

suspect that there was a great number of hamlets and villages, but a relatively small total population. The pattern was probably very close to that of the Texcoco region. During the Late Horizon this region was the most densely settled part of the Basin due to the presence of Tenochtitlan–Tlatelolco, located on islands and artificial lands within the lakes, a growth related primarily to the increasing political importance of that center and to the expansion of chinampa agriculture.

The Ixtapalapa Region

The Ixtapalapa region is essentially a low, secondary range of volcanos that begins at the foothills of the Sierra Nevada and extends west to form a peninsula between Lake Texcoco and Lakes Xochimilco–Chalco. The range is

TABLE 6.4
Ixtalpalapa Region: Population in Percentages, by Community Types

Period	Population	Area (km²)	Density	Hamlet	Small village	Large village	Small center
EH	480	200	2.4	56	44	—	—
1I1	855	200	4.27	24.5	75.5	—	—
1I2	9,864	200	49.32	4.5	6	27	62
1I3	8,886	200	44.43	4	7	42	47
1I4	Small	200	—	—	—	—	—
1I5	5,528	200	22.64	22	30	47.5	—
MH	5,528	200	—	—	—	—	—
2I1	7,539	200	37.69	7	6	20	67
2I2	2,154	200	10.77	75	25	—	—
2I3	4,923	200	24.61	—	—	—	—
LH	16,040	200	80.20	9	13	13	66

one of the most recent, geologically, in the formation of the Basin and is therefore rugged, with numerous areas of surface rock and steep slope. Good agricultural land is essentially limited to a few stretches of lake shore plain. The plain is generally small in proportion to the volcanic massif, and nearly everywhere situated close to the lake shore. The combination of runoff and subterranean seepage maintains a relatively high water table, thus ameliorating the problem of frosts in the plain, since the high water table would permit early planting. What this means is that site location in terms of ecological zone is basically irrelevant; all sites were within easy access of the key resource, the alluvial plain. (The reader is referred to Tables 6.4 and 6.5 and Figure 6.6 to clarify the discussion to follow.)

The region was settled early. In fact, the earliest ceramics in the history of the Basin have been found only at Tlapacoya. The Early Horizon population nevertheless remains small, less than 500 people, and furthermore, only

TABLE 6.5
Ixtapalapa Region: Population in Percentages, by Ecological Zones

Period	Alluvial plain	Lower piedmont	Middle piedmont	Upper piedmont
EH	100	—	—	—
1I1	75.5	24.5	—	—
1I2	76	22	.5	—
1I3	25	16	57	1
1I4	—	—	—	2
1I5	35.5	32	32	—
MH	—	—	—	1
2I1	23	75	2	—
2I2	36	50	13	—
2I3	—	—	—	1
LH	73	16	9.5	1.5

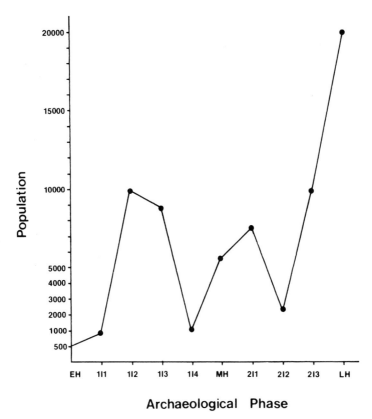

Figure 6.6. Population history of the Ixtapalapa region.

increased slightly by the end of the First Intermediate One phase. We are somewhat suspicious of our First Intermediate One population estimates, however, since the population, if our survey is definitive, increased by a factor of 10 by Phase Two, a unique growth rate for these two periods. It should be noted that the survey region was already heavily urbanized when Blanton conducted his survey, and one additional large village site would make the growth rate closer to the average for the Basin as a whole.

The population leveled off during Phase Three, suggesting ecological factors at work. During Phase Four the region was virtually abandoned, and this was followed by a substantial recolonization during Phase Five times, when the population level approximated 50% of the First Intermediate Two high. It increased further to a level almost as high as the Phase Two–Three peak during the Second Intermediate One phase. Then, in common with the rest of the southern portion of the Basin, the population underwent a sharp reduction during the Second Intermediate Two phase, followed by a very rapid growth, to reach an all-time high during the Late Horizon.

We suspect that the population of 7000–10,000 achieved during the First Intermediate Two–Three and again in Second Intermediate One phases was probably the maximum population supportable by the land resources of the region. The increase to over 16,000 during the Late Horizon was made possibly by the development of chinampa agriculture in the lakebed. In fact, the Late Horizon population undoubtedly exceeded 16,000, since only portions of the large town of Ixtapalapa were available for survey. We would add at least 5000–6000 to Blanton's estimate of 2800 for the population of this community, based on documentary sources.

With respect to the distribution of the population by community type, following the Early Horizon–First Intermediate One phases, when all settlements were small, and excepting the First Intermediate Five–Middle Horizon period, when population was rather evenly distributed by community type, there was a strong tendency for population to be concentrated in a few large centers (from 78–88%). With respect to distribution by ecological zone, the following generalizations can be made. The upper piedmont is virtually nonexistent as an agricultural resource. During all phases, with one exception, the population was located either on the plain or at the lower edge of the piedmont, within easy access to the plain. The exception is the First Intermediate Three phase, when most of the population was located in several sites, well upslope, in defensible locations, a trait apparently conditioned by the political environment.

The Southern Region—Summary

In summary, the demographic profile of the southern portions of the Basin may be summarized as follows: It was settled early, went through an explosive growth during the First Intermediate Phases One and Two, when it was the demographic heartland of the Basin, and stabilized during Phase Three. It was generally a marginal area demographically during the period of Teotihuacan supremacy, with the exception of the cluster at Azcapotzalco, had a brief recovery during the Second Intermediate One phase, declined again as Tula emerged in the northwest as a major power, and then went through a major population growth phase during the First Intermediate Three and Late Horizon, when it became the demographic, political, and economic heartland of the Basin.

THE TEXCOCO REGION

The Texcoco region is a well-defined topographic unit bordered by high ranges to the north, east, and south, and by Lake Texcoco to the west. It is characterized by a north–south orientation of ecological zones and by extensive zones of both alluvial plain and gently sloping piedmont. The original survey strategy used by Parsons involved a series of east–west strips traversing the ecological zones and covering perhaps one-third of the total area. When these strips were completed, it was noted that most sites, virtually all

TABLE 6.6
Texcoco Region: Population in Percentages, by Community Types

Period	Population	Area (km²)	Density	Hamlet	Small village	Large village	Small center	Supra-regional center
1I1	2,520	600	4.20	43	—	57	—	—
1I2	10,800	600	18.0	12	9.5	40	39	—
1I3	24,150	600	40.25	5	26[a]	16	53	—
1I4	Small	600	—	—	—	—	—	—
1I5	4,800	600	8.0	45	20	12.5	22.5	—
MH	4,055	600	6.76	58	9	—	33	—
2I1	38,280	600	63.8	2	4	9	85	—
2I2	7,938	600	13.23	39.5	26.5	11	23	—
2I3	Substantial	600	—	—	—	—	—	—
LH	140,520	600	234.20	3	6	17	53	21

[a] Thirteen percent live in Tezoyuca hilltop communities, 13% in lower peidmont villages.

pre-Second Intermediate Two sites, in fact, were located on the piedmont, and the intervening areas between these strips were also included in this survey. This means that our survey error of 20% is probably greater than that in the alluvial plain during the last two phases of prehispanic occupation. While Gonzalez's map helps to resolve this problem for the Late Horizon, we still have no reliable way of calculating population from his map. With these deficiencies in mind, we will now summarize the demographic picture for the region (see Tables 6.6 and 6.7 and Figure 6.7).

The initial colonization occurred during the First Intermediate One phase, presumably from ths Ixtapalapa region, and the population reached a figure of 2500 by the end of the phase. This population quadrupled by Phase Two times, doubled again by Phase Three, so that by the end of Phase Three it had increased to a figure 10 times that of Phase One. Following this period of sustained and rapid growth, the region was virtually abandoned during

TABLE 6.7
Texcoco Region: Population in Percentages, by Ecological Zones

Period	Alluvial plain	Lower piedmont	Middle piedmont	Upper piedmont	Saline lakeshore
1I1	59	18	18	5	—
1I2	8	9	82	2	—
1I3	14	11.5	71.5	3	—
1I4	—	—	—	—	—
1I5	4	77	14	5	—
MH	4	92	4	—	—
2I1	1.5	98	.5	—	—
2I2	39	53	4	4	—
2I3	—	—	—	—	—
LH	30	32	24	14	—

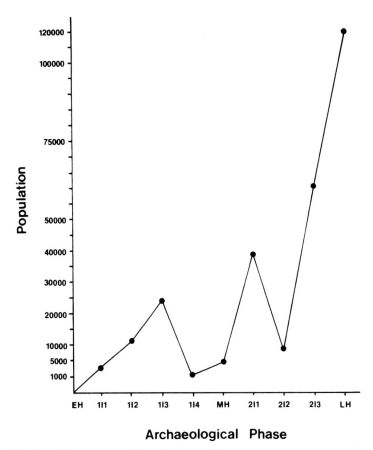

Figure 6.7.   Population history of the Texcoco region.

the First Intermediate Four phase. Minor growth occurred during the succeeding Phase Five and Middle Horizon, to a level about one-fifth of the
Phase Three high. It increased sharply during the Second Intermediate One
phase by a factor of almost 10, when it reached a level 50% above the First
Intermediate Three high. During the Second Intermediate Two phase, it
underwent a sharp decline, to a figure 20% of the Second Intermediate Phase
One peak. Even assuming some population in the unsurveyed portions of
the alluvial plain, the population certainly declined sharply. During the final
200 years of the prehispanic occupation of the area, the population rose
spectacularly, to a high 56 times that of the First Intermediate One phase
and 3.7 times the previous Second Intermediate One high.

   This profile was clearly the product of a complex interplay of ecological–
political processes. The profile during the First Intermediate One–Three
continuum has all the characteristics of internal growth. The low during the
First Intermediate Five–Middle Horizon, and subsequent high during the
Second Intermediate One phase, clearly relates to the ebb and flow of

urban–rural migration to and from Teotihuacan, and the Second Intermediate Two decline is related to the movement of population northward
toward Tula. Finally, the Late Horizon high is part of the overall process of
population growth and urbanization that affected all regions of the Basin of
Mexico.

With respect to population distribution by ecological zone and community types, the pattern is of considerable interest. During Phase One the
majority of the population resided in a single large village located at the base
of Cerro Chimalhuacan, the balance in hamlets on the lower and middle
piedmont and the Papalotla floodplain. During Phase Two, two striking
processes occurred, one of differentiation into more community types (but
with a heavy bias towards large settlements), the other one of intensification
of settlement on the middle piedmont. Many of the settlements are located
such that the only easily accessible agricultural land is, in fact, the piedmont,
and the focus of the agricultural activities was certainly in that zone. Illustrat-
ive of these two processes, 80% of the population lived in large villages, and
the one regional center, and a corresponding 80% lived in the middle piedmont. These conditions persisted during Phase Three with 70% of the population residing in large communities and on the middle piedmont, the only
major changes being an increased number of communities and in population
density.

This process is sharply interrupted during the Middle Horizon, when
65% of the population resided in small villages and hamlets, and 77–92%
resided in the lower piedmont. It should be noted also that many of these are
at the lower edge of the lower piedmont in the immediate vicinity of the
alluvial plain. This shift persists during the Second Intermediate One phase
with 98% of the population residing in the lower piedmont within easy
access of the plains. Nearly 95% of the population, in contrast to the Middle
Horizon, however, were located in large communities. During the First
Intermediate Two phase, this process of downslope movement continues,
but now 40% of the population resided within the riverine floodplains, and
53% on the lower piedmont. During this phase there was also a shift of
population to a more equitable distribution by hamlet, small village, large
village, and small regional center.

The Late Horizon, the phase of maximum population, was also one of
maximum utilization of all zones, including the first substantial use of the
upper piedmont. The population was distributed almost in direct relationship to the relative sizes of the various ecological zones. Although on survey
one's impression is that of an almost continuous distribution of small sites,
in fact our calculation of population distribution shows the reverse. Over
20% of the population resided at the supraregional center of Texcoco, and
50% in the six smaller centers. An additional 17% lived in large villages, or
80% of the total population resided in large settlements. It should be noted,
however, that most of the large villages were very dispersed, and several of
the piedmont centers had large areas of low-density peripheral settlement,

thus accounting for our impression of continuous distribution during survey.

THE TEOTIHUACAN–TEMASCALAPA REGIONS

One of the difficulties of the type of analysis we are attempting to do here is that our survey regions do not always conform to natural environmental divisions, and this is particularly true of these two regions. The Teotihuacan Valley forms a convenient natural unit defined as the basin of the San Juan River. During the course of our Teotihuacan Valley regional survey, however, we also surveyed the north slope of a chain of hills that defines the north flank of the Valley, where drainage flows north and west to Lake Xaltocan. Most of this strip, which we will refer to here as the north periphery, lies in the middle and upper piedmont in terms of our ecological zones. The Temascalapa region is essentially the lower end of this zone, that is, its lower piedmont–alluvial plain sectors. For some purposes it would have been more convenient to reassemble our data and include the north periphery as part of the Temascalapa region, most particularly when we discuss the later phases of prehispanic occupation; however, for the earlier phases it is more convenient to discuss the north periphery with the Teotihuacan Valley. (See Tables 6.8–6.12 and Figures 6.8 and 6.9 for clarification of the discussion to follow.)

With respect to overall population history, the Teotihuacan region was first settled in the First Intermediate One A phase, with several hamlets established in the drainage of the Barranca de San Lorenzo, in the middle–upper piedmont. This initial population increased by a factor of 8 during the Phase One B and then six-fold during Phase Two. There was an apparent decline during Phase Three A, but this is probably an artifact of our survey. Preliminary papers by Millon's Teotihuacan Mapping Project indicate that substantial amounts of Tezoyuca ceramics occur at the city of Teotihuacan and we suspect that the largest settlement was located there. At any rate, during Phase Three B, the Valley went through a spectacular growth phase, 10 times the Phase Two level, and this, on the basis of comparison with nearby areas, would seem to have been an internal process.

It then doubled during Phase Four, after which the rate of growth slowed considerably. Between Phase Four and the Middle Horizon, it increased by only 50%. It then declined to a level less than 30% of the Middle Horizon high during the Second Intermediate One phase, and was reduced further to only 25% of the Middle Horizon high during Phase Two. By Late Horizon times it had returned to a point at least 80% of the Middle Horizon figure, the only area in the Basin where the Late Horizon population did not exceed that of the earlier peaks by a wide margin.

The Temascalapa region, in contrast, was not inhabited by a sedentary agricultural population until the First Intermediate Four phase. The process

TABLE 6.8
Teotihuacan Valley: Population in Percentages, by Community Types

Period	Population	Area (km²)	Density	Hamlet	Small village	Large village	Small center	Large center	Supra-regional center
11A	81	600	.13	100	—	—	—	—	—
11B	683	600	1.14	22	78	—	—	—	—
112	3,994[b]	600	6.66	35	47	18	—	—	—
113A	2,000[b]	600	3.33	—	Tezoyuca: 100	—	Teotihuacan?	—	—
113B	43,601	600	72.67	4	1.5	1.5	—	94	—
114	93,792	600	156.32	2	—	.5	—	97	—
MH	147,807	600	246.34	1.5	3	7.5	3	—	85
MH[a]	10,163	600	50.80	5.5	21	55	18.5	83	—
211	39,262	600	65.44	2	1	13.5	—	83	—
212	33,001	600	55.50	16	20.5	25.5	38	—	—
213	Substantial	600	—	—	—	—	—	—	—
LH	110,000	600	183.3	3	27	30	31	—	—

[a]Population within valley of Teotihuacan proper, excluding Teotihuacan.
[b]Population at Teotihuacan not included.

TABLE 6.9
Teotihuacan Valley: Population in Percentages, by Ecological Zones

Period	Alluvial plain	Lower piedmont	Middle piedmont	Upper piedmont	Saline lakeshore
1I1A	—	—	40	60	—
1I1B	—	—	89	11	—
1I2[a]	20	5	59	16	—
1I3A	—	—	100	—	—
1I3B	—	25	56	19	—
1I4	—	43	38	19	—
MH	—	7	60	33	—
MH[b]	—	17	76	7	—
2I1	8	91	1	—	—
2I2	13	65	21	1	—
2I3	—	—	—	—	—
LH	See separate chart				

[a]For periods 1I2 through 2I1, population at Teotihuacan not included.
[b]Population within Valley of Teotihuacan proper, excluding Teotihuacan.

TABLE 6.10
Teotihuacan Valley: Population in Percentages, by Ecological Zone, Late Horizon

Lakeshore	2
Alluvial plain—permanent irrigation	4
Plain–lower piedmont junction—permanent irrigation	24
Plain–lower piedmont junction—floodwater irrigation	7
Plain–middle piedmont junction—floodwater irrigation	8
Alluvial plain—floodwater irrigation	8
Lower piedmont	11
Middle piedmont	28
Upper piedmont	8

TABLE 6.11
Temascalapa Region: Population in Percentages, by Community Types

Period	Population	Area (km²)	Density	Hamlet	Small village	Large village	Small center
1I4	675	200	3.37	100	—	—	—
MH	6,648	200	33.24	12	44	44	—
MH[a]	19,292	325	59.36	—	—	—	—
MH[b]	12,644	125	101.14	—	—	—	—
2I1	3,198	200	15.99	8	6	—	86
2I2	5,778	200	28.89	28	49	23	—
2I3	Uninhabited	200	—	—	—	—	—
LH	15,939	200	76.69	28	56	16	—

[a]Temascalapa region and northern periphery of Teotihuacan Valley.
[b]North periphery of Teotihuacan Valley only.

TABLE 6.12
Temascalapa Region: Population in Percentages, by Ecological Zone

Period	Alluvial plain	Lower piedmont	Middle piedmont	Upper piedmont
1I4	42	53	5	—
MH	21	61	18	—
MH[a]	6.5	18.5	37	38
MH[b]	—	—	—	—
2I1	26	74	—	—
2I2	11	75	14	—
2I3	—	—	—	—
LH	12	31	57	—

[a]Temascalapa region and northern periphery of Teotihuacan Valley.
[b]North periphery of Teotihuacan Valley only.

of northern expansion during the First Intermediate period is very strikingly illustrated by the comparative histories of the two regions. For example, the earliest settlement on the north periphery of the Teotihuacan Valley occurs as a single hamlet during Phase One, only one hamlet was located there during Phase Two, and this increases to several small hamlets during Phase Three. The first major occupation did not occur on the north periphery until Phase Four when some 40 hamlets were established in the area. Even during Phase Four, the population in the Temascalapa region was very small, certainly less than 1000 people, and all of it was located in hamlets. There is even the possibility that some of these were exploitation sites, rather than permanent settlements, since they had very light scatters of surface artifacts. During the First Intermediate Five–Middle Horizon, the Temascalapa region had a substantial population, 10 times the figure we have estimated for Phase Four. The population was reduced to half that size during the Second Intermediate One phase, was restored to the Middle Horizon level during Phase Two and then, as elsewhere in the Basin, reached an all-time high in Late Horizon times, when it was three times the size of the Middle Horizon population.

The distribution of population by geographic regions during the Middle Horizon is of particular interest. Of the 154,455 people we estimate as living in the two regions, 125,000 resided in Teotihuacan, 10,163 in lesser communities within the Teotihuacan Valley proper, 12,644 on the north periphery and 6,648 in the Temascalapa region. In terms of ecological zones, most of the Middle Horizon city lies formally on the lower piedmont but is positioned on a tongue of basalt that intersects and divides the great alluvial plain of the Valley. As we noted in Chapter 5, approximately two-thirds of the population were farmers and at least two-thirds of them, or half the total population of the city, obtained their livelihood by farming the alluvial plains of the valley.

Excluding the city, the 10,163 remaining population in the Valley proper were distributed as follows: 16.7% on the lower piedmont, 75.6% on the

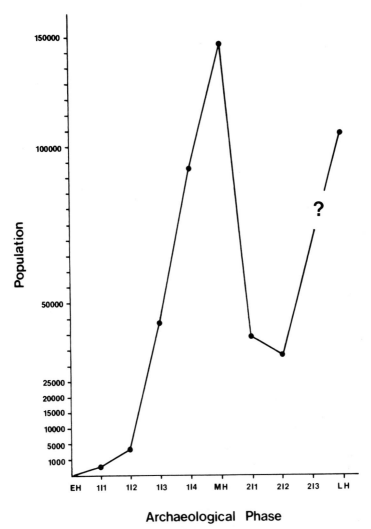

Figure 6.8. Population history of the Teotihuacan region.

middle piedmont, and 6.8% on the upper piedmont. In the Temascalapa–
north periphery sectors the population was distributed as follows: alluvial
plain 6.4%, lower piedmont 18.5%, middle piedmont 37.2%, and upper
piedmont 37.8%. This heavy focus towards recolonization of upper elevations almost certainly is the product of competition and monopolization of
the better lands by the farming population of the city itself.

The heavy focus on the alluvial plain as the major agricultural resource is
even more marked during the Second Intermediate One phase, and the
sharply reduced population abandoned the higher ground areas and re-
trenched entirely along the edge of, or within, the alluvial plain. During Phase

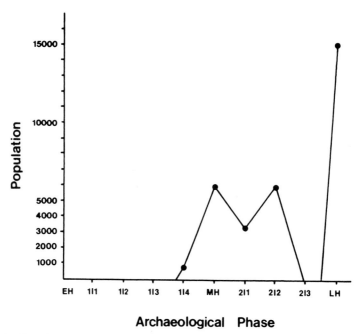

Figure 6.9.   Population history of the Temascalapa region.

Two the heavy focus of activity on the plain continues but is accompanied by a recolonization of the piedmont areas. During the Late Horizon, this process continues, and ultimately all of the ecological zones of the two regions are intensively utilized. This process of filling in, colonization, and recolonization even includes the eastern portions of the Temascalapa region, where annual rainfall falls below 500 mm, an area that was completely uninhabited until Late Horizon times.

With respect to distribution by community types, the following pattern emerges. Most of the population resided in hamlets during the First Intermediate One and Two phases. During Phase Three A all the population, excluding the city of Teotihuacan, was located in hilltop centers that were about the size of small villages. Following this, during Three B, over 94% of the population (accepting Millon's estimate of 40,000 for the city) resided at Teotihuacan; of the remainder, 4% resided in hamlets, 3% in villages. This process of nucleation continues during Phase Four when 97.4% of the population of the Valley resided at Teotihuacan, the balance in hamlets, many of which were within a few kilometers of the edge of the city. Even if we added the Phase Four population in the Temascalapa region, the figures would not change appreciably.

During the Middle Horizon, this process was reversed, and a great number of small settlements were established in the Valley itself, but most particularly on the north periphery and in the Temascalapa region. Excluding

Teotihuacan itself from our analysis, approximately 10% of the population of these three sectors combined resided in hamlets, 25% in small villages, 47% in large villages, and 17% in small regional centers. The contrast between the Teotihuacan–Temascalapa regions and the Ixtapalapa–Texcoco–Chalco–Xochimilco regions is striking, in the tendency of the Middle Horizon population to reside in large settlements.

In the Second Intermediate One phase, most of these settlements were abandoned, including all of those on the north periphery. Virtually all of the population in the Temascalapa region resided at one regional center, near Lake Xaltocan. In the Teotihuacan Valley proper, 83% of the remaining population continued to reside within the borders of the Middle Horizon city, but were distributed in several, spatially separate barrios; nearly all the balance of the population was located in several large villages along the edge of the lower valley plain. The total population of the two regions declined from the Middle Horizon high to 45,040, a loss of approximately 75%. Even if we included the Temascalapa region, 78% of this population resided at Teotihuacan itself.

The succeeding Second Intermediate Two phase witnessed a revolutionary change in the pattern, marked essentially by the dispersion of the population into a great number of sites, many small in size; and a broader ecological distribution into virtually all of the zones of the survey region. In the Teotihuacan Valley 16% of the population resided in hamlets, 20.5% in small villages, 25.5% in large villages, and 38% in centers. Most of the last resided at Teotihuacan itself. The corresponding figures for the Temascalapa region are 28%, 49%, 23%, and 0%. In terms of total population, 5778 resided in the Temascalapa region and 33,000 in the Teotihuacan Valley, approximately the same proportions as in Phase One and the same total population.

With respect to ecological zones the distribution technically was as follows. In the Teotihuacan Valley 13% lived on the alluvial plain, 65% on the lower piedmont, 21% in the middle piedmont, and 1% in the upper piedmont. The majority of the population residing in the lower piedmont, however, including Teotihuacan with its estimated maximum 10,000 people, were located on the edge of the piedmont within easy access of the alluvial plain, and this was clearly the major agricultural resource for that population. At least 50% of the population probably derived most of their subsistence from the cultivation of the lower valley irrigated plain. In the Temascalapa region approximately 11% resided in the alluvial plains, 75% on the lower piedmont, and 14% on the middle piedmont.

The population of the Teotihuacan Valley during the Late Horizon was approximately 110,000, of which approximately 100,000 resided within the drainage basin of the Valley and the balance on the north periphery of the Valley. This is the only case in all of our survey where the Late Horizon population did not exceed earlier populations in the same region by a wide margin, in this case due entirely to the presence of the Middle Horizon center of Teotihuacan.

With respect to distribution of population by community type, 31% resided in the six provincial centers, 30% in large villages, all of which were dispersed, or 61% in all resided in large settlements; 27% resided in small villages, all but a few of which were dispersed, and 3% in hamlets, or a total of 30% in small settlements. The remaining 8% resided in settlements we located on the basis of ethnohistoric accounts, and hence their typological identification is uncertain.

The pattern with respect to distribution by ecological zones is a much more complex one to summarize because of the peculiar topographic situation in the region. To recapitulate, the Valley has a fan-shaped delta of alluvial plain at its lower end; a relatively narrow plain bordered by an even narrower piedmont on the south, and a much more extensive piedmont on the north, in the sector we have referred to as the lower valley; has a narrow piedmont, bordering both sides of the plain, in the middle valley; and then fans out to an extensive piedmont in the upper valley which borders a very small area of alluvial plain. Contemporary settlement in the lower and middle valley usually occurs near the edge of the plain and hence is technically located on the piedmont. Much of the agricultural land of such settlements, however, occurs within the plain. A specific locality of a settlement therefore is not always a good indicator of the land base for its support. We have previously noted this problem in connection with the Second Intermediate Two phase occupation of the Valley. In our analysis of the Late Horizon settlement we will make, therefore, much finer distinctions in terms of the geographic patterning than we have in the discussion of the occupation of the other regions, although we did take into account problems of this nature in their assessment.

Approximately 2% of the population resided on the lakeshore, and on the basis of documentary sources, we know that the settlements had a mixed economy that included cultivation of the permanently irrigated lower valley plain and the manufacture of salt. Approximately 4% resided within the irrigated plain itself and an additional 24% resided on the lower piedmont near the edge of the plain. On the basis of ethnohistoric accounts and analogy with twentieth-century patterns of settlement they probably received most of their food supply by cultivation of the plain. Nearly one-third then of the total population of the Valley were involved in some way with cultivation of the lower valley irrigated plain, an area that comprises only 15% of the surface area of the region. In the middle and upper valley, approximately 15% of the total population of the survey region resided along the edge of the floodwater irrigated plain (about evenly divided in terms of location in lower or middle piedmont positions), an additional 8% resided within the plain, or 22% in all had an economy based essentially on the cultivation of the plain. Adding the two populations together, approximately one-half the total population of the area received most of its food supply from the alluvial plain, and the total surface area of the plain involves only about 25% of the survey region.

Approximately 11% of the population resided on the lower piedmont in positions that suggest that the piedmont was the major resource of the community, 28% on the middle piedmont, and 8% on the upper piedmont, all in localities that suggested immediate use of the adjacent area as the primary source of food. The vast majority of this population resided on the piedmont of the upper valley and along the north periphery of the valley.

THE TENAYUCA–CUAUTITLAN REGIONS

As in the case of the Teotihuacan–Temascalapa regions, this unit forms a compact geographical entity with two major zones. The Cuautitlan region is essentially the drainage basin of the Cuautitlan–Tepotzotlan rivers. Formerly, the two rivers had entirely separate courses, the Cuautitlan draining into Lake Xaltocan, the Tepotzotlan into Lake Zumpango. In the fifteenth century, a ruler of Cuautitlan diverted the Cuautitlan River northward to drain into the Tepotzotlan River. The old eastward course of the Cuautitlan continued to function subsequently as the Acequia del Molino, a major irrigation canal, after the Conquest.

The Cuautitlan region consists of a very extensive alluvial plain, bordered to the south by the narrow piedmont of the north slope of the Sierra de Guadalupe, to the east by the salt lakes of Xaltocan and Zumpango, by the low isolated hill of Tultepec and the Tepotzotlan range to the north, and the extensive piedmont of the Sierra de Las Cruces to the west. This last is the most extensive stretch of piedmont in the Basin. The agriculturally useful part of the Tenayuca region consists of a narrow piedmont and small areas of alluvial plain that ring the Guadalupe range to the east and south and lie along the shore of Lake Texcoco to the west and north. Topographically, it appears as a strip of numerous small valleys traversed by seasonal streams. (The reader is directed to Tables 6.13 and 6.14 and Figure 6.10 for clarification of the discussion to follow.)

The initial colonization of the region was during the final centuries of the Early Horizon, and virtually all of the population lived at the small village of El Arbolillo in the Tenayuca region. This population quadrupled in size during the First Intermediate One A phase, increased by a factor of 5 during the First Intermediate One B phase. At this point it stabilized. During the First Intermediate Four phase, the two regions suffered a striking reduction in population, in common with events in the southern part of the Basin of Mexico and the Texcoco region. During Phase Five and the Middle Horizon, there was a substantial recolonization and the population, at its peak, was 10 times the Phase Four level, and 2½–3 times the First Intermediate One–Two levels. It then stabilized for nearly 800 years from approximately A.D. 500 to 1350, after which it quadrupled.

With respect to distribution by community types, the pattern is as follows: Although hamlets made up the majority of the sites (50–88% according

TABLE 6.13
Tenayuca–Cuautitlan Regions: Population in Percentages, by Community Types

Period	Population	Area (km²)	Density	Hamlet	Small village	Large village	Small center	Large center
EHB	173	400	.43	13	87	—	—	—
1I1A	828	400	2.07	17.5	—	82.5	—	—
1I1B	4,088	400	10.22	10.5	21	68	—	—
1I2A	5,217	400	13.04	5	16	79	—	—
1I2B	6,222	400	15.55	3	27	70	—	—
1I3	4,060	400	10.15	5	30	—	65	—
1I4	1,368	400	3.42	56	—	44	—	—
MH	15,422	400	38.55	7	23	43	27	—
2I1	12,010	400	30.02	7	30	25	38	—
2I2	15,900	400	39.75	20	44	17	19	—
2I3	Substantial	400	—	—	—	—	—	—
LH	61,717	400	154.44	12	20	22	46	—

to the various phases), with the exception of the First Intermediate Four, when 56% of the population resided in them, the range of population, by phase, actually residing in such settlements is low, 3.3–19.9%. Excluding Early Horizon B, which was the pioneering phase of occupation of the two regions, 36–82% of the population resided in large settlements. In fact, the relatively low figure of 36% refers to the Second Intermediate Two phase, a phase of marked ruralization of population all over the Basin, and the next lowest figure of 44% is for the First Intermediate Four phase, a phase of population reduction. If we exclude these two phases, then the range of population, by phase, living in larger settlements is 62–82%.

In terms of distribution by ecological zones and regions, the pattern is as follows. With the exception of the First Intermediate Three phase, when 65%

TABLE 6.14
Tenayuca–Cuautitlan Regions: Population in Percentages, by Ecological Zone

Period	Alluvial plain	Lower piedmont	Middle piedmont	Upper piedmont	Saline lakeshore
EHB	—	100	—	—	—
1I1A	—	100	—	—	—
1I1B	3	97	—	—	—
1I2A	1	99	—	—	—
1I2B	24.5	75.5	—	—	—
1I3	75	25	—	—	—
1I4	—	100	—	—	—
MH	11	88	.5	—	—
2I1	18	82	.5	—	—
2I2	4	95	1	—	—
2I3	—	—	—	—	—
LH	32	61	4.5	—	2.5

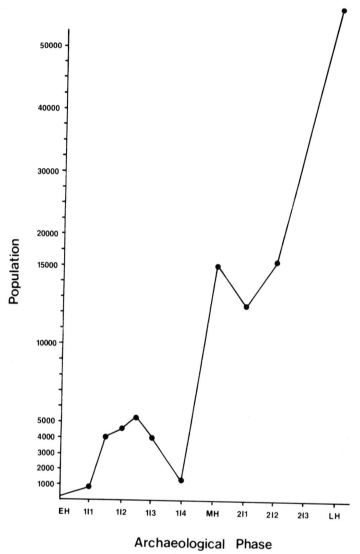

Figure 6.10. Population history of the Cuautitlan and Tenayuca regions.

of the population was nucleated at the site of San Jose in the alluvial plain near Cuautitlan, most of the population lived in settlements on the lower piedmont, usually below the 2300-m contour line. The balance resided within the plain, and in sharp contrast to the other described regions, virtually no settlements are found above 2350 m. The middle and upper piedmont were not even occupied during the Late Horizon.

The history and distribution of population does suggest the operation of ecological factors. For example, twice in the history of the two regions populations leveled off for long periods of time (i.e., for 700 years during the First Intermediate One–Three continuum, 800 years during the First Intermediate Five–Middle Horizon–Second Intermediate One–Two continuum). One could argue that in each case some upward limit was reached in terms of the then functioning ecosystem. The avoidance of the middle and upper piedmont also is a case example. On the other hand, the population was not stable in its spatial distribution over the time periods in question; and with respect to the avoidance of the upper elevations, Sanders' surveys of the middle and upper piedmont in 1977 indicate the soil, rainfall, and availability of springs for irrigation were all highly favorable to maize cultivation in those areas.

It is much more likely that the peculiarities of the history and distribution of population had something to do with the regions' relationship to surrounding regions. Although the Cuautitlan sector, particularly, is one of great agricultural potential, historically it has always been a marginal region. The Tenayuca section is much smaller, and with a very reduced area of good agricultural land, and it too was historically marginal except during the First Intermediate One phase when it was one of the more precocious regions. The result of this marginality was the constant diversion of population and energy elsewhere. There is an essential instability about the occupation of the regions in terms of specific spatial locations that contradicts the appearance of stability implied in our general summary of population distribution by community types and ecological zones.

For example, during the First Intermediate One phase virtually all of the population was concentrated in a narrow band of piedmont bordering Lake Texcoco in the Tenayuca region, presumably the product of colonization from the densely settled Tacuba region to the south. During Phase Two a substantial concentration of population occurred near Cuautitlan. During Phase Three virtually all of the population resided there and the Tenayuca region was almost depopulated, and during Phase Four both regions were almost depopulated.

Of considerable interest, in terms of subsequent events, is the fact that nearly all of the population that was in the two regions during Phase Four was concentrated on the narrow north piedmont of the Guadalupe range, the first time that this strip was well-settled, and was the major focus of subsequent settlement. There was a massive recolonization, as we have noted, during the Phase Five–Middle Horizon time period but located very differently from the earlier population. Virtually all of it was amassed along the edge and within the middle and lower alluvial plains, along the Cuautitlan River, a fact we have interpreted as part of a scheme, organized at Teotihuacan, to develop the Cuautitlan River irrigation system. There was also a concentration at Ecatepec, apparently to exploit the salt resources. In other words, the only way to explain the population size and distribution is in reference to the economic and political needs of Teotihuacan. This focus

on the Cuautitlan plain continues during the subsequent Second Intermediate period. During the Late Horizon, with the diversion of the river, the
population shifted northward and was heavily concentrated in an 80 km² area
drained by the middle and lower courses of the joint rivers Tepotzotlan–
Cuautitlan. At least half the population of the two regions resided in this
small area and had an economy based on intensive irrigation of the plain.
The lower Cuautitlan plain, however, was at least as densely settled as it was
during the Middle Horizon.

In summary, what our data suggest is that the normal processes of
internal growth, fissioning, and colonization characterize the area only during its early phases. Subsequently, much of what we see relates to the
political and economic decisions made in centers elsewhere. Our ecological
reconstruction is that of a population shifting from specific sector to sector
through the history of the two regions, but during most of its history having
an orientation of residence on the lower piedmont. The agricultural economy
until the Late Horizon was based on a combination of piedmont cultivation,
plus restricted use of the nearby plain. During the Late Horizon the plain and
lower piedmont are ultimately fully utilized.

THE ZUMPANGO–PACHUCA REGIONS

With respect to prehispanic agriculture, these two regions, particularly
Pachuca, are clearly marginal. A very high percentage of both regions consists of thin soil alluvium, with very extensive plains in the northwest and
northeast. Here the flat terrain, low annual rainfall, and thin soils all combine
to exacerbate the frost–humidity problems previously discussed. Along the
shore of Lakes Zumpango and Xaltocan are found extensive stretches of deep
soil alluvium, the most productive portion of the two regions. Masses of low
hills, including the oldest geological formations in the Basin, delimit the two
regions to the northwest and east. Some of these are lime-bearing deposits of
Cretaceous age (in the northwest), others are younger and have extensive
deposits of obsidian (in the northeast). A single major stream, the Avenidas
de Pachuca, drains all of the Pachuca and a portion of the Zumpango region.
This river has few permanent sources of water, so that it has little value for
permanent irrigation. Rainfall, as is characteristic of arid regions, however,
is highly variable, and the stream has frequently been the source of disastrous flooding. As a product of this variable volume, it has built up an
extensive delta of deep soil on the edge of the lakes.

Our defined Zumpango Survey Region in reality includes a substantial
area that is not, correctly speaking, part of the Basin of Mexico—the upper
Salado drainage basin. The Salado River ultimately joins the Tula River and
is part of the Tula basin. The river flows through a wide valley, but most of
the terrain of the valley consists of undulating, high ridges with very thin soil

TABLE 6.15
Zumpango Region: Population in Percentages, by Community Type

Period	Population	Area (km²)	Density	Hamlet	Small village	Large village	Small center
1I2	30	600	.005	100	—	—	—
1I3,4	900	600	1.5	100	—	—	—
MH	6,400	600	13.0	42	31	12	15
2I1	5,500	600	9.16	30	20	17	33
2I2	16,000	600	32.50	33	33	3	31
2I3	5,000	600	8.25	—	—	—	100
LH	41,000	600	70.0	20	21	38	21

cover. The river system has dissected this surface and built a series of small floodplains. Most of these floodplains can be irrigated from the numerous springs.

With respect to the overall pattern of population history, we have data only from the Zumpango region (see Tables 6.15 and 6.16 and Figure 6.11). The earliest settlement occurred during the First Intermediate Two phase, when a hamlet, with an estimated population of 30 people, was established on the lower piedmont of the northern ranges. During Phase Three or Four, the population increased by a factor of 30 with a scatter of hamlets dispersed on the piedmont and a tight cluster on the shore of Lake Zumpango in the delta of Avenidas de Pachuca. It was during the First Intermediate Five–Middle Horizon, however, that we have the first substantial population in the region, approximately 6000 people. This, in terms of geographic distribution of the sites, was rather evenly distributed among the various zones.

During the Second Intermediate Phase One, the population declined only slightly, but much of it was distributed at the one center at Mesa Ahumada. Following this, there was a substantial growth of population during the Second Intermediate Phase Two, three times that of the previous Middle Horizon high, and the distribution of sites in geographic space and

TABLE 6.16
Zumpango Region: Population in Percentages, by Ecological Zone

Period	Alluvial plain	Lower piedmont	Middle piedmont	Upper piedmont	Salado basin	Saline lakeshore
1I2	—	100	—	—	—	—
1I3,4	40	20	—	—	—	40
MH	10	55	6	—	17	11
2I1	11	38	4	34 (town)	12	1
2I2	34	25	10	0	25	7
2I3	—	—	—	—	—	100 (island)
LH	25	29	19	—	25	2

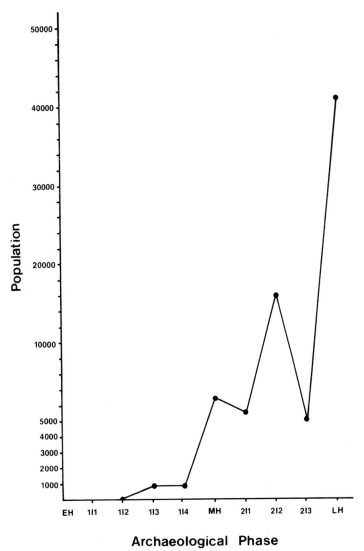

Figure 6.11. Population history of the Zumpango region.

by site types was roughly comparable. During the Second Intermediate Three phase population declined drastically, to a level comparable to the Second Intermediate One phase, and all of it was located at the regional center of Xaltocan. Finally, during the Late Horizon, the population reached its maximum, over double that of the Second Intermediate Two phase (and ethnohistoric data suggest somewhat higher figures). Again, the population distribution was comparable to that during the two previous peaks.

More specifically, the distribution by types of site by phase was as follows. During First Intermediate Two and Three, all of the population lived in hamlets. In Middle Horizon times, 50% lived in hamlets, 36.5% in small villages, and 14% in one regional center. (In summary then, 86.5% lived in small settlements, a pattern comparable to the southern valley during this phase.) During Second Intermediate One, 30% lived in hamlets, 20% in small villages, 17% in large villages, and 33% in the one regional center. During Second Intermediate Two, 40% lived in hamlets, 39% in small villages (in summary, 79% in small settlements), 3.5% in large villages, and 15% in two regional centers. During Second Intermediate Three, 100% lived in one regional center. During Late Horizon, 20% lived in hamlets, 20% in small villages (or 40% in small settlements), 38% in large villages and very small provincial centers, and 21% in two large provincial centers.

In terms of geographic zones, the distribution was as follows. All the population lived in the lower piedmont during the First Intermediate Two phase. During Phases Three–Four, the population was distributed as follows: 39% on the lake shore, 32% in the deep and thin soil plains, and 29% on the lower piedmont. During the Middle Horizon, 9% resided on the lake shore, 8% on the plains, 65% on the lower piedmont, 5% on the middle piedmont, and 13% in the Rio Salado drainage. During the Second Intermediate One phase these figures shift to 11% on the lake shore, 39% on the lower piedmont, 4% on the middle piedmont, 34% on the upper piedmont (but this last case involves the placement of the regional center on a high defensible plateau) and 12% in the Rio Salado. During the Second Intermediate Two phase, 30% lived on the lake shore, 37% on the lower piedmont, 8% on the middle piedmont, and 23% in the Rio Salado drainage. During Phase Three all the population lived on an island in Lake Xaltocan. Finally during the Late Horizon, 27% lived on the plain, 29% on the lower piedmont, 19% on the middle piedmont, and 25% in the Rio Salado drainage.

SUMMARY

Because of the striking variety in the history of settlement it is very difficult to easily summarize it. A glance at Tables 6.17 and 6.18, which show population history by region, in terms of absolute population and density, illustrate this variety. The two tables demonstrate variation in the date of colonization of the respective regions, and subsequent changes in population distribution. They graphically illustrate our conclusion that the southwestern third of the Basin was demographically precocious during the initial 1000 years of occupation by sedentary, ceramic-using farmers, and that the process of expansion was essentially the product of internal growth and gradual colonization of increasingly more marginal areas of the Basin. This part of the history would seem to be representative of a "normal" process of ecological adaptation, stimulated by population growth. The succeeding 1000 years, however, were a period of major spatial dislocations of population,

TABLE 6.17
Basin of Mexico: Population Density (per Square Kilometer) by Phase and Region[a]

Region	EH	1I1	1I2	1I3	1I4	1I5/MH	2I1	2I2	2I3	LH	Area (km²)
Chalco–Xochimilco	1.0	10.15	44.77	36.15	Inap.	8.92	18.15	14.85	103.23	137.85	650
Ixtalapala	2.4	4.27	49.36	44.43	Inap.	27.64	37.69	10.77	24.61	79.69	200
Texcoco	—	4.20	18.0	40.25	Inap.	8.0	63.8	13.23	Medium	234.20	600
Teotihuacan	—	1.14	6.66	72.67	156.32	246.34	65.44	55.50	Medium	183.3	600
Teotihuacan Valley (rural)	—	—	—	—	—	50.80	—	—	—	—	—
Temascalapa	—	—	—	—	3.37	33.24	—	—	—	—	—
Temascalapa and N. Periphery, Teotihuacan	—	—	—	—	—	59.36	15.99	28.89	Uninh.	79.69	200
Teotihuacan, N. Periphery	—	—	—	—	—	101.14	—	—	—	—	—
Tenayuca–Cuautitlan	.43	10.22	15.55	10.15	3.42	38.55	30.02	39.75	Medium	154.44	400
Zumpango	—	—	.0005	1.5	1.5	13.0	9.16	32.50	8.25	70.00	600
Cuicuilco	Very low	12.5	50.0	100.0	25.0	Low	—	—	—	—	200
Tacuba	Low	Low	Low	?	?	Medium	Medium	?	Medium	(800)	400
Pachuca	—	—	—	—	Very low	Low	Uninh.	Medium	Uninh.	High	1000
Tula	—	—	Low	?	?	Medium	Medium	120.	?	Heavy	1000
Sierra	No permanent population										1000
Saline lakebed	Scanty resident population										800
											7650

[a]Inap. = inappreciable; Uninh. = uninhabited.

TABLE 6.18
Basin of Mexico: Population by Phase and Region[a]

	EH	1I1	1I2	1I3	114	MH	211	212	213	LH (Survey)	LH (Documentary)
Chalco–Xochimilco	650	6,600	29,100	23,500	Very small	5,800	11,800	9,650	67,100	89,600	(125,000)
Ixtapalapa	480	855	9,864	8,886	Small	5,528	7,539	2,154	4,923	16,040	(22,000)
Texcoco	0	2,520	10,800	24,150	Small	4,850	38,200	7,938	Subs.	140,520	(140,000)
Teotihuacan (1)	0	683	3,994	43,601	93,792	147,807	39,262	33,001	Subs.	110,000	
Teotihuacan (2)	—	—	—	—	—	10,163	—	—	—	—	115,000
Temascalapa (1)	0	0	0	0	675	6,648	3,198	5,779	Uninh.	15,939	
Temascalapa (2)	—	—	—	—	—	19,292	—	—	—	—	
Teotihuacan (3)	—	—	—	—	—	12,644	—	—	—	—	
Tenayuca–Cuautitlan	173	4,088	6,222	4,060	1,368	15,422	12,010	15,900	Subs.	61,717	(85,000)
Zumpango	—	—	30	?900	?900	6,400	5,500	16,000	5,000	41,000	(110,000)
Cuicuilco	(?)2,500	5,000	10,000	20,000	5,000	—	—	—	—	—	
Tacuba	Small	Small	Small	?	Very small	Moderate	Moderate	?	Moderate	—	(350,000)
Pachuca	—	—	—	—	?	Small	Very small	Moderate	Very small	—	(100,000)
Tula	—	—	Small	?	?	Moderate	Moderate	120,000	?	—	(110,000)

[a]Subs. = substantial; Uninh. = uninhabited.

with only minor total growth, and the pattern may be said to have been conditioned primarily by the emergence of major centers and their impact on resource utilization.

If we exclude Teotihuacan and its immediate hinterland from our analysis, an interesting pattern in terms of population density emerges for the first 2000 years. Nowhere does population density exceed 65 people per square kilometer and most peak local values are in the 30–50 range. The consistency of the patterns suggests that these figures represent some kind of carrying capacity limits that were fairly constant throughout the first 2000 years of occupation. The final 500 years, primarily the final 150 years, witnessed a major change in the pattern, with the Basin as a whole ultimately achieving an overall density of 200 people per square kilometer. This figure probably represents a ceiling in terms of some new carrying capacity limitations. Of considerable interest is the fact that the same ceiling was achieved only once in pre-Late Horizon times, in the immediate hinterland around Teotihuacan during the First Intermediate Four–Five–Middle Horizon continuum, suggesting that the subsistence strategy characteristic of the Late Horizon was established in a limited way in that portion of the Basin at that time. Something approximating these densities was also achieved in the immediate hinterland area of Tula during the Second Intermediate Phase Two.

7
Resource Exploitation

In Chapter 1 we stated that the settlement survey of the Basin was designed on the basis of a few very broad premises. One of these was that a materialist theoretical approach was the one most conducive to an explanation of cultural evolution. A major focus of the project, therefore, was the study of resource exploitation. For all preindustrial cultures, the basic power sources are human and animal. In ancient Mesoamerica, of course, the animal component was quite secondary. Our main concern, then, has been with plant cultivation. In this chapter we will detail our understanding of prehispanic exploitation of soil and water in the Basin of Mexico. We will also consider the utilization of other resources, but in a more secondary way.

A striking feature of Central Mexico is its great environmental diversity, and this feature is reflected in the environment of the Basin of Mexico. Our ecological map (Map 1) was designed to capture much of this diversity and includes in its design the variables of hydrography (including the lacustrine element), elevation (the effects of which are primarily on temperature), rainfall, and topography. These features heavily influenced wild and artificial plant life, and derivatively, animal life, but do not represent all the diversity. Variations in surface geology must be added to the picture, since this feature, along with the variables noted above, indirectly affects soil characteristics, and directly affects mineral resources. We have therefore included an adaptation of Mooser's geological map of the Basin (Mooser 1975). Together the two maps (Maps 1 and 3) offer a useful picture of the environmental diversity of the region.

221

In Chapter 6 we presented a detailed discussion of the demographic history of the Basin. It is a record of major population growth and expansion that clearly indicates a highly successful adaptation to those environmental characteristics of the Basin that affect food availability and production. Therefore, we will begin our discussion of resource exploitation with subsistence, first with agriculture, followed by hunting and gathering.

AGRICULTURE

Although we did make a number of references to the basic problems of agricultural adaptation in Chapter 4, we will begin this topic with a recapitulation and further clarification of the points made. The Basin's staple crop has been and continues to be maize. Although the most productive varieties require a 6-month growing season, there are faster growing, less productive varieties, that mature in 4 months. Because maize originated at elevations lower than those in the Basin of Mexico, it has little resistance to frost and is particularly vulnerable at the critical phases of germination and ear formation, two stages, furthermore, when moisture requirements are high. The major problem, therefore, is the relative timing of the rains and frosts: A late rainy season and early frosts are fatal for the maize crop. The frost–rainfall problem varies considerably in significance from area to area within the Basin, however. Above 2700 meters, an area that constitutes 15% of the total land surface, the frost season is so prolonged that maize cannot be grown except in a few localized warm spots. Within the elevation band where maize can be grown (2240–2700 m), the frost–rainfall problem is most severe in the upper piedmont (2500–2700 m) and the outer alluvial plain (2250–2300 m)—two areas which together make up 40% of the surface area. The problem is less severe in the south, where the precipitation is both more abundant and more regular. Of the remaining 45% of the Basin, 20% lies below 2250 m (two-thirds of this was lake, and the rest a narrow band along the lakeshore); the other 25% lies between 2300 and 2500 m, the lower-middle piedmont. Both the immediate lakeshore plain and the lower-middle piedmont are relatively free of the frost problem (see Table 7.1).

Wholly aside from the timing of frosts and rainfall, deficiencies in the total amount of rainfall can be a problem in some portions of the Basin. Theoretically, since the rain that does fall occurs during the 4 or 5 months of the summer, when thermal conditions are ideal, it should be sufficient in the drier portions of the Basin for successful cropping. It must be remembered, however, that 450–650 mm of rain, which we recorded as the annual rainfall on the northern and central plains, is an average, which means that in many years, values fall far below this amount. On the neighboring piedmont of these plains, rainfall values are 20–50% higher, thus presenting somewhat more favorable conditions. Unfortunately, however, the thinner soils and more rapid runoff nullify this advantage. Figure 7.1 summarizes the relative

TABLE 7.1
Agronomic Potential of Ecological Zones in the Texcoco Region

Ecological zone	Soil fertility	Soil texture	Soil depth	Susceptibility to erosion	Frost problems	Rainfall conditions	Drainage	Special problems
Inner lakeshore plain								
Interfluve — Salinized		Clay Clay–loam	Deep	None	Moderate	Poor	High water table	Salt drainage
Interfluve — Salt–free	High	Clay Clay–loam	Deep	None	Moderate	Poor	High water table	Drainage Heavy soil
Riverine Flood Plain	Very high	Loam Sandy–loam	Deep	None	Moderate	Poor	High water table	Occasional flooding
Outer lakeshore plain								
Riverine Flood Plain	Very high	Loam Sandy–loam	Deep	None	Severe	Poor	High water table	Occasional flooding
Interfluve	High	Clay Clay–loam	Deep	None	Severe	Poor	Moderately high water table	Heavy soils Localized sod
Lower–middle piedmont	Moderate	Sandy–loam Loam Clay–loam	Moderate	Moderate	Moderate	Fair	Rapid drainage Small, semipermanent, possibly permanent brooks	Generally good conditions
Upper piedmont	Low to moderate	Clay–loam Clay	Shallow to moderate	Moderate to high	Severe	Good	Rapid drainage Small, semipermanent, brooks	Frosts, heavy soils Erosion severe
Sierra	Low	Loam Sandy–loam	Shallow	High	Cultivation impossible	Excellent	Abundant, rapid runoff Deeply incised streams Numerous springs	Fertility Problems Nonagricultural resource

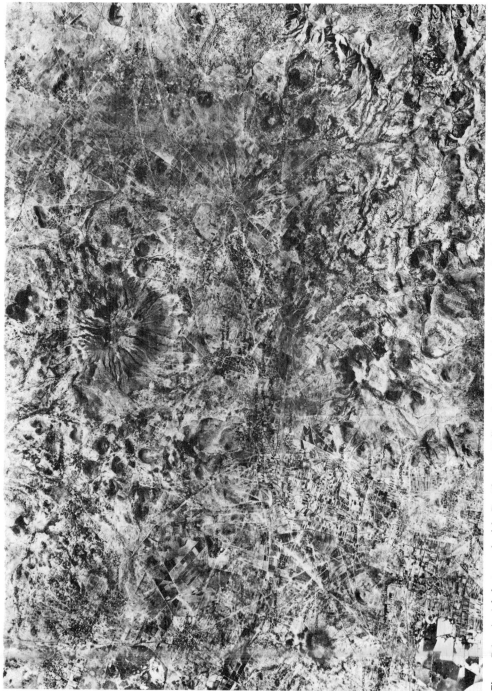

Figure 7.1. Aerial photograph of the Teotihuacan Valley, showing variations in topographic features. Note preponderance of rugged terrain and small size of the alluvial plain. (Courtesy of CIA Mexicana Aerofoto S.A.)

value of agricultural conditions by ecological zones in the Texcoco region for further clarification of these points.

Although the rainy season has never failed completely in the Basin (at least not since meteorological stations were established near the end of the nineteenth century), midseason droughts lasting up to several weeks are by no means rare, and rainfall is highly variable from year to year, frequently falling below the requirement for a good maize crop. For example, we have a 60-year record of rainfall at the Tacuba station, a relatively favorable locality, in which the rainfall dropped below 500 mm 13 times. A recent publication, by Obras Hidraulicas (1975), provides a graphic way of summarizing this situation. Climatologists have designed a number of systems of climatic classification. One of these is the Koeppen system, which utilizes precipitation and temperature as major variables. A critical boundary for successful agriculture is that between what Koeppen refers to as a C and a B climate, the former, a climate with a temperate thermal regime and moderate annual rainfall, the latter defined primarily in terms of deficient rainfall. A particular region is classified on the basis of the average calculated over a number of years. In the noted publication are a series of maps which take 1 year as the data base for climatic classification, and show the shift of the B–C boundary from year to year over the Basin for a selected number of years. Figures 7.2–7.4 illustrate the variability using this approach.

A third major problem of cultivation is the relatively high percentage of land that is susceptible to erosion—45% of the agricultural land in the Basin. Fourth, in the early phase of colonization, an additional problem was drainage in the lower-lying areas. Approximately 3200 km of land surface (lake bed, 1000 km^2; inner alluvial plain, 600 km^2; outer alluvial plain, 1600 km^2) lies below 2300 m. Excluding the lakes, we estimate that all of the inner plain and at least half the outer plain (excluding most of the northern outer plain) was an area of high water table and hence characterized by drainage problems.

In prehispanic cultivation two other problems must have been of primary concern: soil texture and soil fertility. Most soil maps classify soils of the central and southern parts of the Basin (within the area of agricultural exploitation) as "Chernozems," and those of the north as "Chestnut." Both are associated with subhumid to semiarid climates, both fit into a major soil grouping called "soils of calcification," and both generally have great natural fertility. The overall impression is that local differences in soil types within the 2240-to-2700-m contour are minor in relation to agricultural productivity. Of greater importance is variation in soil depth and texture—characteristics that are most closely related to the problems of water conservation and friability.

Because of variations in intensity of erosion and angle of slope, soil depth varies considerably and has a striking effect on agricultural productivity, particularly in the drier central and northern Basin. The least productive part of the Basin is undoubtedly the north. Because the mean annual rainfall is

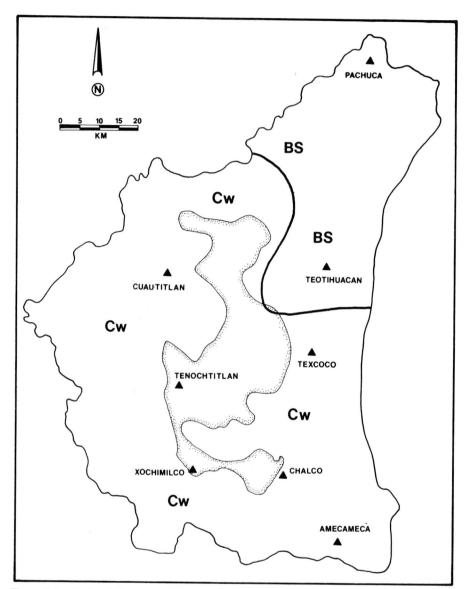

Figure 7.2. Basin of Mexico, C–B climatic boundary during average year.

lowest, and because erosion has reduced the thickness of the soil mantle, maize cultivation is exceedingly precarious in that area. Soil texture is another critical factor. Although loamy, friable, loose-textured soils are the most common (see Figure 7.5), and ideal for agriculture, they are extremely susceptible to erosion. Other soil types occur in localized areas in the Basin: Sandy soils are found on eroded slopes where the finer soil particles have been washed out, and clay-textured soils are especially common near the

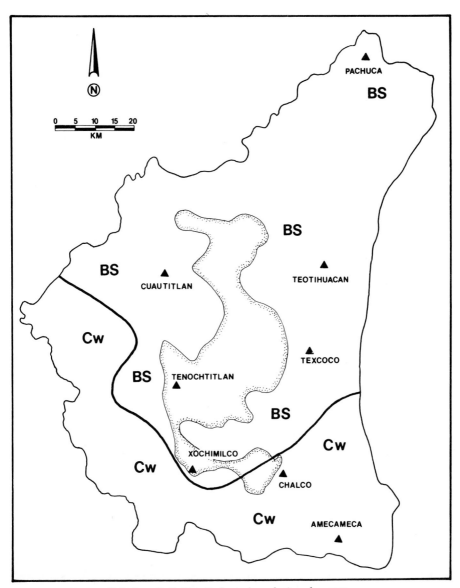

Figure 7.3. Basin of Mexico, C–B climatic boundary during dry year.

lakeshore. Above 2600–2800 m podzol soils predominate, but they are notoriously poor for agriculture, a factor further limiting upward agricultural expansion.

With hand tools of stone and wood for tillage, sandy-textured soils would seem to be ideal, but lack of moisture would present a problem. Clearly, some kind of compromise would have to be struck between soil workability and the need for humidity retention; thus, sandy loams or loams would seem

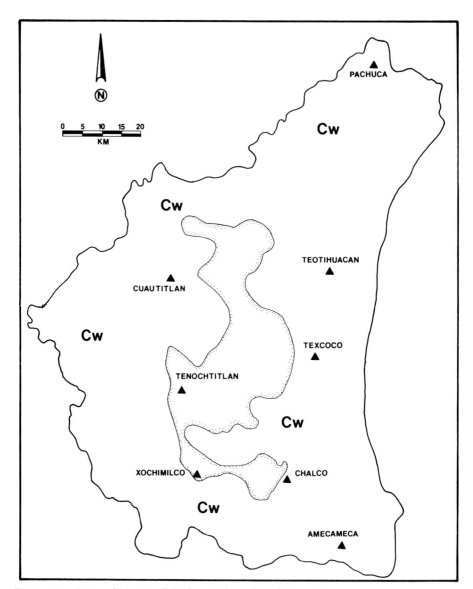

Figure 7.4. Basin of Mexico, C–B climatic boundary during wet year.

to be the preferred soil type, not a high-clay content soil that was probably unworkable with prehispanic tools. Regarding the problem of maintaining soil fertility, the loam-textured soils would again represent a kind of compromise—too sandy a soil would not have sufficient cation exchange capacity to maintain soil fertility. Our soil samples from the Texcoco area suggest that while the natural process of cation exchange of bases in the loams and clays is substantial, the major problem is the replacement of

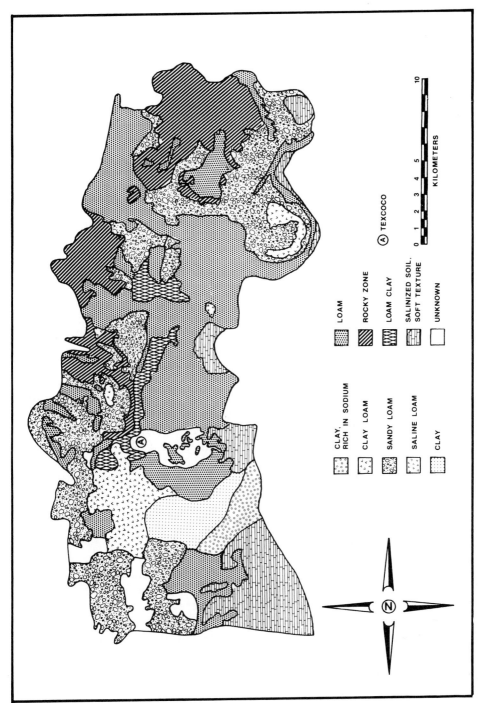

CLAY,
RICH IN SODIUM

CLAY LOAM

SANDY LOAM

SALINE LOAM

CLAY

LOAM

ROCKY ZONE

LOAM CLAY

SALINIZED SOIL,
SOFT TEXTURE

UNKNOWN

Ⓐ TEXCOCO

0 1 2 3 4 5   10

KILOMETERS

Figure 7.5.   Soil texture distribution in the alluvial plain and lower piedmont of the Texcoco region. (Redrawn from Mullan 1973.)

nitrogen and organic matter. Since the Spanish Conquest the primary source of these elements has been animal fertilizers, a resource in very short supply in prehispanic times. In most systems of agriculture, where domestic animals are few in number and small in size, the solution lies in fallowing, a process whereby a successional stage of the natural ecosystem is allowed to reoccupy the field for a specific period of years. The only significant exceptions to this general problem in the Basin of Mexico may have been (*a*) during the Late Horizon when the high population density and numerous large concentrations of people could have provided substantial quantities of human excrement for use as agricultural fertilizer over large areas, particularly in the Greater Tenochtitlan region; and (*b*) during the Middle Horizon when a similar situation could have prevailed in the region surrounding Teotihuacan.

To reconstruct the natural vegetation of the Basin would be difficult, since at least 4000 years of agricultural exploitation have completely removed it from the belt of agricultural occupation. However, small areas of relatively unaltered vegetation can be used as a guide. There was probably a gradual shift from broadleaf forest in the south to xerophytic or scrub forest in the north, in areas below 2600 m. Between 2600 and 4500 m, coniferous forest was the dominant vegetation; above that were strips of alpine meadows or tundra, and finally, in the uppermost southeast, snowfields. With respect to human occupation and land use, two important points should be stressed. The permanent removal of the vegetation between 2240 and 2700 m (in contrast to the tropical lowlands of Mesoamerica) presented no serious obstacle to the Mesoamerican farmer, even with his primitive technology. Above 2700 m the prehispanic population had an easily available source of forest products for construction, household technology, transportation, and medicine. On the basis of documentary, archaeological, and ethnographic data from the contemporary population, we know that the many and very real agricultural problems were and are effectively met. But the various solutions clearly involved enormous differences in labor input and crop output.

Today the major solution to the frost–rainfall problem is preplanting irrigation, in other words, to irrigate the land and plant it before the rainy season begins. Although the southern portion of the Basin has a relatively high annual rainfall, this technique is useful even in this area. Preplanting irrigation, however, is particularly effective in the central and northern portions of the Basin, where most of the soils, because of their loamy texture, have an unusually high water retention capacity. Here, preplanting irrigation can begin as early as January or February and the succeeding planting delayed as late as May. The ideal arrangement, in terms of seed germination and early plant growth, is to irrigate in March or April and plant in April or early May. After planting, the crop growth can then depend entirely on natural rainfall. The preplanting irrigation season, therefore, can be as long as 4 or 5 months, thus allowing a small amount of water to be very widely distributed.

Furthermore, because of the microvariability of the temperature and rainfall regime within the Basin, the ideal dates for planting vary, from February to March in the upper piedmont (theoretically, there is considerable risk in planting this early in the upper piedmont because of the long frost season, but early fall frosts are a much greater threat than the spring frosts), to March and April in the outer plain, to April and May in the lower piedmont and inner plain. An irrigation system based on water sources in the sierra, and following the altitudinal gradients, could therefore be effectively organized to irrigate lands in succession from the heights to the Basin floor. The same system could be used to resolve the problems of a midseason drought, but in a much more limited way, since only a fraction of the lands could be provided with water during a short period. It should be pointed out, however, that rainfall is highly localized in the Basin so that one area may have a highly favorable rainfall–temperature regime in a particular year while another suffers a disaster, even though the two are only 15–20 km apart. As a result, it would be unlikely that drought phases would be generalized in timing and duration over the entire area served by a large irrigation system.

In the alluvial plain, where the water table is high and the major initial problem is drainage, the solution is simple: the construction of a network of drainage ditches linked to the natural waterways of the area. These networks would range in size from those serving the lands of an entire village or several villages, to ditches on the peripheries of, or within, the holdings of a single family. As the water table is lowered, the same canal system can serve for permanent or floodwater irrigation. In sloping terrain the main solution to the problem of soil erosion is the construction of retaining walls around the fields. On low gradients simple earth embankments will serve, while on steeper slopes terraces faced with stone, blocks of *tepetate*, or some volcanic conglomerate are used. Additional defense can be provided by planting maguey, nopal, or sometimes fruit trees along the defensive works and even in widely spaced rows, parallel to the slope, within the field. Terraces, of course, retain not only the soil but also the moisture; in addition, to further improve the moisture level in the soil, the terraces could be connected with floodwater or permanent irrigation systems.

In summary, the major aspects of agriculture adaptation to the Basin were as follows.

1. The soils are not only easily cultivated using Neolithic tools, but they are generally fertile and capable of sustained cultivation with modest application of simple soil restoration techniques (i.e., animal and vegetable fertilizers, crop rotation, short-phase fallowing, intercropping, floodwater and permanent irrigation, and terracing). There is, however, a high percentage of

sloping terrain where soils are markedly susceptible to erosion, and constant effort is required to control this destructive process.

2. The plant cover is fragile and easily controlled with simple tools.

3. The rainfall–temperature regime is favorable to maize cultivation only in the south. In the central and northern parts of the Basin the combination of early frosts and retarded rains, plus internal droughts, make maize production difficult and crop loss frequent.

4. In a number of areas, local permanent water resources are available for permanent irrigation, and the numerous barrancas provide water for flood-water irrigation. Such systems, however, require intensive land use, heavy expenditures of labor per man and suprafamily (and often supracommunity) cooperation to maintain, construct, and operate.

5. Since the summer rains generally provide adequate moisture in areas with moderately deep to deep soils, the primary need is preplanting irrigation. Using this method, the farmer can get a head start on the rainy season, and the plants have more time to grow before the fall frosts. Even in areas of permanent irrigation, however, most of the humidity for plant growth comes from rainfall, which means that a small amount of irrigation water goes a long way.

6. The lakes were a tremendously significant resource for the prehispanic and Colonial populations. Not only did they provide a natural highway system for a people lacking beasts of burden, but they also linked all parts of the Basin—in fact, most of the major population centers in 1519 were located near lakeshores. In addition, the lakes were important sources of protein foods for a population with few domestic animals, and they provided other products, especially salt. The freshwater Lake Xochimilco was nearly covered by artificial, island-like gardens called chinampas, which were the most intensively cultivated and productive lands in Mesoamerica; the chinampas provided much of the surplus foods needed to support the urban communities in 1519.

7. Internally, there is considerable variability in geographical characteristics within the Basin, a condition that stimulated local specialization and trade. Variations in vegetation, topography, soil depth, water resources, amount and distribution of rainfall, and elevation and spatial position regarding mountain passes and lakeshores, along with the distributions of specialized resources (for example, salt, clay, obsidian, lumber, lime, and stone) all acted as factors promoting this specialization and trade.

8. Ranges of small hills within the Basin tend to isolate parts of it into smaller topographic and hydrographic units.

In this chapter we will consider the means by which the prehispanic populations adapted to these environmental features, with particular focus on water and soil conservation systems. It was only by using such systems as permanent and floodwater irrigation, swamp reclamation, and terracing that a regional population of sufficient size and density to support urban civilization was attained.

The basic subsistence crop of the contemporary peasant population of the Basin today is maize (*Zea mays*), consumed primarily as tortillas. Our surveys indicate that at least 65% of agricultural land is annually planted in maize, a figure that ranges from 80% in the better watered regions to perhaps 30% in the drier northeast. It is, however, literally grown anywhere and everywhere, even in sectors where soil depth and moisture are clearly inadequate. There is a tendency to extend maize cultivation to the limits of the tolerance of the plant, particularly when the inception of the rainy season occurs earlier.

With respect to problems of cultivation, the various races of the plant fall into two major types. One is referred to variously as *tres meseño, cuatro meseño, maiz chico,* or *maiz abrileño,* a lower yielding, faster maturing class, adapted for later planting, since it produces ears in 3 or 4 months. It is planted in fields where irrigation is not feasible or where natural soil humidity is low. Although ideally this type is planted in April, in fact, planting occurs frequently in May, and in some years even as late as June. The most common race of this type planted in the Basin of Mexico is *maiz conico.*

A second type is referred to as *seis meseño, maiz grande,* or *marzeño;* this type matures in 6 months, has a higher yield, and is planted where soils are deep and have either high natural humidity, or where irrigation can be practiced. Although the name suggests a March planting, in fact much of this maize is planted in April, dependent on the scheduling of irrigation. The most common race of this type planted in the Basin of Mexico is the *chalqueño.*

Approximately 50–75% of the diet of peasant cultivators consists of tortillas or other maize products. Along with maize, beans (*Phaseolus*), and maguey (*Agave*) are widespread cultigens, the former providing important amounts of vegetable protein, the latter the source of the fermented beverage called *pulque.* Most farmers plant at least some of these crops and supply some of the family's needs from their own holdings. Although maguey is generally planted on thinner soils, it occurs commonly as a field border, or as the only cultigen in the very thin soils on sloping terrain in the drier portions of the Basin. Beans may be interplanted with maize, but another common practice is to plant them in thinner soils on sloping terrain, conditions where maize planting involves a high risk.

A number of other prehispanic cultigens are consumed regularly, but not universally planted. Nopal (*Opuntia*) or prickly pear is primarily a cash crop in the northeast. Both the fruit, or *tuna,* and the tender leaves, or *nopalitos,* are consumed, the latter as a cooked green vegetable. Prior to 1970, most nopal was grown in house lot orchards, but with the recent growth of Mexico City, and the expansion of the urban market for fruit, large fields of nopal are now common sights in the Teotihuacan Valley, even in areas of deep soil. In recent years nopal has also been a major crop in the rugged piedmont south of Lake Xochimilco. Here its principal function is to supply the huge Mexico City market with nopalito leaves.

Squash (*Cucurbita*), tomatoes (*Physalis*), and chile peppers (*Capsicum*) are significant secondary foods, the former eaten both fresh and dried, the latter two consumed together primarily as *salsa* or sauce; all tend to be restricted in planting to deeper, more humid soils; most particularly they are found on irrigated land. Other less commonly consumed prehispanic cultigens are avocados (*Persea americana*), capulin (*Prunis capuli*), chayote (*Sechium*), huauhtli (*Amaranthus*), quilites (*Chenopodiun nutalliae*), epazote (*Chenopodium ambrosioidae*), and *verdolaga* (*Portulaca*). Although a grain, *huauhtli* is consumed today primarily as a fiesta candy called *alegria*; *quilites, verdolaga,* and *chayote* are cooked as green vegetables (along with *ejotes,* or green beans), *epazote* is used as a condiment, and avocados and *capulin* are consumed as fruit.

As the product of the Spanish Conquest, and the recent growth of the capital, a number of other cultigens have been added to the indigenous crop complex, most of which are cash crops. Wheat, because of its capacity to withstand frost, is double cropped with maize on irrigated land, and is a relatively minor crop. Barley, on the other hand, because of its higher tolerance of drought, is extensively grown as a cash crop in the drier portions of the Basin, most particularly on thin soil slopes, but in the northeast it is grown even on the plains. In the northeastern quadrant of the Basin, perhaps half of the agricultural land is planted in this crop. European vegetables are planted on irrigated or naturally humid land, particularly on the chinampas in the southern portions of the Basin. The heartier European fruit crops, such as apples, peaches, and pears are grown in a few places in irrigated orchards. Finally, alfalfa is increasingly replacing grain crops on irrigated land as forage for dairy cattle, as the urban market for dairy products has expanded.

With respect to livestock, most farmers have chickens and turkeys, and poultry products are both consumed and sold; a few keep pigs for sale and many farmers have sheep and goats, all primarily used as a cash resource. Animal protein consumption, although we have no quantifiable data, is undoubtedly very low, but probably substantially higher than it was at the time of the Spanish Conquest, since much of the pastureland available today was intensively cultivated at the time of the Conquest.

On the basis of the *Relaciones Geograficas* of 1580, and other Spanish sources, we can provide a reasonably clear picture of the crop complex at the time of the Spanish Conquest. Compared to regions at lower elevations, the list of cultigens reported is not a long one, attesting to the rigors of the high elevation, but it covers a respectable range in terms of nutritional value. Besides maize, *amaranth* was more widely cultivated and consumed as a basic grain, perhaps as much so as maize, along with an additional grain crop, *chia* (*Salvia*). All of the other prehispanic cultigens listed in our discussion of contemporary agriculture are reported, along with additional fruit trees called *tejocote* (*Crataegus mexicana*) and *zapote blanco* (*Casimiroa eduus*).

Aside from its use as *pulque,* the sap of the maguey was consumed as a syrup, and boiled off to make sugar. Until very recently, we had very little archaeological data on cultigens for the pre-Late Horizon period and we relied heavily on parallel data from the well-documented Tehuacan Valley sequence for our models. Unfortunately, the Tehuacan Valley lies at an elevation of 1500–1600 m above sea level, well below the frost line, and hence the data were not directly applicable.

Considering the fact that maize was one of the two major sources of caloric energy (with *amaranth*), we will focus on the evolution of this plant in some detail. Three ancient indigenous races of moderately high productivity were defined by Wellhausen *et al.* (1952) in their pioneer study of contemporary Mexican maize: *nal tel, chapalote,* and *toluqueño.* Prior to the appearance of these three types in prehispanic times, there were a series of low productivity, indigenous races that have not survived to the present time. These latter were apparently cultivated in the Basin of Mexico from the Early Horizon to as late as the First Intermediate Two phase, whereas the *nal tel–chapolote* complex was already in common use at lower elevations. This statement is based upon Tolstoy's excavation at Early Horizon—First Intermediate One sites, and Santley and Reyna's (Santley 1977) excavations at the First Intermediate One–Two A site, Loma Torremote. They also uncovered great numbers of truncated conical storage pits, a feature also reported by Tolstoy and Fish (1973) and Piña Chan (1958) at Coapexco and Tlatilco, both Early Horizon sites. These early primitive races of maize were characterized by small ears and small, hard kernels, with a relatively low moisture content, presumably sufficiently low to permit storage in these underground pits. Recent excavations at Cuanalan by Manzanilla and Frangipani (unpublished) indicated that this early maize was still cultivated as late as the First Intermediate Two B subphase.

The next bit of information is from First Intermediate Five–Middle Horizon Teotihuacan, when the *toluqueño* and *cónico* varieties were cultivated (McClung and de Tapia 1977). The *toluqueño* is a modern primitive race, with a 4-month growing season, which makes it adaptable to the long frost season and short growing season of those areas in Mesoamerica above 2240 m. *Conico* is a hybrid type, a cross between *toluqueño* and a larger kerneled, more productive Columbian variety called *cacahuacintle*. It is the major variety cultivated today, in areas above 2240 m, and our production figures of modern maize are based primarily upon yields of this type. It also has a 4-month growing season, which makes it adaptable to the high elevation. A reasonable hypothesis then is that the *toluqueño* variety appeared sometime during the First Intermediate Three phase and that the *cónico* appeared during Phase Four or Five. The implication is that modern production figures were approximated by the First Intermediate Five phase, and certainly by Middle Horizon times.

Another race, which apparently appears in Second Intermediate times (to judge from the Tehuacan sequence), is *chalqueño,* which matures in 6 months, has very high productivity, and can be effectively planted only on land where moisture availability, either through irrigation or where natural water seepage is high (to permit pre-rainy season planting), and where the soils are highly fertile, or have a frequent fertilization regime.

With respect to the other cultigens, we have data from some sources which indicate that *Phaseolus vulgarus, Phaseolus lunatus, amaranth, Opuntia, Cucurbita,* and *Sechia* were all utilized and probably cultivated by the Early Horizon–First Intermediate One time period; *Capsicum annum, Physalis,* and *chia* were present by First Intermediate Two times; and *Phaseolus coccineus, Chenopodium portulaca, Prunis capuli,* and *Crataegus mexicana* were all present by the Middle Horizon. Considering the fragmentary nature of this data, it would seem that the Conquest period crop complex was well established by the First Intermediate period and possibly even earlier.

Tools and Techniques

In this section, we will be concerned with tools used in the agricultural cycle and in the variety of techniques involved in the preparation of the soil, the planting, protection, and harvesting of the crop; in other words, the annual round of activities necessary for a successful harvest. A useful distinction can be made between this set of activities, which relate primarily to the crop itself, and those involved in what we would refer to as capital labor, investment of work energy and activity for the maintenance of the land as a resource, that is, wells, reservoirs, dams, canals, and terraces.

The quality and detail of information on tools and techniques expectably varies widely with the time period involved. We have considerable information on the contemporary patterns, a substantial base of data for the sixteenth century, and only scattered information for the periods prior to the Late Horizon. We will, therefore, work backward from the present, where our information is most detailed, and hopefully these data will provide us with models for the earlier periods.

Sanders initiated his studies of contemporary agriculture in 1953–1954 in two areas, the chinampa area in the south, and the Teotihuacan Valley in the north. The data from the latter area were amplified by Charlton in his studies in 1963–1964. Sanders also conducted an agricultural study of the Texcoco region in 1972 and some data were collected by McBride for the Cuautitlan region in 1968. Extensive data on agriculture were also collected as an adjunct to the archaeological studies of the Cuautitlan and Temascalapa regions. Concurrent with these projects, Angel Palerm and his students have conducted research on contemporary and prehispanic agriculture in the Texcoco region since 1966. The various studies provide us with very uneven coverage in terms of the environmental variability of the Basin; we lack data most particularly for the southern and northern thirds of our area. Bearing in mind these deficiencies, the following generalizations can be made.

During the period of the various studies, from 1953 to 1977, a series of significant changes have occurred in the economic life of the rural population that have had a striking effect on agriculture in terms of crops, tools, and techniques. This has been the product, primarily, of the growth of the capital from a city of two million to over eight million inhabitants. In the 1950s, most villages in the Texcoco and Teotihuacan regions were still occupied essentially by peasants, who derived their livelihood primarily from the agricultural production of small land holdings. Since then many, although continuing residence in the villages, have increasingly turned to wage labor in the city and have decreased their dependence and work input with respect to agriculture.

During the 1950s virtually all farmers utilized the Spanish plow, or relatively minor modifications of it, for the preparation of the soil, for planting, and for cultivation during the growing season. A variety of hand tools such as the hoe, and shovel, or *coa,* were used for planting or hilling the maize in large fields, and for the complete cycling of soil preparation in household gardens, small terraces, and chinampas. The major advantage of a plow over hand tools in these activities is, of course, in labor input. Our field studies show that it takes about four times as long to prepare a field for planting with hand tools as compared to plows. This labor saving is counterbalanced to some extent, of course, by the substantial feed requirements of draft animals.

The annual round of activities for maize cultivation in its most complete form involved the following:

Barbecho (deep plowing of the field after the fall harvest)	November–December
Rastrillo (leveling of the field with a mold board)	Immediately after *Barbecho*
Cruzada (shallow plowing of the field at right angles to the barbecho)	January–February
Rastrillo	Immediately after *Cruzada*
Zurcada (plowing of field for planting)	March–May
Siembra (planting, done with hand tools)	March–May
Primer Labor (weeding, with the plow)	When crop is 10 cm high
Segundar (weeding, with the plow)	When crop is 30–50 cm high
Aterrada (hilling, with hand tools)	Late summer
Cosecha (the harvest)	September–November

To these activities would be added irrigation of the field where this was feasible and, in some years, fertilization.

The sequence of activities noted above is most generally applied to maize fields with fairly deep soils, that is, exceeding 50 cm in depth, since the preplanting plowing serves as a dry farming technique to store moisture, and is inappropriate to shallower soils. On such fields, a *barbecho,* but not a *cruzada,* may be applied, or both eliminated. On the better lands, beans, squash, and other plants may be intercropped. During the 1960s, and most particularly since 1970, the absorption of many villagers into the urban labor market has had striking effects on agricultural practices. Many farmers rent their lands to others and this has resulted in a process of increased size of land holdings, at least in terms of use, if not ownership. Men who have access to these larger holdings frequently use mechanized equipment for virtually all of the observed activities. Even men who continue to use their small holdings will often hire such equipment, and invest virtually no labor in cultivation themselves.

Contemporary land use can be classified as intensive, in the sense that land is rarely intentionally fallowed, and is generally planted annually. This was particularly true in the 1950s when villages were still basically agricultural communities. Fertility of the fields at that time was provided primarily from animal waste, and most farmers had some livestock. With the recent shift to mechanized agriculture, farmers have correspondingly shifted to the use of commercial fertilizers. Along with these mechanisms of soil restoration, which are primarily post-Conquest in date, a number of practices survive in some villages that undoubtedly reflect prehispanic practices. In the southern volcanic region around Milpa Alta, where rainfall is high and wild vegetation more exuberant, farmers use woody weeds, growing on the rocky margins of fields, as green fertilizer. Farmers in the chinampa area use aquatic vegetation for the same purpose. Human refuse accumulated in house lots is often combined with that of livestock and used as fertilizers as well, although most farmers would deny the use of human fertilizers, if one asked that question directly.

All of the documents indicate that agriculture was at least as intensive during the Conquest period as it is today; most of the data indicate a more thorough application of technological knowledge and more intensive land use in 1519 than at present. Even allowing some exaggeration, the Spaniards' descriptions of the population of the Basin of Mexico at the time of the Conquest demonstrate that it was much denser then than today. More reliable and detailed tax data for the period 1550–1580 indicate that in 1580 approximately 400,000 people (roughly the size of the 1940 rural population) resided in the Basin. The tax documents, without exception, emphasize a major decline between 1519 and 1580 to at least one-third, possibly one-quarter, of the 1519 population. To the observer, even to the anthropologist, the standard of living of the present-day rural population seems low, and probably below average for the country as a whole. The major question to resolve then is: By what means was the Basin exploited in 1519 so as to permit a population at least triple, probably quadruple, the present rural population?

Before discussing agricultural techniques, several nontechnological explanations may be offered as an answer:

1. The standard of living was even lower than today, and the average farmer produced only a small surplus for sale above subsistence needs.

2. A more efficient, highly organized, government regulated and controlled agriculture existed. This point is so crucial to the theoretical arguments to be presented later that the following statement is quoted in full:

> En el tiempo de Moctezuma eran apremiados a muchas cosas especialmente a dos
> que eran muy buenas, la una que cada uno hiciese su oficio e lo ususase forcib-
> lemente y lo otro que todos generalmente sembrasen e fuesen labradoes por sus
> personas o por sus dineros por manera que se podian sembrar por todos los
> pueblos e provincias de su reino se habian de sembrar por fuerza e habia veedores
> a su tiempo para que las viesen si estaban sembradas y si no el cacique era puesto
> en prision tal, que era peor que muerto e ansi parecen agora los cerros e laderas en
> gran cantidad que se solian labrar e por provincias tenian cargo de proveer de
> maiz e de todas las cosas necesarias a Mexico asi de maiz como de aves e cacao, e
> de leña|e ansi de todas las mas cosas que se podian pensar ser necesarias tenian
> por provincias cargo de las proveer abastadamente, esto demas de lo que cada
> uno queria vender por su voluntad de su cosecha en manera que esta cibdad era la
> mas abastada del mundo [Paso y Troncoso, ENE: Volume 4, pp. 169–170].

[Many things were esteemed in the time of Moctezuma, especially two which were very good, one that each person should follow his trade and should do so energetically, and the other, everyone generally should plant, and that they should be farmers, either personally, or by investment, by whatever means they were able to plant. Through all the villages and provinces of his kingdom they were required to plant, by force, and there were inspectors in his time, to insure that the lands were planted, and if not, the lord was put in prison, which was worse than death, and thus can be seen today the great quantity of hills and slopes that were once worked, and they (the inspectors) had charge, by province, of providing maize and all necessary things to Mexico, thus maize as well as birds and cacao, and firewood; and thus most other things that one would think to be necessary, they had charge of, by provinces, to provide them abundantly. This, besides that which each one wanted to sell, on his own will from his harvest; in this manner the city was the best provisioned in the world.]

3. There is a considerable area today where erosion has reduced excellent to relatively good agricultural land to denuded *tepetate* and miserly pasture.

Even allowing for such differences between the Late Horizon and recent situations in the Basin, the Late Horizon demographic picture argues for an extremely efficient agriculture.

Considering the fact that the land was cultivated intensively, a major problem confronted by the Aztec peasant must have been soil fertility. As we noted previously, the soils of the Basin have high natural fertility, because of the combination of a semi-arid climate and richness in nutrient elements of the volcanic bedrock. The only major problem is the maintenance of nitrogen and organic matter. We suggest several ways in which this problem was resolved. First, intercropping, and in particular the interplanting of maize and beans, which is today a rapidly declining practice, would have helped to resolve the problems since beans have the capacity to fix atmospheric nitrogen. Contemporary farmers, when they harvest a crop, remove the entire plant from the field to use as animal forage. In prehispanic times, in all probability, only the ears of the maize and pods of the beans were removed and the residue of the plants hence returned to the soil. Irrigation, particularly floodwater irrigation, since the water contains sediments in solution, would also act as a soil restorative measure. The use of green fertilizers in the manner we described in the southern Basin was probably a prehispanic practice. Another probable practice was short period fallowing.

Finally, a number of researchers—Angel Palerm (1955) for Elosuchitlan, in northern Puebla, and Stadelman (1940) for the northwest highlands of Guatemala—describe a special use of limited available animal fertilizers that was undoubtedly a prehispanic technique. The village of Elosuchitlan is somewhat dispersed, with each house placed within a rather large house lot, on the average about half a hectare in size. The land adjacent to the house is called *calmil* and is cultivated intensively, usually planted in maize. Besides this, the householder has a much larger, or several equal sized fields, outside of the residential area of the village, which are cultivated using a short fallowing system. The house lot is used to keep small livestock, mostly poultry, and is used for a family latrine and garbage disposal area. The result is a relatively high level of informal and continuous fertilization that enables the occupant to plant maize on a year to year basis. Considering the dispersed nature of Late Horizon rural settlement, in which residential area densities were very similar to that of the highland Pueblan and Guatemalan communities noted, it seems almost certain that this practice is prehispanic. Wolf (1966) refers to it as infield–outfield cultivation. In the case of some portions of the Basin of Mexico, however, the *calmil* land in the Late Horizon was located on piedmonts adjacent to floodwater irrigated plains, so that the outfield was also cultivated intensively.

Various sixteenth-century sources indicate that the principle of fertilization was well understood by Aztec peasants, as the following data illustrate. One of the Spanish Conquistadores, Bernal Diaz del Castillo, describes a system of collecting and selling of human refuse that must have approximated the extraordinarily careful husbandry of such a resource so characteristic of modern China (Bernal Diaz 1927: 177). Sahagun presents a long detailed discussion of types of land according to the current native classification (ca. 1550), in which several types of fertilized lands are mentioned:

Quauhtlalli	Soil fertilized with rotten wood.
Tlazotlalli	Soil fertilized as a result of vegetation being converted to fertilizer and turned over in the soil. (This technique is still used in the southern part of the Basin, not only in chinampas, but also on hillside terraces.)
Callalli	Land located on old house sites.
Tlalauiac	Soil fertilized with animal fertilizer.

Also distinguished in the native system were soils affected regularly by alluviation. Apparently, the enriching aspect of this natural process was well understood by the Indian population (see Sahagun 1946: Volume II, pp. 476–477).

A major question is whether the basic set of cultivation practices we described for contemporary peasant agriculture is applicable to the Late Horizon.

Since the plow is used today to prepare the soil, and since the preplanting activities are clearly linked with European dry farming practices, in which the soil is thoroughly turned over, one could question their appropriateness to the prehispanic period. Studies of hoe cultivation today in highland Guatemala by Stadelman (1940) indicate, however, that the hoe can be used to produce the same kind of soil texture needed for dry farming, the major difference being the work cost.

The following, again from Sahagun, would suggest that the basic agricultural routine we have described, was, in fact, used in the mid sixteenth century (it should be noted that the verb used in the description in the preparation of the soil is *cavar*, 'to dig', not *arar*, 'to plow').

> *El labrador es dispuesto, recio, diligente y apto para la labranza. El buen labrador es fuerte, diligente, y cuidadoso, madruga mucho por no perder su hacienda, y por aumentarla deja de comer y de dormir, trabaja mucho en su oficio, conviene a saber, en romper la tierra, cavar, desverbar, cavar en tiempo de seca, desmontar, allanar lo cavado, hacer camellones, mollir bien la tierra, arreglarla en su tiempo, hacen linders y vallados, y romper tambien la tierra en tiempo de aguas, saber escoger la buena tierra para labrarla, hacer hoyos para echar la semilla y regarla en tiempo de seca; sembrar derramando semillas, agujerar la tierra para sembrar los frijoles, cegar los hoyos donde esta el maiz sembrado, o ocohombrar o allegar la tierra, a lo nacido: quitar el vallico, entresacar las canas quebrandolas, y apartar las mazorquillas, y quitar los hijos de estas y los tallos, porque crezca bien lo nacido, entresacar a su tiempo las mazorcas verdes; al tiempo de la cosecha, quebrar las canas cogiendolas, recoger maiz cuando esta ya bien sazonado; desollar o desnudar las mazorcas, y atar las unas con otras, anudando las camisillas una con otra, y hacer sartales de mazorcas atando unas con otras, y acarrea a casa lo cogido y ensilarlo; quebrar las canas que nada tienen aporrean- dolas, trillar, limpiar, aventar, levantar al viento lo trillado. El mal labrador es muy negligente, haragan, y a el se le hace grave y molesto todo trabajo; en su oficio es tosco, bruto grosero, villanazo, comilon, escaso, enemigo de dar, y amigo de tomar* [Sahagun 1946: 210–212].

[The farmer is prepared, strong, diligent, and apt for farming. The good farmer is strong, diligent, and careful; rises early so as not to lose his holding, and works to increase it; he eats and sleeps little; he works hard at his trade; it is useful for him to know how to break the soil, to dig, to weed, to dig in the dry season, to clear, to level that which he has excavated, to make raised beds, to pulverize well the soil, to arrange it at its time, to make boundaries and fencing, also to break the soil during the rainy season, he knows how to select the good land and work it, make holes to toss in the seed, and irrigate it in the dry seasons; to scatter the seeds; to puncture the earth, to plant the beans; to close up the holes when the corn is planted, or to mound or concentrate the soil around the sprouted plant: to remove the weeds; to prune the canes by breaking them; to separate the small ears, and remove the seedlings from them, and the small sprouts, so that what has sprouted will grow well; to prune at the proper time, the green ears; at the time of the harvest, to break the canes, collect them, harvest the maize when it is well ripened; to strip the ears, to tie them together, tying the little sheaths with each other, and to make strings of the ears, tying them together; to carry home that which is harvested and to store it; to break the canes that have nothing, pounding them; to thresh, to clean, to throw into the wind that which is threshed. The poor farmer is very negligent, lazy, and is one who makes all work sorry and irritating; and in his trade he is coarse, dumb, obscene, villainous, gluttonous, stingy, enemy of giving and friend of taking.]

With respect to tools used to prepare the soil in prehispanic times, several pictorial manuscripts, including that of Sahagun, show farmers working the soil (and the illustrations suggest that the entire field was thoroughly turned over and the soil preparation as complete as that accomplished today with the plow) with an all wooden shovel-like tool called a *coa*. Theoretically, in pre-Late Horizon times, a wide variety of techniques could have been practiced. It is conceivable that the populations were small enough to permit a much more extensive practice of land use, possibly even a long fallow swidden system. Most swidden systems that have been studied usually involve no preparation of the soil. Cutting tools are used for the removal of the vegetation, and crops are normally planted directly in the burned ash of the vegetation, or in the exposed soil, with a dibble stick. Short fallowing and permanent cropping, however, require turning over the soil to control the growth of grasses and herbaceous plants. The Aztec *coa* and the post-Conquest metal hoe, and plow, of course, performed these functions. The use of the wooden *coa*, illustrated in the sixteenth-century codices, would be very difficult to establish on the basis of archaeological data. A common artifact, however, that we did find in the Teotihuacan and Temascalapa regions, on First Intermediate Five–Middle Horizon and Late Horizon sites, both in excavations and survey, and in the Texcoco region on Late Horizon sites (from survey data), were ground basalt hoes. These have been identified as hoes on the basis of their shape, the hafting arrangements, edge polishing, and the fact that they are frequently found in modern fields without associated house sites, as well as within excavated houses. Unfortunately, we were not aware of the possible use of these tools until very recently. We had recognized them in our excavation of village sites during the Teotihuacan project but were uncertain as to their use. They appear in the northern and central portions of the Basin at a time when we record the first substantial buildup of population, justifying our assumption that they are related to agricultural intensification. Theoretically, such tools should appear in the south by First Intermediate Three times. Recent excavations by the UNAM, Instituto of Anthropologia (unpublished), in a Phase Three (Islote de Terremoto) site in the lake bed of Lake Xochimilco, in fact, recovered implements almost identical to those from late sites in the central and northern Basin.

Contemporary Terracing

Generally speaking, in the Mesoamerican Highlands the term *temporal* refers to agriculture in which the humidity for plant growth is derived primarily from rainfall. In the Basin of Mexico, this type of cultivation occurs in one of two contexts. First, it occurs all over the valley in areas of deep soil, primarily the plains, but also in areas of very gently sloping piedmont, where irrigation resources are either unavailable or unneeded. Under these conditions, cropping success, with respect to maize, is moderately high in the central portion of the Basin and high in the better watered south. In such areas, erosion is not a problem and the only approximation of its control is the use of maguey as a field border. Temporal cultivation also occurs all over the central and northern portions of the valley in areas of sloping terrain and thin soil where a rather casual kind of cultivation is practiced, characterized by low labor input, low and variable productivity. In such areas, adequate terracing would result in a deeper soil profile, higher level of humidity conservation, and more dependable cropping.

The primary difference between terrace agriculture and the second type of temporal cultivation lies in the degree of application of certain soil conservation practices known to the present-day peasant population. The degree of application of such techniques is linked with a variety of factors, mostly demographic in nature. The sixteenth- and seventeenth-century decline in population and consequent abandonment of fields, recent population growth and urban migration, and changes in ownership of lands between villages and haciendas are important factors. The borderline between terrace cultivation on the one hand, and temporal cultivation on the other is a vague one. The term *terrace agriculture* is applied here to situations where the terrain is sloping; where erosion is being checked by stone, earth, or maguey structures to the degree that soil depth in slopes exceeds 20–30 cm; and where down-slope drainage is controlled (see Figure 7.6 for an aerial view of contemporary terracing).

As the archaeological data will demonstrate, there is reason to believe that most of the sloping terrain in the central and northern portions of the Basin was covered by complex and carefully constructed terrace systems in 1519. Following the Conquest, several processes occurred that resulted in the deterioration of many terrace systems and their conversion to marginal temporal land. Between 1519 and 1720 there was a disastrous demographic decline all over Mesoamerica, the product of the introduction of European diseases. In the Basin of Mexico, the population declined at least to one-third of its former number by 1580, to one-fourth by 1600. Accompanying this population decline, a second process called *congregación* occurred in which the Spaniards, to facilitate conversion and taxation, moved small communities or dispersed populations into former towns, large villages, or new population centers. In the Basin of Mexico this occurred in the early decades of the seventeenth century.

Population decline and *congregación* caused considerable cultivated land to be abandoned during the latter sixteenth and seventeenth centuries. On sloping ground, this abandonment resulted in intensified erosion as terrace systems, which require constant care, ceased to be maintained. Furthermore, the rapidly expanding use of domestic sheep and goats, and the conversion

Figure 7.6. Aerial photograph of the dispersed village of Amanalco. Note terracing. Many of the terraces adjacent to the houses are irrigated. Late Horizon rural settlement is very similar in nature. (Courtesy of CIA Mexicana Aerofoto S.A.)

of much former agricultural land to pasture, accelerated the erosional process. Once initiated, the process of erosion is rapid, and there are no large areas of sloping terrain in the Basin that have completely escaped it. It is probable that 40–60% of the gentle to medium sloping terrain in the northern and central portions of the Basin of Mexico has a soil cover of less than 20 cm of soil today. During the nineteenth and early twentieth centuries, most of the land of the Basin was gradually incorporated into large haciendas, practicing a basically extensive rather than intensive system of farming. However, the hacendados did partially canalize the barrancas and develop elaborate maguey terrace systems that have partially restored the area.

As erosion progressed in the seventeenth and eighteenth centuries, only terrace systems located near villages managed to survive. Today, terrace systems near relatively isolated villages tend to be better preserved and more thoroughly utilized than those in the more accessible areas. Such communities are more dependent on agriculture than those close to Mexico City, where the urban labor market absorbs a growing proportion of the peasant population into nonagricultural activities. Ambitious attempts at land reclamation on slopes are most commonly found in the most isolated areas. Apparently when recent population growth produces pressures, the more isolated communities respond by building terrace systems; where facilities for commuting to the city are available, the population responds by working part- or full-time in the city.

There are a variety of types of terracing practiced in the Basin today. The most common type we have referred to as bancal terracing. On gentle slopes, earth banks, accompanied by maguey planting, are sufficient to control erosion. These banks are usually constructed on all sides of the field, and larger fields may have a more complex topography with internal banks as well. The embankment may vary from 10 to 50 cm in height. Even fields in relatively flat terrain often have peripheral embankments, particularly if the area is to be irrigated as well, and most fields have at least a maguey border. Since maguey is an economically useful plant, the purpose of this kind of planting becomes a complex matter; it can be considered as a cultigen, as a field border, and as a method of controlling erosion. On very steep slopes maguey is often the only cultigen and is planted in closely spaced rows (usually only a few meters apart) parallel to the slope contour.

Very often, masses of *tepetate*, volcanic conglomerate, or stone laid in earth fill, are incorporated in the fill of these banks so that structurally speaking they involve more than simply embankments of soil. Well-constructed stone terraces are also found in a variety of contexts. At the villages of Tlaixpan, Tlaminca, and Purificacion, east of Texcoco, superbly constructed stone terraces are irrigated from the springs of Amanalco, to grow flowers, medicinal herbs, and fruit orchards. A huge area around Milpa Alta in the southern valley, an area of recent volcanism, is characterized by the most contorted terrain in the Basin, and masses of surface rock, soil-filled depressions (called locally *canadas*), and tongues of lava provide a chaotic topography. Each depression, and the majority of these are less than a hectare in size, is surrounded by rocky terrain that is elaborately terraced, in many cases by constructing above-ground stone walls. This technique of building stone walls around fields is also found in house lots over many portions of the Basin.

One of the most impressive systems of terracing is located near the modern villages of Maquixco Alto and Colhuacan on the north slope of Cerro Gordo (on the north flank of the Teotihuacan Valley). Topographically, the area appears as a series of long, gently sloping ridges, extending outward radially from the main mass of the hill, each separated from the next by barrancas. Because of the height of Cerro Gordo and the closeness of the agricultural area to the upper flank of the hill, considerable runoff is available for floodwater irrigation. The ridges are covered with terraces and the lower and middle segments of the barrancas are frequently partially absorbed by check dams. The total area today presents a very complex picture of deep gullies; sedimented barrancas; large patches of bare *tepetate;* sections of new lands reclaimed from *tepetate;* old, disintegrating terrace systems; and well-maintained, productive terraces.

Partly because of the wealth of archaeological remains in this area, and partly because of the highly developed terrace system, it was decided to survey intensively a test area of 8 km² near Maquixco Alto. Data were collected on both modern land use and ancient settlement patterns. On the basis of this survey the present-day land use and land characteristics may be summarized as follows.

	Percentage of survey strip
1. Steep uncultivated slope (isolated hills); pasture; scattered maguey cultivation	10%
2. Exposed *tepetate;* gentle to medium slope; unused; some pasture	20%
3. Marginal agricultural land; gentle to medium slope; much erosion, thin soil; new terraces, old disintegrating terraces, or unterraced areas; some in agricultural use, much of it used for pasture	35%
4. Good agricultural land; well-kept terraces; medium soil depth (30–100 cm)	25%
5. Deep soil (over 100 cm)	10%
	100%

Terraces in all stages of growth, construction, and deterioration may be seen. There is considerable variation in soil depth, slope angle, crop use, effectiveness of erosion control, and water conservation. Where terraces are carefully maintained, there is practically no free-flowing drainage. The terraces are arranged in vertical strips of parallel lines running downslope with very shallow main canals running between the strips. The upper corner of each terrace is equipped with a low bank of earth that projects into the main canal and automatically diverts part of the flow into the terrace, a self-flooding system. All water derives from flash floods that follow showers.

The most effective terracing occurs just east, north, and south of the village of Maquixco Alto. In these areas soil frequently exceeds 1 m in depth. The lower edge of the terrace has a high earth bank, frequently planted in fruit trees or maguey. The surface of each terrace is completely level, and the sides have earth banks to prevent lateral erosion or loss of water. In the most developed terraces the water is not directly diverted into the field, but into a ditch, located along the upper edge of the field, and situated just below and parallel to the lower bank of the terrace. The ditch breaks the force of the water as it enters the field, holds it, and prevents gullying of the field. Terraces generally vary from 5 to 20 m in width, but this is a highly variable feature depending primarily on slope angle.

Most of the deep-soil terraces are planted in maize, frequently interplanted with wheat, habas (a Spanish bean), or squash. Such lands are as productive as floodwater irrigated plains. This part of the survey area had a lush, almost jungle-like appearance in 1963 (with the maize crop 2 to 4 m high, fruit trees, and maguey along the terrace banks, closely packed, interplanted secondary crops, and natural vegetation) in startling contrast to the vegetation-bare *tepetate* wastelands only a few meters distant. There is little doubt that careful terracing is an extraordinarily effective solution to the problem of hillside agriculture in the Basin. The controlled drainage, use of earth banks, and deep soil, with high water storage capacity, all act to reduce crop loss to a minimum.

Much of the land in the survey test zone today has a soil cover of 0–50 cm with large areas of exposed *tepetate*[1] (approximately 55%). Traces of old terraces are found all over this area. Scattered throughout this part of the zone are numerous recent reclamation projects, all small in size and constructed by groups of only familial size, many occurring even in areas of bare *tepetate*. Techniques of recovery involve the following steps:

1. Excavation of a trench 30–100 cm deep into the *tepetate*, parallel to the slope, the length of the future terrace.
2. *Tepetate* extracted from the ditch is then pulverized to manufacture soil.
3. A series of shallow pits is excavated at 1- to 2-m intervals, about 30–50 cm deep in a row just above the trench and paralleling it.
4. Young maguey plants are planted in each pit, which is then partially filled in with crushed *tepetate*.
5. Blocks of *tepetate*, adobe, chunks of rock combined with earth are used to build a low wall between the maguey plants to form a terrace facing. Crushed *tepetate* may also be heaped over this to form a continuous bank.
6. A lateral bank is constructed on each side of the terrace using the same method.
7. In some cases the surface of the *tepetate* for a width of 5 to 10 m behind the bank is worked over with a pick to manufacture a layer of soil.

[1] The word *tepetate* refers to a layer of compacted volcanic ash that underlies much of the organic soil horizon in the Basin of Mexico.

Once completed, the banks trap free-flowing drainage as it moves down the slope. Such water contains fragments of tepetate and coarse soil particles which are gradually heaped up behind the banks to form a delta of new soil. After a few years, a layer of soil 10–20 cm deep forms behind the bank for a width of 2 to 5 m, depending on the quantity of soil particles available on the slope above, and the steepness of the slope. At this time beans or barley are frequently planted. The texture of the soil in this early phase is usually quite loose, sandy, and very light in color. The maguey has, meanwhile, grown to the height of 1–1-½ m, and new terraces are being constructed above. After 5 to 10 years, the planting of barley and beans, and growth of weeds, adds organic matter to the soil; the soil depth has increased to 30–50 cm and the *tresmeseño* maize may be planted. After 10–20 years, highly productive terraces with deep, loamy, dark-colored soils have formed. The technique described is extraordinarily effective; it is doubtful that any land is completely unreclaimable using this technique in the test zone.

The majority of the terraces today have soil depths varying from 20 to 100 cm. One can see such terraces in all stages of growth and deterioration. Some are obviously new, others are abandoned and still disintegrating. Such disintegration takes place both laterally and vertically. In cases where the lateral banks have not been carefully maintained, the terrace gradually washes away from either side into an adjacent barranca, gully, canal, or down into a lower terrace. Breaches in the lower banks form easily. If a breach occurs in the lower bank of one terrace the flow of water erodes gullies in the terrace immediately below, first washing out the soil, then cutting deeply into the underlying tepetate, forming a miniature barranca. Once this process has advanced, the surface of the terrace presents an undulating appearance; water flow becomes uneven, much of it lost laterally; and the water flowing through the tiny barrancas begins to tear down the next bank below, and the process is repeated down through the terrace system. A deteriorating terrace is therefore a menace to the entire system. Terraces in a relatively advanced state of decline are usually planted in barley, if used at all, and are frequently less productive than new terraces, even with their more fertile soils, because of the loss of water. Well-kept, but still relatively new terraces (5 to 10 years old) are usually planted in barley but may have several rows of maize at the front end, where soils are deeper, and barley at the upper strip.

Another, similar technique of land reclamation which, according to local informants, was initiated approximately 50 years ago, is that of constructing check dams in the barrancas. The idea is similar to terrace building on *tepetate* slopes, except that accumulation of soil in a barranca bed is much faster than that on slopes. A low stone and earth wall is constructed across a barranca bed. In a single year enough soil accumulates behind the wall to permit barley planting. Each year the height of the wall is increased; the soil layer behind this wall increases in depth and fans back to form an increasingly more extensive delta. Finally, a wall 30–40 feet high may result and the entire barranca may be filled in with soil for distances of 30–50 m upstream behind the wall. The completed walls are impressive works, yet are the product of the labor of one farmer and a few assistants. Such check dams, if isolated, are very unstable. The erosive force of water flowing through a barranca is great and even well-built *presas,* as they are called, can be torn apart and washed downstream in a few seasons. Stability can be maintained only if a series is built, one directly below the other, so that each terrace acts as a buttress for the one just below. Once this process is completed, erosion is no more serious a problem than in ordinary terracing. There are several barrancas near Maquixco Alto and Colhuacan that have become completely silted in by this method and converted into lands as productive as any in the deep soil plains. Not only do the check dams permit the accumulation of deep soils, but such soils have higher humidity because of their location in depressed areas.

Terrace maintenance is an arduous and never-ending task. Erosion is a constant threat. Although no detailed study was made, there seems to be a very close relationship between the condition of terraces and the distance from house to land, population pressure, and degree of dependence of the landowner on agriculture for subsistence.

Prehispanic Terracing

The nature of the settlement patterns we described in Chapter 5 produces serious problems of associational dating for terracing in pre-Late Horizon times. During much of the pre-Late Horizon period the population lived in large nucleated settlements, so that virtually all of the agricultural land lay outside of the residential area. In some periods, most particularly the Late Horizon, the rural population was relatively dispersed, and one could establish a very close house to terrace association, and date the terraces, with relative ease. Theoretically, if we had a large nucleated pre-Aztec settlement in an area surrounded by remnants of abandoned terraces we could assume that the terraces dated from that time phase, but complicating the picture is the inevitable presence of a substantial Late Horizon population over and around the pre-Late Horizon site. In fact, pre-Late Horizon sites in the Basin without Late Horizon components are in a minority.

Another complication is that much of the population during the First Intermediate period resided in very gently sloping piedmont areas, and under these conditions erosion is a relatively minor problem. It is controlled today by the bancal type of terracing—a type of terracing that is very difficult, although not impossible, to detect archaeologically. We are not quite sure how the process works, but apparently terracing does have a sculptural effect on the *tepetate* below the soil layer. When soil is completely eroded off of the surface, traces of the original terrace can be detected in the underlying *tepetate* surface. In the southeast, the problem of erosion is even less, with the more abundant rainfall; weed and crop growth is sufficiently rapid to protect the soil surface much of the year; and the possibilities are high that terracing was unnecessary.

Finally, the contemporary and posthispanic populations are using the same area. This complicates terrace dating since posthispanic history involves a long period of population depression, regrowth, and recent diversion of labor to the Mexico City labor market. As a result, there has been a complex history of cycles of rebuilding and abandonment of terraces, both of the stone and earth type, and very often prehispanic terraces have been incorporated into modern terrace construction.

Vaillant (1930, 1931) reported evidence of stone terracing at the First Intermediate Phase One site of Zacatenco and at the Phase Two site of Ticoman. We have some positive evidence of stone terracing at a Phase Two site in the Patlachique range, in an area of substantial First Intermediate and very scanty Late Horizon settlement. If it does pertain to the earlier phase, it occurs relatively early in the colonization process since the region as a whole was lightly settled then. However, this particular local zone, where the site is located, is much more densely settled than average, and the site is a small village, whereas most sites at this time were hamlets. Definite stone terracing occurs at the large First Intermediate Phase One–Two community of Ecatepec, but this almost surely relates to the domestic architecture and ceremonial construction on the site rather than to agricultural land use per se.

The first convincing evidence of agricultural terracing comes from Tezoyuca complex hilltop sites and the large central communities of the Patlachique complex in the Ixtapalapa–Texcoco regions. Both types of sites date from First Intermediate Three times. The latter settlements are rather dispersed, very much in the way that Late Horizon villages are dispersed, and each house on the site has a relatively large terrace associated with it.

For the long period of Teotihuacan's dominance (First Intermediate Phase Five and Middle Horizon), we have little evidence for the presence of erosion control techniques. Within the Teotihuacan Valley there is little rural occupation outside sizable, nucleated communities. It is thus difficult to date remnants of ancient agricultural terraces by their association with datable occupational features. The only convincing evidence of stone terracing dating to this period is from the slopes of Cerro Paula in the Temascalapa region, where there are several Middle Horizon hamlets in which single house compounds are apparently associated with large terraces. These features could relate exclusively to architectural constructions, and may have little to do with agricultural practices. Elsewhere in the Basin we have failed to locate terrace remains that can be linked to the dispersed occupation of this period. This apparent dearth of terracing probably reflects the tendency for cultivators of this era to reside in gently sloping areas of maximal agricultural potential, where erosion was minimal.

For the succeeding Second Intermediate One and Three phases the problem is identical to that for the Middle Horizon. Virtually all of the population lived in a few large nucleated villages or small towns, in the case of Phase

One population, sometimes on the same site as the Middle Horizon. For the Second Intermediate Phase Two phase, when rural population was dispersed, there are numerous sites with associated terrace remains, but most of the sites have much heavier and more extensive Late Horizon occupation mixed with them, and only in a few cases do we feel reasonably sure that the terracing relates to the earlier phase.

For the Late Horizon, the evidence is conclusive, and we would estimate that virtually all the areas defined as the lower, middle, and upper piedmont, throughout the northern and central portions of the survey area, were covered with bancal or stone terraces. The Late Horizon rural settlement pattern consists of houses directly associated with terraces. In terms of the specific topographic situation, settlement within the terraced areas varied in plan and layout. The Teotihuacan Valley, for example, has a linear northeast–southwest plan; running down the center of the valley is a strip of alluvial plain bordered on each side by gently sloping piedmonts, which are flanked in turn by steep-sided hills. The northern range consists of a series of separate elevations, whereas the southern range, the Patlachique, is a solid phalanx of hills. There is virtually a continuous strip of settlement, on terraces, along the lower piedmont on the south flank of the Valley, but along the north flank the strip is discontinuous and the terraced settlements completely encircle the hills.

The topographic layout differs considerably in the Texcoco area, where there are very broad, parallel, north–south zones, ranging from the lakeshore to the flat alluvial plain, to the lower–middle piedmont, and finally to the upper piedmont and the sierra. The zones that we have defined as piedmont are covered by a continuous blanket of dispersed housemounds and terraces, with only occasional ceremonial centers breaking the continuity of what looks essentially like a single, large, rural community. The only area where the settlement pattern compares with that in the Teotihuacan Valley is on the piedmont, along the southern flank of the Patlachique Range, where the topographic situation is comparable.

The rugged piedmont south of Lakes Chalco–Xochimilco remained virtually without occupation until Late Horizon times. Even Late Horizon settlement is relatively sparse, except at the far eastern end of this zone, southeast of Lake Chalco. In this latter area there are many remnants of stone-faced terraces in close association with dispersed Late Horizon occupation in the lower–middle piedmont. Further to the west, principally in the Milpa Alta region south of Lake Xochimilco, there are large areas of well-maintained stone terraces, intensively cultivated today in nopal and other crops. We cannot be sure of the age of these terraces. However, since archaeological remains of Late Horizon are limited, we suspect that many may be posthispanic. East of Lake Chalco we encountered few terrace remnants, and virtually none are found in the Amecameca uplands far to the southeast.

The general pattern of Late Horizon terracing in the far southern piedmont seems clear enough: Terraces are numerous in zones of substantial occupation, and less significant in sparsely settled areas where land was presumably cultivated less intensively. The relatively low development of Late Horizon erosion control in the far south may also be linked to the more humid climate and heavier vegetation, with a consequent decline in the erosive power of the rains.

Irrigation: General

Canal irrigation in the Basin of Mexico has a primary and a secondary function. The primary function is to enable the cultivator to get a head start on the rainy season. The most important environmental variable that endangers crop security is the autumn frosts. In normal years when several substantial showers fall in May and the frosts are delayed until October, even the 6 months variety of maize can be squeezed into the frost-free season. The difficulty is that this ideal condition occurs only in a minimal number of years, particularly in the northern half of the Basin, and most particularly in the northern third. The areas that suffer most from the frosts are the lakeshore plain and the upper piedmont zones. The lower and middle piedmont is generally a favorable zone, with the exception of the far north, where conditions are comparable to those on the alluvial plain. Rainfall also tends to be earlier in the southern part of the Basin, and the average precipitation is higher, thus reducing the risk of frost damage to a relatively minor one, over a long period of time. The second function of irrigation is to supplement moisture, derived primarily from rainfall, during the growing season. This function is increasingly important as one moves from the southwest to the northeastern portions of the Basin, or from areas of deep to shallow soil.

Today, the basic irrigation pattern in the Basin is one in which water is conducted directly from sources to the agricultural field, and storage techniques are relatively rare and undeveloped. This system is a distinctly inefficient use of a resource. The technology is generally simple and involves the use of dams of earth and rock, brush, or masonry, along with simple ditches excavated into the soil layers or the tepetate subsoil. According to the nature of the water source, two types of irrigation exist: permanent spring based irrigation and floodwater irrigation.

The floodwater system may, at times, be unreliable. For example, most of the natural drainage of the Basin is seasonal, and a stream will frequently flow for only a few hours during and after a heavy rain shower. In the southeast, where rainfall is heavier, and where meltwater from the glaciers of Popocatepetl and Iztaccihuatl adds to the flow, streams may be permanent, or flow for several months of the year, but these conditions occur precisely where irrigation is least needed to ensure crop production.

A number of springs, however, do occur in areas where irrigation either markedly improves productivity or is necessary for dependable cropping. The largest concentration is at San Juan Teotihuacan, where 80–100 springs are located within an area of a few square kilometers; and in the 1920s these springs provided an annual average flow of approximately 1000 liters per second. Additional major sources occur above Texcoco at Amanalco, at the junction of the upper piedmont with the sierra (34 springs with a total output, in the 1920s, of 423 liters per second); along the lakeside edge of Cerro Chimalhuacan; at the sources of the Rio Cuautitlan; the Rio Tula, and above Coyoacan. The major sources of the water needed to maintain Lakes Chalco and Xochimilco at adequate levels for chinampa cultivation during the dry season were numerous springs strung along the south edge of the lakes. All of the springs just mentioned were sources for Late Horizon irrigation systems. The Texcoco and Coyoacan systems provided water for terraces on the piedmont, as well as for lands on the lakeshore plain; the Tula, Teotihuacan, and Cuautitlan systems provided water almost entirely for irrigating the alluvial plain.

The second type of irrigation in the Basin draws on numerous floodwaters from the barrancas. Floodwater irrigation can be described in terms of two basic subtypes, one in the plains and the other on the piedmont. Today, much of the piedmont is badly scarred by sheet and gulley erosion; therefore, there is an enormous volume of runoff that ultimately reaches the major portions of the river systems in the alluvial plain. In a number of areas, large terrace complexes constructed on the piedmont trap the runoff from the steeper slopes above them. Some of these arrangements are rather ingenious and sophisticated, as we noted in our descriptions of the Cerro Gordo test survey.

Because of the reduced area covered by these terraces today, much of the piedmont runoff reaches the major tributaries in the alluvial plain, where it is available for floodwater irrigation of the deep soils in the plain. A series of masonry dams with wooden gates have been constructed across the streams on the plain. When the gates are closed, the water is backed up into a large pond and immediately diverted by canals to the fields. When fields served by the canal have been irrigated, the gates are opened and the water is allowed to flow down to the next dam.

Our most detailed information on contemporary irrigation was obtained from our studies of agriculture in the Teotihuacan Valley and a more detailed analysis of irrigation is presented in what follows.

Contemporary Floodwater Irrigation in the Teotihuacan Valley

This sytem is most highly developed in the middle valley alluvial plain, but is practiced all over the Valley, where the combination of shallow barrancas and deep soil plains or gently sloping terrain occurs. In the lower valley it is a desirable auxiliary method to permanent irrigation. For effective application of this system a minimal soil depth of 50–60 cm is required and at least 1 m is desirable. The most careful preparation of the land in the entire Valley is applied with this system, because of the combination of fertile soils and irregular water resources.

Dams of loose stone, earth, or masonry are built across barrancas at selected spots where the latter are relatively shallow. Following a torrential shower, a considerable flow of water runs in the barranca. This is blocked by the dam and a temporary pond forms behind it. In most dams the water is diverted immediately into one or two primary canals. Secondary canals feed the water to the individual fields. Small temporary earth dams are built across the primary canals to divert water into the secondary canals in succession, and across the secondary canals to divert water into the individual fields (see Figure 7.7).

The individual dams and primary canals are generally small and do not provide water for more than 50–100 ha of land each. A major barranca may have a chain of five or six such dam–canal complexes. Each dam has portable wooden floodgates which are closed and opened in succession as the water moves downstream. A single dam and its canal may serve lands belonging to residents of one or two villages, and/or a hacienda, and is constructed and maintained by cooperative labor. Such cooperative groups, therefore, crosscut village membership. The variability and uncertainty of water flow made formal regulation of water distribution impractical. It is probably

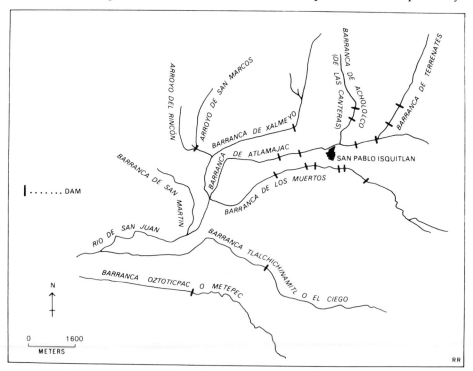

Figure 7.7. Contemporary floodwater dam system, Teotihuacan Valley. (Redrawn from Gamio 1922.)

unnecessary anyway since there is normally either no water in a barranca or more than is needed. Lands further upstream, of course, have an advantage in that water from even brief showers may be utilized. Units located well downstream are those most affected by droughts. Most haciendas in the nineteenth century were located near the headwaters to insure first rights, either for irrigation or to supply reservoirs for livestock. Quarrels and even fights over water rights, although infrequent, have occurred.

The success of the system is based on the localized nature of rainfall in the Basin and the fact that slope areas receive more rain than the plains. Therefore, by an efficient use of the system the effectiveness of the scanty rainfall is considerably improved. The system collects water from areas of marginal agricultural use and diverts it to areas of high productive capacity. Dams and primary canal construction and maintenance are cooperative tasks frequently involving people from different social communities. One of the major problems is the removal of silt. Secondary canals are maintained by small groups of farmers who use them.

Since water resources are uncertain, special techniques of working the soil have been developed to conserve the humidity. The most intensive preparation of the soil is for maize. Fields may be irrigated several times during the rainy season, but irrigation during May and the autumn months is especially valuable for the success of the system; the May irrigation to give the present year's crop a start, the autumn irrigation to store water for the following year. During the growing season, the soil is cultivated several times to keep the texture loose, facilitating downward drainage.

The depth of the soil, presence of the relatively impervious *tepetate* below, use of earth banks, careful plowing and *rastreo*, floodwater irrigation, and loose crumbly soil texture all facilitate the storage of water in the lower soil levels. The upper soil level acts as a dry mulch protecting the humidity below and by spring has the appearance of talcum powder.

Prior to 1950, these techniques were combined with a special planting method called a *cajete* or a *todo costo*. In March or April, possibly as late as May, depending on soil depth and frequency of irrigation the previous year, the land was given a *zurcada* or final plowing to loosen it for planting. Following this, small pits or *cajetes* were excavated with shovels, in the loose soil, at 50–100-cm intervals down to the level of humid layer of soil. Seeds were then planted in the humid soil and the pit partially filled with dry surface soil to seal off capillary action. The shallow depressions that remained served as catch basins for rain or irrigation water. The technique is extremely effective, but laborious. Even with metal tools it requires 80–160 man hours per hectare. Under reasonably good conditions crops may be planted as early as March or April and can withstand 60 days of drought. If water is available for at least one good irrigation in May, crop loss is very rare, even with a retarded rainy season.

Since 1950, the *cajete* technique has been rapidly replaced by a new faster method called *al tubo*. After the *zurcada*, a special steel plow, with a deeper excavating share, is used in combination with a *tubo*, as a planting drill. The *tubo* or tube is a cylinder manufactured from two maguey pencas lashed together and tied to the plow. The farmer drops the seed into the cylinder as he manipulates the plow. The plow theoretically slices down to the humid subsoil, the seed rolls down the tube to this level and the soil falls back over the seed. Most farmers feel that the *cajete* system is more dependable (since the humidity level varies and in dry years the plow probably does not reach it) but the *al tubo* method is more economical. Only 30 man hours of work are needed to plant 1 ha.

Along with these humidity-conservation practices, soil conservation is practiced as well. Much of the area where the system is applied is gently sloping so that some erosion control is necessary. Maguey is planted around most of the fields as a defense against erosion. Fields are rarely rested and most of them are in continuous cultivation. The technique of floodwater irrigation not only brings water to the field, but fresh soil in solution as well. Animal fertilizers are sparingly used, applied every 3 to 6 years. Maize is the dominant crop with wheat or barley as secondary crops frequently rotated with it. Beans are commonly interplanted with maize and, in exceptionally fertile soils, barley and wheat are sown broadcast between the rows of maize.

The result is a highly productive, intensive system of agriculture. At San Pablo Izquitlan, one of the informants stated that in a 10-year period, in 7 years a field yielded fair to good maize crops with production ranging from 900 to 1500 kg (kilograms) per hectare; 3 years were considered poor, with yields ranging from 600 to 750 kg (during these years unirrigated lands were a total loss). The average yield over a 10-year period is probably around 1000 kg per hectare. The same informant also stated that the mentioned 10-year period (1945-1954) was the poorest in the 30 years he had cultivated the land.

Specific data from other fields at San Pablo and San Martin tend to confirm these figures. The Secretario Ejidal of San Martin in 1953 estimated that if the floodwater system was managed with maximal efficiency, the alluvial plain of the Middle Valley (called locally "La Vega") should yield an average of 1200–1500 kg per hectare. This figure, then, would represent a theoretical maximal productivity in terms of present-day technology and climate.

Permanent Irrigation in the Teotihuacan Valley Today

Approximately 80 springs, with a permanent water flow, are located at San Juan Teotihuacan, in the two barrios of Puxtla and Maquixco. Gamio's field group (Gamio 1922) estimated an annual flow of 31,000,000 m^3 of water. The measured flow of water in December at that time (1922) was 1500 liters per second (at the end of the rainy season). They estimated a probable average flow of 1000. In 1954, the output had dropped to an average of 588.6 liters per second. The decline is apparently due to perforation of artesian wells up-valley by large landowners. In 1963, the flow further declined to 450 liters and a recent study by Recursos Hidraulicos (1975) reported a further decline to 382 liters. (The reader is referred to Figure 7.8 for the following discussion.)

The system is primarily one of drainage and is technologically simple. Water is collected from the springs by means of small earthen ditches and

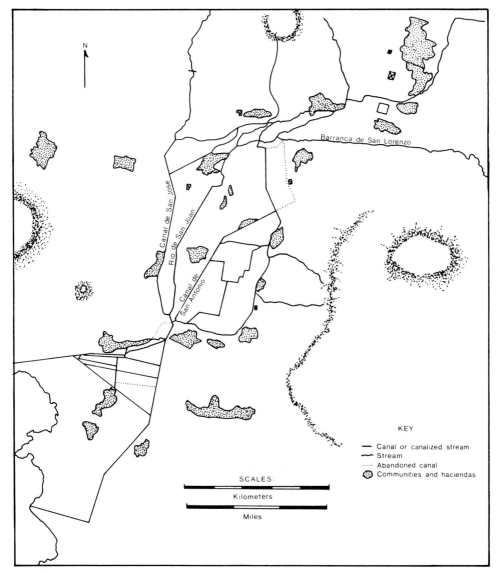

Figure 7.8. Contemporary permanent irrigation system, lower Teotihuacan Valley. (After Millon 1962.)

diverted into a single canal immediately above Maquixco. Below Maquixco, at a place called "La Taza," the canal divides into two main branches, the canal of San Antonio, with an average flow of 200.26 liters per second, and San Jose Canal, with 287.32 (in 1954). There are also two smaller canals that derive their water from local springs at Maquixco, the canal of Texcalac (50.36 liters per second), and Cadena (12.66 liters per second). Near Atlatongo are some very small springs at a place called "El Tular" that provide an additional 2 liters.

Before the agrarian reforms, the water was controlled by the four big haciendas of Cadena, San Jose, San Antonio, and Santa Catarina. After the reform, it fell under the jurisdiction of the Mexican government, and a set of water regulations was designed to administer the system. Fifteen villages or barrios and five haciendas or ranchos cultivate lands supplied by the system, with a total area under irrigation in 1954 of 3652 ha, of which 3373 were assigned to the villages and barrios. Two barrios of San Juan Teotihuacan also use the water directly from the springs before it reached La Taza. The 15 villages and the haciendas and ranchos are organized into a Junta, called the *Junta de Los Pueblos de los Aguas de los Manantiales de San Juan*, with its center at Calvario Acolman. The primary function of the Junta is to implement the water regulation laws established by the federal government. It does not have the power to change them.

The holdings of each village are divided into two divisions, *pequeña propiedad* and *ejido*. These broad divisions may also be broken up into water distribution units depending on which canal supplies the water. The Junta meets monthly and consists of one elected representative from each hacienda or rancho and two from each village and barrio (one for the *ejido*, the other for the *pequeña propiedad*), who in turn elect a president. Water is assigned on a day, hour, minute schedule from each canal for each of the large units, such as the *ejido* or *pequeña propiedad* of a particular village. The large units in turn have an internal regulation system by land holdings. In 1954 it required approximately 4 hours to irrigate 1 ha of land from the San Antonio Canal.

As we have emphasized previously, most irrigation in the Teotihuacan Valley involves a single preplanting flooding of the field to give the crop a head start on the growing season. Most of the humidity for plant growth is derived from the summer rains. The importance of this preplanting irrigation is clearly demonstrated by the concern of the individual farmer over his share, especially the timing, and the almost continuous disputes between villages over water theft. Since most of the moisture used by the crop is based on rainfall, however, the relatively small amount of water flowing from the springs goes a long way, and involves a far greater number of people and communities than would be the case in a desert valley.

Each farmer in the valley receives water normally once or twice a year. Using the figure of four hours of water needed per hectare from one of the main canals, theoretically the system could be used to irrigate 6570 ha of land. Actually the situation is not quite as favorable, as far as maize or other prehispanic crops are concerned. Maize is ordinarily planted no earlier than March 1 and no later than June 1 for maximum efficiency, or over a period of 3 months. If preplanting irrigations for maize were confined to that period this would mean only 1640 ha of land could be irrigated for maize per year. Actually, lands can be irrigated as early as January 1 or as late as June 15 and still be planted in maize. In the case of the former, the lands are flooded in January or February, but planting is delayed until March. The soil is thoroughly worked and prepared to store the water in the manner noted for the Middle Valley. Each farmer receives his share at a different time each year to avoid unfair assignments, since the ideal time for planting is May and that for irrigation is March. The total amount of irrigable land for maize then ascends to 3005 ha. The amount of land classified by the Junta as *tierra de riego* is close to these figures. The situation is further alleviated by the fact that some prehispanic crops, such as beans, mature faster than maize, and can be irrigated as late as June or July. It is very probable that in prehispanic times lands that were irrigated as early as December or January or as late as June were planted with crops that were less demanding than maize. If Gamio's data are to be trusted, all of these figures would need revising upward 80% with the former greater flow of water (1000 liters per second).

Today a number of farmers raise small herds of dairy cattle and plant their fields in alfalfa or clover. Some European crops, such as wheat, are frost resistant and are therefore grown during the winter season so that there is a high percentage of land that is double-cropped. The usual pattern is to plant maize in the spring, followed by wheat in the fall, followed by a single summer barley crop the second year, without irrigation. The exact order is a highly flexible one based on the number and timing of irrigations in a given year. If maize and wheat are to be grown in a single year, at least three rations of water are required, since wheat grown during the dry season would require two irrigations (during preplanting and again during the growing season). One of the villages, Atlatongo (Figure 7.11) had special rights to a continuous flow of water (38.0 liters per second) from the San Jose Canal. This claim was apparently based on a resurrected colonial document and is a constant source of dispute.

The alluvial plain below the springs is traversed by a vast network of secondary and tertiary canals, each of which must be cleaned annually. The main canals and springs are cleaned by all of the villages, under the direction of the Junta, in September and October. Each village sends its own allotment of men, and the total number of workers may be as high as 800. Secondary and tertiary canals are cleaned by smaller work gangs involving farmers who use the particular canal. On this level the work is as informally organized as in the Middle Valley.

Characteristic then of the system is a pyramid of cooperative work gangs that acts as a powerful integrative factor on the infracommunity, community, and supracommunity levels. The system also, however, has disruptive qualities that produce community rivalry and conflict. Water theft is the primary source of conflict, and verbal disputes are frequent, at times turning into physical conflict, as Millon and his coworkers have demonstrated (Millon *et al*. 1962). This combination of integrative and disruptive effects of the administration of the system has theoretical significance, as we shall demonstrate at a later point.

Techniques of preparation of the soil are similar to those used with floodwater irrigation, including multiple plowing, use of earth banks, crop rotation, fertilizers, *cajete* or *al tubo* planting, and interplanting. An additional technique for fertilizing the land was once used by the haciendas. This involved annual flooding of the land with water from the barranca system, to introduce fresh soil, since the spring water was relatively free of sediments. It was called *enlame* (see Gamio 1922).

Yields of maize vary considerably, depending on the date of planting and the quality of the rainy season. At Atlatongo, the most favorably located community, production ranged from 900–2700 kg per hectare with a probable mode of 1500–2250 over a 10-year span. Over a 2-year period, a 1-ha field in the irrigated plain near Atlatongo averages 1875 kg of maize, 1400 kg of wheat, and 1400 kg of barley, plus small quantities of interplanted beans and squash. At Acolman, at the mouth of the Lower Valley, average maize yields drop to 1350 kg and wheat to 1200. These figures are undoubtedly more applicable to the irrigated plain as a whole.

Prehispanic Irrigation

With respect to the Late Horizon we have abundant documentary data to rely on. Palerm (1955) and Palerm and Wolf (1961b, 1961c, 1961d) have summarized the information on permanent, spring based irrigation systems in the Basin of Mexico at the moment of the Spanish Conquest. The evidence is convincing, first that all of the major resources were fully utilized, and second that the basic structure, in terms of major canals, areas served by them, and villages participating in their use, was very comparable to the contemporary systems.

Taking the Teotihuacan system as a case example, according to the data from the Relaciones Geográficas, the system, in 1579, extended from the springs all the way to the lakeshore. The following is a series of quotes from the Relación de Tecciztlan (Paso y Troncoso 1905b):

> 4. *Esta asentada la cauesera de aculma en un llano, al pie de una loma alta, es raso no tiene nengun fuente, pasa per el dicho pueblo el rio que dizen San Juan, dividido en tres asequias de agua con quien riegan gran pedaza de tierra casi una legua en largo e medio en ancho; es fertil de pastos y de mantenimyentos.*
> 19. *Pasa por el dicho pueblo de aculma el rio que llama de San Juan, partido en quatro asequias, illeuara cada una de ellos dos bueyes de agua, rriegase an ella un legua de tierra.*
> 4. . . . *beben las naturales de jagueyes, acepto la Cabecera ques abuindosa de agua, tiene muchos fuentes an poco trecho de que procede un rio grande en la qual tienen las naturales un molino, rieganse con el agua del dicho rio dos leguas de tierra, que toda su corriente hasta entrar en la laguna, pasando per los pueblos de*

*aculma, tepexpa y tequisistlan, termino con tescuco; es tierra abundosa do pasto
y mantenimyentos.*

   3. *El temple de tequisistlan es frio y umido por estar asentado serca de la
laguna grande entre asequias de agua.*

   19. *Pasa par la parte de leuante del dico pueblo de tequisistlan el rio que
llama de San Juan, en una asequia onda dos tiros del dicho pueblo; rriegan con el
casi medio legua de tierra.*

   3. *El temple y calidad de la cauesera de tepexpa es frio y umydo por estar
asentado en baxo la major parte del, y entre asequias de agua. . . .*

   19. *No thiene rrio ny fuente, solo pasa por el pueblo el rrio que llaman de
San Juan, deudido en dos asequias de agua, con que se rriega distancia de media
legua de tierra del dicho pueblo de tepexpa.*

[4. The town of Acolman is located in a plain; at the foot of a high ridge;
it is cleared land; does not have any permanent water sources; a river called
the San Juan passes by the town; it is divided into three canals of water,
from which they irrigate a large piece of land, almost a league long and half
a league wide; it is fertile in pasture and crop land.

   19. The river, called San Juan, passes by the said town of Acolman, is
divided into four canals, each of which carries two bueyes[2] of water, a
league of land is irrigated from them.

   4. The natives drink from jagueys[3], except in the town (i.e., San Juan
Teotihuacan), which has an abundance of water; it has many springs
within a short distance of each other, from which flows a great river within
which the natives have a mill; two leagues of land are irrigated from the
same river; along its entire length before it reaches the lagune, it passes by
the towns of Acolman, Tepexpan, and Tequisistlan; it borders with Texcoco; it is a land abundant in pasture and crop land.

   3. The climate of Tequisistlan is cold and humid, because it is situated
near the great lagune, among canals of water.

   19. A river called the San Juan passes to the east of the town of
Tequisistlan, through a deep canal, which runs two crossbow shots from
the town; from it almost half a league of land is irrigated.

   3. The climate and quality of the town of Tepexpan is cold and humid
because the major part of it is situated in a low area among canals of water.

   19. It has no river or spring, only the river called San Juan passes by the
town, divided into two canals of water, from which is irrigated a half a
league of land of the said town of Tepexpan.]

From the "Abecedario de las Visitas" (Paso y Troncoso 1905a), dating
from the 1540s, we have a description of the town of Tepexpan: "This town is
located on a little hill; it has little irrigated land; it extends 800 brazas in
length by 640 in width, which are in total 1200 [sic] brazas."

The total population utilizing the Teotihuacan system in 1580 was, we
estimate, only 8000 persons. The town and nearby villages of Atlatongo
possessed approximately 1200 ha of irrigated land at that time, and had 1500
tributaries—that is, 0.8 ha per tributary. This would amount to approximately 2.4 ha per extended family of seven persons, a reasonable holding in
terms of our estimates of labor costs and crop yields. The fact that com-

---

[2]A buey of water was a colonial Spanish measure of flow of water 1 yard in diameter.
[3]Reservoirs used to store rainwater.

munities as far below the springs as Tequisistlan were using the system suggests that it was built for a much more substantial population. Our calculation of the population of the same area at the time of the Conquest is approximately 24,000 people, with 7300 tributaries. Supposing that in all of the villages utilizing this system, the average household held 0.8 ha, as in 1580, then there were 5840 ha under irrigation in 1519. These figures also suggest the production of a substantial surplus. If we estimate the average yield per hectare as 1400 kilos, then the total production of this land would be 8,176,000 kilos, enough to supply a population of 51,000 people with their daily maize requirements. These figures check very well with our experimental studies of work input and productivity, and they demonstrate the unusual significance of the irrigated land in the Basin in terms of the support of large urban communities. In contrast to permanent irrigation, we have virtually no documentary references to floodwater irrigation. This is hardly surprising since much of our information on permanent irrigation is the accidental product of legal disputes over water in situations where the water supply could be controlled, or in the form of geographic surveys, where the interest of the crown was in controllable resources.

With respect to archaeological evidence of irrigation the problem of dating is both simpler and more complex than the dating of terracing, and some of the factors that complicate the problem are the same. For example, the tendency of populations in some phases to live in large nucleated centers complicates the problem of association, as does the common association of Late Horizon occupation with the pre-Late Horizon sites where the canals are found. As we pointed out, abundant ethnohistoric documentation indicates that irrigation was highly developed in the Late Horizon. The major question is the date of its inception and the relationship of its development to cultural evolution in the Basin as a whole. We will address ourselves to this latter question in the succeeding chapter. Here we are concerned only with the archaeological evidence for its appearance.

With respect to overall field strategy we decided to follow a lead suggested by René Millon (1957) in his analysis of a small floodwater system north of Atlatongo in the Teotihuacan Valley. Millon argued that the population of the Teotihuacan Valley would first have utilized the big permanent lower valley system because of its dependable water supply; only at a later date would the people have harnessed the more marginal floodwater sources. If we could date the marginal systems, therefore, it would provide us with a minimal antiquity for the main system. This approach was most attractive, since the technical problems of trying to locate and excavate ancient settlements and canal systems in the deep soil plain, still being intensively cultivated today, were many and complicated. Furthermore, the principal canals in the main system, which probably have not shifted position since they were first utilized, have been periodically sedimented and dredged, thus presenting enormous problems for stratigraphic control. We would have been forced to locate secondary or tertiary canals of the system that would relate to landholding units, which obviously would change from period to period. This is a virtually hopeless task without sophisticated aerial photography.

One problem with Millon's assumption is the possibility that some of the smaller systems might have had permanent water supplies in the past. Hence, they might have been utilized before the main system, which would have involved a considerably greater input of manpower resources to build and maintain. This would be particularly true of the smaller systems that served areas of higher, better drained, and fertile soils, where the cost of cultivation would be minimal.

The piedmont seemed an ideal area to search for small, marginal systems, since erosion would have exposed any ditch systems cut into the tepetate and conceivably would have left some remains of dams along the streams. The major problem lay in the strategy of associational dating. Late Horizon occupation is widespread, and since most pre-Late Horizon sites have Late Horizon occupations as well, the dating of an abandoned hydraulic work is always difficult. The fact that the Late Horizon witnessed the peak population for the Valley only intensifies the problem. As we have already noted, Late Horizon piedmont settlement is of the type that enables us easily to date terraces, and in some cases their associated canals. In general, pre-late Horizon settlements were comparable to those found today—compact settlements with the agricultural land lying almost entirely outside the settlement. On the piedmont, therefore, the neat house-to-terrace-to-branch canal type of associational dating cannot be used. Furthermore, most of the systems were so small that they served a single settlement, and the longer ones were preserved only in fragments. Thus, the technique of dating by settlement alignment to canal was generally not possible. Finally, to complicate the problem, many of the systems have gone through multiple uses and modifications, including use by the present-day population. Millon's (1957) excavation of one of these systems exemplifies the problem, and he does suggest a possible pre-Late Horizon use of this system.

An indirect, but more equivocal method of estimating the use of hydraulic resources is to study population history in small local areas. In other words, the closer a prehispanic population size, within a small area (say, 10–20 km^2) approximates the modern size, then the greater the likelihood that a comparable system of land use was in vogue. There are, of course, numerous technical problems in reconstructing population size from archaeological data, and furthermore, as we shall see in Chapter 9, this type of reconstruction tends to lead to circularity of argument.

In a number of cases the particular archaeological situation was such that a convincing case could be made for a pre-Late Horizon dating of a system. In order to acquaint the reader more fully with the methodological problems, we present a detailed description of one of these systems, on the north slope of Cerro Gordo (Figure 7.9).

It begins with a major tributary barranca that flows between Cerros

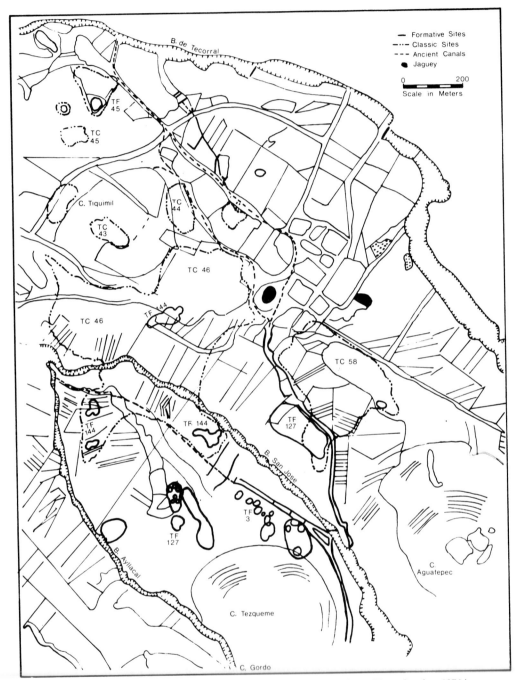

Figure 7.9. Prehispanic irrigation system on Cerro Gordo, north slope. (From Sanders 1976.)

Aguatepec and Tezqueme. Below the hills the barranca goes north for a distance of approximately 1 km, then swings to the west and, after an additional kilometer, joins another major barranca that begins between Cerro Tezqueme and Cerro Tlacuache Grande. All drainage in this area ultimately flows into a main stream called the Barranca de Tecorral, which runs below the village of Maquixco Alto. Between Cerros Aguatepec and Tezqueme, the barranca has a depth of nearly 20 m and is 40–60 m wide. At this point a canal intake (the west canal) departs from the barranca and runs parallel to it. The canal can be traced for a distance of 500 m before it vanishes in an extensive area of *tepetate* wash. On aerial photographs (but not on the ground) it can be traced across the wash until it joins another barranca east of Cerro Teclalo. Since the canal, at and for a distance of 100 m from the intake, is 2–4 m deep, it could only have functioned as a canal when the barranca was a shallow stream. There must have been a dam across the stream when the canal was functioning, but the lateral erosion that occurred when the stream widened has destroyed any traces of it. Following the downcutting of the barranca, the canal apparently continued to function as a natural drainage tract; today it is 10–20 m wide and has an undulating plan. It appears, therefore, more like a barranca than a canal; in fact, it is considered and treated as such by the contemporary peasants, who have constructed a series of check dams within it. The lower portion of the canal, that is, the portion where it shifts direction, runs along the southern or upper edge of the big Middle Horizon village site TC46. Below the last check dam and before entering the *tepetate* area, the canal widens and decreases in depth.

A second canal (the east canal) departs from the same barranca between Cerros Aguatepec and Tezqueme, but on the opposite side and at a point 100 m upstream from the west canal. It flows northeast and is easily traced for a distance of 800 n to the upper edge of the village of Maquixco Alto. For the first 500 m the east canal appears as a narrow, shallow trench that could still function today if the barranca had not incised its bed so deeply. It then enters a wide, deeply scarred wash between two functional modern–Aztec terrace systems. At the point where the canal enters the village, it has deeply incised its bed.

Two large contemporary check dams have been constructed within the east canal bed and, as in the case of the west canal, it looks more like a small barranca than a canal. Below the check dam the water enters a great tepetate wash area near the village jaguey, to which some of the drainage is diverted. Below the jaguey the drainage diverges to follow two tracts, each presently serving as a village street–road. We are convinced that these streets are old canal beds that became floodwater drainage tracts after they ceased to function as permanent canals. Today, they are utilized not only as streets, but also as floodwater canals for the terraces in the west and northwest edge of the village. The lower one is of particular interest. It flows 150 m northeast and makes a sharp turn to the northwest, where it flows for 300 m. It then angles across several modern fields. In passing across one field, the canal has incised its bed deeply—in fact, two contemporary check dams have been constructed over it. The canal, cut down into the *tepetate,* can be seen, distinctly, running under the check dam wall. In its course through the fields it is 280 m long. Once out of the fields, the canal appears as a shallow barranca running between a set of contemporary terraces on the west, and a large unterraced field on the east; it then enters the Barranca de Tecorral. This last section is 250 m long. The total length of the lower canal is a little over 2 km.

After leaving the jaguey area, the upper canal parallels the lower, with the distance between the two varying from 100 to 150 m. It flows about 800 m, then enters the same barranca as the lower canal, but downstream. Sections of it, as in the case of the upper canal, serve as contemporary village roads and floodwater drainage tracts; the lower portion is still used to supply the set of terraces noted above in our description of the upper canal. The terraces are bordered on both sides by the two ancient canals. The entire drainage pattern is easily traced on aerial photos, particularly on large-scale photos. With respect to morphology, the canals are clearly nonfunctional over most of their lengths in terms of the present-day terrace–floodwater systems. In fact, as we pointed out, they are treated as barrancas. It is equally obvious that they are not natural, since they flow diagonally, and connect parts of the natural stream systems.

The present system of cultivation in the Cerro Gordo area was described on page 246. Basically, it involves the construction of sets of vertical terraces separated by shallow floodwater canals. Water is diverted from the canals into each terrace by small earth embankments that enter the canal; the system is self-flooding. The older portions of the contemporary systems are in part remnants of the Late Horizon system, which functioned in much the same way. Although a great deal of the old system has been obliterated by erosion, its remnants are visible everywhere. In some cases, the contemporary villages are recolonizing these eroded areas and building new systems that are morphologically identical with the old ones.

The ancient canal system we have described is quite different in character, since the canals led water directly from major streams and were presumably filled by means of a dam built across the barranca. In this respect, the system is more like the floodwater irrigation system of the Alluvial Plain in the Middle Valley or the permanent system in the Lower Valley. It could only have worked at a time when the barrancas were shallow, narrow, semipermanent or permanent streams. Not only is the system morphologically different from the Late Horizon and contemporary systems, but, to judge from Colonial documents pertaining to the area, many of the deep barrancas were already formed in Late Horizon times. The canals therefore must be pre-Late Horizon. Assuming this to be the case, the precise dating remains the major problem.

Second Intermediate Phase Two occupation is considerable in the area; in fact, the upper part of the east canal flows through the center of TT36, and the lower part through the largest Phase Two site in the area, TT35. There are Second Intermediate Phase Two sites associated with the west canal.

By far the most massive occupation of the area served by the two canals is that of the Middle Horizon. The east canal runs along the southwest edge of TC58, a densely settled village site measuring 8 ha. Flowing along the northeast edge of TC46, a huge village of 25 ha, is the lower part of the canal, with each of its lower branches running past two Middle Horizon hamlets, TC64 and TC45. Immediately before the canals enter the Barranca de Tecorral, the upper branch flows by the cluster of Middle Horizon hamlets TC63, TC60, TC62, and TC61. The lower portion of the west canal flows along the entire south edge of the large village site TC46. In view of the very heavy Middle Horizon occupation of the area and the closeness of the canal system to it, the canals probably date from this period. There is, however, a good possibility that they date from as early as First Intermediate Phase Four times, since at least five Phase Four hamlets have been found within a short distance of the canal system (TF3, TF72, TF144, TF127, and TF202).

Great numbers of similar canals were located in the piedmont, particularly in the Teotihuacan Valley, Temascalapa, Cuautitlan, and Tenayuca regions. The remnants of canal systems found in these regions were primarily parts of floodwater systems, with few possible exceptions, and were of less economic and political significance than the large, permanent irrigation systems in the alluvial plain, but at least they provide evidence that there was manipulation of water resources.

By the method of associational dating described in the case of the Cerro Gordo–North Slope system, those systems we located seem to pertain to the Late Horizon, Second Intermediate One, First Intermediate Five, and Middle Horizon. In only a few cases would it be possible to verify this associational dating by excavation. Most of the systems, since they are in the eroded piedmont, involve canals that are deeply cut into the tepetate. In the case of a system excavated by Millon, the lower reaches of it enter the alluvial plain and hence excavation was feasible. In the 1974 season, we located a small floodwater irrigation system in the alluvial plain on the west shore of Lake Texcoco, near the village of Santa Clara Coatitlan (Sanders and Santley 1977). In the profile of a huge modern earth extraction pit were a series of stratified canals. They appeared at depths of 1 to 5 m below the present land surface. Above the uppermost canal was an occupation layer that included material from the Second Intermediate One to the Late Horizon. Excavations in 1977 revealed that all of the canals were of the First Intermediate One B phase, considerably earlier than our expectation, although one of the largest sites in the local area does date from that phase.

Near the Late Horizon town of Otumba, again in the plain, a road cut has exposed a series of stratified floodwater canals. Small scale excavations conducted by Thomas Charlton in 1977 suggest that the system was initiated in First Intermediate Three times and was reused in the Middle Horizon,

Second Intermediate Two, and Late Horizon phases, although the excavations, and the samples associated with the canals, are small, so that this dating must be accepted with caution.

With respect to the permanent irrigation of the alluvial plains, the problem is, as we have pointed out, acute. Several lines of data suggest strongly that the Teotihuacan system dates at least as far back as the Middle Horizon, and possibly as early as First Intermediate Phase Four times. First, the city covered about 20 km² at its peak and was traversed by a network of natural tributaries, as well as by the San Juan River itself. This entire network was canalized and accommodated to the rather rigid plan of the city, suggesting large-scale manipulation of water systems by the Teotihuacanos. Second, the location of the city at the head of the spring system (and, as Mooser, in Lorenzo [1968] postulates, some springs were entirely within the city) in a comparable position to the Late Horizon town is highly suggestive. Third, the Tepantitla murals show canals and small rectangular gardens, structured similar to the chinampa-like fields that are found today near the springs. Finally, the large size of Teotihuacan suggests intensive use of agricultural resources.

Millon's latest surveys (Millon *et al.* 1973a,b) have located a system of reservoirs and canals that would have served the needs of the urban population, again confirming the fact that the Teotihuacan population did engage in hydraulic works on a large scale. The Middle Horizon settlement pattern, in which the bulk of the farming population apparently lived in the city and traveled back and forth to outlying fields, of course complicates the problem of dating canal systems. The modern, Second Intermediate Phase One and, to a certain extent, the Late Horizon populations formed a series of settlements along the edges of the alluvial plain and an additional string of settlements down the center. Although we did not locate any Middle Horizon settlements, we did find suggestions of use of the irrigation system in the form of light surface concentrations of Middle Horizon pottery along several of the major contemporary canals.

The strongest argument for the use of the irrigation system prior to the Late Horizon, however, lies in our pollen graphs from El Tular (see Figure 7.10), a small spring near Atlatongo, and from Cuanalan, at the lower end of the irrigation system. Our reasoning was that in the area around the springs, before the construction of the irrigation system, there must have been a vegetation adapted to swampy conditions. Today this area of high water table has been converted to a system of chinampas, which covers a maximum of only 100 ha. Since the El Tular spring is located well down-valley from the contemporary high-water-table area, the pollen profile suggests that this environmental niche was once considerably larger, perhaps having a maximal extent of about 1000 ha.

Particularly significant in the graph is the behavior of a group of plants called *Cyperaceae*, or sedges, which live under swampy conditions. In the lower levels of the graph (from 3 to 6 m below the surface), *Cyperaceae* make up

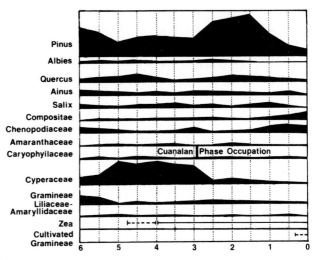

Figure 7.10. Pollen profile, El Tular, Teotihuacan Valley. (After Kovar 1970.)

to 30% of the pollen sample, leading us to conclude that sedges were the dominant plants all over the spring area before its drainage for irrigation. At the 2.5–3-m level the percentage suddenly and dramatically drops to perhaps 7% of the total sample, then gradually declines to reach a low point of 3% in the uppermost level. The most likely explanation for such a reduction is artificial drainage of the swamps. El Tular is a small spring located 2.5 km down-valley from the main cluster of springs at San Juan, indicating that the drainage project had evolved to include land at least that far down-valley. Following the initial reduction, the rest of the profile shows a steady decline in moisture around the springs up to the time of the Spanish Conquest, a reflection of further change and expansion of the irrigation system down-valley.

By comparing the pollen profile from El Tular with one taken at Cuana-lan, which can be directly correlated with the First Intermediate Phase Two occupation there, we have been able to relate the El Tular graph to the history of settlement in the Valley. The rapid reduction of sedge pollen at El Tular apparently dates from the First Intermediate Three phase, thus strikingly agreeing with the known history of settlement in the Valley. Also supporting this interpretation is the fact that maize pollen appears slightly before the time of the sudden reduction of the frequency of sedges.

Our impression is that much of the intensively cultivated land in the Teotihuacan Valley in the First Intermediate Phase Three was probably similar in morphology to the chinampas presently found near the San Juan springs. Today, because of the overall desiccation of the Valley, only 100 ha of land can be cultivated as chinampas. During Phase Three and the succeeding Phase Four, and even into the Middle Horizon, the area of high water table could have been considerably greater.

In summary, therefore, our data suggest (*a*) an inception of chinampa cultivation in the spring area and possible irrigation down-valley in the vicinity of Cuanalan during the First Intermediate Phase Two; (*b*) a striking expansion of chinampa cultivation in First Intermediate Phase Three times; and (*c*) a rapid expansion, possibly to the maximal size of the main irrigation system, down-valley during the First Intermediate Phase Four, and most certainly by Tlamimilolpa times (Early Middle Horizon).

With respect to the Cuautitlan river irrigation system, there is indirect evidence that it was utilized during the Middle Horizon. In the fifteenth century the ruler of Cuautitlan diverted the river northwest into Lake Zumpango to protect the town against flooding and to divert water for irrigation in the vicinity of the town. According to recent ethnohistoric studies the river once flowed due east into Lake Xaltocan (Rojas *et al.* 1974). A striking feature of the Middle Horizon settlement is the heavy concentration of sites parallel to the old middle course of the Cuautitlan River. This includes one of the regional centers, two large nucleated villages, one large dispersed village, and two small nucleated villages. Some distance to the north, but nevertheless within easy access of the alluvial plain crossed by the river, is a provincial center, on Cerro Tultepec. In fact if one compares the settlement distribution during this period it corresponds very closely to the Second Intermediate, Late Horizon, and modern settlement distribution in the lower part of the Teotihuacan Valley (see Figures 7.11 and 7.12). It is important to note here that in the case of the Teotihuacan Valley these occupations are clearly related to the use of the lower valley alluvial plain for permanent irrigation. The pattern involves two strings of villages on each side of the alluvial plain, plus several villages on high spots in the center of the plain. The Teotihuacan occupation of the Cuautitlan Basin reproduces this pattern and there is a strong probability that the Cuautitlan irrigation system functioned on a large scale during this period. Additional confirmation of our conclusion lies in the fact that the First Intermediate population distribution is completely unlike the Middle Horizon one, indicating revolutionary changes in the exploitive strategy.

We have no direct evidence on the history of the Amanalco system above Texcoco, but our settlement history strongly suggests that permanent irrigation appeared in the area during the First Intermediate Three phase. The problem of dating here is complicated by the technical simplicity of the system. In the 1920s the total flow of water from the various springs amounted to 423–433 liters per second. Two clusters of springs, one with a flow of 280 liters per second and the other with 23 liters per second, were located at the headwaters of the Papalotla River and would normally flow into this tributary. An additional two clusters of springs, at the headwaters of the Jalapango River, produced a flow of 68–78 liters per second; and four clusters of small springs, with a total flow of 52 liters per second, are at the headwaters of the Coxacuaco River (see Figure 7.13). In Late Horizon times the water from the Papalotla sources was collected, the flow divided in half and only half allowed to enter the river

Figure 7.11. Aerial photograph of the lower Teotihuacan Valley irrigation system. (Courtesy of CIA Mexicana Aerofoto S.A.)

system. The balance was diverted into an artificial canal, into which was also collected the water from the other two river systems. The water was ultimately diverted into two major canals, each providing water for a separate set of communities.

The headwaters of these streams today, as was probably the case in Late Horizon times as well, are all deeply incised barrancas, and the movement of

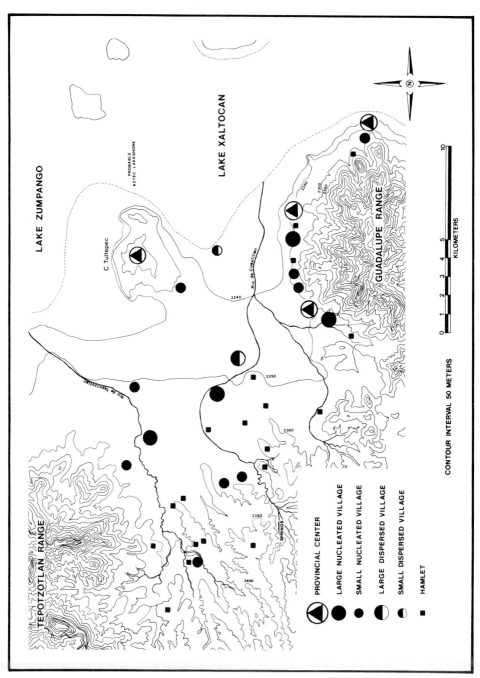

LAKE ZUMPANGO

LAKE XALTOCAN

TEPOTZOTLAN RANGE

GUADALUPE RANGE

C. Tultepec

PROBABLE
AZTEC LAKESHORE

Rio de Cuautitlan

Rio de Tepotzotlan

SPRINGS

2240

2250

2300

2350

2400

2250
2300
2350

PROVINCIAL CENTER

LARGE NUCLEATED VILLAGE

SMALL NUCLEATED VILLAGE

LARGE DISPERSED VILLAGE

SMALL DISPERSED VILLAGE

HAMLET

CONTOUR INTERVAL 50 METERS

0 1 2 3 4 5   10
KILOMETERS

Figure 7.12. The Cuautitlan region, showing Middle Horizon settlement.

water from the sources to the fields below requires a complex network of artificial canals, in some cases massive aqueducts, to carry water across ravines. We suspect that much of this erosion is recent, and, that in First Intermediate times, these barrancas were shallow streams. If this was the case, all that the First Intermediate population had to do was to divert water directly from the three streams, by short feeder canals, into the lower piedmont areas, where most of the cultivated land was found. Under these conditions the majority of the flow would have entered the Papalotla River.

In the First Intermediate Three times there were approximately 25,000 people living in the Texcoco region. Approximately 60% of this population lived in the lower–middle piedmont, or the alluvial plain of the Papalotla River, areas which could have been served by the irrigation system. A much smaller cluster of population was located near the village of Coatepec where there are small springs today, used primarily by households. A substantial increase in flow would have provided significant water resources for irrigated land for this cluster. A substantial percentage of the Phase Three population also resided at Chimalhuacan, where there were considerable opportunities for drainage agriculture. Only one cluster of Phase Three settlements, east of Coatlinchan, is unrelated to any present day hydraulic resources. However, there has been substantial erosion of the slopes in this latter area, and it is conceivable that there were springs in the past, which no longer function. In fact, the recent history of the Amanalco system shows a steady loss of small springs as a product of the erosion process and the consequent aridization of the valley.

Finally, Palerm and Wolf (1961) report canal traces under the lava flow at Cuicuilco which they have dated as no later than the First Intermediate Two phase. This dating was based on the assumption that the lava flow dated from that phase. Later research, however, has shown that the lava did not cover the entire area and parts of the Cuicuilco area were still agriculturally viable as late as the First Intermediate Five, so that the canals could have dated from this later period. On the other hand, the maximal population was achieved during Phase Three and the probability is therefore very high that the canals date from that phase.

Drainage Agriculture

Another type of hydraulic agriculture practiced in the Basin today, and during the Late Horizon, is drainage agriculture. Immediately along the lakeshore, and in some areas removed from the shore, much of the alluvial plain was characterized by a serious drainage problem at the time of agricultural colonization of the Basin. Local situations varied from swampy conditions, to lands which would be classified by farmers today as *tierra de humedad,* lands that have sufficiently high water table to maintain adequate soil moisture most of the year. These lands can be converted to very productive agricultural lands by a system of drainage ditches, using the seasonal

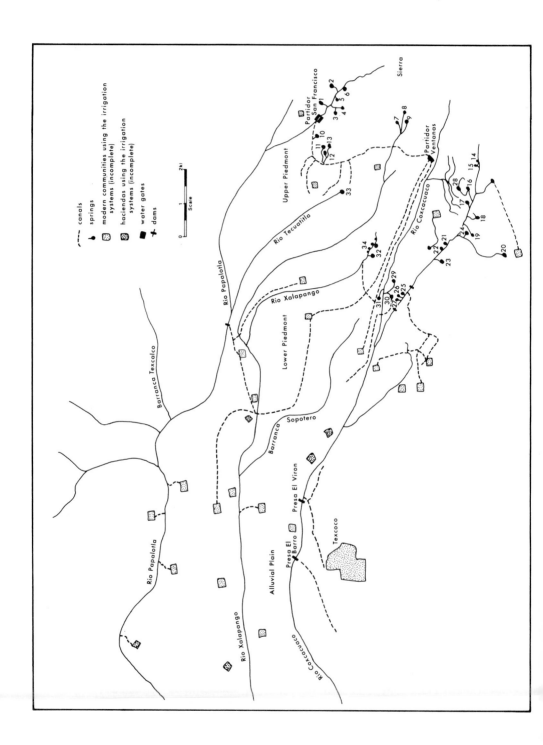

streams as outlets. Once the water table is sufficiently lowered, the same set of ditches can often be used to supplement moisture by floodwater irrigation.

This type of cultivation, however, requires substantial labor input on the part of the individual farmer, and the construction of large scale, complex ditch networks—what we have described as capital works—that would have required a considerable degree of organization as well. One would expect therefore, that colonization of such areas would be retarded, compared to the more easily controlled adjacent piedmont. Since the Spanish Conquest, and most particularly since 1900, as the product of further deforestation, erosion, drainage projects, capture of springs for the urban water supply, and the perforation of deep wells, the water table all over the Basin has steadily dropped and the zone of *tierra de humedad* has correspondingly been reduced to insignificance.

Extensive areas of this type of terrain in the Basin of Mexico lie east of Lake Texcoco, along the lower and middle course of the Cuautitlan River, north of Lake Xaltocan, and east to Lake Chalco. Most of these areas were virtually unoccupied throughout the First Intermediate and Middle Horizon periods. The reasons seem clear: drainage problems, more severe frosts, lower rainfall, and heavier soils. Theoretically, the plain would not be culti- vated until the supply of land became short, and this, in fact, is what the population profile suggests. On the other hand, once these problems were resolved, the alluvial plain had enormous agricultural potential; the high water table would ameliorate the problems of lower rainfall and more severe frosts; the soils are more fertile than on the adjacent piedmont; and erosion, of course, is no problem.

In this discussion we will focus on the Texcoco region as an example of the process of colonization and summarize briefly the situation in the other regions. Except for a few First Intermediate Phase Two and Three sites on the lakeshore, the initial substantial occupation of the alluvial plain in the Tex- coco region took place during the Second Intermediate Phase Two. It is interesting that this occurred in linear strips along major riverine flood plains, in the northern and central sectors, presumably because of the com- bination of more friable soils and the high water table. By the time of the Spanish Conquest, all of the northern and central portions of the plain had been brought under cultivation. The major question concerns the process by which this was achieved. Sanders' unpublished studies of contemporary agriculture at Atenco and Tocuila (on the east shore of Lake Texcoco) have provided some interesting clues in this regard.

Today the plain is traversed by a network of canals that depart from the rivers in the area and either drain back into the main river or enter other streams. This system was in full use 50 years ago when the haciendas were at their apogee and had multiple functions; to provide adequate drainage and floodwater for irrigation; and to bring silt to fields, to enrich the soil. At that

---

Figure 7.13 (facing page).   The Amanalco permanent irrigation system, Texcoco region. (From Sanders 1976.)

time, the water table was within a few meters of the surface, at least in the immediate lakeshore plain section. Since 1930, however, the water table has dropped dramatically all over the area, to 10 to 20 m below the surface, and drainage is no longer a consideration or a problem. Today, those sections of the system that still function are used primarily for irrigation and to flush salt from the dessicated lakebed.

Although the nineteenth-century haciendas remodeled and built new parts of the system, there are numerous references to the major canals in the sixteenth-century literature (Palerm, 1961b), verifying that much of the system is Late Horizon in date. Because of the greater extent of the Late Horizon lake, the alluvial plain during this period would have been narrower. Consequently, the water table conditions of 1920 around the Atenco and Tocuila communities were probably generalized over much of the plain. The major problem in Late Horizon colonization would have been drainage. Once drained, the same canals could have functioned to bring floodwaters to the fields for irrigation. Even more important, with the floodwaters came coarser sediments, which changed the texture of the soil and made it amenable to tillage with simple, wooden digging tools. Sanders is still in the process of tabulating the data, but at least 30% and possibly 50% of the lands of Atenco could be classified as loams rather than clays, apparently the result of this process. An added bonus would be annual increments of fertility, permitting intensive cropping. The lack of major watercourses in the southern plain probably explains the dearth of Late Horizon sites in the area.

Another major area of comparable soil and moisture conditions occurs east of Lake Chalco, where, according to the settlement history, drainage problems were not resolved. On the other hand, the smaller plains south of Lakes Chalco–Xochimilco were occupied as early as First Intermediate Phase One times. By the Late Horizon, this entire southern plain was apparently completely and continuously cultivated. Of interest here is the fact that a major river system, the Rio Amecameca, crosses the plain with a very heavy sediment load, the heaviest of any river in the Basin of Mexico. Presumably, the process of alluviation here, because of the volume of water and soil transported, not only produces a more friable soil over a larger area, but reduces drainage problems as well

The situation in the Cuautitlan Basin is very complex. The river originally flowed between the contemporary towns of Cuautitlan and Tultitlan, ran parallel to and approximately 1 or 2 km north of the Sierra de Guadalupe, ultimately to empty into Lake Xaltocan. The plain east of Cuautitlan was uninhabited until Middle Horizon times and even the adjacent Guadalupe piedmont had a scanty population until this phase. Much of the plain below Cuautitlan, prior to this Middle Horizon colonization, was probably swamp land, and the presence of the dense Middle Horizon population within and on the edge of the plain would suggest massive reclamation at this time, as we noted in our discussion of canal systems. Substantial First Intermediate Two or Three population centers located on the edge of, and within the plain, in the vicinity of Cuautitlan, suggest that this process was probably initiated up-valley at this earlier date.

In the fifteenth century, the river was diverted, near Cuautitlan, canalized, and much of the flow redirected north to Lake Zumpango. The old river bed, however, continued to function as an irrigation canal and by 1915 the entire plain had been converted to productive agricultural land.

With respect to the plain on the north shore of Lake Xaltocan, colonization did not occur until the First Intermediate Phase Four, and remained light until the Late Horizon. In all probability, substantial drainage projects in this plain were retarded until the Late Horizon. Most of the pre-Late Horizon occupation seems to have occurred in the well-drained alluvial strips produced by a delta of the Avenidas de Pachuca, a situation which parallels pre-Late Horizon occupation of the Texcoco region. In the case of the Teotihuacan Valley we presented evidence that an area of perhaps 1000 ha, near the springs, was characterized by swampy terrain, and that this region was reclaimed during the First Intermediate Phase Three. How much of the lower portion of the Valley required initial drainage projects to convert to agricultural land is not known, but if our model of Middle Horizon agriculture is correct, all of this would have been completed by the First Intermediate Phase Four.

The most impressive prehistoric drainage project of all was carried out within the confines of Lakes Chalco–Xochimilco (see Figures 7.14 and 7.15). Before summarizing Armillas' more recent evaluation of the system, a quote from Sanders (1965:44) indicates our conception of the system early in the course of our own project.

> This system, called chinampa cultivation, is probably the most intensive and productive kind of agriculture practiced in the New World in pre-Hispanic times. The main characteristic of the system, as practiced in the south, includes the construction of artificial islands within freshwater lakes. These islands are built of alternate layers of mud scooped from the lake bottom and vegetation collected from the surface. After the island has reached a height of a few inches above the lake surface, huejote trees are planted along the edge to retain the soil. The islands are usually in the form of long, narrow rectangles, which facilitate bucket irrigation and natural inward seepage of water from the lake. The soil is very rich in organic matter, porous, very dark in color, and land use is extraordinarily intensive; no chinampas are rested for more than 3 to 4 months of the year. By the use of seedbeds a continuous succession of crops, in all stages of growth (mostly vegetables for the Mexico City market) may be seen on a single chinampa. To maintain such a demanding cycle of cropping, fertilizers, in the form of fresh mud and floating vegetation, are periodically added to the chinampa. Crops are irrigated by scooping or splashing water onto the chinampa from canoes, or by poles and buckets from the chinampa itself. All preparation of the soil is done by hand tools.
>
> As the system was expanded, most of the surfaces of Lake Chalco–Xochimilco and Lake Mexico (a part of Lake Texcoco diked off from the main lake) were reduced from open lake into a network of chinampas and canals. An added advantage of this system is that produce could be loaded

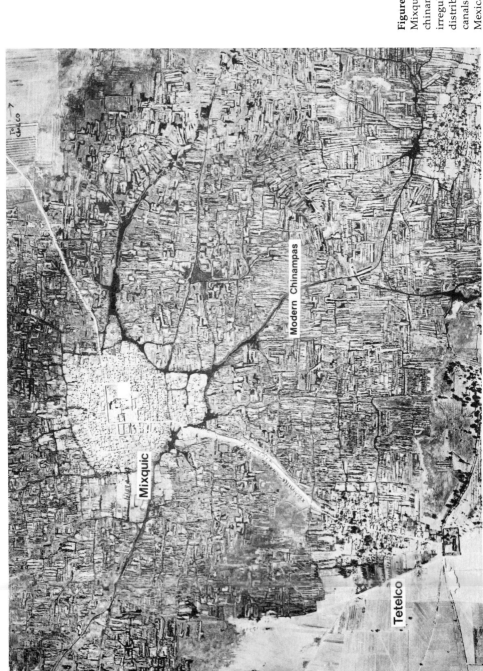

Figure 7.14. Village of Mixquic and surrounding chinampa fringe. Note the irregularity of the pattern and distribution of the major canals. (Courtesy of CIA Mexicana Aerofoto S.A.)

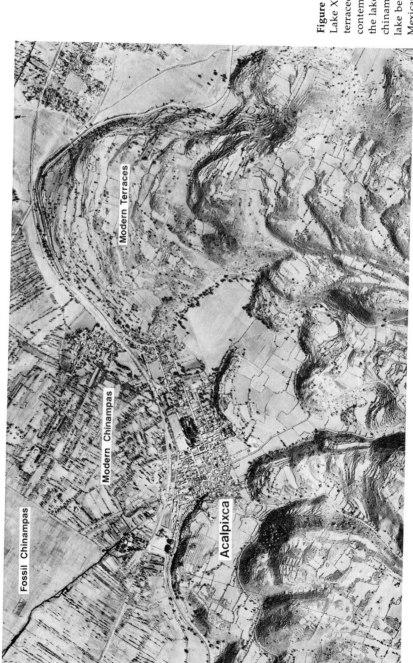

Figure 7.15. South shore of Lake Xochimilco. Note steep, terraced volcanic slopes, contemporary chinampas in the lake bed, and fossil chinampas on the dessicated lake bed. (Courtesy of CIA Mexicana Aerofoto S.A.)

from chinampas into canoes, and poled directly to the urban markets, along the lakeshores or in towns within the lake, such as Aztec Tenochtit- lan and colonial Mexico City. The growth of urban centers in and on the lakes in the Aztec period was, in part, correlated with the evolution of this system of agriculture.

Armillas' (1971) surveys of the chinampa area demonstrated that al- though some chinampas may have been constructed as Sanders described, the process of chinampa formation as a whole was very different from that which was previously thought. First, he points out, the lake bottom was shaped like an "exceedingly shallow saucer" and confined by a low bank around almost the entire perimeter, with the exception of the east. The break of angle of this bank was 2240 m above sea level, and most of the elevation readings of the lakebed itself were between 2238 and 2239, with a few spots as low as 2236. Even allowing for a certain amount of subsidence since the Conquest, the overall depth of the lake apparently did not exceed 1 to 2 m over most of its surface area. During the dry season, the area would resemble a vast swamp, of varying hydrological conditions, interspersed with localized deep ponds and areas of high ground. Of interest is the fact that the deep pools were never converted to cultivation and are present on maps of the area throughout Colonial and Republican periods.

Armillas believes that chinampa formation was essentially produced by the construction of a vast network of drainage ditches, which gradually reduced the water content of the soil to the point where cultivation was possible. In addition, his survey data suggest that the process of colonization proceeded from natural islands and offshore peninsulas on the mainland. The major ditches, used to drain the area, were also utilized as transportation arteries; ultimately large dikes were constructed to further regulate the water distribution, most probably to restrict flooding during the rainy season. The extraordinary regularity of the chinampa plots (see Figure 7.15; it should be noted that the highly irregular patterning visible in Figure 7.14 is unique to Mixquic and the chinampa construction here was clearly not centrally or- ganized) indicates centralized direction or planning. As we saw in Chapter 5, the evidence is strong that the bulk of the Chalco–Xochimilco lakebed area was colonized in Late Horizon times, and that most probably this coloniza- tion was planned by a central government. This could have been carried out by local states such as Tlahuac, Mixquic, or Xochimilco, but some of it may actually have been organized by the Tenocha themselves.

The continuous application of rich lakebed mud and vegetation would have elevated the chinampas somewhat more and reduced the danger of flooding. Since it takes a considerable period of time before the vegetation consolidates in the soil, the cross section of a chinampa would suggest artificial construction, and in essence, the upper portions of the profiles of these plots were artificial. Small, localized areas of chinampas apparently were found in Lake Texcoco at the base of Cerro Chimalhuacan and in Lake Xaltocan (in the community of Xaltocan), where local springs provided enough fresh, new water to reduce the salinity of the two lakes. In the fifteenth century, the Tenochca of Tenochtitlan converted the western one-third of Lake Texcoco into a freshwater lake by constructing a network of dikes equipped with sluice gates. They also brought fresh water from the nearby mountains into the diked basins to convert them more rapidly to fresh water, opening much of this area for chinampa cultivation. Palerm (1973) discusses the structure of the system in considerable detail.

From Early Horizon times until the Late Horizon, our settlement surveys indicate the presence of nucleated settlements in the immediate lakeshore, on peninsulas and islands within the lake. It is possible, and in some cases, highly probable, that some of these communities were practicing small-scale chinampa cultivation, but to date there is no direct confirming evidence. Nevertheless, in the case of some settlements, such as the Second Intermediate Phase One regional center on Xico Island in eastern Lake Chalco, it is difficult to imagine an adequate subsistence base without chinampa agriculture.

Regardless of the possibility of some small-scale chinampa cultivation in earlier times, Armillas' surveys, and our own, clearly demonstrate that there was a rapid, planned, massive colonization of the lakebed during the fifteenth century. This conclusion is based upon a number of lines of evidence. First, the canal system is very regular, and it involved highly planned integration of natural waterways with a network of ditches of varying size. It seems unlikely that this could have been accomplished without centralized planning. With respect to the date, as in the case of terrace systems, rural settlement is dispersed among the fields, the fields are directly associated with house mounds, and almost all are of Late Horizon date. Each grid unit consists of a set of tiny rectangular plots often only 2 or 3 m wide and 10 to 20 m long, and a house mound is located on one of the plots in each grid unit. In fact, the population is even more dispersed than in the case of terraces, and in all probability all the land available to a particular household occurs within one of these grid units.

ANIMAL DOMESTICATION, HUNTING, AND GATHERING

Animal Resources

One of the most serious archaeological deficiencies in the Basin of Mexico is direct evidence bearing upon the role of animals in prehispanic subsistence. Only very recently have a few systematic efforts been made to recover and identify animal bone in excavations. A better understanding of meat consumption is critical because of potential amino acid deficiencies in a diet based primarily upon grains. Although we are beginning to have some reasonable basis for quantifying the dietary significance of hunted and domesticated animals, this is still quite tentative, especially for post-First Intermediate times. We do know that a wide range of animals were exploited in prehispanic central Mexico: deer, dog, peccary, rabbit, rodents, turkey, waterfowl, fish, and various reptiles. These species represent a broad range of habitat types. Unfortunately, because of intense hunting and habitat destruction, in both ancient and modern times, most of these species are now extinct (or nearly so) in the Basin of Mexico.

The range of utilized meat resources is depicted in Table 7.2. The faunas are not directly comparable for a number of reasons. First, there are enormous differences in sample sizes, and a number are obviously incomplete, because of the small numbers of specimens involved. Second, excavation contexts vary greatly. Some samples, like the large fauna from Teotihuacan, come from extensive lateral excavations. Others, like the fauna from El Arbolillo or San José, derive from small test excavations, and very few have been obtained from kitchen middens. Third, for a number of samples, only nominal data are available. Fourth, the summary tabulations involve raw counts. In most cases, these counts have not been transformed into the minimum number of individuals (m.n.i.) represented by each fauna. Transformation to m.n.i. estimates enables the calculation of dietary contributions, and only for the Tlachinolpan and Teotihuacan faunas are such estimates available. These are summarized in Table 7.3.

When conversions of this type are attempted (Starbuck 1975:76; Flannery 1967:171), it is quite clear that faunal exploitation in precolumbian Central Mexico focused on the selective use of a few key species: White-tailed deer (*Odocoileus virginianus*), cottontail rabbit (*Sylvilagus* spp.), domestic dog (*Canis familiaris*), domestic turkey (*Meleagris gallopavo*), and several varieties of wild migratory waterfowl, principally duck. Of these, white-tailed deer are by far the most predominant, surpassing 90% (and sometimes 95%) of the edible food value in many cases. White-tailed deer occur in almost every habitat in Mesoamerica, but their optimal habitats are in the pine–oak woodlands of the Basin of Mexico, Puebla, Toluca, Oaxaca, and Guerrero (Flannery 1968:73). Their density in this habitat is high, circa 13–15 individuals per square kilometer (Leopold 1959:508). The approximately 6000 km² of forest and open woodland formation in the Basin would consequently seem to have been a likely habitat for this species. White-tailed deer are also extremely fecund breeders, commonly being able to withstand an annual culling rate of 20–40% (Leopold 1959:513; Shelford 1963:28–29). Deer also thrive in areas of secondary grassy and weedy growth—on fallow agricultural land in particular—which probably accounts for their persistence near human communities, even under severe hunting pressures. White-tailed deer have relatively small home ranges, frequently traveling known trails, and are therefore very susceptible to daylight hunts by individual males using the spearthrower and the bleeding–trailing technique (Flannery 1968:73; MacNeish n.d.). They are also liable to intense predation by mountain lions (*Felis concolor*) and wolf–coyotes (*Canis* spp.). Thus, of all deer that are potentially

TABLE 7.2
Selected Prehispanic Faunas from the Basin of Mexico[a, b]

	Zohapilco	Ayotla	Zacatenco	El Arbolillo	Atoto	Ayotla	Atlamica	Cuanalan	Loma Torremote	Tezoyuca	Tlachinolpan	San Jose	Teotihuacan	Maquixco	Tenango	Mixcuyo	Tlatenco	La Nopalera	Venta de Carpio	Oxtotipac
White-tailed deer	xx	70	28	60	37	15	31	1	xx		19	43	296	47	2	3	1	26	1	472
Mule deer									x	33								26		
Antelope														1				20		
Cottontail	x								x		8		834					201		92
Jack rabbit	x		3					1			12		177	7				23		10
Misc. lagomorphs							3					1		8						
Pocket gopher	x		1							1			28	14	2	1		19	11	21
Small rodents								3		1			63							
Misc. small mammals							5		x			2								
Misc. large mammals							13					16	160	25	23			35	7	24
Squirrel													21					5	1	5
Badger																		1		
Skunk								1					1					20		
Peccary	x																			
Armadillo													3							
Weasel											1		2							
Cat	x								x			1			1			3		
Wolf							2													
Domestic dog			7			4	1	7	x	6	5		165	73	12			38	1	74
Canis spp.			7				9					2								
Domestic turkey													70	14	1					2
Duck	x									1			112	4				1		
Coot		2		7		15														
Grouse											10									
Quail													76	1						
Hawk–eagle	x												8							
Misc. Aves	x	36		51	4		8	3	x			4	13	10	1	4	8			
Fish	xx												132	3				14	6	
Turtle	x	182	3	61		45	2		x	7	2		56	1						
Snake																				
Misc. reptiles	x								x									9	8	
Totals		290	49	179	41	79	74	16		49	57	69	2217	208	42	8	9	441	35	700

[a] After McBride 1974; Niederberger 1976; Santley 1977; Starbuck 1975; Tolstoy et al. 1977; and White n.d.

[b] x = present; xx = present in substantial amounts.

TABLE 7.3
Pounds of Usable Meat from Tlachinolpan and Teotihuacan[a]

Species	Tlachinolpan			Teotihuacan		
	Minimum number of individuals	Pounds of meat	Percentage of weight	Minimum number of individuals	Pounds of meat	Percentage of weight
White-tailed deer	19	1425	93.94	98	7350	80.14
Domestic dog	4	40	2.64	84	840	9.16
Cottontail	8	16	1.05	218	436	4.75
Jack rabbit	12	36	2.37	94	282	3.07
Domestic turkey				38	152	1.66
Duck				51	102	1.11
Quail				40	10	0.11

[a] After Starbuck 1975: Table 3.

consumable each year, only about 44% will probably end up available to the human population. (See Appendix D.)

Rabbits seem to have been caught using small traps or snares (Flannery 1968:73–74). Recent studies have demonstrated that cottontails are such fecund breeders that virtually no amount of trapping is likely to wipe them out. In twentieth-century southwestern Missouri alone, over 250,000 cottontails were harvested annually without even remotely depleting the total available population (Leopold 1959:358). Data from the Tehuacan Valley suggest that certain species were most at home on the alluvial valley floor, while others predominated in areas of sparest grass and weed-patch ground cover (Flannery 1967:147). The series of substantial alluvial plains in the Teotihuacan Valley, the Cuautitlan Valley, the Texcoco and Chalco regions, and in the northern basin would therefore seem to have been the major habitat for this genus. Although cottontails are frequently the most common mammalian genus represented in prehistoric faunas, their food value by weight is extremely low, so it is doubtful that they ever accounted for a significant portion of the diet.

The procurement of waterfowl (largely migratory) provides an added dimension to subsistence. Until recently, the Basin of Mexico was covered by an extensive series of saline and freshwater lakes. This lacustrine niche was one of the terminal points for the Central Flyway: a migratory route for ducks coming down from the prairie marshes of western Canada during the Fall (Flannery 1968:83). Even as late as 1952, over 33,000 migratory ducks spent the winter in Lake Texcoco (Leopold 1959:Table 4). Given the much larger size of the precolumbian lake system (ca. 1000 km²), the number of waterfowl that annually visited the Basin must have run in the millions. Netting seems to have been the most effective hunting technique. Another possibility is the use of the bow and arrow. The scores of minute projectile points found at First Intermediate Two Loma Torremote (some of which weigh only a gram or two) may have been used for this purpose (Santley 1977:256). As the food value by weight for most species of aquatic fowl is also quite low, their total dietary contribution likewise was probably never very great.

Virtually no data exist concerning the habitat distribution of either dog or turkey in the wild. In fact, it is not certain that domestic dog was intentionally fattened and eaten before Late Horizon times. The excavated specimens of *Canis* show no evidence of butchering, though, as Starbuck (1975:106–107) notes, few examples of meaty parts of the animal were recovered. For turkey the evidence for consumption would seem to be unequivocal. Turkeys today are left to range freely about the houselot, bursting into plumage at the sight of unsuspecting passersby. They typically consume almost everything edible on the houselot grounds and therefore may not have been fed deliberately in antiquity.

Based on the selected prehispanic faunas presented in Table 7.2 the following general patterns of animal utilization are suggested. White-tailed deer comprise the single most important meat resource during all periods although through time their relative frequency tends to decrease. Species of secondary import include waterfowl, mud turtle, and cottontail rabbit. Mud turtle is unusually abundant during the Early Horizon and First Intermediate Phase One but declines substantially during later periods. Waterfowl demonstrate a similar tendency. Coot (*Fulica americana*), a perennial resident of the Basin, is especially common in Early Horizon deposits. "This may point to more fowling outside the winter season and thus to a greater year-round importance of fowling than in later times [Tolstoy *et al.* 1977:100]." Strangely absent in most samples are fish. This may signify dietary unimportance, but it is more likely that the cartilaginous skeletal tissues have not been preserved over the millennia. Domestic animals increase in numbers through time. At Tlachinolpan dog accounts for 2.6% of all animal meat, but by Middle Horizon times more than 9%, if dog was indeed eaten, comes from this domesticated species (Starbuck 1975:Table 3). In general, the pattern appears to be one of progressive decline in hunted resources and their gradual replacement by domesticated species.

Thus far, no mention has been made of the absolute contribution of meat to the precolumbian diet. One of the coauthors explores this subject in some detail in Appendix D, so only a few summary statements will be presented here. Animal exploitation is considered in energetic terms, since the calorie is a convenient measure for comparative analysis. As already mentioned, white-tailed deer are greatly predominant in many prehistoric faunas, commonly accounting for at least 90% of all meat consumed. Because of this preponderance, especially in food value, the level of deer consumption can thus be used as a reliable indicator of the potential amount of meat consumption. Basically then, the model postulates that deer were present in high densities (ca. 13 per square kilometer), that this density was fairly uniform through the zone of procurement (ca. 6000 km^2), that cropping occurred at the highest possible levels without upsetting equilibrium conditions (ca. 40% per year), that each deer was capable of yielding approximately 22 kg of edible meat, and that roughly 1460 kcal (kilocalories) of useable energy were available per kilogram of edible portion. Estimates of prehispanic population size are derived from the Basin of Mexico survey, with extrapolations for small sections of the Basin which have received little or no systematic coverage. Per capita daily human energy needs are assumed to be about 2000 kcal. Accommodations have also been made for interspecific predation by wolves and cats, and an increase in deer has been forecasted for disturbed habitats (i.e., for cultivated and fallow agricultural land).

The following sequence of meat consumption levels is therefore proposed (Table 7.4). Prior to the second millenium B.C., population densities were low (about 0.5–1.0 persons per square kilometer, to judge from ethnographic analogy), so that white-tailed deer could have contributed 13.5% of all energy consumed on an annual basis. These figures correspond quite nicely with hunting levels reported for non-Arctic hunter–gatherer societies (Lee 1968:42). In fact, even when total faunal biomass is exceedingly high—for example, among the Hadza of Tanzania—meat does not account for more than 20% of all energy needs (Woodburn 1968:51). By Early Horizon times the shift to an agricultural economy, with its commensurate population increase, began pushing consumption levels to near capacity limits, thereby greatly intensifying the danger of overkills if hunting remained at Aceramic levels. Beginning during the First Intermediate Phase One, rapid population growth, coupled perhaps with the first severe overkills, resulted in a significant decline in meat consumption, and by Phase Two times probable consumption levels dropped below 1%. Tolstoy *et al.* (1977:100) note a comparable trend, not only for deer but for turtle bone and waterfowl as well.

TABLE 7.4
Dietary Contribution of White-tailed Deer in the Basin of Mexico

Archaeological phase	Maximum number of deer	Number of cullable deer per year	Number of deer culled by other predators	Maximum contribution to diet
Early Horizon	78,663	31,465	17,620	13.5%
First Intermediate One	80,873	32,349	18,115	2.8%
First Intermediate Two	88,205	35,282	19,758	0.9%
First Intermediate Three	94,705	37,882	21,214	0.5%
First Intermediate Four	92,261	36,904	20,666	0.6%
Middle Horizon	107,718	43,087	24,129	0.3%
Second Intermediate One	98,800	39,520	22,131	0.4%
Second Intermediate Two	93,470	37,388	20,937	0.6%
Late Horizon	130,000	52,000	29,120	0.1%

Some increase in deer numbers would be expected on cultivated land, but this added increment was probably not of much consequence, especially when viewed in terms of the size of population increase by First Intermediate Phase Three times. Prey switching, both by the human population and by other competing predators, could have relieved this situation somewhat, but at best this situation was very momentary. By the Middle Horizon there was a marked drop (from 94% to 80%) in the amount of deer consumed in terms of all edible faunal resources (Starbuck 1975:91). More than likely, overkills had become so acute in the vicinity of Teotihuacan that hunting in this area (and perhaps about most of the Basin as well) was no longer a very efficient subsistence strategy. Even without overkills, however, total meat consumption from wild sources could not have exceeded 0.3% of the annual requirement. Consumption levels thereafter remained below 1%. Interestingly enough, it is during the Middle Horizon that beans (*Phaseolus* spp.) and domestic animals become well represented in the archaeological record (Flannery 1967; Kaplan 1967; Starbuck 1975; White n.d.). It is very tempting indeed to view this increased reliance on alternative protein sources as the direct result of significant declines in hunting levels.

Gathered Resources

Reliance on wild plant foods constitutes a third means of energy production. Data from three sites—Zohapilco (Niederberger 1976), Loma Torremote (Reyna Robles and Gonzalez 1976; Santley 1977), and Teotihuacan (McClung de Tapia 1977)—have provided clues concerning the range and type of gathering activities. In all three cases the analyses are still in progress, so total quantitative counts are not available. The following presentation must therefore be regarded as most tentative.

Without a doubt the best documented evidence comes from Loma Torremote. Here storage of both domestic and wild foodstuffs was in underground bell-shaped (tronco-conical) pits. More than 90 of these features were excavated during the 1974–1975 season, and floatation of the earth fill from the pits yielded literally pounds of botanical remains. The samples analyzed thus far (from 18 pits) date largely to the First Intermediate Phase One, though a few may be as early as the Early Horizon Phase Two. Maize and amaranth predominate, but wild plants, including weedy species, are consistently present in moderate amounts. Wild vegetable species include members from the following genera: *Eragrostis, Oxalis, Monarda, Helianthus* (girasol), *Opuntia* (nopal), and *Crataegus* (Reyna Robles and Gonzales 1976). Wild grasses like *Setaria* (fox tail grass) and *Oryziopsis* (wild rice) occur infrequently (Reyna Robles and Gonzales 1976) but consistently. Wild rice in particular indicates some use of naturally humid zones for gathering (Santley 1977:262–267). Ruderal plants such as *Ambrosia* sp., *Amaranthus* sp., *Argemone* sp., *Bidens* sp., *Chenopodium* sp. (epazote), and *Solanum rostratum* (papita) may have been collected on fallow agricultural land, perhaps even from the calmil garden plots (Reyna Robles and Gonzalez 1976). The presence of *Distichilis* sp. and *Portulaca* sp. denote collection in areas of high surface salinity, probably from the western shore of Lakes Xaltocan and Zumpango (Reyna Robles and Gonzalez 1976). The species occurrent at Loma Torremote come from several different environment zones: the lakeshore, naturally humid localities near perennial streams, the alluvial plain, and the piedmont. Gathering activities therefore appear to have sometimes ranged far afield. The vast majority of all collected foodstuffs, however, probably could have been obtained within a 5-km site radius (Santley 1977:293).

At Zohapilco a fossil pollen sequence provides all the information available on possible gathering activities published to date (Niederberger 1976). The excavated sequence covers several thousand years of prehistory: from the Aceramic and Initial Ceramic periods to the Early Horizon and First Intermediate period. The genera represented include *Typha* (reed), *Celtis, Zaluzania, Ambrosia, Bouvardia, Agave, Hecthtia, Polygonum* (chilillos), *Dactylis, Echinochloa, Mimosa, Acacia, Quercus, Pinus, Alnus, Abies, Salix,* and *Taxodium* (Niederberger 1976). A number of these genera (e.g., *Quercus, Pinus, Alnus,* and other tree species) are probably not food resources, whereas others, *Agave* and *Acacia,* for example, undoubtedly are. Many of these genera derive from the lake itself and its immediate shoreline, implying a possible heavy emphasis on lacustrine and riparian resources. Available data on faunal utilization from Zohapilco suggest a similar conclusion. This should not be overly surprising, given the location of Tlapacoya directly adjacent to the north shore of Lake Chalco.

The botanical data from Teotihuacan span the First Intermediate Phase Four, First Intermediate Phase Five, and Middle Horizon. Most of the analyzed specimens come from domesticated species (McClung de Tapia 1977). *Chenopodium* sp., *Opuntia* sp., *Portulaca* sp., *Prunus capuli* (capulin), *Crataegus mexicana,* and *Ficus* sp. (amate), however, would seem to be wild (McClung de Tapia 1977). *Crataegus mexicana* and *Prunus capuli,* both planted perhaps at field borders or near the houselot, are trees bearing edible fruit (Sanchez 1968). *Chenopodium* and *Portulaca* are herbaceous plants common on fallow agricultural land. *Ficus* produces the fibrous type of bark used in making *amatl* paper. (McClung de Tapia 1977). Both the stem and fruit of *Opuntia* have long been important dietary items for the inhabitants of the Basin of Mexico. Whether the fruit was simply gathered wild or collected from cultivated varieties is an unanswered question at present.

To estimate the dietary contribution of wild foodstuffs is a much more difficult matter. The natural flora of the Basin has been greatly modified by more than 3000 years of agricultural land use. It is thus impossible to assess concretely either the habitat or distribution of specific resources collected in the wild. Moreover, the lack of adequate subsistence remains prevents any clear understanding of the full range of gathering activities, especially during earlier periods.

A number of inferences may be drawn, however, if we rely on comparative data. Studies of ethnographically known hunting and gathering societies indicate that the amount of collected foodstuffs is commonly two to three times that obtained from hunted game, even in areas where the fauna is exceedingly plentiful (Lee 1968:42–43). The values assigned to gathering for the Basin are therefore a simple multiple of the percentage of reliance of hunting times the subsistence ratio (Table 7.5, column 4). Unfortunately, modern hunting and gathering bands rarely exploit game animals at carrying capacity levels, so the meat values suggested earlier should be taken as theoretical maxima, not actual hunting rates. What this does is reduce the total contribution of wild plant food resources. The figures, nevertheless, are very suggestive.

A related method involves the calculation of carrying capacity limits for the natural ecosystem. As already indicated, virtually no data exist concerning the density distribution for collected plant foodstuffs. One species for which there is some information is mesquite (*Prosopis juliflora*). Near Mitla in the Valley of Oaxaca mesquite commonly produces an estimated 160–180 g of edible pods per hectare (Flannery 1973:298). Mesquite, however, is a circumscribed resource: Abundant in certain alluvial locations, absent in others, so productivity per unit area is probably considerably less. *Prosopis* is also not an inhabitant of the Basin of Mexico, and the only wild resources of comparable yield—*Setaria* and *Oryziopsis*—were doubtlessly also restricted in distribution. In lieu of this probable variability in resource productivity (i.e., from virtually nothing to as high as 180–200 kg), we suggest a "ballpark" figure of 25 kg for each hectare of collection space. Of this, about 12.5 kg must be considered as inedible waste. Each hectare of gathering space consequently produces the equivalent of 18,750 kcal of consumable energy, assuming a yield of 1500 kcal per kilogram of edible portion (Santley n.d.b). Approximately 15,500 collectors can therefore be supported in the Basin at the carrying capacity level. Wild game can accommodate for an additional 1000 persons, making the maximum limit for hunting and gathering about 16,500. The critical population density is thus about 2.7 persons per square kilometer. This figure compares favorably with population densities reported for central California, a mixed deciduous forest setting, where aboriginally the economy was based on intensive acorn collection supplemented by some hunting.

Table 7.5 plots these estimates through time. Excepting the Early Horizon and First Intermediate One and Two phases, it should be readily apparent that gathered plants played a very insignificant role as a food resource in the Basin of Mexico. A high contribution is theoretically feasible during the earliest phases of occupation, but this is only possible because of the small size of the resident agricultural population. From the First Intermediate Phase Three onwards, the total potential contribution remains in the 2–9% range. Faunal utilization, as already mentioned, follows a similar path. Obviously, therefore, the vast majority of all consumed energy had to come from domesticated cultigens: hence our emphasis on maize-based agricul-

TABLE 7.5
Possible Dietary Contribution of Hunting and Gathering

Archaeological phase	Population	Maximum contribution of meat (percentage)	Possible[a] contribution of gathering (percentage)	Maximum[b] contribution of gathering (percentage)	Maximum contribution of hunting and gathering (percentage)
Early Horizon	4,500	13.4–13.5	23.2–69.6	86[c]	99.5
First Inter-mediate One	22,400	2.7– 2.8	4.8–14.4	46[d]	48.8
First Inter-mediate Two	80,000	0.8– 0.9	1.2– 3.6	17	17.9
First Inter-mediate Three	145,000	0.4– 0.5	0.6– 2.1	9	9.5
First Inter-mediate Four	120,000	0.5– 0.6	0.8– 2.7	9[d]	9.6
Middle Horizon	250,000	0.3– 0.3	0.4– 1.5	6	6.3
Second Inter-mediate One	175,000	0.4– 0.4	0.6– 2.1	9	9.4
Second Inter-mediate Two	130,000	0.5– 0.6	0.4– 1.5	6	6.6
Late Horizon	1,000,000+	0.1– 0.1	0.2– 0.6	2	2.1

[a] Assuming that gathering is two to three times hunting.
[b] Assuming a critical density of 15,500 persons.
[c] Assuming that only one-quarter of the Basin was occupied by sedentary farmers.
[d] Assuming that only two-thirds of the Basin was occupied by sedentary farmers.

ture, irrigation in particular, in our reconstruction of subsistence. In this regard, we are painfully aware of the inadequacy of our understanding about amaranth cultivation. We know that in prehispanic times this grain was comparable to maize in dietary significance. However, its near-disappearance from modern agriculture has made it very difficult to study and evaluate. If its requirements, productivity, or nutritive value are radically different from maize, then some of our inferences about subsistence may need revision.

One gathered wild product, although its energetic contribution to the diet was probably small, may have played an unusually important role in the diet—the lake product referred to by the Aztecs as Tecuitlatl. A number of sixteenth-century documentary sources refer to this as an important food. It is apparently an algae (*Spirulina geitleri*) that thrives in salt lakes and was a major food for the migratory waterfowl. The algae was collected in nets from canoes, transported to the shore where it was laid in layers, sun dried and cut up into bricks. Critical characteristics of *Spirulina* as a food resource are its storability, abundance, rapid growth rate, and its high protein value. Furst (1978) estimates that 70% of *Spirulina*, by weight, is protein, and furthermore, all eight essential amino acids are well represented. Considering the very dense Late Horizon population, it probably would not be stretching the point to argue that this resource may have been critical to its maintenance.

MISCELLANEOUS RESOURCES

The native population of the Basin of Mexico at the time of the Conquest used a great variety of artifacts, particularly if one includes in this assessment the great number made from exotic resources, and to a great extent restricted in use to the upper and middle levels of the society. A quick glance at the Mendoza Codex, Moctezuma's tax list, dramatically illustrates this fact. Such items as copal gum for incense; tropical bird feathers for insignia and clothing ornament; cacao; cotton cloth for clothing; jade and other hard stones for body ornaments; gold and copper, used primarily for body ornaments; honey; paper made from the inner bark of the fig tree; were all exacted as taxes from lower-lying, more tropical regions. Added to this would be a variety of tropical food stuffs. All these items, however, were limited in consumption to a rather small segment of the population. Here we will focus heavily on those resource items that were used by the majority of the population and consumed at relatively high consumption rates, all of which were obtained from the Basin of Mexico itself. Perhaps the best point of departure for such a discussion, would be, in fact, the needs of the ordinary household, since this type of consumption unit made up the vast majority of the population.

The average family lived in a house of walls built of adobe brick, or some kind of volcanic conglomerate that has the consistency of adobe, or of roughly trimmed blocks of stone. The roofs were primarily manufactured from maguey leaves or wood; and the floor of either clay-textured earth, or crushed *tepetate*, or some other volcanic conglomerate. Walls were frequently plastered with mud. The use of these basic materials began back in the First Intermediate period, and they were used with little significant change until the Late Horizon. The particular material used in a Late Horizon house depended on the location of the house, with respect to these various materials. Most village houses were constructed of cheap, readily available materials that were universally distributed, although today the actual construction may be carried out, or supervised, by a specialist. In the case of houses of more well-to-do families, beginning with the First Intermediate Phase Five, lime plasters and stuccos were extensively used in the larger communities. This resource has a highly limited distribution, primarily to the Cretaceous outcrops in the northwestern corner of the Basin and in the vicinity of Tula. In the sixteenth century, villages in both areas specialized in the production of lime (Gibson 1964). Another use for lime was for the cooking of maize, in preparation for the making of pozol and tortillas, and this would be a basic need of families on all social levels.

Peasants in 1519 were clothed primarily from fibers extracted from the leaves of the maguey plant, a material which was also used as cordage. Since most farmers probably planted maguey as field borders, some material of this type was available from the holdings of most agriculturists. But maguey generally tends to grow best in the drier northern portions of the Basin so some deficit was undoubtedly made up through the process of regional specialization and exchange.

A major item in all households, from Early Horizon times onward, was the ceramic culinary vessel. No careful study of the distribution of ceramic clays has ever been undertaken in the Basin of Mexico, but it is clear that the better quality clays, at least, are relatively restricted in distribution, and numerous communities were located in areas where good ceramic clays were unavailable. We know from the sixteenth-century documentary sources that major ceramic clay deposits were found around Coyoacan, Texcoco, and Cuautitlan, and these towns specialized in the manufacture of ceramics at that time. There are also major deposits at Teotihuacan, and the village of San Sebastian specializes in ceramic manufacture today. Presumably, much of the pottery of Teotihuacan was manufactured from these same local clays. The fine quality clays were used for the manufacture of other ceramic artifacts, such as figurines (apparently used in household ritual), musical instruments, and body ornaments.

Aside from its importance as a building material, stone was also universally present in all agricultural households as smoothing, grinding, hoeing, chopping, cutting, piercing, and scraping tools. The two major materials used were various grades of basalt, primarily used for hoeing, grinding, and smoothing; and obsidian, for most other activities. The distribution of fine quality basalt coincides roughly with the distribution of late Tertiary volcanic rocks on Mooser's map, and it is particularly abundant in the Teotihuacan Valley and the Temascalapa region.

Obsidian, on the other hand, has a much more limited distribution. The restricted availability of this key resource provided critical economic and political leverage for those groups that controlled it, not only in terms of local supply, but in terms of foreign trade as well. Major sources occur in two localities within the Basin: above the town of Otumba, on the eastern periphery of the Teotihuacan Valley; and in the northeast corner of the Basin, in the vicinity of Pachuca, where the very fine-grained green obsidian is found (Spence and Parsons 1972). This latter material was in high demand all over Mesoamerica during and after the Middle Horizon when large polities had the capacity to organize and control its exploitation and exportation. Occasional substitutes such as chert, found in the limey Cretaceous deposits in the northern Basin, and quartz, found primarily in the Sierras de Guadalupe and Tepozotlan, were also sparingly used.

A major item of peasant consumption was salt, and the archaeological evidence suggests that this was an item of steadily increasing demand through the history of the Basin. Presumably the Late Horizon salt production peak relates to dense population and very reduced animal protein intake, since salt can be obtained through meat in the diet. As we noted in Chapter 5, there is particularly good evidence for the location of salt production in the Late Horizon. We found that the most intensive productivity was focused on the western shore of Lake Texcoco, at the northern and southern edges of the Tenochtitlan urban center. Salt extraction was also carried out, on a somewhat reduced scale, around the remainder of the Lake Texcoco shoreline, and along the edges of Lake Xaltocan. There may be some natural basis (e.g., variability in the distribution of concentrations of salts most suitable for human consumption) for this observed distribution of Late Horizon salt production, although the presence of the huge Tenochtitlan urban mass was undoubtedly a primary factor in the intensity of salt making around its peripheries, so as to achieve maximal proximity to the greatest concentration of consumers.

Wood was another major resource needed by virtually all households. Uses included handles for tools, particularly for agricultural digging tools, and roofing materials for houses. Some villages in the lacustrine area required wood for canoe construction, and the upper- and middle-class households used it for stools. The two most important trees in the Basin were *encino,* or evergreen oak, and the various species of pine. Pine was used primarily for building materials and oak for tools. Both resources must have been abundant during the initial occupational phase of a particular region, but would have become increasingly scarce as population levels rose. The availability of this resource, then, would have shifted spatially with the passage of time.

Finally, major household items were baskets, used as containers, and mats for sleeping. Both were manufactured of the reeds that were probably abundant throughout the lake region. Again, this would be a resource that, although widely distributed, would be of steadily decreasing accessibility as population in a particular area increased, particularly as large-scale drainage of low ground was carried out.

In summary, the resources discussed here fall into several categories: those of a highly localized nature, some of which (such as obsidian) have almost unique distributions; broadly distributed resources that would always have been available to nearly everybody (e.g., rock and soil for building supplies); and resources that had initially broad distributions, but under the influence of population growth, would have the characteristic of increasingly restricted access (e.g., wood and reeds).

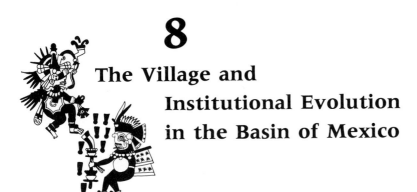

8

The Village and
Institutional Evolution
in the Basin of Mexico

SOCIOECONOMIC TYPOLOGY

In Chapter 1 we stated that one of the objectives of the Basin of Mexico surveys was to describe the socioeconomic evolution of the prehispanic culture of the area. In Chapter 5 we presented a detailed summary of the history of settlement systems. In this summary we intentionally avoided the use of higher level interpretive and analytical sociological terminology and adhered for the most part to a descriptive typology. In this chapter, we will attempt to characterize the prehispanic societies that were responsible for the archaeological remains in terms of social or economic typologies. The major question is: What kind of typology? In the field of social science, typologies have been defined for entire socioeconimic systems, and for relatively small scale analytical units.

Among the broad types of social systems defined by cultural evolutionists are Service's band, tribe, chiefdom, and state; Fried's egalitarian, ranked, and stratified societies, and the state; all of which have been used by one of the authors of this study (Sanders and Price 1968; Sanders and Marino 1970; Sanders and Webster 1978) as models for prehistoric societies. These schemes have been widely used in recent years in the archaeological profession generally. The major problem with large taxonomic categories of this type is not, as many researchers have said, that they tend to divert the user from considerations of process, but rather that they assume too close a functional relationship among the various aspects or categories of human behavior. For example, in Service's definition of chiefdom as a general type, the economic behavior of redistribution is included as part of the definition, yet the chiefdom is essentially a political type that may be associated with a variety of economic behavioral patterns. It would seem more useful, therefore, to use somewhat more restricted taxonomic categories than whole socioeconomic systems, and this is the approach that will be followed generally here.

As Flannery has pointed out, in a brilliant essay "The Cultural Evolution of Civilizations" (1972), the fundamental changes in the socioeconomic sphere of culture can be subsumed under two processes, centralization and segregation. Socioeconomic systems have evolved from small, decentralized, homogeneous societies to large, centralized, heterogeneous ones. One could, and this would be a useful procedure for many purposes, simply measure these two processes quantitatively, a particularly attractive approach for archaeologists. On the other hand, there is substantial evidence that qualitative changes—that is, changes in structure—are functionally related to quantitative changes, so that both approaches are useful. To be even more useful, however, the two processes should be dissected into more specific processes and used as analytical tools, in both qualitative and quantitative terms. For example, the process of segregation includes such subprocesses as economic specialization, stratification, exchange, and urbanization. Centralization primarily includes the process of politicization but may include others, such as militarization, as well.

Economic specialization is one of those variables that can easily be quantified, at least in the ethnographic context. Chapple and Coon (1948) defined a series of levels of evolutionary complexity in economic specialization that has never been extensively used by either ethnographers or archaeologists, but which has considerable merit. Much of the polemic, for example, about this process could have been avoided if the quantitative approach suggested by these writers had been used. The range is from societies characterized by no specialization, other than age and sex, to various grades of part-time specialization (and these levels could be quantified in terms of how much time is spent by what percentage of the population, in what kinds of specialized tasks) to full-time specialization. The process, as in many cases of cultural evolution, is an additive one rather than one of replacement; that is, as societies evolve, specialization by age and sex continue as well as part-time specialization, even when full-time specialization is highly developed. Structurally, the shift would be from village part-time specialization, in which occupational groups are not socially differentiated and where production is organized on the basis of the household, to the highly organized craft guilds associated with urban residence and full-time craft specialization.

Exchange, like economic specialization, is an easily measured variable. Chapple and Coon suggest calculating the percentage of consumption goods in a sample of households that were obtained from outside the household as a measure of the process. Obviously variations in this percentage are in direct relationship to the quantitative value of economic specialization. One could also break down these calculations more finely in terms of distance from which goods were procured.

For example, in highland Oaxaca today (see Cook and Diskin 1976) there is a stratified exchange system that operates on four territorial levels. Some exchange occurs between households but within the same community. Exchange also occurs between households from a group of communities that focus on a central market (redistributive place) that meets once a week and can be referred to as a local market system. A group of such local market systems, however, with market days staggered through the 7-day week, form a regional market system. Professional middlemen move goods in a weekly circuit from one local market town to another, so some goods are purchased that originate outside of the local market system. Finally, via middlemen, goods from other areas of Mexico, and from outside the country, find their way into the regional market area. Berg (1976) tabulated types of goods in terms of their origin in the stratified market system. Even more useful would be data on consumption rates of each item and the energetic costs of its production. By this method we could quantify exchange in energetic terms.

Structurally, exchange systems have been analyzed in terms of three basic kinds of distribution: reciprocation, redistribution, and marketing. Reciprocation involves paired interaction between two producer—consumers and the exchanges are generally balanced, that is, the energetic costs of the objects exchanged are equivalent, and the exchange is directly between the two individuals. Ideologically, the exchange is often conceived as a gift, although reciprocation is, of course, expected. Such exchanges are often described by anthropologists as essentially social in function. They serve to strengthen already existing kin ties, or establish new ties with nonkin. Economic specialization, where present in this type of exchange, is part-time, and even then usually involves a minimal investment of time and labor on the part of the producer in the production process.

Redistributive economies are more clearly economic in nature and generally involve community level part-time specialization; that is, most of the families in the given village spend a considerable part of their work input in the production of one or a few particular goods for exchange. They are usually agriculturally self-sufficient, or nearly so. The major purpose of exchange is to even out imbalances in resource distribution produced by the heterogeneity of the natural environment. Let us suppose, for example, that village A is located in an area where there are good ceramic clays, village B is near a basalt outcrop, and village C near an obsidian deposit. All three villages need ground stone and chipped stone tools, and pottery to maintain their lifestyles. Each village then specializes in a particular product, produces a surplus of these products, and exchanges them.

In many cases the energetic cost of production of the various goods is roughly equivalent and hence no profit is involved in the transaction. The economic system, therefore, does not involve, strictly speaking, a market economy. In order to make the exchange, the common arrangement is for each producer to carry his product to some central point. This central point may be a person or a place. In Service's classic chiefdom it is a person, the chief, who receives the surpluses, often ideologically received as gifts to an elder kinsmen, and he then redistributes them to the villages that lack the particular product. This is done periodically in a series of public festivals in which large numbers of the villagers gather at the central community. A more effective system, which probably develops when the volume of such exchanges reaches a particular point, involves a central place, where the particular producers can make their exchanges directly. In contemporary Mesoamerica, these are frequently referred to as markets or market places. In lieu of the absence of a profit aspect, it is best to consider these as redistributive places. Since specific transactions are dyadic and reciprocal, one could also refer to these as reciprocation places, except that usually reciprocation involves a considerable overlay of ceremonial behavior; whereas the exchange in this case is more comparable, in its impersonal character, to marketing.

Finally, market economies, involving the concept of profit, and including as institutional elements professional merchants or middlemen, full-time craft specialization (often organized into guilds), and permanent wholesaling and retailing establishments, are characteristic, and form another kind of economic system. Such systems may include market places, in which the exchanges occur, that are identical in physical appearance to the redistributive or reciprocation places just noted. In terms of evolutionary process, the progression is clearly from reciprocation to redistribution to marketing, but the process is essentially an additive one, rather than one of replacement. This means that in highly evolved economic systems all of these three elements may be contained, as in the case of contemporary Oaxaca, and this combination was undoubtedly true in prehispanic Mexico at the time of the Spanish Conquest.

Stratification is a complex process that involves the tendency for status positions to become hierarchical, or assume different values of worthwhileness and accessibility to those things that society has determined valuable. It is in fact the product of several other processes, but there is a value in treating it as an independent process as well. In terms of variation in the structural characteristics of stratification, writers like Service and Fried have used broad definitional categories such as egalitarian, ranked and stratified societies, but considerable controversy has developed over the use of these terms. It is not our intention to summarize all of this debate; rather what we propose here is that the stratification process is best viewed as an expansion of the application of the hierarchical principle of status differentiation. What this means is that all societies have some degree of stratification, even hunting and gathering bands. In societies that Service calls bands and tribes, and Fried refers to as egalitarian, however, inequities of access involve women primarily. As the social system evolves, inequities increase to include access to highly prized, but nonutilitarian, technology and nontechnological items such as titles; finally to include goods that are basic to the energetics of the ecological system, in most preindustrial societies meaning primarily access to agricultural land.

Since the process of stratification is usually accompanied by other processes, such as economic specialization, "more economic" patterns of distribution of goods, and politicization of social interaction, it is also marked by an increasing tendency of whole groups of people to share the same rank and form well-defined classes. It is essentially to the latter condition that Fried and Service would apply the term *stratified society*, and contrast it to earlier kinds of stratification, where there is more of a continuum of differentiation of rank. In highly evolved examples of stratified societies, the classes may be characterized by endogamy, and concepts of ritual purity, to form relatively rigid structures normally referred to as castes.

In either case, whether the society is characterized by classes, which permit some vertical mobility, or castes, where vertical mobility is virtually nil, all preindustrial societies, because of the limits of productivity and transportation technology, have at the base of the pyramid a large and socioeconomically deprived class of food producers, who are terminologically referred to as peasants. A *peasant*, using Wolf's definition (1966), is a food producer with access to a small amount of agricultural land. This access may be direct, in cases where he owns the land, or it may be indirect, in which case he is a tenant on land belonging to someone else. In either case a lien is attached to his production, referred to as tax in the first case, or rent in the second. Because of his limited technology and access to land, his production is small and devoted primarily to providing him with a bare caloric minimum and a small surplus, for replacement of technology (what Wolf calls the replacement fund), for ceremonial obligations in cases where he is a participant in a corporate community organization (the ceremonial fund), and for payment of the rent or tax. It is the presence of this class that is the critical element in what evolutionists have referred to as stratified societies.

The process of politicization refers to the evolution of formal status positions and institutions involved in the legitimate exercise of power. Basically, the process is one of expansion of the role of such institutions in social control and integration, at the expense of familial and sodality type institutions. Social control in the latter case tends to operate primarily in the form of public opinion or censure, and is therefore highly decentralized. Structurally and functionally, as political systems get more complex the process involves an elaboration of status positions, and more explicit definition of the roles of these positions. Intermediate levels in the process tend to be characterized by general purpose status positions with only vaguely defined delimitation of roles. The climax of this process lies in the bureaucratic structures of industrial societies, where status positions are not only highly specific in terms of duties and obligations, and the definition of power very explicit, but specialized training is required in order to prepare people for occupying such positions. As part of this process, a well-defined chain of command and specialized functions become increasingly characteristic of political institutions.

Another way of measuring politicization would be in terms of expanded functions. Leaders in "egalitarian" societies do little more than arbitrate disputes, or assume short-term leadership roles over samll groups, in the exploitation of resources or defense of territory. In higher level political systems, arbitration becomes adjudication; and the political institution may be increasingly involved in managing economic production and distribution. Expansion of these activities, of course, augments and amplifies the amount of power available to the high status positions. The process that Flannery refers to as centralization involves primarily this type of expansion of function.

The process of militarization is comparable to politicization and stratification in the fact that it is found at all stages of sociocultural evolution. What is involved essentially in the evolution of militarization is a process of increasing significance of warfare in terms of its impact on socioeconomic systems. All groups wage war, but in the case of simpler societies the major function of warfare is as a spacing mechanism, to reduce competition over resources, and as a mechanism of achieving access to the one resource that is unequally distributed, women. Much of this kind of warfare is of the quick raid type, and the result is little change in the sociocultural structure and size of the societies that are involved. At the other end of the evolutionary continuum, warfare is characterized by having an increasing effect on the mechanisms and processes of politicization and social stratification. The results of warfare in this case involve substantial changes in the nature, structure, and size of competing societies.

We have intentionally left urbanism for last because of the complexity of the process, and the fact that it is difficult to discuss it without reference to the other processes. Basically, it is the process whereby population and certain activities, such as production and distribution of goods and political administration, become increasingly concentrated or nucleated at one locality. Highly urbanized communities are therefore characterized by large populations, high population densities, and extreme socioeconomic heterogeneity, characteristics that are functionally interrelated. All of these features can, of course, be quantitatively measured both in the ethnographic and archaeological context. The urban community is perhaps the best example in human society of a cybernetic system, that is, one in which changes in any of the variables will automatically and significantly change the others.

The broad schemes of social taxonomy, of the Service and Fried type, involve assumptions as to the functional interrelationships among these various processes. Service's band society, for example, is essentially a society where the processes of politicization are developed only to the level of informal leadership involved with arbitration, and occasionally in the organization of small groups for resource exploitation and defense. Stratification and economic specialization are based entirely on age and sex, and warfare functions only as a spacing mechanism and to procure women. Exchange is quantitatively insignificant and involves primarily a pattern of balanced reciprocation. At the other end of the scale, what he would call the state includes well-defined social classes or castes, with differential access to the basic means of production; formal bureaucratic political organization, often involving ownership or tax rights over agricultural land; full-time craft specialization; market economies, etc. The problem, as we pointed out, is that these processes are broadly correlated, but not in such a precise way as the social typology would suggest.

ARCHAEOLOGY AND SOCIOECONOMIC RECONSTRUCTION

The reconstruction of the institutions of a prehistoric population is a formidable task when such reconstructions are based entirely on survey data. Basically, the problem is to what degree are settlement pattern and artifact distributions correlated with socioeconomic behavior. Posing it another way: What kinds of technology are most intimately related to what kinds of social organization? As was apparent from our previous discussion, all human societies are organized on the basis of a few fundamental principles, such as rank, kinship, age, sex, and coresidence. All these principles have technological reference. Gross differences in rank are usually reflected in the quality and quantity of dress, housing, or burial furniture; sex and age may be reflected in either the first or last category; and territorial divisions, along with some types of kin-based groups, are usually expressed in the physical plans of houses and communities. Furthermore, we believe that the degree of significance of an organized group within a society is closely correlated with the degree to which physical discreteness is expressed. For example, if lineages are definable in a given society but have very limited or minor functions, the possibility of mutual residence of its members is probably much less than a case where lineages are highly organized and well-integrated corporate groups possessing a variety of functions.

The functions of these defined social groups—economic, political, or social—can be ascertained by a statistical analysis of artifact distribution, and specific architectural features of structures—particularly when the analysis of artifacts includes a wide range of techniques now available to archaeologists, such as the analysis of wear patterns and trace element analysis to locate the sources of raw material.

In our opinion, given ideal conditions, the archaeologist can reconstruct the social and economic behavior of a prehistoric people almost to the degree of specificity that an ethnographer can study contemporary populations. By ideal, we mean perfect site preservation and complete excavation of all sites.

Obviously, neither condition is feasible and the problem is essentially one of sampling. Large-scale settlement survey of the type conducted in the Basin of Mexico is obviously one research strategy that is feasible in terms of time and money, but surveys cannot resolve all of the problems of institutional reconstruction that the archaeologist poses. To do this, excavation is needed. Over the years, large-scale excavations have been conducted at major sites like Teotihuacan and Tula and at a number of smaller centers, and ethnohistoric data on Tenochtitlan are abundant. Only a fraction of this research has involved the excavation of residences and an even smaller fraction has been oriented toward the reconstruction of institutions. Virtually all of this latter research is unpublished. Ideally, we would like to include in this volume a chapter on the results of excavations in the major centers, where the evolutionary stage of the social system is best indicated, to complement and expand the survey data, but the status of these projects makes this unfeasible. We can, however, summarize some of the preliminary results of survey, ethnohistoric research, and excavations at major centers, such as Teotihuacan, Tula, and Tenochtitlan—sites that span the final 1800 years of the cultural evolution of the Basin.

What these data demonstrate is that the general process of centralization and segregation, including all the component processes, were highly evolved at Middle Horizon Teotihuacan and in these later centers. Societies that resided in these centers and their sustaining areas were all characterized by highly evolved patterns of economic specialization, including full-time specialists, organized on a suprafamilial level (in the case of Tenochtitlan in barrio guilds); exchange systems had evolved in the point where all three kinds of exchanges were present; society was highly and complexly stratified, with a well-defined peasantry; political institutions were elaborated and involved a variety of functions; and urbanization was highly developed. In broad typological terms, all were centers of states and all were cities.

There were also differences that reflect points along the evolutionary process, with Teotihuacan representing the beginning, Tenochtitlan the end of the process, and Tula, in most cases, occupying an intermediate position. In the case of Teotihuacan, and in this case it contrasts with both Tula and Tenochtitlan, many of the peasants (approximately 40% of all of those residing in the Basin of Mexico in Middle Horizon times) resided physically at the city and made up two-thirds of the population of the city. The presence of this large class would tend to blur somewhat the socioeconomic distinction between urban and rural, and the relatively low percentage of the non-food-producing population at this city, compared to the later centers, suggests an appreciably lower index of urbanization.

The maximal size of organized craft groups at Teotihuacan was less than at Tenochtitlan, and the plans of the compounds would suggest a more kinlike structure. The barrio organization of crafts at Tenochtitlan would indicate a more guild-like organization as does Sahagun's description of some of the craft groups. In this connection it is of interest that production for export at Teotihuacan, at least of obsidian, was organized by the state. The presence of much larger craft groups at Tenochtitlan presumably meant that such production could be accomplished without the direct involvement of the state. Where Tula lies in terms of this difference is not known, but there are large continuous areas of obsidian workshops not specifically associated with public buildings that suggest a barrio-like organization of this craft.

Recent studies would suggest that Teotihuacan and Tula were not the capitals of very extensive territorial domains, at least not comparable to that of the Aztec Empire. Assuming that the Ciudadela was the palace at Teotihuacan, the residential portions of this structure were much less monumental than the palace of Moctezuma, and what evidence we have suggests lesser internal differentiation of functions of the residential structures. These characteristics would correlate with the lesser political importance of Teotihuacan and suggest that the state was much less highly developed in terms of structure. If the unexcavated structures south of Temple B at Tula are the remains of the royal palace, it too represents a much less monumental structure than that of the Aztec ruler. In connection with the process of politicization, the evidence suggests the presence of a professional warrior class in all three centers, and yet it is only at Tenochtitlan that this class seems to have been a significant element in social stratification. Finally, using architecture as a guide, Teotihuacan society seems less sharply stratified than the Aztec, that is, the quality of housing is on the average higher in the early period and a higher percentage of the population resided in living structures of high quality.

Data on all of the noted processes are noticeably poorer for the Early Horizon—First Intermediate One—Three phases, primarily because none of the centers have been extensively excavated. The only major center during this long period, other than Teotihuacan, which could be classified as a large center, is Cuicuilco, and the data on this site are very scanty. Data from the First Intermediate Three and Four phases at Teotihuacan would suggest that urbanization and its corollary process, economic specialization, was not very highly evolved. Politicization, however, as measured by monumentality of temples, was a vigorous process, at least at Cuicuilco and Teotihuacan. It is not quite clear to what degree Teotihuacan at this time was a highly stratified society. Virtually all of the population of the Basin resided at the center, which would indicate that the differentiation into well-defined socioeconomic classes was not characteristic, certainly the differentiation was not to the degree that one would suggest the presence of a peasantry class. Scattered data from smaller centers do not suggest full-time craft specialization, well-defined socioeconomic classes, marketing economies, and professionalization of warfare, but the data are admittedly scanty. There is some evidence of community level, part-time economic specialization and substantial evidence of hierarchical differentiation of statuses, primarily in the form of burial furniture, and in the differentiation between centers and small settlements during the First Intermediate Phases Two and Three. Keeping in mind the admittedly poor quality of the data, the evidence would suggest that societies during the period of time from Early Horizon to the First Intermediate Four phase would generally fit into the broad range of types Service calls tribes and chiefdoms, and Fried calls egalitarian and ranked societies.

Although the results of major excavations at the major centers are generally unavailable to us, we do have a rather large body of partially analyzed excavated data from several small sites that we excavated in conjunction with our project. Such small sites are as much a product of overall regional organization as are larger centers. In this chapter we will supplement and amplify the data on social evolution by discussing two small sites which we excavated in considerable detail. In so doing, we want to provide more complete descriptions of settlement systems than has been possible from surface remains alone. In particular, we want to more adequately reconstruct population, intracommunity social structure, and function in order to more precisely measure critical changes in segregation and sociopolitical centralization. Our fairly complete regional perspective should now permit us to understand the roles of individual excavated sites much more fully than during earlier stages of our project when such a regional perspective was much more limited. Conversely, the mass of excavated data available to us from these two sites can make the totality of our regional surface material much more comprehensible. Ideally, of course, we should have such excavations for several representative site types from each time period and each major stage of evolutionary development. One day, in a revised edition of this book, this may actually be possible. For the present, however, we must make do with what we have: two major excavations of two communities, spaced about 1000 years apart, and representing two quite different stages of evolutionary development.

One site is Loma Torremote (QF-50), excavated by Rosa Reyna and Robert Santley in 1974–1975, and dating principally from the First Intermediate Phase Two A. The entire occupation of the site runs from Early Horizon Phase Two to First Intermediate Phase Two B, but the excavated houses date primarily to First Intermediate One–Two A times. The second site is the Middle Horizon component of Maquixco Bajo (TC8), excavated by the Teotihuacan Valley Project in 1961–1962. Once again, there are several occupational components: First Intermediate Phase Four through the Middle Horizon, with Second Intermediate Phase Two and Late Horizon components as well. However, the excavated houses discussed here date from the Middle Horizon exclusively. We have selected these two sites for discussion here for two main reasons. First, the excavations in both cases were large, lateral exposures, especially designed for the purpose of reconstructing house plans and artifact distributions for a single phase. Second, the two sites represent occupations at two very different developmental stages in the Basin of Mexico: the First Intermediate Two A, in the mid-first millenium

B.C., when political organization was fragmented and when there were no major centers; and the Middle Horizon, a millennium later, when Teotihuacan was the capital of a large, highly centralized state organization. Loma Torremote was the central community of a small settlement cluster on the piedmont and alluvial plain west of Lake Xaltocan–Zumpango. Maquixco Bajo was a large, nucleated Middle Horizon community, less than 2 km west of the western border of Teotihuacan. The results are compared to less accessible or at least less complete data from a number of other dependent sites for a series of phases during the long period of occupation of the Basin.

LOMA TORREMOTE: A FIRST INTERMEDIATE PHASE TWO VILLAGE

Loma Torremote is located approximately 4 km west of the modern town of Cuautitlan in the State of Mexico. In 1974 the site was found to be in imminent danger of destruction, and from August 1974 until February 1975, an intensive surface survey, 22 stratigraphic excavations, and one large lateral excavation of three adjacent household units were carried out by I.N.A.H. in conjunction with personnel from the Pennsylvania State University (see Figure 8.1). The results of this study, plus information gathered by Harold McBride (1974) in 1968, are the basis for the following reconstruction.

Natural Setting

The site of Loma Torremote is situated on the tip of a long, low ridge which parallels the headwaters of the Rio Cuautitlan. It is centrally placed in terms of the large expanse of piedmont land which bounds the western part of the Cuautitlan Region. A large, deep soil, riverine floodplain occurs to either side of the Rio Cuautitlan, and directly to the south of the site there are a series of substantial, well-drained alluvial fans. A linear strip of humid, river bottom land flanking the Rio Cuautitlan provides an additional, readily accessible resource zone. Average precipitation is about 700 mm per year: an amount sufficient for a subsistence system based on rainfall agriculture. Palynological evidence suggests that much of the area around the site was originally in broadleaf forest (predominantly oak). Absolute elevation is about 2275 m above sea level.

The Archaeological Remains

Although the site was occupied from Late Early Horizon onward, the most substantial settlement dates to the early part of the First Intermediate Phase Two A (Atlamica subphase), and it is to this occupation that comment is directed. The First Intermediate Two A community covered an estimated 30 ha. Excavation and a grid of modern roadway cuts (laid out by a housing

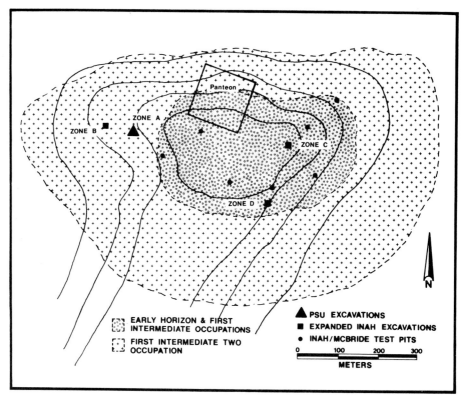

Figure 8.1. The Loma Torremote site.

contractor and providing 12 km of profiles) indicate that within the settlement zone two residential levels occurred: (*a*) the individual house compound; and (*b*) clusters of these compounds (Santley 1975, 1976a, 1976b, 1977, n.d.). Localized distributions of surface pottery suggest the possibility that some kind of barrio grouping might have existed as well, but this level does not seem to be represented by any clustering tendency in residences. A fourth level of analysis, of course, is the site as a whole.

The house compound was the fundamental unit of settlement at Loma Torremote. Each compound contained a wattle and daub, *tepetate* floored residence; one or more compacted earth, patio activity areas adjoining the dwelling; and a small garden, all enclosed by an adobe wall (see Figures 8.2, 8.3, 8.4, 8.5, 8.6, 8.7, and 8.8). Truncated conical storage pits—filled with trash after falling into disuse—abound in the patio and within certain sections of larger residences. Abundant refuse is present in the patio and sometimes within the house, but is rarely found in the garden area. Hearths also tend to be a patio phenomenon, although in one instance a small roofed-over kitchen was appended to the main structure. Burials, of all ages and sexes, generally occur in the patio but are occasionally found under

Figure 8.2. View of crushed *tepetate* house floor, post hole, and two bell-shaped storage pits. Depressions in upper right-hand part of photograph are rodent burrows, Loma Terremote.

Figure 8.3. Junction of house floor and patio. Note the difference in soil texture and shade between the floor and patio, Loma Terremote.

Figure 8.4. Profile showing superimposed crushed *tepetate* house floors. Post hole is associated with uppermost floor, Loma Terremote.

Figure 8.5. View of bell-shaped storage pit. Note high density of refuse within pit, Loma Terremote.

Figure 8.6. Junction of two adobe compound walls, Loma Torremote.

Figure 8.7. Adobe compound wall, showing offset orientation of individual bricks, Loma Torremote.

Figure 8.8. Mass of cut *tepetate* slabs noted in bulldozed roadway profile, Loma Torremote.

house floors. All three excavated compounds were continuously and contemporaneously occupied for nearly 100 years (ca. 650–550 B.C.). Residences
were frequently rebuilt in the same location, many of which assumed the
same configuration after subsequent rebuildings.

Individual house compounds were grouped into a settlement unit that
we are calling the house compound cluster. Each cluster consisted of from
three, to as many as six, spatially adjacent house compounds which shared
common walls. No differences were evident in the quality of house construction between member compounds in the same cluster or between clusters.
No distinctive exterior wall associates with the cluster; each is defined by the
outermost compound walls of the member households. In the excavated
cluster each compound has a surface area of about 300–450 m², the residence
itself covering about 30–40 m² of roofed-over space. Compound A-1, however, appears to have been larger (ca. 550–600 m² in size), and it contained a
series of more substantial dwellings. For these structures, roofed-over space
is usually greater than 100 m² and may be as high as 135 m². Attached to these
buildings are one or more annex-like constructions. Annexes typically have
different wall orientations, contain all subfloor burials associated with the
larger residences, and exhibit little evidence of purely domestic use.

Whereas surface occupation is distributed over an area approximately
30 ha in extent, the area physically occupied by residential structures is somewhat less, circa 24–25 ha. In the southwestern part of the site, the roadway
cuts have bisected a 2.5 ha area where occupational debris is abundant on the

surface and in the roadway profiles, yet where features such as house floors, bell-shaped pits, adobe walls, and burials are absent. We interpret this area as a village midden where household refuse was periodically dumped in antiquity, but where there was little or no permanent residential architecture to speak of. There is also an area 1–2 ha in size near the modern cemetery which may have functioned as the village plaza. The remaining 0.5–1.5 ha of surface occupation we attribute to the scattering effects of plow agriculture and/or to erosion.

Our data indicate that residential compounds at Loma Torremote were tightly packed. In and around the Zone A excavations, the density of contemporaneous households is from 16 to 19 per hectare. In the central part of the site (near Zones C and D) the density of compounds appears to be greater, perhaps as high as 30 households per hectare. The total size of the First Intermediate Two A community, therefore, approached 400–475 households. This qualifies Loma Torremote as a large nucleated village.

Social Structure

Any reconstruction of the kind of social grouping(s) associated with the house compound or house compound cluster is predicated on deriving reliable estimates of the number of individuals occupying the residential units in question. As we observed in Chapter 3, the burial data suggest that each compound contained a social group numbering five individuals on the average. The excavated First Intermediate Two A structures at Loma Torremote, however, were rebuilt at least five to seven times, and residence size tended to increase (and sometimes decrease) with each successive building level (see Table 8.1 and Figures 8.9, 8.10, 8.11, 8.12, 8.13, and 8.14). This we propose is the result of short-term changes in population size within each household unit.

Fluctuations in population size can be determined if variations in

TABLE 8.1
Estimates of the Number of Occupants in Each Excavated Compound and in the Residential Cluster[a]

Building level	Compound A-1	Compound A-2	Compound A-3	Residential cluster
IV B	3	2	4	6–9
IV A	4	2	6	6–12
III B	6	3	—	14–22
III A	6	8	4	28–39
II B	6	8	6	29–40
II A	5	7	???	20–27
I	5???	—	—	5
Mean	5	5	5	15–22

[a] After Santley 1977.

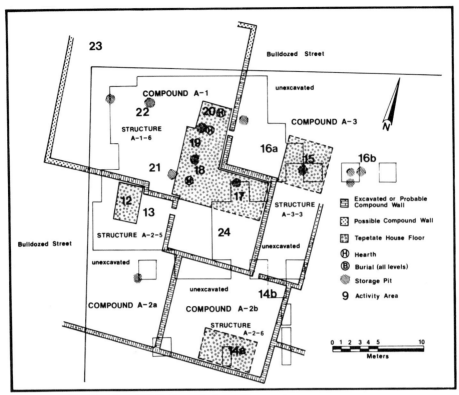

Figure 8.9. Building Level IV B, Zone A, Loma Torremote.

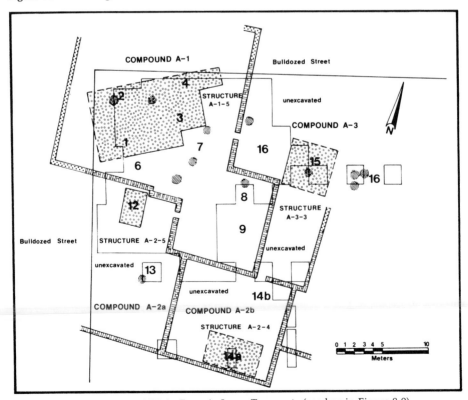

Figure 8.10. Building Level IV A, Zone A, Loma Torremote (see key in Figure 8.9).

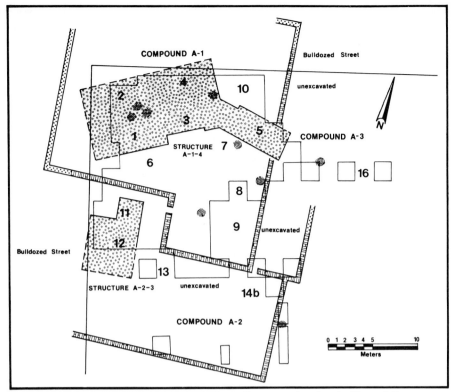

Figure 8.11. Building Level III B, Zone A, Loma Torremote (see key in Figure 8.9).

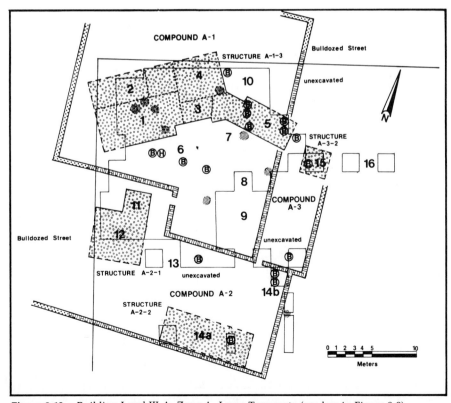

Figure 8.12. Building Level III A, Zone A, Loma Torremote (see key in Figure 8.9).

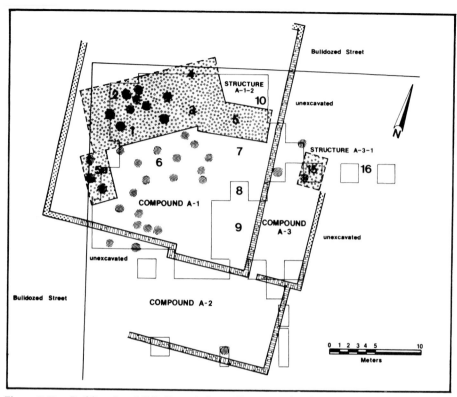

Figure 8.13. Building Level II B, Zone A, Loma Torremote (see key in Figure 8.9).

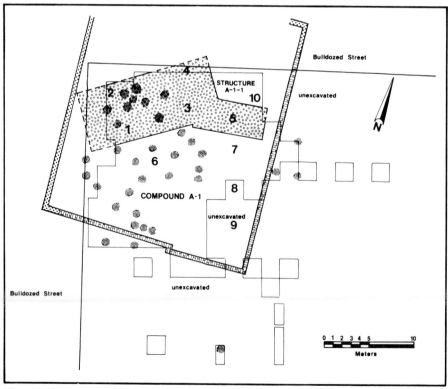

Figure 8.14. Building Level II A, Zone A, Loma Torremote (see key in Figure 8.9).

roofed-over space can be shown to covary with population. At Loma Torremote, increases in the rate of artifact consumption, our measure of the
number of implement-consuming individuals, vary directly with increases
in house size, so roofed-over space appears to be an excellent indicator of
population size. Therefore, while the earliest compounds (Level IV B) were
inhabited by no more than three individuals, a population of 7–8 occupants
is suggested by Level III. Compound cluster size changes accordingly: from
8–12 individuals to a maximum of 28–32 individuals by Level II A. To judge
from our estimate of 400–475 contemporaneous compounds, the population
of the site as a whole at its maximum growth ranged from a minimum of 2000
to a high of 2850 individuals (see Figure 8.15).

The demographic estimates, the small size of most structures, and the
low density of artifacts imply that each of the earliest compounds was
inhabited by a single nuclear family. In two of the three excavated compounds the evidence from later building levels indicated occupation by a
larger familial grouping: presumably one organized on a more extended
basis. In the third case (i.e., Compound A-3) the nuclear family seems to
have remained together as the characteristic social group, although only for
two successive building levels. In Compound A-2 (and possibly in Compound A-1 as well) the component nuclear families making up the extended
unit appear to have split during their later history. In fact, offspring from
these households may have been responsible for the founding of two compounds to the west of Zone A by Level II. This process fits both the ethnographic and the ethnohistoric record where extended families, once they
begin to develop, are rather short-lived phenomena (see Table 8.2).

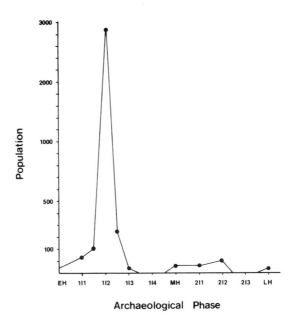

Figure 8.15. Population history
of the Loma Torremote site.

TABLE 8.2
Kind of Family Grouping Occupying Three Atlamica Phase House Compounds[a]

Building level	Compound A-1	Compound A-2	Compound A-3
IV B	Nuclear	Nuclear	Nuclear
IV A	Nuclear	Nuclear	Nuclear
III B	Nuclear–extended	Nuclear	—
III A	Extended	Extended	Nuclear
II B	Extended	Extended–fraternal joint	Nuclear
I	Nuclear ???	—	—

[a] After Santley 1977.

With regard to the next residential level, we have data on the history of four house compound clusters (see Figures 8.16 and 8.17). In three out of the four cases, the house compound cluster was founded as a full-blown unit (Santley 1976b:17–18). House size gradually increased through time, and a few additional compounds were later added to the cluster. The population estimates (i.e., 6–9 persons) indicate that the earliest clusters were occupied by a single extended family. Growth thereafter is quite explosive, with an estimated 29–40 persons residing in the cluster by Level II B. Although this latter figure is within the demographic range for the extended family in several West African societies (e.g., the Nupe), the fact that house location and configuration remained relatively constant for a period of nearly 100 years strongly implies the formation of a residential group which could reckon descent for four or more generations (Santley 1976a:7).

The key variable affecting our assessment of the kind of social grouping occupying the excavated residential cluster is the successive appearance of four ceremonial shrines in Compound A-1. That the house annex was a shrine is indicated by the covariant occurrence of a great number of ritual objects, plus all subfloor burials. In societies dominated by lineage organizations, ritual shrines, when found, occur frequently in association with the residence of the lineage head. Although individual families may have their own ceremonial area, that associated with the lineage head is usually more impressive. Further, ritual at the shrines is often devoted to the welfare of the entire suprafamilial group, and it is of interest here that the vast majority of all ceramic figurines found in the house annex have exaggerated sexual features, perhaps for emphasizing fertility and growth. Therefore, because of residential continuity and growth over nearly a century and because of the presence of a ceremonial shrine in a particular household, we propose that the ancestry of the residential group could be traced for at least four and possibly five or more generations, and hence, that our later compound cluster was occupied by a lineage of minimal size.

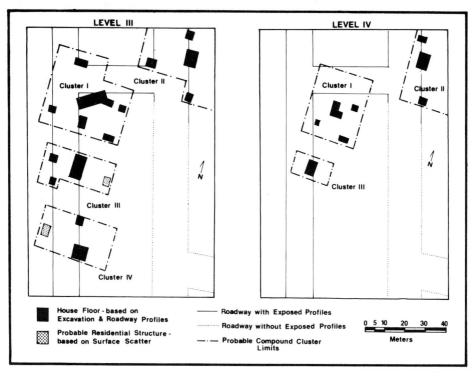

Figure 8.16. Distribution of structures during Building Levels IV and III in the vicinity of Zone A, Loma Torremote.

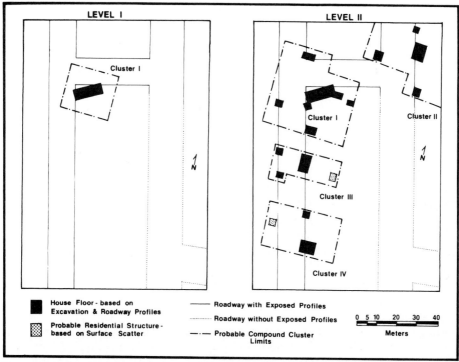

Figure 8.17. Distribution of structures during Building Levels II and I in the vicinity of Zone A, Loma Torremote.

Whether or not there were residential groupings above the level of the house compound cluster is still a moot point. A number of ceramic wares (e.g., whiteware and buffware) exhibit localized biases in our surface samples. It is conceivable that these distributions reflect the presence of some supracluster kinship grouping, one which both manufactured and consumed particular wares to a greater extent than its neighbors. Alternatively, it may be suggested that this kind of variation is related to part-time specialization in pottery manufacture, to differential consumption of certain wares along status lines, to sampling biases, or to one or more of these. Another line of evidence comes from the surface survey. In the Cuautitlan region there is a tendency for First Intermediate settlements to fission, followed during the next phase by reaggregation back at the parent community (Santley n.d.). The size of these fissioned segments is quite variable, but most seem to contain from 50 to 150 persons. Since, in several cases, the budded grouping comprised 100 or more persons, we can conclude that kinship linkage to the parent community occurred above the level of the residential cluster. From this, it might be suggested that some kind of segmentary lineage organization provided the mechanism through which incorporation back into the mother settlement was achieved. On purely circumstantial grounds, therefore, it can be argued that the next level in the kinship hierarchy involved a larger lineage grouping which connected the level of the house compound cluster with that of the social system (i.e., site) as a whole. But because this level does not appear to be correlated with any differences in residential patterning, its demonstration must await further testing.

Rank Differences

Our next consideration involves the manner of social relations between households in the same residential cluster. In other words, can rank differences be detected within the cluster, or is the basis of compound articulation essentially egalitarian in nature? The data from our earliest compounds (Level IV) indicate that the status position of each household was comparable. This pattern is reflected in a number of areas: (a) by the similar frequencies of chipped and ground stone tools in each compound; (b) by the relatively narrow range in pottery vessel consumption per person per year; (c) by the fact that all compounds were engaged in a similar intensity of ritual–ceremonial activity, as measured by the quantity of ceremonial artifacts; (d) by the inability of any compound to store unusually large grain surpluses; and (e) by the relatively small size of all residences in comparison with later building levels. The only observable difference is the larger size of structure A-1-6, the result, perhaps, of occupancy either by the extended family head (suggesting gerontocratic status) or by a slightly larger nuclear family group.

Beginning in Level III B and extending through Level II A, the social group occupying the house compound cluster increased greatly in size and became internally differentiated. Although in these later compounds there is still little variation in manner of burial treatment and mode of house construction, a number of other criteria do serve to distinguish Compound A-1 from neighboring households. First, the structures associated with this household are consistently larger in size, and per capita roofed-over space is twice that noted throughout the rest of the cluster. The ceremonial shrine, the house annex, is a characteristic feature in Compound A-1. In Compound A-2 this construction seems to be absent, as is likely for Compound A-3 as well. The shrine therefore associates with a particular household, specifically, the one residing in the larger dwelling. Third, at least twice as many ceramic vessels are available for use by the occupants of Compound A-1, and the intensity of ritual activity is two to three times that noted in adjacent compounds. Obsidian is more common vis-à-vis chert, as are artifacts made from exotic materials (i.e., greenstone, shell, and golden-green obsidian), and evidence of fluted core preparation is wholly confined to this household. Also, by Level II times approximately 2.2 times as much grain than was annually needed could have been stored in subterranean pits located in Compound A-1, whereas annual needs were just barely met in neighboring compounds. Finally, when Compound A-1 expanded in size (from an estimated 469 m² in Level IV to more than 600 m² by Level II), it was able to do so at the expense of adjacent households, thereby forcing these residences to relocate. All of these differences appear on a progressive basis. They are manifested to a greater degree than rises in population levels, so that variations in the number of occupants do not seem to be a likely explanation. Gerontocratic status can also be rejected because here we would expect variation to occur only within a single building level and the overall pattern should be more cyclical in nature, corresponding to the growth and decay of individual extended families. In contrast, if these patterns are related to emerging ranked distinctions, then they should appear to a greater extent over several generations and remain in evidence regardless of fluctuations in population size. This seems to be exactly what the trajectory for Compound A-1 suggests.

In sum, it appears that differences were not well-developed in the earliest First Intermediate Two A compounds. By Level III, differentials in prestige have become increasingly apparent in Compound A-1, while neighboring households continued to resemble the earlier compounds. It is suspected that these positions of higher prestige were ranked, since the aforementioned variation cannot be attributed to changes in population size and/or to momentary positions of gerontocratic status in certain households. Moreover, the fact that the ranked household is always found in the same compound strongly implies that the higher status position of this family was maintained by some hereditary rule of succession. The extent of this status differentiation, however, does not seem to have been very extreme, at least to judge from the overall uniformity in type of interment and in mode of house construction.

At Loma Torremote the ranked compound performed a number of partially specialized activities, which shed some light on the dynamics of household economic interaction during the First Intermediate Phase Two. One major function of the high status household was obsidian procurement and blade manufacture. Obsidian appears to have been obtained in some way from the source deposits in the Teotihuacan Valley. Before being distributed throughout the residential cluster, some obsidian nodules were preformed into finely prepared fluted cores. The fact that no fluted cores or small trimming flakes were found in neighboring compounds indicates that the blades, themselves, were distributed rather than cores. Irregularly shaped obsidian nuclei and primary flakes, however, do occur in low status compounds, implying that the raw material for more crudely prepared implements (possibly obsidian of lower quality) was available for immediate use throughout the cluster. It is also possible that some of the blades manufactured in Compound A-1 were passed up the ranked hierarchy in exchange of other commodities from residential clusters of similar rank within the village. In the high status compound we also find a great amount of obsidian in comparison with other chipped stone, while neighboring compounds appear to have been consuming a greater proportion of chert. This suggests that obsidian was a relatively highly valued commodity and that it was differentially distributed according to either the relative status position or buying power of each individual compound. Another possibility is that the ranked compound carried out some partly specialized, implement-consuming activity.

In societies dominated by lineage organizations individuals of greater rank frequently occupy positions of high religious standing (Fried 1967:137). The ritual function of the lineage head is intimately related to his position as the closest living relative of some deceased common ancestor. This position entitles him to be a major figure in performing a series of religious ceremonies on behalf of the lineage, many of which relate to group welfare, the agricultural cycle, and fertility. Among societies where ancestor worship dominates much of the religious hierarchy, the lineage head commonly also has a small altar or ancestral shrine built near his residence. Such also seems to be the case for the compound of the lineage chief at Loma Torremote.

Another function of the ranked compound is the storage of agricultural surpluses. Storage pits were 2.2 times as numerous in Compound A-1 than in adjacent compounds, even after correcting for the variable size of the domestic units. These surpluses are viewed not as individual gain but as a necessary prerequisite for insurance against crop failures. It may be that the ranked compound had access to a greater amount of humid land along the Rio Cuautitlan so that surpluses could be expected to occur more commonly in association with the high status household for that reason. On the other hand, surpluses from the entire cluster may have been stored in a central repository simply to facilitate redistribution to needy compounds during lean years. We suspect that some of this surplus passed into the ranked compound in exchange for obsidian products. It is also likely that another amount left the compound of the lineage head in exchange for commodities procured nonlocally. Last, we believe that a small part was siphoned off for exclusive use by the high status compound (perhaps for services rendered) and thus may have represented accumulated wealth.

To recapitulate, the ranked household seems to be involved in the performance of group ritual and in the specialized production of fluted obsidian cores and obsidian blades. It also seems probable that this same household was engaged in the procurement of raw obsidian and that it served as a central place for the storage of agricultural produce. It would appear, therefore, that high status households operated primarily as agents of local redistribution: a function that is wholly consistent with our evaluation of the house compound cluster as the local segment of a ramage-like lineage grouping (see the following discussion).

The Social System

The ethnographic record points out that ranked social systems may take one of two general forms :(a) a series of large unilineal descent groups, often called sibs; and (b) the conical clan or ramage. In unilineal descent groups members of each sib can trace their ancestry back to a different common ancestor. One sib or lineage is typically ranked above all the others, while for the remainder there is no overall system for ranking individuals or lineages. Chiefly functions include leadership in war and dispute arbitration. On the other hand, in ramage systems, all descent groups are ranked in terms of their degree of geneological distance from some deceased, semimythical common ancestor, the chief, of course, being the most closely related living descendent (Service 1962). Descent in the ramage is reckoned bilaterally and includes the principle of primogeniture, so every member of a particular ramage occupies a unique position of rank that is determined by calculation of the degree of closeness (or distance) to the chief (Service 1962). The function of the chiefly personage is not restricted to dispute arbitration or war leadership, as in many unilineal systems, but he is also redistributor of goods from one kinship grouping or localized segment of the chiefdom to another.

The kind of ranked structure manifest at Loma Torremote is closely akin to the ramified organization discussed above (see Figure 8.18). Ranked compounds were involved in low-level redistribution of both agricultural and obsidian products. Evidence of status differentiation was also present on the most local level, the minimal lineage. Such a pattern is not expected in unilineal systems where the relative status of most households should be very similar and where there should be little if any evidence of redistribution. Further, the ranked compound exhibited remarkable continuity both in residence location and residence configuration, suggesting that the higher status position of this household was maintained by some rule of hereditary

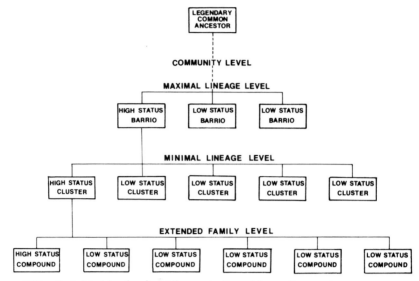

Figure 8.18. Postulated levels of social organization at Loma Torremote.

succession (e.g., primogeniture). Moreover, ramage-like social systems appear to have had a very widespread distribution in Mesoamerica at the time of the Conquest. The Aztec *calpulli* bears a close resemblance to the ramage (Sanders and Price 1968: 155–156), as does the structural organization of Mixtec society (Spores 1967: 10–13) and of the Cuicatec *cacicazgos* (Hunt 1972). In the Valley of Guatemala a ramage-like chiefdom seems to be present at Kaminaljuyu from First Intermediate Phase Two times onward (Michels 1976).

One major difference between the ramage organization in Polynesia and First Intermediate Two society at Loma Torremote was the relatively minor role that sumptuary rules played in sanctifying, legitimizing, and separating the chief and other high status personages from the remainder of the population. Interestingly, evidence for displays of material wealth associated with individuals of high rank (i.e., lavish interments) are particularly characteristic of the Early Horizon in the Basin. Extraordinary amounts of burial furniture (e.g., pottery, figurines, ground and chipped stone objects) do not continue to accompany grave lots during the First Intermediate period when ranked society was supposedly a Basin-wide phenomenon. This suggests that the degree of isomorphism between the First Intermediate Two–Three polities in the Basin of Mexico and the Polynesian ramage is not that exact. In fact, differential control of particular plots of highly productive land may have led to certain fundamental differences. Nevertheless, the association of ranked distinctions, a stipulated principle of geneological succession, and limited low-level redistribution would seem to indicate that Loma Torremote can be considered as an example of the general chiefdom type.

Economic Structure

Analysis of the excavated animal and plant remains indicates that subsistence was derived primarily from agricultural produce. The data also demonstrate a moderately heavy reliance on hunting and gathering. The kinds of utilized species point out that each of these sources of energy production can be divided further into a number of more specific food procurement systems. Cultivated plants at Loma Torremote included the following species: maize, chili pepper (*Capsicum Annuum*), beans (*Phaseolus* spp.), *tomate* (*Physalis* spp.), *chia* (*Salvia* spp.), and *amaranth* (Reyna Robles and Gonzales 1976; Santley n.d.). Of these by far the most common is maize. The species of maize cultivated is pre-Chapalote, and ear size is quite small (ca. 4–5 cm in length), so the variety planted must either have had multiple ears or have been closer spaced than modern varieties in order to attain a yield value worthy of cultivation. A larger type (similar in morphology to the small-eared variety) also occurs, but only in very small amounts.

We infer that agricultural subsistence at Loma Torremote contained three components: the garden plot, humid land agriculture along the adjacent bottom lands flanking the Rio Cuautitlan, and temporal cultivation on the nearby lower piedmont. Gardens were apparently located both within individual compounds and between residential clusters. Intracompound gardens were extremely small (70 m² or less), but separating compound clusters larger areas were available for cultivation. Our estimate, however, is that no more than *approximately* 10–15 ha of the site area could have been potentially utilized as garden space—only enough to have provided about 3% of the village maize requirement (Santley n.d.). Analogy with contemporary land use patterns suggests that much of this area was probably planted in vegetables, not maize.

An area of high natural humidity parallels the Rio Cuautitlan and comprises one category of agricultural land. Such zones are extremely favorable for agricultural exploitation because periodic floodings maintain a friable soil texture and restore nutrient levels, and because the high level of subsurface moisture precludes complete dependence on rainfall. Crop security, in consequence, is high, as are yield levels. It is presumed that much of this area was intensively cultivated, probably in maize and *amaranth*. On the basis of analogy with twentieth-century peasant villages in Mesoamerica, we would suggest a sustaining area for subsistence crops of no more than a 5-km radius from the village. Within this radius at Loma Torremote were all three categories of agricultural land. Humid lands were quite circumscribed in distribution within the suggested radius, however. At best, we estimate that some 200–250 ha were readily available for cultivation, of which approximately 100 ha were probably lying fallow or under standing water. This would have been sufficient to contribute about 17% of the total annual subsistence requirement.

That a substantial amount of the lower piedmont was cultivated is strongly suggested by the fact that produce from the gardens and naturally humid lands could not sustain the energy needs of the resident population at Loma Torremote. Because of its slightly higher precipitation (vis-à-vis the alluvial plain), its reduced frost problem, and its forest vegetation (principally oak), the lower piedmont is ideally suited for cultivation using extensive techniques. In the central highlands today this system of land use is known as *tlacolol*. A land use factor of 5 to 6 is common, and simple digging sticks would be the only tool required. Under conditions of greater demographic pressure such as occurs over much of the Central Plateau today, plows or hoes are used for preparing the soil and the ratio of cultivated to fallow land reduces to 1:2, 1:1, 2:1. This system is frequently referred to as *temporal* or *barbecho* cultivation. Either system could have been used at Loma Torremote, dependent on the population pressure. The large size of the village would suggest a shorter fallowing system. Maize and *amaranth* again appear to have been the major cultigens, perhaps interspersed with beans and squash. The most serious problem for agricultural land use is the amount of effective moisture, which varies considerably from year to year. As a result, since agriculture here is rainfall dependent, yield levels fluctuate widely—from complete failure to values comparable to those from intensively cultivated plots. Because of the relatively small amount of humid lands available to Loma Torremote, we estimate that perhaps as much as 40% of the community's caloric needs were obtained from parcels of land cultivated in this manner.

To date, there is no evidence suggesting the widespread application of more intensive forms of land use at Loma Torremote during the First Intermediate Phase Two. First Intermediate Two A settlements consistently prefer piedmont locales, and it is not until Phase Three times that hydraulic agriculture was probably introduced as a major subsistence alternative. Data pertaining to agricultural terracing are similarly wanting. If either of these techniques were employed as a part of the subsistence economy, then it would seem that they only accounted for an extremely small fraction of all agricultural production.

Game animals are a year-round source of energy production. Three categories of game appear to have been exploited on a regular basis: white-tailed deer (*Odocoileus virginianus*); cottontail rabbit (*Sylvilagus* spp.); and various species of waterfowl. Species of secondary import that were occasionally consumed include dog (possibly domesticated), mud turtle, jaguar–puma, and mule deer (McBride 1974: 221–222). In the Mesoamerican highlands generally, deer appear to have been the single most predominant source of meat during the First Intermediate period, surpassing 90% of the game food value in many cases (Flannery 1967: 171; Tolstoy and Paradis 1970: 350; Starbuck 1975: 76; White n.d.). White-tailed deer occur in almost every habitat in Mesoamerica but are most abundant in pine–oak woodland situations (Flannery 1968: 73). Deer are also exceptionally prolific breeders, commonly being able to withstand a 30–40% cropping rate (Leopold 1959: 513). Ethnographic analogies suggest that hunting was performed by individual males using the spearthrower and tracking technique (MacNeish n.d.). At Loma Torremote, although deer are amply represented in excavated contexts, our conclusion is that they could not have contributed any more than 5% of total energy needs on a continuing basis (Santley 1977; and see Appendix D).

Great numbers of rabbit and bird also occur in our excavated samples. Rabbits seem to have been caught using small traps or snares (Flannery 1968: 73–74). Waterfowl, on the other hand, seem to have been procured either by netting or with the bow and arrow. Whereas rabbits are a nearly inexhaustable perennial source of meat, waterfowl are mainly available during the winter months when literally tens of thousands of migratory ducks travel southward along the central flyway. Despite their common archaeological occurrence, the food value of individual birds and rabbits is extremely low, so it is very doubtful that these genera ever provided a significant portion of the diet.

Wild plants are a third food source. The species recovered at Loma Torremote illustrate the full range of gathered resources. Included in our samples are *nopal* (*Opuntia* spp.), *tejocote* (*Crataegus mexicana*), fox-tail grass (*Setaria* spp.), wild rice (*Oryziopsis* spp.), *Potamogeton*, *girasol* (*Helianthus* spp.), *verdolaga* (*Portulaca* spp.), and possibly various members of the Chenopodiaceae (Reyna Robles and Gonzalez 1976). The species exploited come from a variety of environmental zones—the lakeshore, humid locales near perennial streams, the alluvial plain, and the piedmont—so it seems that gathering activities ranged very far afield. Also represented are weedy plants, presumably collected on fallow agricultural land. Regrettably, particular gathered species cannot be ranked at present in terms of their relative dietary contribution. Taken as a whole, however, an estimate of 30% does not seem unreasonable, in lieu of data from elsewhere in the Central Plateau (MacNeish 1967).

Craft Specialization

Data from Loma Torremote also permit a reconstruction of household activity patterns. The activities discussed here are primarily technological in nature, that is, they are represented by variations in the distributional patterning of different kinds of artifacts and features. There must be a broad spectrum of pattern activity which has no artifact analogues, at least none that were preserved in excavated contexts. These we make no attempt to address. Our reconstruction considers only that segment of patterned human behavior for which there is material evidence.

All of our data clearly indicate that most of the village's technology was produced at the site. On the level of the individual household each appears to have manufactured its own pottery, chipped its own crude obsidian, chert, and basalt tools; produced, prepared, stored, and of course consumed its own food; built, swept, and repaired its own dwellings, and engaged in some woodworking, scraping, and ritual activities. Both female-related and male-oriented tasks are represented in each household. The patio, an irregular compacted-earth area outside the house, was the main focus of domestic activity. Within the house the number, kind, and spatial segregation of activities varies directly with residence size. Structures of 30 m² or less exhibited little evidence of activity patterning. By the time the residence approaches 40 m², spatially distinct activity loci begin to appear. These are well-marked by the time the dwelling reaches 70 m². Above 100 m² ritual loci become well-defined. Our largest structures (130–135 m² in size) contain at least five areas of behavioral import: (1) an obsidian workshop, (2) a probable sleeping room, (3) a zone where grinding implements and utilitarian pottery are extremely common, (4) a locus where decorated service wares are unusually abundant, and finally (5) a ritual–ceremonial shrine—the house annex (Santley 1976a:3).

Within the excavated residential cluster a number of activities have more localized distributions. Obsidian blade manufacture, as we have seen, only occurs in Compound A-1. This household, we believe, had fluted core preparation as a part-time specialty. In fact, given the very low rate of implement usage, enough blades could have been produced in a day or two to accommodate the total domestic needs of the residential cluster. For the entire site (an estimated 400–475 households) perhaps no more than one man-month of labor would be needed to satisfy the total community's requirements.

There is also some evidence to suggest that pottery manufacture had become a part-time specialization. As we have noted, ceramic manufacture was a domestic endeavor: Data pertaining to pottery making occur in each of our excavated Atlamica phase households. A number of ceramic wares, however, do distribute nonrandomly in our surface samples. We have already mentioned that this kind of variation might reflect the presence of supracluster kinship groupings. Decorated pottery wares tend to have variable percentage spatial distributions, yet they are wholly complementary in terms of vessel function. It is conceivable, therefore, that particular lineage segments each produced their own series of decorated wares for immediate local consumption. A similar interpretation of ceramic variability—this time using decorative motifs—has also been proposed by Longacre (1970:28) for the Carter Ranch site in east–central Arizona.

The procurement and distribution of house foundation building material is our third example of part-time craft specialization at Loma Torremote. House foundations at the site consist of cut *tepetate* slabs, and the kind of *tepetate* selected for foundation material appears to have been quarried at source deposits some distance away from the community (Santley 1976:19). Near the Zone A excavations a deep modern sewer trench had cut through a mass of shaped *tepetate* blocks at least 2 m in depth. The disjunctive way the blocks associate with one another, plus the depth of feature, suggest that the deposit was a stockpile of building material rather than the remains of a destroyed structure or wall foundation. The sheer quantity of material exposed by the trench indicates an activity that required considerable labor input. As no other features of this type were recognized in the bulldozed profiles, the associated household may have been totally responsible for quarrying, shaping, and redistributing this material on a site-wide basis.

It should be emphasized that we do not believe that craft specialization at Loma Torremote was tied in with a market economy. The exchange system that we envision is based on low-level redistribution, so that rather than exchange *quid pro quo*, commodities are passed up the ranked hierarchy for allocation by lineage chiefs to needy households. Whether redistribution occurred above the minimal lineage level is not clear. It is possible that unprocessed obsidian was redistributed from some higher level in the segmentary system to the lineage chief, but it is also possible that each lineage chief procured obsidian for his followers.

Religious Organization

Another significant result of the Loma Torremote Project concerns the data it has produced on First Intermediate phase religious activity. A factor analytic study of "ritual–elite" objects found during the excavations indicates several different categories of ceremonial behavior (Santley 1977). These include ritual food consumption (polychrome and other decorated vessel forms), magico-religious petitioning connected with fertility and growth (ceramic figurines and squinch pots), bloodletting (golden-green obsidian microblades), and general ceremonial activity (ceramic drums, censers, masks, and crescents). With the exception of bloodletting, all of these activities occurred in each household unit, although their intensity in Compound A-1 was considerably greater. Bloodletting, on the other hand, was only found in association with the house annex.

Variations in the kind, amount, and context of ritual objects suggest that the residential cluster organized its ceremonial activity on several conceptual levels. The most basic level is that of the individual household. The northern section of structures A-2-1 and A-2-3 (Area 11) appears to have functioned as these households' ceremonial locus, since figurines and censer fragments were more common here than in any other excavated part of Compound A-2 and evidence of most other kinds of activity was characteristically lacking. The same may be said for the patio (Area 6) in Compound A-1, although the number of ritual objects that occurred at this locus suggests a more intense kind of religious involvement. This higher occurrence of ceremonial artifacts (especially figurines) we believe reflects both individual family ritual and in some instances joint participation by the entire residential cluster. Some of the religious activities carried out in this patio area therefore constitute a second level in ritual organization, one that was devoted to the welfare of the local lineage group.

A third level is represented by the ancestral shrine. Inside this structure

more than 200 figurines and censer fragments have been found, along with
several complete ceramic masks, most of the shell found during the excavations, and five subfloor burials. As already mentioned, there is reason to
believe that the shrine served in suprafamilial ritual. Second, and perhaps
more importantly, we believe that the occurrence of the shrine in association
with the ranked household aided in legitimizing this compound's high
status position vis-à-vis the remainder of the cluster. In many ethnographically known chiefdoms, specialized ceremonial structures are erected as
memorials to particular personages and descent lines. Worship of particular
individuals or lineage segments tends to reinforce status distinctions, because those persons who are most closely related to a particular descent line
are frequently accorded the privilege of playing the major role in worship,
and because those of high ritual standing are also the same persons responsible for overseeing dispute arbitration and redistribution. At the same time,
the local lineage patriarch is related to an even more distant series of common
ancestors whose genealogical ties form the basis for integrating the entire
social system. In this way the system of descent group ranking receives
ideological justification.

Summary

In this section we have presented a reconstruction of a society at Loma
Torremote—a First Intermediate Phase Two site in the Basin of Mexico. Our
reconstruction has principally considered two levels of domestic organization, the individual household and the residential group. Each excavated
household appears to have been founded by a small nuclear family, and in
two cases it seems that these family groups evolved gradually into social
units organized on a more extended basis. Concomitant with this development was the transformation of the residential cluster into a lineage grouping
of minimal size. Within the lineage segment one household is ranked above
the others, its higher position being maintained by some hereditary rule of
succession. Lineage heads have a number of redistributive functions: obsidian procurement, the manufacture and distribution of obsidian blades, and
the storage and allotment of agricultural surpluses. It also seems likely that
ranked individuals also functioned as ritual specialists. The simultaneous
appearance of ranked distinctions, a prescribed mode of descent, and low-
level redistributive exchange suggest that First Intermediate society at Loma
Torremote structurally resembled the Polynesian ramage. However, the degree of congruence does not seem to be exact, due to the relatively insignificant role played by sumptuary rules in isolating chiefly personages.

Household economics was based on subsistence agriculture. Included
here are three components: gardening, humedad agriculture, and temporal
cultivation. In addition, moderate dietary inputs are provided by hunting
and gathering. Hunting appears to have focused on white-tailed deer procurement, whereas gathering had as its objective the collection of a wide

variety of resources. Craft specialization at Loma Torremote appears to have been incipient. What evidence we do find is closely tied in with exchange along redistributive lines. Several levels of ritual–ceremonial activity have also been suggested. These seem to reflect the basic levels of domestic organization.

Comparisons with Other First Intermediate Sites

Certain parallels may also be drawn with excavated First Intermediate sites elsewhere in the Basin. It should be strongly emphasized at this juncture that the quality of this comparative material is often quite variable. To a large extent this is because relatively few research projects have had as their objective the delineation of household residential patterns and by extrapolation the sociocultural, political, and economic underpinnings responsible for archaeological patterning. A large number of projects have focused on the excavation of civic–ceremonial–elite architecture. Equal effort has also been devoted to chronological considerations. Both of these are of course very legitimate undertakings, but unfortunately they do not lend themselves to yielding much data of the type pertinent to the central theme of this chapter. Nevertheless, a number of general comparisons may be made.

Regarding residential groups, we have data from Coapexco (Tolstoy and Fish 1973, 1975) and from Cuanalan (Sanders *et al.* 1975; Fletcher 1962). At Coapexco (an Early Horizon Phase One village) and at Cuanalan (a First Intermediate Phase Two B village) residential structures are small—about 15–25 m^2 of roofed-over space per dwelling—so that each was probably occupied by a single nuclear family (see Figures 8.19 and 8.20). Associated with each of the excavated structures is the full range of the debris of the processing of domestic technology, suggesting that, as at Loma Torremote, most of the household's material needs were produced locally, if not by the individual household itself. In both cases the residence is located next to or surrounded by an irregular area of compacted earth, the patio, where most domestic activities were carried out. At Cuanalan, excavations and accidental profiles suggest that houses were closely located, but no definite indications of household clusters of the Torremote type were present. Household clustering is also not evident at Coapexco.

To come by data concerning social structure is a much more difficult matter. Perhaps the best evidence, at least for the Early Horizon and First Intermediate period, is from Tlatilco, a site long famous for its spectacular, lavish burials. In the literature this site is frequently referred to as a cemetery, but the association of interments with abundant domestic refuse and tronco-conical pits—features which at Loma Torremote invariably occurred near domestic structures—indicates that Tlatilco definitely had a substantial residential occupation. The fact that earthen platforms, some with frontal steps, and fragments of adobe plaster could be discerned in the profiles of recent brick-making pits provides added support for this point of view

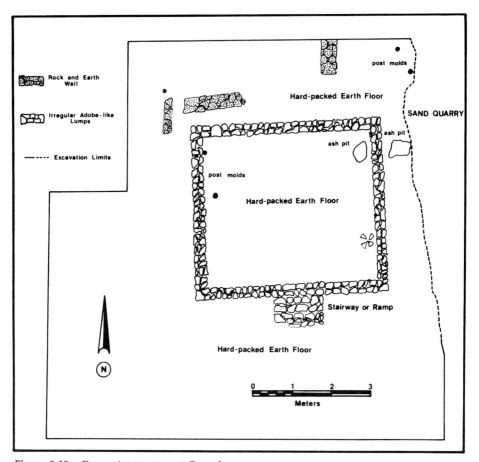

Figure 8.19. Domestic structure at Cuanalan.

(Porter 1953:34). The burial sample (more than 500 altogether) is marked by extraordinary diversity in the kind and amount of burial furniture. Some are accompanied by only a few ceramic vessels, while others contain literally scores of offerings, including pottery, jade ornaments, figurines, and stone implements (Piña Chan 1958). Some of the more lavish interments involve women as the central figures along with sacrificed men and children (Piña Chan 1955:69). Also occurrent are infant burials, again with extensive offerings. All of this points to a social system with significant variations in ascribed rank and prestige. The degree of status differentiation exhibited by the Tlatilco "cemetery," at least in terms of numbers of associated grave goods, stands in obvious contrast with the relatively impoverished burial sample found at Loma Torremote. However, ranked distinctions at Loma Torremote are expressed by other lines of evidence, not sumptuary displays of funerary wealth. Both sets of data, therefore, are consistent with the

Figure 8.20. Oblique view of Cuanalan excavation.

variations in rank and status noted by Sahlins (1958:11–12) for Polynesian Chiefdoms.

Another body of information comes from George Vaillant's excavations at Zacatenco, Ticoman, and El Arbolillo (Vaillant 1930, 1931, 1935). Although no residential structures were excavated, the burial sample is substantial (134 individuals), and all three sites have been surveyed by members of the Basin of Mexico Project. The burials, though not as extravagant as at Tlatilco, still manifest low-level gradations in status. Most interments contained several pieces of burial furniture; a few had no associated grave goods. The major distinction is in the mode of interment, especially at El Arbolillo and to a lesser extent at Ticoman. At El Arbolillo eight individuals, both males and females, were interred in slab-covered tombs, all within an excavation area of 30 m² (Vaillant 1935:175). Also in the same area was an infant equipped with jade earplugs and a number of pottery vessels. Most other burials were rather modest affairs. Since both adult males and females as well as children occurred at this burial locus, the implication is that statuses were again based on the principle of ascription. On the other hand, there is no evidence of emergent prestige differences at Zacatenco, a contemporary community a few kilometers to the southeast. In fact, the absence of slab tombs coupled with the poverty of all interments suggest that status positions at Zacatenco were essentially egalitarian in character. Mortuary treatment at Ticoman resembles the El Arbolillo pattern, although the tendency for slab-covered tombs to cluster is not very marked.

The variations in social rank noted at Tlatilco, El Arbolillo, and Zacatenco also correlate with settlement type. Tlatilco is a large nucleated community, with a population numbering some 1500 individuals. El Arbolillo is a much smaller site, circa 10 ha in size, though total population was still moderately large (ca. 700–900 persons). We classify Zacatenco as a hamlet. The impression is one of increased site ranking, not only in population but also in social status, as community size becomes larger. It may thus very well be that small settlements such as Zacatenco occupied a relatively low social position *as a whole* with respect to the rank of larger sites like El Arbolillo. The status position of El Arbolillo, in turn, would be subordinate to still larger sites like Tlatilco.

Data pertaining to prehistoric economic patterns and exchange networks for the Early Horizon and First Intermediate are likewise not abundant. Perhaps the best evidence is provided by the kinds of tools found in excavated contexts. As we have already mentioned, this body of information implies that most households tended to produce most of their own technological needs (e.g., pottery, figurines, chipped stone implements, grinding tools, etc.). Nowhere is the kind of localized lineage economic intradependence indicated that we have suggested for Loma Torremote. However, at El Arbolillo, Zacatenco, and Ticoman, the total amount of obsidian is very low, an artifact most probably of Vaillant's sampling methods. The fact that not one piece of obsidian debitage (flakes) was recovered from Ticoman casts further suspicion on the adequacy of Vaillant's samples.

There are also some data suggesting part-time economic specialization by entire villages. For the most part this is a direct result of the fact that many raw materials have very localized distributions in the Basin. Ecatepec, a substantial community throughout the First Intermediate period, thus appears to have been a principal locus of salt extraction and processing (Santley n.d.). Likewise, at Coapexco the density of ground stone tools is so aberrantly high that Tolstoy (personal communication) suspects that this site had as a part-time specialty the manufacture of manos and metates, probably for exchange to Puebla and Morelos. Other sites like Tlapacoya (Zohapilco) may have derived some income from the exploitation and subsequent exchange of lacustrine faunal products (Niederberger 1976). To this we might add the Altica type site, a settlement that may have functioned as a processing station for obsidian nodules during the First Intermediate One A (Tolstoy, personal communication). The way in which other sites located near exploitable raw materials follow this pattern is regrettably unknown at present. It does seem likely, nonetheless, that the sites we have mentioned were tied in with a system of symbiotic exchange, along either reciprocal or redistributive lines.

Not being situated near any localized deposits of needed raw materials, Loma Torremote does not exhibit any craft specialties on the village level.

Concerning interregional exchange within the confines of the Basin, we have excellent data on obsidian consumption for several sites: Tlapacoya (Niederberger 1976); Zacatenco, Ticoman, and El Arbolillo (Vaillant 1930, 1931, 1935); San Jose Cuautitlan (McBride 1974); Teotihuacan (Spence n.d.); and Loma Torremote (Santley n.d.). Taken as a whole, these studies show an increasing preference for the high quality, golden-green obsidian from the Pachuca source throughout the overall Early Horizon–First Intermediate period. There is some disagreement, however, regarding the time period of peak popularity. For example, at Loma Torremote obsidian from the Pachuca source remains low (ca. 5% of the sample) during the Early Horizon and First Intermediate Phase One, but it rises abruptly during the Atlamica B subphase (600–550 B.C.), accounting for nearly one-third of the obsidian sample. At Tlapacoya (Zohapilco) a similar peak is in evidence during the First Intermediate Two A and B times (Niederberger 1976:277). If El Arbolillo and Ticoman are assumed to represent a continuous occupation by a single population (a not unreasonable assumption since the two sites are situated within several kilometers of one another), the maximum popularity (ca. 18%) occurs during the First Intermediate Phase One B (Vaillant 1935:242). At San Jose Cuautitlan, a Phase Two–Three site, the golden-green variety is not represented (McBride 1974:225–226). Obviously part of this variation is the result of differences in sample comparability. A substantial part, however, may be due to internal variability in the trading network itself. Whether this variation is because of changes in the mode of exchange (from reciprocity to low-level redistribution and finally to an incipient market economy), because of shifts in individual trading partners, and/or because of alterations in political alliances, is an unanswered question at present.

Basin-Wide Implications of the Loma Torremote Excavation

In Chapter 5 we argued for the existence of a number of small, autonomous First Intermediate Two polities within the Basin of Mexico, each defined by a settlement cluster more or less apparent on our general map. The Loma Torremote site occurs within the smallest of these settlement clusters, at the far-northern periphery of the intensively occupied part of the Basin. The largest settlement clusters are in the southern Basin, and these include several nucleated communities of more than 100 ha (compared to about 30 ha for Loma Torremote), at least two of which have temple platforms of 5 m or more in elevation (while there is no indication of any ceremonial architecture anywhere near this size at Loma Torremote). We think it is fairly reasonable to assume that the degree of social differentiation, economic specialization, and redistributional complexity which we have outlined for Loma Torremote

represents no more than a simplified version of the more complex developments some 35–50 km to the south and southeast.

In specific terms, we expect that future investigations of First Intermediate sites in the southern Basin will show evidence at two or three
communities of powerful lineage heads acting as paramount chiefs of polities
that may have incorporated upward of 10,000 people. These same
paramounts should be much more intensively involved than their Loma
Torremote counterparts in the underwriting of specialized production, and
the acquisition and redistribution of key materials, such as obsidian and
obsidian tools. Although it is not now very clear to us how such a relationship might actually have been structured, it would not be surprising to find
that the paramount rulers of one major southern center were attempting to
gain a greater degree of control over access to the major obsidian resources
near Otumba and Pachuca, as well as a greater control over the production
and redistribution of obsidian tools and objects. The significance of such
control may have been great enough to have provided the principal impetus
for large-scale habitation of the arid Teotihuacan Valley during First Intermediate Three times. Our data would indicate that such an impulse would
have come from the south.

MAQUIXCO BAJO: A MIDDLE HORIZON VILLAGE

TC8 is located on the gently sloping north piedmont of the lower
Teotihuacan Valley at the base and on the lower flank of a small hill known
locally as the Cerro de Calaveras. It is situated 1.5 km north of the edge of the
alluvial plain and 5 km west of the Sun Pyramid. The site was discovered
during our very earliest surveys in 1960. In 1961 and 1962 major excavations
were carried out in three adjacent house compounds, and in a slightly
detached ceremonial complex, by personnel of the Teotihuacan Valley Project. The site is small and compact, with a formal plan. It may be described as
a rectangle measuring approximately 200 m north–south and 400 m east–
west, the long dimension being at right angles to the slope of Cerro
Calaveras. The upper one-third of the rectangle lies on a small, flat plateau-
like surface, the lower end on gently sloping terrain. The lower, east edge of
the village is defined by a shallow canalized barranca. The total surface area
of the village is approximately 8 ha. The lower 6 ha is densely occupied by
approximately 16 large stone and earth houses arranged in three east–west
tiers; the houses are separated by small plazas forming a grid system of
alternating houses and plazas. Some of the plazas were paved with stucco
and lime plaster, others with earth and gravel. The upper 3 ha is occupied by
a plaza with public buildings (including a pyramid temple), open areas, and
four or five houses approximately oriented to the noted tiers of houses at the
lower portion of the site (see Figure 8.21).

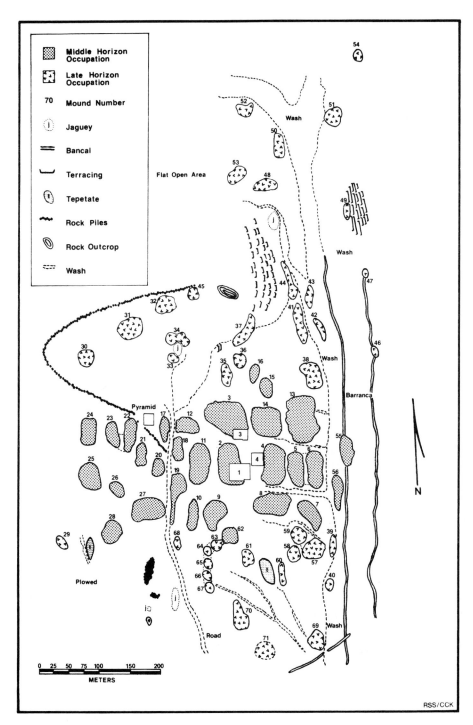

Figure 8.21. The Maquixco site.

Territorial and Kin-Based Groups

TC8 was clearly a corporate community. It is physically compact and separated from the nearest contemporary settlements by distances of 2 km in either direction. TC8 has a religious precinct consisting of one small plaza,[1] that measures approximately 30 by 40 m in area, with a pyramid temple on the north side and three probable civic buildings on the south, west, and northeast sides. The pyramid was partially excavated. It was in poor condition with extensive surface pitting, but some data on its form and dimensions were obtained. It consisted of a single platform, in typical Teotihuacan style, with a talud and tablero facade (possibly without an upper molding) and a balustraded stairway, facing the plaza on the south side. Evidence of lime plaster floor surfaces and portions of temple walls were found on the badly pitted summit. The original height of the platform (above *tepetate*) was 1.3 m, and the basal dimensions were 10.4 by 14.6 m. Trenching along the base of the platform retaining wall did not reveal any ceremonial middens or offerings so that our identification as a temple is based on architectural analogy with Teotihuacan itself.

The temple complex suggests that the community constituted a religious or ritualistic group. Its physical discreteness argues for a sense of social identity as well. There is evidence, to be presented later, that it had political functions also. We estimate the population of the village at approximately 140–150 families or 500–600 people. The estimate is based on the plans of three excavated houses, seriation of surface samples from the others for chronological control, and the comparative size of the unexcavated mounds to those excavated. The village was founded in the final centuries of the first millennium B.C. (First Intermediate Three phase) at which time it consisted of perhaps a dozen widely dispersed small houses scattered over the slope. The population steadily increased through the succeeding periods to reach a peak in Late Middle Horizon times. The artifact sample from the three excavated houses indicates that all three were occupied in the Tlamimilolpa subphase, so that the final form of the village (although probably involving smaller and more numerous housing units) was at least approximated by Late Tlamimilolpa times.

The floor plans (showing well-defined apartment units) and abundant domestic refuse of the 20 large structures argue convincingly for their residential function. Each large house must represent a significant social subdivision of the larger settlement. The size and density (6000 per square kilometer) of the residential occupation, the presence of a distinctive religious precinct, and the well-defined physical limits of the site argue for a corporate character comparable, in some ways, to peasant village communities in many parts of the world. However, its close physical proximity (less than 2 km) to the

---

[1] In the project, open squares between complete buildings are called plazas, central open areas within buildings are referred to as courts, secondary open areas within buildings as patios, and unroofed sunken areas within rooms as light wells.

huge Middle Horizon city of Teotihuacan and the near-identical character of residential and ceremonial architecture at both sites suggest an urban–rural linkage that may have been in some ways different from the urban linkages of historically known agrarian states.

Excavations were conducted in three of the residential mounds, numbers 1–2, 3, and 4 (see Figures 8.22, 8.23, 8.24, 8.25, and 8.26). Prior to excavation mounds 1–2 were considered as separate houses. Excavation revealed that they were parts of a single house with a court occupying the depressed area between them. The debris of rock and sherds that included mounds 1 and 2 and the intervening depressed area covered approximately 1500 m². Of this area 900 m² was excavated. The excavation reveals a large house with a central court, surrounded by a series of platforms, faced with retaining walls (in part with a Teotihuacan style talud and tablero) on varying levels. On the summit of the platforms was a complex series of rooms, alleys, patios, and porches. Specialized features within the rooms included light wells, masonry floor pits, post molds, and benches. The platforms were ascended by balustraded stairways and a small platform was located near the center of the court. The plan bears a striking resemblance to housing complexes in the city, particularly to Yayahuala (Sejourne 1959).

The rooms, patios, and porches occur in apartment-like subdivisions. The number of rooms per apartment in the excavated portions of the house varied between 1 and 3, plus, in some cases, porches and patios. Each of the apartments was probably the residence of a nuclear family. We will summarize the argument in favor of this position shortly. The house contained between 10–15 such units. On this basis, the residential group probably numbered 40–60 persons.

Mound 3 is of comparable size to the mounds 1–2 complex. The excavation involved only 400 m² of floor space that included primarily the central court. Enough of the house was excavated, however, to indicate that its overall characteristics were similar. Within the court was a small central platform, in this case with definite evidence of a partial Teotihuacan talud and tablero retaining wall (including only a lower molding and the sloping talud).

Mound 4 was completely excavated. It was a much smaller structure, measuring only 22 by 23 m, or a total floor space of 529 m². The plan was much more compact and regular than the others but included similar features. It included a central court with a central platform and a set of eight rooms and six porches (two apparently serving as reception halls at the entrances).

The 16 residential mounds in the village varied in size between mounds 1–2 and 4. If the assumption that the apartments were residences for nuclear families is correct, then the house population varied in size between 4 and 15 families or 16–60 persons. The fact that particular families resided together, the variation in the number of the families, and the presence of a communal structure such as the central court and its central platform all point to the

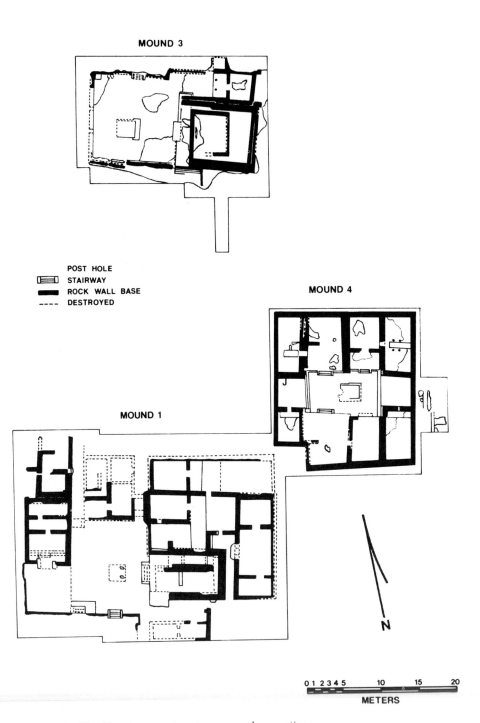

MOUND 3

POST HOLE
STAIRWAY
ROCK WALL BASE
---- DESTROYED

MOUND 4

MOUND 1

N

0 1 2 3 4 5   10   15   20
METERS

Figure 8.22. The Maquixco apartment compound excavations.

Figure 8.23. Maquixco excavation; mound 4, apartment compound. In the center is a central courtyard with its shrine overlain by a Late Horizon wall.

Figure 8.24. Maquixco excavation; mound 3 (background), mound 4 (foreground).

Figure 8.25. Maquixco excavation; mound 4, apartment compound, showing central courtyard shrine with superimposed Late Horizon wall.

Figure 8.26. Maquixco excavation; one of the apartments of mound 4. Note lightwell in the center of the floor of one room.

existence of a corporate group of some kind. In most nonindustrial societies such rural groups are usually based on kinship; the variability and range in size suggest a lineage or true descent group (Murdock 1949). The only unusual aspect of the TC8 lineages is their residence in a single communal house, although this is certainly not unique in the ethnographic record. Spence's skeletal analysis (1974) of a burial population from one comparable compound unit in Middle Horizon Teotihuacan suggests that the adult males in this population were more closely related to each other than were adult females, and that a mode of patrilocal residence may have prevailed. This observation dovetails with our own inferences at TC8, based on architectural configurations alone.

The argument that each of the apartments was occupied by a nuclear family is based on the following considerations. Nuclear families are probably universal in human society. Even in socieites with extended or polygamous families, the nuclear family is usually identifiable as a recognizable subdivison with its own structure, membership, and functions. Very common functions are residence and food consumption. In many societies, where extended families are present, one of the functions of that group is food production, and one of the principal concerns of extended-family heads is the adequate and equitable provisioning of all individuals within the group. In such situations, however, food is usually apportioned to and consumed by the constituent nuclear families. In two apartments at TC8 one of the rooms was clearly identifiable as a kitchen. This is based on the unusual number of complete or restorable pottery vessels and fragments of manos and metates found on the floor. In several other apartments, kitchens have been tentatively identified. Hearths generally were lacking; apparently portable pottery stoves were used instead. Their small size (one to three rooms) and range in area of roofed over space (24–66 m^2) suggest a small residential group comparable in size to a nuclear family. (Using Narrol's formula for egalitarian societies this calculates at a range of 2.4–6.6 persons per apartment.)

In summary, we are identifying at least three levels of social organization at TC8: the village, represented by the entire site; lineage, represented by the house; and the nuclear family, represented by the apartment. The presence of secondary courts or patios and their associated apartments within the larger houses might indicate the presence of extended families (i.e., a level between the lineage and the nuclear family) as well, but a complete excavation of one of the larger houses would be needed to verify this. Only one definite case of a discrete patio complex within a house (in mounds 1–2) was found and the patio lacks a central platform. The patio may simply have been needed to provide air and light, or additional work space.

Rank

The Aztec *calpulli* was a social group comparable in size and probably in many of its functions to TC8. The former was a physical and social community with economic, social, political, religious, educational, and military functions. Many rural communities in Late Horizon times consisted of a single *calpulli*. The population as a whole of such rural communities was clearly inferior in rank to the ruling and merchant class that resided in the towns and to at least some of the craftsmen. Within the rural *calpulli*, however, there seems to have been considerable variation in rank. A formal headman position existed that involved a number of duties and rights. The headman was entitled to services in the construction and maintenance of his house and daily services for his household, including firewood and water. His household was supported by agricultural surpluses produced by communal labor. In return, his duties involved arbitrating disputes, custodianship of the land maps, and representation of the *calpulli* to the higher organization levels. The picture very briefly summarized above for the Late Horizon is easily adaptable to the situation at TC8 during the Late Xolalpan phase. The style and materials of house construction at TC8 are carbon copies of those in the city. There are, however, significant differences that reflect variations in rank of the Aztec type.

Although the overall plan and number of apartments of mounds 1–2 is very similar to Yayahuala at Teotihuacan, the total floor space is less than half the size of that covered by the urban building; rooms and courts are much smaller in size, there are fewer rooms per apartment, construction is inferior, and the plan generally is much more irregular. At Yayahuala nearly every apartment has a patio, the central court is much more spacious, and its central platform is almost as large as the village temple. Even the individual rooms at TC8 are highly irregular. The few Xolalpan phase burials excavated (very few were, since the objective of the excavation was to reveal as much of the floor plan as possible, and vertical trenching was sacrificed to horizontal excavation) were either without offerings or accompanied by one or two vessels. Nothing comparable to the richly stocked urban tombs was found. In mounds 1–2 and 4, one room had a mural painting placed on the wall of the porch of an apartment, and this apparently in simple geometric design. Mural painting in some urban residences is of course one of the great Mesoamerican artistic traditions.

On the other hand, there are residential districts within urban Teotihuacan (e.g., the Tlamimilolpa area, excavated by Linne in the 1930s [Linne 1942]) where residential architecture is much more comparable to that of TC8 than to Yayahuala. In several respects, with its cramped living quarters and poorly defined spatial units, the Tlamimilolpa residential architecture could certainly be regarded as a manifestation of a status level inferior to that of TC8. This complicates any simple urban–rural–suburban rank dichotomy, since the main center apparently contained substantial numbers of people of several widely different status levels. Our data do indicate clearly, however, that the highest-ranking groups resided exclusively in urban Teotihuacan.

With respect to differences in portable household equipment, a comparison with the city is more difficult since a report of the total sample of refuse from an urban house has not been published. In ceramics, along with the array of utility pottery for cooking, serving, and storage of food, such artifacts as figurines, braseros, tripod vases (even including fresco painting) were all present in the peasant household inventory, indicating that rank differences between rural and urban were not reflected in such areas of technology, at least qualitatively; possibly there were quantitative differences. Bodily ornaments were found only rarely, perhaps reflecting significant rank differences in dress. Generally speaking, the archaeological data indicate definite differences in rank between villagers and city folk particularly in the area of housing and dress, thus reflecting the same general type of social stratification present in Aztec times. Also comparable to the Aztec situation was evidence of internal stratification at TC8.

The smallest of the three excavated houses, mound 4, was noticeably superior in quality to the houses in mounds 1–2 and 3. The masonry was of better construction, particularly the plaster finish, the rooms more spacious, the plan much more regular, and such specialized features as courtyard drains, porches, and light wells were generally more common. The central courtyard, particularly, was much more ornate, with six balustraded stairways, a complete talud–tablero facade, and a much more elaborate central platform. Furthermore, there seem to have been two formal entrances with reception rooms associated with two possible porter's rooms. In the debris, we found roof ornaments of baked clay in the form of a row of crouching felines, and one of the apartments had a mural painting. The overall plan furthermore does not suggest division into a series of discrete apartments, but rather the house of a single nuclear, or probably extended family.

Other peculiarities in the house are the lack of evidence of kitchens and the generally lower artifact density relative to the other two houses. In our analysis of the faunal remains, White (n.d.) cites evidence of both butchering and consumption activities in mounds 1–2 and 3, but only consumption in 4. What all of this seems to suggest is that food processing and perhaps technological activities were conducted for the residents of mound 4 by occupants of other compounds. This pattern is described for the Late Horizon period by a number of Spanish sources in which nobles had the right to tribute and tax in the form of processed food (tortillas, for example) and goods, along with housekeeping maintenance (cleaning, provisioning with water, firewood, etc.).

When we first evaluated the TC8 data, we suggested that the mound 4 house was that of the village headman, and compared the position of head of the household to that of the Calpuleque or Calpulli headman of the Aztec. The Aztec *calpulli,* however, was a social unit approximately the size of the entire village of Maquixco. Considering the fact that the house was not located in a central position, and that the temple complex, the probable social center of the community, was located at the upper edge of the village, it is more likely that the village headman's house was one of the mounds associated with the temple plaza complex. The head of the mound 4 residence may have been the head of some internal territorial level below the level of the village. In this connection it should be pointed out that mounds 4, 1–2, and 3 and an additional mound, 14, are grouped around a large unpaved plaza, possibly forming some internal intermediate level territorial group of the type suggested.

To summarize, the settlement pattern at Maquixco includes at least three territorial levels, the apartment, the house compound, and the site. These probably correspond to the nuclear family, the lineage, and the village, in terms of sociopolitical organization. There is a strong possibility of an extended family level between the nuclear family and the lineage and some intermediate group between the lineage and the village. Adding to this picture are obvious differences in ranking of the population of the village as a whole as compared to the city of Teotihuacan and strong suggestions of internal ranking within the village. The structure of the village can easily be accommodated to a ramage model, and was similar to the Aztec *calpulli*.

All of the larger Middle Horizon rural communities in the Basin of Mexico are physically compact, formally planned settlements. This is in striking contrast to the Late Horizon pattern with its great variability of settlement pattern. The latter has a strong ecological bias and variations of settlement types show an extraordinarily close relationship to land form and agricultural systems. In contrast, Teotihuacan settlements seem as nonecological in character as the sixteenth-century Hispanic Colonial pattern. There is an extraordinary resemblance to the communities established as the product of the Congregation policy, in which dispersed populations were collected and settled into large planned nucleated settlements to facilitate administration, particularly for tax collecting and proselytization. The implication here is that of a much greater penetration of urban institutions into rural life or perhaps suggests that the dichotomy between rural and urban is less well-defined in Middle Horizon times.

In his 1966b paper, Sanders discussed the evidence of warfare from the village data. We quote the passage here in full.

> *Warfare.* A surprising result of the excavation in view of the usual picture painted of Classic Mesoamerican society, was the clear indication of a significant militaristic aspect to village life. Obsidian projectile points were common and functioned probably as lance points. Considering the large population of the Valley, it is very doubtful that hunting was of any significance; the rarity of bone other than human and dog in the midden supports this argument. Human bone was common, and scattered through the kitchen refuse. Isolated mandibles were particularly common and several pieces of worked skull fragments were found. In several cases more direct evidence of cannibalism was revealed, i.e., human bone in cooking pots. Warfare with its attendant ritual practices seem to parallel very closely those reported by the Spaniards of the Aztec.

Certain modifications are required on the basis of further examination of the data. First, hunting was probably of somewhat more importance in the diet than we had originally assumed since deer bones make up a substantial part of the TC8 skeletal remains. Our earlier assumption that hunting was of no significance was based on the belief that surveys of the other portions of the Basin of Mexico would reveal Middle Horizon populations comparable in density and size to the Late Horizon. Our surveys (see the preceding chapter) indicate that it was not more than one-quarter the size of the Late Horizon population, which meant that large numbers of deer were still present in the Basin. This conclusion is also supported by the faunal evidence from Teotihuacan itself. On the other hand, the total contribution of wild animals to the diet must have been still a minor one considering the large size of the population (Santley, on page 486, estimates that no more than 0.2–0.5% of the annual caloric intake could have come from deer, 0.6 from all game sources). This still leaves unexplained the unusual number of bifacially flaked points. When Sanders originally suggested their use for warfare, this conclusion presented some difficulties, since the balance of our data argued that Maquixco was a peasant community, and it was surprising to find military equipment in the houses of people of this social type. Furthermore, data from the Late Horizon suggest that the state was the distributor of military equipment (from royal arsenals). Upon reexamination, it appears that many of the bifacial implements actually were used as cutting tools or knives, which means that the number of points would have been well within the range of the modest hunting activity of a Middle Horizon village. We also further suspect that many of the deer were taken in the agricultural fields of the village.

The value of infant remains as evidence of warfare can now be reinterpreted. Recent examination of burials from house compounds at Teotihuacan, for example, show that foetuses and very young children were treated ritually in a different manner from individuals who died later on in life (Serrano and Lagunas 1975). They were often interred in altars. The placing of the infants' bones in a pot on the patio floor of Apartment 2, therefore, may involve some kind of burial ritual rather than cannibalism. In this context it is interesting to note that the Aztecs considered children who died before the age of 4 years as incomplete human beings who went to the paradise of the thirteenth heaven to be nourished from the tree of life until they achieved full humanity. As we noted in the description of religion at Loma Torremote, this differential treatment goes back to the First Intermediate Two phase. The jaws and skull fragments found in the TC8 middens may also reflect some pattern of specialized treatment of the dead within the village itself rather than evidence of trophy taking and ritual cannibalism as we originally suggested. Many societies in the ethnographic present, for example, keep bones of dead kinsmen as mementos.

We do not mean to imply, however, that there was not a military component to Middle Horizon society as a whole. Recently discovered mural paintings, showing warriors, from the city itself, and sculptural scenes of Teotihuacan warriors in other Mesoamerican sites suggest a strong militaristic component to the total society. What we are now deemphasizing is the evidence for this pattern within the peasant village.

Economic Structure

Unfortunately, the Maquixco excavations were conducted prior to the development of flotation techniques for retrieval of botanical remains from exposed sites and no macrosamples were obtained during the excavations. With respect to animal bone the techniques of excavation were not conductive to collection of small fragments but we did obtain a total of 347 fragments of animal bone. Of these 187 were identified, of which 60% were deer or dog bones, the latter presumably domesticated. The fact that the dog bone was found scattered through the midden, plus evidence of butchering marks on the bones, indicates this animal was used for food during the Middle Horizon in a way similar to the Conquest-period Aztec. Turkey bones were also present in small quantities, presumably representing a domestic species, and the balance of the bones consisted primarily of small mammals, birds, reptiles, and a few fish bones. Of the unidentified bones, there were numerous large bones present, presumably representing dog or deer. Recent excavations at Teotihuacan itself shows roughly the same range and proportions of animal bone (Starbuck 1975).

Flotation samples taken recently from the site of Teotihuacan indicate that maize was the staple crop, and that some wild plants were collected as supplements to the diet (McClung de Tapia 1977). The small amount of agricultural plant pollen that we found in our pollen core at the Atlatongo Springs southwest of Teotihuacan indicates that maize was a significant factor in the diet of the Middle Horizon population.

On the basis of the regional settlement pattern during the Middle Horizon in the Teotihuacan Valley, direct archaeological evidence, and analogies derived from ethnographic data, we can make a series of suggestions about the agricultural system at Maquixco. The twentieth-century population of the Valley consists primarily of peasant villagers whose livelihood is based on a combination of subsistence agriculture, the sale of agriculture surpluses, and some local craft specialization. Documentary sources for the Late Horizon suggest a similar situation. One major difference between the two periods is in land tenure. Lands used by rural communities in Aztec times were apparently owned in common by the calpulli and divided for use by families. Although some rental of land did occur and holdings of the various corporate groups somewhat dispersed as a consequence, generally the lands held by a community were situated within a short distance of the residential area. As a result, detailed mapping of Aztec corporate villages would make it possible to roughly define land holdings. Twentieth-century villagers have three types of land: private, which is held by individuals who are free to rent and sell it; ejido land, owned by the federal government, assigned to village use and therefore inalienable; and village communal pasture, with freedom of access to all villagers. Even though much of the land is privately owned, there is still a strong tendency for most of the land used by the contemporary village to lie within a maximum radius of 5 km of the community. In the case of small villages like TC8, it is usually only 1–2 km. With these considerations, the distribution of rural sites in an agricultural society should provide clues as to patterns of land use and tenure.

Although individual Middle Horizon rural communities in the lower Teotihuacan Valley like TC8 were similar in size, population, and density to present-day plain and plainside villages, their number and distribution differed strikingly from both Late Horizon and twentieth-century patterns. Unlike the later patterns, the bulk of the population that farmed the lower and middle sectors of the Valley apparently resided at Teotihuacan and there was a marked attrition of population as one proceeded down valley from the city. TC8 is the last really substantial (in size) settlement below the city. A string of hamlets, or small but physically compact settlements (in one case consisting perhaps of only two or three communal houses), is located on the north piedmont below TC8 but the total population was far below the capacity of the plain to support. There were no settlements on the south piedmont. The same generalization applies to the Middle Valley. The only settlements, in that area, of demographic consequence were pseudopod-like extensions of the city itself. Rural settlements of the size and zonal densities comparable to those of the Late Horizon and twentieth century are found only in areas peripheral to the main valley. The implication here is that the use of most of the alluvial plain, and portions of the adjacent piedmonts, were controlled directly by the urban population, perhaps by major institutions like the temple, or the state, and that a substantial portion of the population in the city were full or part-time farmers.

TC8 is one of the few relatively large rural settlements in the main valley. Tending to corroborate our assertation that access to the alluvial plain was controlled by the urban population is the location of the village. Present-day settlements that own land in the plain are located on the edge of, or within it. TC8 is located well back from its edge; present-day villagers in such settings are primarily piedmont cultivators. In terms of the spacing of TC8 with respect to other Teotihuacan piedmont villages, and assuming that the plain was not available, the village could have had access to 600–700 ha of piedmont, or an average of 4–5 ha per family.

The evidence of an agricultural base for the community is primarily indirect. Excavations in three houses revealed no evidence of craft specialization. The size and location of the settlement, particularly with respect to the city, plus the negative evidence of other economic specialties, argue for an agriculturally based settlement. Obsidian scrapers were unusually abundant in the excavation (approximately 300, of which the majority were of the Tlamimilolpa–Xolalpan phase). The large population of the Basin of Mexico as a whole, and scanty evidence of hunting in the midden, would indicate that the scrapers were not used primarily for fleshing hides.

The form of these tools, and particularly the long handle, is quite similar to modern iron tools used to rasp the interior walls of the cultivated maguey plant so as to facilitate sap flow during the period of *aguamiel* and *pulque* production. The obsidian scrapers, whose steeply angled faces are heavily worn and battered, could well have functioned for such a purpose. If so, maguey cultivation and the production of *aguamiel* and *pulque* must have been important activities at TC8. Maguey is a very hardy plant, which does quite well on thinner, drier piedmont soils where it has been an important cultigen in modern times. On sloping terrain it is now characteristically closely planted in linear strips, parallel to the contours, so as to form a complex of terraces which facilitate the cultivation of maize, barley, wheat, and beans. Such maguey terrace cultivation can be quite intensive and productive when integrated with networks of floodwater irrigation canals. Framentary traces of long-abandoned canals, stone terrace faces, and three possible spring-fed reservoirs occur in the general TC8 area, although all are of problematical date. If these hydraulic features were contemporary with the TC8 Middle Horizon occupation, they would indicate a rather intensive system of piedmont cultivation.

We suggest that TC8 represents a community of peasant farmers, capable of a substantial surplus production (perhaps especially of maguey products), whose major function was to expand and consolidate the productivity of the broad piedmont down-valley from Teotihuacan. TC8's close physical proximity to Teotihuacan, the stylistic similarities between architecture and artifacts of both sites, and the apparent absence of any significant artisan activity at TC8 (see following discussion) all suggest a close, economic relationship between the two. Our reconstruction, therefore, is that of a relatively prosperous rural settlement that supplied itself with staple foods and produced a surplus of agricultural produce, primarily the products of maguey, as taxes to the Teotihuacan state and for exchange in the urban market.

In a prior section we stressed the fact that the degree to which a type of social group is physically expressed is generally correlated with the significance of its functions, particularly economic. If so, the lineages previously defined were probably units of land tenure and agricultural production, and generally functioned as cooperative labor groups. Lineages in many societies do have such functions, and the extraordinarily tightly knit settlement pattern of this group at TC8 suggests vital economic functions.

Craft Specialization and Trade

There is some slight evidence of manufacturing activities on the site but as a whole most of the technology seems to have been produced and obtained outside of the community. This conclusion is based on the excavation of the three houses, plus surface samples from all of the structures of the site. The obsidian sample from Maquixco is still in the process of being analyzed, but some basic patterns can be ascertained at present. The total assemblage of artifacts includes 39 cylindrical cores, 9121 rectangular blades struck from these cores, 255 bifacially flaked scrapers, 4 bifacially flaked drills, 8 large bifacially flaked knives, 92 bifacially flaked points, 174 irregular cores, and 869 irregular utilized flakes. Of interest is the distribution of these artifacts in the three houses and the areas within the houses. The data are summarized in Table 8.3.

The absences of obsidian workshops indicate that the bifacially flaked tools and the cylindrical cores were not produced at the site. The cores were probably obtained at Teotihuacan and the blades manufactured in the village, to judge from the ratio of rectangular blades to cylindrical cores (250:1). The same conclusion applies to the bifacial tools; there was no recorded workshop detritus from this activity. These conclusions coincide with data from Teotihuacan, where a number of households in the city specialized in the production of cylindrical obsidian cores, points, and scrapers, and the villagers apparently obtained these items from the city market (see Spence 1967, n.d.). On the other hand, the presence of irregular cores and utilized flakes suggests that these general purpose cutting tools were manufactured by the individual households at Maquixco. The unusual concentration of irregular cores in the courtyard of mounds 1 and 2 furthermore would suggest some internal specialization within the village.

Bifacial knives, points, scrapers, and rectangular blades are found evenly dispersed throughout the living quarters and open space of each courtyard indicating use as household implements. In the case of mound 3, however, two artifacts were found in unusual quantities, bifacially flaked scrapers and irregular flakes, which suggests that the household was involved in some specialized activity. We believe that this is connected with the pulping of maguey leaves and the processing of the fiber. No evidence of pottery manufacture was found, and only one figurine mold was collected. The Late Xolalpan figurines were all apparently mold made and the collection includes several hundred heads. In two seasons of excavation, only one stone celt was found (from a surface collection) indicating that woodworking was rarely done in the village. Combined with this scanty evidence of craft activities is the extraordinary similarity of the entire array of artifacts from pots to stone tools with those in the city. Thus, all of the data support our contention as to the significance of the urban market in peasant life as a source of this technology.

One technological activity that was probably conducted by the villagers was house building. The noticeably poorer quality of the construction and extraordinary irregularity of room and court dimensions argue for construction by nonprofessionals. The plaster surfaces, however, talud and tablero facades, and balustraded stairways look like professional work. We suspect that the lineage was a cooperative work group that built most of the house and that urban masons were contracted for the more professional construction. This supposition is also supported by the distribution of two distinctive Teotihuacan artifacts. Both are objects of the size that can be held in the hand; one is shaped out of light porous volcanic rock (called *tezontle* locally), in the form of a terraced pyramid; the other is similar in appearance to a clothing iron (but with a rectangular base) and made of a dense heavy,

TABLE 8.3
Distribution of Obsidian in Mounds 1–2, 3, and 4 at Maquixco (TC8)[a]

	Mound 1–2			Mound 3			Mound 4			Totals
	Courtyard (200 m²)	Midden (200 m²)	Apartments (500 m²)	Courtyard (150 m²)	Midden (100 m²)	Apartments (150 m²)	Courtyard (60 m²)	Midden (100 m²)	Apartments (360 m²)	
Drills	—	—	2	—	2	—	—	—	—	4
Knives	—	—	1	4	2	—	—	1	—	8
Scrapers	14	4	53	123	24	2	3	7	25	255
Points	1	3	36	14	21	11	—	2	4	92
Irregular cores	50	0	82	4	0	0	3	9	26	174
Irregular flakes	64	48	49	425	112	60	13	31	67	869
Cylindrical cores	4	3	11	6	3	2	—	1	7	37
Blades	1405	241	2401	2219	883	675	161	296	841	9122

[a] The table does not include artifacts whose spatial provenience was uncertain.

basaltic stone. Both are referred to as plastering tools in the literature. Teotihuacan style buildings are faced with two layers of finishing material, an inner, thicker, layer of earth, gravel, and lime that we are referring to as stucco and a thin, outer layer of slaked lime that we refer to as plaster. We believe that the first type of artifact was used for applying the stucco; the second for plaster. Stuccoing tools are abundant in the Maquixco middens, plastering tools extremely rare, agreeing with the pattern of construction work we have suggested.

Religion

One of the most significant results of the excavation was substantiation and amplification of the evidence from the city as to the importance of religion in the integration of Teotihuacan society. The enormous number and size of religious buildings at the city is mute testimony as to the significance of the public or state ritual. What the TC8 excavation reveals is an extraordinary emphasis on household ritual as well. Every house, to judge from our three excavations, had a central court with a small altar-like central platform. No concentrations of ritual objects were actually found on and near the platforms (nor were they found in the temple excavation) but Linne reports finding a stone Huehueteotl (the Middle Horizon equivalent of the Aztec god of the hearth, in this case carved in the form of an incense burner) and pottery censer (the large chimneyed composite type) fragments on and near the central platform of the Xolalpan court at the city. Spanish eyewitness accounts of Aztec religion emphasize the fact that temples were swept and cleaned daily (it was one of the duties of the novices) in Tenochtitlan so the lack of ceremonial midden is not really surprising. At TC8 an offering, consisting of two pots (one inverted over the other), containing a green stone bead and sea shells, was found under the courtyard floor at the northeast corner of the central platform in mound 3. A second offering under the floor near the same platform may have included a human sacrificial victim or more probably a burial. The central court and its platform at TC8 were probably the scene of lineage ritual.

Each of the two large houses (mounds 1–2 and 3) furthermore possessed a distinctive architectural complex, which opened directly into the court in front of the altar, that probably had ritual functions. Each consists of a bench room or a porch room unit and an alley that ran alongside the unit and connected with a back room. In neither case was kitchen refuse found on the floors. In the case of mound 1–2 the noted frescoed wall was in this complex. The back room in both houses lacked a formal floor. These complexes were clearly not residential in function, and probably had some function related to the lineage as a whole. In part, they may have functioned as rooms to store religious paraphernalia or dressing and rehearsal rooms for courtyard ceremonies that involved the use of the platform. In the large apartment compounds at Teotihuacan itself, there is a direct functional equivalent. Delimiting the central courtyard are a series of large rooms that are placed on high platforms that were apparently not residential in function; Millon refers to them as temples (see Millon 1967).

Great quantities of complete and fragmentary objects were found in the refuse middens of the houses that are thought to have had religious functions. The list includes several thousand figurine fragments; sherds of the typical Teotihuacan composite incense burners; candeleros, usually considered as censers; and numerous sherds of pottery tripod vases that, at Teotihuacan, are associated with burials or ritual offerings (particularly the fresco painted type). A Huehueteotl, carved from *tepetate*, was found in the mound 3 excavation in a rubbish deposit outside of the house. Excavations in another Middle Horizon village, TC46, on the north slope of Cerro Gordo, resulted in the find of a basalt Huehueteotl in the house midden, so that this type of sculpture was apparently involved in household ritual. The Aztec Huehueteotl was a hearth god so that his association with household ritual is not surprising.

The frequent occurrence of religious objects in the house refuse and the fact that figurines are never found intact strongly suggest that they were used once for a specific ritual or ritual season and then discarded. Since the evidence is conclusive that they were obtained in the city, they represent a substantial economic investment and are a good prehistoric example of what Wolf (1966) refers to as the peasant "Ceremonial Fund" in contemporary peasant society. None of the objects were actually found *in situ* in a functional sense, so we can only guess how they were used. Some type of family altar complex, comparable to the twentieth-century Catholic altar, may have been present, involving the candeleros and figurines, since they are abundant and occur all through the room complexes. They were particularly abundant in the patio that served apartments 1–3 and this is our strongest argument for some extended family organization within the compound. The Huehueteotls are rare, and this fact, plus the evidence from Xolalpan, suggests that they were probably used in courtyard ritual involving the entire lineage. We suspect that this was true of the braseros for the same reasons. The frescoed tripod vases were more abundant, but were found in quantity only in the courtyards so that they too were probably used in lineage rather than family ritual.

In striking contrast to the abundant evidence of household ritual, the village temple seems rather unimpressive. Its presence does argue for a well-integrated corporate community but its small size and that of the associated structures would imply that the public aspects of ritual may have involved considerable participation in urban rather than an elaboration of community ritual, at least in those settlements conveniently located with respect to the city. Religious architecture is much more elaborate in the more distant Middle Horizon communities north of Cerro Gordo.

Very little can be said presently about the symbols of religion. The figurines almost certainly represent gods with compartmentalized functions, as in the case of Aztec gods. The Late Xolalpan mold-made heads and bodies can be sorted into approximately 10 male and female deities based on variations in dress. Tlaloc is represented but is found only infrequently and is not included in the tally of 10 deities. Presumably a patron god of the city, perhaps he was more involved in the state religious ritual and functioned rarely in peasant household ritual. The types have not yet been compared with figurines from the city so it is uncertain whether a greater variety of gods were represented there. The gods represented at TC8 were definitely worshipped in the city as well and the household ritual we have described apparently applies to the urban population. This is not to argue, of course, that the peasant who resided at TC8 completely understood all of the conceptual levels of what was obviously a highly sophisticated religious system at the city.

As in the city, shell, in this case brought primarily from the Pacific Coast, apparently had ritualistic use. Great quantities, particularly *Spondylus,* were found in the midden. Artifacts manufactured from shell are rare, and shell fragments generally show no signs of working, so that it was clearly not brought as raw material for artifacts. Although its occurrence in the midden suggests that shellfish may have been eaten, it would seem very unlikely that human porters would carry the shell also, all the way from the Pacific Coast. Furthermore, it must be remembered that the refuse in the houses includes cast-off ceremonial as well as kitchen artifacts. There is abundant evidence of the ritual use and significance of shell at the city and apparently it had the same use in household ritual in the village as well.

Village and City

The Aztec *calpulli,* the socioeconomic equivalent of our TC8 village, was part of a larger territorial unit, the regional state. The population of the rural *calpulli* in Aztec society was obligated to pay tribute to the ruler in agricultural crops, usually produced by communal labor; in corvée labor for the construction of public buildings in the towns, or on public works like dams, dikes, or canals; and in military service. Legal disputes were resolved by especially appointed officials residing in the town so that the legal functions that are characteristic of the rural community in many societies were appropriated by the state. The *calpulli* chief acted as a go-between between village and town. Presumably villagers were also spectators in the elaborate religious ceremonial and made periodic offerings in the temples of the towns. Aside from this formal interaction with the state and temple, Aztec peasants exchanged their surplus for craft products in the urban market.

The above brief summary of the interrelationships between the rural and urban community in Aztec times could easily be applied to the Middle Horizon situation. We have direct or indirect archaeological evidence as to the subordinate status of the villagers, formal political organization, subsistence base, market economy, and close cultural integration with the city. If anything, the impression of the Middle Horizon is one of a greater control and penetration of rural life by the urban ruling class. In part, this undoubtedly reflects the fact that TC8 is located within the shadow of a major city.

Comparison with Other Middle Horizon Villages

Survey and excavation data from the north flank of Cerro Gordo, outside of the Teotihuacan Valley proper, tend to support our argument as to the closer relationship between urban and rural in Middle Horizon times. Approximately 8 km north of the city, on the north slope of Cerro Gordo, a test zone of 8 km^2 was intensively surveyed. During the Tzacualli phase, approximately 30 hamlets were scattered along the barrancas and interfluves. These hamlets varied in size from less than 1 ha up to 1 ha in size and exhibit no planning. No definite ceremonial structure of this phase was located. Probably at the end of the Miccaotli or beginning of the Tlamimilolpa phase, a program of nucleation of the population into large communities was initiated. By the end of the Tlamimilolpa phase, most of the hamlets had disappeared and the population was concentrated into four large nucleated villages and a town. These communities varied in size from 5 to 25 ha. We estimate the density as comparable to that at TC8, which would yield a minimal population per village of between 300–1500 inhabitants. Actually three of these, totalling 42 ha, were almost coterminous. All of these sites exhibit formal planning, but only the town has a substantial ceremonial–civic center. The population climax of the area was achieved in the Late Xolalpan phase. During the Metepec phase there was a rapid reduction of population and a resettlement of the remnants at TC73, a large planned town, with an impressive center, that is a miniature copy of the Main Street complex at Teotihuacan itself.

Excavations at one of the villages, TC46, although very small in scale, suggest similarities to and differences from the TC8 site. Portions of two houses were excavated and each had a central court comparable to TC8. The overall plan, however, seems much less formal with nonconjoined apartments loosely arranged around the courtyard. Virtually no lime plasters seem to have been used in the excavated portions of the houses, although the floors were well constructed, from layers of clay and volcanic gravel, and had well-smoothed mud-plastered surfaces. A test pit at TC49, however, did reveal remains of a lime-plastered residence. Apparently the urban type of house was typical at TC8, whereas only some houses were so constructed at the Cerro Gordo north slope area. Scattered information from the settlement survey suggests that the TC46 pattern was typical of many Middle Horizon villages, particularly those in Zone 2. Data from soil profiles of other Middle Horizon villages and recent excavations, however, reveal that some Middle Horizon village residences were constructed with only hard tamped earth floors and courtyards.

In summary, including houses from the city, at least four levels of housing may be defined for Teotihuacan settlements in terms of the construction material, plan, and skill of excavation. Within the city, furthermore, distinctions in housing in terms of spaciousness of rooms and courtyards, architectural elaborations, floor plans, and quality and subject matter of mural paintings suggest a number of social class levels. The data would point to a much greater elaboration of status levels than during First Intermediate Two times.

With respect to portable artifacts, the evidence from villages like TC46 is that the total range of stone and ceramic artifacts was comparable to TC8, but there seems to be definite differences in the quantity of certain types such as thin orange, frescoed vases, and orange ware cooking pots. What the data apparently show is a gradation of integration of rural communities into the life style of the city, with TC8 falling into a kind of suburban category, and sites like TC46 more definitely rural and peasant.

Basin-Wide Implications of the Maquixco Excavations

Middle Horizon sites comparable to Maquixco, with nucleated populations of several hundred people, overall site planning, and substantial residential and ceremonial architecture are found primarily in Zone Two of our Middle Horizon land use model. They occur very predominantly around the peripheries of the Teotihuacan Valley, in the Temascalapa region, along the edges of the Cuautitlan alluvial plain (with probable extensions southward into the Azcapotzalco area), some 20–30 km west and southwest of Teotihuacan. Among these settlements, the Maquixco community is perhaps unique in the configuration of residential apartments that so closely resemble the compound units at Teotihuacan, and the close physical proximity to the city. These features combine to make Maquixco appear more like a physically detached urban segment than a truly rural community. Future investigations may show that the other large nucleated villages in the Teotihuacan Valley and the Temascalapa region are of similar character, with a strong tendency toward cultural simplification at greater physical distances from the urban capital (e.g., the TC46 data). Similarly, the nucleated villages to the west of Lake Xaltocan–Zumpango may represent physically detached segments of the small Middle Horizon centers in that area, with center–suburb linkages somewhat comparable to those we have suggested for Teotihuacan and Maquixco. Clearly, a very different model must be developed for the much more fragmented Middle Horizon occupation in Zone Three. The small site size, dispersed occupation, and near absence of any architectural remains in these more distant areas are strongly suggestive of significant differences in residential patterns, economic roles, and societal composition relative to the urban–suburban core of the Middle Horizon settlement system.

THE TRIBAL AND THE PEASANT VILLAGE:
A COMPARISON

Cultural anthropologists analyze social groups in terms of two major characteristics, structure and function. A comparison of the tribal and peasant villages shows very close parallels in territorial organization and, derivatively, social structure. In each case the nuclear family is isolatable as a social group and the range in size is very comparable between the two sites. In the case of the First Intermediate Two village, the family resided in a separate house, within a walled compound, that included a patio and garden plot. The Middle Horizon family resided in an apartment within a large multifamily compound.

Above the level of the family, at Loma Torremote, was a house compound cluster in which three to six compounds shared adjacent walls, forming a compact territorial unit. The comparable unit at Maquixco would be the apartment house. This unit at Maquixco was probably larger in size than the cluster at Loma Torremote. We estimate that there were 10–12 nuclear families residing in mounds 1–2, but on the other hand, this was one of the largest apartment houses on the site. Most of the mounds were only one-half to three-quarters the size of mounds 1–2, suggesting smaller resident populations. In all probability, the population mode per apartment house at Maquixco was close to that of the compound cluster at Loma Torremote. In either case, the resident group was within the range of a large extended family, or a small localized lineage, in terms of ethnographic parallels. In both cases there was a religious shrine that served the group of families; in the case of Loma Torremote, located in one of the house compounds; in the case of Maquixco, located in the central courtyard. One obvious difference between the two sites is the more formal plan of the lineage residence in the later site.

In the case of the Middle Horizon village, we suggested the possibility of an extended family group, intermediate in size between the nuclear family and the lineage; and of a maximal lineage, formed by a set of apartment compounds, with a formal chief as leader. There is evidence from the First Intermediate Two village that nuclear families did occasionally grow into extended families, but the group was coresidential, that is, it resided within the same physical house. No definite evidence of the maximal lineage was noted except that there were areas of light occupation over the site that might represent unsettled, probably cultivated zones between sets of house compound clusters. Above all of these levels was the community. The First Intermediate village was considerably larger in population, lacked any indication of central planning, and it is not known whether it had a central ceremonial ground or building complex. The very low density of surface remains in and around the contemporary cemetery on the site suggests a central, nonresidential area. In contrast, the Middle Horizon village is smaller, more compact, has an organized grid arrangement, and a definite ceremonial complex, including a temple and associated structures.

Added to these parallels is clear evidence of hierarchical statuses within the social structure. In our discussion of the Middle Horizon village, we suggested a parallel to the structure of the Aztec calpulli for the village as a whole. The *calpulli* has often been considered as having a ramage type structure, with the two characteristics of segmentary lineage and ranking, a model that could easily fit both of our sample villages. In terms of population size, Maquixco is near the lower end of the range of size for the Aztec *calpulli,* and Loma Torremote is at the upper range. It is in the area of function that we see significant differences between the two villages, differences that reflect overall changes in the institutions of the Basin of Mexico between the First Intermediate and the Middle Horizon periods. The major differences lie in the economic characteristics of the settlements, but involve the political organization as well.

The evidence from Loma Torremote would suggest a relatively self-sufficient community with internal patterns of part-time specialization and redistribution, possibly reciprocation. The redistribution in some cases, most clearly in the case of obsidian, apparently flowed from lineage heads through the various members of the lineage. How raw materials were obtained that were not locally available is not clear. During the period of the earliest house approximately 5% of the obsidian came from the Pachuca mines, the balance from Otumba; by the final period it had shifted to 35% from the Pachuca, and 65% from the Otumba source. Considering the lack of evidence of settlements near either of the quarries, or of large processing centers anywhere in the Basin, it would seem probable that the villagers had direct access to the raw materials. One question would be whether each lineage of the village procured its own obsidian or whether a particular lineage controlled the distribution of the raw materials among the various lineages of the village. Our surface samples do not indicate any such concentration of materials and suggest that each lineage obtained its raw material separately.

The pattern at Maquixco with respect to obsidian is quite different. The bifacially flaked tools, along with the cylindrical cores, were not processed locally and apparently were obtained at a central place. Considering the data from Teotihuacan, they were probably obtained from professional craftsmen at the site, presumably through the central place that Millon refers to as a market. Whether the locality was a redistribution place or a market place is not clear, but the fact that housing, and portable technology generally, at the city, is superior to that in the village, suggests a negative balance in the exchange, and hence a profit element in the transactions. Although the data are by no means conclusive, and our samples less completely analyzed, what we have does suggest that the pattern described for obsidian applies to other crafts as well. The contrast, then, is between a relatively self-sufficient, tribal community, with reciprocation and small-scale redistribution, during the First Intermediate Two A subphase, and a peasant community, linked by close economic ties to an urban center, in which the relationship was clearly inequitable. The economy of Middle Horizon Teotihuacan was probably a mix of reciprocal, redistributive, and market exchanges comparable to the pattern in contemporary Oaxaca.

The contrast between the two systems is most apparent by a comparison of the two houses of the lineage heads, that for Torremote and that for Maquixco. The data reflect clearly the difference between an official who is essentially a senior kinsmen and a source of redistribution, in the case of the earlier village; and an official who not only does not produce surpluses of technological goods for redistribution to kinsmen, but virtually manufactures no goods at all. His position is more explicitly political.

In summary, for the First Intermediate Phase Two we seem to be dealing with an essentially self-sufficient local community in which ranked individuals functioned to redistribute, over short distances, small quantities of certain finished products. At least some of these materials (e.g., obsidian) were locally unavailable, and some of the finished items were manufactured by a few specialized, or semispecialized, producers who resided within the higher-status households. We feel fairly comfortable in generalizing from the economic pattern we infer for Loma Torremote to the rest of the Basin of Mexico for the First Intermediate Phase Two; that is, all the settlement clusters we have identified as First Intermediate Two polities were probably behaving in much the same manner. At Middle Horizon Maquixco, on the other hand, we have a specialized agricultural community which was totally dependent on a neighboring city for most of its necessities, aside from basic food staples. At Loma Torremote the lineage head was a senior kinsman who functioned as the principal focus of community redistribution, and who underwrote some specialized production. At Maquixco, the lineage head was a much more explicitly political figure who had nothing to do with the production of nonagricultural redistributed goods, and whose principal function was probably to relate the entire local community to a higher organizational level at Teotihuacan.

9

Theoretical Implications of the Basin of Mexico Survey

In Chapter 5 we presented a detailed description of the settlement history of the Basin of Mexico over a period of 3000 years. Although we did occasionally offer explanations for some of the changes we described, our intent was to make that section as descriptive as possible. Here we will explore a number of hypotheses that we believe were responsible for the characteristics of settlement systems during the various phases and for the changes in those systems that occurred during the long period of occupation by sedentary farmers.

From the inception of the project we have emphasized a materialist and ecological approach. More specifically we favored and continue to favor Steward's (1955) culture core paradigm as the most useful theoretical structure; that changes in the exploitative system require changes in social interaction; changes in social interaction produce the need for new organizational rules; and these rules require ideological validation. We have, however, modified this scheme in response to recent developments in culture ecology, particularly in demography, energetics, and quantitative geography. These new developments can easily be adapted to Steward's paradigm, particularly if one shifts from a linear concept of change to a more systemic one, a shift that is becoming increasingly popular among anthropologists.

We enthusiastically endorse this change but have not been impressed with recent attempts to apply it to anthropological problems. The difficulty is that most systemic models that have been proposed do not include in the design any way of assigning different weighting values to the various factors. As Robert Carneiro (1972) has pointed out in a recent seminar, it would be a mistake to assume a democracy of variables. Also needed, to make systemic models useful, are quantitative measures of the individual variables in the particular cases being analyzed, a particularly difficult problem if the system is to include factors such as social and political organization. Our suspicion is that if we do assign quantitative values to the variables, and different weighting values for each factor, that the systemic model will assume a unilineal, or at least a multilineal, character (see Sanders and Webster 1978 for a detailed discussion of this problem).

In summary we feel that a systemic frame of reference has great utility, but would add the warning that useful theory must be simple theory; the fewer the variables and the easier it is to assign quantitative values to them, then the more effective the capacity of the theoretical structure for prediction. An ideal objective would be to isolate four or five variables that explain 80% or more of the variety recorded in the archaeological record. We see no way of accomplishing this task at present, and although our own theoretical structure has some systemic elements to it, in essence, it can be described as a multilineal paradigm. Essentially our procedure is first to suggest several lawlike generalizations that we suspect have considerable validity and explanatory power for the cultural evolution of the Basin of Mexico, then to discuss some of the feedback effects of the social system on the operation of these basic propositions. At our present stage of theory we know of only three lawlike generalizations that govern cultural change: the *law of biotic potential*; the *law of least effort*; and the *law of minimization of risk*.

The law of biotic potential simply states that all species of life have the potential to constantly increase in numbers. This potential is enormous; when sufficient time is allowed (and this involves only hundreds, or at most thousands, of years) even the slowest growing and reproducing animal has the capacity to cover the surface of the earth with its progeny. The law of least effort simply states that when choices between two or more alternate responses to a stress are possible, the choice will be that which produces the greatest gain with the least effort. The law of minimal risk means that when faced by choices the decision will be to adopt that solution which produces the minimal risk.

Virtually all previous evolutionists have explicitly or implicitly utilized the operation of these lawlike generalizations in their theoretical arguments. Carneiro (1970) reviewed the various theories and found that they begin with one of two very different assumptions. One position assumes that the evolution of complex societies, or as it is frequently referred to, the evolution of civilization, is a process of overall progress or improvement of human well-being, and the emergence of civilization can therefore be understood as a "volunteeristic" process. Because of the nature of political centralization and economic specialization, both inevitable to the civilizational process, some individuals derive more benefit from the system than others. Since everyone improves his general well-being, however, even those who occupy the base of the system of social stratification will accept a certain amount of negative reciprocity.

The second position sees the process as both a loss of political autonomy, and an increase in economic cost, to the majority of the population, and the process hence is conceived of as a coercive one; people accept the situation because they have no other choice. There seems to be a general trend toward the latter position in the recent literature and we will generally favor this position. Both positions of course can be adapted to the three basic lawlike generalizations we presented previously.

Carneiro's own theory of the evolution of complex societies assumes that they emerge only through a coercive process. The major stimulus is population growth; in other words, the operation of the law of biotic potential. The process he sees, however, is a direct political one, not necessarily mediated through economic processes, and thus it is not a materialist paradigm. His argument assumes that warfare is universal. In areas of large geographic space (areas he refers to as open environments) and low population density, losers in warfare can escape the penalties of exploitation by fleeing to other areas and hence little political evolution occurs as a consequence of war. In cases where the environment is small (referred to by him as a circumscribed environment), and population density relatively high, then the losers cannot escape the penalty of defeat and must accept an exploitative relationship with the conquerers. Accepting his arguments, the population density of an area need not be unusually high, but the density should be high enough to restrict movement, in the form of out-migration. One factor that would limit migration would be major geographic barriers like high, unproductive mountains, or deserts, or areas of such striking differences from the groups' own habitat that ecological adaptation would be inhibited. Even in such areas where such barriers do not exist, if the area is surrounded by areas of comparable, or at least substantial population buildup, then the group would be socially circumscribed. This means that complex societies could emerge under relatively low conditions of population density. It also means that they should emerge first in smaller, socially or environmentally circumscribed areas, and these areas should show a much faster rate of political evolution than the large ones, providing of course that the small area is sufficiently large to permit a population beyond a few thousand people. This final consideration must be added because there is a very close relationship between complexity of social organization and the size of the society, as Carneiro himself has shown. Apparently the law of least effort operates in terms of social systems as well as economic behavior, that is, people will not organize themselves any more expensively than is necessary. Band societies, for example, tend to have populations maximally in the hundreds, tribal societies maximally in the thousands, and chiefdom societies maximally in the tens of thousands, whereas primitive states have populations in the millions.

Netting (1972) has offered another, essentially nonmaterialist explanation to the evolution of complex society, but again with population growth as the major stimulus. In this case he argues that overt coercion, particularly warfare, is not necessarily the mechanism by which a local group or individuals will surrender their autonomy. His argument is that populations increase at an arithmetical rate, but the frequency of conflicts increases at a geometric rate. Finally a point is reached when it becomes less costly to accept the results of arbitration even if occasionally unfavorable to the litigant, than to continue the feud. Although some of these feuds may be over property, they can be over a great range of situations. The theory is therefore not essentially materialistic since some of these conflicts may not involve property at all. In the African case the individual selected as arbitrator is usually a person who already has a position of prestige in the society, usually a religious leader with very limited economic or political power. Through his role as arbiter, and because he receives gifts from the litigants, he gradually builds up a fund of political and economic power. Much of this power may be transferable to his descendants and ultimately a chiefdom emerges from an essentially egalitarian society.

A more materialist explanation of the evolution of complex society, but still within Carneiro's coercive tradition, is that offered by Esther Boserup (1965). In her book, *The Conditions of Agricultural Growth*, her major objective was to explain variations in agricultural systems. Previous researchers, including anthropologists, have recorded a great variety of agricultural systems in terms of crops, tools, techniques, and, most importantly, degree of intensification of land use. One explanation of these variations was cultural evolution, with the basic assumption that agricultural change was a progressive process starting with simple tools, few techniques, and extensive practices of land use, and ending with more complex tools, elaborate techniques, and intensive patterns of land use. When groups still retained a "primitive" agricultural system it was ascribed to cultural backwardness. These conclusions were particularly held by evolutionists, who started with the assumption that cultural evolution generally was a progressive process and that the changes in agriculture stimulate population growth. Another explanation was environmental, that is, each kind of agriculture was an adaptation, a concession, to variations in soil fertility and was hence in static relationship to the land resource.

Boserup reversed the argument, based on a careful comparison of labor input and crop yield, for the various systems of agriculture. She demonstrated that extensive systems of agriculture have a higher input/output ratio, that is, the farmer gets more calories of crops, in terms of calories of work expended, than from intensive agriculture, and what we call agricultural evolution is a process of gradual decline in per capita income, produced by uncontrolled population growth. Following this argument, when new areas are colonized the extensive agricultural systems will be utilized first; as population increases people will first respond by fissioning into nearby unsettled areas. Ultimately, as the region is completely colonized and fissioning inhibited, further population growth will require a shortening of the fallow system, and finally the entire area will be occupied by farmers practicing intensive agriculture. Her theory provides us with a more dynamic view of agricultural systems, and variations in degree of intensification at any point in time are due primarily to stages in the colonization process.

In her book, however, she goes beyond explaining agricultural variety. She sees agricultural intensification as causing changes in land tenure from virtually no clearly defined land rights, even on the village level, until ultimately the level of individual holdings is reached. Another effect of the process is increasing economic specialization and social stratification. Social stratification is primarily the product of the land tenure system, and land holding rights become increasingly inequitable as intensification occurs. In her model she assumes population growth as a universal and independent variable. Her theory is essentially in the tradition of cultural materialism, since social, economic, and political changes are mediated through the system of agriculture.

In all three of these arguments there is the suggestion that population growth is an independent variable; that in general, human populations increase, and that population-regulating mechanisms among human beings are generally ineffective. All these assumptions have been questioned, and the whole issue has excited considerable controversy in recent years (see Blanton 1975; Cowgill 1975a; Dumond 1965, 1972; Lee 1972; Logan and Sanders 1976; Rappaport 1971). Briefly, the counter argument is that the very rapid growth that obviously has affected human populations since the Industrial Revolution has misled us into the philosophical assumption that this is the human norm; while in fact, through most of the human history, population growth has been anomalous or at least unusual. Human beings, it is reasoned, like all animal and plant populations, are parts of an ecosystem characterized by a network of homeostatic controls, which regulate population. Factors that regulate population growth include cultural practices as well as natural factors. Taking this position, population growth, particularly rapid rates of growth, are rare phenomena.

One of the arguments against population growth as a causative factor in cultural evolution is the very low rates of growth prior to the Industrial Revolution, a strange argument since cultural evolution has also been an extremely slow process! In fact one can show that although cultural evolution, in an overall sense, has been slow, the rate of growth has been an accelerative one and, as Dumond's (1965) calculations show, population growth has also occurred at an accelerated rate (he calculates a rate of 0.0007–0.0015% per year for the Paleolithic, 0.1% during the period for 8000 B.C.–A.D. 1750, and 0.15–0.40% for the period between A.D. 0–A.D. 1750). Taking the argument one step further it can also be demonstrated that in the case of very small local regions, both population growth and cultural evolution can be enormously accelerated compared to these average rates.

We also question the assumption that nonhuman ecosystems are balanced, static systems. If they were, biological evolution would never have happened. Most researchers, whether anthropologists or biologists, when they study contemporary systems, have been struck by their functional harmony—an observation that leads to the erroneous conclusion that they are static systems. The major problem is our inability to measure small changes that accumulate in systems when our period of observation has such a shallow time depth as a few months, a few years, or at most a generation or two. It is curious that most archaeologists see the cultures they study as dynamic.

We strongly favor the position that population growth is a general phenomenon and that human reproductive behavior generally is unlike that of most other species only in its tendency towards sustained growth. The validity of these positions cannot be argued philosophically, they must be supported by empirical data, and the data are overwhelmingly in favor of population growth as a universal phenomenon. Very simply, if this was not the case we would still be Australopithecines living in South Africa. It is undoubtedly true that the growth rates prior to the Industrial Revolution were much slower (primarily due to a much higher infant mortality), but the fact is that there has been a steady increase in the human populations since Paleolithic times.

The major reasons why human population growth has on the whole been a more sustained, and even accelerative one, when compared to other animal populations, is because of the tremendous significance of learned behavior or culture, which is capable of constant elaboration and development. This means that responses to population pressure are much more apt to trigger responses in the form of changes in the cultural system than population regulation, and these changes either permit larger numbers of people to live in the same area or allow people to expand into new geographic space with strikingly different environmental characteristics.

With respect to smaller geographic areas and relatively short periods of time, the data show much greater variation in the pace of population growth, and these variations require explanation. Our own data from the Basin of Mexico reflect this variability. With very favorable epidemiological, nutritional, and political conditions, pre-industrial farming populations apparently have the capacity to double every 100–200 years, and this has probably been close to the maximum growth rate until the great reduction in infant mortality in the modern era. This rate has been recorded by archaeological studies in a number of areas, and is particularly characteristic of pioneering populations, occupying new environmental regions, where the colonizing population is small and land is in abundance. Apparently, under these conditions, cultural controls are either absent or completely ineffective, and natural checks are of minor significance, so that the maximal growth rate is achieved. Such populations, even on the local level, ultimately tend to level off, whatever the factors are that reduce the growth rate. The reason why

larger geographic regions show slower rates of growth is undoubtedly because the smaller areas within them, which were first colonized, ultimately
undergo very reduced growth rates or their populations become completely
stabilized. The question is: How does this process of reduction of growth
occur and what are the growth-curbing mechanisms?

It is our opinion that the reduction process is a gradual one, that is, if the
doubling rate, at the initial phase of colonization, is every 200 or 100 years, it
will gradually shift to every 300 or 400 years, and ultimately will reach a point
of stability. This process occurs also in many nonhuman ecosystems and has
been referred to as environmental resistance. It also is in accordance with our
model of how agricultural intensification proceeds. Within a settlement experiencing population growth, the consequent inequities of land distribution will create situations where individual families will be forced to reduce
their fertility or increase their mortality, in order to solve their economic
problems. The mechanisms by which this is accomplished are undoubtedly
numerous and complex. The most effective ways of curbing population
growth are infanticide and retarded age of marriage, and both can be considered as economic decisions. Other factors, not directly controlled by economic choice, would be malnutrition and disease, two conditions that are
mutually interactive. Within a local region, variations in land pressure from
community to community will also produce the same kind of variety in
reproductive behavior.

What the data seem to show is that the mechanisms of population control
operate so slowly and gradually that frequently the process is not even a
conscious one and certainly cannot function to prevent changes in the cultural system. In taking this position then, Boserup's argument, that population growth can be operationally seen as an independent variable, is essentially correct. We have seen virtually no examples in the literature where
population growth has been controlled in cases of an agricultural population
at a very low percentage of carrying capacity. The most effective means of
curbing population growth, and we would argue the only one that can be
totally effective over a long period of time, is infanticide, and this seems to be
resorted to on a sufficient scale to produce equilibrium of population only
very rarely, and under very extreme conditions.

Basically, all of the theories discussed up to this point involve the operation of the noted two laws, the law of biotic potential and the law of least
effort. In Carneiro's (1970) discussion of the various theories of the evolution
of complex societies he classifies Wittfogel (1957) and his hydraulic civilization theory as a volunteeristic theory. Following Carneiro, it is a theory
derived from our third law, the law of minimal risk. We feel that Wittfogel's
hydraulic civilization theory in fact is an example of the operation of all three
laws. There have been a number of attempts by archaeologists in recent years
to apply Wittfogel's ideas to prehistoric evolutionary sequences, generally
with negative results. The reasons for this failure we believe stem from (a) a
basic misunderstanding of the theory, and (b) a very naive research design to

test it. It is not our intention here to review all of the literature, but a brief summary of the problem is necessary to set the stage for our argument.

What Wittfogel did was to demonstrate a correlation between the large, highly centralized political systems, which he refers to as *oriental despotisms,* with very large scale water management, the latter involving both irrigation and transportation systems. The central features of oriental despotisms are a monopoly of political and economic power by the state, with absolute control over the supporting population, a monopoly that prevents the formation of rival power-controlling institutions. Such states tend to have monarchial institutions, weakly developed mercantile classes, and feudal institutions that are subverted by partible land inheritance. The means by which the state achieves this absolute power is essentially control of water, and the management of this resource requires an elaborate bureaucracy. This type of society he felt was characteristic of Islamic Mesopotamia and China from the Han dynasty to the republic, and was the end product of a long process of internal evolution in those areas; in other words, the development was an example of primary state formation.

A final conclusion of Wittfogel's, and perhaps the one that is most responsible for negative reactions to his theory from some anthropologists, is that other states, evolving in areas of nonhydraulic agriculture, particularly those in which some of the features of the oriental despotism type of state were present, were all cases of secondary state formation; that is, the development occurred under contact or stimulus from pristine or primary states that had evolved in hydraulic regions.

Wholly aside from the validity of this last argument, there has been considerable misunderstanding of Wittfogel's primary argument about state formation and its relationship to hydraulic agriculture, and some of the criticism reflects a curious lack of time perspective on the part of the very anthropologists who are most concerned with testing the theory of cultural evolution—the archaeologists. For example, Adams (1965, 1966) rejects the Wittfogel model as not applicable to third millenium B.C. Sumeria. What is almost incomprehensible in Adams' position is that he rejects both Wittfogel's model of the oriental despotism type of state and large scale hydraulic agriculture as applied to Bronze Age Sumeria. If the sociopolitical system was not yet evolved to the degree that Wittfogel himself would classify it as an oriental despotism, and if the agricultural system was not the large scale centralized irrigation system that Wittfogel is talking about, it is difficult for us to understand what Adams is objecting to. In fact one can interpret the political evolution of Mesopotamia as a gradual process that parallels very closely the evolution of hydraulic agriculture in the same area. Sociopolitically we begin with small early Bronze Age chiefdoms, which evolve into small states during the Late Bronze Age period, and ultimately into large empires, with the institutional characteristics of Wittfogel's oriental despotism, at least by Iron Age times, certainly during Islamic times. This evolution goes hand in hand with a process of gradual artificialization of the natural environment, beginning with a system of agriculture consisting of short feeder canals from the numerous natural tributaries of the region; to small scale, artificial, network canal systems; and finally to a point where the entire river system is canalized. In fact the overall process would seem to justify Wittfogel's argument very strikingly.

The same parallel processes between political evolution and increasing control of irrigation resources can be seen in the culture history of the Peruvian coastal valleys, and yet Andean archaeologists have so far taken issue with Wittfogel's major argument (see Lanning 1967). Sites like Las Haldas, Moche, and Chan Chan are points along a continuum of political evolution of the region, and this evolution goes hand in hand with the development of hydraulic agriculture from small scale floodwater systems, to small scale local canal irrigation, to valley wide systems, and ultimately to transvalley irrigation systems. The difficulty seems to be that most archaeologists visualize hydraulic agriculture as an invention rather than a process. They apparently expect to find a chronological sequence in which large complex canal systems precede archaeological evidence of large complex political systems.

An even more naive treatment of Wittfogel's thesis is represented by ethnographic studies, which propose to test this hypothesis by the use of carefully controlled data from studies of contemporary communities. A classic example of the misuse of Wittfogel is Susan Lees' (1973) study of contemporary irrigation in the Valley of Oaxaca. The Valley of Oaxaca, covering approximately 2500 km², is part of a modern republic which covers approximately 2,000,000 km², characterized politically by an elaborate bureaucracy including several hierarchical levels and a complex pattern of departmentalization of functions. The political organization at the lowest levels is predetermined by the national constitution and all of these local groups in the State of Oaxaca conform to the organization of the republic generally.

Within the villages, beside the formal political system established by the Federal Government, there are series of other positions of a quasipolitical, primarily religious function, such as the Mayordomias, and very often, special sets of officials who are in charge of water control within the village. Irrigation in the valley is similar to that in the Basin of Mexico, that is, it is used primarily for preplanting to obtain a head start on the rainy season, and rainfall is the primary source of soil moisture. However, because the valley is situated below 2000 m, continuous cropping can occur, and hence irrigation is of particular significance during the dry season. Unlike the Basin of Mexico, however, the systems are very small in size, very frequently restricted in use to single villages, and at most involve only a few villages and a few thousand people.

Apparently, when Lees initiated her project she expected to find an elaborate bureaucracy of water management, and despotic political power within and between communities, according to the classic model of Wittfogel, and she applied this to the tiny irrigation systems and the small scale organization of the area! This initial hypothesis reached a level of absurdity when she attempted to find out whether there were examples of internal despotism within the village and whether one village would despotize over other villages using the same irrigation system. All of this was supposed to happen within the setting of a modern national state! Most of her effort was spent in an analysis of the formal political positions, those established by the Federal Government, and those that were particular, or peculiar, to the community that she studied. What she found was a great variety in arrangements in terms of the distribution of water (*although water was officially managed in every community*) and no evidence of village "despotism." Consequently she rejected Wittfogel's hypothesis.

In our opinion what Lees' study should have done was to focus on the network of informal *patron–client* relationships *within* the village and the relationships of the patron–client system to differential access to irrigated land. If she had done this she would have seen a close relationship between these two variables and would have found informal as well as formal power manipulation within the village. Sokolovsky (1974) was able to do a parallel study of the village of Amanalco in the Texcoco region of the Basin of Mexico which revealed this process in great detail.

Aside from these methodological problems in testing Wittfogel's ideas it would seem logical that hydraulic agriculture is varied enough in its characteristics to require a series of evolutionary models, each dependent on the specific characteristics of the system. Such variables would include the size of the system (particularly whether it is a single community or a multicommunity system), degree to which the population derived nearly all or most of its crops from irrigated land, ratio of water to irrigable land, whether the system occurs in an environment where the risk of unirrigated cropping is high or low, long-term problems such as salinization, and feedback relationships between irrigation and the sociopolitical system.

We also take issue with Carneiro's identification of Wittfogel's theory as a volunteeristic theory. The effects of irrigation on the cultural system are in fact multifaceted and very complex. An important element in the social relations among users of an irrigation system is in fact competition, both intracommunity and intercommunity, as Millon *et al.* (1962) have pointed out in their study of the contemporary Teotihuacan system. To recapitulate, the contemporary Teotihuacan system involves approximately 20,000 people distributed in 15 villages and 6 haciendas. The system has a single source, approximately 80–100 springs concentrated in an area of a few square kilometers. Water is collected from the springs into a single canal, which then splits into two major canals, running down opposite sides of the valley. Much of the agriculture of the valley is not based on the irrigation system, so a substantial population derives its food supply from nonirrigated land, including people within the irrigation villages. The risk of crop failure in unirrigated land is extremely high, so that a major function of the system is to reduce risk. The situation creates patron–client relationships within the village, between people who have access to adequate amounts of irrigated land, and those who do not. Particularly characteristic of the system is intensive competition among the villagers over the use of the water and this competition has at times come close to open warfare. Upstream villages obviously have advantages over the downstream villages in terms of these conflicts, and this is one of the major kinds of confrontation. The intervillage disputes are regulated by a council made up of all the member villages, but even this would not work effectively if it were not for the fact that the Federal Government has established the water regulations and has the power to enforce them when these conflicts become acute. Only because of periodic intervention of the Federal Government has the Teotihuacan system remained relatively stable over the past 30 years.

In the case of the Amanalco system approximately 30 local cooperatives (villages, ranchos, and haciendas) once received regular water allotments from the system. The history of the system over the past 30 years shows a constant process of downstream villagers losing their water rights to the upstream villages, until today, only a fraction of the former irrigation cooperatives have access to the system. This is the product of population growth in the upstream villages, and a shift from subsistence cropping to more intensive garden crops, which require greater amounts of water.

The water regulations of the Amanalco system are also guaranteed by the Federal Government and we are not sure why such regulation has been effective in the Teotihuacan system and has failed in the case of the Amanalco system. We can, however, offer a probable explanation. The Teotihuacan system is twice as large as the Amanalco system in terms of irrigable land and volume of water, and water is distributed to half as many cooperatives. What this means is that the allotment is used by a greater percentage of the population of each village in the system. This probably makes it easier for upstream communities to take advantage of their position in the case of the Amanalco system, since only a small fraction of the villagers in the downstream villages even received water from the system. Those few users probably cannot effectively mobilize the entire community for resistance to abuse by the upstream communities.

POPULATION PRESSURE AND SOCIOPOLITICAL EVOLUTION IN THE BASIN OF MEXICO

In this section we will test the usefulness of the first two lawlike generalizations, the law of biotic potential and the law of least effort, to the problem of cultural evolution of the Basin of Mexico. In a recent paper Logan and Sanders (1976:31–178) designed a population pressure model, based upon Boserup, and applied it to those areas of the Basin that had been surveyed at the time of the writing of the paper. In essence this study is a second attempt to apply the same model but with data from the entire area. The model was originally presented in outline form followed by a detailed discussion. A reproduction of the model follows.

   I. Population growth depends on certain favorable combinations of three factors:
       A. Fertility
       B. Mortality
       C. Migration

  II. If interaction of factors in I leads to population increase and subsistence stress, the group may respond by:
       A. Physical and social fission
       B. Increase in food production per unit of space by intensifying use of available resources or by exploiting newly incorporated or newly developed resources within the same physical space

 III. II-A will be eliminated as a response and II-B will occur if:
       A. Environment is circumscribed and desirable resettlement locales are either occupied or nonexistent
       B. Environmental factors permit II-B

  IV. If II-B does occur, this will then stimulate:
       A. Sedentary residence
       B. Differential access to both agricultural and nonagricultural resources, first within settlements and then between settlements
       C. Intrasocietal and intersocietal competition

   V. If IV-A, IV-B, and IV-C occur, then the following processes will result:
       A. Occupational specialization in nonagricultural activities
       B. Further intensification of agriculture, including specialization in agriculture in the first stages of the process
       C. Increase in economic exchange networks and the development or elaboration of managerial institutions
       D. Rank differentiation and, ultimately, class stratification
       E. Political linearization, or the emergence of more numerous, increasingly complex political controls

  VI. The rate of development of II-B, IV, and V is affected by:
       A. Population size and rate of growth
       B. Size of the circumscribed area
       C. Resource variability within the circumscribed region
       D. Technological base of production and military spheres of culture
       E. Comparable events and processes occurring in nearby geographical areas

 VII. The stability of, or decline in, cultural complexity will occur when:
       A. Factors in I result in a stable or diminishing population
       B. II-A is operative
       C. III-B does not permit II-B
       D. Circumscribed areas are excessively small or isolated

In order to test the model a necessary step is the calculation of carrying capacity for the various regions of the Basin in terms of different agricultural systems.

Carrying Capacity

Considerable controversy has developed in recent years over the question of carrying capacity (see Hayden 1975), what it is, how to measure it, and the usefulness of the concept to an understanding of cultural adaption. Much of this controversy has occurred because carrying capacity has been conceived of as a static condition rather than as a dynamic process. The biological definition of carrying capacity as the maximum number of a species of living organisms that an area can sustain, without long-range deleterious effects that reduce the capacity of the area to sustain that same population, is probably of limited utility for cultural ecologists. The problem is that humans, through culture, are able to change their exploitative arrangements drastically as their population increases, and these changes allow for increasingly larger populations to reside in the same area. This is not to say that the process never produces long-range deleterious effects, but in most cases the effects can be arrested by new techniques.

If we accept Boserup's thesis, that the initial colonization of any area by farmers should involve an essentially extensive approach to land use, we can then calculate the carrying capacity of this extensive system. Theoretically a population first fills in an area, to the degree that the carrying capacity of extensive agriculture is approached, and only then should there be a shift to a more intensive agriculture system. Prior to this point, as local populations build up to certain levels, the work cost of agriculture increases, and, in response, physical fissioning occurs. When the fissioning process has resulted in colonization of a defined area, then a shift to a more intensive agricultural system would be the response to further pressure. One could then calculate the carrying capacity of the new system. Successive shifts to increasingly more intensive systems of land use can each be evaluated using the carrying capacity concept, and theoretically we should be able to discern quantitative regularities in the process, that is, changes in settlement, agricultural practices, and techniques should occur at some central value or mode of percentage of carrying capacity.

In the previously cited paper (Logan and Sanders 1976) we estimated that fissioning, during the pioneer stage of colonization, would occur at approximately 20–30% of carrying capacity, and overall changes in the subsistence system should occur, to a degree that is measurable, at 50–80%. The main reason for changes to occur at levels well below carrying capacity relate in part to the feedback effects of the sociopolitical system on the process. Within a community, inequities of land rights may result in some farmers shifting to more intensive patterns of agriculture well before others. Apparently even at relatively low levels of population there is a perception of land as a limited good and the process of competition over this resource results in differential access to it. Between communities the same process of competition may operate to create unsafe zones between politically antagonistic populations, and hence reduce the zone of cultivation artificially. Aside from these feedback effects of social structure on the process, Napoleon Chagnon's studies of the demography of the Yanomamo (Chagnon 1968, 1974) show striking variability in demographic behavior of small groups, much of which is idiosyncratic in nature. This means that some settlements in a given region would be expanding in population at a much faster rate than others, and consequently the process of agricultural intensification would be uneven, even within one of our survey regions.

In a very large area like the Basin of Mexico, where colonization proceeded from a few localities, and where large areas were agriculturally marginal or uncultivable, this process would be expectedly even more uneven, and the initial areas of colonization would experience heavy land pressure while other areas might still be in a stage of pioneer occupation. In part this is because of the essential inefficiency of the fissioning process as a means of population dispersion. As we noted before, the fissioning process involves relatively small-scale, short distance, local movements, rather than large-scale long distance treks. What this means is that even lightly settled frontiers may act as buffers and restrict colonization from well-settled areas, and well-settled areas may act as buffers against population movement from overpopulated regions, precisely what Carneiro describes as social circumscription. The steady increase of population density, and consequent agricultural intensification, in the southern third of the Basin during the First through the Second Intermediate time frame can, in part, be explained by the circumscribing effects of population buildup in the central region.

Our model of the agricultural history of the Basin proposed here is derived essentially from Boserup and assumes a process of increasingly more intensive land use as the population increases. In order to demonstrate this process we need to calculate the carrying capacity of the Basin in terms of different agricultural regimes. This is an exceedingly difficult task and what we have done instead is to establish carrying capacity estimates for a very extensive system of farming and then estimates for a fully intensive agricultural system. These two calculations can then act as control points for estimating the process of intensification. In the previously cited paper by Logan and Sanders (1976) we discussed in detail our methods of calculation. A number of charts from that study have been republished here for reference (see Tables 9.1, 9.4, and 9.5).

Basically our method is a direct application of William Allan's (1965) method of calculating carrying capacity, as presented in his classic study, *The African Husbandman*. He uses three variables, the cultivation factor, the land use factor, and the cultivable land factor. We will begin with the cultivation factor. This refers to the amount of land planted in crops in a particular year, necessary to sustain the average person. In our calculations we have changed the unit of consumption to the extended family (in the mid-sixteenth century averaging seven persons), since the extended family was the production unit (see Table 9.1). Allan's calculation was an empirical one, based on the particular economic system being studied. For example, among relatively

TABLE 9.1
Grain Yields and Cultivation Factors for an Extended Family of Seven[a]

Type of cultivation system	Post-First Intermediate Phase 3		First Intermediate Phase 3		First Intermediate Phase 1–2		Early Horizon	
	Yield (in kilograms per hectare)	Cultivation factor (in hectares)	Yield (in kilograms per hectare)	Cultivation factor (in hectares)	Yield (in kilograms per hectare)	Cultivation factor (in hectares)	Yield (in kilograms per hectare)	Cultivation factor (in hectares)
Alluvial plain (permanent irrigation)	1400	0.8	1050	- 0.86	875	1.1	700	- 1.3
Piedmont (permanent irrigation)	1000	1.1	750	1.2	625	1.5	500	1.8
Alluvial plain (floodwater irrigation)	1000	1.1	750	1.2	625	1.5	500	1.8
Piedmont (floodwater terracing)	800	1.4	600	1.5	500	1.9	400	2.25
Tierra de Humedad	1400	0.8	1050	0.86	875	1.1	700	1.3
Tierra de Humedad (riverine)	1200	0.95	900	1.03	750	1.3	600	1.55
Chinampa	3000	0.37	2250	0.4	1875	0.5	1500	0.6
Pseudo-chinampa	2000	0.55	1500	0.6	1250	0.75	1000	0.9
Alluvial plain (temporal)	1000	1.1	750	1.2	625	1.6	500	1.8
Piedmont (temporal)	400–800	1.4–2.8	300–600	1.5–3.0	250–500	1.9–3.8	200–400	2.5–5.0
Bush fallowing (good land)	1400	0.8	1050	0.86	875	1.1	700	1.3
Bush fallowing (poor land)	800	1.4	600	1.5	500	1.9	400	2.25

[a] From Sanders 1976b.

self-sufficient tribal farmers, where craft specialization and social stratification are weakly developed, the cultivation factor is the amount of land needed to provide food to feed the family. In societies where both social stratification and craft specialization are highly developed, the factor must include additional crop production for marketing and taxation. In this study we are concerned only with the demographic capacity of the agricultural system, not with the redistribution network, so our measure assumes relative self-sufficiency in food production by the family, and is therefore an estimate of the amount of land needed to feed one extended family. Considering the large size of the Basin of Mexico, and the primitiveness of transportation, it is very unlikely that any significant foods were exported from or imported to the area. The only complicating question is whether economic specialization does not produce greater efficiency in terms of agricultural production. We feel that the differences are relatively slight, and hence our methodology is, in fact, a good measure of the demographic capacity of the agricultural system.

In Central Mexico today a variety of agricultural systems are practiced, under a considerable variety of environmental conditions. All these variations affect crop yields, particularly maize, the staple crop. We have abstracted from our studies of contemporary agriculture a set of average productivity figures for the staple crop. These averages include extrapolations for the effects of climatic variables (based on yields over 10-year periods); extrapolations for losses of the harvested crop to other living organisms; and we have selected those values from fields where fertilization regimes are relatively light, in an attempt to approximate pre-Conquest conditions. A major variable, over which we have little control, are changes in the maize plant itself that might have affected its yield. We know, primarily from the Tehuacan project, that maize went through a series of major botanical changes from the inception of domestication from its wild ancestor *teocentli*, to the time of the Conquest.

On the basis of the data on the history of maize in the Basin presented in Chapter 7, yields comparable to modern varieties of maize were possible as early as the First Intermediate Five phase. The remaining problem is to estimate yields for the earlier phases. Kirkby (1973) has made calculations, based on a comparison of ear size, for the less productive, earlier varieties, but we feel that her calculated yields are far too low. Using these calculations she obtains a yield of only 200 kilos per hectare, on lands which today yield 1000, in the Valley of Oaxaca. In the paper by Sanders (1976b) we criticized this figure in terms of the labor cost of cultivation. Even assuming that only two-thirds of the food supply was derived from maize, a family of seven would need to cultivate nearly 5 ha of land a year to feed itself. Based on our field studies of labor input, with wooden or stone tools, this would require an annual labor input, depending on the soil texture, of 375–785 man-days. The return is only 1.5–2.0 kilos of maize for each day of labor, an unacceptable return for a stable agricultural economy. In fact they would have had at least as favorable, and possibly a more favorable, ratio of return by gathering wild plants. For example, for every seven Kalahari bushmen only 520 man days are required for the seven people to feed themselves (Lee 1969). Under these conditions it would be very difficult to explain why a group would become agricultural. Among most contemporary farmers using hand tools (see Sanders 1976b), a yield of 400–500 kilos of grain per hectare is a minimal yield for them to consider it to be worth the effort. With plows, of course, lower yields could be accepted, because the labor input per hectare is less and hence more land could be opened up to cultivation.

Another reason that we doubt Kirkby's conclusion is that the wild ancestor of maize, *teocentli,* yields at least as high as her calculated Early Formative maize, and on some lands, even higher, and almost certainly the process of selection that produced the increased ear size would have at least some effect upon productivity. Kirkby does demonstrate that there is a relationship between ear size and yield per hectare in contemporary fields in Oaxaca, but this is expectable since the same variety of maize is planted on most of these fields and the variation in yield is due to variations in climatological factors which correspondingly affect ear size. It is quite another matter, however, to assume that the primitive varieties of maize were planted using exactly the same regime as those today. If the yield per ear was consistently only one-quarter or one-half as much as it is today, what this undoubtedly means is that the individual plant required lesser amounts of nutritional elements and water for its growth. One would assume therefore that the plants were placed closer together to maximize yields. Another possibility, as suggested by Mangelsdorf (1964), is that the more primitive varieties had greater numbers of ears per plant. If this were the case, then the planting regime might have been comparable to that of more productive varieties, but the total yield per plant somewhat less. With these considerations in mind we will assume an average productivity of Early Horizon maize as approximately one-half the values of modern maize and extrapolate values for the intervening phases.

Finally we need to know the entire range of food resources and their quantitative contribution to the diet in order to make a reasonable estimate of carrying capacity. In some ecosystems a short supply of a relatively minor (in terms of caloric intake) but critical food (particularly proteins) may restrict the carrying capacity to levels considerably below those possible in terms of the main calorie producing foods. The Mesoamerican crop complex includes, however, virtually all of the nutritive elements needed, with an added small ingestion of animal proteins. This means that the productivity of the staple crop can be used as reference data for calculation of carrying capacity. Considering the fact that our maximal figures for the Pre-Late Horizon population are only one-fourth the size of the Late Horizon it would seem probable that the animal and plant protein from the lake and land fauna from uncultivated areas were more than sufficient to meet the major protein requirements. Furthermore, intercropping was a common procedure, so that most of the cultivated plant foods were derived from the same field where the basic caloric staple, maize, was produced. What this means is that data on maize yields can be used to estimate carrying capacity, providing we make a calculation as to the percentage of the diet that was derived from maize products. In poor peasant families today in Mexico this figure may reach as high as 80% of the caloric intake, and we will use this figure for the very dense population of the Late Horizon. For the earlier phases we will assume that only two-thirds of the food intake was derived from maize products, or a grain equivalent like *amaranth*.

The second component in Allan's calculation is the land use factor, that is, the number of units of the size of the cultivation factor needed to support the family or individual indefinitely. The calculation therefore includes the land under cultivation in any one year, plus a number of plots of land of the same size, in the various stages of rest or fallow. A world-wide sample includes examples of a land use factor as high as 20 or 30 (meaning 20 or 30 units are needed for each one in production) down to 1 or even 0.5 in the cases of double cropping regimes. Our specific land use model supposes that the process of intensification is a gradual one. On the basis of Lewis' (1951) studies of swidden or extensive agriculture at Tepoztlan we will use a factor of 5 as representing the system during the early phase of colonization. For fully intensive agriculture, which we postulate, on the basis of abundant data, as present during the Late Horizon, we will use land use factors of 1 or 2. These two calculations will then provide us with points of reference.

The third component is more difficult to evaluate, the cultivable land factor. This is the percentage of the landscape that can be classified as agricultural land. This factor varies according to natural conditions, but also according to the cultural characteristics of the population. Allan's method was first to divide the overall region into a series of major ecological zones. Some entire ecological zones, at least in terms of a given level of technology or crop complex, may, as a whole, be uncultivable (examples in the Basin of Mexico would be the sierra zone and the saline lake zone). These areas would then be subtracted from the total land surface. Even within a zone that was cultivated, however, one never finds 100% cultivability. This is due to topographic, cultural, hydrographic, and climatic variability. In the case of the upper piedmont, for example, much of the region is in the form of very steep hillsides, in some cases without any, or a very thin soil cover; also present are areas of exposed volcanic detritus and deep, wide barrancas.

In Sanders' (1976b) study of carrying capacity, he assumed that, when pre-Late Horizon populations avoided completely entire ecological zones for settlement, even though they were occupied in Late Horizon times, the inhibitory forces to their colonization were sufficient to classify these zones as nonagricultural land. We justify this argument on the basis that not only were the zones avoided for settlement for long periods of time, but they were so even when adjacent zones were obviously experiencing substantial land pressure.

Our settlement surveys indicate that most of the area that was culturally defined as agricultural land during the First Intermediate period was settled by Phase One. In the subsequent First Intermediate Two and Three phases the only significant geographic expansion of population was into the alluvial plain of the lower Teotihuacan Valley. Virtually all of the rest of the population growth involved essentially a filling-in process. This restriction of movement suggests very severe limitations on the ecosystem, on the nature of which we can only offer tentative explanations.

To recapitulate, basically the problem of the prehispanic cultivator was how to adapt a crop that required 6 months to mature to an area where only a minority of the land has a frost–rainfall regime that could insure successful cropping in a majority of the years. The key variables are the fall frosts which, as we noted, begin as early as September but generally occur first during the October months and become extremely severe in November, December, and January. Spring frosts also occur, but these offer relatively minor problems, so minor that villages in the upper piedmont of the Texcoco region today will irrigate their land in February and plant as early as March, in some cases as early as February. Apparently the risk of fall frosts in terms of crop failure is substantially greater than the risk of spring frosts. What is important is that only a small percentage of the Basin includes lands where there is a 6-month period free of frosts in a majority of years, and these lands would be highly favored for settlement, particularly during the early phases of the agricultural adaptation to the area. It should also be reiterated that there is a rainfall gradient from southwest to northeast, and the problem of the frost is further compounded by low average rainfall and great variation in rainfall in some sections. In the south conditions are most favorable, in terms of frost and rainfall, and the cultivable land category during the First Intermediate period includes the alluvial plain as well as the lower and middle piedmont. In the central region the operation of the two environmental parameters of precipitation and frosts would effectively restrict occupation during that period to the lower and middle piedmont, or to a few small areas in the alluvial plain, where natural soil moisture would permit plantings as early as April or May. In the Teotihuacan Valley, primarily the middle piedmont and the upper part of the lower piedmont would fulfill these conditions and, for the far north, only a small area of naturally humid lands on the lakeshore plain would permit successful cropping. Even today, with 4-month varieties of maize, many villages in the northeast plant barley rather than maize, and, in essence, are cash farmers. By the end of the First Intermediate period, with the appearance of a 4-month variety of maize, we have the initiation of a substantial colonization of the alluvial plains in the central regions. The northern portion of the Basin, however, seems to have been virtually unoccupied until the First Intermediate Four phase.

Another deterrent in the expansion of population into certain zones would lie in the feedback relationships between the political system and the exploitative pattern. Even with a 6-month growing season, or with the availability of 4-month maize, large scale drainage and irrigation system projects in the alluvial plain probably could not have been carried out until a point in time when the sociopolitical groupings were sufficiently centralized to mobilize the kind of labor required.

For the Late Horizon, applying our model of intensive agriculture, assuming highly centralized political organization, and varieties of maize adapted to all of the various niches of the Basin, we estimate that 80% of the alluvial plain could have been cultivated, two-thirds of the lands in the lower piedmont, one-half of the lands in the middle piedmont, and approximately one-third of the lands in the upper piedmont. This is an average figure for the Basin. In fact, in some lands within these categories the percentage of cultivable land would be substantially higher or lower. For example, in the upper and middle piedmont of the Xochimilco area only a tiny fraction of the land is cultivable; much of it is volcanic waste land. On the other hand in the upper piedmont of the Texcoco region the cultivable land factor is relatively high.

Population Pressure and Agricultural Intensification

Tables 6.17–6.18 (pages 217–218) and 9.2–9.3 provide the reader with a summary picture of the prehispanic demographic history of the Basin by region—the carrying capacity of the Basin of Mexico, with a land use factor of 5 and with intensive agriculture—and should be referred to for clarification of the discussion to follow. Excluding the Pachuca region, where we lack survey data, the sierra, which was above the zone of agricultural utilization, and the lakes, which were not an agricultural resource until Late Horizon times, the total amount of cultivable land in our surveyed region is 2331 km^2 or 233,100 ha. Our estimate of the carrying capacity of the same area, plus the chinampa zone in the lakes, with intensive agriculture, is 1,250,000 people. Our various estimates for the population in 1519 are 800,000 (derived primarily from the archaeological data with documentary estimates added in for the large cities like Tenochtitlan, Texcoco, Tlacopan, and others), and 900,000 to 1,100,000 (from documentary sources alone). This means the population had reached from 65–88% of carrying capacity with intensive agriculture.

Considering these raw figures and particularly considering the fact that the pre-Late Horizon population of the Basin never exceeded 250,000, the theory that population pressure produced sociopolitical evolution would seem to be of very doubtful utility. In fact, if we take into consideration all the variables that limited agricultural expansion during the First Intermediate, and apply Boserup's ideas as to how the process of intensification operates, then the model does provide a powerful explanatory framework for at least the early stage of cultural evolution in the Basin. Assuming an extensive system of cultivation, 47,100 ha would be available for annual cropping, in the area of 2331 km^2. We have included in this calculation the large areas of lower and middle piedmont in the northern third of the Basin

TABLE 9.2
Basin of Mexico: Carrying Capacity, Extensive Agriculture

Categories of land	Basin area (in km²)	Area within survey (in km²)	Cultivable land (in percentages)	Cultivable land (in km²)	Land cropped annually (in km²) (land use factor of 5)
Sierra	1000	200	0	0	0
Pachuca region	1000	0	?	?	?
Area below 2200 m	0	140	80%	112	22
Lake	900	900	0		
Freshwater	160	160	0		
Saline	640	640	0		
Salinized shore	100	100	0		
Deep soil plain	800	800			
Floodplain	200	200	80%	160	32
High water table	200	200	35%[d]	70	14
Well-drained	400	400	80%	320	64
Thin soil plain	400	400	80%	320	64
Upland alluvium	35	35	80%	29	6
Lower piedmont	950	950[a]	65%	617	123
Middle piedmont	1050	950[b]	50%	475	95
Upper piedmont	750	650[c]	35%	228	40
	6000	5125		2331	471

Carrying Capacity

	Basin	Basin and lower middle piedmont	Southern half, lower and middle piedmont	Average cultivation factor
Early Horizon	150,000	70,000	25,000	1.8
First Intermediate 1–2	220,000	100,000	35,000	1.5
First Intermediate 3	250,000	125,000	42,000	1.2
Post-First Intermediate 3	300,000	140,000	45,000	1.1

[a] 670, north half; 280, south half.
[b] 600, north half; 350 south half.
[c] 300, north half; 350, south half.
[d] Without large scale drainage.

which were of doubtful agricultural utility during the early phases of adaptation and the alluvial plain (which was only sparingly used, primarily in the south and west). The total area classified as cultivable lands, assuming that all of these lands were cultivated, would permit a theoretical maximal population of 150,000 people during Early Horizon, 220,000 during the First Intermediate One–Two, and 250,000 in Phase Three. Considering these figures the population of the Basin did not reach carrying capacity in any pre-Middle Horizon phase, even in terms of extensive agriculture.

TABLE 9.3
Basin of Mexico: Carrying Capacity, Maximal Agricultural Intensification

Category of land	Cultivation factor (seven people)	Land use factor	Hectares cultivable land	Land cultivated in 1 year	Carrying capacity
Pachuca region	?	?	?	?	?
Sierra			0		0
Area below 2200 m	1.1–2.2	1–2	11,200	7500	35,000
Lake					
Freshwater	.37	1	10,000	10,000	200,000
Saline lake	.60	1	(Artificially desalinized) 2,500	2,500	30,000
Salinized shore			0		
Deep soil plain					
Floodplain	.95	1	16,000	16,000	120,000
High water table	.80	2	15,000	7,500	65,000
Well-drained—permanent irrigation	.80	1	15,000	15,000	130,000
Well-drained—temporal and flood-water irrigation	1.1	1–2	18,000	12,000	75,000
Thin soil plain					
Floodwater irrigation	1.4	1–2	16,000	12,000	80,000
Temporal	1.4–2.8	2–3	16,000	6,400	20,000
Upper alluvium	1.1	1–2	2,900	2,175	13,800
Lower piedmont					
Permanent irrigation	1.1	1	5,000	5,000	33,000
Floodwater irrigation	1.4	1	20,000	20,000	90,000
Temporal	1.4–2.8	2	36,700	18,500	60,000
Middle piedmont					
Permanent irrigation	1.1	1	5,000	5,000	33,000
Floodwater irrigation	1.4	1	17,500	17,500	85,000
Temporal	1.4–2.8	2	20,000	10,000	35,000
Upper piedmont					
Permanent irrigation	1.1	1	5,000	5,000	33,000
Floodwater irrigation	1.4	2	7,800	4,000	20,000
Temporal	1.4–2.8	3	10,000	3,300	12,000
					1,169,800

If we assume that only the lower and middle piedmont were cultivable lands, and exclude all of the alluvial plains, the carrying capacity drops to 70,000, 100,000 and 125,000. Using these data, by Phase Three the population had exceeded the carrying capacity of swidden agriculture. The carrying capacity of the southern half of the Basin only calculates at 25,000 during the Early Horizon, 35,000 during the First Intermediate One and Two, and 42,000 during the First Intermediate Three. Since virtually all the population of the Basin during the Early Horizon and the First Intermediate One and Two phases was located in that portion of the Basin, and over half the population was located there during Phase Three, quite obviously the population levels of this portion of the Basin were well above carrying capacity for swidden agriculture by Phase Three times, suggesting the need for some level of agricultural intensification. The process is even more dramatically illustrated in a region by region analysis (see Maps 21, 22, and 23 to illustrate the discussion that follows).

The pattern may be summarized as follows. By First Intermediate One times there was a strip of settlement on the plain and adjacent lower piedmont on the south shore of Lakes Chalco–Xochimilco where the population was very close to carrying capacity with a swidden system. Another continuous strip of comparable land pressure rings the Guadalupe range on the east and south. The balance of the population in the Basin consisted of a series of small population clusters widely spaced over the southern two-thirds of the area.

By the end of the First Intermediate Two phase the entire lower and middle piedmont, with adjacent areas of lakeshore plain, in the Lake Chalco–Xochimilco Basin, had exceeded carrying capacity for a swidden system by a factor of 2 to 3. All of the examples of utilization of the alluvial plain occur at the foot of major zones of piedmont occupation or at the bases of very steeply sloping terrain. In the Texcoco region there was a continuous strip of settlement along the lower and middle piedmont from the Ixtapalapa region to the Patlachique range that had now reached carrying capacity, in terms of swidden agriculture. A comparable zone extended along the east and south sides of the Guadalupe range (including both plain and lower piedmont), and probably along the lower and middle piedmont west of Lake Texcoco. Further to the north were small pockets of population in the Cuautitlan region.

During First Intermediate Three times the processes and patterns we have described reached their maximal expression. The Chalco–Xochimilco lake basin, the Ixtapalapa peninsula, and the Texcoco piedmont–Middle Papalotla river basin all reached a point where the carrying capacity of swidden agriculture was exceeded by a factor of 2–4. The south flank of the Teotihuacan Valley had now reached carrying capacity and a large town emerged at Teotihuacan, based, however, on drainage and permanent irrigation of the alluvial plain. Scattered pockets of population were found on the north flank of the Teotihuacan Valley. In contrast, the Tenayuca region apparently underwent a process of rapid population decline (we say apparently because we surveyed only 30% of the region, due to recent urbanization, and one or two large sites in the unsurveyed area would alter our conclusion) and virtually the entire population of the Cuautitlan region was nucleated at the site of San Jose in the alluvial plain, a striking contrast to previous settlement. With respect to the Tacuba region we have no definite sites and have suggested in our model that perhaps this area was abandoned. In our summary of settlement history we have also suggested that this was a phase of major military confrontation between the various political group-ings, particularly between the two large ones at opposite ends of the Basin, Teotihuacan and Cuicuilco, and this region may have been politically unsafe. The northern third of the Basin was still uninhabited.

Our estimates of carrying capacity and of the history of population growth in each of our survey regions, and of the Basin of Mexico as a whole, provide strong support for Boserup's theory. The population levels and the fact that the initial phase of the colonization of the Basin as a whole, and of each of its regions, involved selection of those niches where the risk of crop failure was least, would suggest an extensive approach to cropping. The higher values of our population estimates in those same regions in later times when they exceeded swidden farming would further suggest a process of agriculture intensification. In order to strengthen this latter conclusion, how-ever, we need a variety of data that are independent of our calculations of population, since these are admittedly subject to a relatively wide error, and more importantly, a reliance only on these kinds of data is, in essence, a highly circular argument.

Innovations in the form of a number of specialized tools and techniques of cultivation can be used as indicators of agricultural intensification. As Boserup suggests, long fallow swidden agriculture does not require the labor of turning over the soil; this only becomes necessary with short fallow systems, where competition from grasses and herbaceous plants becomes a serious problem. Soil turning tools would be an indication, therefore, of a process of intensification. In Chapter 7 we summarized the data on tools and techniques for the prehispanic period. Of particular interest was the history of the tool type we described as a hoe. Our admittedly inadequate data do seem to suggest that the hoe appears as a tool in each of the regions when our calculation of population indicated that it had surpassed the levels permitted by extensive cultivation. It appears in the southern Basin as early as First Intermediate Two times but not in the northern regions until the Middle Horizon or later. It should be admitted, however, that no consistent sam-pling of sites to control more thoroughly the distribution in time and space of this artifact has been undertaken.

Other possible indications of intensification are innovations in tech-niques such as terracing, permanent irrigation, floodwater irrigation, and drainage systems. Before we summarize the history of these features, it should be pointed out that under some conditions, intensification need not involve these specialized techniques, so that the absence of such techniques does not preclude intensification. Their presence, however, is certain evi-dence of the intensification process. Contemporary studies of Highland New Guinea agriculture, for example, demonstrate that where land surfaces have only gentle slopes and drainage is good, intensification may involve no new techniques and involves little more than a reduction of fallow (Waddell 1972). In other areas in New Guinea where the potentially productive agricultural land is poorly drained, the intensification process may involve elaborate ditch and ridge systems.

With respect to terracing, to recapitulate, the evidence is incontrovertible for the Late Horizon, when virtually all sloping areas of the Basin were terraced. The association of terraces with sites is made relatively easy by the dispersed nature of the settlement systems. For pre-Aztec times there are a number of periods and phases (Early Horizon, First Intermediate One–Two, First Intermediate Four–Five, Middle Horizon, and Second Intermediate One, Three) when the rural population was nucleated in compact villages or towns and the problem of archaeological association of such sites with nearby areas of prehistoric terracing, from survey data alone, is considerable. We do have evidence of at least residential terracing for sites of the First Intermediate Two and Middle Horizon phases. During the First Intermediate Three and Second Intermediate Two phases rural populations were dispersed and we can, with some confidence, date terracing from those phases. Of course, in a particular area if we have evidence of terracing for two phases of dispersed settlement and the intervening phase of nucleated settlement was of comparable population we can probably safely assume that terracing was present then as well.

The difficulty with all of this pre-Late Horizon data is that the dated terraces are directly associated with residential sites (in fact if they were not we would not be able to demonstrate their contemporaneity), and the areas of terracing that we can actually date are therefore very small. They may be small kitchen gardens associated with houses. This means that it is still possible that most of the agricultural land used by the settlement did not involve terracing as a technique. As we pointed out before, the important data that we need are the amount of land that was actually under terracing, for each of the villages, during each of the time phases, and this is an extremely difficult problem to resolve.

It should be emphasized that our philosophical position with respect to the history of intensification is away from the idea that looks at such techniques as inventions, but rather that intensification is the product of the necessity of increasing labor input, brought about by conditions that require agricultural intensification. In other words, terracing, as we see it, is a process, not an invention. To put it more explicitly, terracing is time consuming and costly, and only resorted to when land availability is reduced to the degree that the fallow cycle must be shortened. As the fallow cycle is shortened, the erosion rate increases, and terracing is adopted to correct the problem. If agricultural land is abundant and erosion rates slow, our argument is that farmers will not invest this heavy labor in terrace maintenance. This means that the appearance of terracing in an area is no indication of its general use in that area, and hence is only a suggestion that some kind of process of agricultural intensification is involved. This warning is directed to ourselves as well as to other archaeologists, and if it seems to our colleagues that we are presenting unnecessary problems in terms of archaeological methods, it is because the process that we are describing is complex and the archaeological methods we use are not always successful in obtaining the data that illustrate the process. What the data on terracing suggest is that as a technique it appears early in our sequence and as a whole its pattern seems to coincide with the phase in a region when population had reached substantial levels. In this sense, the data do justify our argument that the appearance of terracing in the various regions is an indication of population pressure.

With respect to hydraulic agriculture as an indicator of agricultural intensification, the question is more complex. One could argue that its occurrence should occur relatively late in the population history of a region since considerable extra labor input is involved and the law of minimal effort would predict its late appearance. This would be particularly true in an area like the Basin of Mexico, where there are favorable zones of rainfall-based agriculture with reasonably high crop security. On the other hand, in the drier regions of the Basin, risk becomes a major factor and might stimulate its appearance at a very early phase of colonization, as Flannery *et al.* (1967) have argued for the Valley of Oaxaca. Convincing evidence of hydraulic agriculture does seem to appear in the drier regions, however, only when populations reach substantial size, so it seems that the law of least effort does help to explain its appearance. What this means is that the appearance of hydraulic agriculture can be used as a measure of the intensification process. We will return to a discussion of the history of hydraulic agriculture in the Basin since its development also is closely related to the risk factor.

Agricultural Intensification and Sociopolitical Evolution

Our settlement survey, the reconstruction of population levels based on it, and direct evidence of agricultural techniques all strongly support Boserup's assumptions as to the nature of population growth and the impact of such growth on agricultural intensification, and, as such, are an empirical demonstration of the laws of biotic potential and of least effort. Whether the data also support the corollary argument that changes in agricultural systems, and following Netting and Carneiro, the direct effects of population growth, are correlated with changes in social institutions is more difficult to establish from settlement survey data alone, but our data do strongly suggest that the model we presented on page 370 is indeed applicable to the Basin of Mexico in First Intermediate times. The process of physical and social fissioning, as a response to population growth, is dramatically illustrated in each local population and settlement profile, as well as the overall process of settlement of the Basin. The proliferation of hamlets on the frontiers of zones of substantial settlement followed by subsequent shifts in settlement pattern to larger communities in those same frontiers is, in each case, an example of the process.

With respect to political centralization and social stratification, our data from the survey are obviously inadequate but highly suggestive. Fortunately, we do have a substantial body of excavation data that can be combined with the survey to present a reasonably clear picture. Community differentiation between center and outlying settlements seems to correlate very closely with population growth in each of the local regions, beginning as early as the First Intermediate Two phase in the south, appearing as a characteristic pattern in Intermediate Three times in the Texcoco region, and finally appearing contemporary with the rise of Teotihuacan in the northern portions of the Basin. Burial and residential data from a variety of excavated sites—Coapexco, Tlatilco, El Arbolillo, Zacatenco, Ticoman, Loma Torremote, Isla de Terremote, Cuanalan, Chimalhuacan, Venta de Carpio, Tezoyuca, and Tlapacoya—provide interesting data on the process of ranking. What all of these data suggest is that at least some incipient form of ranking began as early as Early Horizon times, and when it appears in a local region it is always in those areas where local populations are substantial and have a tendency to be nucleated at large settlements. These larger settlements, during virtually the entire First Intermediate period, also seem never to have exceeded 2000 or 3000 people, with, of course, the two major exceptions of Cuicuilco and Teotihuacan. This restriction of size probably relates to the limitations of ranking as a mechanism of social integration. The ceremonial construction at these central sites during Phases Two and Three is generally very small and unimposing, again with the exception of the two major centers.

In our opinion all of our data indicate the correlation of a series of processes, population growth, concentration of population in large settlements, intensification of agriculture, and increasing significance of low-level ranking in the sociopolitical system. Most of these political groupings, however, were probably organized along the lines of a simple chiefdom type of organization, with severe limitations in terms of degree of political integration. The restriction of most of the population to zones of relatively low agricultural risk through most of the period also probably retarded the evolution of truly stratified social systems and state formation over most of the Basin of Mexico during this time period.

HYDRAULIC AGRICULTURE AND SOCIOPOLITICAL EVOLUTION IN THE BASIN OF MEXICO

Our present reaction to the data from the Basin of Mexico is that a combination of the laws of biotic potential and the law of minimal effort provide a useful explanation of much of the sociopolitical evolution of the Basin during the First Intermediate One–Three time period. It would be difficult, however, to explain the revolutionary events of the First Intermediate Four phase, subsequent developments during Phase Five and the

Middle Horizon, or the fluctuations in the sociopolitical patterns between the Middle Horizon and the Late Horizon solely on the basis of the operation of these two factors.

The sequences of events that occurred during this long span of time, from the beginning of the First Intermediate Four phase until the Late Horizon, we feel, primarily reflect the operation of the third ecological law, the law of minimal risk, and the effects of the feedback processes of the sociopolitical system itself upon the ecosystem. The major reason why the third law assumes greater significance during this time is because this is the first time in which there was a substantial occupation of the drier regions of the Basin. Boserup's theoretical paradigm was designed primarily on the basis of the data from humid regions and is most useful under the conditions where the risk factor is minimal. In the case of the arid regions the factor of risk probably is more significant than the operation of the law of least effort.

There are two major problems in testing Wittfogel's (1957) theoretical paradigm with the Basin of Mexico data that are very different in nature. The first problem is the evolutionary significance of the various hydraulic agricultural systems. Were they large and economically significant enough to have major effects on the sociopolitical evolution of the area? The second question concerns the archaeological evidence for the history of such techniques. Recently there have been a number of criticisms of the value of Wittfogel's (1957) theoretical concepts as applied to irrigation in the Basin of Mexico. Basically, the criticism is that the irrigation systems were too small and able to supply only a fraction of the food supply; thus, they neither required complex bureaucratic management nor stimulated conflict and competition. In this section we will offer a counterargument to these criticisms.

With respect to permanent spring-based irrigation, we have detailed data on two of the systems—on the San Juan Teotihuacan system and the Texcoco Piedmont (Amanalco) system. The San Juan springs system is apparently dying, according to evidence which shows that the output of water has steadily declined over the past 50 years. To recapitulate, in the 1920s Gamio *et al.* (1922) estimated the flow of water at the springs to be 1000 liters per second. In 1956 Sanders found the springs to have a flow of 580 liters (according to the federal water regulations); at the time the springs regulated 3652 ha of land. In the early 1960s, Millon *et al.* (1962) estimated the flow of water at only 540 liters. Finally, a recent publication shows the output since then has dropped to below 400 liters per second (Comisión Hidrológica de la Cuenca del Valle de México 1968). (Current data also show greater month-to-month variability than previously.)

The major cause of the declining output of the San Juan springs in the twentieth century has been the perforation of artesian wells, both within the Valley of Teotihuacan and in the bed of Lake Texcoco. Between 1519 and 1920, enormous amounts of land eroded in the Valley as a result of population decline from disease, the abandonment of agricultural lands on the piedmont, and their conversion to grazing lands. What effect this erosion has had is unknown, but there may have been even more water in the system in 1519 than in 1920. Also, the long period of occupation from the First Intermediate Phase One to the Late Horizon witnessed a continuous process of deforestation, which certainly must have affected the drainage in the area to a great degree. (See Figure 7.8, page 257, showing the twentieth-century irrigation system in the Teotihuacan Valley.) Other permanent water resources on a smaller scale were probably available in First Intermediate times; some may still have been functioning as late as the apogee of Teotihuacan. Mooser, in fact, has postulated the existence of a series of springs within the archaeological zone in Middle Horizon times that provided an additional flow of 100 to 200 liters per second (Lorenzo 1968). What this means is that the Late Horizon irrigation system could have been at least 1.7 times larger than the recent system, and the Middle Horizon system approximately twice as large and capable of serving a total of 7200 ha of land. In the Texcoco piedmont 31 springs were still functioning in the 1920s (see Table 9.4). In Table 9.4 we have grouped the springs, not in terms of the present routing of the canal system, but in terms of the natural drainage of the area before canalization. (See Figure 7.13, page 274, which shows the spring locations and the structure of the twentieth-century irrigation system in the Texcoco area.)

What is the agricultural significance of the two systems? On the basis of our studies of the contemporary system, an average yield of 1400 kilos of maize, with minimal or no use of animal fertilizer, is a reasonable calculation. If we assume somewhat lower productivity, because less well-developed varieties of maize may have been used in the Middle Horizon

TABLE 9.4
Texcoco Springs of the 1920s[a]

Irrigation system	Water flow (in liters per second)		Irrigable area (in hectares)
Rio Papalotla			
Cluster 1 (springs 1–6)		280	—
Cluster 2 (springs 10–13)		23	—
	Total	303	1818
Rio Jalapango			
Cluster 1 (springs 7–9)		30	—
Cluster 2 (springs 32–34)		38–48	—
	Total	68–78	408–462
Rio Coxacuaco			
Cluster 1 (springs 14–24)		35	—
Cluster 2 (springs 25–27)		8	—
Cluster 3 (spring 28)		4	—
Cluster 4		5	—
	Total	52	300
	Grand Total	423–433	2526–2580

[a] From Sanders 1976b.

period, this figure might be lowered to 1050 kilos. Another variable to be considered is the percentage of irrigated land that would be devoted to maize production as opposed to other crops. On the basis of patterns of land use in the Teotihuacan Valley today (where land is devoted either to maize or to a humidity-demanding commercial crop like alfalfa), one could argue for 100% maize utilization. However, we have prepared two models, one calculated at 100% and the other at a 65% cultivation in maize.

Finally, to calculate the carrying capacity for the two systems we offer two alternate subsistence models, one based on a 80% caloric intake derived from maize, the other 65%, with the assumption that the former is generally applicable to Late Horizon subsistence, the latter to all of the pre-Late Horizon phases. Assuming an average per capita daily need for a total population, all ages and both sexes, of the size and weight of the prehispanic Mesoamerican, of 2000 kcal, carrying capacity estimates for the Teotihuacan and Amanalco irrigation systems are as given in Table 9.5.

Citing a sixteenth-century source, Palerm (1961b) reports that the Coyoacan system served the needs of 23,000 *vasallos*. It is not clear what the term *vasallos* refers to, but it obviously was a major system, at least comparable to the Texcoco piedmont complex. Although we lack detailed quantitative

TABLE 9.5
Carrying Capacity of Permanent Irrigation, Texcoco and Teotihuacan Regions[a]

| | | 65% Dependence on Maize | | | |
| System | Land area (in hectares) | 100% Planted in maize | | 65% Planted in maize | |
		1400 kg per hectare	1050 kg per hectare	1400 kg per hectare	1050 kg per hectare
Contemporary Teotihuacan system	3,600	39,600	28,800	25,740	18,720
Middle Horizon, Teotihuacan system	7,200	79,200	57,600	49,480	37,440
Middle Horizon, both systems	9,700	116,700	77,600	69,355	50,440

| | | 80% Dependence on Maize | | | |
| System | Land area (in hectares) | 100% Planted in maize | | 65% Planted in maize | |
		1400 kg per hectare	1000 kg per hectare	1400 kg per hectare	1000 kg per hectare
Contemporary Teotihuacan system	3,600	32,400	21,600	21,060	14,040
Middle Horizon, Teotihuacan system	7,200	64,800	43,200	42,120	28,080
Middle Horizon, both systems	9,700	87,300	60,200	56,745	39,130

[a] From Sanders 1976b.

data on the Cuautitlan system, in terms of the sixteenth-century population of the area and distribution of canals on colonial maps and recent aerial photos, it must have been minimally comparable to the Texcoco or Coyoacan complex. Spring flow, according to Recursos Hidraulicos (Memoria de la Obra . . . 1975), exceeds that from the San Juan springs.

Taking the average yields from permanently irrigated land for the Late Horizon (1400 kilos for the alluvial plain and 1000 kilos for the piedmont areas), assuming the permanent water resources were maximized, that all the land was planted in basic grains, and that the population derived 80% of their calories from the grain products, then the permanently irrigated land (20,000 ha) would have sustained a maximum population of 120,000 people.

With respect to floodwater irrigation it is difficult to assess the maximal capacity of this resource. In a recent publication by the Instituto Mexicano de Recursos Naturales Renovables (Mesas Redondas Sobre Problemas del Valle de Mexico, Mexico 1963) the total average annual precipitation for the Basin of Mexico is calculated at 6,717,000,000 m^3. Of this, 4,704,000,000 m^3 filtrates into the soil (of which 133,000,000 m^3 flows to the surface in the form of springs) and 343,000,000 m^3 flows through the barranca–river systems. These figures, however, refer to the present day drainage basin, a combination of artificial and natural drainage systems, that drains an area of 9600 km^2. We have roughly calculated the surface drainage of our smaller region at 70% of these figures, or 240,100,000 m^3. In fact it would be a little higher since those areas that the study includes, which are excluded in our studies, such as the Apan Basin, have an average annual precipitation that is comparable to the drier regions of the Basin. Since irrigation water is used for very different purposes, dependent on the season, we must break this total figure down by seasons. The ratio of rainfall in the Basin of Mexico from winter through the fall is approximately 1:4:10:5. This means that approximately 12,000,000 m^3 flows during the winter, 48,000,000 m^3 during the spring, 120,000,000 m^3 during the summer, and 60,000,000 m^3 during the fall.

The winter flow would have little use for agriculture. The spring flow could theoretically be used for the same purpose as the permanent irrigation, that is, preplanting (with the difference that the local variability year to year would be very high). Taking the average measure of 1200 m^3 per irrigation, theoretically, the spring flow in the Basin could be used to irrigate 40,000 ha of land. Summer irrigation is primarily used as a supplement, and the flow for this function could be used to provide water for 100,000 ha. During the fall, contemporary farmers use floodwater, not so much for the standing crop, but as a technique of water storage for the spring planting. We estimate that 50,000 ha of land could theoretically be irrigated for this purpose. What the data suggest is that 40,000 ha of land could be provided with water for preplanting irrigation, and that the same land could be given two–three irrigations during the growing season, to supplement the rains, and an additional irrigation in the fall for water storage in the subsoil for the following year. In actual fact the figures for preplanting irrigation would be considerably lower than this since some of the rainfall during the spring season would fall at widely spaced intervals and in such small amounts that there would not be enough buildup of water behind dams to allow simple gravity irrigation. Furthermore, much of the rain falls in areas where irrigation is either unnecessary or topographic situations make it unfeasible with prehispanic technology.

Finally, also falling under the rubric of hydraulic agriculture is what we have referred to as drainage agriculture, including the chinampas of the lake system—the most productive kind of agriculture in the Basin. Considerable areas along the lakeshore were probably characterized by swampy conditions, the water table lying within a few meters of the surface. As a result of increased cultivation, erosion, and development of irrigation–drainage ditch networks, this zone undoubtedly went through a process of gradual lowering of the water table between Early and Late Horizon times. Much of the immediate lakeshore plain was probably still characterized by a relatively high water table at the time of the Spanish Conquest and hence was characterized by high yields and crop security. The extent of this zone is not known. In the case of the chinampas, however, on the basis of Armillas' survey of the southern lakes and Palerm's analysis of the dike system in Lake Texcoco, we estimate that there were approximately 12,000 ha of chinampas in 1519.

On the basis of Sanders' study of productivity, the 12,000 ha of chinampas could have sustained at least 228,000 people. This means a total population of 348,000 or at least one-third of the population of the Basin of Mexico in 1519 could have been supported from either chinampas or permanent irrigation agriculture. When one adds to these figures the area of unknown size of drainage agriculture along the lakeshore and the use of floodwater irrigation, then the economic significance of hydraulic agriculture in terms of the Late Horizon population can hardly be overemphasized, and was undoubtedly critical.

Aside from the matter of demographic capacity and crop security, hydraulic agriculture has another equally important economic effect—productivity—as measured by the input–output ratio. In our discussion of Boserup's model of agricultural dynamics we noted that the intensification process commonly leads to a gradual decline in input–output ratios, or per capita income, as an economist would put it. This decline can be measured energetically, in terms of kilocalories, of work expended to produce kilocalories of food, or in a less precise measurement, of work hours or days in proportion to yield. In all cases Boserup cites, intensification results in an increase in work input per unit of land cultivated. In some cases this is accompanied by a decrease in yield, the product of losses in soil fertility. Even in cases when special practices may stabilize or even increase yield however, she argues that the increases do not entirely compensate for increased work input, and the result is still a decline in ratio.

The input–output ratio has obvious significance in terms of the capacity of households to produce surpluses to sustain non-food-producing elements in the population. We suggest that in humid environments, where soil fertility is a general problem, the process of intensification may result in a decline of income to the degree that the capacity of the system to support non-food producers, and hence complex social systems, is seriously impaired. In semiarid and arid environments, where soil fertility is a less serious problem, the same difficulty may arise because of the insecurity of cropping with extensive practices. Hydraulic agriculture has such a striking effect on productivity in semiarid and arid regions (because of the added nutrients brought in with the water) that the increased yield and regularization of such yields may in fact compensate for the increased labor input.

The problem of providing sufficient surpluses for market exchange and taxation is exacerbated with a Neolithic technology. Our experimental studies with Neolithic tools, intensive use of the land, but no irrigation, show a work input that varies from 70–150 man days per hectare, dependent on soil texture. Dry farming yields vary from 400 to 800 kilos per hectare, with contemporary races of maize, and with adjustments for crop losses during bad years. An extended family of seven would require approximately 1120 kilos of grain for its basic needs during the Late Horizon. This means that approximately 200 man days of input into agricultural work would be necessary to provide the caloric minima. In terms of the demands of other kinds of work, and the limitation of work input imposed by this climatic regime, it is doubtful that this work input could be increased by more than 50%. By adding irrigation, the increase in yields almost doubles, with only a slight increase in labor input. Chinampa agriculture would result in a yield of four times the maximal yield of dry farming, with little extra labor input, thus enhancing enormously the capacity of the food producer to support a non-food producing population. What our data suggest is that when agriculture did expand into the higher risk areas of the Basin of Mexico, particularly when the process was accompanied by increasing social stratification, then the stimulus to develop technology to increase and regularize yields would have been considerable.

With respect to the evidence for the history of hydraulic agriculture, the data in Chapter 7 may be summarized as follows. During the Late Horizon, on the basis of ethnohistoric and archaeological sources, all hydraulic resources, floodwaters and permanent water resources, and virtually all naturally humid lands were fully utilized throughout the Basin. Floodwater and permanent irrigation appear as early as the First Intermediate period in the southwestern and west central portions of the Basin, at times when population densities reached relatively high levels. Small-scale drainage agriculture along the southern lake shores may also have begun that early. In the central portions of the Basin, drainage agriculture, on a fairly substantial scale around the San Juan springs, dates from the First Intermediate Three phase, and permanent canal irrigation on a large scale was probably present during the First Intermediate Four–Five, Middle Horizon time period. Floodwater irrigation was also apparently widely distributed in the central portions of the Basin as well. Although drainage agriculture probably began early, and was of considerable significance during the early phases of the growth of Teotihuacan, the major expansion of this system of farming was during the fifteenth century, with the large-scale conquest of the southern lakes.

In summary, the economic significance of hydraulic agriculture would seem to be considerable. As we have argued previously the indirect effects of the various hydraulic systems on social stratification could have been revolutionary. Whether the irrigation systems were large enough to have required, in Wittfogel's terms, an elaborate managerial bureauocracy is perhaps debatable. The settlement system during the period of the emergence and growth of Teotihuacan in the Teotihuacan Valley–Texcoco regions very clearly suggests the presence of centralized control, but this control, we believe, would not have necessitated a separate managerial administrative set. We rather suggest the presence of a single power-holding institution—what the Hunts (1976) have referred to as role embeddedness. This is not to deny that almost certain presence of lower level officials who functioned to distribute water and organize labor for maintenance.

The organization of the drainage of the lakes and their subsequent conversion and use as cultivated land during the sixteenth century was clearly a state organized and administered project, as were the subsequent public works involved in the protection of the system—the network of dikes (a system minimally 80 km in length) to regulate the flow of water (Palerm 1973). These projects were of a scale, and the skill needed to maintain them of such a nature, that it is likely that there was a professional class of administrators to safeguard the system. Bearing in mind the limitations of our data and the character of irrigation in the Basin of Mexico we present the following tentative model for the functional relationship between the development of hydraulic agriculture and the state in Central Mexico.

HYDRAULIC AGRICULTURE AND STATE FORMATION IN THE BASIN OF MEXICO

The emergence of Teotihuacan in First Intermediate Three times as a large town, its explosive growth in Phase Four, and its ultimate climax during the Middle Horizon reveals a process of state formation and urbanism unparalleled in prehispanic Mesoamerica until the rise of Tenochtitlan and the Mexica state in the fifteenth century. Although one can trace many aspects of the Teotihuacan culture back through the various phases of the First Intermediate period in the Basin of Mexico, its emergence represents a revolutionary break with the past, and a complete redesign of the ecosystem of the Basin. This redesign involves major changes in population distribution, settlement types, and environmental exploitation.

In Chapter 5 we presented an analysis of the Teotihuacan ecosystem in terms of basic zones of resource utilization. Zone 1 was the city and its immediate agricultural resource, basically the middle and lower alluvial plain of the Teotihuacan Valley and the middle and lower Papalotla plain. In this area there were virtually no rural settlements, and we argued, on this basis, that a substantial percentage of the population of the city were farmers. In the cited paper by Sanders *et al.* (1976) we presented an agricultural model for this nuclear zone. We assumed full use of hydraulic resources (the two major spring sources at San Juan and Amanalco) and calculated the total potential of permanently irrigated land in Middle Horizon times at 9700 ha. Physically the two irrigated regions were separated by the Patlachique range through most of their extension, but merged at the lakeshore, to form one continuous zone. Assuming 100% cropping of grain on such lands, 65% per capita caloric intake from grains, and a yield of 1400 kilos per hectare, the irrigated land could have supported 116,700 people. Even if we assume a lower yield, to the First Intermediate Three level of 1050 kilos, then it still would have the capacity to support a population of 79,200 people. In either case much of the support of the city, with respect to staple crops, could have come from this zone of intensive cultivation, which lay within a radius of 15 km of the city. Differential access to the land and control of the water could have been a major factor in the patterning of the Teotihuacan class structure and political organization.

This pattern of land use is clearly an inconvenient one from a purely agricultural point of view, but we must remember that Teotihuacan was also a major craft and mercantile center. In the model of Teotihuacan economy, Sanders, Parsons and Logan suggested a parallel to the contemporary Yoruba of Nigeria, who also live in large nucleated settlements, and where the household has a multifaceted economy, involving agriculture, craft, and mercantile activities. Under these conditions the household is faced with the options of what kind of settlement arrangement is most convenient. Among the Yoruba it is apparently more convenient to reside in the nucleated community and travel out to the outlying fields, and this is the model we are suggesting for Teotihuacan. The remainder of the agricultural food supply for the city could have been provided from the surplus production of the numerous settlements in Zone 2, particularly if those populations were using the irrigation resources of that region. We noted in our previous discussion that virtually all of the population in this area is distributed in close relationship to hydraulic resources.

We admit that this model goes far beyond the data, but the various data that we have described previously at least suggest it as a very strong hypothesis, and it would be very difficult to design an alternative one to explain the population distribution and settlement types for the period in question. The events prior to and after the establishment of the First Intermediate Five–Middle Horizon ecosystem also offer strong support for the model's validity. For example, the large First Intermediate Three population in the Papalotla basin vanishes during Phase Five and the region continues to be unoccupied during Phase Five and the Middle Horizon. A reasonable explanation of this settlement change is that the First Intermediate Three population moved to Teotihuacan, but continued to cultivate land in this area. As soon as Teotihuacan lost its extraordinary preeminence as a major political and commercial center, the Second Intermediate Phase One population immediately reoccupied the same zone. Presumably the colonists were the same people who formerly lived at Teotihuacan and cultivated these lands.

In the case of the Teotihuacan Valley the process is similar, but also different in some respects. During First Intermediate Three times a large town emerged at the head of the irrigation system and its growth is directly related to the initiation of canal irrigation and drainage agriculture in the vicinity of the springs. After Teotihuacan declined as a major center, the population of the city dropped back down to the First Intermediate Three level and the balance of the population, the farming class of the city, was distributed along the edge of and within the irrigated plain, precisely the contemporary settlement system.

Basically our evolutionary and historical model of the impact of canal irrigation on the institutions of the Basin of Mexico involves the following stages.

(1) During the First Intermediate period a number of local groups began to experiment with hydraulic agriculture. Many of these experiments involved small-scale drainage and permanent canal irrigation. Most of the cases occur in the drier central portion of the Basin. The immediate effect of this shift was to cause a change from a ranked to a stratified social system. At Teotihuacan, the zone of highest agricultural risk, the process was faster than elsewhere and was large in scale. The result was the emergence of a town of approximately 40,000 people by the end of the phase. As we have noted previously, this was also a phase of intensive conflict among the various political groupings.

(2) Teotihuacan, with its advantage of size, and location near the largest permanent irrigation system in the Basin, emerged as the major power. As a result of the conflicts that emerged during Phase Three, the population of the Basin of Mexico was substantially reduced during Phase Four. For reasons as yet unclear, the remnants were not only ruled by Teotihuacan, but nucleated at the city itself. This would, if our model is correct, be the phase of maximum expansion of the irrigation resources of the core area.

(3) During the successive First Intermediate Five and Middle Horizon phases Teotihuacan became a Mesoamerican as well as a local Basin of Mexico political and economic power. The city now had a secure agricultural base, conveniently located in terms of distance and ease of control, had developed a major extraregional commercial trade network, and had completely redesigned the ecosystem of the Basin.

The subsequent history of the Basin of Mexico involved a number of phases of political decentralization (Second Intermediate Phases One–Three) and centralization (Second Intermediate Two and the Late Horizon). In the case of the two phases of political centralization, the relationships between the center, its sustaining area, and hydraulic resources are a virtual reproduction of the Teotihuacan pattern (see Figure 9.1).

FEEDBACK MECHANISMS AND PROCESSES

Up until this point we have focused heavily on the operation of the three basic laws of cultural evolution as prime movers, primarily in terms of their economic and ultimately political effects. However, as these laws operate to stimulate the emergence of new sociopolitical institutions, the institutions themselves become part of the cause and effect system, and may act in a systemic way as motivators of change.

This point was heavily stressed by Flannery (1972) in his paper, "Cultural Evolution of Civilizations." As social stratification becomes more intense, along with other kinds of intrasocietal differentiation, more elaborate and complex political controls and organization are necessary. Ultimately a professional managerial class emerges, with little direct relationship, and often only a very general knowledge, of the means of production at the base of the system. Decisions as to how the environment is to be used are increasingly made by people who are not directly exploiting it. Decisions are often made for self-serving reasons, in terms of their own needs rather than in terms of the functioning of the total system. Sometimes the process even creates ecological disasters, as in the case of salinization in lower Mesopotamia, and possibly soil erosion in the Classic Maya Lowlands. We would argue, however, that the decisions made by the ruling class are based upon our three basic laws—but in terms of their own subsystem—not the system as a whole. It is for this reason, we believe, that many anthropologists often see decision-making in complex societies as nonecological.

We have previously discussed the effect of stratification on carrying capacity in terms of the process of competition, both internal and external, to the societal system. In Oscar Lewis' (1951) study of contemporary Tepoztlan, for example, he asserts that the village is land deficient. In fact, if one were to take the agricultural resource of this community and divide it up equally among the various families, there would be no land shortage. The system of stratification, in which a substantial percentage of the land holdings are private, produces inequities in land distribution, so that, with respect to the bulk of the population, there is in fact land shortage. What we are assuming is that a process comparable to this operated in prehispanic times to create inequities of land availability to lineages or to villages.

Another kind of feedback effect relates to the character and nature of capital works in agriculture such as canal and dam construction. In our previous discussion of hydraulic agriculture, we suggested that the retardation of colonization of alluvial plain in several of our regions may have

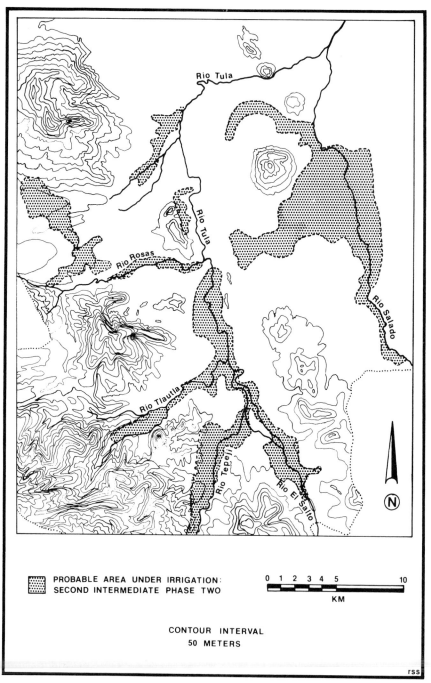

Rio Tula

Rio Tula

Rio Rosas

Rio Tula

Rio Salado

Rio Tlautla

Rio Tepeji

Rio El Salto

(N)

PROBABLE AREA UNDER IRRIGATION:
SECOND INTERMEDIATE PHASE TWO

0 1 2 3 4 5   10

KM

CONTOUR INTERVAL
50 METERS

rss

Figure 9.1.   Probable area under irrigation in the Tula region during the Second Intermediate Phase Two. (After Mastache 1976.)

occurred because the level of sociopolitical organization that would be needed to construct and to maintain such systems had not yet evolved. More specifically, our reference was to the emergence of large-scale drainage works in the alluvial plain of the Texcoco region, which may have been delayed until a level of sociopolitical organization emerged that was capable of mobilizing the labor for such a project. This is obviously a complex process since the organization was available by the First Intermediate Four phase, yet it still was not undertaken. This, however, can be ascribed to the major reshuffling of population during that phase and use of the labor elsewhere (i.e., the Teotihuacan Valley). It is no accident that the first large-scale application of a system of drainage agriculture was carried out in the Teotihuacan Valley, where both the population and political organization were available to carry it off successfully.

It may seem to the reader that we are reversing our arguments since previously we have argued that the emergence of the state at Teotihuacan was a product of hydraulic agriculture. In fact, we are doing precisely that, since the relationships really are systemic in nature and it would be very difficult to sort out the direction of cause and effect. This is particularly true of archaeological case examples, but we have strong doubts that this can be done even with ethnographic data. Our argument is that if such systems are constructed by the political leaders, then the control of the water distribution is very apt to be a politically centralized one. Even in the cases of gradual accretion of such systems some kind of political solution is needed to resolve disputes and to maintain the system. As the system grows in size and includes greater numbers of separate physical and social communities, the potential for conflict will increase proportionately, and customary law ultimately will need to include some kind of more forceful sanctions in order for the system to function.

A more dramatic example of a feedback process of this type is the effect of large demographic and political centers on their sustaining area. As a generalization we would argue that the larger a political center becomes, the greater its effect on the overall system, and this is dramatically illustrated by the effects of Teotihuacan, Tula, and Tenochtitlan on the ecosystem of the Basin of Mexico. In the case of Teotihuacan, what is involved is a complete restructuring of the ecosystem, accompanied by revolutionary changes in settlement pattern and population distribution. Major patterns that took 1500 years to evolve were suddenly and dramatically reversed or altered. This begins with the massive relocation of at least 80% of the population of the Basin at the city during Phase Four and ends with the reestablishment of a new settlement system in the countryside during Phase Five and the Middle Horizon. While it can be argued that a variety of ecological processes stimulated and made possible these changes—that is, the rapid evolution of hydraulic agriculture and consequent colonization of the alluvial plains, and the appearance of new varieties of maize—it would be difficult to argue simple linear causation here. The location of the city and its early growth are clearly related to a set of ecological factors and processes as we have described, but our argument is that the presence of the city in First Intermediate Three times produced its own dynamic of change. Millon (1976) has made a similar argument, influenced by points made by Jane Jacobs (1969) in her book *The Economy of Cities,* in which she discusses the dynamic effects of the city on the countryside.

In this book Jacobs' major thesis is that the growth of the city causes intensification of agriculture in its immediate area. She takes the argument one step further and insists that agriculture itself was created by a people living in nucleated settlements (therefore classified by her as urban settlements), whose economy was based on hunting and gathering of unusually rich local resources. Obviously, this is simply a restatement of some of Binford's (1968) early arguments about the origin of agriculture but with the concept of nucleation of population added to his model. The thesis is not supported by recent data on the history of agriculture in Mesoamerica, where agriculture was clearly developed by populations not living in large nucleated settlements. This is not, however, to deny Jacobs' basic argument that cities have an enormous effect upon rural settlement and the way in which land is used in their vicinity. Her theoretical argument is of course strongly supported by our model of Teotihuacan economy, with the various zones of exploitation, and the role of these zones in the city's economy. The Middle Horizon land use and settlement system in the Cuautitlan, Temascalapa, and Zumpango regions, and the northern flank of the Teotihuacan Valley, can hardly be explained in terms of our population growth, population pressure, or our hydraulic models. In all of these areas there were very small pre-First Intermediate Five populations, and this condition was followed by explosive growth over a very short period of time. This growth also involved planned settlements and major use of the hydraulic resources of the area, in the form of floodwater and permanent irrigation. Outside of Zones 1 and 2, the balance of the population distribution and nature of settlement makes little sense except in terms of the needs of the city.

The effects of Teotihuacan on the rural areas, however, go even further afield than the Basin of Mexico, and if our model is correct we should have included a larger region for our analysis. To explain further, we noted, in Chapter 2, that the Proyecto Aleman included a large-scale settlement survey of the Tlaxcala–Puebla region, under the direction of Angel Garcia Cook. At the Paris meetings of the International Congress of Americanists we presented a comparative study of the settlement history of the Basin of Mexico with this region. The Tlaxcala–Puebla region appears to be more precocious in its evolution during the Early Horizon and First Intermediate periods as compared to the Basin of Mexico. This is indicated by differences in population size, size of major sites, evidence of site stratification, and intensification of agriculture. In general, the evolution of the Puebla–Tlaxcala region is approximately 300 years ahead of the developments in the Basin of Mexico. For example, the levels that were reached in the Late Early Horizon phase in the former region were hardly achieved in the Basin of Mexico until the First Intermediate One phase; developments characteristic of the First Intermediate One phase were not achieved in the Basin of Mexico until Phase Two, etc. While the explanation for this variation is undoubtedly complex, we believe that it does relate primarily to environmental differences between the two regions. All of central Tlaxcala, along with a large section of west Puebla, even in areas above 2240 m, has a shorter frost season, and this favorable situation is combined with approximately 25% more rainfall than the Basin of Mexico (see Figure 4.1, page 83). This means that the Puebla–Tlaxcala region was much more favorable in terms of early agriculture than the Basin. During the long First Intermediate period, and considering limiting factors previously described, this region had a much higher percentage of cultivable land, and hence could support substantially larger populations. By First Intermediate Three and Four times this advantage is gone and the Basin reaches the same level as the Tlaxcala–Puebla region and ultimately surpasses it.

Interestingly, the drier, cooler, northern area around Calpulalpan and Apizaco had virtually no population during the First Intermediate period, yet this area was densely settled during the First Intermediate Five–Middle Horizon. Of even greater interest is the fact that the architectural and ceramic styles of sites in this colonized region are identical to those at Teotihuacan, whereas the old First Intermediate population in the south still retains independence in ceramic styles. It seems difficult to escape the conclusion that this northern zone was colonized directly by Teotihuacan. The distance from Teotihuacan is comparable to that of the Cuautitlan region and should be included as part of our Zone 2. One purpose of this colonization was probably to provide further agricultural support for the city, but a more important function was probably to secure trade routes to the Gulf Coast (see Map 20).

Another example of Teotihuacan colonization is the Tula region. This region also had a very small pre-First Intermediate population, and yet by the First Intermediate Five and Middle Horizon times, there was a very substantial population in the area, living in large nucleated settlements, some of which were larger than any towns in the Basin of Mexico (excluding, of course, Teotihuacan itself, and probably Azcapotzalco). When all of the population of the Basin of Mexico and the surrounding regions is plotted on a map, Teotihuacan assumes a central position in terms of its distribution, rather than a peripheral one.

This pattern of rural–urban relationships and the processes involved are virtually duplicated in the case of Tula. The northern third of the Basin (including the Zumpango, Cuautitlan, Teotihuacan, and Temascalapa regions) are comparable in terms of settlement densities and sizes of settlements to our Zone 2 during the Teotihuacan phase period, and the Texcoco, Tenayuca, Tacuba, and Xochimilco regions are comparable to Zone 3 during Middle Horizon times. Presumably, settlement surveys north, east, and west of the Tula region will show a substantial concentration of population thinning out toward the peripheries. This model would agree very closely with ethnohistoric statements about the domain of Tula, in which a large region north and west of the city was considered part of its political domain. To what degree the presence of Tula changed the agricultural economy of the immediate region is not clear, but recent studies by Mastache (1976) and Crespo (1976) reveal that a substantial percentage of the Tula region can be permanently irrigated. Our estimate from their maps is that approximately 10,000 ha of land are capable of irrigation from several independent, permanent, water resources (see Figure 9.1). Their studies also show a striking correlation of the Middle Horizon and Second Intermediate Two settlement with the distribution of irrigated land. Our calculation is that at least half the population of the Tula region could have been supported, during the maximum prosperity of the city, by the production from these irrigated lands.

Tenochtitlan illustrates similarities and differences in the rural–urban relationships when compared to Teotihuacan and Tula. A major distinction is the fact that the intensification process had been completed over the entire Basin of Mexico. Nevertheless the growth of the city is closely and clearly related to the expansion of drainage agriculture on the lakeshore, and most particularly, to the colonization of the lakes themselves. Much of this colonization was organized by the state, which, throughout the Late Horizon, was a major entrepreneur of irrigation works. As Calnek (1972) has pointed out, based on his analysis of documentary sources, and the indirect evidence from Armillas' (1971) surveys of the chinampas, the expansion of chinampa agriculture was essentially a fifteenth-century phenomenon and was a planned colonization. Calnek's major point is that existing state organizations were the entrepreneurs that created the chinampa area as an agricultural resource, and the evolution of chinampa agriculture did not produce the Late Horizon states. Once created, however, it is equally clear that the use of these lands enormously modified the Aztec political system, its economic institutions, and the stratification of Aztec society, a classic example of our suggested feedback process. Furthermore, although intensive agriculture was practiced all over the Basin of Mexico in 1519, approximately 40% of the population was concentrated in an area of 600 km^2 around the city, thus reproducing the pattern of population imbalances we described for the earlier cities. This was made possible by the evolution of drainage agriculture, and it must have been a powerful factor in promoting stability to the political system.

In recent years there has been an increasing focus on foreign trade as a mechanism in state formation. We do not see this as a productive line of research, at least for prehispanic Mesoamerica, for a variety of reasons. In a book by Howard Odum (1971) a very important theoretical point is made about human energy systems. Virtually the entire continuum of societies studied by anthropologists, from bands to preindustrial states, can be classified into one type of energetic system, one in which the great majority of the energy produced is consumed within the local community, and conversely most of the energy consumed is produced within that community. Even within communities a substantial percentage of energy utilized and consumed is within the family. Energy flow between families, and particularly between physical communities, therefore, has a relatively low value. The actual range is probably from 5% to 30%. To the cultural evolutionist, of course, this is a significant variation, and is thus the focus of this analysis. The range, however, does seem insignificant when one compares it to modern industrial societies where energy flow from and to communities probably everywhere exceeds 95%. The larger the geographic region the greater the contrast between industrial and nonindustrial societies. The limiting factor in nonindustrial societies clearly relates to the *human* energetic costs of production and distribution.

The meaning of these points to studies of the ecosystem of ancient states and their centers seems obvious. First, the major determinants of social stratification must be sought in terms of differential control or access to basic resources within a relatively short radius of those centers. Even in societies where animal power is utilized, the major source of power is still human energy; hence the *control of agricultural land* is the most significant single factor affecting stratification. Second, the life support radius for central places, whether urban or nonurban, must be a relatively short one for those goods that are both bulky and consumed at a rapid rate. Lightweight goods, with low consumption rates and limited use, can of course be brought from considerably greater distances, but these goods have only a marginal effect on the functioning of the ecosystem.

Obviously, following this model, the significance of long-distance trade, in an energetic sense, will be proportional to the efficiency of the transportation and production systems. The case of Mesoamerica involves primitive transportation, in most cases the human back, and equally primitive production systems. To take the specific case of Middle Horizon Teotihuacan, accepting Spence's estimate of the number of people at Teotihuacan who produced obsidian for the long-distance market, assuming that a comparable ratio of local to foreign producers was characteristic of the other crafts, then maximally 20,000 people should be involved in foreign trade, or less than 10% of the population of the Basin of Mexico. In fact this number was undoubtedly much less since we know that many of the major crafts, such as ceramics and ground stone, were nearly entirely for local consumption. It is doubtful that more than 10,000 people actually derived a substantial percentage of their incomes from the long-distance trade, at the peak of Teotihuacan's history.

With respect to local or internal trade, on the other hand, the movement of goods from household to household was undoubtedly considerable, and, in Odum's terms, the transfer of energy was close to the maximal of the range for preindustrial societies. In a previous section we have described the Aztec redistribution system in which a substantial percentage of the goods used by the average household was obtained through the market system, or through the tax redistribution network.

In two papers Sanders (1956, 1968) has argued that the great microgeographic complexity of Mesoamerica both permitted (in the sense of the short distance to zones of differential production) and stimulated (in the tendency of localization of resources) an intensive pattern of economic symbiosis, particularly in highland regions. Following this theoretical argument, out of the need to safeguard these exchange networks, political centralization developed. Beside the need to safeguard the system, its control, like hydraulic agriculture, altered the political positions themselves that were designed to regulate them, and provided added opportunities for status occupants to expand this political power. An additional aspect of the theoretical argument is that the great frequency and regularity of market encounters would reduce the parochiality of local group feeling and act to validate the large political system. The model was designed on the basis of contemporary and Late Horizon patterns of the settlement, population, and resource utilization, where all environmental zones were inhabited, and one would expect very clearly defined territorial rights over such resources by the local community.

The model is probably very useful in explaining the degree of integration achieved by local and supralocal states during the Late Horizon. In Sanders' original formulation, however, the purpose was to explain how centralized political systems emerged in earlier times. It was seen as a mechanical process brought about by the need for exchange. The very divergent settlement system from earlier times, particularly during the First Intermediate period, when the first stages of political centralization were achieved, weakens considerably the explanatory value of this model. For example, not only was virtually all of the First Intermediate population distributed in a narrow band along the lower–middle piedmont, but much of it was in a dozen or so communities. Each of these central communities presumably had control of a territory that extended upslope and downslope from the zone of cultivation, in many cases from the sierra to the lakeshore. The location of settlements is such that nearly all resources are readily accessible. If economic specialization and symbiosis were important it would be among segments of the same physical community. Local specialization therefore would not seem to be a variable that stimulated the evolution of simple chiefdoms or small states during this period. The growth of large central communities, however, would act as a stimulus toward internal specialization, particularly as the overall population in the agricultural strip approached carrying capacity.

The localized distribution of resources with respect to the Basin as a whole, however, could have been a factor in the evolution of the larger centers and states during the First Intermediate Three–Four–Five, Middle Horizon, Second Intermediate Two, and Late Horizon phases and periods, since a number of key resource have very limited distribution in the Basin, and would not be locally accessible to small states. Among these would be obsidian, lime, basalt, chert, fresh water reeds, protein foods, salt, and fine quality ceramic clays.

SPATIAL ANALYSIS AND CULTURAL EVOLUTION IN THE BASIN OF MEXICO

Recently a number of archaeologists have attempted to apply spatial models, derived from quantitative geography, to prehistoric situations. The major effort has been the application of central place theory to prehistoric societies that show clear evidence of social stratification and economic specialization. To do this they have borrowed models directly from the geographers and have applied them with very unconvincing results. We suggest that these efforts will continue to meet with marginal success until they return to the huge ethnographic literature to generate their own spatial models. The basic theory behind such models in geography is undoubtedly sound and to a great extent derives from maximization and minimization principles in economics. The point is that the geographers' models are all drawn from much more complexly organized socioeconomic systems than the prehistoric societies that we have tried to apply them to. Most particularly they derived from marketing economies and the distribution of central place relates very closely to the market principle of competition and profit.

Our best documented data derive from the Late Horizon, and this was also the phase of greatest institutional complexity in terms of the prehispanic time range. At the time of the Conquest one could define three definite levels of community stratification. The first level included the great conurbation of Tlatelolco–Tenochtitlan and its constellation of lakeshore towns. Including only those communities that were probably more urban than rural in their lifestyle (Azcapotzalco, Tlacopan, Coyoacan, Huitzilopochco, Mexicaltzingo, and Ixtapalapa), the total population of this cluster was between 200,000–300,000 people, about 20% of the population of the Basin.

The next level includes all of the dependent centers that had resident *tlatoanis*. If one counts separate physical communities this would involve approximately 40 settlements. Counting the multiple *tlatoani* communities as separate communities would raise the number to 60. These centers had populations of 2000–20,000 people and were relatively evenly distributed throughout the Basin, but with a strong tendency toward a lakeshore and alluvial plain orientation. Below this level were the thousands of rural settlements, varying in populations from a few score to a thousand or two. We would estimate that perhaps 20–30% of the population lived in the second-level communities, and the balance, 40–60%, in the rural settlements. This distribution is a reasonable one in terms of principles of social stratification, particularly if one assumes, as the data suggest, that a substantial percentage of the population of the second-order communities were farmers. Texcoco's position, in terms of the pattern, was peculiar in that it formally ranked with

Tenochtitlan politically, and exercised suzerainty, even up to the time of the Conquest, over a substantial number of communities in the Teotihuacan–Texcoco regions. Its political power, however, had suffered a serious decline after the death of Nezahualcoyotl, and Tenochtitlan was rapidly emerging as the only first-order center by 1519.

Although we have described the system as though it were a neat political hierarchy with discrete administrative domains, in fact the social system of the Basin was exceedingly complex and highly fluid. At the upper end were a number of royal families with access to the surplus labor of the balance of the population. The domains that served these families varied considerably in size, and the dependent populations of individual *tlatoanis* were in many cases physically interdigited. The relationship between the noble class and the commoners was essentially an exploitative one, although the rulers did provide economic and political services.

Much has been made of the state organized redistributive economy in the recent literature, and certainly there was a redistributive aspect to the political system of the Basin of Mexico. The degree to which taxes of agricultural surpluses were redistributed during the years of poor agricultural harvest is not clear, but considering the energetic limitations of Aztec agriculture, we doubt that the tax in agricultural produce was sufficiently large to sustain the entire population of one of the local states through an entire harvest year. In the case of the larger political systems, of course, this process could work more effectively, since small quantities of surpluses from large areas could then be diverted to small, crisis areas that were suffering from agricultural deficiencies. The highly localized nature of rainfall in the Basin would make it very likely that small areas would suffer crop crises, but unlikely that a very large area would undergo this stress. One could therefore argue that the larger political groupings did have some redistributive functions, and that this would be a major stimulus toward centralized political organization.

Another economic function of the *tlatoani* was to organize and safeguard the marketplace. What is not clear from the documentary sources, however, is whether all of the *tlatoani* centers had marketplaces. All cases of marketplaces that are known seem to have occurred at political centers, so there was a coincidence in these two functions in terms of central place. What little data we have seem to indicate that the entire range of crafts was not found in each of the market centers and that there was considerable local specialization of markets. For example, Ecatepec was a center of salt manufacture, and Acolman had a major dog market; most of the ceramics seemed to have been produced at Cuautitlan and Texcoco. Tenochtitlan–Tlatelolco had the largest market, the only one that served the entire Basin of Mexico and included the entire range of products.

Another characteristic of the market system is that most transactions really were not profit oriented, and so in this sense it was not a market economy. Recent studies of contemporary markets in Oaxaca show that most exchanges, even though they are mediated by money, are not profit oriented (Cook and Diskin 1976). The object is for people from one village who do not have ready access to a particular resource or product of that resource necessary for the maintenance of their lifestyle to obtain products from a village which is located in a favorable situation. Basically, therefore, it is a system by which a population residing in a region of great environmental diversity can obtain all of the raw materials or finished products that are necessary for its needs. As such the only marketplace that could concentrate all the necessary resources was in a major political center. Analyzing the system from an economic point of view, the prehispanic market was a special type of redistributive system.

Considering the character of the natural environment, the distribution of raw materials, the character of the market, and of the political institution, it seems obvious that the central place models produced by geographers are of only marginal value, even when applied to the Late Horizon settlement system. What we need are spatial models that derive from contemporary socioeconomic systems that are comparable to the Aztec one. When we move to the pre-Late Horizon periods the applicability of known spatial models is considerably less. What spatial model, for example, is useful for the Middle Horizon situation in the Basin of Mexico, in which over one-half of the population resides in a single central place, and the rest of the population is very unevenly distributed in the surrounding area? One could argue, as we did previously, that the significant regional unit for the understanding of the Middle Horizon settlement system should be expanded to include some areas outside of the Basin of Mexico; but, of course, as one moves further from the central city, transportation costs rise to a point where these areas can no longer be considered an important part of the immediate sustaining area of the center. Even including these areas, we do not obtain a consistent hierarchical ordering of communities. The major reason why the Late Horizon settlement system approximates most closely the known central place models is precisely because of the considerably denser population and the location of the central city at a very convenient spot in terms of transportation, particularly involving the use of the lake system. What this does is to increase the efficiency of transportation considerably beyond that of the Middle Horizon, and to provide a better geographic setting for the operation of central place principles.

Moving to the First Intermediate One period when the Basin was politically fragmented, but where we do have evidence of site hierarchy, one of the curious characteristics of the settlement system is that each of the small polities (for example, in First Intermediate Two–Three, and Second Intermediate One and Three times) reproduces the Middle Horizon pattern on a smaller scale. By this we mean that over half, in some cases nearly all of the population, is concentrated in the central community and the satellite settlements included only a small percentage of the total population. As in the case of small Aztec centers, the small First Intermediate centers were essentially large agricultural settlements. They were larger than the dependent rural settlements most probably because they were located closer to more productive agricultural land. What all of this points out is the essentially agrarian character of early states, and hence central place models will have to be adapted to this very different context.

ENVIRONMENTAL CHANGE AND CULTURAL EVOLUTION IN THE BASIN OF MEXICO

A major question that obviously would have a significant effect on the process of prehispanic adaptation to the Basin of Mexico is the possibility of significant changes in the environment, either natural or man made. Unfortunately, most of the studies that have been addressed to this question have focused on the macrochanges that occurred during the final stages of the Pleistocene. What is needed is information on relatively minor cycling in rainfall and temperature over the past 3000 years. From our previous discussion it is clear that over much of the Basin even minor variations would have striking effects on crop productivity and security.

In his 1970 report Sanders summarized the current opinion as to the possibility of minor fluctuations in rainfall. This summary was based on pollen cores described by Sears (1952) and Kovar (1970), and changes in lake levels described by Lorenzo (1956). The following sequence of events was postulated.

1. During the Early Horizon and First Intermediate One phase lake and rainfall levels were high, and environmental conditions were quite favorable for extensive agriculture.
2. During the First Intermediate Two phase the decline in *Quercus* pollen and the lowering of the lake level indicate that conditions were becoming progressively more arid.
3. During the First Intermediate Three–Four phase oak pollen and the lake level had reached a nadir, suggesting a corresponding decrease in precipitation.
4. An upswing to more favorable conditions occurred by the First Intermediate Five phase.
5. Rainfall and lake levels then dropped during Middle Horizon and Toltec times, but rose again to the First Intermediate One level during the Late Horizon.

It should be mentioned that this reconstruction of climatological events has not met with universal acceptance. For example, Kovar (1970:24) notes that the rate of evaporation of the lakes was greater than the annual contribution of precipitation. Thus, over time one would expect the lake level to decrease. Counteracting this process, as population densities increased throughout the Basin, the stripping of the original forest canopy exacerbated the rate of soil erosion, and the net result might have been a later rise in lake levels. Unfortunately, these considerations do not explain why the lake level dropped during the Second Intermediate period.

More importantly, the reconstruction is contradicted by recent studies of the climatological history of the Puebla–Tlaxcala area, a region adjacent to the Basin of Mexico, and situated at the same elevation. One would expect close correspondences between the two areas and yet the sequence is almost reversed. Conditions are described as warmer and drier than today during the Early Horizon, gradually become colder and wetter during the First Intermediate, reaching a peak about the time of Christ, become increasingly drier and warmer to about A.D. 900, when the trend is reversed, to achieve another maximum of rainfall and minimum of temperature by A.D. 1519 (Heine 1973). Although the Valley of Oaxaca is considerably lower in elevation, (1500–1600 m), and much further from the Basin of Mexico, a recent study of climatic conditions during the Early Horizon–First Intermediate shows a close parallel to the Puebla–Tlaxcala profile (Flannery and Schoenwetter 1970). Data from the Tehuacan Valley, at the same elevation as the Valley of Oaxaca, in contrast, suggest that the present day climatic regime has been fairly constant since about 7000 B.C. (Smith 1967:249), but we wonder whether minor pulsations of a few hundred years or less would have had much of an effect on faunal–floral species composition and distribution.

It should be emphasized in all of this discussion that the changes involved are relatively minor ones, 20–30% increases or decreases in rainfall, and variations in average annual temperature of a degree or two. Such variation would not alter the basic problem of adaptation in the Basin of Mexico, but they would have significant effects on crop productivity and security. By way of evaluation, we would raise a question as to Heine's assumption that the post-Pleistocene climatic cycling necessarily involves a combination of colder temperature with wetter conditions and drier conditions with warmer temperature. This is undoubtedly the case for the major Pleistocene fluctuations, but there is a strong suggestion, from meteorological data gathered at the Tacuba station in the Basin of Mexico, that over the past 100 years there has been a correlation of low average annual temperature with dry years. A combination of this nature would of course put even more severe stresses on agricultural utilization of the Basin.

A very close correspondence between minor climatic cycling and settlement history for the Basin of Mexico should exhibit the following pattern (see Figure 9.2 for a graphic presentation of the following correlation).

1. An Early Horizon environment both cooler and drier than present; this would limit agricultural population to a very restricted area and explain the initially slow rate of population growth.
2. A succeeding period of increasing rainfall and increase of mean annual temperature through the First Intermediate One–Three period. This is a period of rapid population growth and spatial expansion.

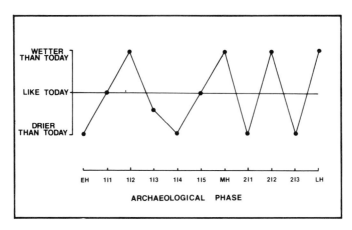

Figure 9.2. Graph showing perfect correlation between population history and climatic change in the Basin of Mexico.

3. A brief phase of cooler, drier conditions during the First Intermediate Four phase. This is a phase of rapid evolution of irrigation agriculture, relocation, and contraction of population.
4. A phase of increasingly wetter and warmer climate, coincident with population expansion into the drier portions of the Basin—the First Intermediate Five and Middle Horizon.
5. A cool, dry phase coincident with the Second Intermediate One phase, a phase of population reduction and contraction to the more favorable portions of the Basin.
6. A warm, wet phase coincident with the explosive growth of Tula, large population concentration in the drier portions of the Basin, and general expansion of the Mesoamerican frontier northward—the Second Intermediate Two phase.
7. A drier, colder phase, which coincides with the Second Intermediate Three phase, a phase of population reduction and retraction southwest to the more favorable portions of the Basin.
8. A warmer, wet phase corresponding to the Late Horizon, a phase of maximum population growth.

Unfortunately, the postulated climatic cycling does not correspond closely with this profile, but again it should be emphasized that very few excavations have been conducted to specifically define minor climatic phasing in the Central Plateau.

Another major question is that of possible environmental changes produced by the human utilization of the landscape. The most significant variables that might have feedback effects on human adaptation would be changes in soils and the water table. If swidden agriculture was widespread during the earlier phases of colonization, one would expect some erosion, both gully and sheet, to result, particularly in the drier portions of the area, since rainfall tends to be more torrential in character, and weed and crop growth is less exuberant in such areas. It is possible that many of the deep barrancas in the area were formed as the product of this early removal of protective vegetation

Along with intensification of cropping regimes the emergence of terracing would decelerate this process considerably, perhaps even stabilize it. The most massive sheet erosion clearly occurred during the Early Colonial period, when a combination of population decline and introduction of grazing animals led to abandonment of many hillside lands from cultivation, and their conversion to pasture.

During the early phase of colonization when forests, fields, and secondary bush covered the area, many streams may well have had shallow beds and, if not permanent flows, at least periods of steady, prolonged runoff, in contrast to the present day pattern, where even the runoff from heavy rains flows only a few hours through the barranca system. The removal, first of vegetation, ultimately of some of the soil cover, would probably also affect the water table in such a way as to lower it in the adjacent plains and reduce the flow of water in the springs. In all probability there were numerous springs that no longer function. Mooser has suggested that there were springs within the limits of the Middle Horizon city that provided a flow of 100–200 liters per second. Recent measurements of the water flow for the Amanalco and San Juan springs show a steady decline since 1920, in this case brought about primarily by the perforation of deep wells.

Armillas in his study of the chinampas of Lake Chalco–Xochimilco (1971), has suggested that the sudden and explosive growth of chinampas in the lakes during Late Horizon times may have been made possible by a change in the hydrographic conditions; namely, a process of sedimentation that reduced a body of open water to a swamp. Conceivably this sedimentation could have been produced by the three major cycles of swidden agriculture: during the Early Horizon–First Intermediate One phase; during the First Intermediate Four–Five, Middle Horizon; and finally, during the Second Intermediate Two phase, when the southern Basin had a very small population.

10

The Basin of Mexico
and Future Research

The Basin of Mexico provides one of the few places in the world where the evolution of preindustrial states in their heartland zones can be studied. Our investigations have served to outline some aspects of the general stages of this long evolutionary process in central Mexico. In the early years of our work, it is probably fair to say that we expected to produce some definite answers about how and why cultural evolution had occurred in our study area. More recently, we have come to realize that our principal success has been in the realm of posing better questions to which future research can be most usefully directed, that is, a better definition of a dynamic, multifaceted research program whose ultimate objective is to help explain cultural evolution in the Basin of Mexico, in Mesoamerica, and ultimately, at a more general level. At this point we want to outline our perspectives on the general directions along which such a program should proceed during the next decade or so in the Basin of Mexico.

Before getting into specifics, however, we should stress a critical factor of immediate and overwhelming concern: *Time is rapidly running out* as archaeological remains are daily consumed and forever obliterated by the astonishing, and accelerating, industrial and urban growth of modern Mexico City. In 1920 this metropolis had about 1,000,000 people. In 1975, at the end of our survey work, there were more than 8,000,000 inhabitants. Some current predictions forecast an incredible urban megalopolis of some 20,000,000 by the end of the century. This growth has meant, and will continue to mean, an accelerated engulfment in the course of a few decades of a countryside where the destructive impact of more than four preceding centuries of posthispanic activity has been miniscule by comparison.

For example, the entire western and southern two-thirds of Lake Texcoco, along with the adjacent lakeshore plain and piedmont, is now virtually completely covered by nucleated complexes of residential and industrial architecture. The wealth of archaeological sites along the entire western shoreline of old Lake Texcoco from Ecatepec south to Tepeyac, westward through the former villages of Zacatenco, Ticoman, and Tenayuca, southward again through Azcapotzalco, Tlatilco, Copilco, and Cuicuilco is now virtually unavailable for study. The area north of Mexico City, within a great triangle formed by Tepozotlan, Lago de Guadalupe, and Ecatepec, is presently undergoing *very rapid* urbanization and industrial growth. On the south and southeast, the urban metropolis has already extended over the western and northern halves of the Ixtapalapa peninsula (including areas where complete survey was possible in 1969), and over the western third of the bed and piedmont slopes of Lake Xochimilco. Easterly encroachment onto Lake Xochimilco is proceeding rapidly, and even the pedregal, in the far southwest, is being built up. On the eastern side of the lake system, growth and destruction are less massive, but substantial outliers of the modern towns of Chalco and Texcoco have already covered over sizable areas of lakeshore and piedmont terrain that we were able to survey with no problem as recently as 1972.

Completely apart from the problems of modern urban growth is the matter of agricultural mechanization in this area where subsistence agriculture is increasingly giving way to commercial dairy farming. Even in the rural countryside, sites that have easily resisted more than 450 years of posthispanic cultivation are now being rapidly destroyed by a shift from horses to tractors in plowing. We have seen that sustained tractor plowing levels even large ceremonial mounds.

The implications are clear: If archaeological research is not continued and greatly intensified during the next few years, within another decade there will be little left to study, and many key questions, of significant applicability to general problems of cultural evolution, will remain forever unanswered in the Basin of Mexico. So what? we hear some readers ask. Why not just abandon the Basin of Mexico to its inevitable fate, and intensify research in the relatively untouched surrounding areas which also have strong claims upon the energies and attention of archaeologists? Does it not make more sense, we hear even more readers ask, to do just this in view of our lower level of knowledge about the prehistory of the Toluca Basin, the Morelos valley, the Pachuca–Queretaro frontier, or Tlaxcala–Puebla?

The core of our argument for continued and intensified research in the Basin of Mexico is that this region, because it was a natural heartland region for the two largest prehispanic Mesoamerican states, provides unique insights into the development of these states that cannot be obtained elsewhere. Furthermore, if action is taken promptly, we still have enough time to carry out a great deal of research that can be directed at problems and questions which our antecedent work has defined as particularly important. We now understand rather well what specific sites it will be most useful to consider for excavation and intensive surface collection, programs already pioneered within this framework by Santley (1977) and Brumfiel (1976b), designed to cope with well-defined interests. Should we find that any such sites no longer exist at particular localities, we would usually have a fair idea of what surviving sites could be approached for similar purposes. This level of insight and flexibility is rare in archaeological research and should not be lightly discarded.

Clearly needed is a well-planned, vigorous program which can guide and facilitate the interests and energies of all investigators concerned with what, of necessity, must be the *final* stages of large-scale archaeological fieldwork in the Basin of Mexico. Our view is that such a program should involve a separate institutional structure dedicated exclusively to archaeological investigation in the Basin. Presently, the central office of the Mexican Instituto Nacional de Antropología e História functions in this capacity. However, with its heavy administrative burden, it would be difficult for this unit to effectively run a large research program in the Basin itself. We suggest that a separate regional center of the I.N.A.H. be established, whose areal concerns would be limited to the Basin of Mexico, and which would be comparable in status to the several other I.N.A.H. regional centers established to expedite archaeological investigation elsewhere in Mexico. Ideally, this regional center might comprise a small staff of permanent personnel who could act as advisors and colleagues for Mexican and foreign archaeologists carrying out specific field projects. The regional center should have its own physical plant with a library, artifact type collections, laboratory facilities, extensive storage space, and living quarters for transient investigators. Such a facility would be fairly expensive, but without it, it will be correspondingly difficult to attain our objectives. It might also be useful, in some instances, to have long-term understandings with foreign institutions that would commit themselves to sustained research within the Basin.

KEY PROBLEMS FOR FUTURE RESEARCH

The fundamental contribution of our research has been to establish a sound space–time framework for some aspects of prehistoric occupation in the Basin of Mexico (exclusive of preceramic periods). The framework has served as a data base from which to generate inferences about the organization of polity, economy, and society during several time periods. The observed changes over a 2500-year period in population and settlement configuration have provided a series of plausible generalizations about the complex processes of cultural evolutionary change in prehispanic central Mexico. For all this, there still remain unanswered many really fundamental questions, some of which we posed at the very beginning of our fieldwork, but even more of which have arisen in the course of our investigations: What is the role of canal irrigation, or population growth, or exchange, or technological innovation, or warfare in the development of political centralization and societal differentiation? In a very real sense, a great deal of what we have done consists of refining these questions so as to make them more specific, more realistic, and more operationalizable within the Basin of Mexico setting.

We are well aware that our research has not actually explained very much about processes of evolutionary change, in terms of demonstrating cause and effect. We have been able to work toward improved descriptions of what is changing into what, and we are able to correlate certain kinds of variables in a general way (e.g., population growth with cultural complexity). It is also true that over the years we have grown increasingly modest in our expectations of what our research can actually accomplish in terms of scientific explanation. Nonetheless, we still see such explanation as the ultimate objective of our work.

Two general needs stand out as particularly critical for future archaeological research aimed at the explanation of evolutionary change in the Basin of Mexico: *chronology* and *function*. Any truly significant advances in the ability to describe and explain cultural evolution can only come when we are better able to perceive what people were doing within relatively short blocks of time.

Artifact Chronology.   It is no secret, of course, that the correct temporal association of archaeological features is absolutely basic to any interpretation of their sociological meaning. We have already noted that more refined ceramic chronologies recently worked out in some parts of the Basin have begun to suggest the complexity of demographic processes that can be largely camouflaged within any one of our fairly long periods. Our own surveys have indicated that some significant spatial variation may occur within contemporary ceramic complexes throughout the Basin. This is apparently particularly true during the First Intermediate Phases Three and Four, and during the Second Intermediate. This variability remains poorly described, and we are far from understanding its chronological or sociopolitical basis. The potential chronological value of lithic artifacts has been only minimally explored. Future research must involve a great deal of basic stratigraphic work, in all parts of the Basin, as well as the application of valid seriational techniques to existing and forthcoming artifact collections. Until this is done, our inferences about site size, population, and settlement dynamics within each of our general time periods (usually some 200–300 years in length) must remain inadequate. This would probably be particularly the case within periods where settlement was unusually unstable or undergoing great change. Thus, for example, what now appears to us as a long period of great rural settlement stability and continuity in the Middle Horizon could conceivably, when examined at a finer chronological scale, turn out to be an era of significant subphase settlement dislocation. Similarly, because we cannot usually differentiate occupation at a level much below a unit of time representing some 8 or 10 generations, the specific sociological bases for community formation, expansion, contraction, and fragmentation remain largely invisible to us. This is unfortunate since such processes must certainly involve sociological units of basic organizational importance.

Site Classification. Our basic analytical unit is the site. Ideally for our purposes, the site should be considered as a composite artifact, capable of being defined and classified by means of its many component attributes and traits, and which can be subjected to analysis in a fashion comparable to common analyses of lithic and ceramic artifacts. In practice, however, such site analysis is very difficult for us. This is principally because the "site" is a very complex artifact, whose proper recognition, definition, and classification depends upon the proper recognition, definition, and classification of a whole series of component artifacts. Our site classification is a subjective one, based upon intuitively logical judgments. Nevertheless, our site classification is analytically weak because we have only limited control over some of the attributes most critical to an adequate site typology: the kinds of material remains that will inform us about the role of a specific site in a regional settlement system. Up to now, we have measured only settlement size, location, general density of surface remains, general occupational chronology, and to a more limited degree, general architectural complexity. A few limited excavations have convinced us that most of the surface remains which we define as sites do, in fact, represent residential occupation. However, we still have no real basis for systematically defining spatial or temporal variation in ceramic, lithic, or subsistence remains. Consequently, our ability to measure systematically the spatial and temporal variation in activity and status remains quite limited.

The *primary* objectives of future research in the Basin of Mexico should be related to this general question of site function. It is only in this way that the "site" will become useful for spatial analyses that can take us beyond the level of subjective and impressionistic generalization. An example or two might be useful by way of illustrating our point. For the Middle Horizon, we have one very distinct supraregional center, a handful of poorly defined smaller centers (poorly defined in terms of their political and economic roles), and a great mass of small rural sites, most of which we call hamlets or villages. Although we have made some predictions about the roles of these smaller sites in the general Middle Horizon settlement system, there are several viable alternatives, none of which can be evaluated with available data. In many cases we are not even confident that these sites represent full-time, or significant, residential locations. A *systematic* program of intensive surface collecting and small-scale excavation, which could probably be done in a single 6-month field season, might readily permit us to compare artifact variability and infer any basic functional–status variation that might exist within and between rural Middle Horizon sites throughout the Basin. Our typology of Middle Horizon rural sites could then be systematically modified so as to provide a better basis for spatial and chronological analyses of political and economic structure. Comparable programs could be developed for any time period, and for both rural settlements and centers. An ideal investigation of this sort might proceed at the main Teotihuacan center where Millon's reconstructions (based mainly on surface remains and limited excavations carried out for different purposes many years ago) of barrio organization, household organization, and social distinctions could be evaluated and elaborated by selective excavation at a moderately large scale.

Closely related to the general matter of function and improved site typology is the question of subsistence and diet. It now seems almost unbelievable that there is so little information about prehispanic diet for the Basin of Mexico. What little is available is mainly useful because it indicates the great promise of a systematically applied excavation program with emphasis on the careful recovery of faunal samples and flotation of plant remains. A convincing demonstration, for example, of significant spatial or chronological dietary differences could provide useful insights into status variation (e.g., elite versus subordinate, rural versus center) that might validate or modify comparable insights gained from other lines of archaeological evidence. Similarly, indications of significant dietary changes during particular time periods might reinforce hypotheses, developed from other lines of evidence, about the demographic impact of the development or introduction of new cultigens.

We have stressed, implicitly and explicitly throughout this book, that the ability to infer the presence and organization of specialization in the archaeological record is basic to any success we might have in describing and explaining evolutionary change. And yet, with the exception of salt making in the Late Horizon, we have made only a minimal contribution to the substance of prehispanic specialization. We have made a series of suggestions and speculations, reasonable in light of available knowledge, but undemonstrated assertions nonetheless. The whole problem of demonstrating the existence, distribution, and organization of specialization still lies almost wholly before us in the Basin of Mexico. So too, in consequence, does a large part of the study of cultural evolution.

The Amplification of Regional Perspective in Central Mexico.   One of the least ambiguous results of our research has been to demonstrate that any future success in explaining cultural evolution in the Basin of Mexico is dependent upon an expanded view of regional occupation in adjacent parts of central Mexico. This is particularly the case as regards the impact upon our survey area of major centers that developed outside the Basin from the Middle Horizon onward. We have had occasion to refer to Tula, the Morelos area, Cholula, and the entire Tlaxcala–Puebla region. We understand something of all these areas, but usually only just enough to know that they all played a role in what happened in the Basin of Mexico. In no case do we have regional settlement data comparable to our own, and in no case (although the information gap is least serious for Tula) can we describe the developmental sequences of these neighboring regions in a satisfactory way. Most serious of all, perhaps, is our continuing ignorance about the major center of Cholula. Time after time (particularly during the Second Intermediate Period), we have come up against the potential significance of Cholula, and time after time we have been unable to reach any satisfactory conclusions about how this center influenced cultural development within our survey area. From our point of view, Cholula should be a major focus of intensified research in the near future. Other adjacent areas in central Mexico are only slightly less critical in this regard.

One specific example can suffice to illustrate our meaning here. Hirth's (1974) survey in eastern Morelos has suggested (on the basis of the frequency and distribution of ceramic spindle whorls on Middle Horizon sites) a great expansion of cotton production and spinning during this period, with direct stimulation and control from Teotihuacan. This is a fascinating suggestion, and a proper understanding of the development and organization of this cotton production would be extraordinarily useful in illuminating the organization of the Middle Horizon economy focused on Teotihuacan. As it now stands, nearly all of what substantive insight into this economy we possess derives from the obsidian industry. Our understanding of Middle Horizon cotton production in Morelos still remains vague and imprecise. Badly needed are excavations and intensive surface collections at a representative sample of Hirth's suspected cotton-producing sites, together with an expansion of regional survey in Morelos so as to better define the specifics of time depth, intensification of production, organization, and relationship to Teotihuacan.

An Expanded Synthesis of Archaeological and Ethnohistoric Data Bases for the Late Horizon. Archaeologists, ourselves included, have long utilized ethnohistorically based studies of indigenous fifteenth- and sixteenth-century society to aid their research. However, there has seldom been a large-scale sustained, cooperative effort in which archaeologists and ethnohistorians have pooled their complementary realms of expertise for common purposes. It seems almost certain that such long-overdue cooperation could result in new levels of comprehension of Late Horizon society not hitherto attained. Perhaps one of the best examples we could give here would be the sociology of chinampa agriculture in the southern Basin. Here, a few areas of extraordinarily well-preserved archaeological features (remains of field systems and associated residences) could probably be directly related to early sixteenth-century sources on the specifics of household composition, land tenure, and productive output. Certainly, Calnek's recent archival studies of Aztec Tenochtitlan suggest that such high-quality documentary data may well be available.

Paleoenvironmental Studies. Despite some early and scattered attempts to reconstruct prehistoric environment, the great bulk of our appraisal of subsistence productive potential and demographic carrying capacity has derived from extrapolations backward from modern conditions. This is probably fairly reasonable for later prehispanic periods, but it becomes increasingly less so for more remote eras. We suspect that our evaluation of Early Horizon, First Intermediate, and even Middle Horizon environmental resources may be farther off the mark than desirable. More systematic palynological investigation, together with greatly expanded studies of ancient and modern soils, fauna, and flora are necessary to rectify this situation.

Designation of Immediately Threatened Areas as Zones of Top Priority for Archaeological Investigation. We presently feel that there are three areas where archaeological remains still survive in some abundance, but where the threat of their destruction is imminent and overwhelming: the bed of Lake Xochimilco and its surrounding piedmont; the western half and northern side of the Ixtapalapa peninsula; and most of the entire Cuautitlan–Tenayuca region on the north side of Mexico City. Top priority should be given to work in these zones, and every effort should be made to encourage and facilitate research which concentrates in these localities. Within a few years, only small-scale salvage operations will be feasible. The bed and shoreline zone of Lake Chalco, plus the entire eastern shoreline zone of Lake Texcoco should also be given high priority in this regard.

Permanent Preservation of Selected Sites. The past decade has witnessed impressive innovations in archaeological methodology throughout the world. It is likely that comparable innovation will occur in the future. Just as we now regard some of the techniques of the 1950s as woefully inadequate today, archaeologists of the early twenty-first century will probably look back in a comparable manner on our own era. Since many important sites in the Basin of Mexico are not going to survive long enough on their own so that new research techniques can be applied to them, it seems reasonable and necessary for the Basin of Mexico regional center to initiate a program of permanent protection for selected numbers of sites. Ideally, this protection should include a representative number of different categories of sites from all periods. Such a protection program should first focus its attention on the zone threatened with immediate destruction and proceed from that base.

APPENDIXES

A
Site Survey Form

Descriptive Data

Site Number _____   Recorder _____
Aerophoto Mosaic Number ____   Location–Municipio _____
Date _____   Village _____
Checked by _____   Owner _____

I. Natural Setting of Site: Cuautitlan Area
  a. General—Lake Bed   North Hills   Cuautitlan Plain
        Sierra de Guadalupe Piedmont   Sierra de Guadalupe
                  Sierra Las Cruces Piedmont

  b. Topography—Alluvial Plain (Main)   Small Alluvial Fan
        Gentle Slope   Steep Slope   Hill Top   Ridge Top

  c. Soil—(based upon exposed cuts: roads, canals, ravines)
        Depth (cm)   Texture—sand loam clay
        Color   Amount of erosion

  d. Hydrography—Permanent Streams
                  Springs
                  Barrancas—depth, location, width
                  Washes

  e. Vegetation—Type, abundance

  f. Special resources (clay, lime, obsidian, basalt, tezontle, salt, chert,
              tezontle gravel)

Site Number _____   Date _____

Aerophoto Mosaic Number _____   Recorder _____

Amplification of Aerophoto of Site

Site Number ————————————   Date ————————————————

Aerophoto Mosaic Number ————   Recorder ——————————————

Map of Site Based on Tracing of Aerophoto

Site Number _____

II. Modern Cultural Features:
    a.   Structures (Note number and location with respect to site features)

    b.   Jagueyes

    c.   Agricultural use
         1. Crops, state of growth

         2. Erosion control (bancals, terraces)

         3. Humidity control (canals, dams, drainage ditches, cajetes)

         4. General classification—temporal, humedad, riego

    d.   General relationship of site to agricultural and other land use today

Site Number _____

III. Prehistoric Features:
   a. General condition of site—erosion, excavation, pitting

   b. Mounds—number, size, height, classification (ceremonial, domestic) (location map) (clustering, plaza-like plans)

Site Number _____

  c. Specialized features—(walls, floors, canals, dams, burials, forts, moats, quarries, workshops)

  d. Pottery—Quantity, description

Subjective		*Objective*
None	Even	Take several 1 × 1 m counts—on residential mounds, between them, empty areas between mound clusters
Sparse		
Moderate	Localized and variable	
Heavy		
Very heavy		

  e. Miscellaneous artifacts—relative abundance

Obsidian

    Scrapers   Points   Workshop detritus

    Blades   Cores   Miscellaneous

Ground Stone

    Manos—metates   Figurines

    Celts   Spindle whorls

    Pestles and mortars   Pottery discs

        Pottery discs—perforated   censers

Bone—human

  Worked
  Unworked

Bone—animal
  Worked
  Unworked

Shell—worked, unworked

Site Number _____

    f. Depth and nature of archaeological deposit (stratification, stone–shell–midden layers, soil changes, total depth)

IV. Miscellaneous Data

Site Number ————————————   Date ——————————————
Aerophoto Mosaic Number ————   Recorder ——————————

Photographs

1. General photos—showing ecological setting

Site Number _____   Date _____
Aerophoto Mosaic Number _____   Recorder _____

Photographs

2. Photographs of modern and ancient terracing, irrigation, stream beds

Site Number ———————————

Photographs

3. Archaeological features (mounds, mound clusters, profiles of walls and floors, etc.)

Site Number _____   Date _____
Aerophoto Mosaic Number _____   Recorder _____

Problems, Summaries, Impressions

These three sheets [sic] are designed to permit the recorder to make tentative summary statements about nature, plan, and function of site, its relationship to environment and land use, problems of dating, relationships to other sites nearby, problems of relating structures to various periods of multi-period sites, desirability and need of further work to define the characteristics of the site, or any other problems or impressions he may wish to record.

B

Field Survey Form

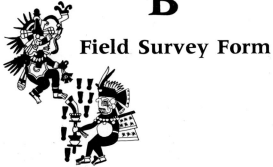

Field Number _____ Recorder _____ Site—No Yes
Aerophoto Number _____ Date _____ Sampled—No Yes

Topography 1 plain, 2 gentle slope, 3 medium slope,
4 steep slope, 5 hilltop

Soil depth 1 5–10 cm, 2 10–25, 3 25–50, 4 50–100, 5 100+

Soil color 1 lt brown, 2 brown, 3 grey, 4 pulverized *tepetate*

Soil condition 1 wet, 2 damp, 3 dry

Erosion 1 generalized, 2 extensive areas, 3 small localized areas

Barrancas 1 none
  position—1 north 2 south 3 east 4 west
  width—1 5–10 2 10–25 3 25–50 4 50–100
  depth—1 less than 1 m 2 1–3 m 3 greater than 3 m

Surface cover 1 sod grass, 2 scattered grass sod,
3 scattered nopal and/or maguey, 4 pirul trees,
5 thorn forest, 6 compact bare earth, 7 dense crop cover,
8 sparse–light crop cover, 9 industrial–domestic refuse

Modern features 1 none, 2 house, 3 jagueyes, 4 field houses,
5 factory, 6 street

Crops   1 none, 2 fallow, 3 maize, 4 maize and beans,
             5 maize–beans–squash, 6 maize–beans–haba,
             7 maize–beans–squash–haba, 8 beans, 9 squash, 10 haba,
             11 barley, 12 oats, 13 alfalfa, 14 wheat, 15 maguey,
             16 nopal, 17 fruit tree orchard, 18 vegetable garden

Maize height   1 less than 10 cm, 2 10–20, 3 20–50, 4 50–100,
                 5 greater than 100 cm
condition   1 pretassle, 2 tassle, 3 ear, 4 ripe, 5 harvested

Erosion control   1 lateral and front and back earth banks,
                     2 front and back earth banks, 3 front earth banks,
                     4 peripheral ditches, 5 internal ditching, 6 internal banks,
                     7 stone terrace, 8 maguey with banks, 9 nopal with banks

Humidity control   1 wells, 2 irrigation canals, 3 drainage ditches,
                     4 dams, 5 cajetes, 6 interior banking and ditching

Prehistoric features   If occupation is scanty or absent check below. If Aztec is
                         light also check below. If heavier, fill out site report.

1 absent	AZTEC	NON AZTEC	POST CONQUEST
	2 scanty	8 Middle Formative	18 scanty
	3 scanty–light	9 Terminal Formative	19 scanty–light
	4 light	10 Late Formative	20 light
	5 Aztec II	11 Early Classic	21 moderate
	6 Aztec III	12 Late Classic	22 heavy
	7 Aztec IV	13 Early Toltec	
		14 Late Toltec	
		15 Formative	
		16 Classic	
		17 Toltec	

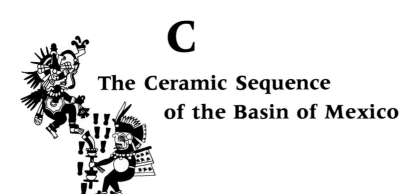

C

The Ceramic Sequence
of the Basin of Mexico

EARLY HORIZON–FIRST INTERMEDIATE
ONE–FOUR
(1550 B.C.–A.D. 100)

General Considerations

In viewing the period of time from 1500 B.C. to A.D. 100 there are a number of overall generalizations one can make about the ceramic chronology. A number of basic vessel forms are found during the period: jars, tecomates, basal break bowls with flat bases, basal break bowls with round bases, and hemispherical bowls. Variations in their popularity have diagnostic chronological value. Over the first two-thirds of this sequence (i.e., from Early Horizon A to the First Intermediate Two A subphase) there is a distinctive ware, which Vaillant referred to as bay ware, that has a well-burnished, reddish brown surface. During the latter one-third of the sequence it is replaced by a lightly burnished, buff, or tan ware.

The Early Horizon stands out in the presence of flat bottom, flare sided bowls, a form not to reappear to any degree until the First Intermediate Five phase. Characteristic of the entire time segment is a form that Vaillant referred to as a composite silhouette bowl, which we have redescribed as a basal break bowl with a round base. This begins in the Early Horizon but increases in popularity through the First Intermediate One until Phase Three, and then decreases sharply in popularity during Phase Four, and virtually

435

disappears by Phase Five. It goes through a series of changes in terms of the upper wall height ratio to the total vessel height (from a high to a low ratio); lip forms vary from well-rounded bolsters in the First Intermediate One phase to small bolsters in Phase Two B, to rounded and bevelled forms in Phase Three, and direct rounded in Phase Four. Along with these changes there are changes in surface texture varying from well-burnished bay ware in Phase One, and into the early part of Phase Two, and then shifting to a buff ware throughout the rest of the sequence. During Phase Two B, decoration includes red on buff, polychrome, and negative painting. Generally the form is undecorated during the earlier and late phases.

Hemispherical bowls have a curious history, being very common in Early Horizon and First Intermediate One and Two A phases, almost disappearing during Phase Two B, and becoming the most important decorated ware during Phases Three and Four. During the First Intermediate One phase they are characterized by great variety in lip form including bevelling, flanging, and eversion; and in decoration, with cream slipping as a common diagnostic. Forms during the late phase, however, tend to be simple.

Tecomates generally are early in the sequence and virtually disappear by Phase Three. They also go through a series of lip modifications, starting with a direct rounded rim during the Early Horizon and the First Intermediate Subphase A, shifting to flat, large bolstered rims during Phase One B and Two A, then occurring with small rounded bolsters during Phase Two B, and finally shifting to simple rounded rims in Phase Three.

Large utility jars also go through a series of well-defined changes. Nearly all of them are bay ware during the first two-thirds of the sequence and vary slightly in stylistic characteristics. Generally they have large, well-rounded, bolstered lips. During Phase Two B jars shift to the buff ware, have small lip bolsters, and are still well-burnished vessels. During Phase Three A bay ware continues and the lip form shifts to a simple rounded lip. During Phase Three B the vessels almost entirely lose their burnishing and lips tend to be bevelled, a form which persists into Phase Four.

Early Horizon Phase One
(1500–1300 B.C.)

In the Basin of Mexico ceramics dating to the Early Horizon Phase One are equivalent to what Tolstoy calls the Coapexco and Ayotla phases. Radiocarbon determinations indicate that materials from this phase fall into the time span from 1500 to 1300 B.C., sidereal time (see Figures C.1 and C.2). Phase One ceramics have been defined from three principal excavations: Tlapacoya (Niederberger 1969, 1976), Tlatilco (Tolstoy and Paradis 1970), and Coapexco (Tolstoy and Fish 1975, 1977). The hallmarks of Early Horizon Phase One pottery include the following: ". . . the flat-based dish, which is the prevailing form, and tends to be dark in color, well burnished and, when decorated, to bear incised, excised, rocker-stamped and or zoned motifs;

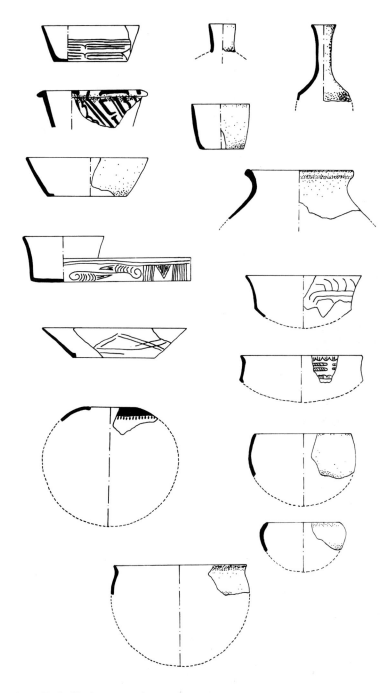

Figure C.1. Early Horizon ceramic vessel types.

Figure C.2. Early Horizon decorated sherds.

elaborate red-on-buff painted decoration, sometimes combined with resist painting; white ware with elaborate interior incision, often of 'Olmec style,' sometimes also combined with resist painting; differentially-fired ware; figurines of the 'baby-face,' D and K varieties; and small pointed stem projectile points [Tolstoy n.d.:12]."

Early Horizon Phase Two
(1300–1150 B.C.)

Early Horizon Phase Two materials are typologically equivalent to what is called Manantial by Tolstoy (n.d.:16). It succeeds the Ayotla phase in Tolstoy's sequence and is noted for carryovers from the Early Horizon Phase One (see Figures C.1 and C.2). Distinctive characteristics include an "imitation" differentially fired ware with painted white rim bands and a generally nonspecular red ware which appears in moderate abundance (Tolstoy n.d.: 16). Also found are split diamond designs on olla shoulders, flat or near flat-based white dishes with the double-line break motif and interior base incision, the Tlatilco panel design, gashed bowls, gadrooned bottles, and figurines of the D-1 and D-2 traditions (Tolstoy 1976).

According to Tolstoy (1975), sites having Manantial characteristics date from 1300 to about 1150 B.C. Although Tolstoy would assign this phase a First Intermediate Phase One date, we have used 1150 B.C. as the cutoff point for the Early Horizon, since it agrees with the existing chronologies for the Valley of Oaxaca (Winter 1974: Figure 2), for the Tehuacan Valley (Johnson and MacNeish 1972: Table 7), and for the Amatzinac region near Chalcatzingo (Grove *et al.* 1976:5). On temporal grounds, therefore, Manantial phase materials belong to the latter part of the Early Horizon. The lingering of many Early Horizon Phase One attributes (many of which are not present in succeeding phases) would seem to justify our Early Horizon placement of this phase.

First Intermediate Phase One A
(1150–950 B.C.)

The First Intermediate Phase One A corresponds to what is called Altica in the Teotihuacan Valley (Sanders 1965; Sanders *et al.* 1975) and Bomba and El Arbolillo elsewhere in the Basin of Mexico (Tolstoy and Paradis, 1970; McBride, 1974) (see Figures C.3 and C.4). This phase is coeval with the decline in "Olmec" or "Olmecoid" ceramics and accounts for that block of time from 1150 to 875 B.C. Since there is still some disagreement over whether or not Bomba reflects a mixture of El Arbolillo ceramics and Early Horizon refuse, we will only consider El Arbolillo traits as definitive of this phase (Tolstoy n.d.:16).

Typologically this phase is defined by material in which ". . . a stiff geometric style of incision prevails, accompanied by relatively large amounts of round-bottomed, often brown-paste, white vessels with parallel lines incised on the upper rim or lip (the double-line break motif), and sunburst or panel designs cut into the interior base [Tolstoy n.d.:17]." Bay ware vessels predominate, but with vague neck jars being the most common form (Vaillant 1930: Table II; Sanders *et al.* 1975: Table 39). Bay ware bowls are also characteristic, representing about 25% of the collection from Zacatenco (Vaillant 1930: Table II). Hemispherical bowls typically have bevelled lips, and direct rim tecomates and molcajetes are present. C-1 figurines are especially commonplace, but C-2 and C-3 variants also occur.

First Intermediate Phase One B
(950–650 B.C.)

First Intermediate Phase One B materials are identical to what has been termed Chiconautla in the Teotihuacan Valley (Sanders *et al.* 1975). It is also equivalent to the La Pastora and Cuautepec phases in the Tolstoy-McBride sequence and therefore dates from 875 to 650 B.C. (Tolstoy 1975) (see Figures

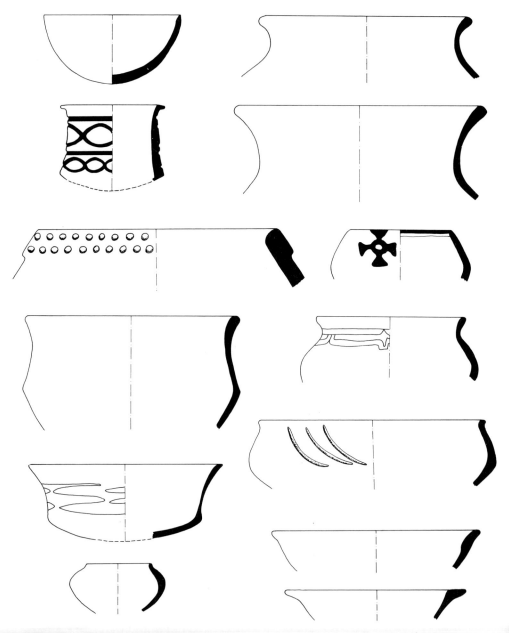

Figure C.3. First Intermediate Phase One ceramic vessel types.

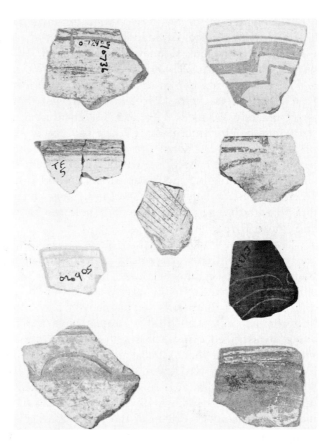

Figure C.4. First
Intermediate Phase One
decorated sherds.

C.3 and C.4). Bay ware sherds again predominate, as during the preceding
First Intermediate Phase One A, but now there is a relatively equal frequency
of bay ware jar and bowl forms, at least at Zacatenco (Vaillant 1930: Table II).
Other diagnostics include the emergence of red-on-white painted decoration, a high percentage of sherds with a cursive style of incision, a distinctive
"yellow-white" ware, and figurines styles C-3, C-5, B, F, and A (McBride
1974: 250; Tolstoy n.d.: 17–18). Hemispherical vessels with wide everted lips
are characteristic of the white and red-on-white wares. Cursive incision is
prevalent on incurving rim hemispherical bowls and high, vertical wall,
basal break bowls (McBride 1974: Plate 8). Other First Intermediate Phase
One B traits include the peak frequency of lacquer ware and the beginning of
a red-on-black ware (Vaillant 1930: Table II).

First Intermediate Phase Two
(650–300 B.C.)

On stylistic grounds the First Intermediate Phase Two refers to what has
traditionally been called the Late Formative or Preclassic (see Figures C.5 and

C.6). Elsewhere in the Basin of Mexico ceramics dating to Phase Two have been variously termed Ticoman I–III (Tolstoy n.d.; McBride 1974), Cuicuilco I–III (Bennyhoff 1966), Cuanalan (Sanders *et al.* 1975), and Atlamica–Cuautlalpan (Santley n.d.). Tolstoy (1974) places the First Intermediate Phase One B to Phase Two transition at about 650 B.C. Radiocarbon dates, mainly from First Intermediate Phase Three sites, suggest that this phase endures to approximately 300 B.C. (McBride 1974). A number of authors also stress the point that the First Intermediate Phase Two can be split into at least three and possibly four subdivisions. These we have only been able occasionally to sort out in our surface collections. Based on our recent surveys in the Cuautitlan and Tenayuca regions, we propose a two-fold breakdown, Ticoman I and Ticoman II–III, which should be of assistance in chronologically separating this phase into time periods comparable to the First Intermediate Phase One and Phase Three.

"Taken as a whole, Ticoman pottery tends to be relatively light in color, and includes a higher proportion of red ware than Zacatenco Phase (First Intermediate Phase One) ceramics [Tolstoy n.d.: 20]." During the earlier part of this phase (Ticoman I) bay ware is still common, contains a preponderance of deep, everted rim basins and vague neck jars, and is about as abundant as undecorated buff ware. Buff ware jars have a pronounced shoulder–neck angle, a restricted orifice, and a short, relatively straight neck, frequently with a bevelled or slightly bolstered lip. Tecomates consistently appear, albeit in low frequencies, and have a flat bolstered rim with deep punctate designs. Basal break bowls have a low wall in relation to the height of the base, greatly outleaning walls, usually with drooping lips, and hollow, conical-shaped, mammiform supports. Much of the painted pottery is red-on-buff, generally occurring on hemispherical bowls. The red-on-buff decoration is sometimes accompanied by shallow incision lateral to the painted areas. Polychrome ceramics (red and white-on-buff) make their first appearance as does a distinctive black-brown ware. Figurines of the E-2 style are very common, however; examples of the H-5, I, A, and B traditions also occur in moderate frequencies.

During the second part of the First Intermediate Phase Two (Ticoman II–III), buff ware becomes the predominant ceramic ware, and polychrome increases in frequency with respect to red-on-buff. Well-burnished red ware reaches a peak in popularity, especially during Ticoman III (Vaillant 1931; Table II). With regard to specific vessel forms, jars still have a sharp shoulder–neck angle, but the height of the neck is much greater, and jar lips are frequently slightly bolstered (Sanders *et al.* 1975: 130). Jar necks, which are burnished during Ticoman I, are generally unburnished by Ticoman III times. Tecomates occur with rounded, well-bolstered rims, and they are without the punctate incision. Basal break bowls typically have an upper segment ". . . placed almost vertical to the plane of the base, have a small rounded bolster very comparable to that found in the contemporary jars, and are very well burnished [Sanders *et al.* 1975: 132]." At Cuanalan, red-on-buff, white-on-buff, punctated, and incised decoration occur (Sanders *et al.*, 1975:

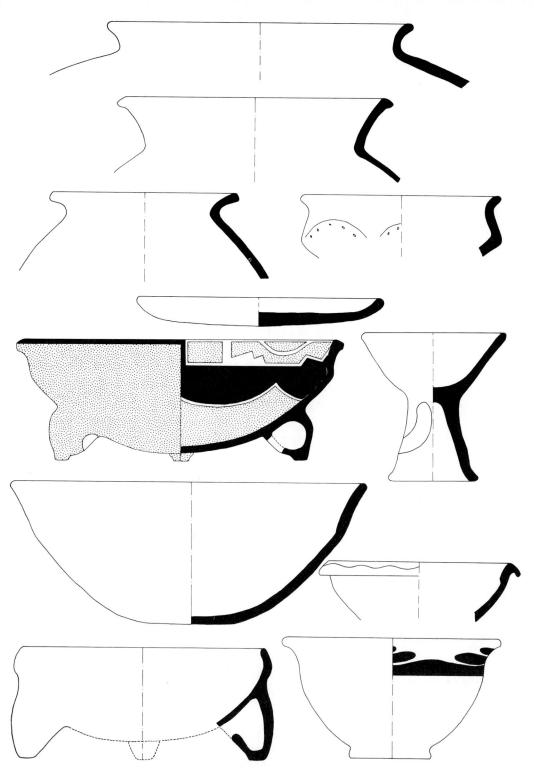

Figure C.5. First Intermediate Phase Two ceramic vessel types.

Figure C.6. First Intermediate Phase Two decorated sherds.

132). Tripod supports are most characteristic and include large hollow conical and bulbous supports, large, well-made, semiglobular legs with pinched tip, and knee and foot supports (Sanders *et al.* 1975: Figures 41–42; McBride 1974: 363). Figurines of the H and G traditions predominate, with the latter peaking somewhat earlier (Vaillant 1931; Table I). I and L figurines tend to occur in Ticoman II contexts (Vaillant 1931: Table I; McBride 1974: 254).

First Intermediate Phase Three
(300–100 B.C.)

The First Intermediate Phase Three has been designated as Tezoyuca–Patlachique (Sanders *et al.* 1975) and Cuanalan IV (Blucher 1971) in the Teotihuacan Valley, Cuicuilco IV–V at the sites of Cuicuilco (Bennyhoff 1966), and San Jose Cuautitlan (McBride 1974), and the Early Chimalhuacan, Ticoman IV, and Tultitlan phases elsewhere in the Basin (Tolstoy n.d.: 22–23; Santley 1977) (see Figure C.7). In the Cuautitlan region McBride suggests that Cuicuilco V ends somewhere near the time of Christ. In the Teotihuacan

Figure C.7.   First Intermediate Phase Three decorated sherds.

Valley, the Tezoyuca–Patlachique subphase lasts to around 100 B.C. (Sanders *et al.* 1975: Table 38). On the basis of a number of pottery seriations it seems likely that at least two subphases are present, as McBride (1974) and Heizer and Bennyhoff (1972) suggest for excavated lots. Surface survey and excavation have also shown that the Tezoyuca and Patlachique ceramic complexes are quite distinctive, and the two have very contrasting patterns of settlement. Because of these differences, which may be both temporal and cultural, Tezoyuca and Patlachique are discussed separately. The problems of dating the Tezoyuca complex have been discussed in Chapter 5.

Tezoyuca pottery is distinguished by a great amount of buff or tan pottery, usually with a highly variable surface color, which most frequently occurs on jar forms (Sanders *et al.* 1975:130). Tezoyuca jars are similar to those from the First Intermediate Phase Two, except the lip form seems to be much more variable. Included here are jar forms containing simple rounded lips, slightly thickened lips, rims with small lip bolsters, and wedge-shaped rims. Basal break bowls are similar to their First Intermediate Phase Two counterparts but with a higher frequency of insloping upper segments. In fact, of all basal break bowl forms, the vast majority are undecorated (Sanders *et al.* 1975:131).

The hallmark of Tezoyuca pottery is a distinctive white-on-red ware. The exterior surface is covered with a red slip and is well burnished (see Figure C.8). Geometric designs, often quite complex, are rendered on this surface using a glossy white, thickly applied paint. The predominant vessel form is the hemispherical bowl, usually with a simple rounded lip. A red-on-buff ware is also present, often occurring both in hemispherical bowls and basal break bowl forms. A polychrome ware is found on hemispherical bowls and pedestal-based drinking goblets. Negative painted, polished black, and appliqué pottery also occur in Tezoyuca contexts.

Patlachique is defined by the presence of a great amount of buff-colored pottery (see Figure C.9). Jars are again common, but the rim is frequently wedge shaped, sometimes with a lip groove. Patlachique basal break bowls resemble those found in the Tezoyuca complex, but with bevelled lips now characteristic (Sanders *et al.* 1975:133). Hemispherical bowls decline in popularity; many of these have a much flatter curvature to the wall (Sanders *et al.* 1975:135) and perhaps should be called dishes rather than bowls. A large, deep crater form with a wide, everted lip, equipped with shoulder lugs and possessing a lightly burnished tan surface, is also definitive. Patlachique sherds are further marked by a very low incidence of painted decoration; the most common variety is red-on-buff, followed by small occurrences of white-on-red, negative painting, and polychrome (Sanders *et al.* 1975:136).

In the Cuautitlan region, mainly at the site of San Jose, the First Intermediate Phase Three is defined by a slightly different set of ceramic markers. Tezoyuca–Patlachique characteristics include the distinctive white-on-red; channeled and everted–channeled jar rims; hemispherical and medium-walled red-on-buff, black-brown bowls; grooved, wedged and everted rim ollas; red-on-buff, shallow, hemispherical bowls with large globular semi-spherical, or conical legs; and red-on-buff, low-wall, composite-silhouette bowls with small saddle, duckhead, large complex knee and foot, or conical supports (McBride 1974:366–368). Traits peculiar to the assemblage, perhaps coming from Cuicuilco, are channeled necks on high cylindrical-neck jars; thin, granular, white ware jars; cream and red-on-cream ceramics; and a polished red ware (McBride 1974).

First Intermediate Phase Four
(100 B.C.–A.D.100)

Tzacualli or Teotihuacan I comprises the block of time that we distinguish as the First Intermediate Phase Four (see Figures C.10 and C.11). This phase is coeval with the emergence of Teotihuacan as the preeminent center in the Basin of Mexico. Radiocarbon dates from the Teotihuacan Valley indicate that the First Intermediate Phase Four begins around 100 B.C. and

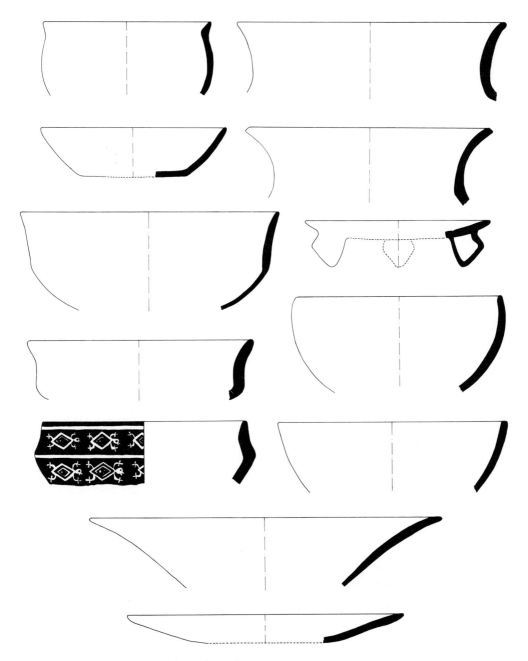

Figure C.8. First Intermediate Phase Three A ceramic vessel types.

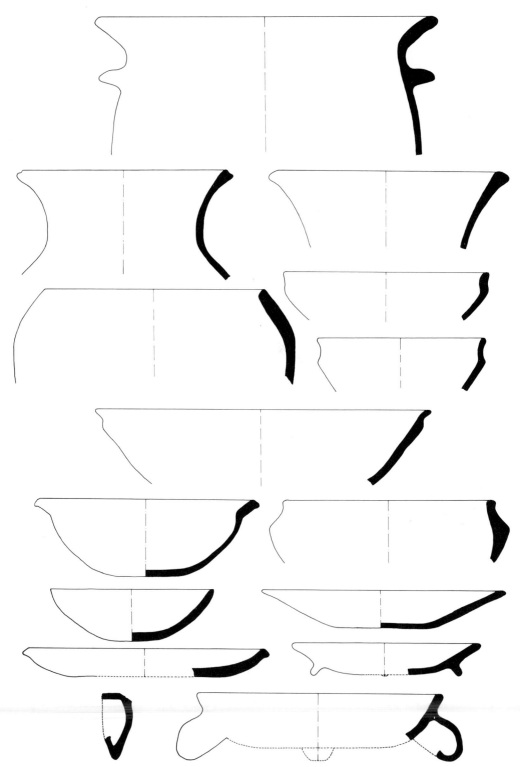

Figure C.9. First Intermediate Phase Three B ceramic vessel types.

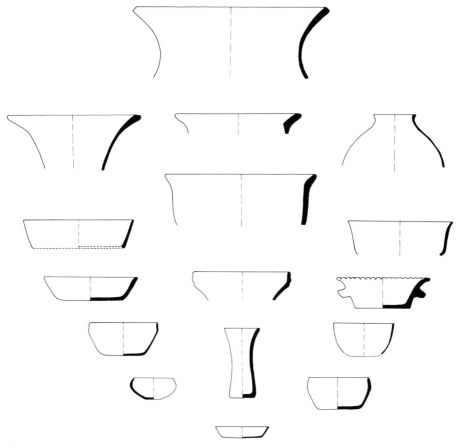

Figure C.10.   First Intermediate Phase Four ceramic vessel types.

lasts until about A.D. 100 (Sanders *et al.* 1975:Table 38). Throughout much of the rest of the Basin this phase seems to be a somewhat later manifestation, beginning around A.D. 1 (McBride 1974:Table 24). It has also been pointed out that at least three subphases may be defined within the First Intermediate Phase Four (Rattray 1973).

Buff ware continues in abundance, appearing mainly on jar forms. Jar rims are commonly bevelled, although wedge-rim and everted-rim vessels are also present (Parsons, 1971:272). The upper surface of the lip of Tzacualli jars tends to be much flatter than First Intermediate Phase Three jars (Sanders *et al.* 1975:131). Hemispherical bowls with flat bases and flat-bottomed, basal break bowls with flaring walls predominate in the red-on-buff and red-on-orange wares. White-on-red, white and red-on-buff, and white and red-on-orange wares also occur in Phase Four contexts. The paste of much Tzacualli pottery is also quite distinctive, with large angular pieces of quartzite being used as tempering material.

Figure C.11. First
Intermediate Phase Four
decorated sherds.

FIRST INTERMEDIATE PHASE FIVE – MIDDLE HORIZON
(A.D. 100–750)

The ceramics from the period of time from A.D. 100 to 750 contrast sharply
with those from the 1500 B.C. to A.D. 100 time frame. In terms of our overall
Mesoamerican chronology this is the First Intermediate Five phase and the
Middle Horizon. A very refined chronology has been established from Millon's excavations at the city of Teotihuacan with six phases: Miccaotli, Early
Tlamimilolpa, corresponding to Phase Five (see Figure C.12); and Late
Tlamimilolpa, Early Xolalpan, Late Xolalpan, Metepec, corresponding to the
Middle Horizon (see Figures C.13, C.14, C.15 a and b, and C.16) (Millon,
1973). To date only the Tzaqualli (First Intermediate Four) and First Inter-
mediate Five ceramics have been described in detail (Rattray 1973). On the
basis of our excavated samples from rural sites and the surface samples, we
have divided up the period into three phases corresponding to Miccaotli–
Early Tlamimilolpa, Late Tlamimilolpa–Early Xolalpan, and Late Xolalpan–
Metepec. In our preliminary analysis we had divided the period into two

Figure C.12. First Intermediate Phase Five ceramic vessel types.

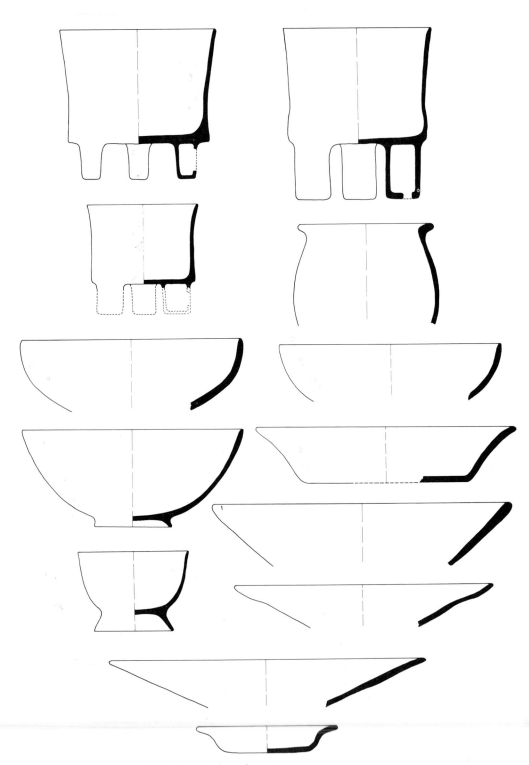

Figure C.13. Middle Horizon bowls and vases.

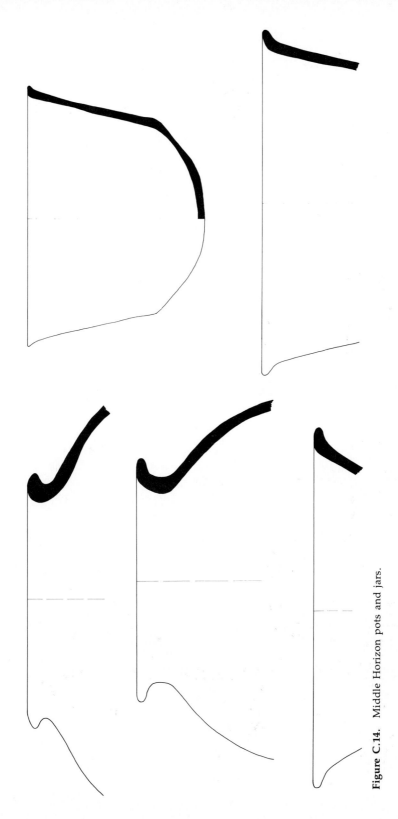

Figure C.14. Middle Horizon pots and jars.

a

b

Figure C.15 a and b. Middle Horizon decorated sherds.

Figure C.16. Middle Horizon
decorated ceramics.

major phases and unfortunately have not had access to all of the surface
samples in order to refine our dating either by our more recent tripartite
phasing, or Millon's more refined phasing.

With the rise of Teotihuacan there is a corresponding increase in the
complexity of ceramics, with a great variety of types and forms with
specialized functions. Many of these specialized vessels are rarely represented in our surface collections and hence have little chronological value, at
least with our method of surface sampling. More rigorous and more extensive sampling would probably capture many of these rarer types since they
are well represented in our excavated rural samples. Basically our preliminary dating of the surface samples as Early or Late was based on the occurrence of three basic ceramic types and their variability, and occasionally on
some of the minor types. The three major types are the large utility jars, the
monochrome bowls, and the red-on-buffs; all of which are heavily represented in our surface samples. Minor types which have been useful in dating
are San Miguel Orange cooking pots, thin orange, thin matte ware, and

monochrome hemispherical bowls. We have also used figurines and variations in supports as criteria for dating. Of occasional significance in our dating technique have been the heavy matte wares, primarily used for braziers and censers; and monochrome vases, primarily a ceremonial ware.

A utilitarian form which occurs throughout the time sequence and which was of considerable value in phasing are the utility jars. They go through a sequence of changes from well-burnished, relatively high neck jars, with bevelled or slightly everted lips (Early phase), to vessels with lower necks and either strongly everted lips or recurved necks (Middle phase), and finally to poorly burnished, almost neckless, jars, with simple direct rims or heavy, beaked, thickened rims (Late phase). The monochrome basal break bowls with flat bases also provided an excellent guide to internal phasing. These shift from a vessel with nubbin supports, highly burnished dark brown or black surface, and with a wall profile that is nearly vertical in its lower section, and then shifting to a sharply flaring upper wall; to vessels with a dull tan surface, without supports, and with a relatively concave, gradually flaring wall profile. Also present commonly in the Early phase are larger, deeper variants of the same basic form, often with everted or bolstered lips. Another characteristic difference between the phases is surface decoration, including incision, pattern, and zone burnishing in the Early phase, all of which disappear or are uncommon at the end of the sequence. Monochrome tan hemispherical bowls, often with ring bases, are limited to the Late phase.

Another major type that is useful in phasing is the red-on-buff. Red-on-buff, along with other kinds of painting, seems to be entirely absent during Miccaotli and very rare in Early Tlamimilolpa, so that its absence or low frequency in a site sample would suggest occupation during this earlier phase. It became only popular during the Middle phase when virtually all vessels are deep, flat bottom, basal break bowls with everted or bolstered lips. During the Late phase large hemispherical basins, small hemispherical bowls, and deep, comal-like vessels appear.

Among the minor types, the thin matte ware is relatively uncommon until the Late phase when it is used for comals, saucers, covers, and miniature jars. Prior to this phase it is not only rare but seems to have been used primarily for covers. Thin orange is relatively uncommon in all of our surface samples but is most common in the later phases. Miccaotli examples all have well-burnished surfaces, are undecorated, and restricted to the hemispherical bowl form. During the succeeding Early Tlamimilolpa phase the same form persists, the surface finish declines, and incised design is common. By the final phase other techniques such as punctation, stamping, and molded additions are incorporated in the decorative repertoire, and besides the hemispherical bowls there are a number of forms that duplicate the forms in other Teotihuacan wares, such as vases, basal break bowls with flat bases, and jars.

Another minor type which has some diagnostic value can be briefly mentioned. These are the comals, which tend to be very thick walled and have highly burnished upper surfaces in the Early phase, continue to have the burnished characteristic but with much thinner walls in the Middle phase, and finally are replaced by matte ware variants during the Late phase. Monochrome vases generally increase in frequency through the various phases and one of the variants, a small, thin walled vase, tends to be limited to the late phase.

On the basis of these criteria our samples from sites of the First Intermediate Five–Middle Horizon time frame show a consistent patterning. We have very few early sites that were not occupied later, and numerous sites with only late occupation. In nearly all cases multicomponent sites have their maximum density of surface refuse late in the sequence. For this reason we have decided to map our settlement data only for the Late Middle Horizon.

SECOND INTERMEDIATE PHASE ONE
(A.D. 750–950)

By Second Intermediate Phase One we mean that block of time between the decline of Teotihuacan and the rise of Tula, roughly from A.D. 750 to 950, when the Basin was apparently split into a number of small competing states (see Figures C.17, C.18, C.19, and C.20). Throughout the Basin this phase is generally known as Coyotlatelco or Early Toltec (Rattray 1966) after the type site, located at the western edge of the town of Azcapotzalco, and first excavated by A. M. Tozzer (Tozzer 1921). In the Teotihuacan Valley two discrete subphases appear to be present, Oxtotipac and Xometla (Sanders *et al.*). Although Oxtotipac-like ceramics have been reported near Santa Clara Xalostoc (Sanders and Santley 1977), it still remains to be seen whether or not this subphasing will be borne out in other parts of the Basin. Here we will describe the ceramics of the phase as a whole.

The hallmark of Coyotlatelco pottery is a distinctive red-on-buff ware. Common vessel forms include upright-wall or flaring-wall bowls with flat bases and hemispherical bowls (the most common form). Lip forms are usually simple though some may be bevelled or slightly everted. The red painted decoration, most commonly found on the vessel interior, is typically in the form of complex, fine-lined geometric design rendered within the borders of an outlined panel running around the middle or upper part of the vessel wall. Painted surfaces are characteristically well burnished, but where decoration is absent, the surface is more poorly finished and much rougher in texture. Other decorated ceramics include red-on-white, red-on-buff (in the form of simple lip or medial bands), and vessels with red slipped interiors or exteriors, and a few vessels with negative painting. Another important ware found in this phase is a monochrome buff, tan, or pale brown ware. Five basic vessel forms are typically represented in this ware: jars, hemispherical bowls, basins, flat bottom bowls with flaring sides, and comals.

Jars occur in three basic forms: a low necked type bearing some re-

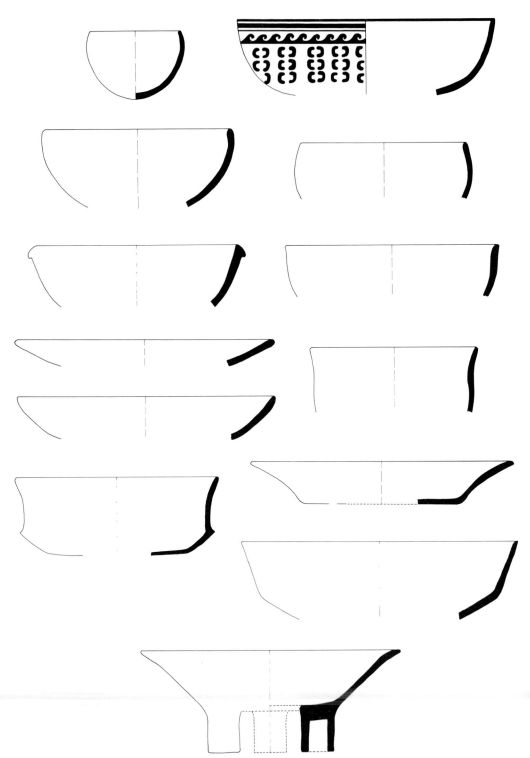

Figure C.17. Second Intermediate Phase One bowls.

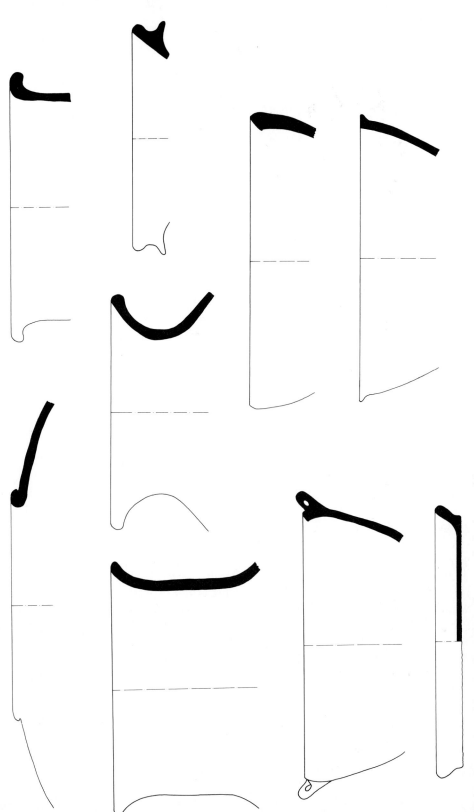

Figure C.18. Second Intermediate Phase One comals, basins, and jars.

Figure C.19. Second Intermediate Phase One decorated sherds.

semblance to the Xolalpan and Metepec jars; a medium high neck jar with vertical or slightly flaring neck and everted lip; and a high neck, red slipped jar with a well developed, round bolster. Large hemispherical vessels, which we refer to as basins, are another form. The rims of these vessels are everted, wedge shaped, or bevelled. In the case of the wedged and bevelled rims, the vessel interiors or exteriors are typically red-slipped. In the case of the vessels with the everted lip there is a red lip band. Another form which is found in the monochromes are comals, a relatively rare vessel form, but with a typical roughened base and a relatively flat profile.

The flat bottom, monochrome bowls are very similar to those from Xolapan–Metepec phases at Teotihuacan (except for a variant which has a more rounded basal angle, nearly vertical walls, and a slightly everted lip). This new form is almost identical to one of the forms found in the Coyotlatelco red-on-buff. A very common form is the simple hemispherical bowl.

Figure C.20. Second Intermediate Phase One decorated sherds.

A distinctive form, but found in very small quantities, is a composite silhouette vessel very similar to First Intermediate One vessels, with a nearly vertical upper wall, a sharp break at the basal angle, and a round base. A number of bowls have stamped designs, occurring in both hemispherical and the flat bottomed variants. Other features of the First Intermediate One ceramic complex are small, solid, conical supports, annular ring bases, and trough handle ladles. Molcajetes, on the other hand, are not present. A very distinctive support type, but occurring in very small frequencies, is a tubular support with an open base.

SECOND INTERMEDIATE PHASE TWO
(A.D. 950–1150)

The Second Intermediate Phase Two is contemporary with Tula's ascendancy as a major political center and population locus. In the Basin this period is more popularly known as Mazapan or Late Toltec (see Figures C.21, C.22, and C.23). In terms of sites excavated it is without a doubt the most poorly understood period in the prehistory of the Basin. Data from the Teotihuacan Valley, perhaps the most substantial body of information from the Basin pertaining to the Late Toltec, indicate that at least two subphases

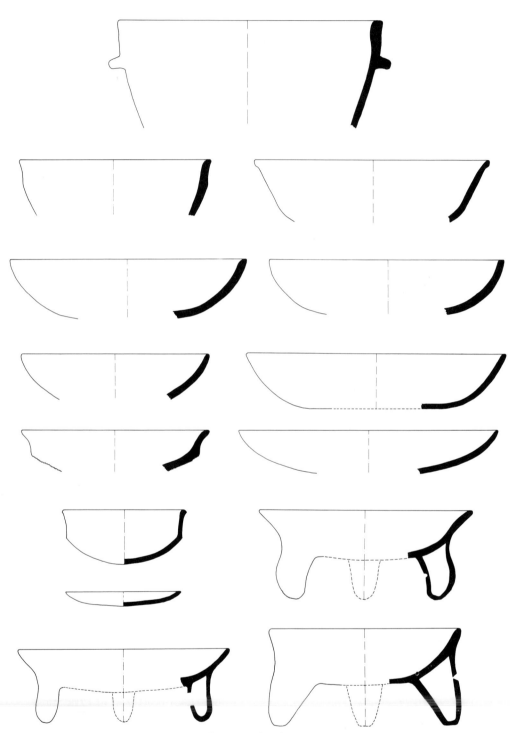

Figure C.21. Second Intermediate Phase Two bowls.

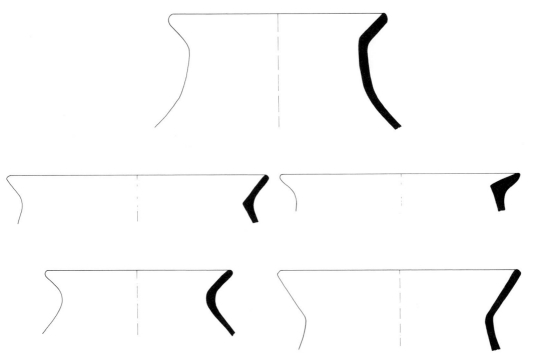

Figure C.22.   Second Intermediate Phase Two jars.

are present: an earlier Mazapan subphase, and a later Atlatongo subphase (Sanders n.d.). The dating of Phase Two, here assumed to extend from A.D. 950 to 1150, is based almost exclusively on chronometric dates from neighboring phases, combined with some evidence from ethnohistoric sources. Toltec pottery from the Tula region is closely related to the Atlatongo and Mazapan complexes in the Basin of Mexico, but there are a number of important differences (Cobean 1975: personal communication). First we will describe the ceramics from the Basin of Mexico.

Decorated red-on-buff pottery continues as a common service ware. Most vessels are simple hemispherical bowls with direct rims and convex walls. Bases are rounded or slightly flattened. Three distinctive decorative variants have been recognized: wavy-line red-on-buff, "Toltec" red-on-buff, and wide-band red-on-buff. In the wavy-line variant, decoration consists of sets of parallel lines, generally wavy, but also occasionally straight, occurring at several localities on the interior vessel wall and applied with a multiple brush technique. This mode of decoration, most common in the Teotihuacan and to a lesser degree in the Texcoco region, does not appear in abundance in the rest of the Basin. Likewise at Tula wavy-line red-on-buff is uncommon, and it seems to predate Tula's emergence as a major center (Cobean 1975: personal communication). This suggests that the wavy-line variant may eventually prove to be a local stylistic tradition, perhaps emanating from the site of

Figure C.23. Second Intermediate Phase One and Phase Two decorated sherds.

Teotihuacan, but found to any great extent only in the northeastern and central-eastern parts of the Basin.

Late Toltec red-on-buff ". . . features red designs in the form of irregular splotches, crude concentric circles, irregular linear elements, and broad splashes of red color [Parsons 1971:290]." Burnishing seems to have been applied before the painted decoration had been allowed to dry, as in many cases the designs appear quite smeared. This variety has a similar spatial distribution to the Mazapan wavy-line. Throughout most of the Basin and at Tula itself the wide-band red-on-buff decorative variant occurs in abundance. The painted decoration consists of a wide red-painted or slipped band or bands on the interior rim and interior vessel wall. On the exterior, decoration features a single narrow rim band. Large, hollow, conical, tripod supports are generally associated with wide-band vessels, in some cases the supports having a circular blob of red paint on the upper exterior part. In most cases a lattice of oblique cross-hatched incisions has been cut into the interior base and lower wall, indicating that these vessels functioned primarily as molcajetes. Vessel walls tend to be smoothly burnished, but the quality of the burnish is not as fine as that found on red-on-buff bowls from Phase One. Mazapan–Atlatongo wide-band red-on-buff bowls have a mass-produced appearance about them and data from Tula indicate that they were mold-made, probably by full-time specialists residing in the city (Cobean 1975: personal communication). Characteristic of many surface samples, in sites outside of the Teotihuacan–Texcoco regions, are hemispherical bowls with a narrow red lip band. These are very difficult to distinguish from comparable vessels from the First Intermediate Phase One.

With respect to Late Toltec monochrome service wares, there are two distinctive complexes, a burnished tan complex that is very similar to that from the First Intermediate One phase and an orange ware complex that is distinctive of this phase. The former is found in abundance all over the Basin and at Tula. It occurs primarily in the form of thick, mold-made hemispherical bowls with poor surface finish: but a consistent, small percentage are flare-sided, flat-bottom bowls, comparable to those in Phase One. The major difference between the two phases is the fact that the hemispherical bowls are a vastly more important form.

The orange ware complex includes a great variety of bowls, although most of them are comparable to the forms found in the red-on-buff and the monochrome bowls in the same phase. New forms include vessels with flaring or vertical sides, a rounded base, and hollow tripod supports. Surfaces vary from dull matte to well-burnished orange and cream slipped. The complex is very common in the Tula region and in the northern part of the Basin of Mexico, is well represented in the central part of the Basin, and is virtually absent in the south. Finally, there is a set of distinctive utility vessels which are found over the entire Basin of Mexico as well as Tula. These include jars with a medium-high neck, which flares sharply from the shoulder, and with a squared off, tapered lip; basins with a vertical upper wall segment and round base, and comals with vertical, upright rims.

On the basis of a study of excavated ceramics and surface samples from the Teotihuacan Valley we have subdivided the phase into two subphases, Mazapan and Atlatongo. The early phase includes the red-on-buff ceramics, monochrome brown service ware, and the utility ware. All of these carry over into the Atlatongo phase but with a decline in popularity of the red-on-buff, which is apparently being replaced by the orange ware complex. An exception to this would be the continuing popularity of the wide band red-on-buff. At Tula, the red-on-buff complex is always uncommon and the maximum growth of the city coincides with the great popularity of the orange ware complex.

The situation is obviously very complex, in which the variation in ceramics is the product of two separate factors, space and time. It is our conclusion, and this is based on consultation with Diehl, on the basis of his work at Tula, and with Cobean, the ceramicist of Diehl's Tula project, that the Mazapan wavy-line and the Toltec red-on-buff probably originated at Teotihuacan, whereas the orange ware complex undoubtedly originated at Tula. It is also probable that the orange ware complex represents a very short period of time, no more than 100 years, and perhaps less. What this may mean is that Tula's emergence as a major political center was an extremely brief period, in all probability so short that its major ceramic styles had not yet completely replaced the local styles in the Basin of Mexico before the collapse of the city occurred.

SECOND INTERMEDIATE PHASE THREE AND LATE HORIZON
(A.D. 1150–1519)

General Considerations

Vaillant (1941) defined the Aztec period as beginning in A.D. 1247 and extending until the Spanish entry into Tenochtitlan in 1519. He divided this block of time into four phases, based on rebuildings of the Tenayuca pyramid every 52 years: Aztec I (1247–1299); Aztec II (1299–1403); Aztec III (1403–1507); and Aztec IV (1507–1519). Our data suggest a number of revisions in this sequence. First of all, we extend the Early Aztec period back to the fall of Tula, around A.D. 1150. Our surveys also indicate that Aztec I and Aztec II are probably at least partly contemporary with one another. Aztec I is found exclusively in the southern Basin, principally in the area around Lake Xochimilco–Chalco. Aztec II, although present in the south, is found predominantly in the central third of the Basin. If we accept Vaillant's contention that the two phases are sequential, we are confronted with a population loss of unprecedented magnitude, since Aztec I sites, even in the south, are few in number. The explanation for this apparent decline could be climatic in nature, but we find it difficult to imagine a climatic change severe enough to cause the abandonment of the Basin's major irrigation systems along the Cuautitlan, Teotihuacan, and Papalotla rivers. On the other hand, if the Aztec I and Aztec II styles are coeval, then the degree of population loss, in comparison with the Second Intermediate Two, is only slight. The period embraced by the Aztec I–II style is dated as A.D. 1150–1350 and, in terms of our overall Mesoamerican sequence, this would be the Second Intermediate Three.

The reasoning outlined above departs rather significantly from our earlier belief that there was chronological overlap between the Late Toltec and Aztec I ceramic complexes (e.g., Parsons 1971). Prior to our surveys in the southern Basin of Mexico, we felt that the Aztec I complex would largely replace the Late Toltec there. However, this proved not to be the case, and we found a well-defined regional Late Toltec ceramic assemblage throughout our Chalco–Xochimilco region. Although the situation is still not wholly clear, and there may still be some chronological overlap between Aztec I and Late Toltec, we now feel that our data make more sense if we view Aztec I and II as more or less equivalent in time.

We define the Late Horizon as extending from A.D. 1350 to A.D. 1519. Ethnohistoric sources tell us that the political fragmentation of the Second Intermediate Phase Three ends about A.D. 1350 with the unification of most of the Basin, and a large territory outside of it, under the hegemony of Texcoco (i.e., during the reign of Techotlala). Azcapotzalco replaces Texcoco, for a decade, early in the fifteenth century, and then in 1428 Azcapotzalco was overthrown by a coalition of Texcoco and Tenochtitlan. These two cities, plus Tacuba (or Tlacopan), designed the triple alliance. This ultimately led to the domination of a large area of Mesoamerica, approximately 160,000 km², and with a total population of at least 5–6 million. The period could therefore be divided into two phases: Phase One, 1350–1428; and Phase Two, 1428–1519. We cannot as yet sort out these phases archaeologically, and the Aztec III (or Tenochtitlan phase) ceramic complex probably characterizes most of the period.

We originally thought that Aztec III pottery persisted until the early sixteenth century, after which it ceased to be manufactured in any significant quantity (e.g., Parsons 1971). We also formerly accepted Griffin and Espejo's (1947, 1950) suggestion that Aztec IV black–orange pottery came into existence during the early sixteenth century and persisted through the early decades of the Colonial period. However, Charlton's work (1972b) on Colonial pottery suggests rather clearly that some of the material we designate as Aztec III actually continued to be manufactured well into the Early Colonial period, while the Aztec IV complex may be largely a Colonial phenomenon. It is possible that Aztec IV was a very late Late Horizon phenomenon that did not spread widely into rural areas. This means, of course, that our map of Late Horizon settlement actually includes some Early Colonial occupation as well. However, because of rather substantial population losses after the mid-sixteenth century, we do not believe this results in any significant error in our estimates of population size and distribution for Late Horizon times.

Second Intermediate Phase Three
(A.D. 1150–1350)

The Second Intermediate Phase Three comprises that period of time when pottery known either as Aztec I–II, Culhuacan–Tenayuca, Zocango, or as Early Aztec was in common use in the Basin (see Figures C.24 and C.25). The phase dates roughly from A.D. 1150 to 1350: a period when the Basin was again divided into a number of petty states each vying for regional control. With the exception of excavations at Tenayuca (Noguera 1935a), Culhuacan (Griffin and Espejo 1947, 1950), Chalco, Xico (O'Neill 1956–1957), and Cuanalan (Sanders 1965; Parsons 1966), plus our surveys, the period is not well known archaeologically. Because of the relative scarcity of Culhuacan material in most of our surface samples, the Early Aztec component that we

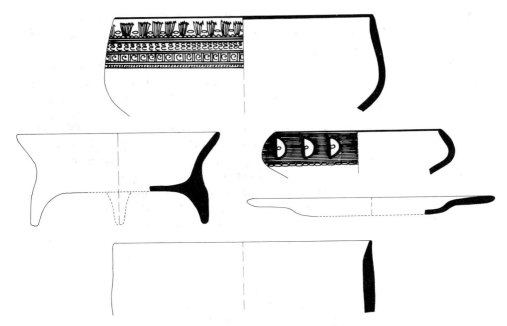

Figure C.24. Second Intermediate Phase Three ceramic vessel types.

describe is based primarily on ceramics pertaining to the Tenayuca or Aztec II complex. One serious problem is the character of Early Aztec undecorated pottery. Although unpainted pottery is very definitive for the Aztec period as a whole, we have been unable to employ it—with one noticeable exception, the large jars—in differentiating the Second Intermediate Phase Three from the Late Horizon. All Aztec undecorated materials are consequently described in the section dealing with Late Horizon ceramics (see Figure C.26).

Three decorated service wares are in common use during Early Aztec times: black-on-orange, black-on-red incised, and black-on-red. The black-on-orange ware is most characteristic. Surface color, the result of the natural clay color rather than slipping or painting, varies from light orange, orange-brown, and yellowish-brown, to reddish-orange and reddish-brown. The basic form variants in black-on-orange ware include basins, dishes, *molcajetes* (Chili grinders), plates, and bowls. Rim forms are generally simple, sometimes with interior tapering. In comparison with the Late Horizon, Early Aztec black-on-orange vessels are slightly thicker as a whole. Basins typically have small horizontal loop handles or small solid lug handles (Parsons 1971:298). Dishes and *molcajetes* have thick, stubby, tripod conical supports (Parsons 1971). *Molcajetes* also have cross-hatched incisions on the interior base. Plates lack appendages of any kind.

The exterior painted decoration on bowls and basins is in the form of black designs applied to the vessel surface. Motifs ". . .are characterized by relatively thick lines, hastily applied in complex geometric and curvilinear

Figure C.25.   Second Intermediate Phase Three decorated sherds.

forms. A particularly diagnostic element is the *zacate* motif, comprised of one or more rows of thick, short lines of grassy appearance [Parsons 1971:298]." In the case of bowls and basins, painted motifs generally occur in a band about the outer upper vessel wall. All other vessel forms lack exterior decoration. The *molcajete*, dish, and plate forms have painted decoration on the interior surface only. Both surfaces tend to be smoothly burnished, although the quality of burnishing on painted surfaces is more carefully done. There is also a tendency for the upper part of vessel exteriors to be better smoothed and burnished than the lower section (Parsons 1971).

Early Aztec black-on-red incised pottery is consistently found in small percentages in our surface samples. Two vessel forms are diagnostic: upright-wall bowls and incurved-wall bowls. A thickly applied, red-painted or slipped band, outlined by thin black lines, generally occurs on the upper segment of the exterior vessel wall. Curvilinear and geometric black designs, bounded by crude shallow incision, have been applied to the surface of the

Figure C.26. Second Intermediate Phase Three and Late Horizon ceramic vessel types.

red band (Parsons 1971:298–299). The interior surface is commonly undecorated. Both surfaces are well smoothed and burnished, and on the decorated
areas the surface may be highly polished.

Black-on-red and black-and-white-on-red vessels are also present in
Early Aztec contexts. Most vessels are simple bowls, with flat bottoms and
upright or slightly recurved walls (Parsons 1971:299). The red surface is
similar to that found on black-on-red incised bowls. The black decoration is
different, typically consisting of vertically placed wide bands at intervals of
4–5 cm around the vessel exterior (Parsons 1971). The design frequently occurs
with contrasting bands of thick white paint to form a polychrome. The

interior surface is either black, black-brown, or natural clay color (i.e., orange-brown to reddish-gray). Both surfaces are well burnished, particularly in the case of black interiors. Jars from the Early Aztec phase have bevelled lips, nearly vertical to flaring, medium high necks, and a well-burnished, orange surface.

The Late Horizon
(A.D. 1350–1519)

The Late Horizon corresponds to that block of time when the Basin was subordinate to a single political power. As a chronological period it begins around A.D. 1350 and lasts up until the Spanish Conquest in 1522. The period is also known by the phase names Chimalpa–Teacalco in the Teotihuacan Valley, Tenochtitlan–Tlatelolco in the southern Basin, and Late Aztec or Aztec III–IV in most of the literature (see Figures C.27 and C.28). Although excavations at Late Horizon sites are few in number, there is a great abundance of documentary evidence pertaining to the period.

The black-on-orange ware persists as the major ceramic tradition during the Late Horizon. Surface color generally varies from yellowish-orange to reddish-orange. As in Early Aztec black-on-orange the basic form variants are basins, dishes, *molcajetes,* plates, and bowls. Rim types are simple, and bases are typically flat or slightly rounded. Basins have small horizontal loop handles or small solid lug handles, while dishes and *molcajetes* occur either with spindly, slightly arched, solid, conical, tripod supports, or wide, thin, slab tripod supports (Parsons 1971:308). Technologically the ware is characterized by uniform surface and paste color, and is one of the hardest wares in Mesoamerica, often ringing like porcelain when struck.

According to Parsons (1971:308) ". . .Late Aztec black-on-orange differs from Early Aztec pottery of this same type in three main characteristics: (a) generally thinner vessel walls; (b) slightly finer paste; and (c) black decoration whose principal design elements are groups of thin parallel lines, simple combinations of dashes, circles, and dots, and simple curvilinear motifs." The designs are usually precisely and expertly drawn, but the range of design is monotonous.

On the vessel exterior only basins and hemispherical bowls have painted decoration. This characteristically occurs as a thin band of parallel lines, often incorporating lines of dashes, dots, or circles, about the upper part of the vessel. Only slab supports are decorated, again with linear motifs. On the vessel interior, decoration is restricted to dishes, *molcajetes,* and plates. The painted motifs resemble those occurring on the exterior surface of basins and bowls. On plates the decoration commonly extends over the whole of the vessel interior (Parsons 1971:309). Vessel walls are well smoothed and burnished, particularly on the upper exterior wall and on the interior surface.

Black-on-red and black and white-on-red (Aztec polychrome) also occur at Late Horizon sites, especially in the Cuautitlan and Tenayuca regions. All

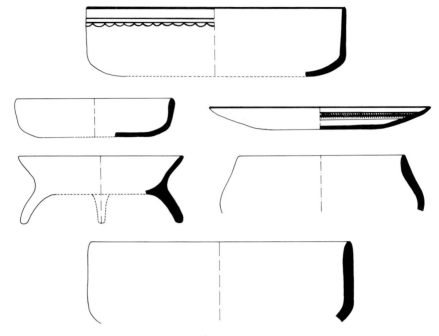

Figure C.27. Late Horizon ceramic vessel types.

vessels are simple bowls, with upright walls, simple direct rims, and flat bases (Parsons 1971:309). In most cases the painted decoration has been applied to the exterior surface only. A thickly applied red paint rings the upper part of the vessel wall. Onto this background clusters of 2–10 thin vertical black lines are repeated about the circumference of the vessel in the black-on-red ware.

In the cases of Aztec polychrome, the red-painted surface is again present, onto which have been rendered thick black lines outlining rectilinear and triangular areas, which, in turn, have been filled in with a thick, fugitive white paint (Parsons 1971:311). This variant is much more common in Early Aztec sites but continues into the Late Aztec. Occasionally, more complex curvilinear–rectilinear motifs occur, sometimes on the interior surface. Both surfaces are well smoothed and burnished, but this variant lacks the mirror-like polish found on the black–red.

Aztec plain ware is especially common both during the Second Intermediate Phase Three and during the succeeding Late Horizon, and there is evidence to suggest that this ware continues in popularity well into the Post-Conquest period (Charlton 1972a,b). Although the modal color is orange, there is a marked tendency for utilitarian vessels to be differentially fired. The full range of vessel forms is represented: jars, basins, comals, and bowls. Parsons (1971:299) describes several jar–basin form variants: high

Figure C.28. Late Horizon decorated sherds.

necked vessels, with simple, direct rims, and large vertical loop handles (only jars); vessels with upright walls and flat, wide rims (both jars and basins); and flaring-mouth vessels, with bolstered rims, and a distinctly bevelled exterior edge, often with a pronounced overhang or drooping lip (both jars and basins). Comals are typically flat, with direct, bevelled, and grooved rim form types. Bowl forms include hemispherical wall bowls with direct rims, and shouldered vessels. Except for jar handles, appendages and supports seem to be absent. Only bowls and the interior surface of comals are well burnished. Comal exteriors appear to have been deliberately roughened, and they have generally been blackened from use over a fire.

A distinctive fabric-marked ware is frequently present in lakeshore locations. Surface color is generally quite variable, ranging from light orange-brown to reddish-orange and grayish-brown. The exterior surface is very rough, its texture apparently being the result of impressing coarse fabric or basketry on the wet clay surface (Parsons 1971:313). The most common vessel form is a deep, vertical-wall basin, with a bolstered or bevelled rim, and a flat bottom. Fiber tempering is very abundant. In general this pottery is not very well made, in many cases crumbling to the touch. A number of authors have argued that this ware was used in the salt-making process (Charlton 1969, 1971; Parsons 1971). The fact that fabric-marked pottery only predominated at mounds ringing the saline lakeshore strongly supports this point of view.

D

Prehispanic Meat Consumption Levels in the Basin of Mexico

The reconstruction of prehistoric subsistence patterns has been a subject of much recent concern in Mesoamerican archaeology. Research in this direction has resulted largely from the pioneering efforts of Richard S. MacNeish and associates in Tamaulipas and Tehuacan, Mexico (MacNeish 1958, 1964, 1967, 1972). Since the mid 1960s a wealth of subsistence information has come to light from virtually every nook and cranny of highland Mesoamerica (Drennan 1976; Flannery 1967; Flannery *et al.* 1970; Niederberger 1976; Reyna Robles and Gonzalez 1976; Santley n.d; Tolstoy and Paradis 1970; Tolstoy *et al.* 1977; White n.d.). The quality of this information is quite variable, depending on the effects of differential preservation, prehistoric activity patterning, and kind of excavation on the composition of the recovered samples. Much of this research has focused on tracing agricultural developments in various parts of Mesoamerica, while only a few of these studies have attempted to tackle the question of animal utilization during precolumbian times. It is to this latter topic that this appendix is directed.

In prehispanic Central Mexico faunal exploitation involved the selective use of a few key species: white-tailed deer (*Odocoileus virginianus*), cottontail rabbit (*Sylvilagus* spp.), domestic dog (*Canis familiaris*), domestic turkey (*Meleagris gallopavo*), and several species of wild migratory waterfowl (*Anatidae*), principally ducks. Of these, white-tailed deer are by far the most predominant, surpassing 90% (and sometimes 95%) of the edible food weight in excavated faunas (Flannery 1967; Starbuck 1975; White n.d.). Because of this preponderance, frequently in numbers but especially in food value, the percentage of deer consumption can thus be used as a very reliable indicator of the level of total meat consumption.

THE EQUILIBRIUM MODEL

The simplest way to evaluate the role of meat as a prehispanic food resource in the Basin of Mexico is to forecast an equilibrium model of deer energy availability at various time periods. The model offered here assumes total optimality, that is (a) that deer were present in high densities, (b) that this density was fairly uniform throughout the zone of procurement, and (c) that cropping occurred at the highest possible rate without upsetting equilibrium conditions. The estimates suggested below are presented in energetic terms. The model makes no suggestion that energy capture was the major reason for hunting. The kilocalorie is used only for comparative purposes, and since all foodstuffs contain some consumable energy, the use of the kilocalorie as analytical measure is justified in this case. The model also has its drawbacks. The assumption that deer densities were uniform is especially unrealistic, since numbers per unit area are known to vary greatly in different environmental zones. In addition, densities probably were rarely as high on the average as the model would predict, and the fact that white-tailed deer are nearly extinct today indicates that prehispanic hunters certainly culled the species in excess of the maximum rate of annual replacement. The figures suggested by the model should therefore be taken as theoretical maxima.

The test area is the Basin of Mexico, a hydrographic unit roughly 7000 km² in extent (Sanders et al. 1970:71). Depending on elevation, soil depth and texture, and the rainfall regime, at least nine major ecological zones traverse the Basin. Aboriginally the floor of the Basin was partially covered by a series of five shallow interconnected lakes. Flanking the saline lakeshore is a band of alluvial deposition, the deep soil plain. At an elevation of about 2260–2300 m the terrain begins to slope upward. At first, the slope angle is gentle, but at 2350 and 2500 m the gradient becomes increasingly more steep. Above 2750 m is the sierra, a zone of rugged precipitous relief. Before deforestation much of the piedmont (2260–2750 m), the sierra (2750–5000+ m), and the southern alluvial plain (2240–2260 m) was in forest: an oak broadleaf forest at lower elevations, a mixed pine–oak formation starting at about 2500 m, and finally a coniferous forest from 3000 m to the 4000-m timberline. At lower elevations in the northern Basin the reduction in precipitation apparently affected a transition to a more open association composed of scrub oak, various grasses, and forbs.

White-tailed deer occur in almost every habitat in Mesoamerica, but their optimal habitats are in the pine–oak woodlands of the Basin of Mexico, Puebla, Toluca, Oaxaca, and Guerrero (Flannery 1968:73). Their density in this habitat in high, circa 10–13 individuals per square kilometer (Leopold 1959:508). The approximately 6000 km² of forest and open woodland formation in the Basin would consequently seem to have been a likely habitat for this species. Deer are also extremely fecund breeders, commonly being able to withstand an annual culling rate of 30–40% (Leopold 1959:513). White-tailed deer also thrive in disturbed areas of secondary grassy and weedy growth, on fallow agricultural land in particular, which probably accounts for their persistence near human communities even under severe hunting pressures (Flannery 1968:73). White-tailed deer have relatively small home ranges, frequently trailing known trails, and are therefore very susceptible to daylight hunts by individual males using the spearthrower and the bleeding and trailing technique (MacNeish n.d.).

In order to estimate the amount of energy that could potentially be extracted from deer populations living in the Basin, four variables need to be measured: (a) the total number of deer, (b) the cropping rate, (c) the amount of edible meat per deer, and (d) the energy value per kilogram of edible meat. Application of a density of 13 individuals per square kilometer suggests that maximally 78,000 deer could be expected in the Basin under equilibrium conditions. Of these, about 31,200 would be available for immediate predation, assuming a killing rate of 40% per year. The mean weight for adult white-tailed deer today in the Central Plateau is around 44 kg (Leopold 1959:508). Since only about one-half of this mass is actually consumable as meat, an energy value of 1460 kcal per edible kilogram indicates that each deer was capable of providing 32,000 kilocalories of usable energy (Wu Leung 1961). The total energetic yield from white-tailed deer in the Basin would thus be approximately 998,400,000 kilocalories during any given year, assuming that harvest rates did not exceed replacement rates.

With respect to the energy requirements of the human population, two additional variables must be assigned quantitative values: (a) the total human population residing in the Basin at various time periods, and (b) the per capita energy needs. Population figures are based on estimates obtained from the Basin of Mexico survey, with extrapolations for small sections of the Basin which to date have received little or no intensive survey coverage and for sites which have been affected by post-depositional factors (e.g., erosion and alluviation) or have been obliterated by modern settlement. These estimates rise from a low of 4500 persons during the Early Horizon to a peak of more than 1,000,000 persons by Late Horizon times. Daily energy needs are assumed to be about 2000 kcal per person. This figure is derived from recent studies which demonstrate that the 2000-kcal level is a close approximation of individual subsistence needs for moderately active populations of relatively small stature living in tropical or subtropical semiarid settings (Lee 1969; MacNeish n.d.; Sanders 1976; Santley n.d.). Subsistence needs refer only to that segment of total energy production necessary to provide the daily caloric minima. It does not, however, attempt to take into account surplus production from outside the Basin that was collected as taxes to support local elites or that was funneled into trade, market, or redistributive networks in exchange for nonsubsistence commodities.

TABLE D.1
Dietary Contribution of White-tailed Deer in the Basin of Mexico[a]

Archaeological phase	Human population per phase[b]	Energy needs of human population[c]	Edible kilocalories from deer[d]	Maximum contribution to diet
Early Horizon	4,500	$3,285 \times 10^6$	998.4×10^6	30.4%
First Intermediate One	22,400	$16,352 \times 10^6$	998.4×10^6	6.1%
First Intermediate Two	80,000	$58,400 \times 10^6$	998.4×10^6	1.7%
First Intermediate Three	145,000	$105,850 \times 10^6$	998.4×10^6	0.9%
First Intermediate Four	120,000	$87,600 \times 10^6$	998.4×10^6	1.1%
Middle Horizon	250,000	$182,500 \times 10^6$	998.4×10^6	0.5%
Second Intermediate One	175,000	$127,750 \times 10^6$	998.4×10^6	0.8%
Second Intermediate Two	130,000	$94,900 \times 10^6$	998.4×10^6	1.1%
Late Horizon	1,000,000+	$730,000 \times 10^6$	998.4×10^6	0.1%

[a] Assuming no other competing predator species or increases in deer intensity on fallow agricultural land.
[b] Based on probable levels derived from the Basin of Mexico survey.
[c] Based on a daily energy requirement of 2000 kcal. per person.
[d] Based on an equilibrium level of 31,200 deer (32,000 kcal. edible portion per deer).

Table D.1 summarizes the maximum amount of energy that could be extracted from white-tailed deer by agricultural populations living in the Basin from 1500 b.c. to the time of the Spanish Conquest. These figures do not take into consideration (a) competition from other predator species or (b) increases in deer density on fallow agricultural land. It should be readily apparent that, excepting the Early Horizon, hunted game played a quantitatively insignificant role as a food resource in the Basin of Mexico. A high contribution is theoretically feasible during the Early Horizon, but this is only possible because of the small size of the resident agricultural population. From the First Intermediate One onwards the overall contribution of deer declines dramatically, and by the Middle Horizon it is so small that only 0.5% of all energy needs can be met on a continuing basis. During the Late Horizon, when virtually every part of Central Mexico was densely occupied, white-tailed deer would have at best accounted for 0.1% of the Basin's subsistence requirements.

EFFECTS OF NONHUMAN PREDATORS

Thus far, we have assumed that all potentialy cullable deer were consumed by the human population. In actuality, deer are also subject to losses from other predator species. In Central Mexico two species of carnivore are of paramount import in this regard: mountain lion or puma (*Felis concolor*) and wolf (*Canis lupus*). Both puma and wolf subsist primarily on deer, which may make up as much as 50–90% of the total diet (Leopold 1959: 399–405, 476–482), and as both predators are deer-density dependent, their highest populations should closely parallel optimal deer distributions. Predator–prey studies conducted elsewhere in North America point out that wolves and men are complementary, noncompetitive predators: wolves harvesting predominatly young fawns and older, more vulnerable individuals: the human population culling mainly young adults (Pimlott *et al.* 1969; Smith 1974). Central Mexican hunters appear to have followed a similar pattern, though fawns and pregnant does are sometimes represented in prehistoric faunas (Flannery 1967, 1968).

A major problem is estimating the number of top-level predators present in the Basin during prehispanic times. Today wolf and puma are nearly extinct in Central Mexico, and no faunal surveys have been carried out elsewhere in Mexico to establish carnivore densities. Such studies, however, have been conducted in mixed deciduous forest settings in the eastern U.S.A. In this area 3–6 top-level predators (wolf and puma) have been found to occur every 10 square miles (Shelford 1963: 28). In such a setting, small game—rabbits and assorted rodents—are moderately plentiful, as in the Central Mexican Highlands, so about 100 deer are devoured ". . . by five predators (3 wolves and 2 mountain lions) on ten square miles [Shelford 1963: 29]." In the Basin of Mexico predator remains have been only sporadically reported in faunal samples (McBride 1974: 221–222; White n.d.). The reason for their relative infrequency can be attributed to the fact that the ratio of predators-to-deer ranges from 1:67 to 1:133 in deciduous forest situations (calculated from Shelford 1963: 28). The Basin of Mexico and the eastern U.S.A. deciduous forest biome are both composed primarily of oak and pine, a precocious habitat for white-tailed deer, and in both areas the optimal density for deer is comparable. Moreover, wolf and mountain lion are the principal predators in the two areas, both of which feed mainly on deer. A predator–prey ratio of 1:67–133 is therefore assumed to characterize the prehistoric fauna of the Basin.

Predation by wolves and large cats has great impact on the amount of deer biomass reaching the human population. A predator–prey ratio of 1:67–133 suggests that approximately 587–1164 top-level predators were required to keep the Basin's large herbivore population in check in the equilibrium system. While each carnivore kills only about 20 deer annually, on a Basin-wide basis an average of 17,520 individuals would be lost to nonhuman predator food chains. Thus, of the 31,200 deer that are potentially consumable each year, only about 44% are liable to end up available for human exploitation. This means that the figures presented in Table D.1 should be more than halved if they are to account for losses to other predator species.

Higher consumption levels could have been maintained if all competing predator species were selectively killed. Under such circumstances, the ratio of predators-to-deer found in archaeological contexts should drop appreciably during the period when wolves and large cats were intentionally removed from the landscape. The ratio of predators-to-deer found in pre-Aztec contexts in the Teotihuacan Valley is approximately 1:222, indicating that large cats and wolves were not frequently exploited (White n.d.). Certainly the culling rate for these predator species was less than the pyramid of numbers would suggest. And, as Smith (1974) reports, the wolf–human–deer relationship is largely noncompetitive, so little reason would exist for selective killing, except under very severe hunting pressures. The faunal evidence from the Basin, as a result, does not imply that such management techniques were commonplace in Central Mexico during pre-Late Horizon times.

EFFECTS OF CULTIVATED LAND

Another consideration of major importance is the increase in deer numbers on cultivated land. To calculate this increment we need to know (a) the amount of land under cultivation and in fallow at any one moment in time and (b) the additional number of deer per unit area of agricultural land. Both of these variables are difficult to establish quantitatively, due to the lack of much direct data on pre-Aztec land use patterns and aboriginal deer densities. Comparative studies, however, can provide some useful information if used with caution.

The amount of land under cultivation at various time periods is derived form Sanders' (1976b) study of the agricultural history of the Basin. To determine the total area for agriculture one must measure three variables: (a) the amount of land necessary to sustain the subsistence needs of an average family (the cultivation factor), (b) the amount of land under cultivation necessary to provide for family needs besides direct subsistence requirements, and (c) the cycle of cropping and resting (the land use factor). The cultivation factor varies with the level of agricultural intensification, crop yield, and the percentage of the diet derived from agriculture (Sanders 1976b: 145). Four modes of agricultural production, each progressively more labor demanding, are considered here: bush fallow cultivation in piedmont localities, *humedad* agriculture in areas of high subsurface moisture, permanent irrigation on the alluvial plain, and drainage (or chinampa) cultivation. *Humedad* cultivation and bush fallowing are viewed as the major types of land use practiced in the Basin during the Early Horizon and the First Intermediate One–Three, and these are supplemented first by large-scale irrigation during First Intermediate Four times and then by chinampa agriculture, principally in lakes Chalco and Xochimilco, during the Late Horizon (Parsons 1971; Sanders 1976b). Variations in agricultural yield and in percentage contribution of maize agriculture to the diet have already been accounted for in Sanders' (1976b) study. A listing of the changing value for the cultivation factor appears in Table D.2. These figures are average values derived from the range in modes of cultivation practiced during each phase (Sanders 1976b: 147).

The percentage of land required for nonsubsistence needs refers to that fraction of the cultivation factor needed per family to provide for taxes,

TABLE D.2
Additional White-tailed Deer Expected on Cultivated Land

Archaeological phase	Cultivation factor (in hectares)	Land for other funds [a]	Total land under cultivation per family (in hectares)	Agricultural land, assuming intensive cultivation (in square kilometers) [e]	Agricultural land, assuming extensive cultivation (in square kilometers) [f]	Extra deer due to intensive cultivation	Extra deer due to extensive cultivation
Early Horizon	1.43[a]	10%	1.57	10–20	30–51	130–260	390–663
First Intermediate One	1.20[a]	15%	1.38	44–88	132–221	572– 1,140	1,716– 2,873
First Intermediate Two	1.20[a]	15%	1.38	157–314	471–785	2,041– 4,082	6,123–10,200
First Intermediate Three	0.92[a]	35%	1.24	357–514	771–1,285	3,341– 6,682	10,023–16,705
First Intermediate Four	0.85[b]	50%	1.28	219–439	658–1,097	2,847– 5,707	8,554–14,261
Middle Horizon	0.85[b]	50%	1.28	457–914	1,371–2,286	5,941–11,882	17,823–29,718
Second Intermediate One	0.85[b]	50%	1.28	320–640	960–1,600	4,160– 8,320	12,480–20,800
Second Intermediate Two	0.85[b]	50%	1.28	238–476	714–1190	3,094– 6,188	9,282–15,470
Late Horizon	0.73[c]	50%	1.10	1,571–3,143	4,000–4,000[g]	20,423–40,859	52,000–52,000

[a] Average derived from Sanders' (1976c: 147) estimates for bush fallowing ard *humedad* cultivation based on an average extended family of 7 persons.
[b] Average derived from Sanders' (1976c: 147) estimates for bushing fallowing, *humedad* cultivation, and permanent irrigation agriculture; based on an average extended family of 7 persons.
[c] Average derived from Sanders' (1976c: 147) estimates for bush fallowing, *humedad* cultivation, permanent irrigation agriculture, and chinampa agriculture; based on an average extended family of 7 persons.
[d] Other funds include taxes, ceremonial fund, and replacement fund; percentages refer to percentage of cultivator factor.
[e] All cultivated land under intensive cultivation; land use factor, 1–2.
[f] All cultivated land under more extensive cultivation; land use factor, 3–5.
[g] Maximum of 4000 km² of cultivated land.

replacement and technological funds, and ceremonial obligations. A value of 50% (of the cultivation factor) is considered a close estimate for Late Horizon nonsubsistence needs. A comparable percentage is assumed for the First Intermediate Four and for all succeeding periods: a block of time when complex, socially stratified societies were widespread throughout the Basin. For earlier time periods, when the Basin was occupied by sociopolitical systems organized on less complex levels (i.e., tribes and simple chiefdoms), reduced values have been applied.

With regard to the length of time that land must lie in rest, two alternative fallowing regimes are postulated. In the first (Table D.2, column 5), intensive agricultural exploitation is posited. The land use factor, in this case, varies from 1 to 2; in other words, for every year that a particular parcel is cultivated, it is allowed to rest for 0–1 year. The second cropping cycle (Table D.2, column 6) is for a more extensive agricultural system, where for each year under cultivation the plot is placed in fallow for 2–4 years (land use factor = 3–5). The total amount of land needed per family is a simple multiple of the total area being tilled in any one year and the land use factor.

To estimate the amount of increase in deer numbers on cultivated land is a more difficult matter. Taking the eastern U.S.A. deciduous forest biome for example, deer densities in relatively undisturbed areas range from 100 to 840 individuals per 10 square miles, with 400 considered the optimal figure (Shelford 1963: 28). The 40 per square mile figure, as already mentioned, is the optimal equilibrium level postulated for the Basin. What needs to be explained, however, is why in certain areas numbers per unit area climb to more than twice the optimal level.

In the wild, there are great variations in deer numbers from area to area, and the number of deer composing a particular population appears to be highly fluid, passing through periodic cycles of population increase and decline. Fluctuations in population numbers is clearly related to annual variations in predator numbers, periods of reduced predation enabling deer to recuperate demographically (Leopold 1959: 512, Boughey 1973: 95). Areal variations, on the other hand, stem in part from minor cycling in ecosystem precocity, due mainly to oscillating climatic factors. More importantly, they correlate with microenvironmental variability. The exact mix of floral species composing major biomes is very sensitive to minor perturbations in local topographic, pedalogic, edaphic, and associational characteristics. Biome microvariability also creates transitional zones, commonly referred to as ecotones. Biological productivity in such zones tends to be high, and they offer maximum variation in the availability of plant species (Harris 1969: 9). Higher overall productivity and greater plant diversity affect a larger, more densely packed herbivore population, of which deer, in this case, is the principal representative. The high density of white-tailed deer in certain localities, synecological theory predicts, is a result of the effects of ecotone situations on numbers of game animals per unit area.

The effects of agriculture on ecosystem dynamics may be likened to those generated by ecotone situations. Without artifical enrichment, yields decline on cultivated plots because the nutrient levels required for high agricultural productivity become depleted (Donahue *et al.* 1971: 266). The cultivated plot, then, must stand in fallow for nutrients to be replenished by natural means. During the fallow period, the plot is subject to plant invasion: first by a few pioneering species, then by a set of seral plant communities, each of which improves conditions for the succeeding association, and finally by climax vegetation (Daubenmire 1968: 114–115). The fallow plot, therefore, may be viewed conceptually as an ecotone, since the invading species are perpetually in a state of succession, and succession means that species diversity should be high. Variation in and between fallow plots (i.e., length of fallow) enhances species diversity even further. White-tailed deer thrive in dense brushland and scrubby thickets, two formations which appear very early in successional sequences in Central Mexico (Leopold 1959: 508). Deer flourish in such situations because plant species diversity is high, permitting both browsing during the winter and grazing for seeds, grasses, and forbs during the summer. High species diversity also characterizes ecotone situations in deciduous forests: areas where deer numbers rise to approximately 100% above optimum levels. Since rested tracts are rarely allowed to return to climax vegetation, comparable levels of increase likewise may be expected on fallow agricultural land. It is not being argued that the eastern U.S.A. deciduous forest biome and the Central Mexican pine–oak woodlands are identical ecosystems. To be sure they are not. Rather, what is being contended is that there is a set of governing principles which guide and direct species interrelationships, regardless of time or space. An increase of 100% above optimal densities is thus assumed for all lands cultivated and lying in fallow in the Basin during the prehispanic period.

The extra amount of deer due to agriculture is presented in Table D.2. The level of increase rises from a low of 130–663 individuals during the Early Horizon to a high of 52,000 deer by Late Horizon times. However, a significant percentage of this additional biomass cannot be consumed by the human population because of predation from wolves and large cats. A total of from 13,751 to 22,880 whitetail deer is therefore available for human exploitation (Table D.3). While these numbers appear to be quite substantial at first glance, the total added contribution to the diet is not, since the rate of human population increase far surpasses the total rise in deer biomass. The absolute level of meat intake should drop, in consequence.

EFFECTS OF OVERPREDATION

We may now beg the question of the effects of short-term overkills on deer populations. Table D.4 traces three models of hyperexploitation and replenishment during the Early Horizon. Column 2 presents a trajectory in

TABLE D.3
Number of White-tailed Deer Culled by Humans and Other Predators

Archaeological phase	Total number of deer[b]	Total number of cullable deer[c]	Total number of deer culled by other predators[d]	Total number of deer culled by humans
Early Horizon	78,130–78,663	31,252–31,465	17,501–17,620	13,751–13,845
First Intermediate One	78,572–80,873	31,429–32,349	17,600–18,115	13,829–14,234
First Intermediate Two	80,041–88,205	32,016–35,282	17,929–19,758	14,087–15,524
First Intermediate Three	81,341–94,705	32,536–37,882	18,220–21,214	14,316–16,668
First Intermediate Four	80,847–92,261	32,339–36,904	18,110–20,666	14,229–16,238
Middle Horizon	83,941–107,718	33,576–43,087	18,803–24,129	15,182–18,958
Second Intermediate One	82,160–98,800	32,864–39,520	18,404–22,131	14,460–17,389
Second Intermediate Two	81,094–93,470	32,438–37,388	13,165–20,937	14,273–16,451
Late Horizon	98,423–130,000	39,369–52,000	22,047–29,120	17,322–22,880

[a] Assuming a 100% increase above optimal deer densities on cultivated land.
[b] Assuming a 1–5 range in the land use factor (see Table D.2).
[c] Based on a maximum cropping rate of 40% per year.
[d] Assuming that 56% of all cullable deer are cropped by nonhuman predators.

TABLE D.4
Postulated Rates of Decimation and Replacement for White-tailed Deer during the Early Horizon in the Basin of Mexico

	Decimation rate[a]			Replacement rate[b]		
				Base population of deer		
Year	14.5% of diet	18.5% of diet	23.5% of diet	1000	5000	10,000
1	78,663	78,663	78,663	1,000	5,000	10,000
2	76,953	70,087	61,532	1,400	7,000	14,000
3	74,103	55,793	32,980	1,960	9,800	19,600
4	69,353	31,970	00,000	2,744	13,720	27,440
5	61,437	00,000			19,208	38,420
6	48,243			5,379	26,891	53,790
7	26,253			7,531	37,647	75,310
8	00,000			8,320	52,706	78,663
9				11,648	73,788	
10				16,307	78,663	
11				22,830		
12				31,962		
13				44,747		
14				62,646		
15				78,663		

[a] Assuming that 56% of all cullable deer are cropped by nonhuman predators.
[b] Assuming no cropping by nonhuman predators.

which deer provide 14.5% of the diet (i.e., 1% above the equilibrium level) and where the annual growth rate for whitetail deer is about 40%. In column 3 the model assumes that deer accounted for 18.5% of the diet (i.e., 5% more than the equilibrium system can replace at a rate of 40% per year). The third model (column 4) assumes that deer provided 23.5% of all energy consumed and that the rate of replenishment was around 40%. Columns 5, 6, and 7 plot the length of time that three decimated deer populations need to return to optimal levels in a area roughly 7000 km^2 in extent. All three simulations demonstrate that even with a modest amount of overkill deer populations diminish rapidly. If the consumption rate of meat is constant, it takes only 4–8 years to remove the entire deer population, the most extreme rate being the 23.5% consumption level. Columns 5–7, however, illustrate the astonishing fact that optimal levels can be restored very quickly, if predation by carnivores is minimal.

Recent biological ecological studies have observed that there is a direct relationship between the density of prey species and the frequency of predation in some predator–prey systems (Boughey 1973: 95). In many interspecific cases, the rate of predation is prey-density dependent. But in situations where overkills have dramatically reduced the prey density, a phenomenon known as prey switching comes into play. Here, rather than exploiting the decimated species, predators increasingly rely on other more abundant prey until the density of the original prey species has returned to its former high level. In energetic terms, therefore, switching behavior occurs because of the rising costs of procurement.

We may conclude that on a short-term basis deer could have accounted for more than 13.5% and perhaps as much as 23.5% of all dietary needs during the Early Horizon. Diminishing returns would have acted as an effective stimulus for brief periods of increased reliance on alternative sources of animal protein (e.g., cottontail rabbit or waterfowl). Switching thus functions as the regulatory mechanism by which overexploited prey populations recuperate demographically. It must be emphasized, however, that such levels of increased consumption are at best very momentary and must be balanced by decreased consumption for at least equivalent lengths of time if optimal density levels are to be restored. Moreover, overpredation is only feasible when the size of the predator population is relatively small. For populations of the magnitude present in the Basin from First Intermediate Three times onward, overexploitation, even to a modest degree, would result quickly in the wholesale elimination of white-tailed deer as a food resource. Since as late as the Middle Horizon deer still accounted for a significant percentage of all meat consumed (Starbuck 1975: 91), overpredation does not appear to have had a major long-term impact on prey densities. Nonetheless, there is a slight reduction in overall consumption (14% of all meat consumed), suggesting that overkills had reduced deer numbers drastically in the immediate vicinity of Teotihuacan.

LEVELS OF PREHISPANIC MEAT CONSUMPTION

Estimation of prehispanic meat consumption levels in the Basin of Mexico may now be undertaken. The results, presented in Table D.5, imply the following. During the Aceramic period (ca. 7000–1800 B.C.) human population densities were low (about 0.5–1.0 persons per square kilometer), so meat could have accounted for perhaps 15–20% of all energy consumed on an annual basis. By Early Horizon times (ca. 1500–1150 B.C.) the shift to an agricultural economy, with its commensurate population increase, began pushing consumption levels near carrying capacity limits, thereby greatly exacerbating the danger of overkills if hunting remained at Aceramic levels. Beginning during the First Intermediate One (ca. 1150–650 B.C.) rapid population growth, coupled perhaps with some harvesting in excess of reproductive rates, resulted in a significant decline in meat consumption, and by Phase Two times (ca. 650–300 B.C.) probable levels of dietary intake dropped below 1% for the first time. Tolstoy *et al.* (1977: 99–101), using independent data from excavation, come to a similar conclusion. Not only does the contribution of deer decline by a factor of 2.5, but also mud turtle and waterfowl drop by significant margins. The total amount of animal bone in the Tolstoy samples decreases roughly five-fold, and this stands in marked agreement with our postulated drop of from 13.5% to 2.8% during the Early Horizon and the First Intermediate Phase One. Both studies clearly indicate major declines in hunting levels during the overall Early Horizon–First Intermediate One period, therefore.

Some increase in the number of deer would be expected on cultivated land, but this added increment was not of much consequence, especially when viewed in terms of the magnitude of population increase by First Intermediate Three times (ca. 300–100 B.C.). Prey switching, both by the

TABLE D.5
Dietary Contribution of White-tailed Deer in the Basin of Mexico[a]

Archaeological phase	Human population per phase	Energy needs of human population	Edible kilocalories from deer	Maximum contribution to diet
Early Horizon	4,500	$3,285 \times 10^6$	$440.0–443.0 \times 10^6$	13.4–13.5%
First Intermediate One	22,400	$16,352 \times 10^6$	$442.5–455.5 \times 10^6$	2.7–2.8%
First Intermediate Two	80,000	$58,400 \times 10^6$	$450.8–496.8 \times 10^6$	0.8–0.9%
First Intermediate Three	145,000	$105,850 \times 10^6$	$458.1–533.4 \times 10^6$	0.4–0.5%
First Intermediate Four	120,000	$87,600 \times 10^6$	$455.3–519.6 \times 10^6$	0.5–0.6%
Middle Horizon	250,000	$182,500 \times 10^6$	$485.8–606.7 \times 10^6$	0.3–0.3%
Second Intermediate One	175,000	$127,750 \times 10^6$	$462.7–556.4 \times 10^6$	0.4–0.4%
Second Intermediate Two	130,000	$94,900 \times 10^6$	$456.7–526.4 \times 10^6$	0.5–0.6%
Late Horizon	1,000,000+	$730,000 \times 10^6$	$555.3–732.2 \times 10^6$	<0.1–0.1%

[a] Assuming complementary predation by nonhuman predators and a 100% increase above optimal deer densities on cultivated land.

human population and by other predators, could have relieved this situation somewhat by allowing decimated deer populations to return to density-dependent levels, but at best this solution was short-term. By the Middle Horizon (ca. A.D. 300–750) there was a marked drop (from 94 to 80%) in the amount of deer consumed in terms of all other edible faunal resources (Starbuck 1975:91). More than likely, this was because overkills had become so acute in the vicinity of Teotihuacan that hunting in this area was no longer an efficient subsistence strategy. Consumption levels thereafter remained below 1%.

IMPLICATIONS FOR OTHER STUDIES

The problem posed by this Appendix is the estimation of the amount that meat (particularly deer) could have contributed to the precolumbian diet. Although prehistoric faunal remains are commonly cited in the literature, few investigators have attempted to delimit prehispanic consumption levels. Virtually the only complete study is MacNeish's comprehensive reconstruction of changing subsistence patterns in the Tehuacan Valley, on the border between the modern states of Puebla and Oaxaca. In the Tehuacan Valley MacNeish (1967: 298) suggests that the percentage of meat consumption in the diet decreased through time as follows: 60% (7000–5000 B.C.), 34% (5000–3400 B.C.), 30% (3400–2300 B.C.), 27% (1500–850 B.C.), 25% (850–150 B.C.), 18% (150 B.C.–A.D. 700), and 17% (A.D. 700–1519). These calculations are based on the straightforward comparison of liters per consumable resource, the floral products being further corrected by a preservation factor (MacNeish 1967: 299). This method, which attempts to compare liters of edible meat with liters of agricultural or gathered foodstuffs, has serious shortcomings.

Most importantly, it does not take into account plant food products not channeled into the human population. For example, all edible seeds (in particular grains) found on an occupation floor must be construed as resources that were lost sometime during the food preparation–storage process. They *do not* represent food products that were physically consumed by the human population, or they would not have been found on the living surface in the first place. Scattered data from contemporary rural agricultural populations in Mesoamerica indicate that approximately 10% of all grain harvested in any given year will be lost to nonhuman food chains (Steggerda 1941). What this suggests, therefore, is that any calculation of the amount of edible seeds associated with any prehistoric living surface must be raised at least 10 times that amount observed in the field if the volume estimates are to be considered representative. A consideration of the variable effects of preservation may then be made, and, as MacNeish (1967: Tables 37–38) notes, this value may be as high as 50. This problem does not directly pertain to the number of animal bones found in archaeological contexts, so the edible weights per game animal still remain a good indicator of type of meat consumption. It does, however, have a tremendous effect on the bulk percentage of all meat consumed, since grains and other edible seeds would contribute much more volume to the diet. The volume percentages of meat consumption suggested by MacNeish should therefore be lowered, perhaps considerably, if they are to genuinely reflect probable levels of dietary intake.

More recent is Starbuck's (1975) study of man–animal relationships in precolumbian Central Mexico. This study, primarily derived from data collected by the Teotihuacan Mapping Project, deals with changing patterns of animal exploitation in the Basin of Mexico during the First Intermediate Three–Middle Horizon phases. It has as its major working hypothesis ". . . that: (1) even if irrigation agriculture was practiced, it was probably only at a small scale and was not the sole subsistence base for the Classic city, as is normally implied; in which case; (2) the Classic Teotihuacanos would more logically have been forced to rely upon a broad spectrum base of both wild and domesticated plant and animal resources, developing specialized adaptations which permitted them to greatly increase their food supply as the city's population grew [Starbuck 1975: 3]." Starbuck then proposes that although wild food resources may not have been the major source of foodstuffs, hunted and gathered products certainly provided an important secondary component to Teotihuacan's subsistence system. Following this, he postulates that most hunting was performed either by specialized hunters residing at Teotihuacan or by agriculturalists who rescheduled their subsistence activity for hunting primarily during the late fall and winter months (Starbuck 1975: 101–102).

In order to test Starbuck's hypothesis that hunted game animals ". . . served as essential supplements to a highly variable and uncertain diet of domesticated plant staples [1975: 24]," it is necessary to examine the level of meat consumption in terms of the total diet. Inspection of Table D.5 indicates that at most white-tailed deer could have provided 0.3% of all energy consumed on an annual basis during the Middle Horizon. In fact, at no point in Teotihuacan's history (from the First Intermediate Two to the Late Horizon) could deer flesh have contributed more than 0.9% of all yearly subsistence requirements. And if we assume that nonhuman predators were in fact deliberately eliminated at some point early in the history of the Basin, then levels of dietary intake could conceivably have been double those forecasted in Table D.5 (e.g., from 0.3% to 0.6% during the Middle Horizon). Inclusion of small hunted game (i.e., rabbits, rodents, waterfowl, etc.) might raise the Middle Horizon figure to perhaps 1%. Clearly, *meat was a scarce resource* throughout the history of Teotihuacan. The hypothesis that hunted game was an important secondary component in Teotihuacan's subsistence system is wholly untenable in energetic terms.

The hunting levels offered by MacNeish for the Tehuacan Valley are also greatly at odds with the maximum levels of dietary intake suggested in Table D.5. We have already noted that the bulk estimates used in calculating the

Tehuacan percentages are suspect, since food products not routed for human consumption have not been taken into consideration. Our figures support the assertion that the Tehuacan percentages should be reduced substantially, at least from Santa Maria times onwards. Calculation of the exact amount of reduction will not be attempted here, though comparability with the hunting levels suggested above does not seem an unreasonable guess.

CONCLUDING REMARKS

The model put forth here strongly suggests that population, as early as the First Intermediate Phase One, was already dense enough to put heavy pressures on the wild fauna of the Basin. Succeeding population growth would have caused a steady reduction in the total dietary contribution of hunting in the Basin of Mexico. Hunting is nutritionally advantageous because meat is protein-rich; for deer, 29.5 gm of protein may be obtained from each 100 gm edible portion (Wu Leung 1961). This explains its persistence during late periods when the contribution of hunting to the diet of the population was minimal. Maize is also high in protein but deficient in certain amino acids, particularly lysine (Kaplan 1967: 202). For moderately active populations in Latin America the average daily protein requirement is approximately 40–50 gm per person (Gross 1975: 543). Assuming that maize made up 75% of all energy consumed throughout the year, at least 12 gm per person per day would have to be procured from other sources. In order to have a diet that fulfills the minimum protein, only 3–4% of all energy consumed would have to have requirements from hunted game. If half of this total was furnished by beans, another cultigen high in protein, hunting levels which provided only 1–2% of the total energy requirement could have been tolerated on a continuing basis.

Problems, however, would occur when hunting levels dropped below 1% during the First Intermediate Two, certainly by Phase Three times. The most obvious solution would have been increased reliance on alternative sources of protein, beans and domestic animals in particular, to bank against the diminishing role of hunted game. Interestingly enough, this is precisely what the subsistence data for Central Mexico suggest. Beans appear quite early in the Tehuacan sequence (Coxcatlan Phase), but it is only by Palo Blanco times (First Intermediate Four and Middle Horizon) that they begin being recovered archaeologically in substantial numbers (MacNeish 1967: Table 38). Domestic dog and turkey, virtually absent in the Basin of Mexico during the Early Horizon and First Intermediate One–Three, also appear abruptly during the First Intermediate Four–Five and Middle Horizon. It is tempting, indeed, to view these dietary shifts as the direct result of significant declines in hunting levels.

The major conclusion of this appendix is that the role of hunting in prehispanic Central Mexico has been greatly exaggerated. The hunting levels suggested above stand in sharp contrast with those commonly cited in the literature; for sure, they do not bear out the assertion that hunting was an important secondary component in Teotihuacan's subsistence system. The figures utilized in the model are in many ways hypothetical, since direct data from the Basin are frequently lacking. However, it is their order of magnitude that is important; deer densities three to four times higher than those postulated above would make little difference as far as absolute levels of consumption are concerned. As a result, not only are the theoretical maxima low, but when other predators are introduced into the model, the amount of energy being channeled for human consumption becomes minor indeed. Thus, while estimates as high as 15–40% are acceptable for societies practicing hunting and gathering, they appear to be unwarranted for agricultural populations of the size present in the Basin of Mexico from the First Intermediate Period onwards.

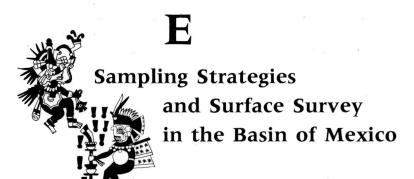

E
Sampling Strategies
and Surface Survey
in the Basin of Mexico

Probability sampling has been recognized in recent years as a useful tool for selecting units of investigation and for generalizing to larger units of analysis (Mueller 1975:ix). Archaeologists sample frequently because they have neither the time nor the funds to completely study a site or region. The degree of confidence to be placed in such inferences can be evaluated by objective tests which measure sampling efficiency (Mueller 1974; Plog 1976). Estimation of sample predictability, however, is contingent upon having available a target population to which the sampled population can be compared.

The Basin of Mexico is an ideal area to test the ability of various sampling strategies to predict certain settlement characteristics. First, the area has been intensively surveyed, and the recovered settlement data have been organized into a hierarchy of site types, many of which have behavioral significance. Second, preservation at the time of the surveys was relatively good, so we are reasonably sure that our inventory of prehistoric sites is complete. Negative data (i.e., the absence of sites) can thus be weighed and interpreted in meaningful ways. Finally, major environmental parameters affecting settlement distribution in the Basin are fairly well conceived, making stratification of the landscape into a number of natural zones a relatively straightforward matter.

To evaluate the predictability of various sampling strategies using data from the entire Basin of Mexico survey would be a major undertaking in itself; one clearly beyond the scope of this appendix. Consequently, data from only one section of the Basin, the Cuautitlan region, are considered here. Moreover, the settlement data are restricted to one archaeological phase, the Middle Horizon. Predictability is evaluated in terms of the ability of each sampling technique to adequately measure the following five variables: (*a*) total number of sites, (*b*) percentage of distribution of sites by settlement type, (*c*) total population size, (*d*) percentage of distribution of population by settlement type, and (*e*) general settlement pattern. These are variables we have considered at length in preceding chapters. Presumably also, they are variables to which the sample data should have bearing. The most successful sampling technique, therefore, is simply the one which provides the most accurate and precise estimation of the greatest number of variables.

The sampling procedures used in this study in no way constitute the only designs that could have been applied. The utility of numerous other techniques could have been explored, but because of the time limitations at this writing, a more in-depth consideration has not been attempted. The experimental results which follow, and the guidelines suggested from them, must be considered as most tentative, not established fact. Hence, their major value is heuristic, serving as hypotheses for further inquiry. A comprehensive reappraisal of the results presented in this appendix, this time using data from the entire Basin, is planned for the near future.

SAMPLING DESIGNS

Two different types of sampling designs are applied in this study: (*a*) simple random sampling, and (*b*) stratified sampling. Definitions of these designs abound in the literature (Haggett 1965; Taylor 1977), so only a few brief comments will be made here. In *simple random sampling* the study area is divided into a set of units of equivalent size, and the units are numbered consecutively. A set of random numbers is then drawn arbitrarily from prepared lists, and the unit ". . .whose number coincides with the chosen random number is selected for the sample [Taylor 1977:74]." The number of units to be selected varies with the sampling fraction. The basic property of random sampling is independence of unit selection. Thus, the fact that one unit has been selected has no effect on the selection of any other unit (Taylor 1977:74).

"In *stratified sampling* the study area is divided into segments (such as cropland and woodland) and the individuals in the sample are drawn independently from each segment [Haggett 1965:195]." Within each stratum units are selected using the same randomization procedure as in simple random sampling. The number of units selected within each segment is proportional to total stratum size. This insures that ". . .the strata sampling fractions approach equality [Mueller 1974:34]." The sampling fractions within each segment may also be unequal. Such a disproportional stratified sampling scheme has not been applied here.

Three methods were used to divide the study area into sampling units. In the first, the survey region was gridded into units of equal size called *square quadrats* (see Figure E.1). Two different square sizes were selected. The smaller units were 1.0 km on a side, the larger 2.0 km on a side. These have been termed small square quadrats and large square quadrats, respectively. The second type of sampling unit involved *rectangular quadrats*. Unit size again varied; small rectangular quadrats measured 1.0 by 4.0 km, large rectangular quadrats 2.0 by 8.0 km. Transects, each 1.0 km wide, were the third type of sampling unit. No attempt was made to apply transecting units of variable size; however, transect orientation (i.e., north–south, east–west) was changed to investigate the effect of unit alignment on sample predictability. Transect orientation paralleled the grid established for small square quadrats. The long axis of rectangular quadrats was aligned east–west. The size of all sampling units was chosen arbitrarily. Both sampling designs employed small and large quadrat units. Transect sampling, on the other hand, only used the simple random design, since topographic variability made accommodation of major environmental zones to the transect sampling grid exceedingly difficult.

For samples using the simple random design, the study area was divided into units, and each unit was assigned a number running from west to east (left to right) and from north to south (top to bottom). Transects were allotted numbers either from left to right (in the case of north–south orientation) or from top to bottom (in the case of east–west orientation). The appropriate number of sampling units was then selected from a random number table. The sampling fraction for all random designs was 20%. Each sampling strategy was run 10 times.

For all samples using the stratified design, the study area was first split into major environmental zones: in this instance, the lakebed–lakeshore, the alluvial plain, and the piedmont–sierra. Stratification criteria were derived from the major environmental–topographic parameters discussed in Chapter 4. Units from each stratum were then selected using the same procedure already described for simple random sampling. The number of units chosen from each stratum was set equal to the sampling fraction (20%) whenever possible. Due to variations in the actual number of units within each stratum, sampling intensity varied somewhat: from 18% to 22%. Also, a number of sampling units bisected two strata. In these cases, stratum designation was based on which environmental zone accounted for more than one-half of the area within the unit. A few times the sampling unit crosscut all three major environmental strata. Here, areal preponderance formed the basis for stratum assignment.

To classify sites, the settlement typology described in Chapter 3 was used. Two modifications were introduced, however, to correct for levels in the settlement hierarchy that contained few sites. The dispersed village–nucleated village dichotomy, a basis for measuring population density, was discarded. As only two dispersed villages (one large, one small) occurred

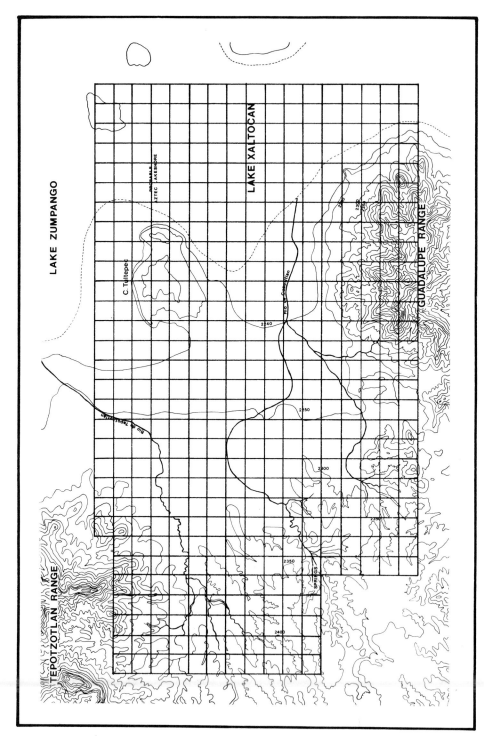

Figure E.1. The Cuautitlan region showing the superimposed sampling grid.

within the survey area, the chances that such sites would be found at a 20% level of sampling intensity appeared not great. Likewise, all provincial centers and large villages were considered as representing a single settlement type. The fact that most of these sites had populations numbering 800–1200 persons seemed to justify this view. Thus, the community typology used here employed a three-tiered hierarchy: provincial centers–large villages, small villages, and hamlets.

Finally, sometimes only parts of sites occurred within the sampling units. Unit borders, in other words, occasionally did divide sites in half. This was a particularly annoying problem, for if we were to adhere strictly to the sampling program, such sites, and these were frequently large communities, would be misclassified, both in terms of population and in terms of settlement type. Moreover, site tallies would be inflated, since neighboring sampling units could conceivably capture parts of the same site. As a result, it was decided that all sites affected by bisection by unit borders would be totally surveyed. This procedure introduced a certain level of error into the experiment, especially in terms of estimating absolute population size. At the same time, however, it greatly facilitated comparisons using settlement type distributions and proved to be a more sensitive indicator of total site number. The benefits derived from use of this procedure, it would appear, outweighed the drawbacks.

TESTS FOR SAMPLE PREDICTABILITY

The purpose of statistical generalizations is to say something about various characteristics of the population being studied on the basis of known facts about a sample drawn from that population or universe. The population or universe is the aggregate to which most research is directed. Samples of that population are generally selected as a matter of convenience. One's objective, therefore, is to make ". . . inferences about various population parameters on the basis of known, but intrinsically unimportant, sample statistics [Blalock 1972:110]."

In this study, predictability is defined as the ability to consistently measure a variable within specified statistically bounded limits. For adequate determination both accuracy and precision must be considered. Following Plog (1976:140) accuracy is defined ". . . as the difference between the mean of the distribution of sample estimates and the true population mean." Precision, on the other hand, refers to ". . . the squared standard error of the mean of a distribution of sample estimates obtained by repeated applications of a sampling procedure to a group of data [Plog 1976:140]." An accurate technique, then, yields a set of estimates whose mean approaches the target value. A precise sampling scheme, however, repeatedly generates estimates whose degree of dispersion does not differ significantly from expected value or population. For a technique to be highly predictive then, it must consistently have both a high accuracy and precision rating.

To determine whether or not the mean frequencies obtained empirically from the sampling programs differed significantly from values obtained from the complete survey, two statistical techniques were applied. For two variables, total population size and total number of sites, chi-square (χ^2) was used. The chi-square statistic was computed using the formula

$$(\chi)^2 = \sum \frac{(O_i - E_i)^2}{E_i}$$

where Σ is summation, o_i is the mean observed frequency (derived from the sampling programs), and E_i is the expected frequency (derived from the complete survey). Statistical significance was ascertained by comparing the calculated values of χ^2 with the critical value of χ^2 in a chi-square table. If the calculated value of χ^2 at a particular confidence level (in this case, 0.05) exceeded the critical value, then the amount of difference between the mean sample estimate and the target value could be expected by chance only 5 times out of 100. Hence, the null hypotheses, that there is no difference between the value of the sample and target data, would be rejected. If, on the other hand, the calculated value did not exceed the critical value, then the null hypothesis would be accepted.

To evaluate the distribution of population and site number by settlement type, the Kolmogorov–Smirnov test was used. K–S is a very useful test when the data being examined have been divided into a number of ordered categories. The basic principle behind the K–S test is as follows:

> If the null hypothesis that independent random samples have been drawn from identical populations is correct, then we would expect the cumulative frequency distributions for the two samples to be essentially similar. The test statistic used in the Kolmogorov-Smirnov test is the maximum difference between the two cumulative distributions. If the maximum difference is larger than would be expected by chance under the null hypothesis, this means that the gap between the distributions has become so large that we decide to reject the hypothesis. We can take either the maximum difference in one direction only (if direction has been predicted) or the maximum difference in both directions [Blalock 1972:262–263].

In this study direction has not been predicted, so the test applied is two-tailed.

To apply the K–S test, two values of D, the test statistic, must be computed. Calculated D was obtained by first summing the class percentages cumulatively for each sample (in this case, the average sample and the target distributions). The amount of difference between the percentages within each class was then determined, the largest value regardless of sign being the calculated D. The ordered classes were settlement type categories: provincial centers—large villages, small villages, and hamlets. Critical D, at the 0.05 level, was derived using the formula:

$$\text{Critical } D = 1.36 \sqrt{\frac{n_1 + n_2}{n_1 n_2}}$$

where n_1 is the frequency of the target population and n_2 is the frequency extrapolated from the sample population. If the value of calculated D was at least as large as critical D, then the null hypothesis that there was no significant difference in the population distributions could be rejected. Otherwise, it could not, at least at the 0.05 level. To establish whether or not the level of difference between the sampled and target populations is statistically significant is not to say which technique is the most predictive. To answer this additional tests must be performed. Determining variance and standard error is a convenient way to address this problem.

In this study, variances and standard deviations were calculated for each variable (except settlement pattern). Variance ($Var(x)$) was determined using the formula

$$\text{Var } (x) = \frac{\Sigma (x_i - \bar{x})^2}{n}$$

where Σ is summation, x_i the sample value, $\bar{x}$ is the sample mean, and n is the number of cases. Standard deviation (σ), a measure of the amount of dispersion about the sample mean, involved taking the square root of the variance. Thus, sampling techniques displaying low standard deviations, if the one-sigma range contained the target value, were weighed highly in a predictive sense, while those having a relatively large range of dispersion, even if the one-sigma deviation included the expected value, were predictably of lesser import.

When a number of sampling techniques appeared to be accurate predictors, the F-test was used as the basis for evaluating precision. The F-test is a way of assessing precision by determining whether or not the squared standard errors of the two samples approach equality. If they do, then both techniques would appear to be equally precise predictors of the variable in question. But if the F-value is statistically significant, then the technique yielding the lowest squared standard error would have the highest precision rating. Estimation of standard error involved dividing the standard deviations by the square root of the sample size. The F-value was then computed using the formula

$$F = (S_1)^2/(S_2)^2$$

where S_1 is the standard error of the first sample and S_2 is the standard error of the second sample.

Determination of settlement pattern was based on visual inspection. All sites found using a particular sampling program were plotted on a map and the resultant distribution compared with that generated from the complete survey. If a technique consistently yielded a pattern that conformed generally to the expected settlement pattern, then the technique was assumed to be predictive. But, if the results were greatly at odds with the expected pattern or varied greatly from run to run, the sampling technique was assumed to be inadequate.

In assessing four variables, total population, total number of sites, distribution of population by settlement type, and distribution of sites by settlement type, the basic testing procedure was to use either the chi-square statistic or the Kolmogorov–Smirnov test to determine whether the mean estimates generated by each sampling program differed significantly from the target data produced by the complete survey. Standard deviation was used to determine the amount of dispersion about the sample mean and whether or not the range evinced by each sampling program captured the desired target value. When a number of techniques appeared to be "predictive," the F-test was applied to evaluate sampling precision. Appraisal of a fifth variable, settlement pattern, was based on direct visual comparison of the sampled and complete site distributions. The technique that best predicted the greatest number of different variables was considered to be the best sampling program.

THE STUDY AREA

The Cuautitlan region is located in the west–central portion of the Basin of Mexico. To the north and east the region is bounded by Lakes Zumpango and Xaltocan, to the south by the Guadalupe Range, and to the west by the high mountain massif of the Sierra de las Cruces. Environmentally, the region has been split into a number of different zones. The central part of the region is defined by an extensive, deep-soil alluvial plain that is bisected by two major perennial stream flows, Rios Cuautitlan and Tepotzotlan. To the north and east the plain abuts Lake Zumpango–Xaltocan. To the south and west are zones of sloping terrain that we have termed the piedmont and sierra. In the Guadalupe Range these zones extend east–west, but in the Sierra de las Cruces, a general north–south orientation is indicated. The eastern boundary of the Las Cruces piedmont is quite distinctive, consisting of several long, low ridges that extend out into the alluvial plain. In the north is Cerro Tultepec, a broad, gently sloping volcanic dome. Average annual precipitation today is about 700 mm. Rainfall, however, increases steadily on an east–west gradient.

In 1973–1974, systematic surface survey was carried out by members of the Basin of Mexico project. The results of this survey produced a listing of more than 900 spatially isolatable communities spanning the prehispanic period from the Early Horizon Phase Two onwards (Parsons 1973; Santley 1977; Sanders and Santley n.d.). A site hierarchy, from individual family homesteads to provincial centers with civic–ceremonial architecture, only becomes well established by Middle Horizon times, the period under consideration here. This pattern continues virtually unchanged to Late Horizon times.

Thirty-eight Middle Horizon sites, representing a population estimated at 11,598 persons, occur in the Cuautitlan region (see Figure E.2). In terms of classification by settlement type, 23.6% of all sites are provincial centers–large villages, 26.3% are small villages, and 50.0% are hamlets. Population, on the other hand, is weighted toward the top of the settlement hierarchy: 78.7% residing in provincial centers–large villages, 16.4% occupying small villages, and 4.9% inhabiting hamlets. These two variables, the distribution of site numbers and population, appear to be inversely related phenomena. That is to say that as the percentage of sites found in each level of the settlement hierarchy increases, there is a decrease in total population represented by those sites. In the Cuautitlan region the vast majority of the Teotihuacan period occupation thus resides in a few key sites. To miss or overrepresent these important sites would greatly skew any reconstruction of prehispanic settlement patterns during Middle Horizon times.

The Middle Horizon settlement pattern in the Cuautitlan region may be described as follows. Prehispanic communities, especially large sites, are consistently oriented to alluvial areas. On the north slopes of the Guadalupe Range, sites are typically situated at the base of the lower piedmont where they occur as an almost continuous band from Chilpan (near the modern Mexico City–Queretaro Cuota Highway) to Coacalco. Centers, with evidence of both civic and ceremonial architecture, are interdigited with both large and small villages and hamlets. From Coacalco to Ecatepec very few permanent residential sites occur. At Ecatepec, however, there is a large provincial center, containing minimally several large Teotihuacan-style apartment compounds; a number of smaller, less conspicuous occupations are also situated in the immediate vicinity. Along Rios Cuautitlan and Tepotzotlan, large substantial sites occur at regular intervals. Middle Horizon settlement in the Las Cruces piedmont has a more dispersed character, and the size of most sites is considerably smaller. With the exception of Ecatepec and its outlying barrios, few lakeshore sites have been found. A large site, in this case a provincial center, is also situated atop Cerro Tultepec.

RESULTS

An evaluation of sample predictability may now be undertaken. In the sections that follow each of the variables discussed above is treated singularly. An assessment of the ability of various sampling strategies to measure multiple variables appears in the concluding section.

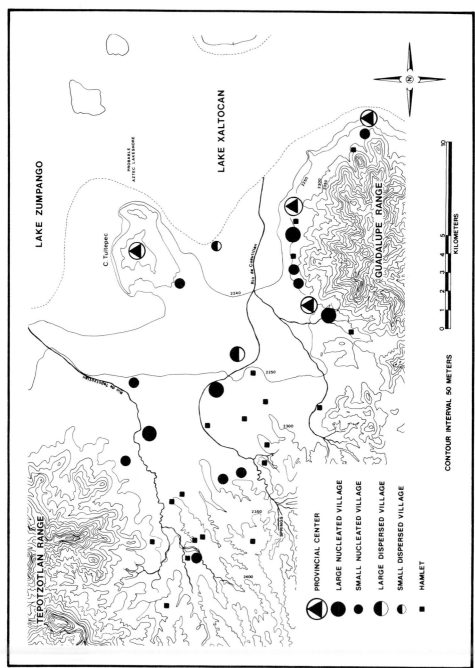

Figure E.2.   The Cuautitlan region showing Middle Horizon settlements.

Total Population Size

The results presented in Table E.1 indicate that *no sampling technique consistently provides a precise estimate of total population size.* Although high levels of accuracy are sometimes encountered, the amount of dispersion about the sample mean is consistently very great (see Figure E.3), producing substantial standard deviations. To a large part, this pronounced inability to adequately measure population size is attributed to the fact that the Middle Horizon occupation is nucleated on a few large sites. As already mentioned, to over- or undersample these important sites enhances sample aberrancy. Random designs, it appears, generally underrepresent all sites, resulting in lower mean estimates, while stratified designs repeatedly indicate greater numbers of large sites. The sampling techniques employed in this study, one might argue, are best suited for populations that reside in a great number of small communities (e.g., during the Second Intermediate Two or Late Horizon). For all time periods marked by a high incidence of population agglomeration, the use of simple random and stratified sampling procedures is not recommended. A stratified systematic unaligned design, at a 20% level of sampling intensity, might yield better results in this regard.

TABLE E.1
Sample Data for Total Population Size

Sampling technique	Mean	Variance	Standard deviation	Chi-square	Null hypothesis[a]
Simple random, small square quadrats	11,172	47,012,380	6,856.6	19,534.8	S
Simple random, large square quadrats	9,944	32,121,536	8,015.2	15,029.6	S
Simple random, small rectangular quadrats	9,748	14,104,176	5,311.2	7,554.7	S
Simple random, large rectangular quadrats	15,042	38,139,050	8,733.7	21,554.4	S
Simple random, east– west transects	11,448	10,188,921	4,514.2	1,877.2	S
Simple random, north– south transects	10,576	30,560,790	7,818.0	13,625.9	S
Simple stratified, small square quadrats	14,880	25,234,685	7,104.2	15,520.4	S
Simple stratified, large square quadrats	11,852	37,478,266	8,657.7	16,185.0	S
Simple stratified, small rectangular quadrats	14,680	89,448,927	13,375.3	42,661.5	S
Simple stratified, large rectangular quadrats	15,204	16,986,967	5,828.7	12,926.6	S

[a] S indicates that the null hypothesis may be rejected; the difference between the sampled and target data is statistically significant at the 0.05 level.

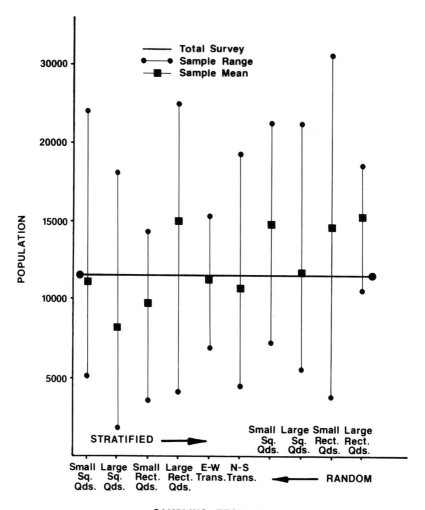

Figure E.3. Sample data for total population size.

Total Number of Sites

Table E.2 suggests that *a number of different sampling strategies are accurate predictors of total site number.* If proximity of the sample mean to the target value, in conjunction with standard deviation, is used as a guide, simple random, small rectangular quadrat sampling is the most accurate technique, followed by (*a*) simple random, east–west transect sampling, (*b*) simple random, large square quadrat sampling, (*c*) simple random, north–south transect sampling, and (4) simple stratified small square quadrat sampling (see Figure E.4). Samples using the random design (in four out of six cases) are clearly the most accurate. Stratified sampling, interestingly, is not a

TABLE E.2
Sample Data for Total Number of Sites

Sampling technique	Mean	Variance	Standard deviation	Chi-square	Null hypothesis[a]
Simple random, small square quadrats	28.8	213.8	14.6	39.3	S
Simple random, large square quadrats	36.0	36.0	6.0	4.8	NS
Simple random, small rectangular quadrats	35.2	73.6	8.6	9.0	NS
Simple random, large rectangular quadrats	44.0	140.8	11.9	23.3	S
Simple random, east–west transects	36.8	34.6	5.9	4.8	NS
Simple random, north–south transects	35.2	28.2	5.3	4.8	NS
Simple stratified, small square quadrats	32.0	25.6	5.1	8.1	NS
Simple stratified, large square quadrats	28.8	53.8	7.3	18.2	S
Simple stratified, small rectangular quadrats	33.6	266.2	16.3	37.6	S
Simple stratified, large rectangular quadrats	53.6	221.4	14.9	48.0	S

[a] S indicates that the null hypothesis may be rejected; the difference between the sampled and target data is statistically significant at the 0.05 level. NS indicates that the null hypothesis cannot be rejected at the 0.05 level.

particularly accurate design for estimating total site number, except for the technique using small square quadrats.

With the exception of one instance, F-test values for all possible pairs of accurate strategies are not statistically significant. Statistically significant F-values are obtained only when simple random, small rectangular quadrat sampling is compared with the other "accurate" schemes, indicating that there is loss in sampling precision when a technique utilizing small rectangular units selected randomly is applied. This particular procedure, one might conclude, is the least precise predictor of total site number. For the remainder, the amount of difference is not significant, suggesting that each is an equally precise indicator of total site number.

When individual procedures are merged by sampling design, transect sampling is clearly the only predictive strategy; both random quadrat and stratified quadrat sampling do not appear to be overly precise. Moreover, when quadrat size is used as the basis for comparison, a significant gain in sampling precision is evident when units of intermediate size (i.e., 4 km²) are used. Thus, *the most predictive design appears to be one using transects, the*

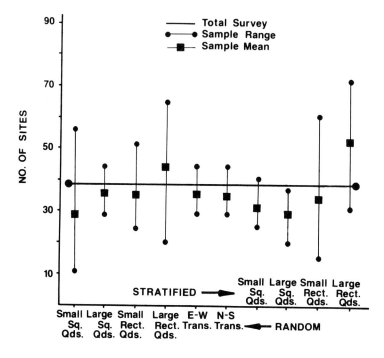

Figure E.4. Sample data for total number of sites.

most predictive unit size is one roughly 4 km² in area, and the least precise individual technique is one utilizing randomly selected, small rectangular quadrats.

Population Distribution

Of the 10 techniques applied in this study, *six sampling strategies accurately predict population distribution* (see Table E.3 and Figures E.5, E.6, and E.7). When proximity to expected values and standard deviation are used as bases for evaluation, simple random, large rectangular quadrat sampling (Figure E.8) and simple stratified, large rectangular quadrat sampling (Figure E.9) appear to be the most reliable techniques. Simple random, small square quadrat sampling; simple random, small rectangular quadrat sampling; simple random, east–west transect sampling; and simple random, north–south transect sampling also yield predictive results, though standard deviations are consistently greater. In contrast, simple random, large square quadrat sampling; simple stratified, small square quadrat sampling; simple stratified, large square quadrat sampling; and simple stratified, small rectangular quadrat sampling are not particularly accurate techniques for assessing population distribution. With respect to estimating the percentage of population residing in provincial centers–large villages and small villages, simple random,

TABLE E.3
Sample Data for Population Distribution

Sampling technique	Provincial centers–large villages			Small villages			Hamlets			K–S test of null hypothesis[a]
	Mean	Variance	Standard deviation	Mean	Variance	Standard deviation	Mean	Variance	Standard deviation	
Simple random, small square quadrats	85.0	127.9	11.3	11.7	88.0	9.4	3.2	5.6	2.4	NS
Simple random, large square quadrats	77.5	1,250.4	35.4	17.2	183.1	13.5	5.3	573.4	23.9	S
Simple random, small rectangular quadrats	75.3	73.1	8.5	19.0	71.1	8.4	5.6	4.0	2.0	NS
Simple random, large rectangular quadrats	79.7	31.9	5.6	17.5	34.2	5.8	2.8	38.6	6.2	NS
Simple random, east–west transects	77.0	46.4	6.8	18.5	55.6	7.5	4.5	14.6	3.8	NS
Simple random, north–south transects	82.1	124.1	11.1	10.4	87.7	9.4	7.4	84.3	9.2	NS
Simple stratified, small square quadrats	90.0	50.6	7.1	7.3	58.1	7.6	2.7	6.1	2.5	S
Simple stratified, large square quadrats	85.2	25.3	5.0	11.5	37.0	6.1	3.2	6.7	2.6	S
Simple stratified, small rectangular quadrats	86.2	1,545.5	39.3	12.3	1442.1	38.0	1.5	3.4	1.8	S
Simple stratified, large rectangular quadrats	77.7	36.8	6.1	17.4	10.4	3.2	4.8	10.2	3.2	NS

[a] S indicates that the null hypothesis may be rejected; the difference between the sampled and target data is statistically significant at the .05 level. NS indicates that the null hypothesis cannot be rejected at the .05 level.

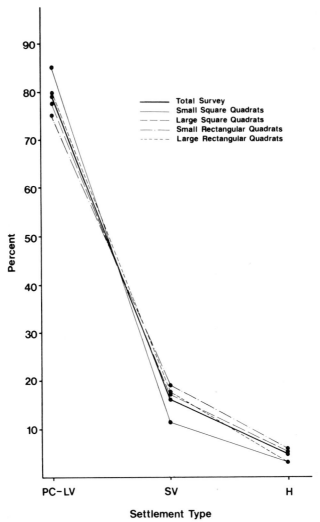

Figure E.5. Distribution of sample means for population distribution by settlement type using various sampling techniques; quadrats selected randomly.

large rectangular quadrat sampling and simple stratified, large rectangular quadrat sampling both provide accurate indices. However, for hamlets which contain less than 5% of total momentary population, the stratified design appears to be more successful.

F-test values indicate a statistically significant gain in sampling precision when simple stratified, large rectangular quadrat sampling is employed. Sampling schemes using east–west transects and large rectangular, randomly chosen quadrats appear to be more precise than procedures using small square quadrats. Small square quadrat sampling, be the selection procedure totally random or stratified by environmental zone, consequently appear to be the least precise "accurate" strategies.

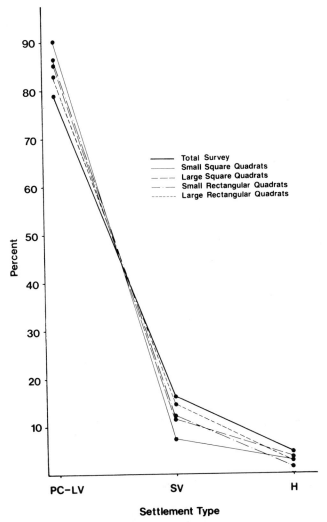

Figure E.6. Distribution of sample means for population distribution by settlement type using various sampling techniques; quadrats stratified by environmental zone.

In general, therefore, *random designs produce more predictive results than do stratified designs, transect sampling emerges as the most precise general strategy, and there is an increase in sampling precision and accuracy when units of large size are used. The best procedure is one involving the use of large rectangular quadrats.*

Site Distribution

Output from the K–S test suggests that *all sampling programs are accurate predictors of site distribution.* The number of sites occurring in each settlement category, however, is extremely small, so the results of the K–S test, the

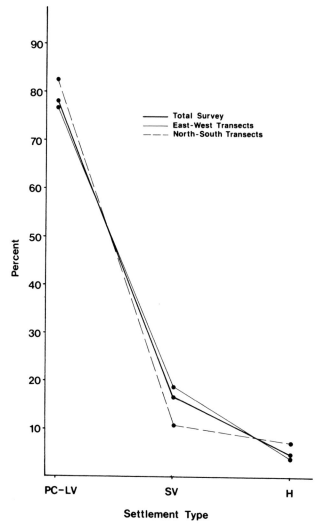

Figure E.7. Distribution of sample means for population distribution by settlement type using various transect sampling techniques; transects selected randomly.

values of critical D in particular, should not be weighed very highly. Inflation of the observed site numbers yields the following suggestive results. In seven instances the difference between the sample and target data is not statistically significant, indicating that accurate prediction is achieved (see Table E.4 and Figures E.10, E.11, and E.12). Simple random, small rectangular quadrat sampling appears to be the most reliable individual technique, followed closely by simple stratified, large rectangular quadrat sampling (Figure E.13). Simple random, small square quadrat sampling; simple random, large rectrangular quadrat sampling (Figure E.14); and simple random, north–south

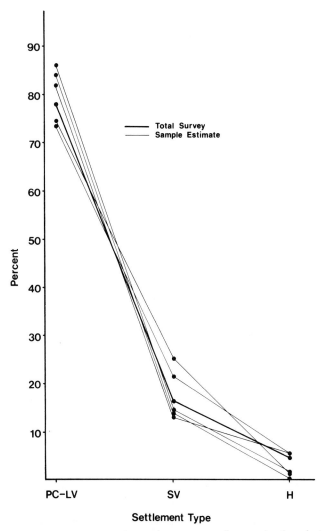

Figure E.8. Population distribution by settlement type; five randomly selected runs using simple random, large rectangular quadrat sampling.

transect sampling are somewhat less accurate, to judge from the sample means and standard deviations. Simple random, large square quadrat sampling and simple random, east–west transect sampling appear to be the least accurate of the seven strategies.

F-test values indicate a consistent gain in sampling precision when simple random, small square quadrat sampling and simple stratified, large rectangular quadrat sampling are applied, though the increase in precision over simple random, north–south transect sampling can be attributed to chance. Moreover, simple random, large rectangular quadrat sampling and

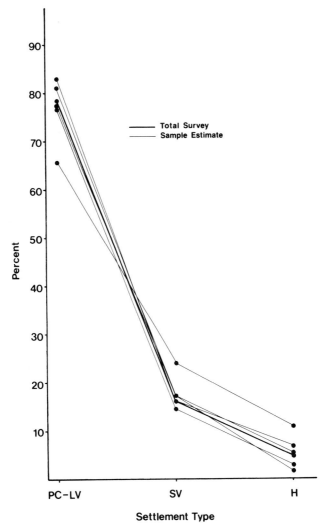

Figure E.9. Population distribution by settlement type; five randomly selected runs using simple stratified, large rectangular quadrat sampling.

simple random, north–south transect sampling are more precise than simple random, large square quadrat sampling and simple random, east–west transect sampling.

To conclude, *it appears that random designs in general yield more accurate results than stratified designs, that transect sampling is the most accurate sampling strategy, and that there is a slight gain in sampling precision and accuracy when units of larger size are used in the analysis. The most precise individual technique is one using either small square quadrats selected randomly or large rectangular quadrats stratified by major environmental zone.*

TABLE E.4
Sample Data for Site Distribution

Sampling technique	Provincial centers—large villages			Small villages			Hamlets			K–S test of null hypothesis[a]
	Mean	Variance	Standard deviation	Mean	Variance	Standard deviation	Mean	Variance	Standard deviation	
Simple random, small square quadrats	27.8	165.9	12.9	22.2	156.1	12.5	50.0	65.9	8.1	NS
Simple random, large square quadrats	25.8	338.8	18.4	22.5	235.0	15.3	51.6	932.7	30.5	NS
Simple random, small rectangular quadrats	18.2	16.4	4.0	27.3	68.6	8.3	54.5	94.9	9.7	NS
Simple random, large rectangular quadrats	27.3	168.6	13.0	32.7	119.1	10.9	40.0	457.6	21.4	NS
Simple random, east–west transects	24.4	670.9	25.9	26.7	205.8	14.3	48.9	806.2	28.4	NS
Simple random, north–south transects	25.0	70.7	8.4	18.2	141.5	11.9	56.8	299.2	17.3	NS
Simple stratified, small square quadrats	40.0	31.6	5.6	17.5	293.9	17.1	42.5	262.3	16.2	NS
Simple stratified, large square quadrats	33.3	82.8	9.1	22.2	205.4	14.3	44.4	536.7	23.2	NS
Simple stratified, small rectangular quadrats	35.7	417.7	20.4	26.2	562.2	23.7	38.1	152.9	12.4	NS
Simple stratified, large rectangular quadrats	22.4	77.5	8.8	23.9	44.2	6.6	53.7	211.2	14.5	NS

[a] NS indicates that the null hypothesis cannot be rejected; the difference between the sampled and target data is not statistically significant at the 0.05 level.

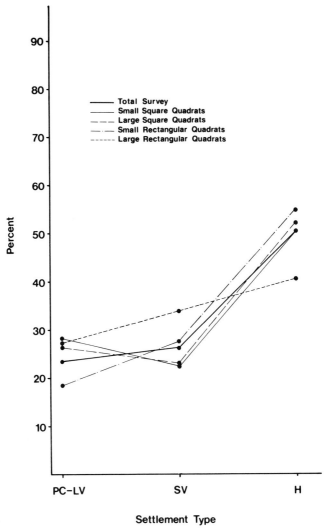

Figure E.10. Distribution of sample means for site distribution by settlement type using various sampling techniques; quadrats selected randomly.

Settlement Pattern

Determination of general settlement pattern is discussed in this section. Since the ability of each technique to adequately measure areal pattern was based on visual inspection of the site distributions, each sampling technique is treated separately. A comparison of the precision of different sampling techniques is then made.

Simple Random, Small Square Quadrat Sampling (see Figure E.15). In 8 of the 10 runs, a substantial population is depicted in the upper Cuautitlan

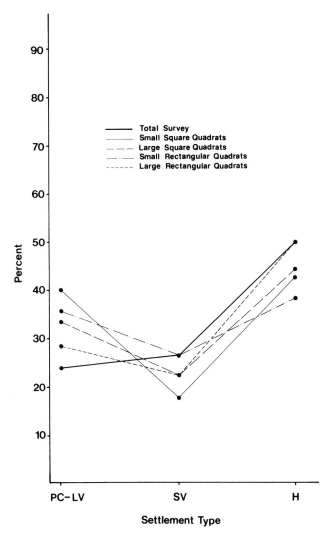

Figure E.11. Distribution of sample means for site distribution by settlement type using various sampling techniques; quadrats stratified by environmental zone.

Valley, principally along the middle and upper courses of the Rio Cuautitlan and Rio Tepotzotlan. In only two instances is the dense band of Middle Horizon settlement on the lower piedmont immediately to the south of the lower course of the Rio Cuautitlan predicted. By and large, population is nucleated in large sites, though in several cases a dispersed, hamlet-centered settlement pattern is indicated. In general, this sampling strategy does not produce reliable results.

Simple Random, Large Square Quadrat Sampling (see Figure E.16). Two general settlement patterns are indicated by the sample runs. On the one

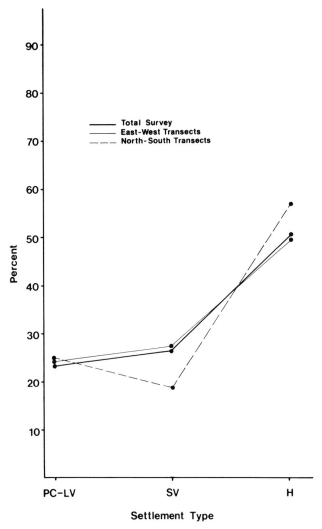

Figure E.12. Distribution of sample means for site distribution by settlement type using various transect sampling techniques; transects selected randomly.

hand, the ribbon of dense settlement on the piedmont adjacent to the lower Rio Cuautitlan is predicted. Settlement in the upper Cuautitlan Valley, in these cases, occurs in small villages (generally nucleated) and in hamlets. On the other hand, four sampling runs indicate the upper Cuautitlan Valley as the preferred locus of settlement. Moreover, the settlement pattern is dispersed, with at best 60% of the population residing in centers and large scattered villages, the remainder in small hamlets. Because of this variability, this technique is not considered to be overly predictive.

Simple Random, Small Rectangular Quadrat Sampling (see Figure E.17). In eight cases, a substantial population is forecasted in the upper

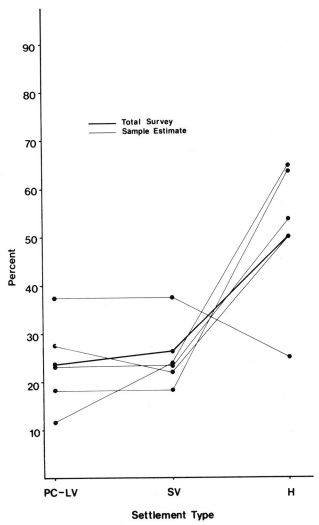

Figure E.13. Site distribution by settlement type; five randomly selected runs using simple stratified, large rectangular quadrat sampling.

Cuautitlan Valley. Only a few sites occur downstream. In only one run is the dense band of Middle Horizon settlement from Chilpan to Ecatepec indicated. In general, the settlement pattern is highly nucleated, the vast majority of population being aggregated in a few large sites. Thus, neither precision or accuracy in predicting overall settlement configuration is suggested.

Simple Random, Large Rectangular Quadrat Sampling (see Figure E.18). In 8 of the 10 cases, this sampling technique captures the ribbon of dense piedmont settlement paralleling the lower reaches of the Rio Cuautitlan. Large settlements in the upper Cuautitlan Valley are generally situated along major perennial streams. Sites not located near major stream flows are

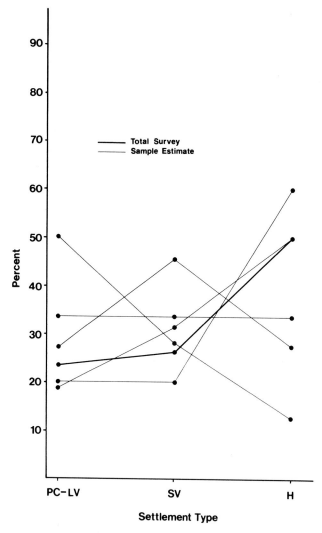

Figure E.14. Site distribution by settlement type; five randomly selected runs using simple random, large rectangular quadrat sampling.

typically small hamlets. Most large settlements, in contrast, are highly nucleated. This sampling technique, as a result, measures general settlement pattern with a high level of accuracy and precision.

Simple Random, East–West Transect Sampling (see Figure E.19).   In general, this technique is predictive. In 7 of 10 cases, the band of dense piedmont settlement encircling the Guadalupe Range is indicated. Settlements in the upper Cuautitlan Valley are nucleated and parallel major stream flows. Hamlets typically occur upstream, larger sites farther downstream.

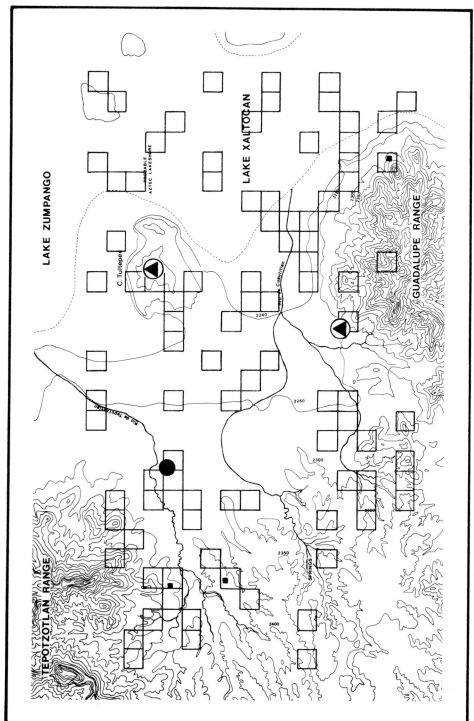

Figure E.15. The Cuautitlan region, showing sites found using simple random, small square quadrat sampling.

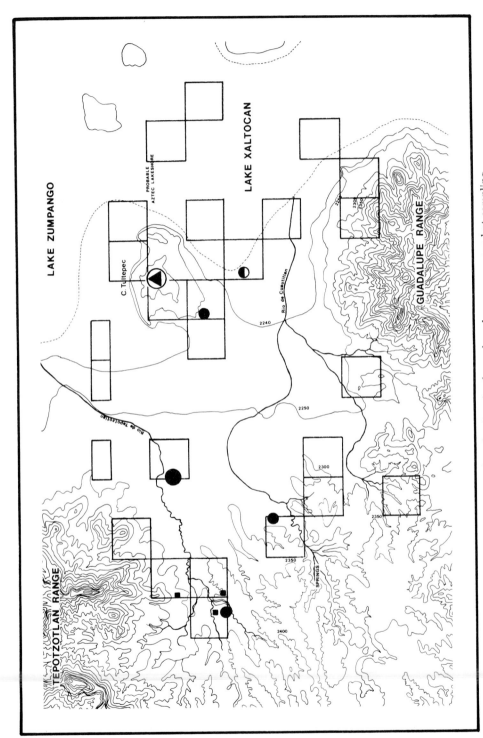

Figure E.16. The Cuautitlan region, showing sites found using simple random, large square quadrat sampling.

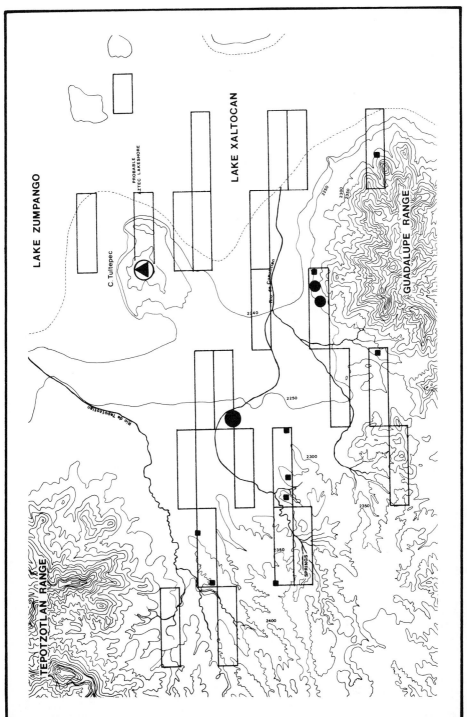

Figure E.17. The Cuautitlan region, showing sites found using simple random, small rectangular quadrat sampling.

LAKE ZUMPANGO

LAKE XALTOCAN

C. Tultepec

PROBABLE AZTEC LAKESHORE

GUADALUPE RANGE

TEPOTZOTLAN RANGE

SPRINGS

Río de Cuautitlan

Río de Tepotzotlan

519

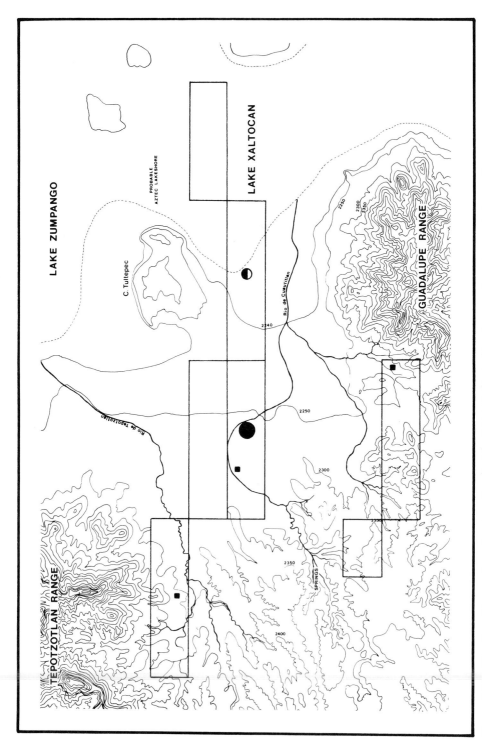

Figure E.18. The Cuautitlan region, showing sites found using simple random, large rectangular quadrat sampling.

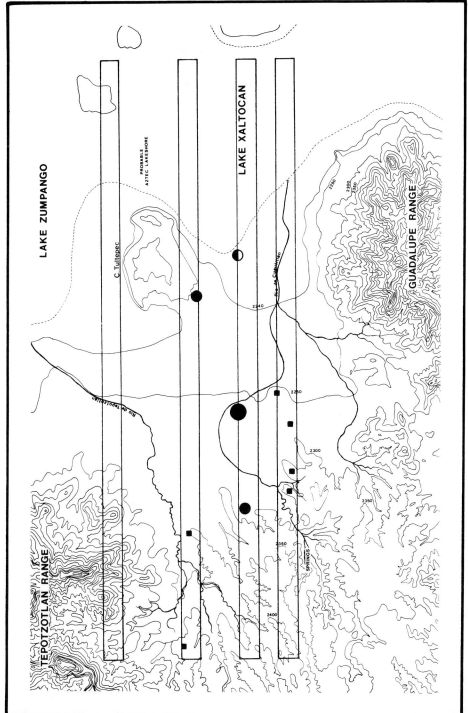

Figure E.19. The Cuautitlan region, showing sites found using simple random, east–west transect sampling.

Simple Random, North–South Transect Sampling (see Figure E.20). As expected, general settlement pattern is again predicted with precision. In 9 of 10 cases, a ribbon of settlement at the base of the Guadalupe Range is suggested. In eight instances, sites found in this band are large and highly nucleated; in one case, a hamlet-centered pattern is indicated. Settlements in the upper Cuautitlan Valley generally flank major streams. Sites in this subarea are large and densely occupied. In upstream localities, a few small hamlets occur.

Simple Stratified, Small Square Quadrat Sampling (see Figure E.21). This technique is moderately predictive. In six cases, the band of large nucleated settlements situated about the base of the Guadalupe Range is indicated; otherwise, no sites occur. In the upper Cuautitlan Valley, large sites frequently parallel major stream flows, but in two cases no large sites are predicted. Farther upstream, a hamlet-centered settlement pattern appears characteristic.

Simple Stratified, Large Quadrat Sampling (see Figure E.22). This technique is also moderately predictive. In seven cases, a band of large nucleated sites is found encircling the base of the Guadalupe Range. In the upper Cuautitlan Valley, six runs suggest that large sites follow major stream courses; in four runs, however, only hamlets are predicted. Hamlets are largely restricted to upstream localities. Villages appear to become more common at slightly lower elevations.

Simple Stratified, Small Rectangular Quadrat Sampling (see Figure E.23). In 6 of 10 cases, general settlement pattern is predicted. A band of dense piedmont occupation is found occurring at the base of the Guadalupe Range, and in the upper Cuautitlan Valley sites are confined to localities near major streams. The settlement pattern is highly nucleated, especially at lower elevations. Farther upstream, a more dispersed, hamlet-centered pattern is indicated. In four cases, however, either no sites occur in the upper Cuautitlan Valley or the bulk of the population resides in this subarea. This technique, then, predicts general settlement pattern with a moderate level of precision.

Simple Stratified, Large Rectangular Quadrat Sampling (see Figure E.24). In eight cases, the dense band of settlement at the base of the Guadalupe Range is predicted. Large nucleated sites are found to occur at regular intervals. In the upper Cuautitlan Valley all 10 runs depict large sites paralleling major streams, with hamlets frequently occurring upstream. In general, this sampling technique consistently yields precise results.

In comparing the sampling strategies applied in this study, several general points may be made. First, *there appears to be an increase in sampling precision when units of larger size are used.* Small quadrats, be they square or rectangular in shape, repeatedly yield geographical distributions which are at considerable variance with the pattern generated by the complete survey,

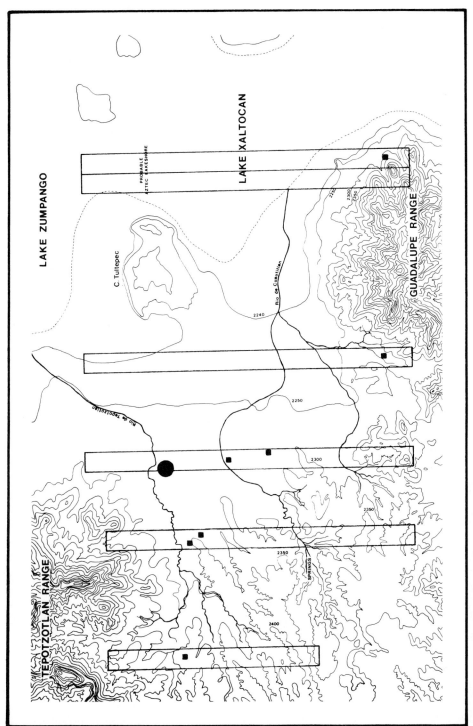

Figure E.20. The Cuautitlan region, showing sites found using simple random, north–south quadrat sampling.

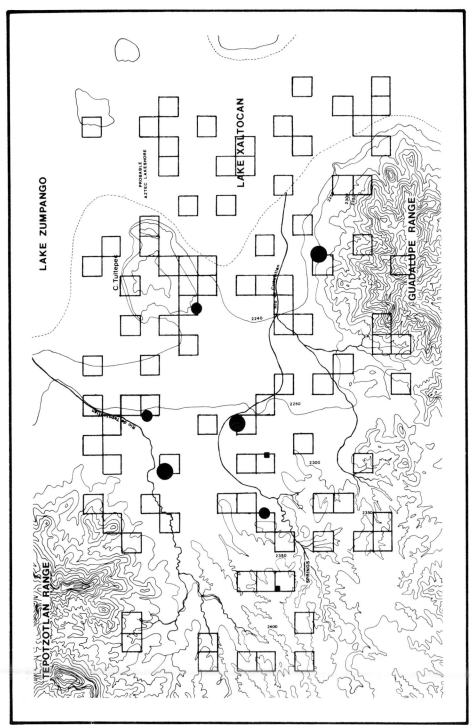

Figure E.21. The Cuautitlan region, showing sites found using simple stratified, small square quadrat sampling.

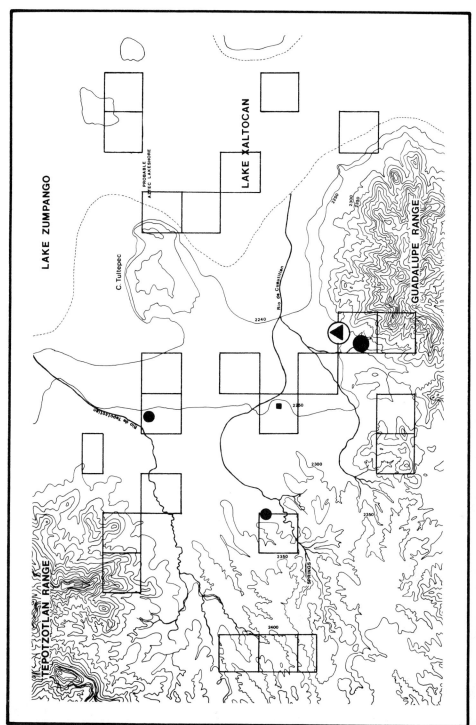

Figure E.22. The Cuautitlan region, showing sites found using simple stratified, large square quadrat sampling.

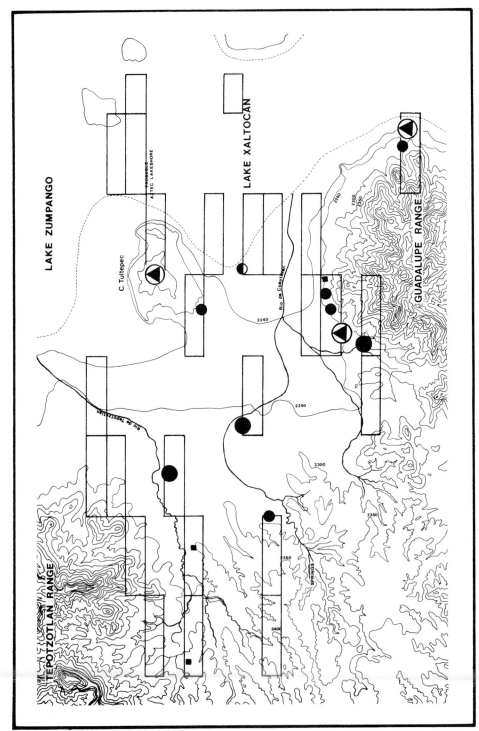

Figure E.23. The Cuautitlan region, showing sites found using simple stratified, small rectangular quadrat sampling.

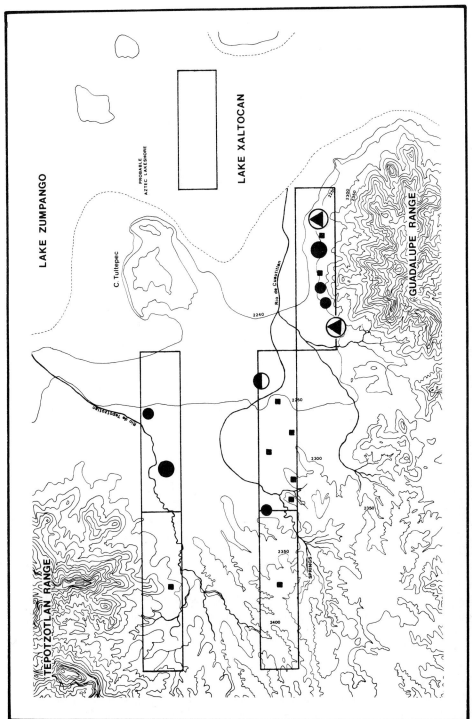

Figure E.24. The Cuautitlan region, showing sites found using simple stratified, large rectangular quadrat sampling.

while transect and large rectangular quadrat sampling are consistently highly predictive, both in terms of the spatial distribution of sites and in terms of the highly nucleated character of the sampled sites. Second, *there appears to be some increase in precision when stratified quadrat sampling schemes are applied, regardless of unit size.* The amount of gain is small, at best moderate, but it is present nonetheless. Thus, simple stratified, small square quadrat sampling is somewhat more precise than simple random, small square quadrat sampling. The same applies to the designs employing large square and rectangular quadrats. *The highest level of precision, however, appears to be achieved when the stratified design is used in conjunction with large rectangular quadrat sampling units.*

Multivariate Prediction

Ability to simultaneously measure multiple variables may now be determined. The results of the sampling experiment are presented in Table E.5 in summary form. Measurement of individual variables is evaluated using a rank scale of estimation. An empty cell indicates lack of prediction within specified statistical limits. Occurrence of the alphabetic character "X" indicates that accurate prediction is probable at the 95% confidence level. The character "XX" denotes that highly predictive results have been repeatedly obtained at the 0.05 significance level. Also tabulated in Table E.5 are the number of accurately predicted variables (column 7) and the number of variables predicted with accuracy and precision (column 8).

With respect to measuring the greatest number of variables, the following hypotheses are offered. First, *transect sampling clearly appears to be the most accurate individual technique.* Excepting estimation of total population, both transect schemes adequately predict (*a*) total number of sites, (*b*) population distribution by settlement type, (*c*) site distribution by settlement type, and (*d*) general settlement pattern. Of these, only general settlement pattern is estimated with precision. Individual variables, it would appear, can be more precisely assessed using alternative sampling procedures. Moreover, both transect strategies consistently provide accurate results, indicating that transect orientation has little effect on sampling reliability.

Large rectangular quadrat sampling, regardless of unit selection procedure, results in the next largest and most consistent gain in accuracy. Although general settlement pattern is again the only variable predicted with precision, three variables, population distribution by settlement type, site distribution by settlement type, and general settlement pattern, are reliably estimated. Simple random, small square quadrat sampling, simple random, large square quadrat sampling, simple random, small rectangular quadrat sampling, and simple stratified, small square quadrat sampling are assigned a tertiary position, since each accurately predicts only two variables.

TABLE E.5
Prediction of Variables

Sampling technique	Total population	Total number of sites	Population distribution	Site distribution[a]	Settlement pattern	Number of predicted variables	Number of variables predicted with precision
Simple random, small square quadrats	—	—	X	XX	—	2	1
Simple random, large square quadrats	—	XX	—	X	—	2	1
Simple random, small rectangular quadrats	—	X	—	—	—	2	—
Simple random, large rectangular quadrats	—	—	X	X	XX	3	1
Simple random, east–west transects	—	XX	X	X	XX	4	2
Simple random, north–south transects	—	XX	X	X	XX	4	2
Simple stratified, small square quadrats	—	XX	—	—	X	2	1
Simple stratified, large square quadrats	—	—	—	—	X	1	—
Simple stratified, small rectangular quadrats	—	—	—	—	X	1	—
Simple stratified, large rectangular quadrats	—	—	XX	XX	XX	3	3

[a] Derived from the inflated cells.

Regarding prediction with precision, it is clear that simple stratified, large rectangular quadrat sampling is the most precise scheme. Of the three predicted variables, population distribution by settlement type, site distribution by settlement type, and general settlement pattern, each is estimated with precision. Application of transect sampling strategies yields the next largest gain in precision. Full randomization, it appears, produces a slight increase in sampling precision. Stratified designs, in three of four cases, do not generate overly precise results.

Thus, random designs appear to accurately predict more variables than do stratified designs, and there appears to be a gain in sampling accuracy when units of larger size are employed in the analysis. Random transect sampling is the most predictive design, though the gain over techniques using large rectangular quadrats is small. Gains in precision, on the other hand, seem to be closely related to increases in survey unit size. Stratification, regrettably, appears to have little effect on sampling precision, despite the fact that the most precise individual technique utilized the stratified design. *Prediction with accuracy and prediction with both accuracy and precision may consequently require alternative procedures of estimation.*

Additionally, there is considerable variation in terms of which sampling technique most precisely measures which variable. Population distribution by settlement type, for example, is precisely estimated using simple stratified, large rectangular quadrat sampling, yet this technique cannot adequately determine total site number. Similarly, population distribution and site distribution are consistently measured with accuracy by the same set of techniques, though none of these strategies reliably answeres the question of total population size. As Cowgill (1975:266) notes, "a grain size and sampling fraction quite adequate and efficient for settling the question of whether sites are substantially more abundant in one ecological zone than in another may be very inadequate for revealing settlement systems." *Different sampling techniques, this likewise suggests, adequately measure different sets of variables.*

Finally, one problem became painfully apparent during the course of this study. By this we are alluding to the tremendous range in variation displayed *within* each set of sampling runs. Even when a particular sampling scheme turned out to be highly predictive, a few trials were aberrant, sometimes by substantial margins. In probabilistic terms, such aberrations can be accounted for by conducting 50, 100, or 1000 repeated applications of the same sampling procedure on the group of data. In practical terms, regrettably, such deviations cannot be discounted, for archaeological surveys are "one shot" opportunities. Given only one chance, therefore, one cannot estimate error, and with no inkling of the error factor, one may never be able to tell whether the sampling program has predictably captured the variables in question. This is a point of major importance, one which we contend only complete surveys can concretely resolve.

PROBLEMS FOR FUTURE RESEARCH

As we stated initially, the purpose of this appendix is heuristic. Some of the results produced by this study are disturbing, and there are other considerations, varying the sampling fraction, for example, which deserve additional attention. The most disconcerting aspect of the present study is the inability of any one technique to reliably estimate total population size. Demographic variables, as we have argued, have major theoretical import in explaining settlement, subsistence, and institutional transformations. Perhaps the problem here is inadequacy in the level of sampling intensity. Likewise, the number of trial runs may not be sufficient; so with 50 or 100 repeated applications, prediction with accuracy and precision may eventually prove to be the case. Systematic and clustered designs have also not been considered, so it may turn out that lack of adequate prediction is related to selecting the wrong sampling designs.

Stratified sampling procedures, as we have seen, are not particularly accurate nor are they overly precise. This is disturbing, for theoretically stratification should improve accuracy as well as precision. Again, the problem may be the inadequate number of trial runs employed in this study. On the other hand, even with 100 repeated applications of the same sampling programs, Plog (1976) found that the gains in precision resulting from stratification were consistently quite small. Thus, ". . . for surveying unknown areas, the simplest sampling designs may well be the most practical [Plog 1976:158]."

There is also a cost factor involved in conducting sampling programs. Moving from one sample quadrat to another is certainly time consuming, and this, combined with logistical problems, may well negate any benefits derived from the reduced cost of fractionally surveying an area. It is equally likely, however, that overall expense will be less, so in terms of cost–benefit, the advantage of surveying by sample quadrats may still outweigh added inconveniences encountered in the field. This, again, is a problem for future research.

CONCLUDING REMARKS

Our conclusion is that sampling techniques *can be* useful, economical means for generating data from which inferences can be drawn concerning a wider set of phenomena. Application of sampling schemes, however, must be problem specific. Hence, if one desires an estimate of total site number, a particular technique must be applied, but if one wants to determine another variable, general settlement pattern, for example, a completely different technique may be necessary. Had our problems been sufficiently well conceived at the beginning of the Basin of Mexico survey, we may have opted for one or more sampling strategies as a convenient means for generating a representative inventory of sites. As it stands, they were not, so we were compelled, both by intellectual curiosity and methodological naiveté, to conduct complete surveys. We believe, in retrospect, that our decision was the correct one. Whether or not this proves to be the case in the long run, only time will tell.

References

Abascal Macias, R.

    Analysis for activación de neutrones: Una aportacíon para la arqueologia moderna. I.N.A.H., Mexico: Tesis profesional.

Abascal Macias, R., P. Dávila, P. U. Schmidt, and D. Z. de Dávila

    1976   *La arqueologiá del sur-oeste de Tlaxcala (primera parte)*. Comunicaciones 11. Puebla, Mexico: Fundación Alemana para la investigation cientifica.

Acosta, Jorgé R.

    1964   *El palacio del Quetzalpapalotl*. Memorial del Instituto Nacional de Antropologia e Historia 10. Mexico.

Acsádi, Gy, and T. Nemeskéri

    1970   *History of human life span and mortality*. Budapest: Akademiai Kiado.

Adams, Robert M.

    1961   Changing patterns of territorial organization in the Central Highlands of Chiapas, Mexico. *American Antiquity* **26**(3):341–360.

    1965   *Land behind Baghdad*. Chicago: University of Chicago Press.

    1966   *The evolution of urban society*. Chicago: Aldine.

Adams, Robert M., and Hans J. Nissen

    1972   *The Uruk countryside*. Chicago: University of Chicago Press.

Alden, J. A.

    1978   A reconstruction of Toltec Period political units in the Valley of Mexico. In *Transformations: Mathematical approaches to culture change*, edited by K. Cooke and C. Renfrew. New York: Academic Press.

Allan, William

    1965   *The African husbandman*. New York: Barnes and Noble.

    1945   *Anales de Cuautitlan, Codice Chimalpopoca*, translation by Feliciano Velazquez. Mexico: U.N.A.M., Imprenta Universitaria.

Anglerius, Peter Martyr
  1628/ *De Orbe Nofo: The eight decades of Peter Matyr d'Anghiera.* Translated and edited by
  1912   Francis A. MacNutt, 2 vols. New York: G. P. Putnam.
Apenes, O.
  1944   The primitive salt production of Lake Texcoco. *Thenos* **9**(1):25–40.
Armillas, Pedro
  1950   Teotihuacan, Tula y los Toltecas. *Runa* **3**(1-2):37–70.
  1971   Gardens in swamps. *Science* **174**:653–661.
Barba de Pina Chan, Beatrix
  1956   Tlapacoya: Un sitio preclasico de transicion. *Acta Anthropologica*, Epoca 2, 1, no. 1.
         México.
Barlow, R. H.
  1949   The extent of the empire of the Culhua Mexica. *Ibero-Americana* **28**. Berkeley: University
         of California Press.
Bennyhoff, J. A.
  1966   Chronology and periodization: Continuity and change in the Teotihuacán ceramic
         tradition. In *Onceava Mesa Redonda: Teotihuacán.* Mexico: Sociedad Mexicana de An-
         tropologia. Pp. 19–30.
Berg, Richard L. Jr.
  1976   The Zoogocho Plaza system in the Sierra Zapoteca of Villa Alta. In *Markets in Oaxaca,*
         edited by S. Cook and M. Diskin. Austin: University of Texas Press.
Bernal, Ignacio
  1963   *Teotihuacán: Descubrimientos, reconstrucciones.* Mexico: Instituto Nacional de An-
         tropologia e Historia.
Binford, L. R.
  1964   A consideration of archaeological design. *American Anthropologist* **29**: 425–441.
  1968   Post-Pleisteocene adaptations. In *New perspectives in archaeology,* edited by S. R. and
         L. R. Binford. Chicago: Aldine. Pp. 313–341.
Blalock, H. M.
  1972   *Social statistics.* New York: McGraw-Hill.
Blanton, Richard E.
  1972a Prehispanic settlement patterns of the Ixtapalapa Peninsula region, Mexico. *Occasional
         Papers in Anthropology*, 6. Department of Anthropology, The Pennsylvania State Uni-
         versity, University Park, PA.
  1972b Prehispanic adaptation in the Ixtapalpa region, Mexico. *Science* **175**:1317–1326.
  1975   The cybernetic analysis of human population growth. In *Population studies in archaeol-
         ogy and biological anthropology: A symposium,* edited by A. C. Swedland. Memoir 30.
         American Antiquity **40**(part 2):116–126.
  1976a Anthropological studies of cities. In *Annual Review of Anthropology*, Vol. 5. Palo Alto,
         CA: Annual Reviews, Inc.
  1976b The role of symbiosis in adaptation and sociocultural change in the Valley of Mexico. In
         The Valley of Mexico, edited by Eric Wolf. Albuquerque, NM: University of New Mexico
         Press.
  1978   *Monte Alban: Settlement patterns at the ancient Zapotec capital.* New York: Academic
         Press.
Blanton, R. E. et al..
  1978   *Prehispanic settlement patterns in the Valley of Oaxaca, Mexico.* Symposium at the Forty-
         Third Annual Meeting of the Society for American Archaeology, May 1978, Phoenix,
         Arizona.
Blanton, R. E., and Steve Kowalewski,
  n.d.   *The Valley of Oaxaca settlement pattern project, a progress report to the National Science
         Foundation.* Instituto Nacional de Antropologia e Historia, México, and the Research
         Foundation of the City University of New York, mimeographed.

Blucher, Darlena
  1971 *Late preclassic cultures in the Valley of Mexico: Pre-urban Teotihuacan,* Unpublished Ph.D. dissertation, Department of Anthropology, Brandeis University, Waltham, MA.
Borah, Woodrow, and Shelburne F. Cook
  1963 The aboriginal population of Central Mexico on the eve of the Spanish Conquest. *Ibero-Americana* **54**. Berkely: University of California Press.
Boserup, Esther
  1965 *The conditions of agricultural growth: The economics of agrarian change under population pressure.* Chicago: Aldine.
Boughey, Arthur S.
  1973 *Ecology of populations.* New York: MacMillan.
Browman, D. R.
  1970 Early Peruvian peasants: The culture history of a Central Highlands valley. Unpublished ph.D. dissertation, Department of Anthropology, Harvard University.
Brumfiel, Elizabeth
  1976a Regional growth in the eastern Valley of Mexico: A test of the population pressure hypothesis. In *The early Mesoamerican village,* edited by Kent V. Flannery. New York: Academic Press. Pp. 234–248.
  1976b Specialization and exchange at the Late Postclassic (Aztec) community of Huexotla, Mexico. Unpublished Ph.D. dissertation. University of Michigan, Ann Arbor.
Brundage, Burr C.
  1972 *Rain of darts.* Austin: University of Texas Press. p. 354.
Bullard, W. R., Jr.
  1960 Maya settlement patterns in Northwestern Peten, Guatemala. *American Anitquity* **25**(3):355–372.
Calnek, Edward E.
  1966 The Aztec imperial bureaucracy. Paper presented at the Sixty-Fifth Annual Meeting of the American Anthropological Association, Pittsburgh, PA.
  1970 The population of Tenochtitlan in 1519. Paper presented at the Sixty-Ninth Annual Meeting of the American Anthropological Association, San Diego, CA.
  1972 Settlement pattern and chinampa agriculture at Tenochtitlan. *American Antiquity* **37**:104–115.
  1093 The location of the sixteenth century map called the Maguey Plan. *American Antiquity* **38**(2):190–195.
  1976 The internal structure of Tenochtitlan. In *The Valley of Mexico,* edited by E. R. Wolf. Albuquerque: University of New Mexico Press. Pp. 287–302.
Carneiro, Robert L.
  1970 Theory of the origin of the state. *Science* **169**:733–738.
  1972 From autonomous villages to the state, a numerical estimation. In *Population growth: Anthropological implications,* edited by Brian Spooner. Cambridge, MA. M.I.T. Press.
Carrasco, Pedro
  1961 El Barrio y la regulación del Matrimonio en un pueblo en el Valle de México en el siglo XVI. *Revista Mexicana De Estudios Anthropologicos 17.*
  1964 Family structure of sixteenth century Tepoztlan. In *Process and pattern in culture.* Edited by Robert A. Manners. Chicago: Aldine.
  1971 The people of central Mexico and their historical traditions. In *Handbook of Middle American Indians,* edited by R. Wauchope. Vol. 11. Austin: University of Texas Press. Pp. 459–473.
Carrasco, P., J. Broada *et al.*.
  1976 *Estratificación social de la Mesoamerica Prehispanica.* Instituto Nacional de Antropologia e Historia, México.
Casselberry, Samuel D.
  1972 How much space do we need: A proxemic approach. Paper presented at the Seventy-

first Annual Meetings of the American Anthropological Association, Toronto, Canada, mimeographed.

Chagnon, Napoleon
1968 *Yanomamo: The fierce people,* New York: Holt, Rinehart and Winston.
1974 *Studying the Yanomamo.* New York: Holt, Rinehart and Winston.

Chapple, Elliot, and Carleton J. Coon
1948 *Principles of anthropology.* New York: Henry Holt.

Charlton, Thomas H.
1969 Texcoco fabric-marked pottery, tlatels and salt making. *American Antiquity* **34**(1):73–76.
1970a Contemporary settlement patterns: The Cerro Gordo–North Slope and Upper Valley areas. In *The natural environment, contemporary occupation and 16th century population of the Valley. The Teotihuacan Valley project final report,* Vol. 1, *Occasional Papers in Anthropology* 3. Department of Anthropology, The Pennsylvania State University, University Park, PA. Pp. 181–236.
1970b Contemporary agriculture of the valley. In *The natural environment, contemporary occupation and 16th century population of the Valley. The Teotihuacan Valley project final report,* Vol. 1. *Occasional Papers in Anthropology.* 3. Department of Anthropology, The Pennsylvania State University, University Park, PA.
1971 On postconquest depopulation in the Americas. *Current Anthropology* **12**:518.
1972a Population trends in the Teotihuacan Valley, A.D. 1400–1969. *World Archaeology* **4**(1):106–123.
1972b Postconquest development in the Teotihuacan Valley, Mexico. Part I: Excavations. Office of the State Archaeologist, Report no. 5. University of Iowa, Iowa City.
1977 Final report of a surface survey of preconquest trade newworks in Mesoamerica. A report to El Instituto Nacional De Anthropologia e Historia and the National Endowment for the Humanities. Department of Anthropology, University of Iowa, mimeographed.

Charnay, Desire
1884 *Les anciennes villes du nouveau Monde.*

Chimalpahin, Domingo, Francisco De San Anton, and Muñon Cuauhtlehuanzin
1965 *Relaciones originales de Chalco-Amaquemechan.* ⸱Traducido del Nahuatl al Español por Silvia Rendon. Fondo de Cultura Económica, México.

Clarke, David L.
1968 *Analytical archaeology.* London: Methuen.

Comision, Hidrológica De Le Cuenca Del Valle De México
1968 *Boletin hidrológico resumen No. 1,* Secretaria de Recursos Hidrológicos, México.

Cook, Shelburne, F.
1972 *Prehistoric demography.* Addison-Wesley Modular Publications 16, Reading, Pennsylvania.

Cook, Scott and Diskin, Martin (Eds.)
1976 *Markets in Oaxaca.* Austin: University of Texas Press.

Cowgill, G. L.
1975a Population pressure as a non-explanation. In *Population studies in archaeology and biological anthropology: A symposium,* edited by A. C. Swedlund. Memoir 30. *American Antiquity* **40** (part 2):127–131.
1975b A selection of samples: Comments on archaeo-statistics. In *Sampling in archaeology,* edited by James E. Muller. Tucson: The University of Arizona Press. Pp. 258–274.

Crespo, A. M.
1976 Uso del suelo y patron de poblamiento en el area de Tula, Hgo. in *Proyecto Tula, Segunda Parte,* editado por E. Matos. Instituto Nacional de Antropologia e Historia, Coleción Cientifica 33, México. Pp. 35–48.

Cummings, Bryon
1933 Cuicuilco and the archaic culture of Mexico. *University of Arizona Social ScienceBulletin* **4**(8).

Davies, Nigel
   1976 *The Toltecs.* Norman, OK; University of Oklahoma Press.
Daubenmire, Rexford
   1968 *Plant communities.* New York: Harper & Row.
DeJong, Gordon F.
   1972 Patterns of human fertility and mortality. In *The structure of human populations,* edited by G. A. Harrison and A. J. Boyce. Oxford: Clarendon Press. Pp. 32–56.
Diaz Del Castillo, Bernal
   1927 *The true history of the conquest of Mexico.* Translation by Maurice Keatinge. New York: Robert M. McBride and Company.
Diehl, Richard A.
   1970 Contemporary settlement patterns: An overview. In *The natural environment, contemporary occupation and 16th century population of the Valley. The Teotihuacan Valley project final report,* Vol. 1. *Occasional Papers in Anthropology* 3. Department of Anthropology, The Pennsylvania State University, University Park, PA. Pp. 103–179.
   1974 Studies of ancient Tollan: A report of The University of Missouri Tula archaeological project. *University of Missouri Monographs in Anthropology* 1, Department of Anthropology, University of Missouri, Columbia.
Donahue, R. L., J. C. Shickluna, and L. S. Robertson
   1971 *Soils: An introduction to soils and plant growth.* Englewood Cliffs, NJ: Prentice-Hall.
Drennan, Robert D.
   1976 Fabrica San Jose and Middle Formative society in the Valley of Oaxaca, Mexico. *Memoirs of the Museum of Anthropology, University of Michigan* 8, Ann Arbor.
Dumond, D. E.
   1965 Population growth and culture change. *Southwestern Journal of Anthropology* **21**:302–324.
   1972 Population growth and political centralization. In *Population growth: Anthropological implications,* edited by B. Spooner. Cambridge, MA. M.I.T. Press. Pp. 286–310.
DuSolier Massieu, Wilfrido
   1949 Ceramica arqueologica de San Cristobal Ecatepec. *Anales del Instituto Nacional de Antropologia e Historia* 3:27–(México).
Earle, Timothy K.
   1976 A nearest-neighbor analysis of two Formative settlement systems. In *The early Mesoamerican Village,* edited by Kent V. Flannery. New York: Academic Press. Pp. 196–222.
Flannery, Kent V.
   1967 The vertebrate fauna and hunting patterns. In *Environment and subsistence, the prehistory of the Tehuacan Valley,* edited by Douglas S. Byers. Austin: University of Texas Press. Pp. 132–177.
   1968 Archaeological systems theory and early Mesoamerica. In *Anthropological archaeology in Americas,* edited by Betty J. Meggers. Washington, Washington, DC: Anthropological Society of Washington. Pp. 67–87.
   1972 The cultural evolution of civilizations. *Annual Review of Ecology and Systematics* 3:399–426.
   1973 The origins of agriculture. *Annual Review of Anthropology,* Vol. 2. Palo Alto, CA: Annual Reviews, Inc. Pp. 271–310.
   1976 *The early Mesoamerican village.* New York: Academic Press.
Flannery, Kent V., A. V. T. Kirkby, M. J. Kirkby, and A. W. Williams, Jr.
   1967 Farming systems and political growth in ancient Oaxaca. *Science* **158**:445–454.
Flannery, Kent V., et al.
   1970 *Preliminary archaeological investigations in the Valley of Oaxaca, Mexico, 1966–1969.* A report to the National Science Foundation, and the Instituto Nacional de Antropologia e Historia, México, mimeographed.

Flannery, Kent, V., and James Schoenwater
1970   Climate and man in Formative Oaxaca. *Archaeology* **23**:144–152.

Fletcher, Charles
1962   *Cuanalan: An archaeological excavation and study of a Ticoman Period site in the Valley of Teotihuacan, Estado de México, México,* Unpublished masters thesis, Department of Sociology and Anthropology, The Pennsylvania State University, Universtiy Park, PA.

Fried, Morton H.
1967   *The evolution of political society: An essay in political anthropology,* New York: Random House.

Furst, P. T.
1978   Spirulina. *Human Nature* (March 1978) 60–65.

Gamio, Manuel
1922   *La población del Valle De Teotihuacan,* 3 vols. Secretariá de Agricultura y Fomento, México.

Garcia Cook, Angel
1972   Investigaciones arqueológicas en el Estado do Tlaxcala. *Comunicaciones, Proyecto Puebla Tlaxcala,* No. 6. Fundación alemana para la investigación cientifica, Puebla, México. Pp. 21–26.
1973   El desorollo cultural prehispánico en el norte del area: intento de una secuencia cultural. *Communicaciones Proyecto Puebla Tlaxcala,* No. 7. Fundación alemana para la investigación cientifica, Puebla, México. Pp. 67–71.
1974   Una secuencia cultural para Tlaxcala. *Comunicaciones, Proyecto Puebla Tlaxcala,* No. 10. Fundación alemana para la investigación cientifica, Puebla, México. Pp. 5–22.

Garcia Cook, Angel, and Elia Del Carmen Trejo
1977   Lo Teotihuacano en Puebla. In *Comunicaciones, Proyecto Puebla-Tlaxcala,* No. 14.

Gibson, C.
1964   *The Aztecs under Spanish rule* Stanford: Stanford University Press.
1974   Structure of the Aztec empire. In *Handbook of Middle American indians, Vol. 1.* Austin: University of Texas Press.

Gonzalez Aparicio, Luis
1973   *Plano reconstructivo de la región de Tenochtitlan.* Instituto Nacional de Antropologia e Historia, México.

Griffin, J. B., and Antonieta Espejo
1947   La alfarería corespondiente al último periodo de ocupación nahua del Valle de México. *Memorias De La Academia Mexicana De La Historia* **6**(2):131–147.
1950   La alfarería del último periódo de ocupación del Valle de México, II: Culhuacan Tenayuca y Tlateloco. *Memorias de Academia Mexicana de la Historia* **9**:118–167.

Gross, Daniel
1975   Protein capture and cultural development in the Amazon Basin. *American Anthropologist* **77,** No. 3.

Grove, David C., K. G. Hirth, D. E. Bugé, and A. M. Cyphers
1976   Settlement and cultural development at Chalcatzingo. *Science* **192**:1203–1210.

Haggett, Peter
1965   *Locational analysis in human geography.* London: Edward Arnold.

Harris, D. R.
1969   Agricultural systems, ecosystems and the origins of agriculture. In *The domestication and exploitation of plants and animals,* edited by P. V. Ucko and G. W. Dimbleby. Chicago: Aldine. Pp. 3–15.

Harris, Marvin
1977   *Cannibals and kings: The origins of cultures.* New York: Random House.

Hayden, Brian
1975   The carrying capacity dilemma in population studies. In *Population Studies in archaeology and biological anthropology: A symposium,* edited by A. C. Swedland. Memoir 30. *American Antiquity* **40**(part 2).

Heine, Klaus
1973 Variaciones mas importantes del clima durante los ultimos 40,000 años en México. In *Comunicaciones: Proyecto Puebla Tlaxcala,* No. 7, edited by Wilhelm Lauer and Erdmann Gormsen. Fundación alemana para la investigacion cientifica, México. Pp. 51–58.
Heizer, R. F., and J. A. Bennyhoff
1958 Archaeological investigations at Cuicuilco, Valley of Mexico. *Science* **127**:232–233.
1972 Archaeological excavations at Cuicuilco, Mexico, 1957. *National Geographic Society Research Reports 1955–60.* Pp. 93–104.
n.d. Preliminary report on excavations at Cuicuilco in 1957. Informe al Departamento de Monumentos Prehispanicos del Instituto Nacional de Antropologia e Historia, México.
Hirth, K. G.
1974 Precolumbian population development along the Rio Amatzinac: The Formative through Classic periods in eastern Morelos, Mexico. Unpublished Ph.D. dissertation, Department of Anthropology, University of Wisconsin at Milwaukee.
Hunt, Eva
1972 Irrigation and the sociopolitical organization of Cuicatec Cacicazgos. In *Chronology and irrigation, the prehistory of the Tehuacan Valley,* Vol. 4, edited by Frederick Johnson. Austin: University of Texas Press. Pp. 162–248.
Hunt, Robert C., and Hunt, Eva
1976 Canal irrigation and local social organization. In *Current Anthropology,* WL 17–203.
Jacobs, Jane
1969 *The economy of cities.* New York: Random House.
Jiménez Moreno, W.
1941 Tula y los Toltecas según las fuentes históricas. *Revista Mexicana De Estudios Antropológicos* **5**:79–83.
Johnson, E. A. J.
1970 *The organization of space in developing countries.* Cambridge: Harvard University Press.
Johnson, Frederick, and R. S. MacNiesh
1972 Chronometric dating. In *The prehistory of the Tehuacan Valley: Chronology and Irrigation,* Vol. 4, edited by F. Johnson. Austin: University of Texas Press. Pp. 3–55.
Kaplan, Lawrence
1967 Archaeological phaseolus from Tehuacan. In *Environment and subsistence, the prehistory of the Tehuacan Valley.* Vol. 1, edited by Douglas S. Byers. Austin: University of Texas Press. Pp. 201–211.
Kirchoff, Paul
1959 The principles of clanship in human society. In *Readings in anthropology,* Vol. 2, edited by M. H. Fried. New York: Thomas Crowell. Pp. 259–270.
Kirkby, Anne V. T.
1973 The use of land and water resources in the past and present Valley of Oaxaca, Mexico. *Memoirs of the Museum of Anthropology, University of Michigan* 5, Ann Arbor.
Kottak, Conrad P.
1978 *Anthropology, the exploration of human diversity.* 2nd ed. New York: Random House.
Kovar, Anton
1970 The physical and biological environment of the Basin of Mexico. In *The natural environment, contemporary occupation and 16th century population of the Valley, the Teotihuacan Valley project final report,* Vol. 1. *Occasional Papers in Anthropology* 3, Pp. 13–67. Department of Anthropology, Pennsylvania State University, University Park, PA.
Kowalewski, Stephen A.
1976 Prehispanic settlement patterns of the central part of the Valley of Oaxaca, Mexico. Unpublished Ph.D. dissertation, Department of Anthropology, University of Arizona, Tucson.

Lanning, E. P.
    1967   *Peru before the Incas.* Englewood Cliffs, NJ: Prentice-Hall.
Lee, Richard B.
    1968   What hunters do for a living, or, how to make out on scarce resources. In *Man the
           hunter,* edited by Richard B. Lee and Irven DeVore. Chicago: Aldine. Pp. 30–48.
    1969   !Kung Bushman subsistence: An input-output analysis. In *Environment and cultural
           behavior: Ecological studies in cultural anthropology,* edited by Andrew P. Vayda. New
           York: The Natural History Press. Pp. 47–79.
    1972   The intensification of social life among the !Kung Bushmen. In *Population growth:
           Anthropological implications,* edited by Brian Spooner. Cambridge, MA: M.I.T. Press.
           Pp. 343–350.
Lees, S. H.
    1973   Sociopolitical aspects of canal irrigation in the Valley of Oaxaca. *Memoirs of the Museum
           of Anthropology, University of Michigan* 6, Ann Arbor.
Leopold, A. Starker
    1959   *Wild life of Mexico: The game birds and mammals.* Berkeley: University of California Press.
Lewis, Oscar
    1951   *Life in a Mexican village: Tepoztlan restudied.* Urbana, Ill.: University of Illinois Press.
Linné, S.
    1934   Archaeological researches at Teotihuacan, Mexico. *Ethnographic Museum of Sweden, new
           series, publication 1,* Stockholm.
    1942   Mexican highland cultures: Archaeological researches at Teotihuacan, Calpulalpan, and
           Chalcihcomula in 1934–35. *Ethnographic Museum of Sweden, new series, publication 7,*
           Stockholm.
    1948   El Valley y la Ciudad de Mexico en 1550. *Ethnographical Museum of Sweden, new series,
           publication 1,* Stockholm.
Litvak King, Jaime
    1964   Estratigrafia cultural y natural en un tlatel en el lago de Texcoco. Departamento De
           Prehistoria, I.N.A.H., México.
Logan, Michael H., and William T. Sanders
    1976   The model. In *The Valley of Mexico,* edited by Eric Wolf. Albuquerque: University of
           New Mexico Press. Pp. 31–58.
Longacre, William
    1970   Archaeology as anthropology, a case study. *Anthropological Papers of the University of
           Arizona* **17,** Tucson: University of Arizona Press.
Lorenzo, Jose Luis
    1956   Notas sobre arqueologia y cambios climaticos en la Cuenca de Mexico, In *La Cuenca de
           Mexico: Consideraciones geologicas y arqueologicas.* Direccion de Prehistoria, Instituto
           Nacional de Antropologia e Historia, México.
    1968   Clima y agricultura en Teotihuacan. In *Materiales para la arqueologia de Teotihuacan,*
           edited by J. L. Lorenzo. Instituto Nacional de Anthropologia e Historia, Serie Inves-
           tigaciones 17, México Pp. 51–72.
McBride, Harold W.
    1974   Formative ceramics and prehistoric settlement patterns in the Cuauhtitlan Region,
           Mexico. Unpublished Ph.D. dissertation, Department of Anthropology, UCLA, Los
           Angeles.
McClung De Tapia, Emily
    1977   Recientes estudios paleo-etnobotánicos en Teotihuacan. In *Anales de Antropologia*
           14:49–61.
MacNeish, R. S.
    1958   Preliminary archaeological investigations in the Sierre de Tamaulipas, Mexico. *Transac-
           tions of the American Philosophical Society, N.S.* **44**(5).
    1964   Ancient Mesoamerican civilization. *Science* **143:**531–537.
    1967   A summary of the subsistence. In *Environment and subsistence, the prehistory of the*

Tehuacan Valley, Vol. 1, edited by Douglas S. Byers. Austin: University of Texas Press. Pp. 290–309.

1972 The evolution of the community patterns in the Tehuacan Valley of Mexico and speculations about the cultural processes. In *Man, settlement and urbanism*, edited by P. J. Ucko, R. Tringham, and G. W. Dimbleby. London: Gerald Duckworth and Co. Pp. 67–93.

n.d. Energy and culture in ancient Tehuacan. Unpublished m.s.

Marquina, Ignacio (Ed.)

1970 *Proyecto Cholula*. Instituto Nacional de Antropologia e Historia, Serie Investigaciones 19, México.

Mastache de Escobar, A. G.

1976 Sistemas de riego en el area de Tula, Hgo. In *Proyecto Tula, Segunda Parte*, edited by E. Matos M. Instituto Nacional de Antropologia e Historia, Colección Cientifica 33, México. Pp. 49–70.

Mastache, de Escobar A. G., and A. M. Crespo

1974 La ocupacion prehispánica en el area de Tula, Hgo. In *Proyecto Tula, Primera Parte*, edited by E. Matos M. Instituto Nacional de Antropologia e Historia, Colección Cientifica 15, México. Pp. 71–103.

1976 Mazapan Period occupation of the Tula Region. Paper delivered at the XLII International Society of Americanists Meeting Paris, France.

Matos Moctezuma, Eduardo (Coordinator)

1974 *Proyecto Tula, Primera Parte*. Instituto Nacional de Antropologia, Colección Cientifica 15, México.

1976 *Proyecto Tula, Segunda Parte*. Instituto Nacional de Antropologia, Colección Cientifica 33, México.

Mayer-Oakes, W.

1959 A stratigraphic excavation at El Risco, Mexico, *Transactions of the American Philosophical Society* **103**(3).

Memoria de la obra del sistema de drenaje profundo del Distrito Federal.

1975 Secretaria de Obras y Servicios Hidraulicos, México.

Mendizabal, M.

1946 Influencia de la sal en la distribucion geografica de los grupos indigenas de México. In *Obras Completas* **2**:181–344. México.

Mesa redońdas sobre problemas del Valle de Mexico.

1963 Published by the Instituto Mexicano de Recursas Naturales Renovables.

Michels, Joseph W.

1976 Kaminaljuyu social structure. Paper delivered at the XLII International Society of Americanists Meetings, Paris, France.

Millon, René

1957 Irrigation systems in the Valley of Teotihuacan. *American Antiquity* **23**:160–166.

1967a Chronologia y periodificación: Datos estratigraficos sobre periodos ceramicas y sus relaciones con la pintura mural. In *Teotihuacan, XI Mesa Redonda I*. Sociedad Mexicana de Antropologia, México. Pp.1–18.

1967b Extensión y población de la ciudad de Teotihuacán en sus diferentes periódos: Un cálculo provisional. In *Teotihuacán, XI Mesa Redonda I*. Sociedad Mexicana de Antropologia, Mexico. Pp. 57–58.

1970 Teotihuacan: Completion of map of giant ancient city in the Valley of Mexico. *Science* **170**:1077–1082.

1976 Social relations in ancient Teotihuacan. In *The Valley of Mexico*, edited by E. R. Wolf. Albuquerque: University of New Mexico Press. Pp. 205–248.

Millon, René, Bruce Drewitt, and George Cowgill

1973a *Urbanization at Teotihuacan, Mexio, the Teotihuacan map*, Part One. Austin: University of Texas Press.

1973b Urbanization at Teotihuacan, Mexico. *The Teotihuacan map, part two: Map*. Austin: University of Texas Press.

Millon, René, C. Hall, and M. Diaz
  1962   Conflict in the modern Teotihuacan irrigation system. *Comparative studies in society and history* **4**(4):394–521.
Molins, Fabregat, N.
  1954   El codice mendocino y la economia de Tenochtitlan. *Biblioteca Minima Mexicana*, Vol. 30. Calle Mesones 14, Mexico.
Montúfar, Alonso
  1897   *Descripcion del Arzobispado de Mexico hecha en 1570.* Jose Joaquin Terrazas E. Hijas, México.
Monzón, Arturo
  1949   El calpulli en la organización social de los Tenochca. *Publicaciones del Instituto de Historia*, Serie 1, No. 6. Universidad Naciona Autonoma de México y Instituto Nacional de Antropologia e Historia, México.
Mooser, Frederico
  1975   Mapa geológico de la Cuenca de Mexico y zonas colindantes. In *Memoria de las obras del sistema de drenaje profundo del Distrito Federal,* Tomo IV. Secretaria de Obras y Servicios, México.
Moreno, Manuel
  1931   *La organización politica y social de Los Aztecas.* Universidad Nacional Autonoma, México.
Mueller, J. W.
  1974   The use of sampling in archaeological survey. *Memoirs of Society for American Archaeology* **28,** Washington, DC.
  1975   *Sampling in archaeology.* Tucson: University of Arizona Press.
Mullan, Elizabeth
  1973   *La evaluacion cuantativa de un levantamiento de suelos.* Tesis de Maestro en Ciencias, Escuela Nacional de Agricultura, Colegio de Postgraduados, Chapingo, Mexico.
Murdock, G. P.
  1949   *Social Structure.* New York: Macmillan.
Naroll, Raul
  1962   Floor area and settlement population. *American Antiquity* **27**:587–589.
Netting, Robert M.
  1972   Sacred power and centralization: Aspects of political adaptation in Africa. In *Population growth: Anthropological implications,* edited by Brian Spooner. Cambridge: M.I.T. Press. Pp. 219–244.
Niederberger, Christine
  1969   Paleoecologia humana y playas lacustres post-Pleistocenos en Tlapacoya. *Boletin del Instituto Nacional de Antropologia e Historia* **37**:19–24 (México).
  1975   Excavations in Zohapilco, Mexico. In *Actas del XLI Congreso Internacional de Americanistas México,* 2–7 Sept. 1974, Vol. 1. México.
  1976   Zohapilco. Colección Cientifica 30, Instituto Nacional de Antropologia e Historia, Mexico.
Noguera, Eduardo
  1935a Antecedentes y relaciones de la cultura Teotihuacana. *El Mexico Antiguo* **3**(5–8).
  1935b *La cerámica de Tenayuca y las excavaciones estratigráficas.* Departamento Monumentos, México.
  1954   *Cerámica de Cholula.* Editorial Guaráni, Mexico.
Odum, Howard T.
  1971   *Environment, power, and society.* New York: Wiley-InterScience.
Olivera, Mercedes
  1976   *Pillis y macehuales: Las formaciones sociales y los modos de producción de Tecali del siglo XII–XVI.* Edicion de la Casa Chata.
O'Neill, Gene S.
  1955– Preliminary report on stratigraphic excavations in the southern Valley of Mexico.
  1957   *Revista Mexicana de estudios anthropologicos. Sociedad mexicana de antropologia.* Tomo Decimocuarto.

Orozco y Berra, Manuel
  1864 *Memoria para la carta hidrografica del Valle de Mexico*. México.
Palerm, Angel
  1955 The agricultural bases of urban civilization in Mesoamerica. In *Irrigation civilization: A comparative study*, edited by J. H. Steward. Pan American Union Social Science Monographs 1, Washington, DC.
  1973 *Obras hidráulicas prehispánicas en el sistema lacustre del Valle de México*. Instituto Nacional de Antropologia e Historia, México.
Palerm, Angel, and Eric R. Wolf
  1960 Ecological potential and cultural development in Mesoamerica. In *Social Science Monographs*, Vol. 3. Pan American Union, Washington, DC. Pp. 1–37.
  1961a La agricultura y el desarrollo de la civilización en Mesoamerica. *Revista Interamericana de Ciencias Sociales*, Segunda epoca, Vol. 1. Pan American Union, Washington, DC.
  1961b Sistemas agrícolas y desarrollo del area clave del imperio Texcocano. *Revista Interamericana de Ciencias Sociales*, Segunda epoca, Vol. 1, No. 2. Pan American Union, Washington, DC.
  1961c Agricultura de riego en el viejo senorio del acolhuacan. *Revista Interamericana de Ciencias Sociales*, Segunda epoca, Vol. 1, No. 2. Pan American Union, Washington, DC.
  1961d Potential ecologico y desarrollo cultural de Mesoamerica. *Revista Interamericana de Ciencias Sociales*, Segunda epoca, Vol. 1, No. 2. Pan American Union, Washington, DC.
  1961e Sistemas de regadio prehispanico en Teotihuacan y en el Teotihuacan y en el Pedregal de San Angel. *Revista Interamericana de Ciencias Sociales*, Vol. 2, No. 1. (México). Pp. 297–302.
Parsons, Jeffrey R.
  1966 The Aztec ceramic sequence in the Teotihuacan Valley, Mexico. Unpublished Ph.D. dissertation, University of Michigan. Ann Arbor: University Microfilms.
  1968 Teotihuacan, Mexico, and its impact on regional demography. *Science* 162:372–877.
  1971 Prehispanic settlement patterns in the Texcoco region, Mexico. *Memoirs of the Museum of Anthropology, University of Michigan*, 3, Ann Arbor.
  1972 Archaeological settlement patterns. *Annual Review of Anthropology*, Vol. 1, Palo Alto, CA: Annual Reviews, Inc. Pp. 127–150.
  1973 Reconocimiento superficial and sur del Valle de Mexico. Temporada de 1972. Report to I.N.A.H.
  1974 The development of a prehistoric complex society: A regional perspective from the Valley of Mexico. *Journal of Field Archaeology* 1:81–108.
  1976a Settlement and population history of the Basín of Mexico. In *The Valley of Mexico*, edited by E. R. Wolf. Albuquerque: University of New Mexico Press. Pp. 69–100.
  1976b The role of chinampa agriculture in the food supply of Aztec Tenochtitlan. In *Cultural change and continuity*, edited by C. E. Cleland. New York: Academic Press. Pp. 233–257.
  1976c *Prehispanic settlement patterns in the Upper Mantaro, Peru: A preliminary report of the 1975 field season*. Progress report submitted to the National Science Foundation and the Instituto Nacional de Cultura, Peru.
  n.d. *Prehispanic settlement patterns in the southern Valley of Mexico: The Chalco and Xochimilco Regions*. Manuscript, Museum of Anthropology, University of Michigan.
Parsons, Jeffrey R., and C. Hastings
  1977 *Prehispanic settlement patterns in the Upper Mantaro, Peru: Results of the 1976 field season*. Mimeograph report to National Science Foundation.
Paso y Troncoso, Francisco del (Ed.)
  1905a *Papeles de Nueva España, segunda serie: Geografia y estadistica*, Tomo I. Est. Tipográfico "Sucesores de Rivadeneyia," Madrid.
  1905b *Papeles de Nueva España, segunda serie: Geografia y estadistica*, Tomo VI. Est. Tipográfico "Sucesores de Rivadeneyia," Madrid. Pp. 226–230.
  1939 *Epistolario de Nueva España 4*. Antigua Libreria Robredo, México.

Pimlott, D. H., J. A. Shannon, and G. B. Kolenosky
  1969   The ecology of the timber wolf in Algonquin Park. Ontario Department of Lands and
         Forests.
Piña Chan, Roman
  1955   *Las culturas preclasicas de la Cuenca de Mexico.* Fondo de Cultura Economica, México.
  1958   Tlatilco. *I.N.A.H. Serie Investigaciones* 1, México.
Piña Chan, Roman *et al.*
  1977   Teotenango: El antiguo lugar de la muralla. Dirección de Turismo, Gobierno del Estado
         de Mexico.
Pires-Ferreira, Jane W.
  1975   Formative Mesoamerican exchange networks with special reference to the Valley of
         Oaxaca. *Memoirs of the Museum of Anthropology, University of Michigan* 7, Ann Arbor.
Plog, Stephen
  1976   Relative efficiencies of sampling techniques for archaeological surveys. In *The early
         Mesoamerican village,* edited by K. V. Flannery. New York: Academic Press. Pp. 136–
         158.
Porter, Muriel N.
  1953   Tlatilco and the pre-classic cultures of the New World. Viking Fund Publications in
         Anthropology, No. 19, Wenner-Gren Foundation for Anthropological Research, New
         York.
Puleston, D.
  1973   Ancient Maya settlement and environment at Tikal, Guatemala: Implication for subsis-
         tence models. Unpublished Ph.D. dissertation, Department of Anthropology, Univer-
         sity of Pennsylvania, Philadelphia.
Rappaport, R. A.
  1971   The flow of energy in an agricultural society. *Scientific American* **225**(3):117–132.
Rattray, Evelyn C.
  1966   An archaeological and stylistic study of Coyotlatelco pottery. *Mesoamerican Notes* 7–8,
         Department of Anthropology, University of the Americas, Mexico. Pp. 87–193.
  1968   A Tzacualli burial from Pueblo Perdido. *American Antiquity* 33:103–105.
  1973   The Teotihuacan ceramic chronology: Early Tzacualli to early Tlamimilolpa phases.
         Unpublished Ph.D. dissertation. University of Missouri, Department of Anthropology,
         Columbia, Missouri.
Reyna Robles, Rosa Maria
  1971   Las figurillas preclasicas. Tesis profesional, Escuela Nacional de Antropologia e His-
         toria, Instituto Nacional de Antropologia e Historia, México.
Reyna Robles, Rosa Maria and L. Gonzalez Quintero
  1976   Resultados del analisis botanico de formaciones tronconicos. Trabajo presentado en el
         Simposio de Ethnobotanica, México.
Riehm, Karl
  1961   Prehistoric salt boiling. *Antiquity* 35:139.
Rojas, Teresa, Rafael A. Strauss, and Jose Lamieras
  1974   Nuevas noticias sobre las obras hidraulicas prehispanicas y coloniales en el Valle de
         Mexico. I.N.A.H., Centro De Investigaciones Superiores, México.
Rowe, John H.
  1960   Cultural unity and diversification in peruvian archaeology. In *Men and culture, selected
         papers of the Fifth International Congress of Anthropological and Ethnological Sciences,*
         September, 1956. Philadelphia.
Sahagun, Fr. Bernardino De
  1946   *Historia general de las cosas de Nueva Espana.* Editorial Nueva Espana.
Sahlins, Marshall D.
  1958   *Social stratification in Polynesia.* Seattle: University of Washington Press.
Salzano, Francisco M.
  1972   Genetic aspects of the demography of American Indians and Eskimos. In *The structure*

of human populations, edited by G. A. Harrison and T. A. Boyce. Oxford: Clarendon Press. Pp. 234–251.

Sanchez Sanchez, Oscar
  1968   *La flora del Valle de México.* México.

Sanders, William T.
  1956   The central Mexican Symbiotic Region. In *Prehistoric settlement patterns in the New World,* edited by G. R. Willey. Viking Fund Publications in Anthropology, No. 23. Wenner-Gren Foundation for Anthropological Research, New York. Pp. 115–127.
  1965   *The cultural ecology of the Teotihuacan Valley,* Department of Sociology and Anthropology, The Pennsylvania State University, University Park, mimeographed.
  1966a Review of W. Borah and S. Cook, The Aboriginal population of central Mexico on the eve of the Spanish Conquest. *Ibero-Americana* No. 45. *American Anthropologist* **68**(5):1298–1299.
  1966b Life in a classic village. In *Teotihuacan: Onceava Mesa Redonda.* Sociedad Mexicana De Anthropologia, México.
  1968   Hydraulic agriculture, economic symbiosis and the evolution of states in central Mexico. In *Anthropological archaeology in the Americas,* edited by B. J. Meggers. Washington, DC: Anthropological Society of Washington. Pp. 88–107.
  1970a The geography of the Valley of Teotihuacan. In *The natural environment, contemporary occupation and 16th century population of the Valley. The Teotihuacan Valley project final report,* Vol. 1. *Occasional Papers in Anthropology* 3, Department of Anthropology, The Pennsylvania State University, University Park. Pp. 69–101.
  1970b Comments to Contemporary settlement patterns: The Cerro Gordo-north slope and upper Valley areas. In *The natural environment contemporary occupation and 16th century population of the Valley. The Teotihuacan Valley project final report,* Vol. 1. *Occasional Papers in Anthropology* 3, Department of Anthropology, The Pennsylvania State University, University Park. Pp. 237–239.
  1970c The population of the Teotihuacan Valley, the Basin of Mexico and the central Mexican Symbiotic Region in the 16th century. In *The Teotihuacan Valley project final report* Vol. 1. *Occasional Papers in Anthropology,* 3, Department of Anthropology, The Pennsylvania State University, University Park.
  1976a The natural environment of the Basin of Mexico. In *The Valley of Mexico,* edited by Eric Wolf. University Albuquerque: University of New Mexico Press. Pp. 59–67.
  1976b The agricultural history of the Basin of Mexcio. In *The Valley of Mexico,* edited by Eric Wolf. Albuquerque. University of New Mexico Press. Pp. 101–159.
  1976c The population of the central Mexican Symbiotic Region, the Basin of Mexico and the Teotihuacan Valley in the Sixteenth century. In *The native population of the Americas in 1492,* edited by William M. Denevan. Madison, WI: University of Wisconsin Press.

Sanders, William T., A. Kovar, T. H. Charlton, and R. A. Diehl
  1970   *The natural environment, contemporary occupation and 16th century population of the Valley. The Teotihuacan Valley project final report,* Vol. 1. *Occasional Papers in Anthropology* 3, Department of Anthropology, The Pennsylvania State University, University Park.

Sanders, William T., and J. Marino
  1970   *New World prehistory.* The foundation of modern anthropology series. Englewood Cliffs, NJ: Prentice-Hall.

Sanders, William T., J. R. Parsons, and M. H. Logan
  1976   Summary and conclusions. In *The Valley of Mexico,* edited by Eric Wolf. Albuquerque: University of New Mexico Press. Pp. 161–178.

Sanders, William T., and Barbara J. Price
  1968   *Mesoamerica: The evolution of a civilization,* New York: Random House.

Sanders, William T., and Robert S. Santley
  1977   A prehispanic irrigation system near Santa Clara Xalostoc in the Basin of Mexico. *American Antiquity,* **42**(4):582–588.

n.d.   Prehispanic settlement patterns in the Cuauhtitlan Region, state of Mexico. Unpublished manuscript.

Sanders, William T., and David L. Webster
1978   Unilinealism, multilinealism, and the evolution of complex societies. Unpublished manuscript.

Sanders, William T. *et al.*
1975   *The Formative period occupation of the Valley. The Teotihuacan Valley project, final report,* Vol. 2. *Occasional Papers in Anthropology* 10, Department of Anthropology, The Pennsylvania State University, University Park.

n.d.   The Toltec period occupation of the Valley. Ms submitted as part of The Teotihuacan Valley project, final report. Occasional Papers in Anthropology. Department of Anthropology, The Pennsylvania State University, University Park.

Santley, Robert S.
1975   Historia del asentamiento formativo en Loma Torremote. Paper presented at XIV Mesa Redonda: Las Fronteras Mesoamericas, Sociedad Mexicana de Antropologia, Tegucigalpa, Honduras, mimeographed.

1976a Form and function of preclassic residential groups: Loma Torremote as a test case. Paper presented at the 41st Annual Meetings of the Society for American Archaeology, St. Louis, mimeographed.

1976b The late Formative community of Loma Torremote: A preliminary report to El Instituto Nacional de Antropologia e Historia, Department of Anthropology, The Pennsylvania State University, University Park, Mimeographed.

1976c Formative settlement patterns in the Cuauhtitlan Region, State of Mexico: A preliminary evaluation. Paper presented at the XLII International Congress of Americanists, Paris, France, mimeographed.

1977   Intra-site settlement patterns at Loma Torremote and their relationship to Formative prehistory in the Cuauhtitlan Region, State of Mexico. Unpublished Ph.D. dissertation, Department of Anthropology, The Pennsylvania State University, University Park.

n.d.a A reconstruction of energy flow in the Tehuacan Valley. Manuscript on file at the Department of Anthropology, The Pennsylvania State University, University Park (1973).

n.d.b Reconstructing a prehistoric society: The Late Formative settlement of Loma Torremote in the Basin of Mexico. Unpublished manuscript (1977).

Sears, Paul B.
1952   Palynology in southern North America I: Archaeological horizons in the Basin of Mexico. *Bulletin of the Geological Society of America* **63**:241–254.

Sejourne, L.
1959   *Un palacio en la Ciudad de los Dioses: Exploraciones En Teotihuacan, 1955–58.* Instituto Nacional de Antropologia e Historia, México.

1966a *Arqueologia de Teotihuacan: La ceramica.* Fondo de Cultura Economica, México.

1966b *Arquitectura y pintura en Teotihuacan.* Siglo XXI Editores, S. A., México.

Serrano, Carlos, and Zaid Lagunas
1975   Sistema de enterramiento y notas sobre el material osteologico de La Ventilla, Teotihuacan, Mexico. *Anales 7a (IV):* 105–144. Instituto Nacional de Antropologia e Historia, México.

Service, Elman R.
1962   *Primitive social organization: An evolutionary perspective,* New York: Random House.

Shelford, V. E.
1963   *The ecology of North America.* Urbana, IL: University of Illinois Press.

Smith, B. D.
1974   Predator-prey relationships in the southeastern Ozarks-A.D. 1300. *Human Ecology* **2**:31–43.

Smith, C. Earle
1967   Plant remains. In *Environment and subsistence, the prehistory of the Tehuacan Valley,*

volume 1, edited by Douglas S. Byers. Austin: University of Texas Press. Pp. 220–255.

Snow, Dean
  1969 Ceramic sequence and settlement location in prehispanic Tlaxcala. *American Antiquity* **34,** No. 2.

Solokovsky, Jay
  1974 The socio-economic basis of political change in Nahuatl pueblo in Mexico, Ph.D. dissertation, Pennsylvania State University, University Park.

Soustelle, Jacques
  1955 *Daily life of the Aztecs on the eve of the Spanish conquest.* Harmondsworth, England: Penguin.

Spence, Michael W.
  1967 The obsidian industry of Teotihuacan. *American Antiquity* **32**(4).
  1974 Residential practices and the distribution of skeletal traits in Teotihuacan Mexico. *Man* **9,** No. 2.
  n.d. The development of the Teotihuacan obsidian production system. Unpublished manuscript.

Spence, Michael W., and Jeffrey R. Parsons
  1972 Prehispanic obsidian exploitation in central Mexico: A preliminary synthesis. In *Miscellaneous studies in Mexican prehistory, Anthropological papers,* 45. Museum of Anthropology, University of Michigan, Ann Arbor. Pp. 1–45.

Spores, Ronald
  1967 *The Mixtec kings and their people.* Norman, OK: University of Oklahoma Press.

Stadelman, Raymond
  1940 Maize cultivation in northwestern Guatemala. *Carnegie Institution contributions to American anthropology and history,* No. 33. Washington, DC: Carnegie Institution.

Starbuck, David R.
  1975 *Man-animal relationships in preColumbian central Mexico.* Unpublished doctoral dissertation, Department of Anthropology, Yale University, New Haven.

Steggerda, Morris
  1941 Maya indians of Yucatan. *Carnegie Institution of Washington Publication* No. 531, Washington, DC.

Steward, Julian
  1955 *Theory of culture change,* Urbana, IL: University of Illinois Press.

Taylor, P. J.
  1977 *Quantitative methods in geography.* Boston: Houghton-Mifflin.

Tolstoy, Paul
  1958 Surface survey of the northern Valley of Mexico: The classic and post-classic periods. *Transactions of the American Philosophical Society* **48**(5).
  1971a Progress report on archaeological investigations of Early and Middle Preclassic occupations in the Basin of Mexico. Report submitted to the National Science Foundation, Washington, DC, and the Research Foundation of the City University of New York.
  1971b Utilitarian artifacts of central Mexico. In *Archaeology of northern Mesoamerica, handbook of Middle American indians,* Vol. 10(1), edited by Gordon F. Ekholm and Ignacio Bernal. Austin; University of Texas Press. Pp. 270–296.
  1975 Settlement and population trends in the Basin of Mexico (Ixtapaluca and Zacatenco Phases). *Journal of Field Archaeology* **2**:331–349.
  n.d. The archaeological chronology of western Mesoamerica before 900 A.D. Unpublished manuscript (1975).

Tolstoy, Paul, and Suzanne K. Fish
  1973 Excavations at Coapexco, 1973. Report submitted to the National Science Foundation, Washington, DC.
  1975 Surface and subsurface evidence for community size at Coapexco, Mexico. *Journal of Field Archaeology* **2**:97–104.

Tolstoy, Paul, S. K. Fish, M. W. Boksenbaum, K. B. Vaughn, and C. E. Smith
  1977   Early sedentary communities of the Basin of Mexico. *Journal of Field Archaeology* **4**:91–106.
Tolstoy, Paul, and Louise I. Paradis
  1970   Early and Middle Preclassic culture in the Basin of Mexico. *Science* **167**:344–351.
Tozzer, A.
  1921   Excavations at a site at Santiago Ahuitzotla, Mexico, D.F. *Bureau of American Ethnology Bulletin 74*. Washington, DC: Smithsonian Institution.
Ubelaker, Douglas H.
  1974   Reconstruction of demographic profiles from ossuary skeletal samples: A case study from the tidewater Potomac. *Smithsonian Contributions to Anthropology 18*. Washington, DC: Smithsonian Institution Press.
United Nations
  1967   *Demographic yearbook.*
Vaillant, George C.
  1930   Excavations at Zacatenco. *Anthropological papers of the American Museum of Natural History,* Vol. XXXII, Part 1. New York.
  1931   Excavations at Ticoman. *Anthropological papers of the American Museum of Natural History,* Vol. XXXII, Part 2. New York.
  1935   Excavations at El Arbolillo. *Anthropological papers of the American Museum of Natural History,* Vol. XXV, Part 2. New York.
  1938   A correlation of archaeological and historical sequences in the Valley of Mexico. *American Anthropologist,* **40**(4).
  1941   *Aztecs of Mexico.* Garden City, NY: Doubleday.
Vescelius, G. S.
  1960   Archaeological sampling: A problem of statistical inference. In *Essays in the science of culture in honor of Leslie A. White,* edited by G. E. Dole and R. L. Carniero. New York: Thomas Crowell. Pp. 457–470.
Waddell, Eric
  1972   The mound builders. *Monograph 53, the American ethnological society.* Seattle: University of Washington Press.
Wellhausen, E., L. Roberts, E. Hernandez, and P. Manglesdorf
  1952   *Races of maize in Mexico.* Bussey Institute, Harvard University, Cambridge, MA.
West, M.
  1965   Transition from Preclassic to Classic at Teotihuacan, *American Antiquity* **31**(2):192–202.
West, R. C. and Pedro Armillas
  1950   Las Chinampas de Mexico. *Cuadernos Americanos* **50**:165–192.
Whalen, Michael E.
  1977   Settlement patterns of the eastern Hueco Bolson. Anthropological Paper No. 4, Centennial Museum. University of Texas at El Paso. 217 Pp.
Whalen, Michael E., and J. R. Parsons
  n.d.   Ceramic markers used for period designations. Appendix I. Prehispanic settlement patterns in the southern Valley of Mexico: The Chalco and Xochimilco Regions. Manuscript, Museum of Anthropology, University of Michigan, Ann Arbor.
White, R. S.
  n.d.   Faunal remains from archaeological sites in the Teotihuacan Valley, Mexico. Unpublished manuscript (1975).
Wicke, C. R., and F. Horcasitas
  1957   Archaeological investigations on Mount Tlaloc, Mexico. *Mesoamerican Notes* **5**:83–85. Department of Anthropology, Mexico City College, Mexico.
Wilkes, H. Garrison
  1967   Teosinte: The closest relative of maize. Bussey Institute, Harvard University, Cambridge, MA.

Willey, G. R.
    1953 Prehistoric settlement patterns in the Viru Valley, Peru. *Bureau of American Ethnology Bulletin 155*. U.S. Government Printing Office, Washington, DC.
Winter, Marcus C.
    1974 Late Formative society in the Valley of Oaxaca and the Mixteca Alta, Mexico. Paper presented at the XLI International Congress of Americanists, Mexico, mimeographed.
Wittfogel, K. A.
    1957 *Oriental despotism*. New Haven: Yale University Press.
Wolf, Eric
    1966 *Peasants*. Englewood Cliffs, NJ: Prentice-Hall.
Wolf, Eric R., and A. Palerm
    1955 Irrigation in the old Acolhua domain, Mexico. *Southwestern Journal of Anthropology* **11**(3):265–281.
Wolf, Eric R. (ed.)
    1976 *The Valley of Mexico*. Albuquerque: University of New Mexico Press.
Woodburn, James
    1968 An introduction to Hadza ecology. In *Man the hunter*, edited by R. B. Lee and I. DeVore. Chicago: Aldine. Pp. 44–49.
Wright, H. T., and G. A. Johnson
    1975 Population, exchange and early state formation in southwestern Iran. *American Anthropologist* **177**(2):276–289.
Wu Leung, Woot-Tsuen
    1961 *Food composition table for use in Latin America*, Inter-departmental Committee on Nutrition for National Defense, Washington, DC.

Index

Thomas F. King, Patricia Parker Hickman, and Gary Berg. **Anthropology in Historic Preservation: Caring for Culture's Clutter**

Richard E. Blanton. **Monte Albán: Settlement Patterns at the Ancient Zapotec Capital**

R. E. Taylor and Clement W. Meighan. **Chronologies in New World Archaeology**

Bruce D. Smith. **Prehistoric Patterns of Human Behavior: A Case Study in the Mississippi Valley**

Barbara L. Stark and Barbara Voorhies (Eds.). **Prehistoric Coastal Adaptations: The Economy and Ecology of Maritime Middle America**

Charles L. Redman, Mary Jane Berman, Edward V. Curtin, William T. Langhorne, Nina M. Versaggi, and Jeffery C. Wanser (Eds.). **Social Archeology: Beyond Subsistence and Dating**

Bruce D. Smith (Ed.). **Mississippian Settlement Patterns**

Lewis R. Binford. **Nunamiut Ethnoarchaeology**

J. Barto Arnold III and Robert Weddle. **The Nautical Archeology of Padre Island: The Spanish Shipwrecks of 1554**

Sarunas Milisauskas. **European Prehistory**

Brian Hayden (Ed.). **Lithic Use-Wear Analysis**

William T. Sanders, Jeffrey R. Parsons, and Robert S. Santley. **The Basin of Mexico: Ecological Processes in the Evolution of a Civilization**

in preparation

David L. Clarke. **Analytical Archaeologist: Collected Papers of David L. Clarke. Edited and Introduced by His Colleagues**

Arthur E. Spiess. **Reindeer and Caribou Hunters: An Archaeological Study**

STUDIES IN ARCHAEOLOGY

Consulting Editor: Stuart Struever

Department of Anthropology
Northwestern University
Evanston, Illinois